Novels
for Students

National Advisory Board

Novels for Students

Presenting Analysis, Context, and Criticism on Commonly Studied Novels

Volume 22

Sara Constantakis and
Ira Mark Milne, Project Editors

Foreword by Anne Devereaux Jordan

THOMSON

GALE

Detroit • New York • San Francisco • San Diego • New Haven, Conn. • Waterville, Maine • London • Munich

Novels for Students, Volume 22

Project Editors
Sara Constantakis and Ira Mark Milne

Editorial
Anne Marie Hacht

Rights Acquisition and Management
Sue Rudolph, Jessica Schultz, Timothy Sisler

Manufacturing
Drew Kalasky

Imaging
Leitha Etheridge-Sims, Lezlie Light, Mike Logusz

Product Design
Pamela A. E. Galbreath

Vendor Administration
Civie Green

Product Manager
Meggin Condino

ISBN 0-7876-6945-8
ISSN 1094-3552

Printed in the United States of America
10 9 8 7 6 5 4 3 2 1

Table of Contents

The Informed Dialogue: Interacting with Literature

When we pick up a book, we usually do so with the anticipation of pleasure. We hope that by entering the time and place of the novel and sharing the thoughts and actions of the characters, we will find enjoyment. Unfortunately, this is often not the case; we are disappointed. But we should ask, has the author failed us, or have we failed the author?

We establish a dialogue with the author, the book, and with ourselves when we read. Consciously and unconsciously, we ask questions: "Why did the author write this book?" "Why did the author choose that time, place, or character?" "How did the author achieve that effect?" "Why did the character act that way?" "Would I act in the same way?" The answers we receive depend upon how much information about literature in general and about that book specifically we ourselves bring to our reading.

Young children have limited life and literary experiences. Being young, children frequently do not know how to go about exploring a book, nor sometimes, even know the questions to ask of a book. The books they read help them answer questions, the author often coming right out and *telling* young readers the things they are learning or are expected to learn. The perennial classic, *The Little Engine That Could, tells* its readers that, among other things, it is good to help others and brings happiness:

> "Hurray, hurray," cried the funny little clown and all the dolls and toys. "The good little boys and girls in the city will be happy because you helped us, kind, Little Blue Engine."

In picture books, messages are often blatant and simple, the dialogue between the author and reader one-sided. Young children are concerned with the end result of a book—the enjoyment gained, the lesson learned—rather than with how that result was obtained. As we grow older and read further, however, we question more. We come to expect that the world within the book will closely mirror the concerns of our world, and that the author will *show* these through the events, descriptions, and conversations within the story, rather than *telling* of them. We are now expected to do the interpreting, carry on our share of the dialogue with the book and author, and glean not only the author's message, but comprehend how that message and the overall affect of the book were achieved. Sometimes, however, we need help to do these things. *Novels for Students* provides that help.

A novel is made up of many parts interacting to create a coherent whole. In reading a novel, the more obvious features can be easily spotted—theme, characters, plot—but we may overlook the more subtle elements that greatly influence how the novel is perceived by the reader: viewpoint, mood and tone, symbolism, or the use of humor. By focusing on both the obvious and more subtle literary elements within a novel, *Novels for Students* aids readers in both analyzing for message and in determining how and why that message is communicated. In the discussion on Harper Lee's *To*

Kill a Mockingbird (Vol. 2), for example, the mockingbird as a symbol of innocence is dealt with, among other things, as is the importance of Lee's use of humor which "enlivens a serious plot, adds depth to the characterization, and creates a sense of familiarity and universality." The reader comes to understand the internal elements of each novel discussed—as well as the external influences that help shape it.

"The desire to write greatly," Harold Bloom of Yale University says, "is the desire to be elsewhere, in a time and place of one's own, in an originality that must compound with inheritance, with an anxiety of influence." A writer seeks to create a unique world within a story, but although it is unique, it is not disconnected from our own world. It speaks to us *because* of what the writer brings to the writing from our world: how he or she was raised and educated; his or her likes and dislikes; the events occurring in the real world at the time of the writing, and while the author was growing up. When we know what an author has brought to his or her work, we gain a greater insight into both the "originality" (the world of the book), and the things that "compound" it. This insight enables us to question that created world and find answers more readily. By informing ourselves, we are able to establish a more effective dialogue with both book and author.

Novels for Students, in addition to providing a plot summary and descriptive list of characters—to remind readers of what they have read—also explores the external influences that shaped each book. Each entry includes a discussion of the author's background, and the historical context in which the novel was written. It is vital to know, for instance, that when Ray Bradbury was writing *Fahrenheit 451* (Vol. 1), the threat of Nazi domination had recently ended in Europe, and the McCarthy hearings were taking place in Washington, D.C. This information goes far in answering the question, "Why did he write a story of oppressive government control and book burning?" Similarly, it is important to know that Harper Lee, author of *To Kill a Mockingbird,* was born and raised in Monroeville, Alabama, and that her father was a lawyer.

Readers can now see why she chose the south as a setting for her novel—it is the place with which she was most familiar—and start to comprehend her characters and their actions.

Novels for Students helps readers find the answers they seek when they establish a dialogue with a particular novel. It also aids in the posing of questions by providing the opinions and interpretations of various critics and reviewers, broadening that dialogue. Some reviewers of *To Kill A Mockingbird,* for example, "faulted the novel's climax as melodramatic." This statement leads readers to ask, "Is it, indeed, melodramatic?" "If not, why did some reviewers see it as such?" "If it is, why did Lee choose to make it melodramatic?" "Is melodrama ever justified?" By being spurred to ask these questions, readers not only learn more about the book and its writer, but about the nature of writing itself.

The literature included for discussion in *Novels for Students* has been chosen because it has something vital to say to us. *Of Mice and Men, Catch-22, The Joy Luck Club, My Antonia, A Separate Peace* and the other novels here speak of life and modern sensibility. In addition to their individual, specific messages of prejudice, power, love or hate, living and dying, however, they and all great literature also share a common intent. They force us to *think*—about life, literature, and about others, not just about ourselves. They pry us from the narrow confines of our minds and thrust us outward to confront the world of books and the larger, real world we all share. *Novels for Students* helps us in this confrontation by providing the means of enriching our conversation with literature and the world, by creating an *informed* dialogue, one that brings true pleasure to the personal act of reading.

Sources

Harold Bloom, *The Western Canon, The Books and School of the Ages,* Riverhead Books, 1994.

Watty Piper, *The Little Engine That Could,* Platt & Munk, 1930.

Anne Devereaux Jordan
Senior Editor, TALL
(Teaching and Learning Literature)

Introduction

Purpose of the Book

The purpose of *Novels for Students (NfS)* is to provide readers with a guide to understanding, enjoying, and studying novels by giving them easy access to information about the work. Part of Gale's "For Students" Literature line, *NfS* is specifically designed to meet the curricular needs of high school and undergraduate college students and their teachers, as well as the interests of general readers and researchers considering specific novels. While each volume contains entries on "classic" novels frequently studied in classrooms, there are also entries containing hard-to-find information on contemporary novels, including works by multicultural, international, and women novelists.

The information covered in each entry includes an introduction to the novel and the novel's author; a plot summary, to help readers unravel and understand the events in a novel; descriptions of important characters, including explanation of a given character's role in the novel as well as discussion about that character's relationship to other characters in the novel; analysis of important themes in the novel; and an explanation of important literary techniques and movements as they are demonstrated in the novel.

In addition to this material, which helps the readers analyze the novel itself, students are also provided with important information on the literary and historical background informing each work. This includes a historical context essay, a box comparing the time or place the novel was written to modern Western culture, a critical essay, and excerpts from critical essays on the novel. A unique feature of *NfS* is a specially commissioned critical essay on each novel, targeted toward the student reader.

To further aid the student in studying and enjoying each novel, information on media adaptations is provided, as well as reading suggestions for works of fiction and nonfiction on similar themes and topics. Classroom aids include ideas for research papers and lists of critical sources that provide additional material on the novel.

Selection Criteria

The titles for each volume of *NfS* were selected by surveying numerous sources on teaching literature and analyzing course curricula for various school districts. Some of the sources surveyed included: literature anthologies; *Reading Lists for College-Bound Students: The Books Most Recommended by America's Top Colleges;* textbooks on teaching the novel; a College Board survey of novels commonly studied in high schools; a National Council of Teachers of English (NCTE) survey of novels commonly studied in high schools; the NCTE's *Teaching Literature in High School: The Novel;* and the Young Adult Library Services Association (YALSA) list of best books for young adults of the past twenty-five years.

Input was also solicited from our advisory board, as well as from educators from various areas.

From these discussions, it was determined that each volume should have a mix of "classic" novels (those works commonly taught in literature classes) and contemporary novels for which information is often hard to find. Because of the interest in expanding the canon of literature, an emphasis was also placed on including works by international, multicultural, and women authors. Our advisory board members—educational professionals—helped pare down the list for each volume. If a work was not selected for the present volume, it was often noted as a possibility for a future volume. As always, the editor welcomes suggestions for titles to be included in future volumes.

How Each Entry Is Organized

Each entry, or chapter, in *NfS* focuses on one novel. Each entry heading lists the full name of the novel, the author's name, and the date of the novel's publication. The following elements are contained in each entry:

- **Introduction:** a brief overview of the novel which provides information about its first appearance, its literary standing, any controversies surrounding the work, and major conflicts or themes within the work.

- **Author Biography:** this section includes basic facts about the author's life, and focuses on events and times in the author's life that inspired the novel in question.

- **Plot Summary:** a factual description of the major events in the novel. Lengthy summaries are broken down with subheads.

- **Characters:** an alphabetical listing of major characters in the novel. Each character name is followed by a brief to an extensive description of the character's role in the novel, as well as discussion of the character's actions, relationships, and possible motivation.

  Characters are listed alphabetically by last name. If a character is unnamed—for instance, the narrator in *Invisible Man*—the character is listed as "The Narrator" and alphabetized as "Narrator." If a character's first name is the only one given, the name will appear alphabetically by that name.

  Variant names are also included for each character. Thus, the full name "Jean Louise Finch" would head the listing for the narrator of *To Kill a Mockingbird,* but listed in a separate cross-reference would be the nickname "Scout Finch."

- **Themes:** a thorough overview of how the major topics, themes, and issues are addressed within

the novel. Each theme discussed appears in a separate subhead and is easily accessed through the boldface entries in the Subject/Theme Index.

- **Style:** this section addresses important style elements of the novel, such as setting, point of view, and narration; important literary devices used, such as imagery, foreshadowing, symbolism; and, if applicable, genres to which the work might have belonged, such as Gothicism or Romanticism. Literary terms are explained within the entry but can also be found in the Glossary.

- **Historical Context:** This section outlines the social, political, and cultural climate *in which the author lived and the novel was created.* This section may include descriptions of related historical events, pertinent aspects of daily life in the culture, and the artistic and literary sensibilities of the time in which the work was written. If the novel is a historical work, information regarding the time in which the novel is set is also included. Each section is broken down with helpful subheads.

- **Critical Overview:** this section provides background on the critical reputation of the novel, including bannings or any other public controversies surrounding the work. For older works, this section includes a history of how the novel was first received and how perceptions of it may have changed over the years; for more recent novels, direct quotes from early reviews may also be included.

- **Criticism:** an essay commissioned by *NfS* which specifically deals with the novel and is written specifically for the student audience, as well as excerpts from previously published criticism on the work (if available).

- **Sources:** an alphabetical list of critical material used in compiling the entry, with full bibliographical information.

- **Further Reading:** an alphabetical list of other critical sources which may prove useful for the student. It includes full bibliographical information and a brief annotation.

In addition, each entry contains the following highlighted sections, set apart from the main text as sidebars:

- **Media Adaptations:** a list of important film and television adaptations of the novel, including source information. The list also includes stage adaptations, audio recordings, musical adaptations, etc.

- **Topics for Further Study:** a list of potential study questions or research topics dealing with the novel. This section includes questions related to other disciplines the student may be studying, such as American history, world history, science, math, government, business, geography, economics, psychology, etc.

- **Compare and Contrast Box:** an "at-a-glance" comparison of the cultural and historical differences between the author's time and culture and late twentieth century/early twenty-first century Western culture. This box includes pertinent parallels between the major scientific, political, and cultural movements of the time or place the novel was written, the time or place the novel was set (if a historical work), and modern Western culture. Works written after 1990 may not have this box.

- **What Do I Read Next?:** a list of works that might complement the featured novel or serve as a contrast to it. This includes works by the same author and others, works of fiction and nonfiction, and works from various genres, cultures, and eras.

Other Features

NfS includes "The Informed Dialogue: Interacting with Literature," a foreword by Anne Devereaux Jordan, Senior Editor for *Teaching and Learning Literature (TALL)*, and a founder of the Children's Literature Association. This essay provides an enlightening look at how readers interact with literature and how *Novels for Students* can help teachers show students how to enrich their own reading experiences.

A Cumulative Author/Title Index lists the authors and titles covered in each volume of the *NfS* series.

A Cumulative Nationality/Ethnicity Index breaks down the authors and titles covered in each volume of the *NfS* series by nationality and ethnicity.

A Subject/Theme Index, specific to each volume, provides easy reference for users who may be studying a particular subject or theme rather than a single work. Significant subjects from events to broad themes are included, and the entries pointing to the specific theme discussions in each entry are indicated in **boldface**.

Each entry may have several illustrations, including photos of the author, stills from film adaptations, maps, and/or photos of key historical events, if available.

Citing Novels for Students

When writing papers, students who quote directly from any volume of *Novels for Students* may use the following general forms. These examples are based on MLA style; teachers may request that students adhere to a different style, so the following examples may be adapted as needed.

When citing text from *NfS* that is not attributed to a particular author (i.e., the Themes, Style, Historical Context sections, etc.), the following format should be used in the bibliography section:

"*Night.*" *Novels for Students*. Ed. Marie Rose Napierkowski. Vol. 4. Detroit: Gale, 1998. 234–35.

When quoting the specially commissioned essay from *NfS* (usually the first piece under the "Criticism" subhead), the following format should be used:

Miller, Tyrus. Critical Essay on *Winesburg, Ohio*. *Novels for Students*. Ed. Marie Rose Napierkowski. Vol. 4. Detroit: Gale, 1998. 335–39.

When quoting a journal or newspaper essay that is reprinted in a volume of *NfS*, the following form may be used:

Malak, Amin. "Margaret Atwood's *The Handmaid's Tale* and the Dystopian Tradition," *Canadian Literature* No. 112 (Spring, 1987), 9–16; excerpted and reprinted in *Novels for Students*, Vol. 4, ed. Marie Rose Napierkowski (Detroit: Gale, 1998), pp. 133–36.

When quoting material reprinted from a book that appears in a volume of *NfS*, the following form may be used:

Adams, Timothy Dow. "Richard Wright: Wearing the Mask," in *Telling Lies in Modern American Autobiography* (University of North Carolina Press, 1990), 69–83; excerpted and reprinted in *Novels for Students*, Vol. 1, ed. Diane Telgen (Detroit: Gale, 1997), pp. 59–61.

We Welcome Your Suggestions

The editor of *Novels for Students* welcomes your comments and ideas. Readers who wish to suggest novels to appear in future volumes, or who have other suggestions, are cordially invited to contact the editor. You may contact the editor via e-mail at: **ForStudentsEditors@thomson.com.** Or write to the editor at:

Editor, *Novels for Students*
Thomson Gale
27500 Drake Road
Farmington Hills, MI 48331–3535

Literary Chronology

1820: Anna Sewell is born on March 30 in Yarmouth, England.

1856: Harold Frederic is born on August 19 in Utica, New York.

1871: James Weldon Johnson is born on June 17 in Jacksonville, Florida.

1877: Anna Sewell's *Black Beauty* is published.

1878: Anna Sewell dies on April 25, just five months after her novel *Black Beauty* was published.

1885: Sinclair Lewis (Harry Sinclair Lewis) is born on February 7 in Sauk Centre, Minnesota.

1896: Harold Frederic's *The Damnation of Theron Ware* is published.

1898: Harold Frederic dies on October 19.

1909: James Agee (James Rufus Agee) is born on November 27 in Knoxville, Tennessee.

1912: James Weldon Johnson's *The Autobiography of an Ex-Coloured Man* is published.

1918: Muriel Spark is born on February 1 in Edinburgh, Scotland.

1920: Ray Bradbury is born on August 22 in Waukegan, Illinois.

1924: Kobo Abe is born on March 7 in Tokyo.

1925: William Styron is born on June 11 in Newport News, Virginia.

1927: Sinclair Lewis's *Elmer Gantry* is published.

1932: Umberto Eco is born on January 5 in Alessandria, Italy.

1938: James Weldon Johnson dies on June 26 in a car accident in Wiscassct, Maine.

1947: Salman Rushdie is born on June 19 to a prosperous family in Bombay, India.

1951: Sinclair Lewis dies of heart disease in Rome, Italy.

1955: James Agee dies of heart failure on May 16.

1957: James Agee's *A Death in the Family* is publishcd.

1957: Ray Bradbury's *Dandelion Wine* is published.

1958: James Agee is awarded the Pulitzer Prize for Fiction for *A Death in the Family*.

1960: Arundhati Roy is born. Roy grows up in Aymanam, a village in the state of Kerala, in southern India.

1961: Muriel Spark's *The Prime of Miss Jean Brodie* is published.

1962: Kobo Abe's *The Woman in the Dunes* is published.

1968: William Styron is awarded the Pulitzer Prize for Fiction for *The Confessions of Nat Turner*.

1979: William Styron's *Sophie's Choice* is published.

1980: Umberto Eco's *The Name of the Rose* is published.

1988: Salman Rushdie's *The Satanic Verses* is published.

1993: Kobo Abe dies of heart failure on January 22 in Tokyo.

1997: Arundhati Roy's *The God of Small Things* is published.

Acknowledgments

The editors wish to thank the copyright holders of the excerpted criticism included in this volume and the permissions managers of many book and magazine publishing companies for assisting us in securing reproduction rights. We are also grateful to the staffs of the Detroit Public Library, the Library of Congress, the University of Detroit Mercy Library, Wayne State University Purdy/Kresge Library Complex, and the University of Michigan Libraries for making their resources available to us. Following is a list of the copyright holders who have granted us permission to reproduce material in this volume of *Novels for Students (NfS)*. Every effort has been made to trace copyright, but if omissions have been made, please let us know.

COPYRIGHTED MATERIALS IN *NfS*, VOLUME 22, WERE REPRODUCED FROM THE FOLLOWING PERIODICALS:

www.About.com, December 28, 2004 for "*Black Beauty*," by Paula Kirman. Copyright © 2004 by Paula Kirman (http://womenwriters .about.com). All rights reserved. Used with permission of About, Inc., which can be found on the Web at www.about.com.—*American Literary Realism 1870–1910*, v. 25, fall, 1992. Copyright © 1992 by the Department of English, The University of New Mexico. Reproduced by permission of the publisher.—*Baker Street Journal*, v. 40, June, 1990. Copyright © 1990 by The Baker Street Irregulars. All rights reserved. Reproduced by permission.—*English Journal*, v. 60, October, 1971. Reproduced by permission.—*Negro Ameri-can Literature Forum*, v. 3, spring, 1969 for "The Politics of Passing: The Fiction of James Weldon Johnson," by Richard Kostelanetz. Copyright © Indiana State University 1969. Reproduced by permission of the author./ v. 4, winter, 1970 for "Contemporary Themes in Johnson's *Autobiography of An Ex-Coloured Man*," by Robert E. Fleming. Copyright © 1970 by Indiana State University. Reproduced by permission of the publisher and author.—*Newsweek*, v. 129, May 26, 1997. Copyright © 1997 Newsweek, Inc. All rights reserved. Reprinted by permission.—*Southern Literary Journal*, v. 22, fall, 1990; v. 25, spring, 1993; v. 28, spring, 1996. Copyright © 1990, 1993, 1996 by the University of North Carolina Press. All used by permission.—*Studies in American Fiction*, v. 3, spring, 1975. Copyright © 1975 by Northeastern University. Reproduced by permission.—*Twentieth Century Literature*, v. 43, spring, 1997; v. 45, fall, 1999. Copyright 1997, 1999, Hofstra University Press. Both reproduced by permission.—*Women's Review of Books*, v. 14, September, 1997 for "The Age of Innocence," by Ritu Menon. Reproduced by permission.

COPYRIGHTED MATERIALS IN *NfS*, VOLUME 22, WERE REPRODUCED FROM THE FOLLOWING BOOKS:

Bardolph, Jacqueline. From "Language is Courage: *The Satanic Verses*," in *Reading Rushdie: Perspectives on the Fiction of Salman Rushdie*. Edited by M. D. Fletcher. Rodopi, 1994. Copyright © 1994 Editions Rodopi B. V. Reproduced by permission.—Bennett, Bridget. From *The Damnation of Harold Frederic: His Lives and Work*. Syracuse University Press, Syracuse, NY 1997. Copyright © 1997 by Syracuse University Press. All rights reserved. Reproduced by permission.—Burke, John J., Jr. From "The Romantic Window and the Postmodern Mirror: The Medieval Worlds of Sir Walter Scott and Umberto Eco," in *Scott in Carnival*. Edited by J. H. Alexander and David Hewitt. Association for Scottish Literary Studies, 1993. Copyright © John J. Burke, Jr. Reproduced by permission of the author.—Carroll, Eugene T. From "Mood and Music: Landscape and Artistry in *A Death in the Family*," in *James Agee: Reconsiderations*. Edited by Michael A. Lofaro. University of Tennessee Press, 1992. Copyright © 1992 by The University of Tennessee Press. Reproduced by permission of The University of Tennessee Press.—Dissanayake, Wimal. From "Self, Place, and Body in *The Woman in the Dunes*: A Comparative Study of the Novel and the Film," in *Literary Relations, East and West: Selected Essays, 1990*. Edited by Jean Toyama and Nobuko Ochner. Copyright © 1990 by the College of Languages, Linguistics and Literature, University of Hawaii at Manoa, Honolulu, Hawaii, 96822. All rights reserved. Reproduced by permission.—Dooley, David J. From *The Art of Sinclair Lewis*. University of Nebraska Press, 1967. Copyright © 1967 by the University of Nebraska Press. Renewed 1995 by The University of Nebraska Press. All rights reserved. Reproduced by permission of the University of Nebraska Press.—Ellerby, Janet Mason. From "Narrative Imperialism in *The Satanic Verses*," in *Multicultural Literatures through Feminist/Poststructuralist Lenses*. Edited by Barbara Frey Waxman. University of Tennessee Press, 1993. Copyright © 1993 by The University of Tennessee Press. Reproduced by permission of The University of Tennessee Press.—Keene, Donald. From *Five Modern Japanese Novelists*. Columbia University Press, 2003. Copyright © 2003 Columbia University Press, New York. All rights reserved. Republished with permission of the Columbia University Press, 61 W. 62nd St., New York, NY 10023.—Kramer, Victor A. From "Urban and Rural Balance in *A Death in the Family*," in *James Agee:*

Reconsiderations. Edited by Michael A. Lofaro. University of Tennessee Press, 1992. Copyright © 1992 by The University of Tennessee Press. Reproduced by permission of The University of Tennessee Press.—Light, Martin. From *The Quixotic Vision of Sinclair Lewis*. Purdue University Press, 1975. Copyright © 1975 by the Purdue Research Foundation. Reproduced by permission.—Lundquist, James. From *Sinclair Lewis*. Frederick Ungar Publishing, 1973. Copyright © 1973 by Frederick Ungar Publishing Co., Inc. Reproduced by permission of The Continuum International Publishing Group.—O'Mahony, Brendan. From "*The Name of the Rose*: 'Tractatus Contra Zelotes,'" in *Italian Storytellers: Essays on Italian Narrative Literature*. Edited by Eric Haywood and Cormac O'Cuilleanain. Foundation for Italian Studies, 1989. Copyright © 1989 Foundation for Italian Studies, University College Dublin. Reproduced by permission.—Pearce, Richard. From "Sophie's Choices," in *The Achievement of William Styron*, Revised Edition. Edited by Robert K. Morris, with Irving Malin. University of Georgia Press, 1981. Copyright © 1975, 1981 by the University of Georgia Press. All rights reserved. Reproduced by permission.—Pollack, David. From *Reading "Against" Culture: Ideology and Narrative in the Japanese Novel*. Cornell University Press, 1992. Copyright © 1992 by Cornell University. Used by permission of the publisher, Cornell University Press.—Portelli, Alessandro. From "The Tragedy and the Joke: James Weldon Johnson's *The Autobiography of an Ex-Coloured Man*," in *Temples for Tomorrow: Looking Back at the Harlem Renaissance*. Edited by Genevieve Fabre and Michel Feith. Indiana University Press, 2001. Copyright © 2001 by Indiana University Press. Reproduced by permission.—Reid, Robin Anne. From *Ray Bradbury: A Critical Companion*. Greenwood Press, 2000. Copyright © 2000 by Robin Anne Reid. All rights reserved. Reproduced by permission of Greenwood Publishing Group, Inc., Westport, CT.—Sirlin, Rhoda. From an Introduction to *William Styron's "Sophie's Choice": Crime and Self-Punishment*. UMI Research Press, 1990. Copyright © 1990 by Rhoda Sirlin. All rights reserved. Reproduced by permission of the author.

Contributors

Bryan Aubrey: Aubrey holds a Ph.D. in English and has published many articles on nineteenth century literature. Entries on *The Damnation of Theron Ware* and *Elmer Gantry*. Original essays on *The Damnation of Theron Ware* and *Elmer Gantry*.

Cynthia Bily: Bily teaches English at Adrian College in Adrian, Michigan. Entry on *The Autobiography of an Ex-Coloured Man*. Original essay on *The Autobiography of an Ex-Coloured Man*.

Laura Carter: Carter is currently employed as a freelance writer. Original essays on *Black Beauty*, *The God of Small Things*, and *The Prime of Miss Jean Brodie*.

Douglas Dupler: Dupler is a writer and has taught college English courses. Original essay on *The God of Small Things*.

Joyce Hart: Hart is a freelance writer and author of several books. Entry on *The Woman in the Dunes*. Original essays on *Black Beauty*, *The God of Small Things*, and *The Woman in the Dunes*.

Diane Andrews Henningfeld: Henningfeld is a professor of English at Adrian College who writes widely on literary topics for academic and educational publications. Entries on *Dandelion Wine* and *The Name of the Rose*. Original essays on *Dandelion Wine* and *The Name of the Rose*.

Catherine Dybiec Holm: Holm is a short story and novel author, and a freelance writer. Original essay on *Black Beauty*.

David Kelly: Kelly is an instructor of literature and creative writing at two colleges in Illinois. Entry on *A Death in the Family*. Original essays on *A Death in the Family* and *The Prime of Miss Jean Brodie*.

Lois Kerschen: Kerschen is a school district administrator and freelance writer. Entry on *Black Beauty*. Original essay on *Black Beauty*.

Melodie Monahan: Monahan has a Ph.D. in English. She teaches at Wayne State University and also operates an editing service, The Inkwell Works. Entries on *The Prime of Miss Jean Brodie* and *Sophie's Choice*. Original essays on *The Prime of Miss Jean Brodie* and *Sophie's Choice*.

Scott Trudell: Trudell is an independent scholar with a bachelor's degree in English literature. Entries on *The God of Small Things* and *The Satanic Verses*. Original essays on *The God of Small Things* and *The Satanic Verses*.

The Autobiography of an Ex-Coloured Man

James Weldon Johnson
1912

The Autobiography of an Ex-Coloured Man, by James Weldon Johnson, was published anonymously by a small New York publisher, Sherman, French and Company, in 1912. The work is a novel, but the author hoped that by remaining anonymous he could persuade readers that it was an actual autobiography. The novel, told in the first person, is the story of a man whose parents were a wealthy white Southern gentleman and the "coloured" seamstress employed by the gentleman's family. The narrator travels around the United States and through Europe, observing how white and black people behave within separate enclaves and with each other. In the end, he decides to "pass," or to live as a white man, and abandon his African American heritage. The story includes many short scenes and didactic digressions, told in a rather flat style with little description or dialogue. When the book was published, only two or three books by African Americans had attracted large audiences, and *The Autobiography of an Ex-Coloured Man* did not sell many copies. Its publisher went out of business, and the book all but disappeared.

With the blooming of the Harlem Renaissance in the 1920s, Johnson became widely known as a writer and an intellectual. His book was re-issued by Knopf, an influential firm that published many of the Harlem Renaissance writers, and for the first time Johnson acknowledged that he was the author. This time, the book was widely sold and discussed, and it has remained in print ever since.

James Weldon Johnson The Library of Congress

Author Biography

James William Johnson was born in Jacksonville, Florida, on June 17, 1871. His father was head-waiter at an expensive restaurant, and his mother was an elementary school teacher and a gifted pianist; neither had been slaves. They saw to it that their children received a good education and lived a secure middle-class life—relatively unusual for African Americans during the nineteenth century. As a teenager, Johnson worked as a secretary to a white physician who took him to New York City and Washington, D.C., tutored him in upper-class manners, gave him books to read, and encouraged him to write.

Johnson attended Atlanta University, created to provide African Americans an education based on the classics and on the idea of public service. Johnson took to heart the call to serve his community, as he demonstrated through a long and varied career in public life. After graduating in 1894, he returned to Florida, where he was principal for the state's first high school for black students. In 1895, he began publishing the nation's first black daily newspaper, the Jacksonville *Daily American*. The paper ran out of money after several months, and Johnson turned to the study of law, becoming the first African American admitted to the bar in Florida. Two years later,

he embarked on a new career, writing songs for musical theater with his brother and another partner in New York City. One of their songs was "Lift Ev'ry Voice and Sing," which came to be known as the Negro National Anthem.

Johnson's next career was in diplomacy. He served as United States consul to Venezuela and to Nicaragua between 1906 and 1913. It was while he was serving in Nicaragua that he wrote his only novel, *The Autobiography of an Ex-Coloured Man* (1912). Johnson published the novel anonymously through a small publisher, in part to help create the illusion that the book was an actual autobiography. At this time, he changed his middle name to "Weldon," believing that a writer needed a more impressive name. Returning to New York in 1913, he became an editorial writer for the *New York Age* newspaper, a position he held for ten years. In 1916, Johnson joined the National Association for the Advancement of Colored People (NAACP), working as a field secretary before becoming executive secretary in 1920. During his ten years as executive secretary, the Harlem Renaissance brought exciting opportunities for African American artists and intellectuals. Johnson edited two volumes of *American Negro Spirituals* and *The Book of American Negro Poetry* (1922), and published his most notable book of original poetry, *God's Trombones* (1927). Also in 1927, *The Autobiography of an Ex-Coloured Man* was reissued, this time by a major publisher and with the author's name, and found the popularity that had eluded it previously.

During the 1930s, Johnson was a professor of creative writing at Fisk University and lectured widely on African American literature and culture. He was killed in a car accident in Wiscasset, Maine, on June 26, 1938.

Plot Summary

Chapters 1–3

As *The Autobiography of an Ex-Coloured Man* opens, a first-person narrator announces that he is about to reveal "the great secret of my life," a revelation that he hopes will ease his mind over a concern he will describe at the end of his story. He then begins the story of his life, from his birth in a small Georgia town a few years after the end of the Civil War.

As a young child, the narrator (who is never named) lives with his mother in a pleasant house, and they are visited often by a tall man with a moustache. One day, the boy and his mother abruptly move to Connecticut, where his mother supports herself by sewing and with money she receives every month in a letter. She teaches her son to play the piano and to read. When he is nine, he begins school, where he has friends for the first time: Red Head, an older boy with red hair and freckles, and Shiny, a dark-skinned boy who is the smartest child in the class.

When the boy is about eleven years old, a comment from the school principal forces him to realize for the first time that he is "coloured." This knowledge changes his outlook. He has vaguely considered his non-white classmates to be inferior; now he feels that inferiority in himself. A year or so later, the man from Georgia comes for a visit and is revealed as the boy's father. His mother explains that she was a young seamstress working for a wealthy white woman when she fell in love with the woman's son, home from college. Although they could never marry, she continues to believe that she is the man's one true love, but by the time the narrator graduates from high school, the man has stopped sending letters, and his mother dies soon after. The narrator performs a piano concert to raise money and boards a train south, to Atlanta University.

Chapter 4

When he arrives in Atlanta, a Pullman-car porter from the train helps him find a place to stay and shows him around the city. For the first time, the narrator encounters large groups of African Americans. The people he sees on the streets are of the lower socioeconomic classes, and he is repulsed by them. He also encounters segregation for the first time. As the two men share an unappetizing meal at a dirty restaurant, among the best that will serve "a coloured man," the porter points out that the narrator's skin color and features would enable him to go anywhere in town because no one would realize he was not white.

The next morning, the narrator hides his money in his trunk and sets out to find Atlanta University. There, he meets the president and several other new students, who seem more intelligent and desirable than the African Americans he saw in town. Eagerly, he returns to his room to fetch his trunk and begin college but finds his money has been stolen. He will not be able to pay his tuition. One of his roommates, another porter, suggests he head for Jacksonville, Florida, and find a job. He lends the narrator fifteen dollars, helps him get his trunk to the train station, and hides him in a closet for the twelve-hour ride.

Media Adaptations

- *The Autobiography of an Ex-Coloured Man* was adapted in 1996 as a sound recording on two audiocassettes, read by Allen Gilmore and accompanied by John Popoulous playing Scott Joplin piano tunes. It is available from MasterBuy.

Chapter 5

In Jacksonville, the narrator goes to work in a cigar factory, where he quickly works his way up to a well-paying job and supplements his income by giving piano lessons. At a public dance, he meets the porter who helped him get to Jacksonville; seeing his missing tie around the porter's neck, he realizes that it was the porter who stole his money in Atlanta. Characteristically, he does nothing about the situation other than observe its "ironical humour." In a few pages, he tells of observing the dance called the cake-walk, meeting and almost marrying a young schoolteacher, losing his job when the factory closes down, and heading back for New York.

This chapter includes a lengthy explanation of what the narrator has observed about African Americans. He divides them into three classes—the desperate class, the working-class servants, and middle and upper classes—and describes their strengths and weaknesses in broad terms. He is clearly drawn to the "better" classes of people and looks down upon the lower.

Chapters 6–8

In New York City, the narrator finds a vibrant African American culture. He visits nightclubs where he learns to gamble and where he hears ragtime music for the first time. Fascinated by the music, he learns to play it and soon becomes the best ragtime pianist in New York. He plays in a club that attracts white patrons out for an evening of "slumming," as well as black customers. One night, he meets a white millionaire, who becomes his friend and patron. The millionaire hires the narrator to play piano at his home, both for large crowds when he is entertaining and for the millionaire alone when he is simply bored and depressed. The narrator also makes the acquaintance of a wealthy white widow. Although she has a male friend, a well-to-do African American man, she flirts with the narrator. When her escort finds them chatting together at a club, he pulls out a handgun and kills her. The narrator flees the club and runs into the millionaire, who invites the narrator to accompany him on a trip to Europe the next day.

Chapter 9

The millionaire and the narrator spend several months in Paris and then in London and Berlin. Although the narrator travels as the millionaire's employee, his duties are few beyond playing the piano on the millionaire's whim. In exchange, he lives comfortably, is dressed in the latest fashions, and has plenty of pocket money to enjoy the clubs and theaters. Europe is remarkably free of racial prejudice, and the narrator is welcomed and treated as an equal wherever he goes. One day at the opera, he notices a young lady sitting next to him. Looking past her, he sees that the man accompanying her is his own father; this young girl must be his sister. He does not speak to them, but stumbles from the opera house, confused. He seeks solace in his music. The Europeans respond enthusiastically to ragtime, and the narrator gets the idea that he could make new arrangements of this and other African American musical forms to turn them into "higher" forms of art. When the millionaire tires of Berlin and is ready to move on, the narrator parts with him and boards a ship for New York.

Chapter 10

On the ship, the narrator spends several days discussing "the Negro question" with another passenger, a well-educated African American man. Back in the United States, the narrator continues the conversation with the Texan and the Northerners who share his train compartment. He concludes that opportunities for African Americans will not improve until whites change their attitudes. He embarks on a months-long trip through the rural South, where he meets African Americans of the poorer classes to learn their songs and "to catch the spirit of the Negro in his relatively primitive state." He is continually discouraged by the people he meets on this trip, disdainful of their poverty and lack of education. He also witnesses a lynching, something he had only heard rumors about. Refusing to stay where he will always be considered inferior, he heads again for New York.

Chapter 11

The narrator takes a clerking job, saves his money, invests in real estate, and eventually is able to mingle with the better social classes. His new friends assume he is white, and he does not correct them. When he meets a young woman and falls in love with her, he realizes that he must tell her about his heritage. At a museum one day, the couple runs into the narrator's old friend Shiny, who has become a college professor. Seeing the woman's apparent lack of prejudice when speaking with Shiny, the narrator tells her that he loves her and that he is black. She breaks off all contact with him. Months later, they meet again, and marry. During the birth of their second child, the young wife dies, leaving the narrator grief-stricken and regretting the choice he made to "pass." For the sake of his children, however, he will continue life as an ex-coloured man.

Characters

The Ex-Coloured Man

The ex-coloured man is the novel's narrator, who never reveals his name. At the novel's beginning, he says that the story he is about to tell will reveal his deepest secret, and it is in the interest of protecting those who would be affected by the secret that he gives no names—neither his own nor the names of those who pass through his life. The secret, as the novel's title hints, is that he is by the end of his story an African American man "passing" as a white man. In other words, his skin is light enough that no one who meets him suspects what he himself did not discover until he was nine years old: his mother is "colored" and his father is white. By the end of the novel, the narrator has married a white woman, fathered two children with her, and lived among white people who believe he is one of them. He maintains this secret for the sake of his children, although he has come to believe that giving up his heritage was a mistake, that he has sold his "birthright for a mess of pottage."

Throughout the novel, the narrator tells the story of his life. As a child in Connecticut, he attends a public school where white and black children seem to mingle rather effortlessly. As a high school graduate in the South, he finds that segregation is a stronger force, and that as a black man he will always be limited in his opportunities for education and career, as well as his options for forming social bonds. Later, he travels to New York City, where music helps bring white and black people together, and then to Europe, where the divisions between the races seem almost non-existent.

As he moves about, the narrator examines the African American people he meets, judging them harshly based on their education, their dialect, and their manners. He feels a strong preference for the "higher" classes of any race, and repulsion for rural and poor African Americans. When he falls in love with a white woman, who has assumed him to be a white man, he confesses his secret to her, marries her, and lives the rest of his life as a white man.

Father

The narrator of *The Autobiography of an Ex-Coloured Man* never knows his father's name. At the beginning of the book, when the boy and his mother are still living in Georgia, the father is just "a tall man with a small, dark moustache" who visits their small house a few evenings each week. He wears a gold watch and chain and has shiny black shoes. Normally, he gives the boy a coin but, on his last visit, gives him a ten-dollar gold piece to wear around his neck and hugs him. The next day, the boy and his mother move to Connecticut. When the boy is nine, he learns for the first time that his father is white and that his mother is not, but he does not yet know his father's identity. Three years later, when the man comes to visit in Connecticut, he learns that the tall man is his father.

The narrator's father is at this point about thirty-five years old. As the boy's mother explains, she and the man had fallen in love when she was the sewing girl for a wealthy family and the man was a college student home for vacation. Because of the racial and class differences, their love had to remain a secret. In fact, the man had sent the boy and his mother to Connecticut because he was about to marry a white woman of his own class. He has been sending the boy's mother money and a letter every month and has promised to help pay for the boy's college education. He does not fulfill this promise, though he does send the boy a new piano shortly after his visit. He breaks off contact with the boy and his mother before she dies.

The narrator sees his father only once more. One night in Paris, he sees his father with his wife and daughter at the opera, but does not speak to them. His father does not recognize him.

The First Pullman-car Porter

The first Pullman-car porter is one of several men who give the narrator advice on his travels. This man makes the narrator's acquaintance on the train on his first trip from Connecticut to Atlanta. Like the narrator, the porter is a student, working on the train between terms to pay for his tuition at a college in Nashville. He is the narrator's first guide in Atlanta, showing him to a boarding house and taking him to inexpensive restaurants that serve African Americans. The porter is the first to suggest to the narrator that his skin is so light he would be able to "pass" for white and eat at any restaurant in the city.

The Girl

The girl is a young woman, "white as a lily," whom the narrator meets in New York toward the end of his story, when his acquaintances assume him to be white. He is first attracted by her singing voice as she entertains at a party and then struck by her beauty. Mutual friends introduce them because of their shared interest in the music of Chopin, and he soon falls in love with her. When he decides to propose marriage, he realizes that he must tell her the truth about his race, but he is afraid. When they meet Shiny by chance and she betrays no hint of prejudice, he decides to tell her his secret. However, he does not get the reaction he had hoped for. She breaks down in tears and goes to visit relatives in New Hampshire for the summer, refusing to see him. In the fall, they meet again at a card party. The girl declares her love for him. They marry, move to Europe for a time, and settle into a happy married life. During the birth of the couple's second child, however, the girl dies.

The Millionaire

The millionaire is one of the white "slummers" who visits the Club in New York City where the narrator plays piano. He is "clean-cut, slender, but athletic-looking," graying at the temples, and with a clear aura of culture. He becomes the narrator's employer, patron, and friend, hiring him first to play piano at a single dinner party and then to be available to play for him at any time of the day or night. The millionaire throws lavish parties, attended by wealthy and beautiful people, but he spends his time at the parties sitting on the sidelines, watching his guests with what looks like boredom. The narrator recalls that he "grew weary of everything, and was always searching for something new."

The millionaire takes the narrator on a tour of Europe, in place of his valet. He intends to stay in Paris until he gets "tired of it," and after a little more than a year, they move to London and then to Berlin. The millionaire asks little of his companion except that he play the piano when asked; in exchange, he provides luxurious housing, fashionable clothing, and spending money. Tiring of Europe, he announces a plan to leave the next day for Egypt and Japan, but the narrator decides to return home instead. The millionaire tries to change his mind, pointing out that a black man in the United States will never be able to realize his full potential, as a musician or as a man.

Some critics have suggested that the millionaire is so comfortable with the company of the narrator and so understanding of his doubts about race and identity because he himself is an African American man "passing" as white. There is nothing in the text to clearly lead to this conclusion, nor to rule it out.

Mother

The narrator's mother, like the other characters in the novel, is never named. She earns her living as a seamstress and is so successful that she has to hire other women to help her keep up with demand. In the evenings, she plays the piano and sings hymns and old Southern songs. She teaches her son to play the piano, to read from her small library, and to do simple arithmetic. She does not seem to have friends but is cordial with the ladies who come to her home bringing sewing.

Mother is beautiful, at least in her son's eyes, with skin that is "almost brown," and hair that is "not as soft" as her son's. Until his revelation at school, however, the boy does not realize that his mother is not white. She has no other children and has never married because the love of her life is the white son of her former employer, a wealthy woman in Georgia. Their love is forbidden, and the man has had the boy and his mother moved to Connecticut so he can marry a white woman of his social class. The boy's mother looks forward to the man's monthly letters and believes his promises to provide for the boy's future. Remembering the day his father came to visit in Connecticut, the narrator comments "that was one of the happiest moments of her life." When she dies shortly after the narrator's graduation from high school, she has not heard from the boy's father for some time but still believes that he loves her and his son deeply.

Red Head

Red Head is the nickname the narrator gives to his closest friend at school, an older, awkward boy with freckles and red hair. Red Head is a slow student and has been kept back several times, so he is four or five years older than the narrator and in the same grade. The boys become friends during a spelling competition soon after the narrator begins school. When Red Head is unable to spell his first word, the narrator whispers the answer to him. By secretly helping him, the boy pulls Red Head

through the remaining years of school. On the day that the narrator learns he is "coloured," Red Head walks him home and shyly demonstrates that he intends to remain his friend. When the boys graduate from high school, the narrator and Shiny plan to attend college, but Red Head declares his intention to get a job in a bank instead. When the narrator leaves Connecticut for Atlanta, he gives a few of his books to Red Head and never mentions him again.

The Second Pullman-Car Porter

The second Pullman-car porter is another man who helps the narrator in Atlanta. He is one of four men who share the narrator's room at the boarding house—the room where the narrator's money and some of his clothes are stolen from his trunk. When the narrator discovers his loss, the second porter comes to his aid. He hides the narrator in a closet on the twelve-hour train trip to Jacksonville, Florida, and lends him fifteen dollars to hold him over until he finds work. Months later, after the narrator has achieved a stable income, he sees the porter again and approaches him so he can return the fifteen dollars. He notices then that the porter is wearing the tie that was stolen along with his money. He was the thief al all along. The narrator does not accuse him of the theft but enjoys the "ironical humour of the situation."

Shiny

Shiny is the casually racist name the narrator gives to a dark-skinned classmate whose "face was as black as night, but shone as though it were polished." The boy calls his dark-skinned friend names like Shiny Face, Shiny Eyes, and Shiny Teeth, and soon all the children—both light- and dark-skinned—refer to the child simply as Shiny. Shiny is universally acknowledged to be the smartest child in the class, the best at spelling, reading, and handwriting, and the hardest worker, and this record continues through high school. He is even chosen to give the speech at graduation, a task he completes admirably. Still, the narrator observes that Shiny is treated with less respect than less talented white students. After the narrator learns that he is "coloured," Shiny emerges as one of his only two close friends.

Toward the end of his story, the narrator and the white girl he will marry meet Shiny at a museum. Shiny is well-educated, cultured, and well-dressed and is a college professor on vacation in the North. As he and the narrator chat briefly, the narrator can tell that Shiny realizes that the girl at his side does not know that her escort is a black man, and Shiny says nothing to betray the secret. But seeing the woman's apparent lack of prejudice in her conversation with Shiny gives the narrator confidence to tell her himself.

Themes

Race Relations

The central theme of *The Autobiography of an Ex-Coloured Man* and the main obsession of its title character is the question of race in the United States at the end of the nineteenth and the beginning of the twentieth centuries. Specifically, the novel deals with the relationships between the white majority and the African American minority—no other racial or ethnic groups play important roles. The narrator is born shortly after the Civil War, which ended in 1865, and the country is newly in the process of deciding and discovering what the roles of African Americans (many of them recently freed from slavery) will be. As a man who lives part of his life in the white world and part of it in the "coloured," and one who lives in the North, in the South, and in Europe, the narrator is uniquely qualified to observe the issues from a variety of perspectives.

Several times, the narrator abandons his narrative to digress for a few pages on matters of race. In these didactic passages the narrator acknowledges that "it is a difficult thing for a white man to learn what a coloured man really thinks . . ." "I believe it to be a fact," he writes, "that the coloured people of this country know and understand the white people better than the white people know and understand them." Therefore, the narrator, a coloured man who has been brought up mainly among whites, sets out to study his people and share his understanding with his readers.

In Chapter 5 he separates African Americans into three classes "in respect to their relations with the whites," judging them with a cynical and detached eye. The lower classes, he points out, are desperate and angry and usually ignored; the "advanced element of the coloured race . . . carry the entire weight of the race question." In Chapter 9, during a discussion of the future of race relations in the United States, the millionaire urges the narrator to remain in Europe, because he "can imagine no more dissatisfied human being than an educated, cultured, and refined coloured man in the United States." And in Chapter 10, the narrator discusses

Topics for Further Study

- Research recent organizations and activities of people whose parents are of different races. How do multi-racial or "mixed race" people today see themselves differently than similar people a century ago? How are they treated differently by others?

- The narrator might have had a different sort of life if his parents had been permitted to marry, but Georgia society in the late nineteenth century could not accept white and black people marrying each other. How is their situation like and different from that of same-sex couples today who wish to marry?

- Compare the white audiences' fascination with ragtime music in *The Autobiography of an Ex-Coloured Man* with the ways in which white audiences today admire musical forms that have originated in African American culture.

- Research the history of Atlanta University, and the role of "traditionally black colleges" today.

- Research the history of the words "colored" and "Negro." How have their denotations and connotations changed?

race with an African American man on the ship to New York, and then in a train smoking car with a Jewish man, a Texan and an Ohio professor. Looking back on these conversations, the narrator concludes that racial problems "could be solved by the simple rules of justice."

The narrator, however, does not have the patience to wait for that solution. Never a courageous or aggressive man, he decides in the end that rather than wait for justice—and rather than join "that small but gallant band of coloured men who are publicly fighting the cause of their race"—he will live a "small and selfish" life as a white man.

Identity

The Autobiography of an Ex-Coloured Man is, in some ways, the story of a man trying to discover who he is. As the narrator travels around restlessly, examining and evaluating other people's lives, he is in search of something, though he does not realize what it is until the end of his story. He is looking for a consistent and holistic vision of himself. Sadly, his understandings come after he has made what he considers irrevocable decisions.

The world he lives in recognizes only two kinds of people—white and black—and has assigned him his role as a "coloured man" because his mother is "coloured." However, as the child of a white father, and as a man with light skin that white society accepts unquestioningly, he has some claim to both races. In the beginning of the novel, he assumes he is white, and casually makes fun of the African American children in his school. When he discovers that he is "coloured," he becomes a new person, or the same person in "another world," and although he stops teasing the dark-skinned children he feels "a very strong aversion to being classed with them." For the rest of the novel he will wrestle with his racial identity, resisting the label "coloured" and finding ways to distinguish himself from darker skinned, or more rural, or less well-off African Americans. In Paris, he can shed labels based on race, for in that city he is accepted simply for "the fact that I was an American." But back in the United States, he is treated differently as he travels, depending on whether or not his "identity as a coloured man [has] yet become known in the town." After witnessing the lynching, he decides to "neither disclaim the black race nor claim the white race," but to "let the world take me for what it would." In the end, he is a man with no identity so far as race is concerned. He feels sometimes that he has "never really been a Negro," and at other times that he has "sold [his] birthright for a mess of pottage."

The narrator's feelings are no less muddled in terms of his professional identity. His strongest passions, his most enjoyable moments, come from his music. Music provides his strongest bond to his late mother, to his millionaire friend, and to the woman he marries. From beginning to end, he recognizes, as others do, that playing music is his talent, his gift. Yet after the lynching, he plays music only at social events, and turns to real estate investment for his livelihood. In the end, he settles for money, leaving his musical career to become only "a vanished dream, a dead ambition, a sacrificed talent." If the ex-coloured man, now a successful businessman, plays for his own pleasure or is passing his love of music to his children, he does not think it important enough to mention.

Style

Point of View

As would be expected from a book that calls itself an autobiography, *The Autobiography of an Ex-Coloured Man* is told by a first-person narrator, or one who tells his own story from the "I" point of view. The first-person point of view is said to be "limited," in that the narrator can describe only things he has seen himself, with minor exceptions including the story his mother tells him about how she came to be involved with his father. An "omniscient," or all-seeing, narrator might reveal insights into actions of which the narrator is unaware; for example, an omniscient narrator looking at the story from the outside would know from the beginning where the narrator's missing four hundred dollars has gone, and might provide clues to the identity of the thief. The first-person narrator, on the other hand, does not know what people are doing when he is not with them, unless they tell him—which, of course, the thieving Pullman-car porter does not. In addition, a first-person narrator is limited in his understanding of others' feelings. Although the narrator of this novel believes that the day his father visited his mother in Connecticut "was one of the happiest moments of her life," he has only her smiles to base his judgment upon. Because the only emotions that can be expressed are the narrator's own, and because the narrator of this novel is particularly unemotional, critics have frequently commented on the remarkably flat tone of the narrator's voice in this novel.

It is easy to forget that this is a work of fiction, not a real autobiography, and the first-person narrator of the novel is a fictional character, not a true author and subject. The narrator of this novel is not speaking for Johnson, but rather is a "persona," a character created by Johnson. To increase potential sales, the novel was originally published anonymously, and most readers accepted it at face value, as a genuine autobiography. When Johnson acknowledged authorship fifteen years later, the first-person voice was so effective that readers still assumed the narrator was Johnson, describing his own life. To avoid being linked with his character, Johnson felt compelled to publish a real autobiography, *Along This Way*, in 1933.

Irony

Irony is broadly understood as a gap, or a "disconnect," between what seems to be true and what actually is true. Critics have long accepted *The Autobiography of an Ex-Coloured Man* as an example of dramatic irony, a situation in which the words given by a character—in this case, the narrator—carry a meaning that he does not perceive, but that the reader, looking over his shoulder, understands.

Most of the dramatic irony in the novel has to do with the narrator's treatment of race. When he is just a child, for example, he joins in the teasing of the dark-skinned children at his school, not realizing that he himself is "coloured." The reader has already guessed this truth, because of the novel's title, so the reader perceives the teasing differently than the boy does. But the narrator's ironic treatment of African Americans does not end when he discovers the truth about his own heritage. He is the one who gives Shiny his racist nickname, and he continues to use it to refer to his friend even when they are grown, successful men. Examples of the narrator's blindness to his own racism abound: He analyzes and labels African Americans in the South according to their economic status; he looks down on the customs and manners of poor rural African Americans; he does not like to see white women in the company of African American men, though he himself marries a white woman; he declares African American women to be beautiful only if their skin is relatively light; he accepts the idea that European music is "art" while African American music is not. The fact that he recognizes American racism when it affects him directly, but perpetuates many of its myths and stereotypes himself without realizing it, is an illustration of dramatic irony.

Realism

Toward the end of the nineteenth century, the literary movement known as Realism emerged as a response to the Romanticism that had dominated the Victorian period. Novels of Realism aimed to capture life as it really is, rather than emphasizing fantasy and the imagination as the Romantics had done. The Realists believed in the value of the normal and the everyday, telling the stories of recognizable characters whose actions had predictable consequences. Politically, the Realists hoped to work toward democracy and equality, rather than flattering upper class or even royal characters.

The Autobiography of an Ex-Coloured Man is typical in many ways of the novels of Realism. Its central character is meant to be seen as a representation of a man of mixed race at the turn of the twentieth century. Although the choices he makes are his own, his experiences and the people he meets are believable and recognizable. There are no dramatic plot twists, passionate outbursts or mysteries, but only events that might happen in a normal life, and the natural consequences of those events. The conflicts faced by the narrator are mostly internal, dealing with moral choices. Realism works to bring people together through the experience of reading, and in fact the novel was heralded as a tool for white people to gain a better understanding of their African American neighbors. In 1912, the movement known as Realism gave Johnson a base from which to create one of the first realistic portraits of African American life for a wide white readership.

Historical Context

Slave Narratives

During the middle of the nineteenth century, a number of biographies and memoirs written by slaves who had won their freedom were published in the North as part of the Abolition movement, the effort to ban slavery in the United States. These were typically the stories of people who had been born into slavery in the South, and who managed to make their way to the Northern states and a new life. The very act of writing a book, and of stating an articulate case for the intelligence and strength of African Americans, was an important tool in the struggle to end slavery in the United States, because it showed that freed slaves had the mental capacity to function independently. Publishers knew that most readers of these narratives would be white, because they made up most of the literate and book-buying public, and so the narrative voices addressed themselves directly to a white audience. The most well-known of these narratives is *A Narrative of the Life of Frederick Douglass, An American Slave*, published in 1845. Most white readers in the North would have acquired their most vivid images of African Americans either from these slave narratives or from novels by white authors, including Harriet Beecher Stowe's *Uncle Tom's Cabin* (1852).

Many of the slave narratives feature common structures and scenes that Johnson adapted in creating *The Autobiography of an Ex-Coloured Man*. For example, many begin with the main characters living in a state of relative calm and innocence until a startling event makes them realize their true condition. Learning to read, and then studying the Bible and other books, is an important part of their awakening. Poignant scenes describe separation

Compare & Contrast

- **1910s:** Only two books by African Americans—both autobiographies—have a wide readership among both white and black audiences.

  Today: Many of the United States's bestselling authors are African American or members of other ethnic minorities.

- **1910s:** White and black people are forbidden by law from marrying each other in most states.

  Today: Since 1967, no state in the United States forbids interracial marriage.

- **1910s:** White and black people in large cities in the North come together to listen to ragtime music, a product of African American culture.

  Today: White and black people in most parts of the country share an appreciation for hip hop and rap music, products of African American culture.

- **1910s:** In what will be called the Great Migration, African Americans move from the rural South to the cities in the North. Between 1890 and 1930, more than two million make this move.

  Today: The Great Migration is reversing, especially among the middle class. African Americans with enough economic stability move in large numbers to cities in the South.

---

from family, through death or another tragic event. Narrators address their readers directly, pointing out injustices and hypocrisies. Brief anecdotes describe other broad types of African Americans, and explain the conditions that lead to their successes and failures. Humorous scenes demonstrate how the slaves deceived and tricked their masters. Often, a sympathetic white character takes the narrator in hand, offering financial assistance and guiding him or her through the complexities of the world of freedom.

Johnson knew that his readers would be familiar with the slave narrative form, and with the successful 1901 autobiography by Booker T. Washington, *Up from Slavery*. This, and the fact that there was no established market for novels by African Americans, led Johnson to present his novel in the form of an autobiography.

Racial Inequality and Mutual Ignorance

Although slavery had ended with the end of the Civil War in 1865, life for African Americans was still difficult more than fifty years later, when Johnson was writing *The Autobiography of an Ex-Coloured Man*. Progress was slow, in large part because white and black people knew very little about each other beyond broad stereotypes. The hardships described in the novel are not fictional. African Americans could not eat or sleep in public accommodations throughout much of the United States; they could not attend most public schools or colleges; they were denied many jobs, and were paid less than white people for the work they did. Many black men were denied the vote (no women of any race could vote in national elections until 1919). As the novel demonstrates, there were differences between the North, where the narrator's elementary school enrolls white and black children, and the South, where white and black people live essentially separate lives. But even in New York City, where whites might go "slumming" and visit African American clubs, African Americans did not enter white night clubs except as service workers and entertainers.

Johnson himself had lived a relatively comfortable middle-class life. His parents were never slaves, and held good jobs, and Johnson was a college graduate. He became part of a small black intellectual movement that worked in the early part of the twentieth century to gain equality for African Americans. Their leaders included Booker T. Washington, who believed that African Americans should achieve economic security independent of whites, and W.E.B. Du Bois, one of the founders in 1909 of the National Association for the Advancement of Colored People (NAACP), who worked for African Americans to be accepted as equals alongside whites. As African Americans began migrating from rural areas of the South to the Northern cities, looking for better jobs and better housing, these intellectuals steered the national conversation in a direction that would ultimately focus on the needs of the new urban black population. A decade after Johnson published *The Autobiography of an Ex-Coloured Man*, the energetic New York City he described would burst into an exciting flame of creativity in the period known as the Harlem Renaissance.

Ragtime and the Cakewalk

One of the most popular new musical styles to emerge at the end of the nineteenth century was called ragtime. The name comes from the "ragged" or syncopated rhythms of the music, written in 2/4 time. In the 1890s, ragtime grew out of traditional rhythms out of Africa brought by people who came to the United States as slaves, and was shaped by minstrel shows, "coon songs," and vaudeville. The first performers were itinerant African American piano players who traveled around the South. The Chicago World's Fair featured a gathering of ragtime musicians, and ragtime attracted a large white following there and in New York City. The most important writer of original ragtime compositions was Scott Joplin, who worked in Chicago. The sheet music to his tune "Maple Leaf Rag" was the first American instrumental piece to sell one million copies. By 1917, when Joplin died, ragtime was losing its popularity, but its influences were felt in an emerging musical form—jazz.

The earliest ragtime compositions were written as dance music, to accompany an existing dance called the cakewalk. The cakewalk came from Florida plantations in the 1850s, when slaves there adapted steps they learned from Seminole Indians, and added movements they remembered from African dances. The cakewalk is performed by pairs of men and women, dressed in their finest, and imitating in a stylized manner a dignified promenade by high-society white couples. On some Southern plantations, owners would stage dancing contests between their slaves, and award a cake as a prize. Later, black minstrels or white performers in "black face" performed the cakewalk in concert halls. By the 1890s, the dance had become popular with white dancers also, the first dance step to make that transition.

Pullman Porter John Baptist Ford in uniform
© Bettmann/Corbis

Critical Overview

When first released in 1912, *The Autobiography of an Ex-Coloured Man* was published by a small firm, and the market for books by and about African Americans was small; it did not sell well or attract much critical attention. Reviewers debated whether the book was fact or fiction and how realistic its story was. In 1913, Brander Matthews included *The Autobiography* in an analysis of "Three Books Which Depict the Actualities of Present-Day Life" for *Munsey's Magazine*. Writing for a white audience, Matthews recommended the book for all "who want to understand our fellow citizens of darker hue." He wondered whether the anonymous story should be considered fiction or "an actual record of fact," and concluded that it "contains what is higher than actual fact, the essential truth." The *Nashville American*, a daily newspaper, accepted the book as fiction, "unhampered by respect of the verities and excited by hate," and called its treatment of white women "outrageous."

Since the novel's reissue in 1927, when Johnson claimed authorship and the work was accepted as fictional realism, it has never been out of print. The central critical question since then has been how one should approach the narrator: Is he a tragic figure, brought to an unhappy choice by an unjust world, or a weak one who makes poor choices because of his own character flaws? Robert A. Bone, in his 1958 study *The Negro Novel in America*, was one of the first to attribute the narrator's ultimate choice to his own failings. Bone acknowledged that the narrator is "overpowered by life," but refers to his "moral cowardice" and calls him "a symbol of man's universal failure to fulfill his highest destiny." Dickson D. Bruce Jr., on the other hand, finds in *Black American Writing from the Nadir* that the narrator's attempts to find his identity among the African American communities he visits "are failures not because of his weakness or blindness but because they increase his sense of the separation of the races."

Another issue for critics has been the unemotional and nondescriptive style of the narrator. Early critics, including Bone, tended to see this as a result of Johnson's unsuccessful attempts to merge fiction with a political agenda. Howard Faulkner, writing in *Black American Literature Forum* in 1985, disagrees, arguing that the ex-coloured man's "inability to feel deeply what is happening to him and to put those events in perspective" is not a failure of the author's narrative skills, but a demonstration of what happens to a character who has been "destroyed from within."

Criticism in the 1990s and beyond has focused on what the novel suggests about race itself, as suggested by the title of a 1996 Martin Japtok essay, "Between 'Race' as Construct and 'Race' as Essence: *The Autobiography of an Ex-Coloured Man*." Roxanna Pisiak, in *Studies in American Fiction*, explores Johnson's themes of the ambiguity of the color line, and the ways in which language shapes our attitudes about race.

Criticism

Cynthia Bily

Bily teaches English at Adrian College in Adrian, Michigan. In this essay, Bily examines the narrator's sexual ambiguity in The Autobiography of an Ex-Coloured Man.

Most readers in the twenty-first century will see something in *The Autobiography of an Ex-Coloured Man* that James Weldon Johnson, the novel's author, could not: A solution to the narrator's struggles with his divided self could be in his simple refusal to be divided. In other words, if he

were alive today he would not need to choose between being a "coloured man" and a "white man." He could recognize, as we do today, that our concepts of race have no basis in biology, that our concept of race is socially, not biologically, constructed. According to this way of thinking, most people are not simply "white" or "black" or "Asian," but exist somewhere along a spectrum of racial identity. The truth about racial identity in the United States, three hundred years after the first slaves were brought to this country, is that a large percentage of Americans could call themselves "multi-racial," or "bi-racial" or "mixed." This does not change the fact that in his own time Johnson's narrator does not have "mixed" available to him as a category to slip into. Although terms such as "mulatto" and "octaroon" were used to describe certain persons of mixed heritage, people with these labels were not accepted into "white" society, and that is where the power was. As the Texan in the smoking car crudely explains it, "it's a question of white man or nigger, no middle ground." The fact that we read the narrator's situation differently than he did—that we can envision a middle ground that did not exist a hundred years ago—is one of the joys of reading novels from earlier times.

Just as we see matters of race differently than people did a hundred years ago, so has our thinking about sex and gender undergone a transformation. Most people today are not as comfortable as people once were with traditional notions of men and women having natural differences in abilities, responsibilities, talents, needs and strengths. Rather than seeing "male" and "female" as distinct categories, some critics called "feminist critics" or "gender critics" have explored the idea that masculinity and femininity are points along a spectrum. Science again shapes our re-thinking, as those studying human genetics tell us that two sexes are not enough to account for all the biological varieties of humans. Sociologists point out that matters of sexual attraction and sexual behavior vary from culture to culture. So while most people will fit somewhat comfortably into the sexual category to which their society assigns them, others will seek a "middle ground" that may or may not be available to them.

In his dealings with women, the narrator seems confused, blocked. Consistently, he feels physical attraction only for women he cannot have. His first love, when he is eleven, is a seventeen-year-old white girl, a violinist from church whom he will accompany in a recital. On reflection, the narrator realizes it was not her playing that aroused his interest, but something having to do with "her eyes almost closing, the escaping strands of her dark hair wildly framing her pale face, and her slender body swaying to the tones." The attraction is physical, sexual, and yet he feels it for someone he can never really have a relationship with, because of the differences in their ages and because the young woman is white. He directs the energy of his passion into such safe outlets as playing the piano and writing poetry, but keeps his love a secret. Looking back on this experience years later, having lost his wife, the narrator describes his love of the violist in passionate terms: "at no time of life is love so pure, so delicious, so poetic, so romantic, as it is in boyhood."

The next woman the narrator is physically attracted to is also unavailable to him. She is the rich widow in the "Club" in New York, "an exceedingly beautiful woman of perhaps thirty-five; she had glistening copper-colored hair, very white skin . . ." This woman is an unsuitable match for the narrator, not only because she is white (and he himself never becomes comfortable with the sight of a white woman escorted by a black man), but also because she is already in a relationship with someone else. The narrator is perceptive enough to see that the widow lavishes attention on him only to make her lover jealous, and yet he continues to spend time with her, rather than seeking out some of the other women in the "Club" who make "no secret of the fact that they admired me as much as they did my playing." Of course, this ends badly, with the widow being murdered and the narrator being forced to flee New York under the protection and guidance of the millionaire.

Only once more does the narrator fall under the spell of a woman's beauty. At the opera in Paris he finds himself sitting next to a young woman "so young, so fair, so ethereal, that I felt to stare at her would be a violation." He strains to hear her every word. He glances at her secretly, and each time his "heart leaped into [his] throat." Again, it is not to be—the young woman is his sister. Again he experiences a physical attraction for a woman who can not return it.

Surprisingly, the narrator does not devote much attention to women who might be thought of as suitable matches. After the violinist, the narrator does not mention any other flirtations during his high school years, Perhaps he is too involved with his music, and with his ailing mother, to be interested in a girlfriend. When he gets to Atlanta and meets his future classmates at the University for the

> In the language of gender critics, the narrator bears some of the markers of a 'male-identified male.' This does not mean that he desires sexual intimacy with men, but rather that most of his emotional energy is directed toward other men; he seeks out male companionship rather than female; he feels more comfortable with men than with women."

first time, he seems more interested in the men than in the women. His description of the girls, many so light-skinned they seemed to be white, is noticeably tepid: "many of the girls, with black eyes and wavy dark hair, were decidedly pretty." He uses much stronger language in admiration of the men: "many of the blackest were fine specimens of young manhood, tall, straight, and muscular, with magnificent heads. . . ." During three years in Jacksonville, he attends dances and parties on the weekends, and presumably meets young women there, but none strike him as worth mentioning until he meets a young schoolteacher and begins "to have dreams of matrimonial bliss." The young woman's appearance is never described, and the narrator betrays no special feelings for her. When the cigar factory where he works is shut down suddenly, even though he "was beginning to plan about marrying the young school-teacher," he chooses to leave for New York. Thinking about New York, "all at once a desire like a fever" strikes the narrator—a feeling stronger than any he has apparently felt for his intended bride. He does not ask her to accompany him.

In New York, he meets many women at the night clubs and dinner parties he attends, but shows no interest in any of them (with the exception of the widow). In Paris, he meets "good-looking,

What Do I Read Next?

- Johnson's most famous and most successful book is *God's Trombones: Seven Negro Sermons in Verse* (1927). The poems in this volume, written in the dialect and rhythm of Southern African American preachers, deal with good and evil in a sinful world.

- In 1933, Johnson published *Along This Way: The Autobiography of James Weldon Johnson*, a reflective and detailed account of his fascinating and varied life. The volume includes nineteen photographs of Weldon and his family and friends.

- Wallace Thurman's novel *The Blacker the Berry* (1929) was the first novel to explore prejudice within the African American community against those of darker skin. Emma Lou Brown's journey to New York City echoes the Ex-Coloured Man's in her enjoyment of the night life but is different because her acceptance is affected by her dark skin.

- Zadie Smith's debut novel *White Teeth* (2000) explores the life of a bi-racial woman in London. The novel, which treats serious themes with a great deal of humor, won Great Britain's Whitbread Award for a first novel.

- Jillian A. Sim's essay "Fading to White," originally published in *American Heritage Magazine* (1999), tells the story of the author's discovery of a family secret: that her great-grandmother was an African American woman who spent most of her career after college "passing" as white.

- In *Who Is Black?: One Nation's Definition* (1991), F. James Davis examines the implications of the "one drop rule," by which any person with the smallest amount of black ancestry is classified as black. As Davis explains, this rule applies only in the United States and only for African Americans—there is no similar rule for Asians, Latinos or other groups.

---

well-dressed young women," but he wants nothing from them except language lessons. On his travels through the South he stays with different families, but does not even mention any women, except for those at the revival meeting, where he notices women "immaculate in starched stiff white dresses adorned with ribbons." The word "immaculate" is revealing, meaning "flawless" or "without sin"—hardly a term one uses to describe the object of one's desires.

In the language of gender critics, the narrator bears some of the markers of a "male-identified male." This does not mean that he desires sexual intimacy with men, but rather that most of his emotional energy is directed toward other men; he seeks out male companionship rather than female; he feels more comfortable with men than with women. In Jacksonville, he mentions that "several of the men at the factory were my intimate friends. . . ." In New York he spends his evenings gambling and smoking with groups of men, and women are incidental

to these excursions. Parting from the millionaire, the narrator remembers him fondly as "the man who was . . . the best friend I ever had, except my mother, the man who exerted the greatest influence ever brought into my life, except that exerted by my mother."

It is fair to question whether these attractions are really significant. After all, many people feel their first love as the strongest. The narrator cannot know in advance that the women who catch his eye will be unattainable. However, it is important to remember that these events are not being narrated in real time, but as memories. The narrator has lived his life, and is telling his story looking back. The words he chooses to describe people, then, are not the spontaneous words of an instant. Reflecting on his life, the narrator sees some old images more clearly than others, and the women whose physical attractions are the most vivid for him are those women he could never have.

In New York again, the narrator finally finds the woman he will marry, and all of his issues over women and attraction come together in one person. She is undeniably beautiful, "almost tall and quite slender, with lustrous yellow hair and eyes so blue as to appear almost black. . . . Indeed she seemed to me the most dazzlingly white thing I had ever seen." But the narrator takes pains to explain that it is her voice, not her beauty, that attracts him; he does not even notice her until she began to sing. As a white woman, she is unattainable, even though the narrator's new acquaintances assume he also is white. Although he is no longer a child, but a man who has traveled abroad, nearly married and held several important jobs, he can not approach her, but resorts to the feelings and mannerisms of "the bashful boy of fourteen."

The narrator comes to realize that if he is ever to escape the millionaire's boredom and achieve something like a normal life, he will have to stop living in the "middle ground" that a black man "passing" as white inhabits, and reveal his secret. If he wishes to raise a family, he must step out of that "middle ground" of the male-identified male and commit to a woman. And so he does. But even attaining the unattainable does not make this man happy. During their brief marriage he lives in "constant fear that she would discover in me some shortcoming." And then she dies, and the narrator withdraws from society. He has no wife, no male friends, no people of his own.

Life in the early twentieth century was hard on people who did not fit well into their assigned roles. Multi-racial people, regardless of their intelligence or talent, faced limited opportunities in a white-dominated country. And men and women who did not fit neatly into their assigned gender roles also struggled to find ways to fit in. In the twenty-first century people in the United States have more choices, more acceptable roles and ways to contribute, regardless of their race, or gender, or faith, or ability, in no small part because of the work of those men the narrator admires, "who are publicly fighting the cause of their race." It is important to read novels of days gone by, so that we can celebrate how far we have come and contemplate the work we still have to do.

Source: Cynthia Bily, Critical Essay on *The Autobiography of an Ex-Coloured Man*, in *Novels for Students*, Thomson Gale, 2006.

Alessandro Portelli

In the following essay excerpt, Portelli examines how Johnson both confirms and complicates the "color line" in The Autobiography of an Ex-Coloured Man.*

Significations

> I laughed heartily over what struck me as the capital joke I was playing. —JAMES WELDON JOHNSON, *The Autobiography of an Ex-Coloured Man*

In the beginning of James Weldon Johnson's *The Autobiography of an Ex-Coloured Man,* we are told that this is going to be the story of a joke. In summing up the motives that led him to write the story, the first-person narrator says, "I find a sort of savage and diabolical desire to gather up all the little tragedies of my life, and turn them into a practical joke on society."

Let us start with a joke, then. The ex-colored man laughs because his success as a white man is enough to "disprove the theory that one drop of Negro blood renders a man unfit"; on the other hand, that drop still defines him to himself, an ex-ed colored man, a colored man under erasure whose identity is defined by the identity he thinks he has shaken off. So let us listen to another joke—a little folk tale about the unshakability of identity.

> Two men walk down the street. One of them is a humpback. As they walk, they talk. Turning a corner, they find themselves in front of a synagogue.

> One of them, the "straight" one, sighs deeply, turns to the humpback, and says, "You know, I once was a Jew." The humpback sighs back, and says: "I know, I know. I, too, once was a humpback."

W. E. B. DuBois had prophetically announced in 1903 that "the problem of the twentieth century is the problem of the color line." Less than ten years later, James Weldon Johnson both confirmed and complicated that statement. On the one hand, by writing a novel about the color line, he confirmed its tragic importance; on the other hand—and this is where the joke lies—he made that line greatly problematic. In a complex game of hide-and-seek, Johnson in one motion drew the line and blurred (*ex*-ed) it to the point that, the harder one looks for it, the harder it is to locate. Yet, invisible and powerful, it's there, like the invisible, tragic hump in the old Jewish joke: you can call yourself an ex-Colored Man, or an ex-Jew, but you can no more discard the burden of cultural identity than the cripple can discard the hump on his back.

In his recent revision of Sterling Brown's image of the "Tragic Mulatto," Werner Sollors points out that "in many cases literary Mulattos were able to cross racial boundaries that were considered fixed, real, or even natural. This ability is what made

> From the very first page, Johnson's text plays a threefold game of signifying: on the racial discourse of racial boundaries; on the literary discourse of the tragic mulatto; on DuBois's political discourse of the color line."

them such ideal questioners of the status quo." This is precisely what Johnson's formulation does: he downplays the tragedy (as in *tragic* Mulatto), and he foregrounds the ironic transgression (literally, boundary-crossing) in the form of the joke. Yet, he also reminds us that the mulatto's ironic crossing would be meaningless without the shadow of the tragedy: just as the mulatto needs to evoke the line in order to cross it (to evoke his "colored" identity in order to erase it), likewise, to play his joke, Johnson needs to evoke and exorcise the tragedy.

This takes place a number of times in the text. For instance, a potentially typical tragic-Mulatto situation arises when the narrator, at a performance of Gounod's *Faust* in Paris, finds himself sitting next to his unknowing white half-sister. "I felt," he writes, "an almost uncontrollable impulse to rise up and scream to the audience: 'Here, here in your very midst, is a tragedy, a real tragedy!'" (*Autobiography*). And yet, although his "feelings [are] divided," he does nothing. While the tragic show goes on on the stage, the potentially tragic hero stumbles out of the theater and never mentions the episode again in his narrative.

The theatrical, and therefore implicitly contrived connotation of *tragedy* already visible in this scene is underlined by the author's definition of himself as a "spectator." This is in fact the role that he plays as he narrates, with an abundance of visual detail, the two most actually tragic episodes in the story: the killing of a widow by a jealous lover (in an interracial love story in which, however, race is ostensibly not a motive); and the lynching that scares him into finally passing for white. The word "tragic" is not used in the representation of either of these tragedies.

We find it, instead, again with theatrical connotations, in two passages in which it is linked to the comic. One is the story of the minstrel with the big mouth who carried in his heart a burning ambition to be a "tragedian." His failure to make people take him seriously is so sad that, indeed, in real life "he did play a part in a tragedy." This episode is so important that it later becomes a paradigm for the quandary of black intellectuals, including himself, and the black middle class as a whole. All black people, the narrator remarks, are fixed in comic stereotypes: "A novel dealing with coloured people who lived in respectable homes and amidst a fair degree of culture and who naturally acted 'just like white folks' would be taken in a comic-opera sense. In this respect the Negro is much in the position of a great comedian who gives up the lighter roles to play tragedy."

In the next move, however, the narrator complicates the line he has just drawn between tragedy and comedy. "In the same respect," he remarks, "the public is not too much to be blamed, for great comedians are far more scarce than mediocre tragedians; every amateur actor is a tragedian." Once again, his feelings are as divided as his ancestry. While he resents black exclusion from the serious art of tragedy, he suggests that the seriousness of black culture may be couched in the joke.

The essential black practical joke and serious criticism of life is called, as we know, *signifyin'*. From the very first page, Johnson's text plays a threefold game of signifying: on the racial discourse of racial boundaries; on the literary discourse of the tragic mulatto; on DuBois's political discourse of the color line. Yet, there may be more: he may also be signifying on the values and texts of the dominant culture at large. In this sense, it might pay to read *The Autobiography of an Ex-Coloured Man* not only in the context of DuBois and Frances Harper, but also in that of his contemporaries, Henry James or Edith Wharton.

The ex-colored man's practical joke on society may or may not allude to Melville's Ishmael's sense that "this strange *mixed* [my italics] affair we call life" is nothing but "a vast practical joke." Yet, there is a curious symmetry, a shared symbolic ground. Ishmael feels that life's joke is upon him, while Johnson's narrator is the perpetrator of the joke on society; but they both share a keen sense of existential absurdity (Ishmael ends his musings by drawing up his will; Johnson's narrator ends his story by lamenting the loss of his heritage).

Again, one hears artfully distorted echoes of the literary canon when reading, "My mother and

I lived together in a little cottage" in New England, where the outcast and unwed mother "was kept very busy with her sewing." When we hear that once a month "she received a letter," the impulse to capitalize that "A" is hard to resist—not because this may be the intention of the text, but because it is another way to remind us that what is going on in that cottage is, although apparently normal, potentially tragic.

These are one reader's inferences. On the other hand, it is a fact that Johnson's narrator is not unfamiliar with the white American canon, as shown by his reference to Mark Twain (another very serious comedian and the author of a comic novel called a "tragedy" on the color line: *Pudd'nhead Wilson*). That Johnson is bent on signifying on white discourse is also made clear by the scene in which the narrator, passing for white, listens unrecognized to the white conversation on race in the segregated parlor car. This is a classic motif in turn-of-the-century African-American literature, and its power lies in the fact that it can be seen not only as a figuration of the absurdity of segregation but also as a metaphor for the presence of the black reader in the white text. The fact that this white discourse is reported by the silent and invisible black narrator is also a figure for the ironic bent that the white discourse takes on when it is filtered by the black voice.

The joke, indeed, is already intimated by the title: *Autobiography* implies a pact of referential veracity with the reader, but then the book is a work of fiction. Or, as Philippe Lejeune suggests, the genre "autobiography" is predicated on the coincidence of the names of the author, the narrator, and the main character—who in this case have no names at all. Of course, the truly savage joke is in the rest of the title—*Ex-Coloured Man*. In a society of rigid biologic boundaries in black and white, how can a colored man become an ex? Once we establish this possibility, no one is safe, no identity is sure.

Let us then go back to that little New England cottage, a "place of purity and safety" created by a mother's arms. This may very well be a late-Victorian cliché of the sanctity of maternal love and affection, and probably is—but what are we to make of the fact that this particular mother—like Hester Prynne—is unmarried and therefore, in the same Victorian cult of sainted motherhood, certainly not a paradigm of "purity"? Johnson's text situates itself on the boundary of indecision generated by this ambivalence: not just between black

and white but also between piety and transgression, between middle-class uplift and popular cultural defiance—between the generation of Frances Harper and that of Claude McKay.

Does this ironic image of purity resonate in the tradition of Harriet Jacobs's statement that southern black women cannot be measured against the standards of conventional society, or does it suggest that there is a type of purity that has nothing to do with sexual mores—or does it mean that *purity* is itself a moot concept in a novel of mixing and passing?

All That Glitters

> I have a dim recollection of several people who moved in and about this little house, but I have a distinct mental image of only two: one, my mother; and the other, a tall man with a small, dark moustache. I remember his shoes or boots were always shiny, and that he wore a gold chain and a great gold watch with which he was always willing to let me play. (*Autobiography*)

This passage, quite early in Johnson's text, introduces the figure that is the cornerstone of tragic mulatto stories, the white father. Rather than as an obsession, however, the paternal image is only a dim recollection; a later encounter generates but little emotion. The meaning of this passage is to suggest one side of the double heritage that the narrator derives from his mixed descent. The black heritage, as we learn in the next page, is represented by his mother's piano and by the talent that will make him a black musician (with a "particular fondness for the black keys"); the white side is represented by his father's shoes, a metaphor of inheritance; by the gold that will make a successful white businessman; and by the "shine" that throws an ambiguous bridge between the inheritance of gold and the inheritance of blackness.

I will return later to the gold. First, I would like to follow the variations that Johnson plays on "shine" throughout the first chapter. "It became my appointed duty," he goes on, "whenever he came to bring him a pair of slippers and to put the shiny shoes in a particular corner; he often gave me in turn for the service a bright coin. . . ." Shine, the eponymous hero of black toasts and signifying, is also a slangy synonym for African-Americans. This is the sense in which the word is picked up a few pages later, when the narrator describes his best friend, a bright black boy, exactly in the same terms as his father's shoes.

> His face was black as night, but shone as though it were *polished* [my italics]; he had sparkling eyes, and

when he opened his mouth, he displayed glistening white teeth. It struck me at once to call him "Shiny Face," or "Shiny Eyes," or "Shiny Teeth," and I spoke of him often by one of these names to the other boys. These terms were finally merged into "Shiny."

Just in case we missed the implications, the author gives the reader the source of these images—ironically, a mocking racist rhyme sung by white children (including the narrator, who thinks he's white) to their black schoolmates:

Nigger, nigger, never die,
Black face and shiny eye.

"My admiration," he writes, "was almost equally divided between the watch chain and the shoes." All that shines is not gold; indeed, the symbolic web is rather intricate and all its terms are "divided." "Shiny" is both a racist slur and a term of endearment. The shoes are both a metaphor of his white father's inheritance and a bright object of blackness—polished black skin, like Shiny's face. Polishing blackness seems to be one of the narrator's missions in life, culminating in his project of polishing black music into classical form. The inheritance of gold, finally, is both a possession and a "chain," an essentially flawed gift that becomes a burden:

I remember how I sat upon his knee and watched him laboriously drill a hole through a ten-dollar gold piece, and then tie the coin around my neck with a string. I have worn that piece around my neck the greater part of my life, and still possess it, but more than once I have wished that some other way had been found of attaching it to me besides putting a hole through it.

Passages

The Autobiography of an Ex-Coloured Man is a double tale of immersion and emersion. Starting from New England, the hero immerses himself in the black world of the South, emerges into New York and Europe, then plunges back into the Deep South to do folklore research, and finally finds refuge from fear in wealth and whiteness. The text hinges on two dramatic passages from one race to another, two dramatic initiations to, and one flight from, blackness.

The first passage coincides with the sudden discovery of his own conventional and institutional blackness. "That day," he writes, "was wrought the miracle of my transition from one world into another; for I did indeed pass into another world." As Sollors points out, Johnson subverts the conventional use of *passing,* by designating a passage from white to black rather than vice-versa. Thus, while he does not belittle the brutal suddenness of the

revelation and its impact on the narrator as a child, this episode is more in the vein of comedy than literary tragedy.

On one day near the end of my second term at school the principal came into our room and, after talking to the teacher, for some reason said: "I wish all the white scholars to stand for a moment." I rose with the others. The teacher looked at me and, calling my name, said: "You sit down and rise with the others." I did not quite understand her, and questioned: "Ma'am?" She repeated, with a softer tone in her voice: "You sit down, and rise with the others." I sat down dazed. (*Autobiography*)

This anecdote is another of the many "jokes" included in the novel. It is part of a family of humorous narratives that circulate, orally and in writing, in different traditions, in which the humor derives more from the brazen suddenness of the revelation than from the racial contents. It is also a revision of the beginning of DuBois's *The Souls of Black Folk.* "In a wee wooden schoolhouse" in New England, DuBois recalls in the very first page of his book, he participated in a children's game of exchanging visiting cards, "till one girl, a tall newcomer, refused my card—refused it peremptorily, with a glance." In this way, DuBois tells his discovery of his own blackness and prefaces the memorable passage on double-consciousness and the veil—a passage to which the ex-colored man also refers when he describes the impact of the discovery on himself.

The episode inflicts also on Johnson's narrator a wound "which was years in healing" (*Autobiography*). Rather than DuBois's dark sense of being locked into place, walled-in in a "prison-house" of blackness, however, he experiences a loss of place, and is dazed. Johnson's narrator is driven not to a philosophical revision of the meaning of blackness, but to a physical revision of his own mirror image (another topos in black literature, but not in DuBois). More importantly, while DuBois must face the discovery and its consequences by himself, the ex-colored man finds refuge and consolation in the arms of his mother. Even the tall white girl who spurns DuBois (there may be a suggestion of a sentimental rejection here, too) reappears in Johnson's novel as the older (and implicitly taller) girl with "dark hair" and "pale face" with whom the boy falls in love and plays music while she "laughingly encouraged" him.

Though painful, this passage into blackness generates no overwhelming need for the narrator to confront his white father, nor does he pine for the white world as he lives his life as a black man.

Racial identity is not a life-or-death concern to him, to the possibly mixed-blood Cubans with whom he associates in the cigar industry in Jackson, to the white sponsor who takes him to Europe, nor even to his fiancée. Unlike Rena in Charles Chesnutt's *The House Behind the Cedars,* who is brought to death by her fiancé's rejection after he discovers her racial identity, here the girl overcomes her initial shock and returns to marry him. All this implies that the barriers that made for tragedy in conventional imagination and literary formulae are not as all-important and as impassable as they are said to be.

The narrator's plunge into blackness, indeed, is clinched less by the loss of identity than by the loss of his money, and is therefore as much a matter of class as it is of race. When his money is stolen in Atlanta, he begins his picaresque journey into the world of the black working class, black "society," and the black underworld. In fact, the chapters that tell this story hinge upon a remarkable contradiction. As a character immersed in the black world, he spends and gambles his money freely; but as a narrator, who tells the story after he has already passed for white and contracted the "money fever," he accounts for it carefully, dollar by dollar. On the one hand, he writes

I was a hail fellow well met with all the workmen at the factory, most of whom knew little and cared less about social distinctions. From their example I learned to be careless about money, and for that reason I constantly postponed and finally abandoned returning to Atlanta University. It seemed impossible for me to save as much as two hundred dollars.

On the other hand, accounting for money, his own and other people's, occurs at almost every page: in New England, "the benefit yielded me a little more than two hundred dollars, thus raising my cash capital to about four hundred dollars"; in Atlanta, "When we finished [eating], we paid the waiter twenty cents each and went out"; in Jacksonville, "a *regalia* workman . . . earned from thirty-five to forty dollars a week. He generally worked a sixty-dollar job," while "I was earning four dollars a week, and was soon able to pick up a couple more by teaching a few scholars at night," and later "I was now earning about twenty-five dollars a week"; in Harlem, "In less than three minutes I had won more than two hundred dollars, a sum which afterwards cost me dearly"; later, "I had more than three hundred dollars, and New York had impressed me as a place where there was lots of money and not much difficulty in getting it." Although he quickly adds that "I did not long hold this opinion," the sense remains that money comes

and goes easily: "Some days found me able to peel ten- and twenty-dollar bills from a roll, and others found me clad in a linen duster and carpet slippers."

A great deal of money was spent here [at the "Club"], so many of the patrons were men who earned large sums. I remember one night a dapper little brown-skin fellow was pointed out to me and I was told that he was the most popular jockey of the day, and that he earned $12,000 a year. This latter statement I couldn't doubt, for with my own eyes I saw him spending at about thirty times that rate.

The spending, then, is as important as the earning; and the earning is as easy as the spending. Thus, while class is very much on the narrator's mind, money is not the only defining factor at this stage. He carefully draws class boundaries: the "desperate class," the servants, the independent workmen and tradesmen, and "the educated and well-to-do" who form a "society as discriminating as the actual conditions will allow it to be." Yet, he points out that discrimination is based as much on respectability and "distinction" as on money:

I know personally of one case in which money to the extent of thirty or forty thousand dollars and a fine house, not backed up by a good reputation, after several years of repeated effort, failed to gain entry for the possessor [into society]. These people have their dances and dinners and card parties, their musicals, and their literary societies. The women attend social affairs dressed in good taste, and the men in dress suits which they own. . . . I belonged to the literary society—at which we generally discussed the race question—and attended all the church festivals and other charitable entertainments.

When he is accepted in this "professional" class, he is still working at a manual job in a cigar factory, but also gains distinction as a piano teacher. His mother's piano, always a symbol of uplift in black culture, is still more important than his father's shoes and gold. There is an important symmetry between the remark that this class has evolved "a social life of which they need not be *ashamed*," and the sense of "*shame*" that finally drives him into passing after he has witnessed a lynching (italics mine). This is an expression of what sociologist E. Franklin Frazier has described as "status without substance": the attempt to comply with white standards of behavior without the corresponding material basis. In the absence of gold, polished manners as an outward sign of education and morals, or culture "in the limited sense of 'refinement' and 'sophistication,'" as Leroi Jones put it, will have to do. An illuminating parallel defines this difference.

When he is preparing to enter Atlanta University, the narrator takes a pledge "to abstain from alcoholic beverages, tobacco, and profane language" (*Autobiography*). When he passes for white in the end, he again renounces alcohol and tobacco ("as much as I enjoyed smoking, I limited myself to an occasional cigar. . . . Drinking I cut out altogether"), but makes no mention of profane language. The fact is that this time the pledge has less a moral than an economic significance: "I denied myself as much as possible in order to swell my savings." Words, profane or not, cost nothing; and in an environment in which real money talks, respectable language is not as strictly required.

In between, there is the interlude with his "millionaire friend." Here, music and money are held in temporary balance. The relationship starts with a nightly tip of five dollars for his piano playing and continues with their travels in Europe, during which he plays music and his sponsor "kept me supplied with money far beyond what ordinary wages would have amounted to."

Johnson here treads the same ground as his contemporary Henry James—the international theme of Americans in Europe, always predicated on the opposition of European cultural pretense and American money: "the Londoner seems to think that Americans are people whose only claim to be classed as civilized is that they have money, and the regrettable thing about that is that the money is not English." The difference between English money and American money, of course, is that the former is old and inherited, the latter is new and just made. In a number of these international narratives, in fact, American characters seem to share the embarrassment, not about money but about its sources: how exactly Christopher Newman and the sponsors of Lambert Strether amassed their wealth is always a bit uncertain. It is the making, not the having, of money that is morally suspect. James solves the problem by having his heroines inherit fortunes made by others; Johnson, by making his sponsor a millionaire whose money flows "like fairy godmother's gifts." In this way, Johnson's millionaire and James's heiresses can be as unconcerned about earning and spending money as the cigar makers of Jacksonville and the gamblers of Harlem.

The difference, of course, is that the protagonist is not the millionaire who already has money, but the piano player, who must get it. Thus, the ex-colored man entirely absorbs the near obsession with money of the moneyless in a money-making world that seems so immoral when Henry James's characters strive to pass from poor to rich: "I had made up my mind that since I was not going to be a Negro, I would avail myself of every possible opportunity to make a white man's success; and that, if it can be summed up in any one word, means 'money'" (*Autobiography*).

> What an interesting and absorbing game is money-making! After each deposit at my savings-bank I used to sit and figure out, all over again, my principal and interest, and make calculations on what the increase would be in such and such time. Out of this I derived a great deal of pleasure. I denied myself as much as possible in order to swell my savings. . . . The day on which I was able to figure up to a thousand dollars marked an epoch in my life.

It is an apt conclusion. As the autobiographical form requires, the narrated and the narrating selves finally join together, at the time when, on the threshold of one thousand dollars, the ex-colored man derives pleasure not from the spending but from the making of money. Gone are the days "when my conception of money was that it was made only to spend." He has "earned [it] by days of honest and patient work," has "carefully watched [it] grow from the first dollar." And from this he derives "a pride and satisfaction which to me was an entirely new sensation."

And yet—the ex-colored man has passed from the "status without substance" of the black middle class, to economic substance and unsubstantial identity as an infiltrator in the white bourgeoisie. Just like the hump on the back in the old Jewish story, his native blackness cannot be leveled out but only hidden from sight. "My appearance was always good, and my ability to play on the piano, especially ragtime, which was then at the height of its vogue, made me a welcome guest"; the fact is, however, that his "appearance" is to some extent a mask, and his familiarity with ragtime derives from his immersion in the black world. "The anomaly of my social position appealed strongly to my sense of humor": just as in the parlor car, he is the invisible, and therefore threatening, black presence in the midst of confident whiteness. This is the "capital joke" he plays—but the joke may be on him, too. He smiles inwardly at the racial slurs he occasionally hears, but the humor is also a way of diffusing the frustration of being unable to speak out against them. The last page of the book is about the men who speak out for black people; the fact that he must keep silent makes him feel "a coward, a deserter," "small and selfish," and fills him with "a strange longing for my mother's people." The price he pays for the mask he wears as a "spy in the enemy's country" is cultural silence: a man can pass for white, but the music can't.

Source: Alessandro Portelli, "The Tragedy and the Joke: James Weldon Johnson's *The Autobiography of an Ex-Coloured Man*," in *Temples for Tomorrow: Looking Back at the Harlem Renaissance*, edited by Genevieve Fabre and Michel Feith, Indiana University Press, 2001, pp. 143–58.

Martin Japtok

In the following essay excerpt, Japtok explores how The Autobiography of an Ex-Coloured Man *presents a dual approach to the question of race being of natural essence or of social construction.*

The Autobiography of an Ex-Coloured Man is the coming-of-age story of an African American who grows up believing he is "white," learns in school that he is "coloured" and repeatedly switches from "white" to "black" identity in the years to follow, retaining throughout an awareness of his "colour." After traveling and experiencing, or rather observing, various facets of African American life in the U.S. and of European American life both in the U.S. and in Europe, the Ex-Coloured Man decides ultimately to "pass for white," being jolted into that decision by witnessing a lynching. He becomes a businessman, marries, has children, but then looks back at his life with feelings of regret.

Even this brief plot summary hints at one of the central problems of the novel—the question of identity. Indeed, Henry Louis Gates, Jr. sees the Ex-Coloured Man as an incarnation of DuBoisian double-consciousness (Introduction xvii). Once he *knows* he is "coloured" according to U.S. racial logic, he cannot be "white" again the same way. In other words, he accepts that logic, internalizes it, and acquires double-consciousness; he cannot simply *be* but is always conscious of being, seeing himself, through a DuBoisian "veil," as "whites" might see him. To quote the famous passage from the *Autobiography:* "He [the African American] is forced to take his outlook on all things . . . from the point of view of a *coloured* man."

What does that mean, though? Does it imply that societal forces alone constrain the Ex-Coloured Man to be a "coloured" man, or is there such a thing as a "coloured" point of view regardless of social constraints? Does the *Autobiography* posit "race" as something socially constructed or as something "natural"?

Answers to these questions have ranged over the entire spectrum of ethnic critical theory from "essentialism" (race as "natural" fact) to constructionism ("the position that differences are constructed, not innate" [Fuss xii]). Eugenia Collier

> " . . . the deployment of this double-rhetoric serves to establish as the overall tenor of the book a double critique of white middle class society while at the same time allowing Johnson to show African America's moral (and artistic) superiority."

sees the Ex-Coloured Man "on the verge of surrendering the part of him which is white and letting the black self emerge victorious"; the "black self" fails to win, however, so the protagonist ends up being "white on the outside as well as on the inside" (371). Collier thus emphasizes essential "blackness" and "whiteness," both in psychological and physical terms. Henry Louis Gates, Jr., however, has no doubt that Johnson critiques essential racial identity: "Johnson's decision to chart his mulatto pilgrim's progress back and forth . . . between black and white racial identities, is intended to establish the fact that such identities are entirely socially constructed" (Introduction xvi). According to Eric J. Sundquist, it is the hybrid forms of "blackness" and "whiteness," especially the musical ones, that the *Autobiography* delineates. However, while the Ex-Coloured Man may have "chosen an art [ragtime] emblematic of his racial hybridity" his lack of cultural connectedness does not allow his hybridity to "[produce] fruitful symbiosis" (16). While Sundquist sees the possibility of cultural amalgamation, hinted at and symbolized through biological hybridity, he describes how, instead, the *Autobiography* illustrates the obliteration of black culture through cultural and biological assimilation, as Johnson might have feared it. Sundquist's analysis thus shows the *Autobiography* as adopting a position between essentialism and constructionism, linking culture to color.

While a variety of rhetorical positions on ethnicity in the novel have been convincingly explored, the duality in Johnson's approach to the question of identity has not been emphasized as of yet. I believe that rather than adopting one specific position on race, the *Autobiography* goes both further and not as far as that: while it shows racial identity as socially constructed, it also insists that certain traits are inherent to "whiteness" or "blackness," thus employing seemingly incompatible strategies. The novel "improves upon" the intent of much of the "mulatto" literature preceding it to point out the absurdity of the color scheme through enacting a kind of "reverse passing" in that its protagonist pretends to be black more than he pretends to be white. This strategy doubles complications by depicting not merely a character who, "knowing" he is black attempts to pass for white, but a character who thinks he is white, learns he is seen as black by whites, attempts to *be* black, does not succeed, decides to be white and now thinks of himself as somebody black passing for white. However, while highlighting the social construction of race, the protagonist's life also serves as an indictment of the European American middle class value system as the novel constructs it through relying on the notion of inherent racial traits. In other words, the protagonist's ethnicity is outlined *both* as something "made up" and arbitrary and as something "real." The *Autobiography* thus partakes in a rhetoric of constructionism *and* in a rhetoric of essentialism. While the novel embraces some aspects of white society and critiques others of its black counterpart, the deployment of this double-rhetoric serves to establish as the overall tenor of the book a double critique of white middle class society while at the same time allowing Johnson to show African America's moral (and artistic) superiority. Johnson himself tells us that he set out to do no less than that. He records in his autobiography *Along This Way* a conversation he had with H. L. Mencken on "Negro literature" and "Negro writers":

> "What they should do," he said, "is to single out the strong points of the race and emphasize them over and over and over; asserting, at least on these points, that they are *better* than anybody else." I called to his attention that I had attempted something of that sort in *The Autobiography of an Ex-Coloured Man.* (305)

Thus, to rephrase Diane Fuss's assessment of a conscious use of essentialism, essentialism and constructionism used side by side also prove to have "strategic or interventionary value."

To understand how this happens, it is necessary to show how the novel delineates whiteness and blackness, how each of these come to be seen as a distinct quality, through the characterization of the protagonist, and how, as a result, the Ex-Coloured Man is indeed passing for black more than he is passing for white. How, then, does the Ex-Coloured Man acquire his whiteness and his middle class values? Usually, the blame has been put on his father, whom the narrator remembers by his gold chain and a gold watch. His mother has been accused of being "an adorer of white values" (Kinnamon 173) and has generally received little sympathy from critics. However, she is not only complicit in teaching her son materialism but is herself a victim of double-consciousness and instrumental in bequeathing it to her son. While she spanks him memorably for uprooting glass bottles stuck in the ground, which marks a violation of African (American) cultural customs, as Robert Stepto has explained (101), she also—in the very same paragraph—scrubs the narrator "until [his] skin ached" in an apparent (symbolic) attempts to make him more white (Fleming 86). It is his father who gives him coins, but it is his mother who "[teaches him] to promptly drop [them] in a little tin bank," showing him the value of deferred gratification which will come in handy in his investment scheme. While she is more comfortable—"freer"—when playing "old Southern songs," she is not assertive about her ethnicity when directly confronted by her son: "'No, I am not white, but you—your father is one of the greatest men in the country." Eugenia Collier has noted that she denies "his [and thus her] blackness but not his whiteness" by commenting only on her lack of whiteness while emphasizing her son's white descent. Through her contradictory behavior, which foreshadows the narrator's own ambiguity, the narrator's mother reveals her own unresolved psychological tensions, her ambiguous acceptance and simultaneous rejection of her own ethnicity.

The way she initially rears the narrator seems to be geared toward avoiding the development of double-consciousness in him—at the expense of his African American cultural heritage. As the narrator says, "She was careful about my associates," and one can assume that they are white: his mother surrounds herself exclusively with white women, and the narrator, throughout the novel, "gives no racial designation to white characters but labels instead the black ones" (Collier 366). She sews for "a great many ladies" and, in a punning transposition of color from the givers of money to the object given, makes a "fair income from her work." Nor surprisingly, "the protagonist assumes that he is white" and, as a consequence, he "[absorbs] the racism of his schoolmates" (Kinnamon 173). His experience of racism as a racist turns out to be the ideal breeding ground for double-consciousness: "I had first learned what their status was, and now I learned that theirs was mine." He understands only too well how

European Americans see him—better than any of the other African American children in his class—because he himself evidently looked at African Americans pejoratively. In one of the few instances in which the narrator uses "we" with an ethnic association, he is chasing after African American classmates: "We ran after them pelting them with stones until they separated in several directions." This persecution is the result of one African American boy's striking back after having been taunted in a racist fashion by a European American crowd of children. What this demonstrates is that double-consciousness results from a racist construction of "whiteness" itself, which is defined in contradistinction to "blackness." The narrator experiences a feeling of ethnic identity (of "we" ness) only when he can see himself as part of a group with an "enemy," that is, when he defines "race" in essentialist terms. The former self-definition then turns itself against the narrator. Ironically, the mother's attempt to protect the narrator from acquiring double-consciousness only ensures that it will be even more pronounced than hers. Through this strategy, then, and, through the portrayal of the narrator's essentializing of race, the novel emphasizes the constructedness both of race *and* racism.

Given his white upbringing, it is fitting that it is by the pen of a European American author that he is initiated into the social significance of being "coloured": "[*Uncle Tom's Cabin*] opened my eyes as to who and what I was and what my country considered me; in fact, it gave me my bearing." This kind of initiation, of course, is likely only to deepen his tendency to see blackness through white eyes. His initiation to his race through a *book* further highlights the constructedness of blackness. At the same time, his having read the book opens up the possibility of instruction by his mother on matters of ethnicity: "As a result, she was entirely freed from reserve, and often herself brought up the subject, talking of things directly touching her life and mine and of things which had come down to her through the 'old folks.'" Although we never learn what those things from the "old folks" are, they do inspire him to become interested in the South, which marks the first time that he takes an affirmative attitude towards his new-found ethnicity.

Uncle Tom's Cabin does leave its traces, though. For example, it strengthens his tendency towards middle class "gentility," what he himself calls, in reference to his childhood days, being a "perfect little aristocrat." This prejudice appears in Stowe's novel in the form of condescension toward those characters speaking vernacular (who are usually dark-skinned) and a more equitable treatment, even admiration for those characters—such as Eliza and George—who are closest to Anglo-Saxon norms in speech patterns, values, education, and looks. The Ex-Coloured Man adopts both the class and color prejudice easily, having been predisposed at least to the former since his childhood. As a result, he becomes a class snob (Faulkner 150), and is alienated from the "darker, poorer members of his ethnic community" through "color and class prejudice" (Bell 90–91). Roger Rosenblatt has ascribed the narrator's stance on class matters to his sense of audience: "The hero . . . shows contempt for dialect . . . [and] notes class distinctions among other blacks to demonstrate to the middle class white reader . . . that he fully shares his reader's notion of what constitutes class superiority" (177). But the narrator goes even further than that: he does not condemn dialect per se but only its occurrence among African Americans, particularly those of a "better class." This becomes apparent when he comments on Southern and Northern middle class African Americans, clearly preferring the latter:

> I could not help being struck by the great difference between them [Bostonian African Americans] and the same class of coloured people in the South. In speech and thought they were genuine Yankees. The difference was especially noticeable in their speech. There was none of that heavy-tongued enunciation which characterizes *even* the best-educated coloured people of the South. (152–53, my emphasis)

The narrator does not object to a white Texan's speech pattern when he overhears a conversation in a railroad car, even though one may assume that the Texan spoke with a type of Southern accent as well. This is the behavior and judgment of someone who is not merely appealing to a specific audience but identifies with it to the point that dialect in middle or upper class African Americans is something to be noted and censured while dialect in middle class European Americans escapes judgment because it is "natural" and therefore invisible—to someone who is white. This sense of identification explains why he does not "take greater issue [in his discussion of *Uncle Tom's Cabin*] with his opponents' charge that there never was a slaveholder as bad as Legree than with their claim that there never was a Negro as good as Tom" (Stepto 110). Much of the narrator's foray into the South confirms that he is passing for black more than he is passing for white and establishes a strong link between the protagonist's classism and racism.

Even before he departs for the South, signals for his reverse passing are loud and clear. When listening to "Shiny's" graduation oration, he speculates on what Shiny's feelings might be:

> What were his thoughts when he stepped forward and looked into the crowd of faces, all white with the exception of a score or so that were lost to view? *I do not know,* but *I fancy* he felt his loneliness. *I think* there must have rushed over him a feeling akin to that of a gladiator. . . . (my emphasis)

The narrator empathizes with Shiny, but he also makes clear that he is making imaginative leaps. In the interpretation of the audience's enthusiastic reaction, he does not take similar caution: "The sight of that boy gallantly waging with puny, black arms so unequal a battle touched the deep springs in the hearts of his audience, and they were swept by a wave of sympathy and admiration." He can be more affirmative about the audience's reaction because he seems to know the audience better than he does Shiny, and he admires its "love of fair play." When the narrator departs for the South, then, he has already chosen sides.

Once in the South, it becomes clear that even though "the protagonist has apparently accepted his membership in the race he is describing, his attitude toward black people is curiously aloof" (Fleming 89). As a matter of fact his "first sight of black people en masse unnerves him" (Collier 367) and can be called racist as a function of his middle class sensitivities: "The unkempt appearance, the shambling, slouching gait and loud talk and laughter of these people aroused in me a feeling of almost repulsion" (55–56). His stance is essentialist in that he makes no distinction between race and class in this encounter which, significantly, has no counterpart in his sojourn in the white world. Even when he witnesses a lynching, he does not judge the crowd according to the standards he applies here. As Eugenia Collier has shown, his observations of African Americans are those of an outsider and in their orientation towards stereotypes—such as his description of an innkeeper as a kind of "Aunt Jemima," his perception of mulatto women as prettier than darker women, and of African American men "as splendid physical specimen[s]"—they resemble the perspective of a patronizing white person (368). Even after having lived in Jacksonville for a while, and "though he begins to appreciate black music and dance . . . [he still] refers to black people as 'they,' not 'we.' He is still an observer rather than a participant" (Collier 368). In this context, his eventual choice of lodging proves to be symbolically significant. His landlady is a "rather fine-looking, stout, brown-skin woman" (67), but it is her interior decorating that appeals to him, as he describes in length the "cane-bottomed chairs, each of which was adorned with a white crocheted tidy . . . a white crocheted cover . . . and several trinkets, each of which was set upon a white crocheted mat" (67). Though the narrator conveys a sense of irony about such middle class tidiness, he does decide to settle in where he can be surrounded by so much whiteness.

Even his subsequent stay in New York with his enthusiastic participation in African American nightlife does not significantly diminish his cultural and emotional distance from African Americans. His reaction to a number of photographs on the wall of a night club reveals this distance:

> . . . the walls were literally covered with photographs or lithographs *of every colored man in America who had ever "done anything."* There were pictures of Frederick Douglass and of Peter Jackson. . . .The most of these photographs were autographed and, *in a sense,* made a really valuable collection. (my emphasis)

The use of relativizing or slightly ironic phrases betrays his unwillingness to commit himself fully to the cultural scene he describes. Significantly, he merely comments on the photographs' collectability, "the value imputed to them more monetary than cultural" (Kinnamon 174). Even when he comments on ragtime music and its artistic value, his yardstick for assessing the music's artistry is not the application of any African American intracultural standards but—in a parallel to his interest in the white audience's reception of Shiny's speech—the appreciation of a European (American) audience: "One thing cannot be denied; it is music which possesses at least one strong element of greatness: it appeals universally; not only the American, but the English, the French, and even [sic] the German people find delight in it."

Though on the one hand, the narrator uses ragtime as proof for African Americans' "originality and artistic conception," he seems eager to pull the music out of its ethnic orbit and give it a "universal," i.e. a non-ethnic and non-essentialist, cast. For the narrator, a true sign of ragtime's success is that in "Paris they call it American music." The same is true for all of the narrator's list of African American accomplishments: they have to pass the test of a white American or European audience, so that essentialism in its eurocentric variety is introduced through the backdoor since white acceptance assumes the place of an absolute standard here. He relates with pride that "the newspapers have already told how the practice of intricate cakewalk steps has taken up the time of European royalty and nobility," or that "the Fisk singers made the public and the skilled musicians of both America and Europe listen." Why it is understandable that popularity abroad is taken as a sign of success and artistic greatness, the narrator's tendency to enlist exclusively European (American) reception as the measure of that success is telling. Ethnicity, for him, carries the mark of inferiority (though, ultimately, the novel embraces the opposite view, as I will show), and African American art, according to that logic, can only disprove inferiority if it appeals to a white audience. Once ragtime, has lost some of its ethnic flavor through universal acceptance or through being "classicized" its greatness is assured. Clearly, the narrator's wish to give ragtime a "higher form" tends to the same end. However, this wish, as well as his perception of Douglass' portrait as valuable in the material sense, not only demonstrates his extreme assimilationism but indicates two of his character flaws which are inextricably connected with his alienation—and "essentially" connected to whiteness.

Character flaw number one is the Ex-Coloured Man's materialism, flaw number two his selfishness. Both are related and intertwined. It has been shown above that the narrator acquires his materialism from his father and mother in early childhood. Here I will attempt to trace what this materialism means in his life. Eric Sundquist has aptly noted that the father's gift, the "gold coin he hangs around his neck," is "the chain of neoslavery" (18). This proves to be true in two ways: on the one hand, the coin is symbolic of "the property of whiteness" (Sundquist 18); on the other hand, it foreshadows the narrator's enslavement to materialism (though the novel shows whiteness and materialism as closely related), the Ex-Coloured Man will stay true to this inheritance from his father for the rest of his life. One way in which this legacy becomes apparent is through his "[equation of] respectability with affluence" (Collier 369). Illustrations are manifold during his stay in the South but the attitude remains the same when he sojourns in New York, where he regrets not having

> become acquainted with a single respectable family. I knew that there were several coloured men worth a hundred or so thousand dollars each, and some families who proudly dated their free ancestry back a half-dozen generations. I also learned that in Brooklyn there lived quite a large colony in comfortable homes which they owned; but at no point did my life come into contact with theirs.

Apparently even the narrator's notion of respectability has a price tag.

But his materialism—and selfishness—may be demonstrated most clearly through his relationship to music. In the following the narrator enumerates advantages garnered by his ragtime playing:

> By mastering ragtime I gained several things: first of all, I gained the title of professor. . . . Then, too, I gained the means of earning a rather fair livelihood. . . . And, finally, I secured a wedge which has opened to me more doors and made me a welcome guest than my playing of Beethoven and Chopin could ever have done.

All of his gains relate to either fame, money, connections, or all three. The doors that open for the narrator through his ragtime playing are the doors of his millionaire friend and of European high society. Ironically, then, his choice of an ethnic music (ragtime) over Beethoven and Chopin distances him further from the African American community, at least initially. Music is a "mine" for him, as he will say later when revisiting the South, and his relation to music is expressive both of his materialism and of the absence of any desire for connection with an ethnic community (Stepto 119).

Even when the narrator seems to connect the reasons are dubious. On board a ship bound for the South, the Ex-Coloured Man befriends an African American doctor whom he clearly admires: "He was the broadest-minded coloured man I have ever talked with on the Negro question." The continuation of the passage reveals one of the reasons for his admiration: "He even went so far as to sympathize with and offer excuses for some white Southern points of view." The doctor's stance resembles the narrator's own apologetic discussion of *Uncle Tom's Cabin* of the Texan's racist opinions. This passage marks another instance in which he uses "we" with an ethnic connotation; significantly, though, he only refers to having used the pronoun in the past rather than "actively" using it in the present, indicating his distanced stance at the time of his narration: "In referring to the race I used the personal pronoun 'we.'" The doctor's detachment seems to have the same foundation as the narrator's: egocentrism. Racism becomes an issue to him only when he is concerned personally (Fleming 93): "'I don't object to anyone's having prejudices so long as those prejudices don't interfere with my personal liberty."

Despite the protagonist's self-constructedness between ethnic groups, his very character flaws highlight "organic" links between ethnicity and behavior. While "the conflict in the narrator can easily be seen as not only one of racial identity but also as one between materialism and spirituality"

(Dickson 256), racial identity helps determine whether one chooses to be materialistic or spiritual in *The Autobiography of an Ex-Coloured Man*, whether one resides in the Du Boisian "sole oasis of simple faith and reverence" or "in a dusty desert of dollars and smartness" (*The Souls of Black Folk* 8). In one of the few moments of discarding his distance—at the camp meeting—the narrator explains the importance of the role of the congregation's lead singer, "Singing Johnson":

> It is indispensable to the success of the singing, when the congregation is a large one made up of people from different communities, to have someone with a strong voice who knows just what hymn to sing and when to sing it, who can pitch it in the right key, and who has all the leading lines committed to memory.

Lucinda MacKethan explains that here, "James Weldon Johnson gives us his own ideal of selfhood through a voice that is freed from the circle of white oppression by its ability to sing and to express its own heritage" (146). Indeed, the narrator seems to overcome his class prejudice for a moment, focusing on the integrative and communal power of the singing leader, whose "one-eyedness" might well be symbolic of having only one consciousness: an African American one. It is through music that African American spirituality and communalism are enacted here, and it seems that the narrator implies that "Black people . . . find their real spirituality only among themselves, outside the purview of whites" (Dickson 257). The Ex-Coloured Man's intense double-consciousness, however, makes it impossible for him to ever be outside that "purview," which explains why for him music is more interesting for what it can get him than for its tradition or communal value.

Nonetheless, his internal conflict is highlighted by the fact that "his gifts and powers and promise are all *as a black man*" (Cooke 52)—at least the novel outlines them in this essentialist manner. We are to understand that, in his youth, he is naturally drawn to music and particularly to the blue notes on the piano keyboard. To underscore the biologism of that inclination, the narrator, when talking about the African American originators of ragtime, affirms that they "were guided by natural musical instinct and talent" while not stressing the "geneticness" of such an instinct in the German musician later in the novel. The narrator does develop his musical talent but, in a "self-protecting disengagement from black rural culture," he rejects the "cultural demands" (Sundquist 12–13) of music in the African American context, which are communalism and spirituality, as the camp-meeting shows.

This rejection becomes utterly clear when, in courting his future wife, he ends "Chopin's Thirteenth Nocturne on a major triad—not the minor it requires" as if he meant to "outwhite" Chopin, "thus silencing the minor key of his black life for good" (Sundquist 45).

What, then, leads to this rejection? Materialism, selfishness, and middle class values, and all are shown to be inextricably connected with whiteness. "In *The Autobiography*, Johnson pairs racial pride and the virtues of the middle class, though reconciling their sometimes conflicting implications occasionally proved difficult" (Levy 139). Indeed, such a position is demonstrated by the narrator's attitude towards African Americans who are not middle class. Except for his "lapse" during the camp-meeting, the Ex-Coloured Man admires those African Americans most who have most successfully erased every sign of their ethnicity but their skin color, such as the doctor he meets on his ship passage to the South or Bostonian African Americans who "[i]n speech and thought . . . were genuine Yankees" (153). To become middle class, in terms of the novel, is to become more white, a fact that is best illustrated by the narrator's wish to "classicize" African American folk music "to insure [its] recognition" (Baker 24). Recognition by whom? For the narrator, "black art is a pawn in the larger struggle for recognition from whites. . ., To aid in this endeavor the protagonist wishes to . . . merge the black and white cultural idiom into one" (Gayle 94), an endeavor of which the narrator's ragging of the "Wedding March" is an apt expression.

It is the ragging of Mendelssohn's music that makes the narrator's fame and allows him to meet the millionaire who proves to be instrumental in the furthering of the protagonist's materialism and selfishness, the former through exposing him to a life of leisure and wealth, the latter through attempting to convince him not to go back to the South "since evil is a force that cannot be annihilated [and] the best one can do is to seek such personal happiness as one can find" (Payne 34). Though the narrator rejects the millionaire's advice at first, he follows it after having witnessed a lynching. The choice of studying music in Europe, not an irrational one if he wants to study classical music, can only be seen as selfish against the implied background of ideas of racial solidarity. Solidarity as an ideal thus comes to be associated with blackness. Significantly, the millionaire commits suicide later on, "as an ironic commentary on his own attempt to escape both personal misery and time" (Payne 34), so that one comes to understand that the wages of selfishness are physical death (for the millionaire) or spiritual death (for the narrator, as I will show). That such selfishness is symbolically linked to whiteness is shown not only through the millionaire but also through the narrator's choice to become white after he sees a lynching, "to ally himself with the persecutors rather than the persecuted" (Fleming 95).

Such an avoidance of the call for personal commitment is facilitated by his middle class sensibilities which allow him to dehumanize the lynching victim as "a man only in form and stature, every sign of degeneracy stamped upon his countenance" (186). The narrator bases this dehumanization on the presupposition of the man's absence of morality and refinement, middle class values which had already caused him to put the widest possible distance between himself and lower class African Americans in his first visit to the South. When deciding to become white, the narrator feels "as weak as a man who had lost blood" (190). In a way, he has left the realm of the living. And it is through rhetoric of this kind that blackness is repeatedly essentially connected to humaneness and forms of spirituality while whiteness represents materialism and a Faustian pact resulting in loss of humanity and spirituality. . . .

Source: Martin Japtok, "Between 'Race' as Construct and 'Race' as Essence: *The Autobiography of an Ex-Coloured Man*," in *Southern Literary Journal*, Vol. XXVIII, No. 2, Spring 1996, pp. 32–47.

Robert E. Fleming

In the following essay, Fleming examines the treatment of themes, including namelessness and racial self-hatred, in The Autobiography of an Ex-Coloured Man *that contribute to its lasting significance.*

A superficial view of the life of James Weldon Johnson (1871–1938) may suggest that as an author, he must belong to a closed chapter of black literary history. A member of the establishment, Johnson taught and served as principal in a segregated Florida school, produced literature and song lyrics which were accepted by the white audiences of his day, served as a consul in Venezuela and Nicaragua, and worked for the NAACP, an organization with which today's militant youth has little sympathy. However, Johnson's only novel, *The Autobiography of an Ex-Coloured Man* (1912), is still worth reading today, not just for its value as a cultural or literary artifact, but for the perspective it can give the reader of later fiction by black American authors. While society has changed and

> ... Johnson's novel can hold its own when it is compared with later works, and many of the problems to which Johnson gave literary expression still concern black writers today."

different specific problems have claimed the attention of later black novelists, certain basic themes have an enduring interest and are found in *Autobiography* as well as in the novels or more contemporary writers. *Autobiography* seems especially modern when it is compared with the rather dated novels of Johnson's contemporaries; for example, Paul Laurence Dunbar's *The Sport of the Gods* (1902), Sutton Griggs's *Imperium in Imperio* (1899) or *Pointing the Way* (1908), Charles W. Chesnutt's *The Marrow of Tradition* (1901), and W. E. B. Du Bois's *The Quest of the Silver Fleece* (1911).

The Autobiography of an Ex-Coloured Man is the story of a quadroon who is light enough to pass for white. Throughout the story, the main character attempts to identify with the race of his mother, whom he loves more than he does his white father. Finally, horrified by the sight of a black man being burned alive by a Georgia mob, he makes the following decision: "I would neither disclaim the black race nor claim the white race; but . . . I would change my name, raise a moustache, and let the world take me for what it would. . . ." In the 1920's passing became a popular theme for black novelists: Walter White's *Flight* (1926), Jessie Fauset's *Plum Bun* (1928), and Nella Larsen's *Passing* (1929) all dealt with the same general problem. Although these three writers employ female protagonists, their treatment of the theme suggests that they were influenced by Johnson's novel of the previous decade. However, the passing novel is now a dead piece of literary history, and Johnson's book emerges as the one example of its type to endure. The *Autobiography*'s lasting significance is primarily due to its importance as a seminal book, one which contains many of the themes found in later black fiction. Four of these themes are namelessness, racial self-hatred, the black mother's ambiguous role, and the characterization of the white patron/white liberal.

The theme of namelessness is ultimately derived from the loss of identity suffered by slaves who were stripped of their names along with their languages and patterns of culture. In place of their African names, slaves were given new names, frequently the family names of their owners; it is to reject these surnames and to symbolize the lost African name that the Nation of Islam has adopted the X, as in Malcolm X. In Johnson's *Autobiography of an Ex-Coloured Man* the main character is nameless in a figurative sense because he is the bastard son of a wealthy white southerner and a mulatto servant; on the literal level, the narrator cannot reveal either his former name or his new name because he has crossed the color line years before. Johnson calls attention to the namelessness of his narrator by using the phrase "my name" and deliberately withholding the name itself at various key points in the story: first, when the main character learns that he is a "nigger" according to the standards of his white schoolmates; second, immediately after the shooting incident that causes him to flee the country; and finally, during the scene in which his future wife "forgives" him his black ancestry and agrees to marry him. The fact that the ex-coloured man is presented without a name underscores the major psychological problem of the novel; that is, in a very real sense the narrator doesn't know who he is, and his autobiography records his futile search for an identity.

Later black authors have continued to employ the theme of namelessness, sometimes casually, as in the title of James Baldwin's *Nobody Knows My Name* (1961), and sometimes emphatically and systematically, as in Ralph Ellison's *Invisible Man* (1952), which shares a number of characteristics with Johnson's novel. Like Johnson's nameless protagonist, Ellison's invisible man engages in a book-length identity search. Not only does the reader never learn the name of the narrator, but he is reminded of the fact that he does not know it at key points in the novel. After the explosion in the paint factory, for example, the main character undergoes painful electric shock treatments while the doctor repeatedly asks him, "What is your name?" The importance of the question is emphasized when the narrator muses, "Perhaps . . . when I discover who I am, I'll be free." Later, in another key episode, the protagonist joins the Brotherhood and is given a new name in a passage that is reminiscent of the renaming of the slave: " 'That is your new name,' Brother Jack said. 'Start thinking of yourself by that name from this moment. Get it down so that even if you are called in the middle of the night you will respond. . . . You are to answer to no other, understand?' "

In their endings the two novels differ considerably. Johnson's narrator, who is treated ironically throughout the novel, suffers from intermittent doubts over his decision to pass for white, and the novel ends with his statement, "I cannot repress the thought that, after all, I have chosen the lesser part, that I have sold my birthright for a mess of pottage." Ellison's main character, on the other hand, seems to have learned to accept himself and has cast off his assumed names and identities.

Black self-hatred is another important theme employed by Johnson. Constantly told that he is a member of an inferior race, the black man may come to believe or fear that he really is inferior. The tragic mulatto of nineteenth century fiction, whether treated by Harriet Beecher Stowe, George Washington Cable, William Wells Brown, or Charles W. Chesnutt, succeeds only if the reader accepts the assumption that to be classified according to the black side of one's ancestry inevitably leads to tragic consequences. Johnson's protagonist foreshadows his rejection of his black heritage even before he knows that he is classified as "colored" by white society. As a small boy he joins white students in throwing stones and chanting rhymes at their black schoolmates. When he learns that he too is black, his first feeling is an aversion to being grouped with the black classmates he has persecuted. As he grows up, he observes that he is not alone in feeling shame for his mother's race; in Washington, D. C., he notes the distinctions based on shades of darkness, and is told by his friend, a Negro doctor, that " 'those lazy, loafing, good-for-nothing darkies . . . are the ones who create impressions of the race for the casual observer. . . . A dozen loafing darkies make a bigger crowd and a worse impression in this country than fifty white men of the same class.' " Finally, after the protagonist tells the girl he loves that his mother was black, his thoughts reveal feelings of loathing for his Negro blood: "Under the strange light in her eyes I felt that I was growing black and thick-featured and crimp-haired." He adds, "This was the only time in my life that I ever felt absolute regret at being coloured, that I cursed the drops of African blood in my veins and wished that I were really white." However, because of Johnson's skillful use of irony in the drawing of his main character, the reader has in fact seen the man's racial self-hatred throughout the novel.

Although current black fiction more frequently expresses the attitude that "black is beautiful," much that has been written since the publication of *Autobiography* reflects the assumption of racial inferiority. One thinks, for example, of the main character of *Invisible Man,* determined to deodorize his armpits carefully and to arrive on time for appointments in order to avoid the stereotypes that whites have of his race. In William Demby's *Beetlecreek* (1950), however, the theme of racial self-hatred is an important one. Demby shows how Mary, a Negro domestic worker, feels when she leaves her own home for that of her employer; the white household is an escape from her own disordered home: "She longed for the dawn that permitted her to leave home and husband to go to the neat, dustless whitefolks' house." Mary's social life is tied to a church missionary guild which is modeled on white women's service clubs, and when Mary goes to the meetings—wearing second-hand clothes given to her by her employers—she likes to think of herself as being similar in appearance to the white women she sees at her employer's bridge parties. The "inferior race" label is also implicitly accepted by a group of loafers at the black barber shop: they express surprise that a black sign-painter has the skill to work at such a trade; and they compare the spending habits of the races, saying, "'[White folks are] thrifty and don't throw their money away like our folks do.'" Although this crowd hates whites, not one of them doubts that the white race is superior. Even the black children in *Beetlecreek* reflect the values of an oppressive white society: Johnny Johnson echoes the white man's "nigger" when he calls the Beetlecreek gang "down-home spooks," and the gang itself, far from rebelling against southern institutions and customs, has formed a group known as the Nightriders, which ironically copies the ceremonies, garb, and activities of the KKK.

Another mid-century author who deals with the theme of racial self-hatred is James Baldwin. In *Go Tell It on the Mountain* (1953) dirt is used as a symbol of Johnny's blackness. From the surname of the family, Grimes, to the vivid account of Johnny's sweeping the front room, enveloped in a cloud of dust, and even to the dust of the threshing floor where Johnny writhes as he undergoes conversion, Baldwin's characters are as enveloped in filth as they are in their skin. Johnny's aunt Florence expresses Baldwin's theme without the aid of such subtle symbolism, berating her husband for his "nigger ways" as she rubs bleaching cream into her skin. Robert Bone has noted that Gabriel's sermons contain the implicit acknowledgement of the black man's inferiority so prevalent in the Negro church, with its emphasis on black as a color symbolizing evil, and its pleas for the sinner to be washed white as the snow.

Another major theme in twentieth century black novels is the important place of the mother in family life. For various reasons, black family life has developed into a matriarchal system: during slavery, when a family was separated by a sale, the children normally went with their mother; in modern times, fathers who are unable to support their families often leave them, either because of shame or because of the way the welfare system works. Black authors have always recognized the great importance of the mother in black life, but the attitude of the novelist toward this warm but dominant character has shifted during the course of the twentieth century. Johnson's treatment of his protagonist's mother points up the difference between the sympathetic depiction of a good, hardworking woman and the more critical, even bitter, analyses by later authors. While the protagonist's absentee father is characterized by material symbols such as his shiny shoes, his gold watch and chain, and his occasional gifts, his mother is presented as a warm, tender, almost saintly individual—the source of all love. The reader sees her angry only once—when her son reports his participation in an attack on some of his "nigger" classmates. Though gentle and kindly, the mother unwittingly contributes to her son's dilemma of straddling two cultures; she refuses to talk to him about race until he brings up the subject, and then she conveys her belief in the superiority of the white race: "'Your father is one of the greatest men in the country—the best blood of the South is in you.'" While there is irony in this statement, it is directed not at the mother but at the father. Though she is fallible, the mother is viewed sympathetically.

Later writers, on the other hand, see two sides to the black mother. True, she is often placed in the position of having to raise her children alone, and she often lavishes all her love on her children, but more recent black authors have recognized that such love may be destructive. Perhaps no writer has shown this paradox as well as Richard Wright. In "The Ethics of Living Jim Crow" (1937), Wright tells how his own mother reacted when he came home bleeding after a fight with white children:

> "How come yuh didn't hide?" she asked me. "How come yuh awways fightin'?". . . . She grabbed a barrel stave, dragged me home, stripped me naked, and beat me till I had a fever of one hundred and two. She would smack my rump with the stave, and while the skin was still smarting, impart to me gems of Jim

Crow wisdom. . . . I was never, never, under any conditions to fight *white* folks again. . . . Didn't I know she was working hard every day in the hot kitchens of white folks to make money to take care of me?

In *Black Boy* (1945) Wright relates another such incident in which his mother, angry because neighborhood toughs had twice robbed Richard of grocery money, locked him out of the house until he single-handedly attached the gang and recovered the money. Although Bigger's mother in *Native Son* (1940) is not so cruel as Wright's own mother, she shows the hard side of her character in the opening pages of the novel as she scornfully tells Bigger, "'We wouldn't have to live in this garbage dump if you had any manhood in you.'"

The contrast between Johnson's view of the admirable black mother and Wright's depiction of a veritable harpy is great, but another writer of the forties bridges the gap by showing why the black mother behaves as she does. Ann Perry's novel *The Street* (1946) is an unsuccessful work in many ways, but her representation of black motherhood is a complete and unbiased analysis of a complex problem. Lutie Johnson is forced to work to support her husband and child, but Jim, her husband, resents the fact that she must do so. To reinforce his feeling of manhood, Jim takes a mistress, and the marriage breaks up. Trying to raise her son Bub alone, Lutie is horrified to find him shining shoes on the street one night when she returns from work. Like the black women Wright depicts, Lutie first reacts by angrily slapping Bub and telling him, "'I'm working to look after you and you out here in the street shining shoes just like the rest of these little niggers.'" However, Mrs. Petry goes on to analyze the complex nature of Lutie's feelings. When they go into their apartment, Bub reminds Lutie that she has repeatedly told him they are short of money and explains that he was simply trying to help. Lutie feels a pang of guilt, "thinking of all the times she had told him no, no candy, for we can't afford it. Or yes, it's only twenty-five cents for the movies but that twenty-five cents will help pay for the new soles on your shoes. . . . Then when he tried to earn some of his own he berated him, slapped him." Lutie explains to Bub that she is harsh only because she wants him to make something of himself, something more than white society will normally allow him to be. Altogether, *The Street* effectively shows both the tender side and the harsh side of the black mother and also probes the conditions which foster such a dual nature.

Finally, another important theme treated by Johnson is the relationship of black people to the self-styled white liberal, who, for reasons of his own, wishes to befriend the Negro. In black literature this type of character is often treated with suspicion, and not without reason. Historically, white people who have offered help to blacks have done so with strings attached. One example is William Lloyd Garrison, who withdrew his sponsorship of Frederick Douglass after Douglass began to differ with his onetime mentor on points of policy. From the black writer's point of view, the white do-gooder always has selfish motives for his deeds; frequently he is trying to wash away his racial guilt by performing token acts of penance (normally not too unpleasant, dangerous, or expensive). Johnson presents a full range of characters who embody different aspects of the white liberal, from the main character's own father to a millionaire who befriends him.

The narrator of *Autobiography* introduces his father as a man who visits his mother in the evening, apparently under cover of darkness. His monthly support checks and occasional gifts are clearly a substitute for the love and recognition which he is unwilling to extend to them. Yet he is equally unwilling to give up the sort of proprietary interest he seems to derive from the relationship. Thus, when he is about to ship them north so that his white fiancee won't find out about his black mistress and bastard son, he drills a hole in a gold piece and ties it around his son's neck. The narrator comments wryly, "More than once I have wished that some other way had been found of attaching it to me besides putting a hole through it." This flawed gold piece serves as a fitting symbol for most gifts the white man has given to the black man. Much later in the novel, the main character attracts the attention of a New York millionaire who befriends him because he is impressed by his piano playing. The millionaire offers him a trip to Europe, but it is significant that he does so in a way that is unwittingly insulting: "'I think I'll take you along instead of Walter' [the millionaire says]. Walter was his valet." The narrator is exposed to other white liberals in the smoking car of a train in Tennessee. Since he appears white, the narrator is able to overhear a debate on the race question between a Texas bigot and three northerners: a young college professor, a Jewish businessman, and an old Union veteran of the Civil War. The Jew and the professor are both masters of fence-straddling, and although they theoretically believe in equality, both concede that the racial question is too complex for them to take a definite stand. The old soldier defends the political rights of black people, but he stops short of admitting them to social equality. The narrator ends his account of the debate with the observation that the bigot at least had complete confidence in his convictions, unlike the liberal northerners.

Later representations of the ineffectual liberal are numerous. In *Native Son,* for example, there are the elder Daltons, who give money to the NAACP, buy ping pong tables for the South Side Boy's Club, and employ a token Negro as a chauffeur; but the Dalton fortune is derived from ghetto tenements. Their daughter is being self-consciously liberal when she asks Bigger Thomas to sit beside her in the car and when she eats chicken with him at Ernie's Kitchen Shack. And finally there are Jan and Max, the white communists who are sure that they can save the world by convincing black and white to unite and fight, but who nevertheless fail to understand the real Bigger Thomas. An interesting variation on the white liberal theme appears in James Baldwin's *Another Country* (1962), in which the liberal is a homosexual. While Baldwin does not satirize the white homosexual or present his relationship with his Negro lover as clearcut exploitation, a later novelist, John A. Williams, goes a step further in *The Man Who Cried I Am* (1967). Williams not only depicts Granville Bryant, a white homosexual, as an exploiter of black men, but also employs the homosexual relationship as a metaphor of America's treatment of the black man.

In addition to these four themes which I have discussed in some detail, there are others that might be mentioned: for example, the flight to Europe as a means of liberation, especially for the black artist; the problem of militance versus accommodation as methods of dealing with white society; and the conflict between white standards of success, which are almost solely monetary, and black standards. Like the themes of namelessness, racial self-hatred, the black mother, and the white liberal, these motifs reappear in many recent works and provide additional evidence of the enduring significance of Johnson's novel.

Thus, in spite of changes in the philosophy and techniques of the Negro American novelist over the past sixty years, James Weldon Johnson's *Autobiography of an Ex-Coloured Man* is still a meaningful and relevant book for the reader who wishes to understand the traditions that underlie the twentieth century black novel. Unlike the work of his contemporaries, Johnson's novel can hold its own when it is compared with later works, and many of the problems to which Johnson gave literary expression still concern black writers today.

Source: Robert E. Fleming, "Contemporary Themes in Johnson's *Autobiography of An Ex-Coloured Man,*" in *Negro American Literature Forum,* Vol. 4, No. 4, Winter 1970, pp. 120–24.

Richard Kostelanetz

In the following essay, now appearing as "James Weldon Johnson" in Politics in the African American Novel *(Greenwood, 1991), Kostelanetz examines how Johnson renders the concept of "passing" and its consequences in* The Autobiography of an Ex-Coloured Man.

James Weldon Johnson's sole novel, *The Autobiography of an Ex-Colored Man* (1912), treats a subject recurrent in early Negro American writing, the experience of a very fair-skinned man of some colored background who successfully passes into white society. Indeed, the theme appears in the first novel attributed to an American Negro author, *Clotel, or the President's Daughter* (London, 1853), by the expatriate abolitionist William Wells Brown. His mulatto protagonist, Clotel, is traced to Thomas Jefferson's lecherous adventures in the original British edition; however, in the later American edition, as Robert A. Bone has observed, "An anonymous senator is substituted for Jefferson, and the plot is altered accordingly." The point of Wells Brown's novel is that once Clotel's part-Negro origins are disclosed, she is still considered a slave and, thus, subject to recapture. Charles Chesnutt, perhaps the first major Negro fiction writer, portrayed in *The House Behind the Cedars* (1900) a young woman, Rena, the master's daughter by a colored mistress, who decides to pass into white society. Upon the eve of her wedding to a white man, her background is revealed, and the marriage is cancelled. Heartbroken, she lets her life disintegrate. The moral of Chesnutt's story holds that the major risk of "passing" is that discovery can ruin one's life. The nineteen twenties witnessed a spate of novels about passing, including Jessie Fauset's *There is Confusion* (1924) and *Plum Bun* (1929), Nella Larsen's *Quicksand* (1928) and Walter White's *Flight* (1926).

Johnson's novel, largely because it is thoroughly unsentimental, is a more complex and masterful exploration of the subject and a superior work of art, although it is aesthetically marred by numerous polemical digressions, sometimes of considerable perception, on the Negro Problem. Originally published anonymously by Sherman, French and Co. in 1912, *The Autobiography of an Ex-Colored Man* was restored to its author when Alfred A. Knopf republished it with Carl Van Vechten's introduction in 1927 at the height of the

> " ... in the political sense, the novel suggests that passing—the Negro's total assimilation into white culture—signifies opportunistic rejection of one's heritage for the meagre 'mess of pottage' of material contentment."

Negro Renaissance. As a novelistic creation, the book is an achieved example of a totally fictional memoir whose first-person narrator is so intimate and honest with his readers that they would, unless warned otherwise, accept his words as an authentic autobiography; a later, equally successful model of autobiographical artifice is Ralph Ellison's *Invisible Man*. In fact, *The Autobiography*, like Ellison's novel, is not in the least autobiographical, except in the sense that certain events have their *symbolic* equivalents in Johnson's own life. Johnson, who was actually quite dark, could sometimes "pass" as a Latin American; for by speaking Spanish with a white friend, he could often manage to stay in the first-class coaches on the Southern train. The effectiveness of the artifice is, of course, a basic measure of Johnson's fictional artistry.

The novel's theme is the ambiguities of passing; and its predominant action is the nameless narrator's shifting sympathies for white or black identity. Born in Georgia, the son of a white man by his family's favorite Negro servant, the narrator grows up with his mother in Connecticut, attending a racially mixed elementary school. He unwittingly identifies with the whites in the squabbles with "the niggers," until a white teacher asks,

'I wish all of the white scholars to stand for a moment.'

I rose with the others. The teacher looked at me and, calling my name, said: 'You sit down for the present, and rise with the others.' I did not quite understand her, and questioned: 'Ma'm?' She repeated, with a softer tone in her voice: 'You sit down now, and rise with the others.'

However, as the community is not aggressively anti-Negro, the narrator remains only dimly aware of his colored origins until high school. There, a dark-colored friend, Shiny, instills in the narrator some awareness of his heritage as a Negro.

I read with studious interest everything I could find relating to coloured men who had gained prominence. My heroes had been King David, then Robert the Bruce; now Frederick Douglass was enshrined in the place of honor.

Thus, when forced to select a college from the two possible alternatives presented to him—his Father's recommendation, Harvard; or his mother's, Atlanta—he decides on the latter. Once he gets there, however, he finds himself unable to register because his "inheritance" (money from his father) is stolen. He thinks of explaining his predicament to the schools' authorities; but as he approaches their offices, "I paused, undecided for a moment; then turned and slowly retraced my steps, and so changed the whole course of my life." In traveling to Florida, he undergoes a symbolic dark night of suffering in a womb-like setting. "Twelve hours doubled up in a porter's basket for soiled linen, not being able to straighten up. The air was hot and suffocating and the smell of damp towels and used linen was sickening." He emerges reborn for a new existence in the Negro community of Jacksonville.

As a cigar-maker, he learns of both the impregnable structure of Southern discrimination and the exclusive habits of the Negro middle class. Finding himself doomed to remain an outsider in the South, unfulfilled in his ambitions, the narrator, like so many analogous characters in later Negro fiction, heads North to New York City. There he gravitates toward the major Negro bohemia of the early twentieth century, in the west twenties between Sixth and Seventh Avenues, first making his way as a successful gambler and then as a pianist of rag-time (Negro) music. The milieu he discovers is full of freedom of movement but little discernible stability—opportunistic drifters, white widows on the make, sports capable of sudden violence. An experience with the last element drives the narrator to befriend a millionaire white man who, out of admiration for his piano playing, offers to become his patron. At the novel's turning point, the narrator and his benefactor go off to Europe; and the narrator, now posing as a white man, enters high-class international society.

Still, he does not claim his white identity at once. At a Paris theatre, he recognizes that the man two seats away is his father; but he refuses the temptation to announce his presence. Later becoming disillusioned with his master's way of life—a constant quest for novelty to assuage the boredom of purposelessness—the narrator remembers his childhood ambition to become a Negro composer and collector of Negro folk materials. Despite the millionaire's not-unperceptive warning that "the idea you have of making a Negro out of yourself is nothing more than a sentiment," the narrator returns to America, to pursue his self-determined task. In each Southern town he visits, he is faced with choice of being white; but each time, he reaffirms blackness:

> In thus travelling about through the country I was sometimes amused on arriving at some little railroad-station town to be taken for and treated as a white man, and six hours later, when it was learned that I was stopping at the house of the coloured preacher or school-teacher, to note the attitude of the whole town change.

Just as an earlier incident of violence propelled him out of Negro bohemia into his white patron's beneficence, so his witnessing a Southern lynching initiates another collapse of personal purpose and integrity; and the narrator undergoes a second rebirth with a new vow: "I would neither disclaim the black race nor claim the white race; but . . . I would change my name, raise a moustache, and let the world take me for what it would." His explanation is a patent rationalization for cowardice and self-interest—"Shame at being identified with a people that could with impunity be treated worse than animals." However, it is still a credible outcome of his experience.

He returns to New York, takes a well-paying job, invests his money in real estate, strikes up a relationship with a Caucasian girl. The specter of his past identity confronts him when he and his fiancee accidentally meet his childhood friend "Shiny" in a museum; but in cutting short Shiny's approach, the narrator rejects his last tie to the past. He marries the girl, she bears him a boy and a girl, only to die suddenly; and he assumes responsibility for his children. The book's final passage conveys his ambivalence to "passing":

> My love for my children makes me glad that I am what I am and keeps me from desiring to be otherwise; and yet, when I sometimes open a little box in which I still keep my fast yellowing [music] manuscripts, the only tangible remnants of a vanished dream, a dead ambition, a sacrificed talent, I cannot repress the thought that, after all, I have chosen the lesser part, that I have sold my birthright for a mess of pottage.

The price of "passing" is not only a loss of heritage and the sacrifice of one's self-chosen mission but guilt over an opportunistic materialism equal to Esau's who, in *Genesis* 25: 29–34, himself so famished from toiling in the fields, frivolously exchanged "his birthright" with his brother Jacob for "bread and pottage of lentils."

Some of the book's meaning stems from its relationship to Negro folk blues, that tightly organized lyric form in which the singer narrates the reasons for his sadness, usually attributed to his failure to attain the ideal role he conceives for himself; and in a successful blues, the singer makes his personal predicament a realized metaphor for the human condition. Here the subject of the "blues" is selling out one's dreams for material reward. Johnson, of course, was aware of the folk blues tradition, not only from his experience writing show tunes with his brother Rosamund, but also from a desire to appropriate the heritage for literature. In his autobiograhy, *Along the Way* (1933), Johnson wrote of his early days: "I now began to grope toward a realization of the importance of the American Negro's cultural background and his creative folk-art, and to speculate on the superstructure of conscious art that might be reared upon this." The statement echoes what Johnson wrote in the introduction to *The Book of American Negro Poetry* (1922):

> What the colored poet in the United States needs to do is something like Synge did for the Irish; he needs to find a form that will express the racial spirit by symbols from within rather than by symbols from without, such as the mere mutilation of English spelling and punctuation.

In the novel, then, Johnson's narrator expresses a disenchantment of a special kind—the blues of being white but black. "Passing" produces the individual's alienation from his natural milieu and feelings of the blues, expressed particularly as a guilty self-identification with Abraham's least-favored grandson, Esau; so in the political sense, the novel suggests that passing—the Negro's total assimilation into white culture—signifies opportunistic rejection of one's heritage for the meagre "mess of pottage" of material contentment.

Source: Richard Kostelanetz, "The Politics of Passing: The Fiction of James Weldon Johnson," in *Negro American Literature Forum*, Vol. 3, No. 1, Spring 1969, pp. 22–25.

Sources

Bone, Robert A., *The Negro Novel in America*, Yale University Press, 1958, pp. 45–49.

Bruce, Dickson D., Jr., *Black American Writing from the Nadir: The Evolution of a Literary Tradition, 1877–1915*, Louisiana State University Press, 1989, p. 258.

Faulkner, Howard, "James Weldon Johnson's Portrait of the Artist as Invisible Man," in *Black American Literature Forum*, Vol. 19, No. 4, Winter 1985, pp. 148, 151.

Japtok, Martin, "Between 'Race' as Construct and 'Race' as Essence," in the *Southern Literary Journal*, Vol. 28, No. 2, Spring 1996, pp. 32–48.

Matthews, Brander, "American Character in American Fiction: Three Books Which Depict the Actualities of Present-Day Life," in *Munsey's Magazine*, Vol. 49, 1913, p. 798.

Pisiak, Roxanna, "Irony and Subversion in James Weldon Johnson's *The Autobiography of an Ex-Coloured Man*," in *Studies in American Fiction*, Vol. 21, No. 1, Spring 1993, p. 83.

Review of *The Autobiography of an Ex-Coloured Man*, in the *Nashville American*, June 23, 1912.

Further Reading

Bell, Bernard W., *The Afro-American Novel and Its Tradition*, University of Massachusetts Press, 1987.

In this history of African American novels from the antebellum period through the 1970s, Bell discusses Johnson as an "Old Guard" novelist along with W. E. B. Du Bois. His analysis of the *The Autobiography of an Ex-Coloured Man* focuses on the novel as an example of psychological determinism.

Johnson, James Weldon, *Black Manhattan*, 1930, reprint, Atheneum, 1968.

Johnson traces the history of Harlem from the seventeenth century to the 1930s. His analysis of African American theater and music in the first decades of the twentieth century shed light both on his own career in musical theater and on the clubs frequented by the narrator of *The Autobiography of an Ex-Coloured Man*.

Levy, Eugene, *James Weldon Johnson: Black Leader, Black Voice*, University of Chicago Press, 1973.

This full-length biography, written with the cooperation and assistance of Johnson's widow, is both scholarly and readable. It includes an extensive bibliography of Johnson's major and minor publications as well as an extensive list of reviews and other secondary materials published through 1970.

Stepto, Robert B., *From behind the Veil: A Study of Afro-American Narrative*, University of Illinois Press, 1979.

This important history of African American literature was one of the first to trace a true literary tradition through the texts, in addition to simple chronology. Stepto's analysis of slave narratives and their influence is particularly illuminating for understanding the structure of *The Autobiography of an Ex-Coloured Man*.

Black Beauty

Anna Sewell
1877

Black Beauty, first published in 1877, is a realistic animal story that focuses on the animal itself, not on a child's interaction with an animal like so many other animal tales. Also unique is the presentation of the story using a horse as the first-person narrator; in other words, as if the horse wrote the story. The original title page for the novel read: *Black Beauty: The Autobiography of a Horse*, translated from the original equine, by Anna Sewell. The genre of animal autobiography had been seen in a limited fashion before, but *Black Beauty* is considered the first novel of this type. The style of presenting an animal as an animal rather than giving it human traits has been followed by similar stories such as *Beautiful Joe*, *The Incredible Journey*, and *Bambi*. Further, Sewell's novel has been an influence on animal stories of all kinds, including those of popular modern writers such as Beatrix Potter and Kenneth Grahame.

Sewell's intention in writing the book was to promote the humane treatment of horses. Called the "Uncle Tom's Cabin of the Horse," *Black Beauty* is credited with having the greatest effect on the treatment of animals of any publication in history. The book resulted in legislation protecting horses and a changed public attitude about animal pain and the traditional and fashionable practices that caused suffering for horses.

Black Beauty was the only book that Sewell wrote, and she sold the manuscript for only twenty pounds. It is still one of the most widely read books in the world, with numerous translations and

Anna Sewell © Mary Evans Picture Library

multiple media versions. Barely a year goes by without a new print edition being published, thus continuing the life of this timeless classic.

Author Biography

Anna Sewell may have written only one book in her lifetime, but *Black Beauty* has proven to be a book of great importance and popularity.

Born in Yarmouth, England, on March 30, 1820, Sewell lived in several cities due to her father Isaac's restlessness and financial misfortunes. She spent summers with her grandparents at Dudwick Farm and based Birtwick Park in the novel on Dudwick House. Until 1832, Sewell's mother, Mary, provided her education, emphasizing natural history, moral virtues, and self-reliance. In school, Sewell had exposure to mathematics, foreign languages, and art. Sewell demonstrated a talent for art, but her mother saw art as a frivolous activity and dissuaded her daughter from painting. At age 14, Sewell had an accident that permanently damaged her ankles and made walking difficult for the rest of her life, even though she was taken to European spas on several occasions to seek rehabilitation.

Around 1850, Sewell's mother began a successful career as the author of moralistic books and verse for children. Sewell served as her mother's editor and was otherwise very interested in literature. Living as an invalid did not prevent Sewell from pursuing a few outside interests. Sewell taught Sunday school and evening classes to workers and participated in her mother's temperance activities. She learned horse driving from her brother Philip and would converse about horses with other drivers she encountered when on errands. It is from this experience and from reading American minister Horace Bushnell's "Essay on Animals" that she developed her knowledge about and sympathy for horses.

When she was 51 years old, Sewell contracted an unidentified illness that left her in great pain and restricted her to her house for the remainder of her life. At this point, she began working on *Black Beauty*, sometimes writing and sometimes dictating the text of the novel to her mother. It was published just five months before she died on April 25, 1878. She never knew the success of her novel, but her mother made certain that the horses pulling Sewell's hearse were not subjected to bearing reins, a device that Sewell preached against. Sewell is buried in Lamas, a village just north of her birthplace.

Plot Summary

Part 1

Black Beauty opens with its main character describing his first memory as that of a "pleasant meadow." The reader is told about his life as a colt, his mother's advice on how to behave as a well-bred horse, and his master's kind care. When Black Beauty is two, he witnesses the brutality of a hunt for a hare and the tragedy of one of the riders being killed in a fall from his horse. At age four, Black Beauty is broken in to the use of the saddle, bridle, and carriage harness. He describes how bad the bit feels as well as getting his first shoes. Then he is sent to a neighbor's pasture near a railroad to get used to the sounds he might hear when out on the road and is thus prepared to start work. He is sold to Squire Gordon and is named by Mrs. Gordon. Birtwick Hall becomes his pleasant home for more than three years. Here he meets the horses Merrylegs, Ginger, and Sir Oliver, and the grooms James Howard and John Manly. He learns that Ginger got her ill-tempered nature from a hard life with previous owners, and that Sir Oliver got a shortened tail when a thoughtless fashion dictated that it be cut. Sir Oliver also reveals the painful practices of bobbing tails and ears on dogs. Merrylegs, a pony, is a trusted playmate of the Gordon and Blomefield children. Squire Gordon and John Manly are both known to take issue with those who mistreat horses. Stable hand James gets an opportunity for a better position elsewhere and leaves Birtwick, but before he goes, he drives the Gordons on a trip to see friends. At a stop on the way, the stable catches on fire, but James calmly and valiantly manages to save Beauty and Ginger. Little Joe Green replaces James. Joe does not know how to properly put up the hot and tired Beauty after an emergency run to get the doctor for Mrs. Gordon, and as a result, Beauty becomes very sick. Joe grieves over his mistake and thereafter devotes himself to learning horse care. He even testifies against a man he sees flogging two horses. Life changes, though, when the Gordons must move to a warmer climate for Mrs. Gordon's health. Joe and Merrylegs go to the Vicar Blomefield's, and Beauty and Ginger are sold to Earlshall Park.

Part 2

The mistress at Earlshall insists on using the bearing rein, which is very painful for the horses, but the stable manager, Mr. York cannot object. One day Ginger rebels and goes wild. She is then used as a hunter. When the Earl and some of the family go to London, the Lady Anne takes to riding Beauty, calling him Black Auster. When she tries another horse on one ride and is thrown, Beauty races for help and is much praised. He thinks he has settled into a good home, but then the stable hand Reuben Smith gets drunk and takes Beauty on a dangerous ride that results in Smith's death and ruined knees for Beauty. Ginger is also ruined by hard riding, but is given a chance to recover. Beauty, however, is sold to a livery stable. As a job horse, Beauty is subjected to being hired by people with poor driving skills and little knowledge of the care of horses. One customer, though, recognizes Beauty's value and arranges for him to be sold to Mr. Barry, a gentleman who hires a groom for Beauty. The groom steals Beauty's feed and has to be arrested. The next groom is too lazy to take care of Beauty and causes him to get thrush. Disgusted by all the trouble of keeping a horse, Mr. Barry sells Beauty.

Part 3

Beauty is sold at a horse fair to Jerry Barker, a London cab driver, and is called Jack. His stable

Media Adaptations

- A 1994 film version of *Black Beauty*, produced by Warner Brothers, is now available in both DVD and VHS formats. It is 88 minutes long and was produced by Robert Shapiro and Peter MacGregor Scott with Caroline Thompson as director and writer.

- *Black Beauty* has been adapted for radio and issued as an audio book on records, cassettes, and CDs. One source is the unabridged *Classics for Children of All Ages* audio book (2003).

mate is Captain, a former cavalry horse. Beauty learns the ropes of pulling a cab in the busy streets of London. The hard life is made bearable by Jerry's skillful and kind treatment. Jerry has a loving family with his wife Polly and children Harry and Dolly. He is a very ethical man who will not drink and will not work on Sundays or take fares that will needlessly overwork his horses. He will, however, take pains to do a charitable act. One of Jerry's friends is a sensible and good-hearted cab driver called Governor Grant who serves as the elder advisor for the other drivers. While many customers are thoughtless, some are considerate of the horses. Similarly, some cab drivers are negligent of their horses because they do not own the horses, but work for shares. For these men, life is nearly as hard as it is for the horses. By chance, one day Black Beauty sees Ginger, who has become one of these leased cab horses and very mistreated. She is in such pain that she yearns for death. Later, Beauty happens to see Ginger's body being carted away. Shortly afterwards, Jerry and Captain are involved in a carriage accident that causes Captain to be put down and replaced by Hotspur. At New Year's, a couple of customers keep Jerry waiting in the bitter cold while they party. As a result, Jerry becomes very ill with bronchitis and cannot work. Grant helps out by giving the energetic Hotspur a half-day's work each day and giving half the fares to Polly. When Jerry recovers, the doctor says that he can no longer work as a cab driver. However, Mrs. Fowler, Polly's former employer, hires Jerry to be her coachman in the country and provides a cottage for the family. They go on to a wonderful new life, but the horses have to be sold. Grant buys Hotspur, and promises Jerry to find a good place for Beauty.

Part 4

Beauty is sold to a corn dealer who is good to him, but the dealer's foreman, Jakes, overworks the horses and uses the bearing rein. However, he takes the advice of a lady who advises that Beauty could work better if the bearing rein is removed. Jakes is so impressed by the lady's concern that he is easier on Beauty after that. However, the dark stables nearly make Beauty blind, and he is sold to a cab business again. This time his owner, Nicholas Skinner, has several shabby cabs and a group of overworked drivers who take out their frustration over their hardships by abusing the horses. When a customer insists on the cab carrying a load too heavy for Beauty, the horse collapses. He is saved from being put down by a farrier who finds that Beauty's wind is not broken. Beauty is taken to auction where he is bought by Farmer Thoroughgood and his compassionate grandson who believe that they can rehabilitate Beauty in their country meadow. They are successful and sell Beauty to Ellen and Lavinia Blomefield. Joe Green is still working for the Blomefield family and recognizes Black Beauty, who then settles into a long, happy life in his last home.

Characters

Lady Anne

Black Beauty is Lady Anne's riding horse for a while at Earlshall Park, but she calls him Black Auster.

Dolly Barker

Dolly is the eight-year-old daughter of Jerry, the cab driver who owned Beauty. Dolly would bring food to her father at the cab stand.

Harry Barker

Harry is Jerry the cab driver's twelve-year-old son. Harry capably helped with the care of the horses.

Jeremiah Barker

Jeremiah, called Jerry, was Beauty's owner for three years. Jerry is a kindly and decent London cab driver. Jerry takes excellent care of his horses and does not believe that either he or they should work seven days a week. He is Sewell's example of honesty and integrity in the working class and is the character she uses to express a number of moral lessons. Jerry finds reward in a job well done and is always willing to perform acts of charity. He loves his wife and children dearly and does not linger in taverns as the other drivers do, since he has been a teetotaler for ten years. When Jerry becomes so ill that he can no longer work as a cab driver, he sells Beauty to a friend he thinks will treat Beauty well.

Polly Barker

Polly is the wife of Jerry Barker. Polly is a merry, kindly woman who provides loving care to all around her. Her former employer thinks so highly of Polly that she keeps in touch through the years and offers Jerry a job and the family a home when Jerry has to give up his cab business.

Mr. Barry

Mr. Barry is one of Black Beauty's owners after his knees are ruined. Mr. Barry is a gentleman who must rely on grooms to take care of Beauty, but after two dishonest grooms, he gives up on having his own horse and sells Beauty.

Black Beauty

Black Beauty is the narrator of the novel and is a "well bred and well born" handsome black horse with one white foot and a white star on his forehead. The character is possibly based on Sewell's brother's beautiful carriage horse Black Bess, or Bessie. Black Beauty is the son of a wise older mare named Duchess and the grandson of the winner of a famous race. Following his mother's advice always to be good of heart and a hard worker, Beauty encounters a variety of good and bad owners and grooms, as well as enjoyable and miserable jobs during his life as a horse in Victorian England. Through Beauty and the other horses he meets, the reader learns about the mistreatment that horses often endure and the difficult nature of some of the work imposed on horses. The character of Beauty is Sewell's device for making the public more aware of the need for more humane treatment of horses and other animals.

Beauty has a good start in life under the skillful care of Farmer Grey, then enjoys a happy time at Birtwick Park where his master is a knowledgeable advocate of humane treatment for horses. But that master must leave England, and Beauty's life takes a downward spiral, thanks to a drunken groom who ruins Beauty's knees in an accident. Fashion dictates that a blemished horse cannot pull a carriage, so Beauty begins an odyssey through a series of middle and lower class labors. While he enjoys three years with a wonderful cab driver, the work is hard and debilitating. Fate sends him to even harder work where he collapses and is almost sent to the slaughterhouse, but is fortunate instead to be sold to a farmer who rehabilitates Beauty's health and finds him a pleasant home for the rest of his life.

The people and horses that Beauty meets in each of his jobs all have stories to tell that illuminate the situation of horses in that time period and reveal the natures of the people who are charged with their care. Beauty's gentility and goodness, even during hard times, make him an enduring favorite among readers.

Blantyre

Blantyre is a guest at Earlshall Park and is riding Beauty when Lady Anne has an accident. He sends a workman and Beauty for help, and later praises Beauty.

Ellen Blomefield

Ellen is one of Black Beauty's last owner. She and her sister employ Joe Green.

Miss Lavinia Blomefield

With her sister Ellen, Lavinia is Black Beauty's last owner and Joe Green's employer.

Mr. Blomefield

Mr. Blomefield is the vicar at Birkwick. He buys Merrylegs and hires Joe Green when the Gordons leave England.

The Butcher

The purpose of the character of the butcher is to give another example of a business owner who must cater to thoughtless customers and whose horse suffers as a consequence.

Captain

Captain is Beauty's companion as a cab horse at Jerry Barker's. Captain was in the cavalry during the Crimean War, and tells Beauty of his experiences as a horse in combat. Captain is injured in an accident caused by a drunk drayman and must then be put down.

Prince Charlie

Prince Charlie is a coster-boy whom Jerry nicknamed because of the loving relationship he has with his cart pony that will one day make him a king of drivers.

Duchess

Duchess is Black Beauty's mother. She was named Duchess but was often called "Pet" by Farmer Grey because she was so amiable. An old horse, she advised Black Beauty to be gentle and good, to do his work with a good will, and never bite or kick.

Lord George

When Ginger refuses to wear the bearing rein at Earlshall Park, she is given to young Lord George for hunting, but he ruins her with hard riding.

Ginger

Ginger is a tall, chestnut mare with a "long handsome neck." Ginger is ill-tempered from having been poorly treated. Beauty first met her at Birtwick Park, and they are sold together to Earlshall Park. There, Ginger rebels against the bearing rein, so she is used as a hunter. Ruined with hard riding, Ginger is put to pasture for a year to attempt a recovery but never completely regains her health and goes through a series of owners until she is reduced to being one of Skinner's cab horses. Beauty finds Ginger so overworked and abused she wants to die. Soon after, Beauty sees her tortured body being carted away.

Miss Flora Gordon

Flora is one of Squire Gordon's two daughters at Birtwick Hall.

Miss Jessie Gordon

Jessie is one of Squire Gordon's two daughters at Birtwick Hall.

Mrs. Gordon

Mrs. Gordon is the wife of Squire Gordon. She named Black Beauty. It was her illness that caused the Gordons to leave England and sell all their horses.

Squire Gordon

Squire Gordon is the owner of Birtwick Park. Squire Gordon is Black Beauty's first owner when he is old enough to be sold away from Farmer Grey's. The Squire is a good man who is known for his advocacy of kind treatment for horses.

Governor Grey Grant

Governor Grant is a fellow cab driver and friend of Jerry Barker. He is peacemaker and advisor for all the cab drivers. Grant helps out when Jerry is sick and buys Hotspur when the Barkers leave London.

Joe Green

Joe Green is the stable boy who replaces James Howard at Birtwick Hall. Joe nearly kills Black Beauty by putting him up improperly after a hard ride but later learns good horse care. Joe reports a man for beating two horses, and the man is jailed as a result. Joe and Merrylegs go to live at the Vicar's when the Gordons leave England. Still working for two of the Blomefield sisters when Beauty happens to be bought by them, Joe recognizes Beauty from Birtwick and rejoices to find him again.

Farmer Grey

Until he is four years old, Black Beauty resides in the meadow of Farmer Grey, who carefully breeds and trains quality horses.

Hotspur

Hotspur is the horse that replaces Captain in Jerry's stable. He is bought by Governor Grant when Jerry moves to the country.

James Howard

James is the stable boy at Birtwick Hall who saved Beauty and Ginger from a barn fire. James is so good with horses that Squire Gordon and John Manly recommend him to be the head groom at another estate. James is then replaced by Joe Green.

Jakes

Jakes is the foreman for the baker to whom Jerry sells Beauty. Jake responds to the admonition of a lady who begs him to take the bearing rein off Beauty when pulling a heavy load.

Justice

At Birtwick Hall, Beauty sometimes chats with Justice, the strong, good-tempered roan cob used for riding or the luggage cart.

John Manly

John Manly is the coachman for Birtwick Hall. He is an expert at and advocate of good care for horses. He gives wise advice to James Howard before advancing his career, and trains Joe to be a good groom. John Manly is one of the first characters that Sewell uses to voice moral opinions.

Merrylegs

Amiable Merrylegs is the fat gray pony who plays with the children at Birtwick Park but will not tolerate bad behavior. This character is possibly based on Sewell's own favorite gray pony. Merrylegs goes to the Vicar's with Joe Green when the Gordons move away.

Old Ba-a-ar Hoo

Old Ba-a-ar Hoo is an old gentleman who delivers coal and is proof, Jerry says, that a horse can be happy even in a poor place if properly treated.

Sir Oliver

Sir Oliver is an older, brown horse at Birkwick Hall. He has a shortened tail that was cut to meet a demand of fashion. His story leads to a discussion of the tail and ear clippings on dogs.

Peggy

Peggy is a pretty, dappled brown mare who works with Beauty at the livery stable. Peggy has an awkward gait because of short legs and mishandling by bad drivers. A gentle horse, Peggy is fortunate to be sold to some ladies for country driving and given a good life.

Rory

Beauty is paired with Rory at the livery stable until they are involved in a carriage accident that disables Rory and sends him to work pulling a coal cart.

Seedy Sam

Seedy Sam is a cab driver who works for the disreputable Nicholas Skinner. He describes to Jerry the wretched lives that men and horses have who must work on shares for owners like Skinner and the compromises he feels he must make to earn a living. Sam dies from overwork.

Nicholas Skinner

Nicholas Skinner is the owner of a low set of cabs and horses that he leases to drivers. Skinner so overworks Beauty that Beauty collapses and is almost sent to slaughter.

Reuben Smith

Reuben Smith is placed in charge of the stables at Earlshall Park when York is gone. Smith is competent with horses but has a problem with drink. On one of his binges, he has a riding accident that kills him and leaves Beauty with the blemished knees that prevent him from being a carriage horse anymore.

Farmer Thoroughgood

Farmer Thoroughgood is convinced by his grandson to buy Beauty at auction and to attempt rehabilitating him. Thoroughgood finds Beauty's final home with the Blomefield sisters.

Topics For Further Study

- Anna Sewell's mother was the author of a number of morally instructive children's books and verse. Research Mary Sewell, describing the content and intent of her works and how they fit into Victorian times.

- Female novelists were scarce during the Victorian period. Research other notable women writers and their works during the nineteenth century in Britain and the United States, and discuss what they did (or did not) have in common.

- The Victorian Age is named after Queen Victoria, who ruled Great Britain longer than any other monarch. Write a summary of the life and reign of Victoria, discussing her impact on the royal families of Europe through the marriages of her children and grandchildren.

- The size and influence of the British Empire peaked during the reign of Queen Victoria. Outline the growth of the empire around the world, including the beginning and ending dates of colonization in the various countries.

- The horse has been replaced in the workforce by modern technology. Write a report on how horses are used today. What is their role in transportation, entertainment, and fields such as ranching?

- Write an opinion piece explaining why you think that *Black Beauty* has remained so popular through the years. What is its appeal for adult and children?

Willie Thoroughgood

Willie is Farmer Thouroughgood's grandson. After convincing his grandfather to buy Beauty, Willie meticulously cares for Beauty and enables him to recover well enough to be sold to the Blomefield sisters. Willie's rescue allows Beauty to have a good life in his last years.

Mr. York

Mr. York is the head of the stables at Earlshall Park. York is good to the horses and soft-hearted enough to hire Reuben Smith despite his alcoholism, but he does not stand up to the mistress when she wants to use the bearing rein on the horses.

Themes

Mistreatment of Animals

In the original introduction to *Black Beauty* that Sewell herself wrote, she seems to indicate that the purpose of the book is that of an equine care manual, and not that of an entertaining story. Education was very important to Sewell, and since she declared, in part, that her intent was to induce "an understanding of the treatment of horses" through her "little book," she had to explain how to treat horses. Consequently, it has been said that one could read *Black Beauty* and come away fairly well prepared to actually care for a horse.

The point of describing appropriate equine care was to provide alternative, replacement behaviors to the practices that Sewell abhorred and wanted to stop. Evidence of abuse that causes pain and suffering for horses is found in nearly every chapter: tail bobbing, blinkers, double bits, check or bearing reins, risky jumps for sport, and long-term confinement in stalls. These practices, and the hope that pointing out their cruelty would bring an end to them, were the real focus of the book. Sewell's audience also learned that mean-tempered horses were not born but made by cruel treatment. It is important to note that Sewell did not lay blame for the mistreatment of horses so much on working men, even though they enacted the mistreatment, as on the owners and customers who exploited these workers and thereby their horses.

Sewell maintains the theme of evoking sympathy and understanding of horses through the different horse characters who appear in the book. Although Beauty experiences several different types of jobs, Sewell couldn't realistically place him in every kind of situation. So, evidencing her storytelling skill, she weaves encounters with different horses throughout the book, and each has a unique story to tell. As a result, Sewell is able to present to the reader the types of mistreatment that arise for horses in the city as well as the country; horses that are used for sport, for individual riding, for pulling carts, cabs, and carriages, and for combat. There are abuses that occur in each of these situations, and Sewell's pointed descriptions bring them to the reader's attention as had never been done before in literature.

Upright Behavior

Sewell was raised as a Quaker, lived in a strict religious house, gave classes to working class men, and did charitable work. Her mother wrote evangelical books for children. As a result, Sewell had a definite opinion about what was and was not acceptable behavior. Sewell was classically Victorian in her beliefs about morality, hard work, self-denial, and charity. These beliefs were expressed frequently throughout *Black Beauty*. Consequently, Sewell's novel was seen not only as a book about the proper treatment of horses, but also about the proper behavior of humans in general. The lessons given by Duchess to Beauty, by the coachman John Manly and the cab driver Jerry Barker, among others, were purposely placed in the novel for the edification of the reader. These lessons include: Duchess teaching that one should always do one's best and work hard; John Manly explaining the value of following an example of kindness by doing the same for others; and Jerry Barker demonstrating integrity, helping others in need, and establishing the family as a priority. Others, such as Squire Gordon, lecture on Sewell's main theme: the need for kindness to animals. There is also a very strong point made repeatedly by Sewell about the evils of drink. The groom who ruins Beauty's knees was drunk when he caused the calamity. Often, those seen mistreating horses are drunk. It is noted that many of the cab drivers waste time and money drinking. Even the good Governor Grant has a problem with alcohol and asks Jerry how he managed to give it up. Sewell was known to be an ardent advocate of temperance, and she used *Black Beauty* to express her view on this subject of moral concern as well as others.

Style

Animal Autobiography

Black Beauty requires the reader to accept the fact that a horse is the first-person narrator. This point of view quickly becomes believable because Sewell so effectively entered the mind of a horse that everything in the text is skillfully presented in terms of the animal's perceptions and observations. Sewell's triumph with this novel is the artful way she gets reader to feel that they are actually getting the story "straight from the horse's mouth." The reader is able to imagine what it is like to be a horse, how a bit feels in the mouth, how humans appear to animals, and so on. Stating on the cover page that the text was translated from the original equine is a clever way to set up the suspension of disbelief. Knowing that the story is a translation somehow gets readers past the problem that horses do not speak "English" and do not appear to talk at all.

The Use of the Novel Structure

Since the message of Sewell's book would have been suitable for a didactic series of essays, and since her mother wrote moral tales and verse for children, it is somewhat surprising that Sewell chose the form of the novel for her book. However, it is likely that Sewell had a repressed artistic talent that needed the freedom and space of a novel for best expression. In a novel she could explore many more areas of the written word than the structure of an essay would have allowed.

Also, Sewell loved the poetry of the Romantics, and it shows in the descriptive background she gives to her story. The opening paragraph is often quoted in references to the novel because it is this entrancing picture of the "pleasant meadow" at Farmer Grey's that captures the reading audience. Sewell makes the meadow a charming place by including details about "a pond of clear water," surrounded by shady trees, rushes, and waterlilies. The reader is also helped to envision a ploughed field, a plantation of fir trees, and "a running brook overhung by a steep bank." Later in the story, when Beauty stands severely injured next to the body of Ruben Smith, his anxiety and pain are comforted by the "calm, sweet April night" that includes a nightingale's song, "white clouds near the moon and a brown owl that flitted over the hedge."

The advice that Duchess gives to Black Beauty in the third chapter of the book establishes the plan for the novel. The introduction of the main character having been accomplished, Beauty's mother tells him that there are "many kinds of men" and describes the different types that a horse might encounter in his work. Of course, Beauty goes on through the course of the book to meet all these different types of men. The plot is built around these various encounters, their circumstances, and the results.

Historical Context

Victorian Life

The values of the Victorians were largely shaped by the Evangelical movement that emphasized salvation and the Utilitarian movement that emphasized efficiency. Both promoted self-control and self-denial. Victorians believed that one should be in total control of oneself at all times. Thrift and usefulness were highly regarded virtues, so people were expected to spend their time and money reasonably and with good purpose. Hard work was the key to success, so laziness and drunkenness were seen as the road to perdition. Self-help was another honored virtue. Even though class structure was rigid in Victorian England, members of the lower classes were expected to make an attempt to better themselves through education, personal development, and temperance. There was little sympathy for those who did not succeed in bettering their lot because failure was assumed to be a result of lack of effort. Other social forces were not given much consideration for the plight of the poor. This attitude was further reflected in the temperance movement that was aimed at the working class, ignoring any problems with alcohol in the other classes, because what was most important was getting the labor force to work in a sober condition for better productivity, which increased the wealth of the middle and upper classes. Victorian England was a society of great poverty existing alongside a still enormously wealthy aristocracy and a growing middle class. This middle class consisted of people whose improved economic status allowed them to afford their own horses, but an improved lifestyle did not necessarily mean that they learned how to take care of horses. Consequently, the abuse of horses became the serious problem addressed in *Black Beauty*. The Industrial Revolution also provided many new jobs and opportunities for rural people, but it led them into urban slums. Naturally, the working class resented the hypocritical effort of the Temperance Movement that diverted attention away from the problems of sanitation, overcrowded housing, poor working conditions, and other social abuses.

The Temperance Movement in Victorian England

A major social reform effort in Victorian England was the temperance movement. In effect, the temperance movement was also a class conflict because it was led by the middle-class but aimed at the working class. Specifically, the reform target was working-class men, because they drank in public and women usually did not. Drinking practices in the home were of some concern to the feminist movement in later years because of the link to domestic violence, but the original intent of the temperance movement was to affect a wasteful behavior that was contrary to the Victorian ideals of self-control and self-denial. Drunkenness caused one to lose control; therefore, it was logical that the consumption of alcohol was destructive. Besides, spending money on liquor was a wasteful form of entertainment; rather, one should save one's money and avoid useless times spent in self-indulgent leisure.

Morality was not the only driving force behind this movement. Industrialization demanded a reliable work force for the factories. At first, the intent of the movement was not to outlaw drinking, but to control it. Nor was there an attempt to "cure" drunks, who were seen as lost causes. Instead, the movement aimed to curb social drinking. Eventually, however, control was enforced through various forms of legislation. In addition, some temperance organizations took the step of requiring members to abstain entirely from alcohol consumption, but this "teetotalism" was a passing phase of the movement, as were attempts at the total prohibition of the sale of alcoholic beverages. Another tactic was to appeal to workers to refrain from drinking liquor because it was unhealthy and could lead to death.

The Church of England Temperance Society was formed in 1862 and became heavily involved by claiming there were two forms of life: church life and pub life. Its Sunday School Movement was an effort to encourage working-class children to attend church and learn about temperance. Eventually, though, a conflict over the appropriateness of sacramental wine led to the waning of church temperance efforts as well. Temperance stories for children began appearing in the late eighteenth century in Britain, and by the mid-nineteenth century temperance periodicals became common in both Britain and the United States. Other Victorian stories, such as *Black Beauty*, added a temperance moral into the plot. Although the Temperance Movement eventually died out as an organized cause, it did have the effect of creating a culture in

Compare
&
Contrast

- **1870s:** The Temperance Movement is in full swing in Britain and other countries. In 1874, the Woman's Christian Temperance Movement is founded in Cleveland, Ohio, and in 1883 becomes an international organization.

  Today: The temperance movement, per se, is no longer viable, but Alcoholics Anonymous is a well-known organization for those with alcohol-related disorders, and rehabilitation centers abound to assist those with drinking and other drug addictions, while multiple laws exist to deal with issues such as public intoxication and driving under the influence.

- **1870s:** Few women have careers other than that of homemakers, and Anna Sewell spends her entire life in her parents' home, though her mother is a bestselling author of children's morality tales.

  Today: Women in the workforce are commonplace in Britain and other developed countries and have a firm place as authors in the world of literature, although there are still fewer female than male Nobel and Pulitzer Prize winners in literature.

- **1870s:** Bedford Park, outside London, is developing as the first modern suburb.

  Today: Suburbs are the largest portions of cities and often cause the demise of downtown and inner-city businesses and lifestyles.

- **1870s:** The phonograph is invented, shortly after the introduction of the telephone and telegraph.

  Today: The phonograph has been replaced by music tapes, compact disks, and digital music formats; fiber optics, wireless devices, and satellites rather than the telegraph are used for communicating over long distances.

Victorian England that no longer tolerated public drunkenness and saw alcohol abuse as dysfunctional, not recreational.

Horses in Victorian Society

Horses played a vital role in nineteenth century life. They provided not only the main means of transportation, but also the labor force for a variety of jobs. They pulled carts, cabs, wagons, and barges on the roads and on city streets, worked as pit ponies in the coal mines, and helped plough rural fields. Writing for *Horsepower*, Margaret Bennett reports that "During the 1890s, there were over 11,000 hansom cabs (the taxis of their day) alone on the streets of London, needing twice that number of horses to operate." Despite their importance, horses were treated miserably. Bennett adds that horses "often died in harness due to overwork and lack of care." As brute labor, they were taken for granted, beaten, and, as Ginger said in the book, simply "used up." Those that pulled carriages were subject to whims of fashion that dictated docking tails or forcing horses to hold their heads up higher than was comfortable or practical. Without a long tail, a horse cannot rid itself of flies. With a head held in a painfully unnatural position by a bearing or check rein, a horse cannot use its full strength for pulling, breathe properly, or move its head from side to side to look about. It was abusive practices such as these that Sewell attacked in *Black Beauty*.

Critical Overview

Sewell saw *Black Beauty* as lessons in equine care more than as a literary story, so it is not surprising that some of the early critics appraised *Black Beauty* as a care guide as well as a novelistic form. Readers often thought that a veterinarian, coachman, or groom must have written the book because it was so accurate in its details. Regardless, *Black Beauty*, classified as "Juvenile" by libraries, is considered a children's classic and one that changed the nature of children's literature. It is true that readers usually first encounter this novel as

Several horse-drawn taxis in a row with their drivers, still from the 1994 film version of Black Beauty

© Warner Bros./The Kobal Collection/Keith Hamshere. Reproduced by permission

children, and there are film versions aimed strictly at a juvenile audience. However, many readers, such as Sewell biographer Susan Chitty, realize that if the book was written to educate those who handle horses, then it was written for working class men, not children.

Furthermore, like so many other readers, Lucy Grealy, who wrote the "Afterword" for a recent paperback edition of *Black Beauty*, has discerned additional elements that adults can appreciate. Sewell's novel, Grealy says, goes "into the darker crevices of human failures and frailties, cruelty and indifference to such cruelty." Grealy admits that *Black Beauty* is "a loving fable in so many ways;" however, despite its happy ending for the protagonist, it is "also a deeply sad novel, a tragic account of human failure."

But first, *Black Beauty* is about a horse. Frances Clarke Sayers, in an article entitled "Books That Enchant: What Makes a Classic?," quotes a child as saying, "The fact remains that when you read *Black Beauty* you feel like a horse." In a piece on Sewell for *Children's Books and Their Creators* (Silvey), the comment is made that "Sewell's careful descriptions let readers feel the bit tearing into Black Beauty's mouth or the chills caused by a stable boy who doesn't know enough to throw

blankets on an overheated horse." Such skillful detail illustrates and strengthens Sewell's message about the need for kind treatment of horses.

Her detail and artistic talent also enliven the novel with elements of excitement. Critics have noted that the reader is captured by the action of the nighttime run to get the doctor for Mrs. Gordon, the flooded bridge, and the stable fire. A review of *Black Beauty* in *The Critic* in 1890 praises Sewell's "skill in the art of narration," writing that the story is more "readable than the average novel of today."

Vincent Starrett, in an essay for *Literary Appreciation*, says that *Black Beauty* "is unquestionably the most successful animal story ever written." He added that it is "certain that more than any other single agency this humane classic has improved the lot of the captive horse."

The book was eventually adopted by both the British and American Societies for the Prevention of Cruelty to Animals, and thousands of copies were distributed for educational purposes. As a result, in the United States, a million copies were sold between 1890 and 1892, and *Black Beauty* continued to sell at the rate of a quarter million copies each year for another twenty years.

While some critics have found *Black Beauty* too sentimental and didactic, its success belies these criticisms. Sewell was not just a novice writer pounding on her pulpit. Critics have praised the way her sincerity and passionate convictions are combined with skillful characterization, clever juxtaposition of human and animal experiences, eloquent descriptions, and overall good storytelling.

Criticism

Lois Kerschen

Kerschen is a school district administrator and freelance writer. In this essay, Kerschen discusses the moral lessons, particularly about temperance, that Sewell incorporates into Black Beauty.

In the first chapter of *Black Beauty*, Anna Sewell provides her hero with a wise admonition from his mother: "I hope you will grow up gentle and good, and never learn bad ways; do your work with a good will." This advice may have come from an equine mother, but it is the kind of moral instruction that humans could use as well. It was Sewell's stated intent to write a book that would "induce kindness, sympathy, and an understanding treatment of horses." That is, the subject was not horses, but the treatment of horses, and therefore the book was a set of instructions for humans. In the process, Sewell set forth not only the proper care of horses, but the proper behavior of humans in other areas as well.

Considering Sewell's intent for the novel, it is reasonable to believe that an appropriate audience would be the adults, particularly men, who worked with and cared for horses. However, the book is traditionally classified as a juvenile novel and was actually used for moral instruction in schools. As Lucy Grealy noted in her "Afterword" to a recent edition of *Black Beauty*, the Education Act of 1870, which legally established public education in England, "meant that a huge amount of educational material was needed, and *Black Beauty*, viewed as a morally correct book, was eventually being sold by the box rather than the volume." After all, the book contains lessons such as the following from Chapter Three: "She told me the better I behaved, the better I should be treated, and that it was wisest always to do my best." This kind of instruction is wise counsel for school children as well as colts, and the schools hoped their pupils would perceive the application to their own lives.

It is also helpful to warn children as well as young horses that

> There are a great many kinds of men; there are good, thoughtful men . . . ; but there are bad, cruel men. . .; there are a great many foolish men, vain, ignorant and careless, who never trouble themselves to think; but still I say, do your best, wherever it is, and keep up your good name.

While much of the book is devoted to exposing the various types of cruelty imposed on animals, Sewell expands the point about animal abuse in Chapter 13 to connect it to a general moral deficiency. The chapter is titled "The Devil's Trade Mark" because the schoolmaster who punishes a boy for torturing flies equates hurting the weak and helpless to the hard-heartedness and cowardliness that is the devil's trademark in a person. The teacher says that "the devil was a murderer from the beginning, and a tormentor to the end." In contrast, God's mark is love. When John Manly hears about the incident from James he agrees that people can talk all they want about religion but: "There is no religion without love . . . if it does not teach them to be good and kind to man and beast, it is all a sham." James later asks John if he holds with the saying that a man should look after himself only and "take care of number one." John replies that such thinking is selfish and heathenish.

Sewell created the character of Jerry Barker to supply most of her lessons on honesty and integrity. In scene after scene, Jerry makes decisions based on his strong moral convictions with statements including: "Every man must look after his own soul; you can't lay it at another man's door like a foundling, and expect him to take care of it"; "If a thing is right, it can be done, and if it is wrong, it *can be done without*; and a good man will find a way." He will not take extra fare for extra effort because he finds sufficient reward in a job well done. Jerry also will not work on Sundays, not only because he believes the day is for church and family, but also because he is sensible enough to know the he and the horses must have a day of rest to stay healthy and work well the rest of the week. When he is criticized by his fellow drivers for turning down a good job just because it is on Sunday, Sewell uses Jerry to voice further lessons: "Real religion is the best and truest thing in the world; and the only thing that can make a man really happy, or make the world better."

Jerry once broke his Sunday rule to drive a friend to her dying mother's bedside. Sewell makes certain that this good deed is rewarded with a refreshing day in the country for Jerry and Beauty. Another good deed with fortunate consequences is that of driving a mother with her sick child to the hospital for no fee. This charitable act results in a chance encounter with Mrs. Fowler, his wife's former employer, that reinforces their relationship and will later tie into the rescue provided by Mrs. Fowler when Jerry becomes too ill to continue work as a cab driver.

Knowing that *Black Beauty* would be her only book, Sewell apparently wanted to include as much as she could on various subjects. Therefore, to express her opinion about the importance of elections, there is a chapter on the heightened activity for cab drivers on election day, and Sewell uses Jerry to teach that: "An election is a very serious thing; at least it ought to be, and every man ought to vote according to his conscience, and let his neighbour do the same."

Sewell inserts other good people into the book to deliver lessons. Jerry's customer who stops an inebriated driver from whipping his horses brutally tells Jerry:

> People think only about their own business, and won't trouble themselves to stand up for the oppressed, nor bring the wrong-doer to light. I never see a wicked thing . . . without doing what I can. . . . My doctrine is this, that if we see cruelty or wrong that we have the power to stop, and do nothing, we make ourselves sharers in the guilt.

One of the strongest themes in *Black Beauty* is that of temperance. A major turning point in the story occurs when Beauty's knees are ruined in an accident caused by a drunken groom. To build up the tragedy of the accident, Sewell describes the groom Reuben Smith in glowing terms concerning his abilities and personality but notes that "he had one great fault, and that was the love of drink." Smith could be fine for weeks at a time, but then go on a binge and "be a disgrace to himself, a terror to this wife, and a nuisance to all that had to do with him." Smith had already been dismissed from another position because of a drunken incident, and it caused his family to have to move out of a nice cottage. York had hired him out of pity when Smith promised never to take another drink. However, Sewell's depiction of the incident with Smith shows how alcoholism causes broken promises and broken lives.

Sewell drops other negatives images of alcohol consumption throughout *Black Beauty*. Sometimes her mention is slight, as when Beauty is explaining that one problem with getting sufficient water is that "[s]ome grooms will go home to their beer and leave us for hours with our dry hay and oats and nothing to moisten them." In the scene in which Joe Green witnesses a man beating his horse, the abuser was described as being in "a towering passion, and the

> Even if Sewell was a little obvious in her intent to preach right conduct, one cannot argue with the positive results, not only for horses but for the cab drivers' situation that she highlighted as well."

worse for drink." When one of Jerry's customers sees a horse being abused and intervenes, the driver is described as someone "who had clearly been drinking." It was a drayman who "proved to be very drunk" who was responsible for the accident that so injured Captain that he had to be put down.

In her description of Governor Grant, Sewell says that he is "generally a good-humored, sensible man." She adds, however, that when he drinks too much, he becomes short-tempered and combative. Sewell has Grant ask Jerry how he overcame the habit of drinking so that she can provide a prescription for a cure. Jerry says that when he realized that he was no longer his own master "I saw that one of us must knock under—the drink devil, or Jerry Barker." He admits that it was a struggle, but with Polly's help and the knowledge that he might lose her and his soul to drink if he did not stop, he succeeded.

A review of *Black Beauty* in *Children's Books and Their Creators* mentions that "[s]ome critics have felt that Sewell's preaching fatally flaws her narrative." Perhaps Sewell anticipated this criticism because she uses a somewhat indirect method to deliver her moral messages. The sermonizing about good conduct is not made as a direct plea but comes as opinions expressed by human characters that the horses overhear. Thus, the horses appear to be objective observers of the human scene and are merely reporting the conversations they have heard.

Even if Sewell was a little obvious in her intent to preach right conduct, one cannot argue with the positive results, not only for horses but for the cab drivers' situation that she highlighted as well. The sympathy that was evoked resulted in the building of shelters for the drivers where they could find respite and instruction in religion and temperance. By adding the element of a human plight in

Black Beauty, still from the 1994 film version of Black Beauty © Warner Bros./The Kobal Collection/Keith Hamshere. Reproduced by permission

a book about the harsh treatment of horses, Sewell provided a balance to the message of the novel and enriched it with a portrayal of the complexity of the relationship between humans and animals.

Grealy studied a number of introductions that have appeared in various publications of *Black Beauty*. As time passed and literary fashion changed, the conclusions about the strengths and weaknesses of the novel also changed. Grealy found that critics began to focus "not so much on the human failings depicted in the book as they did on the high morals of Beauty himself." Beauty's virtues are designed not only to persuade people that animals deserve to be treated well, but are intended to be applied to humans, too, concerning "how we ourselves must value honest and hard work under disagreeable circumstances." Therefore, the early response to the book to use it as moral instruction in schools was an understandable and valid reaction. All literature is intended to help the reader to learn and grow, and there are enough lessons about animals and people, about the challenges of life, to give *Black Beauty* timeless value.

Source: Lois Kerschen, Critical Essay on *Black Beauty*, in *Novels for Students*, Thomson Gale, 2006.

Catherine Dybiec Holm

Holm is a short story and novel author, and a freelance writer. In this essay, Holm looks at how Sewell effectively uses a horse's point of view to address issues of cruelty, morality, and class in mid-Victorian England.

The author who decides to tell a story from the point of view of an animal has some tricky challenges. Somehow, the author must use this point of view so that it enhances, rather than detracts from, the story that the author puts on the page. But having an animal as a story's main point of view character also lends advantages. Because of an animal's assumed innocence (in comparison to humans, in this case), the author might more easily make points in the story that could appear preachy or dogmatic if these points were made through a human character. In *Black Beauty*, Sewell uses circumstance and Black Beauty's point of view to effectively make statements about morality, animal treatment, and class division. Sewell uses the horse's point of view to her advantage, and as a result, none of the book's statements about these issues sound overly dogmatic. These issues would run the risk of sounding too much like the author's opinion, if they were voiced through a human character.

Almost immediately, the reader is made aware of the importance of class in the setting of this story. Even among horses, class and breeding are quite important. Black Beauty's mother tells him that he is "well-bred and well-born," and she warns him not to bite or kick in play, as the cart horses (who have not learned manners) do.

In *Black Beauty*, some members of the upper classes will go to any length to appear fashionable. These people are not above making their horses suffer, for the appearance of an upturned neck. Such people force their horses to walk unnaturally all for the sake of appearance. Sewell's detail makes these examples all the more effective, as in the case of Ginger. Ginger is driven with the painful check rein.

> Fancy . . . if you tossed your head up high, and were obliged to hold it there, and that for hours together, not able to move it at all except with a jerk still higher, your neck aching till you did not know how to bear it. It was worse when we had to stand by the hour, waiting for our mistress at some grand party or entertainment.

Sewell's detail helps the reader imagine just how painful it could be for a horse to hold its head up continuously, even though the same reader may previously have been ignorant of check reining, and may have imagined that the horse simply looked good with its head forced upright. For additional contrast, the horse is forced to suffer to support the mistress's upper class lifestyle and entertainment. Cruel humans can be male or female in Sewell's world, and women who mistreat horses in *Black Beauty* do so for the sake of fashion and appearance.

Fashion, and its effect on horses, shows up in many variations in *Black Beauty*. An old horse has his tail painfully docked, and is outraged that it was done "for fashion!" The horse notes that this is done on dogs' ears and tails, causing the animals great pain. And with the subtle irony that Sewell occasionally slips into this story, the old horse mentions that none of the puppies were drowned, "for they were a valuable kind." Animals that have some value, or are perceived as fashionable, are kept by humans, though they are subjected to the pain of docked tails and ears. Animals that are not valuable, or fashionable, are easily expendable. The old horse sums it up by saying that "fashion is one of the wickedest things in the world." And reasonably—and it does seem reasonable from Sewell's well-portrayed animal point of view—the old horse wonders why humans do not dock their own noses for the sake of fashion or to look "plucky."

Sewell makes it apparent to the reader, via situations that the horses observe or are involved in, that the world includes people who are mean to animals, as well as people who care about animal welfare. In the first chapter, Beauty mentions a ploughboy who purposefully throws sticks and stones at the colts to make them gallop. Sewell contrasts the ploughboy's behavior with his master's. The master admonishes the boy and fires him. Sewell does two things here to effectively convey a message about the treatment of animals; she contrasts the boy's bad behavior with a boss who is willing to fire the boy, and she presents the whole event through the eyes of Black Beauty. If Sewell had made a blunt statement directly to the reader about humans' cruelty to animals, it is likely that the reader would feel preached at. Readers do not appreciate being given a sermon by the author. The event may have seemed preachy if it had been told to the reader through the point of view of the farmer, for example. But because the reader assumes that a horse is naturally more innocent, and less judgmental and cynical than a human, the same event through the eyes of a horse is more effective. The horse is simply observing. Sewell uses this technique throughout the book to show the reader instances of friction among the classes, the

> " … because the reader assumes that a horse is naturally more innocent, and less judgmental and cynical than a human, the same event through the eyes of a horse is more effective."

importance of appearance, and ethical and moral attributes of other people in the story.

Early on, Black Beauty's mother prepares the young horse for the world of humans. She tells him that there are "good, thoughtful men" and "bad, cruel men." Beauty will soon learn this for himself, since Sewell peppers the book with both good and bad people. Throughout this story, Sewell constantly reminds the reader that humans consider themselves superior to the "dumb" animals that live around them. In the hunt that occurs early in the book, Black Beauty and his mother see a horse and a man die. If this incident were told through the point of view of a human, the reader would not find it unusual for more emphasis to be placed on the human's death (rather than the horse's death). But because the event is seen and experienced through the eyes of the horses, the reader realizes that the horses are just as upset (and possibly more upset) about the horse's death. This forces the reader to realize that in a human mindset, man (in this case) is considered more important than horse. The reader also cannot fail to miss the irony that the man is attended much more quickly than the horse is. The horse is left groaning in the field, until the farrier comes to look at the injured animal. Again, because the reader sees this event through the eyes of horses, the reader starts to think from that animal's viewpoint. The reader begins to realize that in this world, humans have power over animals, and humans act as if they are superior to animals.

The reader cannot fail to notice the irony when Black Beauty realizes that the horse killed in the hunt was his brother. Black Beauty says:

> So poor Rob Roy who was killed at that hunt was my brother! I did not wonder that my mother was so

What Do I Read Next?

- *National Velvet* (1935), by Enid Bagnold, was made famous by the 1944 movie starring Elizabeth Taylor. It is a story about a fourteen-year-old girl named Velvet Brown who trains a horse for the top steeplechase competition, the Grand National, and wins against all odds.

- A favorite American horse story is *My Friend Flicka* (1941), by Mary O'Hara. It is about a Wyoming boy, his special relationship with a filly, and the complex marriage of his parents. The book was so popular that it was made into a television series in the 1950s.

- The original story of *Bambi* (1926), by Felix Salten, gives a serious message about the cycle of life and nature's law as told through the viewpoint of the forest animals.

- Probably the best-known animal autobiography following *Black Beauty* is the novel *Beautiful Joe* (1893), by Margaret Marshall Saunders. It depicts the true story of a cruelly abused collie. It was the first book to sell a million copies in Canada.

- Sheila Burnford's *Incredible Journey* (1961), about two dogs and a cat traveling together across the wilderness to get back to their human family, is one of the most popular animal stories of all time and was made into a hugely popular film.

- *The Black Stallion* (1941), by Walter Farley, is an adventure story about a boy, a wild horse, a shipwreck, and a desert island. It was made into a popular movie in 1979.

---

troubled. It seems that horses have no relations; at least they never know each other after they are sold.

Obviously, as shown by this excerpt, Sewell is pointing out that these horses do care about their relations, just as humans do. But she also makes the point that horse families and relations are routinely split by humans, when humans separate horses and sell them at will.

Even though humans in *Black Beauty* often consider themselves superior to "dumb" animals, Sewell also gives the reader instances where animals clearly understand more than humans. When Black Beauty refuses to cross a bridge because he knows something is wrong, Beauty recalls the words of his kind master, one human in this story who does understand the nuances of animals.

> Master said God had given men reason, by which they could find out things for themselves; but He had given animals knowledge, which did not depend on reason, and which was much more prompt and perfect in its way, and by which they often saved the lives of men.

Sewell, through the words of a horse and an enlightened master, makes the point that animals often stand between life and death for a human. Humans lack the ability to sense and read situations as an animal can.

There are many instances in *Black Beauty* when humans intentionally mistreat horses, and there are also many instances when humans are oblivious of their actions and the effects on the horses. These instances of obliviousness are no less cruel—they still cause pain for the horses. Because they are presented from the horses' points of view, the reader feels the greater impact of these events. If Sewell, for example, worked through the point of view of a human, she could mention that this human pulled the horse about, or tugged on the reins to get the horse to turn a certain way. A reader would probably think nothing of these actions through the eyes of the human character. But Sewell's detail and knowledge of horsemanship, along with her sympathetic horse characters, give an entirely different slant on the same situation.

> If people knew what a comfort to horses a light hand is, and how it keep a good mouth and a good temper, they surely would not check and drag and pull at the rein as they often do. Our mouths are so

Black Beauty as a workhorse, still from the 1971 film version of Black Beauty © Paramount/The Kobal
Collection. Reproduced by permission

tender . . . and we know in an instant what is required of us.

Although *Black Beauty* has its share of eye opening situations that effectively illustrate cruelty and obliviousness regarding animals, several of the people in this book demonstrate outstanding moral character. Again, this is a way that Sewell avoids preachiness. The author's message would have seemed too forced and false if all the humans in the story had been bad (or oblivious, or apathetic) people. On the contrary, several characters demonstrate real strength in the defense of their morals. John takes time to tell boys that cruelty is hard-hearted and cowardly. An old man speaks up against the hunt, saying that "a man's life and a horse's life are worth more than a fox's tail." When Joe accidentally makes Black Beauty sick by giving the horse cold water, John is quick to point out that ignorance is "the worst thing in the world, next to wickedness." And Jerry demonstrates many acts of kindness—taking a woman with a sick baby to the hospital and refusing payment; getting a young man to the train on time and refusing payment; and treating his animals in the best way possible.

Through Black Beauty's eyes, the reader is given an effective look at a myriad of social issues of the time; including the treatment of animals,

fashion, and the influence of the class system. *Black Beauty* will always be a classic because all of these issues are portrayed effectively, and uniquely, through the mind of an animal.

Source: Catherine Dybiec Holm, Critical Essay on *Black Beauty*, in *Novels for Students*, Thomson Gale, 2006.

Joyce Hart

Hart is a freelance writer and author of several books. In the following essay, Hart examines Sewell's only novel to find the elements that have created the long-lasting appeal despite the novel's flaws.

Anna Sewell wrote just one novel in her life, most of it composed as she suffered the effects of a debilitating disease. There is a passion evident in her writing, more than likely created by her sense of urgency in communicating a lesson she felt compelled to deliver to the world before dying. In her earnest attempt to appeal to all horse owners to treat their animals in a more humane manner, much of the prose in Sewell's book is recorded in a didactic tone. Messages against animal cruelty are paramount, of course, but there is also other subtle moralizing going on here, making some of the reading, in contemporary times, a little hard to

> So as the story develops, so does the emotional grasp on children's attention, as their feelings deepen and become more complex."

swallow. The author's emphasis on teaching specific lessons has also resulted in characters who fit all too comfortably into stereotypical forms. The good characters, for instance, are very, very good, and the few others who do not match this mold are totally and mercilessly corrupt. But despite the novel's shortcomings, this story has a very specific quality that has allowed it to continue to inspire the very young at heart for more than one hundred years after it was written. So what then is the appeal? Why does this story still engage its modern audience far removed from the times and social issues that plagued the world of the nineteenth century?

The sole purpose of Sewell's novel was to make people take better care of their horses. And one way that Sewell attempts to do this is to make the animals in her story appear more human. She wanted her audience to look at animals as creatures who had thoughts and feelings; rather than seeing them as if they were machines, created to do the work that humans were incapable of doing on their own. As seen through Sewell's eyes, horses were often treated as slaves in her time. Little or no thought was rendered by horse owners as to the effect that their cruelty was having on the physical and mental attitude of their animals. Sewell's hope was that she might change all that.

Another thing that Sewell does in order to open the hearts of her readers is to tell her story through the eyes of a beautiful and sensitive horse. In reading this novel, audiences experience every joyful and every sorrowful moment of Black Beauty's life as if they were living through the same situations of the protagonist. The horse, although he is never made into a cartoon character who talks, does, however, speak his mind in this story. He does so through what might be called his intended thoughts, which he is able to share with other animals. In this way, Sewell makes Black Beauty appear human in his reactions and emotions. This is not a talking-horse gimmick, however, because Black Beauty never exposes his thoughts to the human characters in the novel, except through his gestures, which any horse might make—a nudging with his nose, a neigh, a tossing of his head. Sewell does not, in other words, remove Black Beauty from his "horseness." Rather, she situates him in a very definite horse world but then imbues him with a soul, a spirit that is related to that of every living creature on earth. In this way, Sewell arouses more sympathy or empathy for her protagonist; and this is seen most evidently in children who hear or read the story of *Black Beauty*.

Not only does Sewell provide an avenue into the mind and heart of her protagonist through his thoughts, she also gives her readers quite an extensive biography of Black Beauty. Readers are introduced to him shortly after he is born. There is even mention of his lineage, supplied not just to give readers an account of his pedigree, but to place Black Beauty in a family—to connect him to a mother and father. This provides a subtle reference for young readers. Black Beauty does not just appear out of nowhere. He is not just a horse, he is also a son and a grandson. His mother was, at one time, pregnant with him, just as children have been told that their mothers once carried them. And like their mothers, Black Beauty's mother carried him, gave birth to him, and nursed him. This also provides Black Beauty with a history, which adds more depth to his character. Beginning a story in this way especially grabs the imagination of children, who are still very much attached to their parents. Then, as the story progresses, young readers relate to Black Beauty's youth. For example, they associate with the feelings of Black Beauty as he plays in the field as a young colt. And Sewell masterfully intensifies these feelings when she provides a playground setting (for horses, that is) and even includes a neighborhood bully who throws stones at the young colts. Young readers, once again, are pulled into the story through these details. Every schoolyard has a bully, so every child can connect with the young colt as he faces this challenge. And when the "master" comes to the rescue of Black Beauty and the other young horses by banishing the bully from the fields where the young horses play, children cheer the strength and power of the good master and protector. This master represents a sense of security for children reading this book. They would like to believe that at every moment that they are challenged by a bully, they too would be protected by some powerful master.

Black Beauty's mother hits another nerve for young readers. She is represented as a loving and gentle counsel for the young horse. She provides instructions about life that Black Beauty never forgets. In the very beginning of the story, Black Beauty's mother tells him: "I hope you will grow up gentle and good, and never learn bad ways; do your work with a good will, lift your feet up well when you trot, and never bite or kick even in play." Ignoring the mention of "lifting your feet up," most children reading this story will reflect on similar advice that their mothers have provided them. And as youngsters continue to read the story, they have many opportunities to remember these words of Black Beauty's mother's counsel. Just as children are often heard speaking to their dolls, repeating advice that their parents have given to them, they might also find themselves silently reminding Black Beauty (as the story progresses) that he must always be good no matter what circumstances he finds himself in. And in this way, they, like the master who chases away the bully, take on the role of Black Beauty's protector. So now young readers are relating to the story on two levels: they personally identify with Black Beauty's need to find love, friendship, and a safe home; and on a second level, they take on the responsibility of guiding Black Beauty in the right direction. When Black Beauty gets into trouble or in a tough situation, children have an urge to tell him to always be good and never to bite or kick. So as the story develops, so does the emotional grasp on children's attention, as their feelings deepen and become more complex.

With these two caps on, the first one relating on a personal level with Black Beauty and the second one playing out the role of Black Beauty's protector, young readers are set for the journey that Black Beauty will now take. The next challenge that the horse must face is that of discipline—Black Beauty must be "tamed." The descriptions of this process are reminiscent, in general, of lessons that all children must learn. Black Beauty's training includes wearing things that do not seem natural to him, such as a rein and a saddle. Children can relate to this in a different way, such as perhaps when they are forced to put on raincoats and boots before going outside in a warm summer rain. Black Beauty also has to learn to "go just the way they (adults who ride him) wish and to go quietly." What child has not heard these admonishments? So again, children anticipate what Black Beauty is feeling. They understand how much they are torn when presented with a chance to do something their way but must take into consideration their parents' needs.

They know how difficult it can be when they do not obey their parents and other adults around them; and they also know how thorny the consequences might be if they do not behave according to adults' wishes. This is a process of growing up and learning the rules of society. And even though children might not fully understand all the implications of the discipline they are taught, they know exactly how it feels to go through the "taming."

Black Beauty's next challenge is also one that children know about. That is the act (and fear) of leaving home. Whether, for children, it is going to a babysitter or going to school, leaving home is a trip into the unknown. So when Black Beauty moves away from his mother and is taken to Birtwick Park to his new owners, young readers fully empathize with him again. They completely understand the empty feeling that Black Beauty might be experiencing, as he has to say farewell to the people and the animals that he has known all his young life. And when he arrives at his new destination, as any child would do, Black Beauty assesses his new environment; judges the comfort level of his surroundings and the quality of the food and care; and then searches for friendship. And it is through one of Black Beauty's new friends, especially Ginger, that children experience a new revelation. Ginger gives them a chance to reflect on some of their own behavior patterns. For here, in Ginger, is an explanation that children can handle concerning their own bouts of anger and lashing out that might temporarily corrupt their ordinarily good behavior. While Black Beauty represents the always-be-good aspect of their personalities, Ginger clarifies some of children's other more destructive emotions.

No matter how much he or she is loved or how well she or he is trained, no child is good all the time. Grumpiness or moodiness can invade a child's more pleasant nature from time to time. Seldom do young children fully understand where these moods come from or why they have clouded their minds, but they definitely recognize them. And Ginger provides young readers with a prime example of "naughtiness." Ginger has not been raised well; and so she is not very trusting of the humans or the animals around her. She is known to bite and act unruly. Ginger arouses a lot of questions in children. They want to know why she is acting that way. Why is she not as good as Black Beauty? When adults provide answers such as the fact that someone has not been nice to Ginger, children immediate get it. They understand what it feels like to have someone do something unkind and how that can generate ill feelings in themselves. And as the friendship develops between Ginger and Black Beauty, and Ginger becomes more accepting of her surroundings and thus behaves better, children often nod their heads, comprehending how powerful a good friendship can be. They might not fully understand how good emotions can banish, or at least minimize, bad ones, but they can feel it.

And thus, young readers are introduced to the characters of this story. By the end of the first part of this novel, they are totally entrenched in the life of Black Beauty. On a simple level, their interest is sparked. And on a more complex level, they have fallen in love with the beautiful protagonist. They eagerly want to follow Black Beauty through all his adventures. They want to console him when he falls and hurts his knees or when he must once again say good-bye to friends. They are very cognizant of both of these painful experiences. They feel sorry for him when he must pull heavy weights, stand outside all night, and bear the chill of a winter's harsh storm. Sewell has carefully crafted a story that has pulled them in and will not let them go. The author, through her careful and affectionate rendering of a sad story with a somewhat happy ending, knew how to tug at her readers' hearts. One can only surmise that she was capable of doing this because her own heart ached for the animals that she had learned to love. And although her style of writing may have some flaws, her ability to convey her love of Black Beauty to her audience, especially to a group of readers as sensitive as young children, is a well honed skill.

Source: Joyce Hart, Critical Essay on *Black Beauty*, in *Novels for Students*, Thomson Gale, 2006.

Laura Carter

Carter is currently employed as a freelance writer. In this essay, Carter considers the social and historical relevance of Sewell's document as a treatise on animal rights.

Anna Sewell's Black Beauty served in her time not only as a treatise on animal rights, it is an account closely relevant to the author's personal life, as well as her advocacy for horses in a time where females were not a presence in the equine community, their voices more often than not discounted in a male-dominated society. Examples are sprinkled throughout the novel, in the words and actions of the characters, both animal and female, which demonstrate their ability to provoke responses that expose the very underpinnings of a male-dominated Victorian society.

Strikingly different for a Victorian woman, Sewell knew a great deal about an industry long dominated by men. The novel's cast of characters, from stable boys to groomsmen to proprietors—all are men. It is primarily men who openly speak for Sewell in her quest for animal rights. In one scene, for example, one of the novel's main characters goes out of his way to tip off a neighbor of the abuses a pony is suffering as his son needlessly whips, kicks and knocks a "good little pony about shamefully because he would not leap a gate that was too high for him." In another instance, Joe admonishes a carter for flogging or beating a team of horses for failing to pull a load of bricks that is too heavy for them to manage. When the carter tells him to mind his own business, Joe is compelled to knock on the door of the master brick maker to tell him of the trouble. It is Joe's testimony in front of a magistrate that ultimately leads to the carter's undoing. In these and other examples, Sewell uses the male voice to succinctly or clearly drive home her thesis or call to action with respect to animal cruelty, asserting that "with cruelty and oppression it is everyone's business to interfere when they see it."

However, a few of Sewell's female characters are also a leveling presence in the novel, often interceding in equine matters when abuse of an animal is involved. In one such instance, the daughter of one traveler sees the poor condition Black Beauty is in and offers her opinion, telling her father that she is confident that "this poor horse cannot take us and our luggage so far, he is very weak and worn out." Although the young woman implores or begs her father to consider a second cab to accommodate their luggage, her pleas are dismissed. "Nonsense, Grace, get in at once," her father orders, telling her not to make so much of a "fuss." He chastises her for expecting a "man of business to examine every cab horse before he hired it," insistent that the driver knows his business, "of course." Sewell's words do put into context the true nature of women's roles in nineteenth century England. The daughter is openly criticized for questioning, to the point of harassment, a man who, it is implied by her father, a position of unquestionable authority when it comes to the business of cab horses. This scene also puts into stark perspective the colorless victory Grace realizes when Black Beauty tragically collapses under the extreme weight of the overloaded carriage hired by her father.

In yet another scene, however, the frivolity or thoughtlessness of one woman leads to yet another tragic injury for Black Beauty. When Black Beauty is sold to a new owner, John, his former groom warns the new owner of the dangers of using a bearing rein. Although both the former groom and new coachman reach an understanding, the coachman shares that "my lady" is partial to a certain style, requiring carriage horses to be reined up tight, mindful of fashion rather than the horse's well being. And later, when the horses are reined up to satisfy the lady's request, Ginger rebels, then returns to the barn injured. The coachman responds, "I thought we should have some mischief soon—master will be sorely vexed, but there—if a woman's husband can't rule her, of course a servant can't." First, this passage suggests that it is offensive a woman could be so easily swayed by style that she forgets any concern for the horses in her husband's care. Second, it is clear to the coachman that she has too much to say in household affairs, that her behavior is to be dictated by her husband in order to be deemed acceptable, that she must be managed.

Sewell's life seemingly shifts between two worlds, as aptly demonstrated by the text, that of the perfect Victorian lady and outspoken animal activist. In the forward to Black Beauty, Carol Fenner calls Sewell's only novel "surprising," also noting that "it was an unusual thing for a Victorian woman to know so much about horses." Also unusual is the seemingly unanimous opinion of many critics, including Fenner, who aptly remarked that the novel made "a deep impression on men and women alike." What her novel did so skillfully, that none had considered before, was to go into the psyche of the horse, to portray the noble animal from a different point of view. Black Beauty had feelings and shared insights in such a way as to garner or earn sympathy and also implicate the actions of abusive drivers, in a period during which England was known for its abuse of horses. According to Fenner, most horses "suffered badly in the hands of their human keepers." She adds, "The were underfed, they grew lame and sore, and they worked with overloaded carts in burning heat or freezing cold-over ice and mud." They were also beaten to inspire them to work, and often died in the harness. And, there were abuses in the name of fashion including tail cropping and use of the bearing rein.

According to Professor Waller Hastings, in his summary of Sewell's life, her book garnered or gained sympathy from animal anticruelty groups, and "was widely used as propaganda by groups seeking more humane treatment of horses." The book was passed out freely among horse handlers and drivers, and was seen as the strongest form of propaganda used to curb the abuse of their animals. Part of what makes the book such an effective tool

> **The reader finds in Black Beauty a perfect specimen flawed only by the shortcomings of men who choose to take advantage of his good nature and willingness to work in favor of their own short-sighted, often times brutal agendas."**

in the Sewell crusade, according to some scholars, are veiled references to slavery. Hastings mentions that in the work of at least one critic, through the use of slave language, the horses of the novel are portrayed as slaves rather than servants. For example, Black Beauty relates himself to his handler in the tradition of the servant/master relationship, and is called "Darkie." And, it has been pointed out that the pattern of the narrative itself closely imitates one familiar to slave narratives. The contrast between Black Beauty's acceptance of equine servitude juxtaposed or compared with Ginger's resistance, says Hastings, "reveals the uneasiness with which author and society view overt rebellion, while at the same time revealing the causes of rebellion."

The author introduces readers to a world through the eyes of a horse. And it is from this perspective that Sewell makes a case for the animal, speaking for a horse that cannot advocate or speak for himself. The reader finds in Black Beauty a perfect specimen flawed only by the shortcomings of men who choose to take advantage of his good nature and willingness to work in favor of their own short-sighted, often times brutal agendas. Sewell's passion for the horse, it has been suggested, has perhaps come from deep personal experience with an ankle injury that rendered her an invalid throughout most of her adult life. How closely, too, did the novel manage to parallel Victorian life for women, unintentional or otherwise, with regard to the prevailing notion of her time that women should be seen and not heard. All of the animals in the novel are silenced. They cannot speak up to defend themselves, nor can they possibly fight back given the existing dynamic between animal and handler. It is evident this was a frustration that Sewell herself felt, expressed in the dialogue of her characters. Ironically, it is Ginger who admits to Black Beauty that she has ceased or stopped standing up for herself when she has been ill-used. She tells him,

> I did once, but it's no use; men are strongest, and if they are cruel and have no feeling, there is nothing that we can do, but just bear it, bear it on and on to the end.

Certainly, Sewell, and her mother, for that matter, had their convictions about the abuse of horses in nineteenth century England. Fenner in fact notes in the novel's introduction that Sewell was a devoted activist, brazen or bold enough to stand up to abusive drivers, even in the face of a horse-whipping. Her novel, while it is not the reason for English reform, has been identified as one of the most prominent literary works of its type, influenced by Horace Bushnell's "Essay on Animals," or perhaps, it has been suggested, George Mac-Donald's fantasy "At the Back of the North Wind." According to Hastings, other environmental influences that shaped Sewell's book included knowledge the author gleaned from her brother Philip and from conversations with various drivers. The novel is also strongly influenced by many Christian, moral messages along with Quaker beliefs supporting Sewell's life-long support of the ethical treatment of animals.

To view Anna Sewell's first and only novel, *Black Beauty*, as little more than a charming tale about the trials and tribulations of a gentle-natured animal is a grave oversight. The novel was not written as young adult fiction, but as a treatise on animal rights. What resonates with adult audiences today is its value as a historical document. Asserts Hastings: "Black Beauty's life is a microcosm of Victorian horse experience, with every kind of rider, driver, and event occurring at some point in his life." It also mirrors social conditions during a time in history where women had little autonomy or voice outside of the domestic sphere, despite inroads made in the educational system. Although the author wrote the novel with the fate of the cab horse in mind, it is the horse that somehow advocates for Sewell, revealing her impressions and frustrations with a society long defined by male values.

Source: Laura Carter, Critical Essay on *Black Beauty*, in *Novels for Students*, Thomson Gale, 2006.

Paula Kirman

In the following essay, the reviewer suggests that Sewell's faith and personal "physical difficulties led Sewell to have enormous compassion for horses" and produced a story "with a very important message: that animals do feel pain."

Black Beauty is a timeless classic. It is read by countless children, studied in Children's Literature classes, and loved by readers around the world.

Black Beauty is a horse who goes around from owner to owner in 19th century England. Some owners are kind while others are cruel. Black Beauty also gets to know other horses and their experiences.

This is a book that would make a perfect choice for horse lovers and those interested in the rights of animals. The horses are almost human in their emotions and how they express themselves. What are considered to be tough creatures who are hardened for work or racing, are personified into tender, loving creatures.

Anna Sewell is best known for *Black Beauty*. She brought her own observations and perspective into her writing. During the time period when she was growing up in England, horses were terribly mistreated. They were over-worked, forced to work under horrible conditions, beaten, and improperly groomed and harnessed. Since she wrote from Beauty's point of view, the reader can begin to empathize with the suffering and pain he experienced.

Her faith (she was a Quaker) and her own physical difficulties led Sewell to have enormous compassion for horses, as well as all living creatures. In fact, Black Beauty was based on a horse owned by her brother, named Bessie, and the character of Merrylegs was based upon a favorite gray pony of Sewell's.

Black Beauty was published in 1877, when Sewell was in her fifties. Unfortunately, she died only a year after it was published. However, her work made a great impact in her society and how it treated horses.

Over one hundred years later, over 30 million copies of *Black Beauty* have been printed—a record for a work of fiction. Without a doubt, this novel will continue to reach readers with a very important message: that animals do feel pain.

Source: Paula Kirman, "*Black Beauty*," in *www.About.com*, December 28, 2004, http://womenwriters.about.com.

Sources

Bennett, Margaret, "Who Was Black Beauty?," in *Horsepower*, August/September 1999.

Chitty, Susan, *The Woman Who Wrote Black Beauty: A Life of Anna Sewell*, Hodder & Stoughton, 1971.

Grealy, Lucy, "Afterword," in *Black Beauty*, Signet Classics, 2002, pp. 217–23.

Hastings, Waller, *Northern State University online*, April 12, 2005, www.northern.edu/hastingw/sewell.htm.

Review of *Black Beauty*, in the *Critic*, Vol. XIII, No. 338, June 21, 1890, pp. 305–06.

Sayers, Frances Clarke, "Books That Enchant: What Makes a Classic?," in *Summoned by Books*, edited by Marjeanne Jensen Blinn, Viking, 1965, pp. 152–61.

Sewell, Anna, *Black Beauty*, Aladdin Paperbacks, 2001.

Silvey, Anita, *Children's Books and Their Creators*, Houghton, 1995, pp. 593–94.

Starrett, Vincent, "*Black Beauty* and Its Author," in *Buried Caesars: Essays in Literary Appreciation*, Washington Book, 1923.

Further Reading

Altick, Richard Daniel, *The Presence of the Present: Topics of the Day in the Victorian Novel*, Ohio State University Press, 1991.

This informative companion to British novels of the mid-nineteenth century provides historical context by discussing the people, events, or places of everyday Victorian life and explaining references that Victorians understood but the modern reader may not.

Baker, Margaret J., *Anna Sewell and Black Beauty*, George Harrap, 1956.

Written for children, this biography of Sewell also describes the times in which she lived.

Barrows, Susanna, and Robin Room, eds., *Drinking: Behavior and Belief in Modern History*, University of California Press, 1991.

This book is a collection of social science conference papers illuminating drinking practices and societal responses to the effects of drinking—including the Temperance Movement—at various points in history around the world.

Chitty, Susan, *The Woman Who Wrote "Black Beauty,"* Hoder & Stoughton, 1971.

A full-length biography on Sewell, this book includes a family tree with descriptions of Sewell's family, as well as illustrations, and remains a standard reference on Sewell.

Gavin, Adrienne E., *Dark Horse: A Life of Anna Sewell*, Sutton Publishing, 2004.

Dark Horse: A Life of Anna Sewell is a well-researched biography of Sewell that reviewers repeatedly describe as fascinating and an easy read.

Moss, Arthur W., *The Valiant Crusade: The History of the R.S.P.C.A.*, Cassells, 1961.

Black Beauty heavily influenced efforts for the humane treatment of animals and is given credit for its impact in this history of the Royal Society for the Prevention of Cruelty to Animals.

The Damnation of Theron Ware

Harold Frederic

1896

The Damnation of Theron Ware (London, 1896) by
American novelist Harold Frederic—also published as Illumination in England the same year—
is set in the fictional village of Octavius in upstate
New York in the 1880s. Octavius, which is based
on Utica, New York, as Frederic knew it as a boy
and young man, has a strong Methodist community, and also a large Catholic minority made up of
Irish immigrants. The Reverend Theron Ware, a
young, ambitious Methodist minister is sent to
Octavius, where he is disappointed to find an ignorant, narrow-minded congregation. Not long after his arrival, he meets three people who will have
a profound effect on his mind and emotions: a
learned but worldly Catholic priest who is well
schooled in Biblical study associated with the
"higher criticism," a Darwinian scientist, and a
free-thinking, and very attractive, young Catholic
woman who idealizes art and beauty. Ware's ordered and settled world is thrown into confusion
by these new, unfamiliar intellectual influences,
and his faith in the simple dogmas of Methodism
collapses.

This dramatic tale of a young minister seduced
by ideas and infatuated with a beautiful woman presents a vivid portrait of the intellectual forces in
late-nineteenth century America that were challenging the traditional verities of religion. Although
the novel has not been accorded a place amongst
the very highest achievements of American fiction,
it has nonetheless attracted enthusiastic readers for
more than one hundred years.

Author Biography

Harold Frederic was born in Utica, New York, on August 19, 1856. His father, Henry Frederick, who worked for the New York Central Railroad, was killed in a train accident when Frederic was two. His mother, Frances Ramsdell Frederick, remarried in 1861 to a businessman, and Frederic was raised in a middle-class environment. He showed an early talent for writing and drawing, although his formal education ended in 1871. When he was seventeen he went to live in Boston where he worked as a photographic printer and negative retoucher. In 1875, he was back in Utica, where his long career in journalism began as a proofreader for the *Utica Morning Herald*. Within five years he had risen to the position of editor-in-chief of the *Utica Daily Observer*. He had also started writing fiction, publishing several short stories in the newspaper. In 1877, he married Grace Williams, with whom he had four children.

In 1882, Frederic became editor of the *Albany Evening Journal*, but displeased its owner by supporting a Democratic rather than Republican candidate for governor. Frederic resigned his position rather than alter his views, and moved to New York, where he was appointed London correspondent for the *New York Times*. Arriving in London in the summer of 1884, he quickly forged a reputation based on his weekly dispatches on British affairs, especially British politics, in which he championed the cause of Irish independence.

In addition to his newspaper work, Frederic also wrote a stream of books, essays, short stories and reviews. In 1887, he published his first novel, *Seth's Brother's Wife*, set in the Mohawk Valley of upstate New York where he had grown up. *In the Valley*, a work of historical fiction set during the American Revolution, was published in 1890, as was *The Lawton Girl*, again about life in upstate New York. His fourth novel, *The Return of the O'Mahony* (1892), was set in Ireland. Frederic's ambition was to quit journalism and make a living as a writer. Although his books were favorably reviewed, he never made enough money from them to accomplish this goal, and his extravagant living left him in permanent debt. In 1891, he began living with Kate Lyon, an American woman with whom he had three children. Since his wife was reluctant to divorce him, Frederic divided his time between his two households, which further strained his financial resources.

In 1896, Frederic published *The Damnation of Theron Ware*, which became a best seller in England and was also popular in America. It also brought him financial success. About this time Frederic became friends with Stephen Crane, whose novel *The Red Badge of Courage* (1895) he had reviewed favorably in the *New York Times*.

Frederic's final two novels were both set in England. *Gloria Mundi* was published in 1898; *The Market-Place* appeared posthumously in 1899.

In 1898, Frederic suffered two strokes. He refused to follow his doctor's instructions to give up cigars and whiskey. He died on October 19, 1898.

Plot Summary

Part 1

The Damnation of Theron Ware or *Illumination* begins at the annual conference of the Methodist Episcopal Church, where the Reverend Theron Ware is disappointed that he has been assigned to the poor village of Octavius. He and his wife Alice soon discover how difficult life is going to be for them there. At a meeting with the church trustees, Loren Pierce, Erastus Winch and Levi Gorringe, Ware is told that Alice should not wear flowers in her bonnet, and that his sermons should be full of fire and brimstone, not book learning. Ware also discovers that the trustees hold mortgages on the church property, and that two of them charge an illegally high rate of interest. They also want to charge him for a new sidewalk, but Ware refuses to pay.

Walking home one day, Ware encounters four workingmen carrying a badly injured fellow-worker named MacEvoy. Ware follows them to MacEvoy's house, where he meets Father Forbes, a Catholic priest who administers Extreme Unction to the dying man. Ware is impressed by this Catholic ritual, which is explained to him by a young red-haired woman, Celia Madden.

Ware later visits Forbes, who invites him to stay for dinner with his friend, Dr. Ledsmar. Ware enjoys the ensuing scholarly discussion, which opens his mind to new ideas. Later that evening, he meets Celia again, in the Catholic church. She is friendly towards him, and Ware is intrigued by her.

Part 2

After two months in Octavius, Ware is troubled by the fact that a dominant minority in his church is hostile to him. He is apprehensive about the approaching Quarterly Conference, and wants to ask for a salary increase. He consults Gorringe, whom he feels is an ally, and the lawyer hints that he would help Ware out if he had money troubles. It is clear that Gorringe also has a liking for Ware's wife, but Ware chooses not to notice the fact.

Ware occupies himself reading Renan's *Recollections of My Youth*, a book lent to him by Ledsmar, in which Renan tells of how he lost his religious faith. The book makes a deep impression on Ware, and he feels that meeting Ledsmar and Father Forbes was a turning point in his life.

Sister Soulsby arrives. She is an expert at raising money to pay off church debts. With her husband, she plans a series of revival meetings. Ware is impressed by her efficiency, but he now despises his activities as a minister surrounded by ignorant, narrow-minded people.

Ware endures the first revival meeting with distaste as the Soulsbys exploit the emotionalism of the congregation. He watches as Alice goes to the altar with all the others who declare themselves sinners seeking salvation. Gorringe kneels next to her. The spectacle is too much for Ware, who faints and has to be helped home. At the next meeting, which Ware is too weak to attend, Sister Soulsby raises over $1,500 as Winch and Gorringe try to outdo each other in pledges. Soulsby later explains to Ware that she has manipulated the Presiding Elder, as well as Winch and Pierce, in his favor. He will get his salary increase. Following Soulsby's instructions, Ware refuses to let Winch off his financial commitment even though Soulsby tricked him into making it. Ware feels he has behaved inappropriately toward Winch, but Soulsby tells him that he should do whatever he has to do to accomplish necessary business.

Part 3

Disillusioned and depressed, Ware encounters Celia, who invites him to her home. She takes him to a room that contains marble statues of nude men and women, and pictures of the Virgin Mary. She explains her love of ancient Greek culture, and plays Chopin on the piano. Ware feels as if he has been transported into another world, and asks Celia to tell him everything about her Grecian ideals. He is becoming infatuated with her.

The next day he meets Celia at Thurston's, the large store in town, where she advises him about what piano to purchase for his wife. Coming back from the store, he visits Ledsmar, who shows him his laboratory and explains his experiments with plants and bees. He is also experimenting on his Chinese servant, testing the man's tolerance of large doses of opium. Ware questions Ledsmar about Celia, and finds that the doctor despises her. But when Ware tries to find out more about the relationship between Celia and Forbes, Ledsmar feigns an attack of rheumatism, and Ware has to leave.

Several months later, the annual Methodist camp meeting is held in the woods. Ware preaches well and wins over all the factions of the church. But he loathes the occasion and frequently goes for walks on his own. On one walk, he reaches a different part of the forest, where the Catholics are having a picnic. There is dancing and beer drinking, and everyone is enjoying themselves, in contrast to the Methodists. He meets Celia and Forbes, and is introduced to Michael and Theodore, Celia's brothers. Theodore is drunk and insults Ware. He also lets slip that Celia paid for the piano that Ware thought he was buying himself. Celia is upset by this remark, and she and Ware walk to a different part of the forest, where she explains more of her unconventional views. She believes in freedom for women, and says she will never belong to anyone and will never marry. Ware almost worships her, and makes his feelings plain. They go back to the camp, and Celia allows him to kiss her before they part.

Part 4

Ware convinces himself that Celia is in love with him. Hostile to his wife, he allows himself to believe that something is going on between her and Gorringe. He confronts Gorringe and the two men quarrel bitterly. That night Ware dines with Forbes, and tells him that he plans to leave the ministry. But when Ware tries to probe into the relationship between Celia and Ledsmar, Forbes cuts the meeting short.

Wondering about the relationship between Celia and Forbes, Ware determines to see Celia again, but when he calls at her house, she is unavailable. Instead, he sees her brother Michael, who is sick with consumption. Michael reproaches him, telling him he has degenerated from the man he was when he first arrived in Octavius. Ware learns that Celia is traveling to New York that evening, and he is disturbed when he realizes that she and Forbes are traveling together. He decides to go to New York as well. Traveling by train that night, he follows Celia and Forbes to their New York hotel. When he surprises Celia in her room, she rejects him, telling him how objectionable she and Forbes find his behavior. Ware is shattered by this rejection, and wanders around in New York for days, drinking and contemplating suicide. He seeks refuge at the Soulsbys, and Sister Soulsby consoles him.

The last chapter takes place several months later. Ware has left the ministry, and he and Alice, having benefited from the generosity of the Soulsbys, are ready to depart for Seattle, where Ware dreams of a new career in politics.

Characters

Father Forbes

Father Forbes is a Catholic priest in Octavius. He is an urbane, cultivated man who no longer believes in the literal truth of the Bible or in traditional Catholic doctrine. This does not stop him performing his functions as a priest, although he no longer preaches. Father Forbes is an old friend of Dr. Ledsmar, and he also befriends Theron Ware, who is deeply impressed by his knowledge and his conversation. He is instrumental in Ware's loss of faith. Father Forbes has a close relationship with Celia Madden, even though he is fifteen years her senior. The exact nature of their relationship is never made explicit, but it arouses Ware's jealousy.

Levi Gorringe

Levi Gorringe is a lawyer, money-lender, and a trustee of the Methodist Church in Octavius, although he is not a member of the church. Gorringe is a bachelor in his late twenties or early thirties; the local people regard him as rather odd. He takes a liking to Alice Ware and buys expensive plants for her garden. At first, Ware regards Gorringe as a friend, but he later develops suspicions—not unfounded—that Gorringe has designs on his wife. He confronts Gorringe about the matter and the two men quarrel violently.

Harvey

Harvey is the young boy who works in Levi Gorringe's law office. He also delivers milk to the parsonage.

Dr. Ledsmar

Dr. Ledsmar is an old friend of Father Forbes. He is a middle-aged scholar and doctor but has not practiced medicine for many years. Instead, he has scientific interests and conducts various experiments in his laboratory at home—on reptiles, plants, bees and even his Chinese servant. Ledsmar looks at everything with the cool, appraising eye of the rationalist. He dislikes art and music. He is also a misogynist, or woman hater, who holds Celia Madden in contempt. Ledsmar befriends Ware and

lends him some books about religion, a subject on which he is an expert even though he claims to be an atheist. But Ledsmar turns against Ware when the latter makes the mistake of inquiring about the relationship between Celia and Forbes. After this, Ledsmar never invites Ware to his house again.

Celia Madden

Celia Madden is the beautiful, red-haired, well-educated, independently-minded daughter of Jeremiah Madden. She loves beauty and the arts; she can paint, carve wood and speak foreign languages. She idealizes ancient Greece, contrasting it with Christianity, which she dislikes. Celia has advanced social views, believing that women should be free, and she does not plan ever to marry. Since her father is wealthy she can live as she chooses. Celia is a close friend of Father Forbes, and she plays the organ at the Catholic church. She befriends Theron Ware and, when she invites him to her room and plays Chopin for him on the piano, he becomes infatuated with her. She helps him to select a piano for his wife, but then unknown to him pays for it herself. After she talks alone with Ware in the woods, on the occasion of the religious camps, she allows Ware to kiss her. He takes this as a sign that she is in love with him. But when he goes uninvited to her hotel room in New York, she cruelly rejects him, explaining that she has a low opinion of him, and pointing out all the mistakes he has made in dealing with her, Father Forbes and Dr. Ledsmar.

Jeremiah Madden

Jeremiah Madden is the richest man in Octavius, the owner of several wagon factories. He is an immigrant who fled famine in Ireland. In America, he has had two wives and fathered more than a dozen children. He has a cheerful demeanor and keeps his grief to himself.

Michael Madden

Michael Madden is Celia's brother. He is nearly thirty years old and works as the superintendent of a sawmill. Everyone thinks well of him; he is good-natured, diligent and kind. Father Forbes describes his character as sweet and holy. Michael catches consumption (tuberculosis) and is expected to die quickly. When Ware visits him he reproaches the minister for not living up to the ideals of the religious life.

Theodore Madden

Theodore Madden is eight years younger than his brother Michael. He is a misfit, and had a poor record at all the schools he attended, but this does not stop him running for political office. When he and Ware meet, Theodore is drunk and insults the minister.

Loren Pierce

Loren Pierce is one of the trustees of the Methodist church in Octavius. He is an old man who has become rich through the quarries he owns, and he is respected by the townsfolk. Pierce is a tough, shrewd businessman who knows how to make the best use of his money. A blunt-spoken man who likes his religion simple and old-fashioned, Pierce has no time for erudite sermons and nor does he want an organ or a choir in the church. He does not believe in science, and he is prejudiced against Catholics. When Pierce tries to impose unreasonable financial demands on Ware, the minister stands up to him. Pierce become hostile to him, but over a period of months Ware wins him over.

Brother Soulsby

Brother Soulsby is Sister Soulsby's husband. She is the stronger personality and takes the lead in the revival meetings. Before he met his wife, Brother Soulsby led an eventful if disreputable life as an actor, a medium and a phrenologist, among other things. He also had some trouble with the law. He was "a regular bad old rooster," according to Sister Soulsby. But since they became revivalists, Soulsby has shown himself to be a kindly, charitable man.

Sister Soulsby

Sister Soulsby visits Octavius with her husband to lead the revival meetings that raise money for the church. Ware finds her kindly, quick-witted, capable and charming, and she takes a liking to him too. Well traveled, and entertaining in her conversation, Sister Soulsby dresses in a more stylish way than is usual for Methodists. She also has a colorful background. Born in the South, she has been an actress and a singer in comic opera, a ballet dancer, a clairvoyant, and a medium. She was once within a single vote of being indicted by a grand jury, although she does not say what she was accused of. When she met Brother Soulsby, they both decided that they had enough of living as fakes (as she puts it), and settled down together. When they happened to attend a Methodist revival meeting they soon realized that they could do a better job of it themselves, so they went into the business together. Sister Soulsby knows how to play on the emotions of the congregation and is very successful at raising money. She has no qualms about manipulating

people to get what she wants, and she gives Ware practical, common sense advice about how to get things done. She easily overcomes his objections that some of her actions may not be entirely ethical.

Alice Ware

Alice Ware is the wife of Theron Ware. The lively, self-reliant daughter of a farmer, she received an excellent education at a town seminary, and Ware considered himself lucky to marry her. For some years they are happy together, but when Ware meets his new sophisticated friends, Father Forbes, Dr. Ledsmar and Celia Madden, he becomes emotionally distant towards his wife and tells her little of his affairs. He thinks she is limited in her thinking. She feels neglected and her distress emerges at the emotional service where she joins the self-declared sinners at the altar. After this she becomes full of devotional zeal and seems to accept Ware's treatment of her without complaint. But she is also careful to preserves a distant manner towards him. At the Methodist camp in the forest, he can hardly bear to be with her, and she offers no praise of his sermons. Not long after this, Alice resents Ware's insinuation that there is something improper about Gorringe's interest in her. Ware then lies to her about the reason for his trip to New York. After Ware's escapade in New York, Alice leaves Octavius and stays with her husband at the Soulsbys's home. She remains loyal to Ware, although life has taken its toll on her, and she no longer finds it easy to be cheerful.

Reverend Theron Ware

The Reverend Theron Ware is a young Methodist minister who with his wife, Alice, is sent to Octavius by the elders of the church. This is not the appointment he wished for, and he does not much care for the narrow-minded, tight-fisted Methodist congregation in the village. Octavius is his third appointment. His first was in a rural community, which he enjoyed, since he had himself been raised on a farm. This was where he met and married his wife. Then they moved to the village of Tyre, where they remained for three years. This appointment began well, but in the second year Ware fell deeply into debt, and a kindly benefactor had to come to his rescue.

Ware is ambitious, and believes he has the makings of a great pulpit orator. His talents are largely wasted in Octavius, since the congregation does not appreciate anything other than simple, old-fashioned sermons. At first he is determined to make the best of his life there. He wants to buy his wife a piano, and plans to augment his modest salary with income from a book he intends to write about the Biblical patriarch Abraham. But he is rather naïve and does not realize he lacks the learning to write such a book.

Ware's entire life changes when he meets three people from outside the narrow Methodist community: Father Forbes, Dr. Ledsmar and Celia Madden. These new acquaintances open his mind up to realms of thought that he did not know existed. He loses his simple Methodist faith and begins to despise his congregation. He also becomes conceited and vain, buying a book on the care of the hand and fingernails. Then he becomes infatuated with Celia and grows cool towards his wife. But the people he thinks are his new friends in fact despise him, and when Ware chases after Celia to New York, he loses all his integrity and makes a fool of himself. After this fiasco, Ware leaves the ministry and decides to move to Seattle, where he plans to use his oratorical gifts to make a career for himself in politics.

Erastus Winch

Erastus Winch is one of the trustees of the Methodist church in Octavius. He sells dairy furniture and farm utensils for a living, and he is also a cheesebuyer. He has a friendly manner, but in reality he is cold-hearted, and in financial matters he is even tougher than Loren Pierce.

Themes

Loss of Faith

When Theron Ware is sent to Octavius, he is disappointed because he thinks he deserves something better. He knows he is a fine preacher, and he is far better educated than his simple flock, having been trained at a Methodist seminary. He also possesses quite a high opinion of his own abilities, and shortly after he arrives in Octavius he plans to write a book. He thinks this will be a relatively easy task, since he does not have any difficulty composing sermons. He does not for a moment realize that his education is in fact rather rudimentary. He owns few books, and they are all written from the rather narrow point of view of Methodism. Ware is a man who does not know his own ignorance. When he meets Father Forbes, Dr. Ledsmar and Celia Madden he becomes exposed to contemporary currents of thought that, given his limited background, he did not even know existed. Forbes

is deeply knowledgeable about the "higher criticism," which studied the Bible not as the inerrant word of God, but in the light of modern knowledge of history, literature, mythology, archeology, and other disciplines. Forbes can talk knowingly, for example, about the "Christ-myth," as if it is nothing special and can be found in different forms in many other mythologies of the world. Ware's lack of intellectual sophistication is conveyed when he tells Forbes and Ledsmar that he wants to write a book about Abraham, and he naïvely believes Abraham to have been a single individual. He has to be informed gently that no one believes any more that Abraham was an individual man; the name simply represents a tribe or clan. All this is news to Ware, and for a while he is thrilled by the intellectual world that has been opened up to him.

One of the most crucial events is his reading of Ernest Renan's *Recollections of My Youth*, a memoir of the Frenchman's loss of faith in Christianity. The book was lent to Ware by Ledsmar, and he reads it twice. Shortly after his first reading, he realizes that he has "passed definitely beyond pretending to himself that there was anything spiritually in common between him and the Methodist Church of Octavius." Some time later, Celia exposes him to another intellectual world of which he had known nothing, that of Greek philosophy, the ideals of Greek civilization, and the worship of art and beauty. Ware's horizons expand once more, and the following morning he feels he has emerged from a cocoon and "stood forth, so to speak in a new skin, and looked about him with perceptions of quite an altered kind, upon what seemed in every way a fresh existence."

Far from being a painful experience, Ware's loss of faith in the simple dogmas of Methodism is exciting for him. He thinks he is in a state of illumination, so taken is he with all the new ideas. He avidly reads some "higher criticism" for himself, and he thinks he has a sophisticated understanding of it. Thanks to Sister Soulsby's advice, he believes he can carry on as minister, even though he no longer believes in what he is saying, as long as he keeps up the appearances. This, after all, is what Forbes manages to do. Ware is so keen to ingratiate himself with Forbes that when he meets him at the Catholic picnic, he offers the opinion that religion will die out in the near future: "The march of science must very soon produce a universal scepticism. It is in the nature of human progress. What all intelligent men recognize today, the masses must surely come to see in time." Forbes just laughs, and replies that there will always be religion. What Ware

Topics For Further Study

- When *The Damnation of Theron Ware* was first published in England, the title was *Illumination*. Based on the content of the plot and the substance of the characters, write an essay that explains which title you think is more appropriate.

- Is there a conflict between science and religious faith? Select one contemporary issue (political, social, personal) in which scientific research and progress may clash with religious belief, research that issue, and develop a report to be given in-class that details the conflict and/or agreement between science and religion as related to the issue you choose.

- What is the attitude of Theron Ware and Loren Pierce to the Irish and to Catholicism? Does Ware modify his views? How does the author present Catholicism and Methodism? Which of the two is presented in a more favorable light? What was the real historical context like for the divisions of Christianity in early America?

- Who bears most responsibility for what happens to Ware: Father Forbes, Dr. Ledsmar, Celia Madden, Sister Soulsby, or Ware himself? Is Ware a different man at the end of the novel than he was at the beginning, or is he just the same? If you believe Ware changes during the novel, provide examples to explain how his character develops?

does not realize is that he does not really grasp the new ways of thinking in any depth. He can never hope to match the learning of Forbes and Ledsmar. Having discarded the simple pieties of Methodism, there is no place for him anywhere else within the religious fold. From that point on, it is only a matter of time before he leaves the ministry.

Moral Degeneration

When Ware first arrives in Octavius, he is a man of some moral decency. He may be somewhat snobbish, and a little conceited about his talents, but he fulfills his obligations to the best of his ability. But the more he falls under the influence of others, the more he loses touch with his moral compass. The more enlightened he thinks he is becoming, the darker in fact his character becomes. His exposure to new ways of thinking makes him despise everything that supported his life up to that point. He no longer thinks highly of his wife, and becomes cold and distant toward her, even suspecting her of infidelity. He becomes very puffed up with what he thinks is his superior knowledge, and also becomes insincere, thinking that he can continue as a minister even though he no longer believes the things he is called upon to say. As he drinks beer at the Catholic camp, he openly tells Forbes and Celia that he despises his own congregation and that he regrets having married.

When he becomes infatuated with Celia, and full of thinly disguised erotic desire for her, he loses his integrity altogether. Jealous of her relationship with Father Forbes, and indulging in ridiculous fantasies about their future life together, he chases after her to New York, lying to his wife in the process and stealing money from the church to finance his trip. When Celia rejects him, he has an impulse to murder her, and after he leaves the hotel he wanders around trying to get drunk and contemplating suicide. His moral degradation is complete.

Style

Imagery

Ware thinks he is becoming enlightened through his contact with Forbes and Celia, an idea that is reinforced by repeated imagery of light and darkness. Celia, for example, is always associated with light. When Ware first meets her, "The bright light shone for a passing instant upon a fashionable flowered hat, and upon some remarkably brilliant shade of red hair beneath it." Then as he is about

Compare & Contrast

- **1880s–1890s:** From May to October of 1893, an estimated 27 million people attend Chicago's World's Columbian Exposition (World Fair). The fair introduces many new inventions, from zippers to the Ferris wheel, as well as new architecture and machinery. The exhibition reflects contemporary confidence in human progress.

  Today: The tradition of world fairs continues. In 2000, Expo 2000 takes place in Hanover, Germany. The theme is "Man, Nature and Technology," and 187 countries participate.

- **1880s–1890s:** Irish immigration to the United States continues but is lower than during the 1860s and 1870s. Many Irish, who are also predominantly Catholic, face resentment and discrimination in largely Protestant America.

  Today: More than 43 million people in the United States claim Irish descent. Irish immigration to the United States is only a small fraction of what it was more than a hundred years ago.

- **1880s–1890s:** Conservatives within the Methodist Episcopal Church fight to maintain their traditional faith in the face of progressive ministers who are sympathetic to the "higher criticism," who seek to introduce more liberal interpretations of Christian doctrine into the church, and who bring innovations into church services, such as organs and choirs.

  Today: There are twenty-three branches of the Methodist church in the United States. The largest is the United Methodist Church, which had about 8.5 million members in 1997. The most well-known member of the Methodist church is President George W. Bush.

---

to part from her, "The strong noon sunlight . . . made a halo about her hair and face at once brilliant and tender." As he passes the church where Celia is playing the organ, he sees through the open door "A thin, pale, vertical line of light." As he enters the church and finds his way around it, a series of descriptive passages make careful use of the contrast between light and darkness. It is as if Ware is emerging from darkness into light. Similarly, when he first enters the dining room of Father Forbes's house, "for a moment he could see nothing but a central glare of dazzling light beating down from a great shaded lamp upon a circular patch of white table linen." When he leaves, darkness returns. As he stands still outside, "the sudden darkness was so thick that it was as if he had closed his eyes."

Imagery related to snakes, serpents and other reptiles is also prominent. In the Bible, the serpent plays the role of tempter, enticing Eve to disobey God and eat of the tree of the knowledge of good and evil. In the novel, the tempters of Ware are associated with snakes and serpents. Celia refers to Forbes and Ledsmar as resembling "gorged snakes," and when Ware is drawn to Celia's music in the church he feels as if he is being drawn against his will, "like fascinated bird to python." Ledsmar keeps lizards at his house, and he has written a book about serpent worship. The imagery is also transferred to Ware himself, as when Ledsmar renames one of his lizards that has a "pointed, evil head" after Ware. Ware is also associated with the serpent when he thinks that he has undergone a metamorphosis after spending an evening with Celia. He emerges with "a new skin," just as a snake renews itself by shedding its skin.

Historical Context

Higher Criticism

The "higher criticism" that Forbes and Ledsmar are so familiar with in the novel refers to a method of Biblical criticism that began in Germany in the late eighteenth and early nineteenth century. Higher criticism brought a radically new approach

Charles Darwin, whose ideas influenced the protagonist Theron Ware in Harold Frederic's The Damnation of Theron Ware   The Library of Congress

to the study of the Bible. Using historical research and literary analysis, scholars endeavored to reach accurate conclusions about the authorship, date and place of composition of the Old and New Testaments. For example, traditionally it was believed that the first five books of Genesis, known as the Pentateuch, were all written by Moses. But the higher criticism revealed many inconsistencies and contradictions in the Pentateuch, which led scholars to conclude that it was in fact a composite work by several different authors (none of them Moses), reflecting different religious places and traditions.

Significant books reflecting the new approach to the Bible included *Essence of Christianity* (1854) and *The Life of Jesus* (1863), by a Frenchman, Ernest Renan, who later wrote *Recollections of My Youth*, which was translated in 1883 and produced such an effect on Theron Ware in the novel.

The conclusions of higher criticism put traditional faith to the test, and many believers fiercely resisted it.

Darwin and Scientific Rationalism

In the late nineteenth century, another branch of knowledge that threatened traditional religious faith was associated with the work of the English naturalist, Charles Darwin. In *The Origin of Species* (1859) and *Descent of Man* (1870), Darwin hypothesized that humans evolved over a vast period of time from lower forms of life by a process of natural selection. Natural selection was often popularly known as "the survival of the fittest." Darwin's hypothesis of the evolution of species through random mutations undermined the traditional idea of the fixity of species created by God. According to the religious view, man was a special creation, set apart by God from the rest of nature. God created the world with a beneficent purpose in mind, and everything in it has its fixed place. But the implication of Darwin's argument was that there was no cosmic purpose in life. Life evolves through chance and blind struggle, and has no inherent moral meaning.

In the novel, Darwinism is represented by the scientist Ledsmar, who is testing a Darwinian theory about hermaphroditism and refers to man as Vertebrata, suggesting that he assigns to man no special place apart from the rest of the animal kingdom.

Aestheticism

Another current of thought in the late 1800s was known as aestheticism. It began as a literary movement in France and Britain and was a reaction against the belief that art should have a utilitarian purpose. The aesthetic movement believed that art should express beauty, not take stands on political or social issues. The movement was associated in France with the work of Charles Baudelaire, Gustave Flaubert and Stéphane Mallarmé. In England, it was associated with Oscar Wilde and Walter Pater.

The tenets of aestheticism were popularized in America by Wilde, who visited the country on a lecture tour in 1882. Many of the most enthusiastic advocates of aestheticism in America were women, just as in the novel. Celia Madden, with her belief in the spiritual beauty of art, expresses some of the ideas of the movement.

Critical Overview

When published in March, 1896, *The Damnation of Theron Ware* or *Illumination* became a best seller in England, and was also popular in the United States. Critics considered it to be an important novel. In *Cosmopolitan*, Harry Thurston Peck praised it for its realistic depiction of American life, "the good and the bad, the fine and the crude, the enlightened and the ignorant" (quoted by Scott Donaldson in his introduction to the novel). Leading novelist and critic W. D. Howells, reviewing the novel in *Munsey's* in 1897, declared it to be a "moral" book of "great power." He also commented that at the end of the novel :

> . . . although you have carried a hazy notion in your mind of the sort of man Ware was, you realize, for the first time, that the author has never for a moment represented him anywhere to you as a good or honest man, or as anything but a very selfish man.

The anonymous reviewer in the *Atlantic* admired the characterization of Ware and Forbes, and declared that the Soulsbys were "cleverly drawn and highly entertaining," but he thought Ledsmar was inadequately sketched and Celia Madden did not quite ring true. The masterstroke of the novel, according to the reviewer, was the last page, where Ware is shown as "just the same man he was in the beginning."

Although over the years the novel has not been regarded as one of the greatest works of American fiction, there was another wave of interest in it in the 1960s, when several reissues were published. Everett Carter, in his introduction to the edition published by Harvard University Press, praised the novel for capturing the spirit of the 1890s. In times when "old faiths were meeting new doubts and artists were struggling to find the forms to contain this turbulence [the novel] is an illuminating literary document, and one of the most satisfying aesthetic forms."

Criticism

Bryan Aubrey

Aubrey holds a Ph.D. in English and has published many articles on nineteenth century literature. In this essay, Aubrey discusses the role that Sister Soulsby plays in Ware's fall from grace.

Poor Theron Ware. He goes from being an earnest young Methodist minister, well grounded in his faith and happily married, to a man who reeks of insincerity, embezzles money from the church and makes a complete fool of himself with a free-thinking young woman whom he can never, in spite of his fantasies, possess.

It is easy to see the triumvirate of Father Forbes, Dr. Ledsmar and Celia Madden as the ones who are chiefly responsible for Ware's fall from grace. When

> His notions of intellectual and moral integrity are irrelevant to Sister Soulsby, who wants him to emulate her and become a 'good fraud'—manipulating people for their own good."

a man who is educated only within the narrow confines of the Methodist religion encounters a worldly-wise and learned priest, an atheistic scientist, and a cultured, artistic woman who lets nothing interfere with her personal freedom, it is not surprising that he is torn from his simple moorings and flounders. Stepping out of one rigid belief system, he does not have the intellectual training to join any of the others. The dying Michael Madden explains this to him, telling Ware that he should have stayed with his own people and his own religion; when he strayed into another domain he was ill-equipped to understand it and his character degenerated as a result.

There is obviously much truth in this reading of the causes of Ware's downfall. However, Ware also encounters another key figure, and that is Sister Soulsby. On the surface, the kindly Sister Soulsby seems like a beneficent influence on the minister, as well as being a very lively, entertaining character. She rescues the church from debt, gives the naïve Ware some good, common-sense advice, and in general tells him what he needs to know. This positive view of Sister Soulsby was how early reviewers and critics of the novel tended to see her. But since then, more than a few critics have reversed this interpretation. Rather than being a sympathetic character, Sister Soulsby has been presented as the direct cause of Ware's "damnation," a true Mephistophelean temptress in the guise of a friendly adviser. For example, Stanton Garner wrote in his book *Harold Frederic*, "It is she who touches Theron's weakest point, immobilizing his moral faculties with a vision of petty illusions disguising the sordid 'reality' of the world." Garner calls this a "cynical philosophy of sharp practice and self-indulgent rationalizations." Scott Donaldson, in his article "The Seduction of Theron Ware," also follows this line of argument. Sister Soulsby is a corrupting influence on Ware, since she teaches

What Do I Read Next?

- Several critics have noted the close affinity between *The Damnation of Theron Ware* and Nathaniel Hawthorne's *The Scarlet Letter* (1850), in terms of allegory, symbolism, and the relationship between science and religion. Hawthorne's novel is set in Puritan Boston, where a woman convicted of adultery is forced to wear a scarlet "A" on her clothing.

- Frederic admired Stephen Crane's novel *The Red Badge of Courage* (1895). Like *The Damnation of Theron Ware*, it features a young protagonist who finds himself suddenly thrust into a new situation in which he must learn more about life and about himself. But for Crane's protagonist, Henry Fleming, the scene is not a village in New York but a Civil War battlefield.

- *Elmer Gantry* (1927), by Sinclair Lewis, is a satire of fundamentalist religion that caused a storm of controversy when first published. Set in the Midwest, the novel centers around Elmer Gantry, a salesman turned charismatic revivalist preacher and conman who eventually becomes the leader of a Methodist church.

- *The Reckless Decade: America in the 1890s* (1995), by H. W. Brands, surveys the United States during the last decade of the nineteenth century when it stood on the brink of modernity and was trying to absorb rapid social, political, and intellectual change. Brand covers topics such as economic upheaval, labor unrest, the "robber barons," race, immigration, and the Spanish American war.

---

him to be duplicitous and also manipulates him and his congregation by every means she can in order to obtain her goals. This conclusion has been echoed by other critics since, although it is by no means the universal view. Thomas F. O'Donnell and Hoyt Franchere, for example, see nothing sinister in Sister Soulsby. In contrast, the Soulsbys provide "a sincere but realistic spiritual leadership of the kind that expedience demands."

The crux of the matter is the extent to which moral, ethical and spiritual absolutes can be applied in the complex, day-to-day business of human affairs. Those who condemn Sister Soulsby do so on the basis of her willingness to manipulate others for what she sees as a worthy goal. For her, the means justify the ends, but for her critics, this attitude leaves her open to charges of cynicism and insincerity. Those who defend her see her *modus operandi* as she herself sees it: as a necessary way of accomplishing necessary things in a less than perfect world. In this view, common sense and pragmatism trump moral righteousness.

There is some truth in both these opposing views. There is no doubt that Sister Soulsby is a shameless manipulator. She is cunning, knows exactly what she wants to get out of people, and

plans her actions accordingly, using every trick in the book. When she wants to persuade members of Ware's congregation to part with their money, she invites them to a revival meeting without divulging its real purpose, reasoning with some justification (and over Ware's feeble objections), that if people knew the meeting was a fundraiser, they would be unlikely to come. During the meeting she plays on the emotions of the congregation with ease. With her singing, her dramatic gestures, and her smooth, practiced patter, the meeting is more like a theatrical performance than a church service. And once the second revival meeting is under way, Sister Soulsby has no qualms about locking the church doors and saying that no one will be let out until the money is raised. Her methods of raising that money are dubious, to say the least, since she tricks Winch into making pledges that he thinks he will not be called upon to keep. But to Winch's dismay, Ware, manipulated by Sister Soulsby, insists that he meet his commitments. Ware feels his integrity is compromised by his part in this, but Sister Soulsby's attitude is that she uses whatever means are at her disposal to create a desired outcome.

If this was the extent of Sister Soulsby's influence on Ware, perhaps there would not be a

"View Down the Ravine. At Trenton Falls, N.Y.," painting by Frances F. Palmer of falls located just north of Utica, New York, the basis for the fictional town of Octavius © Museum of the City of New York/Corbis

chorus of critics ready to condemn her. There is a certain justice in the discomfiture of the tight-fisted Winch since earlier it was disclosed that he and Pierce were charging the church a higher rate of interest on the mortgage than the law stipulated. And surely few would quibble that Ware needs a proverbial kick in the seat of the pants from someone who possesses worldly common sense. His own performance during his second ministry in Tyre—where he ran up a debt of eight hundred dollars—his extravagant desire to buy his wife a piano he cannot afford, and his horror at the thought of a "debt-raiser" coming to his church, even though the church is sinking deeper and deeper into debt, all suggest that the Reverend Ware needs some sage advice about how to run his own affairs.

The more serious case against Sister Soulsby is that she encourages Ware to create a double self— a private one and a public one. She tells him that it does not matter what he believes, as long as he keeps up outer appearances and does what his congregation wants him to do. His notions of intellectual and moral integrity are irrelevant to Sister Soulsby, who wants him to emulate her and become a "good fraud"—manipulating people for their own good. It is not that she is an out-and-out hypocrite, since she seems genuinely to believe in the value of her work,

but her religion is undoubtedly of the shallow variety. She and her husband first went to Methodist revival meetings just to kill time, but then found they "liked the noise and excitement and general racket of the thing." In other words, it was a good show and had little to do with matters of sin and salvation. The Soulsbys then went into the revival business for themselves because they thought they could do it better than the preachers they were hearing. When pressed by Ware, Sister Soulsby claims that she was genuinely converted, but this seems to mean no more than that she was caught up in the excitement of the moment.

Overcoming his misgivings, Ware takes Sister Soulsby's advice and becomes a "good fraud" with a clear conscience. It appears to be exactly the solution he was looking for. Even before Soulsby's arrival, he had parted company, at least in spirit, with the Methodist church and was troubled about how to keep up the pretense with others. Sister Soulsby has convinced him that pretending is a perfectly acceptable solution, and for a while this appears to work very well for him. Attendance at the church is up, his congregation appears to regard him highly, he preaches effective sermons, and he feels at peace within himself as he pursues his new intellectual ideas: "He had put aside, once and for all, the thousand foolish trifles and childish perplexities which formerly has racked his brain, and worried him out of sleep and strength." He has no doubt that he can succeed in this double life of believing one thing and saying another. After all, the Catholic priest whom he so admires, Father Forbes, does exactly the same, although Ware forgets that Forbes, while still performing the ritual functions of the church, no longer preaches.

But all the time Ware thinks he is doing so well, he is going downhill morally. For one thing, he despises his own congregation, and he makes the mistake of confiding this to Celia and Forbes when he meets them at the Catholic picnic, as well as hinting to them about his dissatisfaction with his marriage. They are not impressed. However, Ware might have continued for some while in this double vein had it not been for his infatuation with Celia, which is a dizzy amalgam of sexual, romantic and intellectual feelings. This infatuation, which makes him lose all reason and judgment, would have proved costly for him even if he had never met Sister Soulsby and listened to her advice.

It thus seems unfair to put the blame on Sister Soulsby for Ware's troubles. She is merely trying to help a troubled young man remain in the ministry to which he has been called, and it would be hard to argue with the wisdom of much of her advice. For example, she tries to correct his eagerness to pass negative judgements on his own congregation, telling him they are no better or worse than any other. And at the end of the novel, when Ware indulges in an orgy of self-reproach about how in a few months he has gone from being a good man to a bad one, she insists once more that such categories are misleading, because everyone is a mixture of good and bad, and it is unwise to judge others. It is Ware's misfortune that he lacks the maturity and good judgment to take advantage of whatever wisdom Sister Soulsby has to offer him.

Source: Bryan Aubrey, Critical Essay on *The Damnation of Theron Ware,* in *Novels for Students,* Thomson Gale, 2006.

Bridget Bennett

In the following essay excerpt, Bennett traces the real-life events behind Frederic's writing of The Damnation of Theron Ware.

Reading *The Damnation of Theron Ware* is a disquieting process. The title of the novel promises revelation. Initially, the process of this revelation—the illumination of the reader—appears to be linear. It is only late in the novel that its full permutations make themselves known. It is not only Theron who is misled about his "illumination," but the reader, too. The novel is powerfully absorbing because it promises so much yet reveals so little. As a morality tale, it is inadequate, for it lacks a clear moral. It is an embodiment of its own message—the difference between appearance and reality. Almost every significant character provides, within the text, a rereading of the novel, but none of the rival readings have much authority. For instance Michael Madden tells Theron that he is a "barkeeper," his sister, in the most systematic and ruthless rereading, calls Theron a "bore." The chronology of the novel embodies forward movement—its progression is seasonal—but each advance in knowledge proves to be an illusion. The movement toward illumination is not smooth. Like Theron, the reader experiences a loss of faith.

In June 1896 Harold Frederic wrote to his friend Sir Charles Russell, currently Lord Chief Justice of England, describing the Reverend Theron Ware in affectionate terms. Russell had recently finished reading Frederic's latest novel, *The Damnation of Theron Ware.* In response to Russell's comments, which are unrecorded, Frederic writes, "All that you say is charming. I think I like best of all the judgement of those who, like you, feel that our friend Theron was badly treated. I couldn't save him from it, but it was a grief to me none the less" (Frederic to Sir Charles Russell, 15 June 1896). The two men had weighed up the case of Theron Ware and decided it in his favor. Yet neither man could "save" him, as Frederic put it, punning both on Theron's religious calling and on his encounter with the saintly Michael Madden, a consumptive archangel. Both Frederic and Russell had good reason to empathize with the "badly treated" Theron. Frederic had felt victimized for years by his newspaper, by Grace Frederic's refusal to give him a divorce, by the public that was not buying his books, and by his main American publishers, Charles Scribner's Sons, who were not, Frederic believed, marketing his work with sufficient care. Frederic's "grief" that he could not "save" Theron was partly self-pity emerging from his sense of futility when confronted with an oppressive predicament. Russell would also shortly experience a difficult public ordeal. When he first encountered Theron, he may already have had intimations of the scandal that was brewing around him.

It is curious that Frederic should speak of Theron in a way that does not acknowledge his responsibility for his protagonist's fate. Something of his impotence—"I couldn't save him from it"—applies equally to the dilemma that he found himself in, in 1896. His description of writing *The Lawton Girl* compounds this sense of powerlessness. In 1897, Frederic described the act of writing the earlier novel as being like a "spectator" who followed the movements of characters at a distance and was able to participate in their activities only through their courtesy. He had been in control, he writes, of his first two novels, *Seth's Brother's Wife* and *In the Valley,* but in his third the characters took on a life of their own, independent of his authority. It is to this that Frederic alludes when he tells Russell that he "couldn't save" Theron from his downfall. In his letter to Russell, his tone is that of a parent helplessly watching as his offspring "goes to the dogs," becoming, in the penultimate chapter, and after a series of canine images, "just one more mongrel cur that's gone mad, and must be put out of the way." Despite Frederic's affection for "our friend Theron," he maintains that he could not interfere with the inevitability of Theron's downfall, suggesting that, like *The Lawton Girl,* the novel had developed a momentum of its own. Stylistically, Frederic had learned restraint. At the end of *The Lawton Girl* Frederic did, as he says, "assert my authority" in order to kill Jessica. He had planned to do the same to Theron—early jottings for *The Damnation of Theron Ware* suggest that Theron commits suicide at the end of the novel. The penultimate chapter of the finished work leaves Theron's fate tantalizingly open until the last chapter reveals it. To have Theron kill himself would be as "false and cowardly" as Jessica's stage-managed death, but Frederic had seriously considered the possibility. Theron was to have jumped off Brooklyn Bridge, opened a few years earlier in 1883. Two years later, some of Frederic's acquaintances believed that his own death was effectively suicide, and certainly his heavy drinking was self-destructive.

The idea of suicide may have been suggested to Frederic by a famous suicide that took place while Frederic was writing the novel, in 1893, which had an enormous impact. Ernest Clark, a young carpet designer, shot himself in the waiting room of Liverpool Street Station. He left a poem by his body that the *Daily Chronicle* translated from the French, and printed on 18 August: "Life is short: / A little love, / A little dream / And then— Good day! / Life is vain: / A little hope, / A little pain, / And then—Good night!" (Frederic Misc. 1977, 344). George Du Maurier used a version of this in the final lines of *Trilby* after the deaths of Svengali, Trilby, and Little Billee. The novel was published just one year after Clark's suicide. Clark's death prompted, or seemed to prompt, the

> **" It is curious that Frederic should speak of Theron in a way that does not acknowledge his responsibility for his protagonist's fate. Something of his impotence—'I couldn't save him from it'—applies equally to the dilemma that he found himself in, in 1896."**

reporting of numerous suicides, and the affair became one of public concern, not least because of the care with which he made sure that his private death was likely to become public. In what John Stokes calls an "ingeniously modern variation" on the suicide note, Clark advertised his forthcoming death by writing to the *Daily Chronicle* shortly before his suicide and informing them ghoulishly that by the time the letter had reached them he would already be dead. As he no doubt expected it was published in the paper, on 16 August.

Frederic was one of many contributors to the ensuing debate, writing to the *Daily Chronicle* on 20 August 1893. He called suicide a subject so old that no one "can hope to say any more about it," though of course this did not silence him. He writes that the Ancients made their image of death "a beautiful youth, twin brother of Sleep, holding his torch downward," which suggests that it is time to go home. Although the debate that took place in the *Daily Chronicle* largely concerned questions of sanity and insanity (was suicide a result of lunacy or was it rather a sane and rational response to an unbearable world?), what was also at issue, as Stokes argues, was that "the suicidal individual was exceptionally sensitive to the world around him, as the Decadent hero might be"; or indeed as Theron believes himself to be.

So what, then, is the significance of Frederic's decision to keep Theron alive and yet deliberately to give the impression, as he does at the start of the final chapter of the novel, that Theron is dead (though not from the suicidal leap he had originally planned)? Part of what is at stake for Frederic is

Theron's delusion: keeping him alive and sending him off West (lighting out for the Territory, as it were) is a far more ignominious ending both for him and for the future prospects of the United States than killing him off might be. Allowing him the drama of a leap from Brooklyn Bridge is more than he deserved, or, by contrast, might suggest that Theron does indeed have heroic potential—might even be a sort of Decadent hero after all. Finishing the novel with a soggy death through drink would be merely melodramatic and somewhat conventional. Yet the ending that Frederic eventually opted for is far more grimly ironic than suicide and is so brilliantly unexpected that it makes uneasy reading. The eternal hellfire that Michael Madden warned Theron of is the steady suicide of real estate that Theron adopts at the end of the novel.

Frederic's letter to the *Daily Chronicle* is echoed in Celia's outburst to Theron and Forbes at the Catholic picnic, but is at the forefront of the novel in another way, too. When Frederic designed the frontispiece of the English edition of the novel he chose the image of a hand holding an upheld torch. This literally inverts the iconography of suicide, and the image becomes one of light, or *"Illumination,"* the title of the English edition of the novel. It also suggests the most famous of American icons, the Statue of Liberty. The frontispiece of the English edition of the novel adds another dimension to the novel. The Statue of Liberty is the guardian of the entrance to the New World. In the 1890s, its illuminated flame, partly a great overt symbol of welcome and arrival, partly functioning in a double role as a lighthouse beacon, guided the traveler from the Old World into the safe harbor of Manhattan, close to the dominant span of the Brooklyn Bridge. Had Frederic ended the novel with Theron's suicidal leap it would have completed the neat architectural structure of the novel. Although Frederic chose to underplay the possibilities of the New York cityscape, for Theron's stay in the metropolis is short and disastrous, he does explore the idea of new worlds. Early in the novel Theron reflects upon his meeting with Dr. Ledsmar and Father Forbes at the Catholic Pastorate. He decides that Ledsmar and Forbes belong to "an intellectual world, a world of culture and grace, of lofty thoughts and the inspiring communion of real knowledge, where creeds were not of importance, and where men asked one another, not 'Is your soul saved?' but 'Is your mind well furnished?'" Once Theron begins to distance himself from the world that he knows—a process that Frederic questions throughout the novel, in regular registers of mistrust ("was it, after all, an advance?")—and to

propel himself into one in which he is as "curiously alien" as the Irish once were to him, he is as ill-equipped to save his own soul as he is to "furnish" his mind. Theron's conspicuous failure is suggested by his inability even to furnish his house without the regular assistance of generous friends and well-wishers—the marriage "donation" of his first congregation, Abram Beekman's offer to clear his debts, and Celia Madden's gift of a piano.

His romantic fantasy of transition fails to take into account the significance of what he has to lose—the tools he needs to acquire in order to help him survive, and the customs and expressions of a new world. Theron must develop different strategies in order to read and understand its language, whether it is the importance of correctly interpreting a kiss, or of convenient attacks of rheumatism. In the continuation of this passage, one of the most significant in this complex and coded novel, the inevitability of Theron's doom is apparent: "Theron had the sensation of having been invited to become a citizen of this world. The thought so dazzled him that his impulses were dragging him forward to take the new oath of allegiance before he had had time to reflect upon what it was he was abandoning." Although Theron has "the sensation of having been invited," the invitation is never forthcoming, and it is difficult to see what form it might ever take. Each invitation that he is offered is quickly regretted: the scientist, Doctor Ledsmar, and the Catholic priest, Father Forbes, vow not to ask him to their homes again, and Celia admits that she has made a mistake in inviting him to kiss her. Theron is less illumined, as he believes, than literally blinded by the people and ideas that he encounters. It is in this debilitated state of hysterical blindness that he seems most like a moth helplessly circling a source of light that he believes to be the catalyst of his illumination, singeing himself every time he gets too close to it, and inevitably floundering into it. *The Damnation of Theron Ware* is a catalogue of that self-destructive trajectory.

Frederic became increasingly pessimistic in his later years. His youthful belief in the likelihood of progress was gradually shaken. Unlike Hawthorne and James, who retained some "Edenic" sense of American character, Frederic, like Twain, doubted. When Frederic lay dying, John Scott Stokes read to him from Twain rather than from his "literary parent," Hawthorne. Frederic had long hoped to be "a Hawthorne," but on his deathbed he must have realized that in his ambivalent relationship to the world he resembled Twain. Evidence from the *Harold Frederic Papers* in the Library of Congress suggests that Frederic shared Father Forbes's pessimistic view that civilization was constantly in danger of collapsing, taking all moral values with it. Forbes tells Theron that "of all our fictions there is none so utterly baseless and empty as this idea that humanity progresses." Frederic's notes for the novel show his own skepticism: "People do not improve as the world grows older . . . They still fluctuate, as they always did, between imitating good models and then forgetting why they did so . . . [There is] no earthly reason why [we] shouldn't all wallow back into the blackest barbarism. Think electric light [will] save you, do you?" (Harold Frederic Papers).

Frederic's journalistic experiences, which brought him into contact with war, disease, violence, social inequality, and political corruption, had long suggested to him that civilization was simply a veneer. One of his *New York Times* pieces, "A Return To Barbarism," shows a preoccupation shared by many writers of the period, especially the naturalists: "When I was a boy we used to be taught that civilization had at last become the permanent state of man. There remained, therefore, nothing for civilized man to do but go on peacefully and develop his improved civilization indefinitely til the crack of doom with none to make him afraid. But Nobel's discovery of what happened when twenty-five parts of silicous earth were saturated with seventy-five parts of nitro-glycerene has absolutely swept that theory from the human mind" (Frederic *NYT* 1892, 1). That an advance in knowledge can mark a retrograde step is the sort of paradox that is depicted in *The Damnation of Theron Ware*. Nobel's discovery literally blasted away illusions, showing the fragility of civilization. Frederic's youthful belief in the perfectibility of mankind was replaced by a well-founded fear of the consequences of Nobel's discovery.

By the time of the publication of *The Damnation of Theron Ware* some months before his fortieth birthday in August 1896, Frederic was indeed tired of life. In notes in the Library of Congress under the heading of "Man at 40" he writes, "He becomes in essence Grave, if he has any brains." He adds, in an abbreviated sentence, "He still full of humor or wit, seems to himself as young and gay as ever, but he doesn't fool young girl" (Harold Frederic Papers). The passage toward the despondency of his fortieth year had been inexorable. He had learned of the depths of corruption of American political life, as well as of its moments of honor, through watching the careers of two Uticans, Roscoe Conkling, and Horatio Seymour. This early

lesson was reinforced by his days on the *Utica Daily Observer* and *Albany Evening Journal,* where he watched and reported on "machine" politics, and rural murders and suicides, as well as more elevated matter. He was not overly pessimistic in those days, but he could be a cynic in the best tradition of the newsman. His gloomy cogitations upon the moral impoverishment of American life had been challenged for a short time in 1884 with the election of Grover Cleveland as president. Yet the burden Frederic was placing upon a figure that he was obviously idealizing hopelessly was always doomed. The regeneration for which Frederic had hoped did not last. It may have seemed to him that no single man was enough to counter the deterioration of the Gilded Age.

The year of Cleveland's retirement from the political stage, 1896, was also the year in which Theron Ware was to make his appearance and have his "confiding ignorance . . . tampered with." In a scene that resembles a political convention, Theron is first introduced at the "annual Nedahma Conference of the Methodist Episcopal Church," in terms that suggest a familiarity with Lombroso, as "the tall, slender young man with the broad white brow, thoughtful eyes, and features moulded into that regularity of strength which used to characterize the American Senatorial type in those faraway days of clean-shaven faces and moderate incomes before the War." By invoking the Civil War and associating him with a halcyon prewar period, Frederic initially appears to be emphasizing Theron's exemption from the general decline that characterizes the younger Methodist ministers at the conference. Theron certainly looks like an aspiring idealist, a figure with the potential to counter the moral decline that was blighting postbellum America. Yet Frederic had always distrusted idealism, even his own, when it existed without a balance of practicality and good sense, conservative qualities that his mother had tried to instill into him. This early description of Theron, read in the light of the rest of the novel, is undercut by an ironic tone that pervades the novel and warns the reader against making superficial judgments.

Later in the novel Sister Soulsby tells Theron that the performance of a play "looks one way from where the audience sit, and quite a different way when you are behind the scenes." So it is with the novel, in which Theron's character "looks one way" at the Nedahma conference, "and quite a different way" as the novel progresses. Theron eventually leaves the ministry to "go West," to move to Seattle, Washington, and go into real estate: the bleakest ending Frederic could conceive of, worse, even, than suicide. Theron also develops senatorial ambitions: "What Soulsby said about politics out there interested me enormously . . . I shouldn't be surprised if I found myself doing something in that line. I *can* speak, you know, if I can't do anything else. Talk is what tells, these days. Who knows? I may turn up in Washington a full-blown Senator before I'm forty." In this parody of the frontier spirit, Theron's political aspirations reveal his damnation more succinctly than much of the sometimes labored symbolism of the novel. To be "full-blown" is to be past one's best, even rotten. All of Frederic's distrust of the corruption of Gilded Age business and political life goes into Theron's transformation. The circularity of this—from Senatorial look-alike preaching pulpit oratory to potential Senator hoping for a political platform—is complete. Theron moves to Washington State, but his real ambitions are centered upon Washington, D.C., even, as Sister Soulsby jokes, the White House: a political nightmare, but the ultimate American real estate dream.

In the fourth and last of his full-length examinations of life in upper New York State, Frederic questions what has happened to the promise of the Revolution. *In the Valley* had ended on an optimistic note that little suggested that within five years Frederic's attitude toward his native country would be considerably less hopeful. From the description of the ministers in the opening pages of *The Damnation of Theron Ware* it is clear that the moral integrity and genuine worth of the early American settlers and of the generation of people idealistically represented in *In the Valley* with such aching precision and optimistic zeal has not been passed down to their children and grandchildren.

The Damnation of Theron Ware is a novel of loss and of longing, the last novel of American life written by a man who had been out of his country for twelve years. Frederic had carefully charted and created a fictionalized version of rural New York State in his novels, but he had lost contact with the real landscape that it resembled. Although he had written about the harshness of American life, he had idealized the landscape of his native region and, personally, he had perfected the development of an "American" character. Now, owing to the circumstances of his divided personal life, he had been shut out of this idealized vision, just as Theron figuratively loses access to his wife's Eden-like garden. Theron's deteriorating relationship with Alice Hastings is an echo of Frederic's failed marriage with Grace Williams. The first names of the two women

are close, and the name "Williams" is obliquely indicated by Alice's surname, "Hastings." The reference is more significant than this, though. It was Harold who lost the Battle of Hasting to William the Conqueror. In the despair that Frederic experienced in the early 1890s he may have felt that he had lost his long conflict with his wife.

In *The Damnation of Theron Ware* the theme of loss works most obviously through Theron's religious doubt, but this is only one of its most superficial manifestations, since there is never much depth to Theron's belief. Although the novel draws upon the vogue for the novel of religious doubt, in Britain contributed to most famously by Mark Rutherford and Mrs Humphry Ward, this is not its sole, or even chief preoccupation. The most poignant "loss of faith" is the shrinking promise of American life, encapsulated by the shift in attitude and beliefs from those of the early mendicant Methodist preachers to those of the young Theron Ware. The drama of the first chapter of the novel centers upon the issue of which minister will move to Tecumseh. The Tecumseh Methodists are presented "with particularly cutting irony," and Theron's credibility is called into question by their eagerness to associate themselves with him. Austin Briggs argues that Frederic treats the oldest ministers—"venerable Fathers in Israel"—with ambivalence. When Abram C. Tisdale is chosen as Tecumseh's preacher, Briggs points out that, "Brother Abram not only bears the name of the Father in Israel but is one of the church veterans, 'a spindly, rickety, gaunt old man.'" He is the leftover representative of what Frederic calls the "heroic times" of early American Methodism. Briggs's examination of the evasive nature of Frederic's irony is also made by Luther Luedtke, who says that "the reader's perceptions are filtered by constantly sliding screens of irony." The depth and complexity of the irony is suggested by Forbes's revelation to Theron that "The word 'Abram' is merely an eponym—it means 'exalted father.'"

Abraham Tisdale, the feeble old man whom even the Licensed Exhorters laugh at, is one of Methodism's "exalted father[s]." Briggs is right to argue that Frederick is ironic at the expense of both Theron and Tisdale. This does not mean that Frederic is dismissive of the older ministers. The description of the ministers is imbued with a nostalgic sense of loss, of stunted potential. The ministers suggest the history of America itself. The oldest ministers have a dignity despite their physical infirmity and evoke memories of the earliest days of both American Methodism and the United States. In their youth they were fervent idealists who

A Methodist chapel © John Heseltine/Corbis

traveled between "the rude frontier settlements" of pioneers. As survivors of "heroic times" these men embody a masculine virility, attractive to Frederic at least, that is far from evident in their current physical state. In old age they are as simple and humble as ever. Their lack of finesse and their present physical inferiority to the younger ministers is balanced by their clear moral superiority. Frederic is explicit about the younger generation's loss of moral credibility: "The impress of zeal and moral worth seemed to diminish by regular gradations as one passed to younger faces, and among the very beginners, who had been ordained only within the past day or two, this decline was peculiarly marked. It was almost a relief to note the relative smallness of their number, so plainly was it to be seen that they were not the men their forbears had been."

The absence of significant beliefs is the deepest loss that Frederic registers within the novel. Each character seeks to compensate for this loss in different ways. Michael Madden retreats into the mysteries of Catholicism when its dogma perplexes him, Father Forbes develops an interest in etymology and origins when he can no longer believe in "this Christmyth of ours." Celia Madden is determined to behave according to new rules of conduct for women while calling herself a "Greek," yet her philosophy

is unsystematic, and willful at best, and Doctor Ledsmar pursues science through experimentation and empirical observation when he can no longer accept the discipline and ideas of the medical profession. The theme of loss works further through the deaths of Jerry Madden's friends and family, through famine and tuberculosis, through Levi Gorringe's search for a woman to replace the one he "lost" years before, and through Alice's attempt, Eve-like "most worshipful of womankind," to entice her American Adam back into the garden of innocence and prolusion that she has created, only to find that his keenest pleasure comes from watching as it is destroyed by frost. Despite its comedy, which comes, predominantly, from its clever character sketches (particularly in its outrageous presentation of Celia Madden), the novel is pervaded with a deep sense of gloom that reflects Frederic's belief in the impossibility of "returning to the garden."

Source: Bridget Bennett, "*The Damnation of Theron Ware* or *Illumination* (1896)," in *The Damnation of Harold Frederic: His Lives and Work*, Syracuse University Press, 1997, pp. 174–83.

Bruce Michelson

In the following essay excerpt, Michelson explores how The Damnation of Theron Ware

> The novel dramatizes changes underway, even in backcountry New York, regarding what it means to think, to hold opinions, and to reconcile such opinions with identity."

dramatizes societal changes in the relationship between intellect and identity.

The Damnation of Theron Ware was published in 1896 amid a springtide of idea-systems in the Anglo-American world; and as a vigorous amateur in history, religion, politics, economics, and literature, Harold Frederic understood *fin de siècle* turmoil and the quarrels of literary Realism and Naturalism—with older modes and with one another. Yet whether Frederic himself held steady opinions on such matters grows less sure as one treks through the canon. The sheafs of newspaper essays, the private letters, the four novels, the short fiction and satires suggest that the opinions of this man were eclectic and changeful. The Europe he portrays in his Sunday-paper reports is full of corruption, social breakdown, and crosscurrents of extremism; yet the voice always seems nonpartisan, reserved. While much of Frederic's fiction is propelled with naturalistic irony, much of it seems workshop-romantic, even bathetic—and in the midst of his brief career, after a sprawling historical romance and before a weak try at Howellsian Realism, comes *The Damnation of Theron Ware*. Uncertainties about *The Damnation* include even what takes place in it, what happens to whom in the story, and why. Comic or otherwise, this novel is frequently read as a cautionary tale, with Ware as a modern Everyman victimized by some hideous "awakening" which menaces those who sail into adult life with simple values and imperfect faith. Yet perhaps Ware is too much a fool or a cad to signify anything beyond himself, regardless of his New England mainstream background or what kind of "Illumination" (the title of the first British edition) he might undergo. Disagreement also runs deep about the supporting cast: what they might represent, and what hand they play in the young

minister's undoing. Little of importance about Frederic's best novel seems settled.

My own premise is that *The Damnation* dramatizes a failure of one archetype of the American consciousness—innocent or otherwise—to recognize that amid the intellectual disorder of that time, something may have changed in the *relationship* of the individual self to such turmoil—in other words, to modern intellectual experience. In Ware's waning century, bonds are apparently breaking between that life and the personality, between professed belief, everyday conduct, culture, literature and its place within culture. There was no shortage in the nineties of novels about new literary, scientific, or moral systems; yet few seem so engaged with the trauma of life in an amusement park of cultural fads and formulations, *The Damnation of Theron Ware* seems more than a work about one era of aesthetic and cultural crisis, or about the comic or dangerous insufficiency of any given intellectual or aesthetic premise. The novel dramatizes changes underway, even in backcountry New York, regarding what it means to think, to hold opinions, and to reconcile such opinions with identity. Whether or not the novel has lasting force as social prophecy, the structure, energy, and much of the delight in *The Damnation* resonate with this crisis.

I

In structure as well as theme, *The Damnation* dissents from doctrines and evades conventions of Gilded Age Realism, Naturalism, and romantic fiction. It rejects such modes perhaps because they are wholesale, reductive, inadequate representations of experience, with little heed for how such representations are to be read and what the status of realistic narrative can or should be for intelligent readers. In a sense, Theron Ware's disaster is that he reads badly and learns too late that other more-or-less thoughtful people in his world do *not* live by premises more central to his own nature than his Methodist faith. These others do not assume simple connections between creed and conduct, or that selfhood requires continuity among what one accepts as truth and what one does and is. *The Damnation* is a story of catastrophic divorce, in at least one American life, between the self and the intellect. Because Ware fails to recognize new rules governing the way people around him read and act, he cannot understand what they say or how they conduct their lives. Frightened by false fire, Theron Ware fails to see that, in the scientific and ideological revolution at the century's end, these new-looking doctrines and representations may lie all around, but for the new-style intellectual, they lack psychological and moral consequence.

Deepening this novel's pleasure is the way it addresses a problem which such a theme poses for moral fiction. *The Damnation* evades the abyss Frederic pushes his protagonist into: the face-value acceptance of doctrinal representations of experience. If this novel is indeed about the degradation of ideas into poses and entertainments, the hypocritical abuse of systematic thought, and the stupidity of allegiance to codes that others profess and nobody else takes to heart, codes which are always inherently unsatisfactory—then can such a novel keep faith with one representational mode?

It is no surprise, therefore, that *The Damnation of Theron Ware* is a mongrel. The narrative stance not only shifts repeatedly, it manages to do so without recourse to heavy irony as a stand-in for definable perspectives. The novel offers an array of relationships between the spoken word and the conduct of daily life; some scenes and tonal changes in *The Damnation* come as surprises, while others parody conventions in formula novels from the time. *The Damnation*'s structure seems playful, yet wary: in Frederic's fable of intellectual crisis, the form exemplifies suppleness and originality of response to life, non-mechanized integrity, and skepticism about a skeptical age—qualities well-suited to a culture where not even ideas are what they seem. Such is the improvised coherence of *The Damnation of Theron Ware*—like a make-shift identity for a profoundly disordered time.

One misunderstanding about *The Damnation* should be addressed first: the date for the novel's action. Because the story is about the effects of imported ideas upon home-grown American identities, it matters how "new" these imports are, how long they have been circulating before striking the minister's brittle ethos, and how fresh they might seem to American audiences of the mid-nineties. The action seems not to be generally "in the 1870's or 1880's," as John Henry Raleigh proposed when he brought the novel out of eclipse, and as subsequent readers have evidently assumed. Internal evidence fixes the date in the last years of that twenty-year range. The mention of the Murray Hill Hotel in New York, where Celia and Father Forbes take rooms on their suspicious junket, gives one good clue—the hotel was not opened until 1884—as do the publication dates of two books that Ware fixates on. Renan's *Reminiscences of My Youth,* which Ware reads at least twice, was first available in English in 1883, the year which saw the publication of

Bertha Thomas' biography of George Sand in the "Eminent Women Series"—the volume Ware buys with his clergyman's discount at a local bookstore. An emphasized detail which helps fix the year turns up in the account of Celia's father Jeremiah Madden, who is fifty-three as the novel opens; we are also told that he was a boy of ten when the Great Famine of 1845–7 devastated his Irish family and forced him to America—meaning that the action is set around 1888–90. We can also cipher from the history Frederic offers of Ware himself. Ware must be at least in his mid-twenties, having already logged four years' experience as a pastor, not a position he would hold before reaching his majority; further, Celia's brother Michael Madden, who is "nearly thirty," observes to the parson, in their final meeting, that they are about the same age. The narrative also observes that this Ware of twenty-five or thirty was still "in petticoats" during the last days of the Civil War, which would mean a birth date no earlier than 1862. Again the details imply that the action unfolds around 1888, possibly later. Frederic offers but one hint that the time of the minister's trouble is at all remote from 1896, the year of the book's release: a remark in Chapter 11 that the origins of Free Methodism life twenty years back from the time of the action. According to standard histories, Free Methodism began officially at a small meeting in 1860. It is reasonable to assume, however, that Frederic had in mind the fundamentalist fervor which gave Free Methodism its impetus and national attention, in the noisy centennial year of Methodism in America, 1866.

To sum up: evidence in the novel points to a setting in the later 1880s—which does help us evaluate Ware's misfortunes, and specifically his culture-crisis at the hands of Father Forbes, Dr. Ledsmar, and Celia Madden. It means that Arnold's *Culture and Anarchy,* with its abusable model of civilization split between Hebraic and Hellenistic temperaments (Celia's "Greeks and Jews"), has been in the intellectual markets for more than twenty years; that the Pre-Raphaelite movement, from which Celia steals her affectations, goes back three decades, Pater's aesthetic manifestoes more than fifteen years, full-bloom French decadence at least ten. In contrast to Celia's pastiche of yesterday's avantgardism, Father Forbes' heresies about religion, history, and human nature are fresher from the source, if narrower in range. His pronouncements about "Christ-myths" and the origins of ritual and sacred texts are lifted wholesale (and uncredited) from works of Renan, whose histories of Christianity and Judaism were being published in English in the late eighties and early nineties. If Forbes enjoys impressing people with borrowed ideas, at least he stays current, and works one authority hard rather than jumbles them up.

Because Celia's poses are old news at the time of the action, and because Forbes, when showing off, does so as a one-trick intellectual, the comic side of Ware's seduction intensifies: one would-be intellectual is undone by straw-hat sophistication. But one distinction taking shape here, concerning what these people know and how they apply their learning, promotes a contrast among the intellectuals and intellectual-pretenders of Octavius. For attention centers not upon ideas professed across these dinner tables and in these curtained boudoirs, but rather on what ideas are now used *for*—social weapons, rationalizations, play-things for idle hours. Because Ware fails to see that the relationship between ideas and identity is different in these private rooms, his fall into error can seem acutely modern. This is why Ware's troubles matter, why this tale of a botched "conversion" to urbane philandering is still worth reading. What unfolds is a conflict between the American Transcendental faith in the unity of intellectual, moral, and domestic life, and sensibilities sustained by fragmentation, in a world where principles and social ethics have almost nothing to do with one another.

Frederic tells an evasive tale, both in its plot twists and in its escape from one mode into others; yet this novel is not a sequence of ironic rude awakenings, either for Ware or the reader. False leads draw the minister toward more complex and absurd illusions about who he is, where he is, and what the motives are of the people around him, while the narrative slips from mode to mode, rising repeatedly towards some Naturalistic or Realistic accounting for Ware and his miseries—then breaking the promise. The story opens with a multiple false start: the lesson Ware draws from his first surprise proves wrong, and each time he recasts it to account for his troubles he errs again. A parody of the first chapter of *The Scarlet Letter,* the opening pages suggest the irony-laden narratives of Frank Norris or Stephen Crane:

> No such throng had ever before been seen in the building during all its eight years of existence. People were wedged together most uncomfortably upon the seats; they stood packed in the aisles and overflowed the galleries; at the back, in the shadows underneath these galleries, they formed broad, dense masses about the doors, through which it would be hopeless to attempt a passage.

> An observer, looking over these compact lines of faces and noting the uniform concentration of eagerness they exhibited, might have guessed they were watching for either the jury's verdict in some peculiarly absorbing criminal trial, or the announcement of the lucky numbers in a great lottery. These two expressions seemed to alternate, and even to mingle vaguely, upon the upturned lineaments of the waiting throng—the hope of some unnamed stroke of fortune and the dread of some adverse decree.

Ranks of expectations raised here are betrayed. The great event proves to be back-country ministers receiving new assignments, and this rapt audience loses interest when Theron Ware is called to Octavius rather than the more glamorous Tecumseh. Though the ironic tone subsides as well, misdirections continue to mount. Everyone in the hall "knows" that Ware is destined for Tecumseh, everyone except (we learn later) the Presiding Elder who dislikes Ware and makes the choices. We are also told, soon after, that Ware is really not the perfection which Tecumseh's parishioners take him for, having bungled his finances and compromised his repute. But Frederic's satiric adoption here of the Tecumseh perspective readies finer surprises for later on. These complacent rubes, with their wish to show off and face down other congregations, *these* people regard the town of Octavius as a backwater. If Octavius is one of those "remote and pitifully rustic stations" in the judgment of such minds, if its mention can make patient, cheerful Alice Ware burst into sobs, then it must be a place of barbarism. Frederic allows this impression to steep for several chapters before he disturbs it. The first view of Octavius is of a garbage-strewn yard: the town seems a blot on the handsome face of upstate New York, and the metaphor seems ratified in Ware's skirmish with tightfisted Brothers Winch and Pierce, Elders in the new congregation. But the impression has more somersaults to turn. Soon comes Ware's discovery of a little Athens of enlightenment, thriving in the cultural desolation. Thereafter a sadder truth emerges, that Octavius is not a place where cosmopolitan minds hide among ignorant busybodies, but where only small souls flourish, either openly or in dangerous disguise.

Source: Bruce Michelson, "Theron Ware in the Wilderness of Ideas," in *American Literary Realism 1870–1910,* Vol. 25, No. 1, Fall 1992, pp. 54–59.

Thomas LeClair

In the following essay, LeClair examines the dynamic of "seeing and being seen" and its repercussions on the fate of the title character in The Damnation of Theron Ware.

Harold Frederic's *The Damnation of Theron Ware* (1896) presents several large and familiar cultural actions—the temptation of nineteenth-century fundamentalist religion by the new science, aestheticism, and intellectual discoveries, the isolation and failure of the American innocent—but it is the psychological action of the novel which sets Frederic apart from his American contemporaries and gives the book its modernist quality. The psychological condition Frederic explores in *The Damnation* is the complex relationship between being seen and seeing, between the person as object of perception and the person as perceiver of self and others. Black writers of our own time, especially Richard Wright and Ralph Ellison, have demonstrated the importance of this relationship between seen and seeing in their novels revealing the tragedy and comedy of what the social scientists call "high visibility." The blacks in *Native Son* and *Invisible Man* stand out from the norm because of their color; they are highly visible, are seen. However, as Ellison suggests in his title, these characters are really unseen because their high visibility leads others to construct stereotypes which obscure real perception. Whites deprive themselves of knowing the reality behind the stereotype, but, more importantly, the blacks who use the white-defined stereotypes as models of identity deprive themselves of knowing themselves. In Frederic's novel, Theron Ware, as a minister in a small town, has this high visibility which leads to his damnation—the estrangement of the self from itself. Theron's appearance and position draw attention to him, but the other characters are misled by the outer forms of his life. When their limited perceptions turn into complimentary statements, Theron is encouraged to falsify his vision of himself and his relationships with others to correspond with what he is told he is. At the center of the book, then, is a conception of identity as extrinsic and provisional, an identity awarded to the individual by the looks and comments of others, an identity which can lead only to the anguish of what Wylie Sypher has called the "loss of self." To dramatize his psychological theme, Frederic constructs *The Damnation* out of a series of false and partial recognition scenes which he objectifies through visual perspectives and a recurring imagery of eyes and sight, imagery which ultimately extends to include light, darkness, and elevation.

Frederic skillfully establishes the context of seen and seeing in the first chapter, even in the first line of the novel. The scene is the Tecumseh Methodist church; the occasion is the annual

> *" Theron Ware, as a minister in a small town, has this high visibility which leads to his damnation—the estrangement of the self from itself."*

Nedahma Conference of the Methodist Episcopal Church; the first line is "no such throng had ever before been seen in the building during all its eight years of existence." In the small town world of *The Damnation,* significance lies in what is seen, not just in what takes place. If Tecumseh Methodists had filled their church before, no one saw them. This time their success is witnessed, ratified, appreciated: it is real. Outside the walls of the Methodist church lurk Baptists, Presbyterians, Catholics, all watching, counting, judging the success of the Methodists—this is the atmosphere Frederic suggests in this first chapter and elsewhere in the novel. The emphasis on appearance in small town life is familiar, yet this atmosphere is also paradoxical, for it is an ambience of necessary paranoia. Persons need to be seen, welcome being seen, yet deeply fear being seen in failure. It is the atmosphere of a public and competitive religion which has looked to the marketplace for its model of behavior, a confusion of realms—secular and sacred—which Frederic quickly turns into irony. In their collective gaze at the pulpit, the congregation appears to be "watching for either the jury's verdict in some peculiarly absorbing criminal trial, or the announcement of the lucky numbers in a great lottery." In their hypersensitivity to being watched and in the nature of their watching, the congregation defines the general environment of the novel. As Frederic narrows his visual perspective in this beautifully handled first chapter, he introduces the foreground of the novel. Eyes focus on a single representative of the congregation's success: the clergyman, in this case a near-sighted old gentleman who ironically betrays the flock's expectations by awarding them Abram G. Tisdale, "a spindling, rickety, gaunt old man, with a long horselike head and vacantly solemn face, who kept one or the other of his hands continually fumbling his bony jaw." What is essential here is the congregation's passing on the psychological pressure of being watched at their religious duties to a kind of visual lightning rod, a scapegoat-hero who literally stands above them and represents them. Admired for his status, the minister is also resented for his authority and closely scrutinized for signs of weakness. He, of all men in a small town, has high visibility. If provincial, immature, and too concerned with secular success, he may depend too much on others' eyes and voices to provide him with an image of himself. He may become invisible to himself. This is the case with Theron Ware.

When religion becomes a business, as it is in the novel, the minister becomes an advertiser of himself as well as God. His success in the business of religion hinges upon the impression he makes. A "tall, slender young man with the broad white brow, thoughtful eyes, and features moulded into that regularity of strength which used to characterize the American Senatorial type," Theron Ware is physically attractive, and his rhetorical gifts have impressed many people—his wife Alice, a benefactor in Tyre, the people of Tecumseh—on the way to Octavius. Theron does not question the bases of respect these rather naive and simple people have for him, perhaps because he very much enjoys the role of fair-haired boy he has been given by his admirers. When more sophisticated and worldly people—Father Forbes, Doctor Ledsmar, Celia Madden, Levi Gorringe, and Sister Soulsby—superficially judge him capable of more than he can manage as a preacher and as a man, Theron willingly accepts their optimistic but limited or mistaken views of him. Levi Gorringe, the first time he sees Theron, thinks that he is "different," a superior human being, and he tells Theron so. Celia Madden, forming her ideas about Theron from a first impression, also tells him he is different from most men: "'a *man,* and not a marionette or a mummy.'" Even Sister Soulsby, the most perceptive of the lot, seems to exaggerate Theron's potential when she first sees him: "'You've got brains, and you've got human nature in you, and heart. What you lack is *sabe,*—common-sense.'" These characters, all isolates except for Sister Soulsby, see Theron as a possible externalization or mirror of themselves, as a blank sheet upon which they can impress their own hopes or values. Forbes and Ledsmar assume Theron's education has led him to their skepticism. Celia Madden would have Theron a "Greek" like herself even though he is obviously no revolutionary. Gorringe feels that his own independence from social conventions is registered in Theron. And Sister Soulsby would have Theron be the performing fraud she is.

All are wrong about Theron's superiority and potential for transformation, but he accepts their confident versions of his identity, even when the versions are at odds with one another. Because Theron lacks a sense of himself independent of others' characterizations of him, he comes to have an over-blown sense of his capacities for expanding the self. He begins to view the possibilities that other characters suggest as certainties, begins to assume the forms of a collection of identities without having understood what those roles demand and mean. Theron's growing presumption, egotism, and selfishness are the results of his accepting these extrinsic identities and lead to the "tempters'" realization that they have been mistaken about Theron's character, with Celia even admitting that her errors may well have helped lead Theron astray. Frederic uses the "tempters'" original errors in perception to mitigate Theron's failure and to contribute to the moral complexity of the novel, but, most importantly, these errors set in motion the psychological dialectic which begins with extrinsic definition and ends with Theron's breakdown at the conclusion of the novel.

Although Theron is not alone in perceptual error, Frederic reveals through physical details, the non-verbal nuances of human intercourse so skillfully exploited by Henry James, that Theron's blindness was self-inflicted, a willful avoidance of reality. His eye repeatedly drifts from mundane and unpleasant reality to visionary realms. Early in the novel he gazes away from the ashes and cinders of a rank garden to the "great blue dome, radiant with light and the purification of spring." Frederic doubles this episode with the ending of the novel, a passage which demonstrates Theron's inability to escape an extrinsically ratified identity: "Only in the eyes themselves, as they rested briefly upon the prospect, did a substantial change suggest itself. They did not dwell fondly upon the picture of the lofty, spreading boughs, with their waves of sap-green leafage stirring against the blue." Now Theron's eyes summon a "conjectural vision" of uplifted faces:

> Their eyes were admiringly bent upon a common object of excited interest. They were looking at *him;* they strained their ears to miss no cadence of his voice . . . The audience rose at him, as he dropped his hand, and filled his daydream with a mighty roar of applause, in volume like an ocean tempest, yet pitched for his hearing alone.

As they have throughout the novel, eyes and voices provide Theron with the affirmation of yet another illusion, sustain a self that he only imagines. There is also a shift from the spiritual to the secular in this doubling of scenes, a technique Frederic uses frequently in *The Damnation*. At the beginning of his spiritual career, Theron "could not look without blinking timidity at the radiance of the path stretched out before him, leading upward to dazzling heights of greatness." Near the end of the novel, he must blink "his eyes again and again, to prevent their seeing, seated together in the open window above this panel, the two people [Forbes and Celia] he knew were there . . ." Another imagistic doubling which demonstrates Theron's questionable progress also has him shutting out reality. Early in the novel Theron "closed his eyes, to be the more wholly alone with the Spirit, that moved him." Later he finds himself so moved by Celia's music that he "would fain have reclined in his chair and closed his eyes, and saturated himself with the uttermost fulness of the sensation."

Perhaps the most revealing of these visual doublings is Theron's twice blinding himself to an ambiguous reality. When Alice comes to the rail as a sinner during the "season of grace," Theron covers his eyes with his hands: "he drew back and put up his hand, shutting out the strange scene altogether. To see nothing at all was a relief, and under cover he closed his eyes, and bit his teeth together." Shortly thereafter "his blurred eyes" prevent him from reading Levi Gorringe's name on the list of new church members. By blinding himself, Theron tries to evade his wife's presence at the sinners' rail before the eyes of the congregation and his suspicions about her relationship with Gorringe. Further on in the novel Frederic dramatizes Theron's ambivalence toward love through this same imagery. When Celia announces the end of her private concert for Theron, he "put his hands to his face, and pressed them tightly against eyes and brow for an instant." Theron then looks directly into her eyes, as though grasping for some encouragement, yet when his eyes rove to "the canopy and trappings of an extravagantly over-sized and sumptuous bed," he looks quickly away. Theron Ware is a man who literally cannot look at reality straight on for fear that it would dissolve or weaken that image of himself (that extrinsic identity) he has accepted. Because he does embrace his and others' illusions about him, Theron ensures a total breakdown when reality finally insists upon intruding. And again Frederic uses visual imagery to register Theron's internal loss: leading Theron from his final interview with Celia, Forbes notes "what vacuity his eyes and loosened lips expressed." When Theron reaches the Soulsbys, it is his eyes that Sister Soulsby notices: "Out of a mask of unpleasant features, swollen with drink and weighted by the physical craving for rest and sleep, there stared at her two bloodshot eyes, shining with the wild light of hysteria," eyes with "an unnatural glare."

Obviously aware of the subtle effects he can work by a repetition and variation of imagery, Frederic describes the eyes of each of the major characters, uses this physical detail as an index to personality. The squinty, evasive eyes of the miserly Loren Pierce, the bespectacled, sharp eyes of the scientist Ledsmar, and the earnest, unblinking eyes of the dying saint Michael Madden may be rather clumsy, but Frederic avoids stereotyping in his other descriptions. Not surprisingly, Sister Soulsby's eyes are the most prominent in the novel: "The rest of Sister Soulsby was undoubtedly subordinated in interest to those eyes of hers." Her eyes are both the objects of perception (she draws the congregation to her with their expressiveness) and the agents of perception (she probes the sham of herself and others). Being seen does not distort her seeing. She and Father Forbes compromise with the audience they, like Theron, are always aware of. These two frauds give the audience what it wants while reserving a selfhood independent of their religious-dramatic roles. Because Theron lacks that independent selfhood, he cannot entertain the possibility of pragmatic compromise. Others' eyes also furnish Frederic with a vehicle for Theron's projection of his feelings. When he looks into the eyes of Sister Soulsby and Celia, he fuses the carnal and the maternal, thus projecting his ambivalence toward the two women and toward his own sexual identity. While Alice's eyes become more "shallow," Celia's become deeper: "The sight [of skirts and stockings] struck him as indecorous in the extreme, and he turned his eyes away. They met Celia's; and there was something latent in their brown depths which prompted him, after a brief dalliance of interchanging glances, to look again at the swings." Theron Ware does not simply avoid the truth by turning his eyes away from it; he also invents a replacement for reality by projecting his own wishes into the eyes of others.

The imagery of eyes and vision modulates nicely into imagery of light and darkness, height and depth. As the novel progresses, Frederic moves Theron into a number of rooms or structures which represent new ideas. Each of these rooms is dark or poorly lighted; most of them are elevated. First is the Irish laborer MacEvoy's cottage where Theron imperfectly witnesses the Roman Catholic last rites and forms his initial impression of Father

Forbes and Celia. Next is Forbes' sitting room, a hazy, ill-lighted room where Theron is both confused and, he thinks, enlightened. The Catholic church which Theron enters to hear Celia play the organ is also dimly lighted, as is Celia's upstairs chamber in the Madden mansion, a room which Theron never understands. Even Doctor Ledsmar's house is elevated and at least puzzling to the eye in its clutter and strangeness. Theron literally aspires to the life of these elevated rooms, but Frederic demonstrates, through an unobtrusive pattern of physical details, that Theron only partially understands the complexities and the subtleties of life in these rooms. He believes he can be free of past constrictions—the small rooms of his parsonage, the narrowness of his church—but Celia's statement near the end of the novel sums up his visual and spatial limitations: "'You are not by any means free. You are only looking out of the window of your prison, as you call it. The doors are locked, just the same.'" Theron's physical elevation above his congregation should have a corresponding spiritual elevation, his desire for transcendence should be spiritual rather than social. But Frederic illustrates through Theron's alternatives to the clergy—the politician of his final vision, the actor in Sister Soulsby's "life is a stage" speech, the barkeeper at the Catholic picnic whom Theron finds admirable—that Theron wants most of all the attention that physical elevation—whether it be the pulpit, the platform, the stage, or the bar risers—can bring. Theron must be seen, must have his success ratified. He sets himself off from the group, transcends his peers in some individual action, real or imagined. However, his uncertainty about himself and his achievement forces him to look back at the persons he has risen above for admiration and confirmation. Because he has gone beyond the mass, he has little respect for their opinion (he calls his congregation "dogs"), yet he must have their attention or praise. Theron Ware is thus imprisoned within a paradoxical relationship with others, a relationship which lacks respect yet demands it.

Elevation is but one of the images Frederic uses to render the confusion of secular and spiritual values in *The Damnation.* Theron transcends his congregation, only to detest them. He lifts up his eyes to illusion, not to God. A new life for Theron is a transfiguration of social class; the ladder to heaven now leads to success. The fall is sinking into economic helplessness; grace is unforeseen financial aid. *Illumination,* the English title of the book, also loses its religious meaning. Light and gold are now the images of Celia's head rather than

the godhead. She is an ironic angel whose halo is formed by a transparent parasol. Revelation now comes when listening to Chopin or reading Renan, and damnation is just an ironic description of Theron's fate at the end of the novel. As Theron indiscriminately mixes the rhetoric of the pulpit and the marketplace, language itself becomes a subject of the novel. Unable to keep the new specialized languages of aesthetics and criticism discrete from the language of religion and everyday life, Theron misunderstands and misinterprets the motives of others. Thus the eye of the mind, language, becomes as misleading as the naked eye when Theron allows the languages of others to subsume his own.

Theron Ware's story is not one of traditional damnation in which the self stands out against God. The novel's psychological action and its metaphors imply that it is a peculiarly modern story about the abandonment or loss of the self to the other. Obsessed with the messages in the eyes of others, Theron abandons whatever was genuine in him, accepts the identity others provide, and eventually becomes a synthetic person, the makeshift creation of Sister Soulsby. Her response to Theron's condition of loss is also modern, quite unlike the distinctly moral pragmatism of a Howells, with whom Frederic is most often compared. Sister Soulsby advocates picking an illusion, knowing that it is an illusion, and then using it to survive in a time of confusion. This prefiguration of a modern sensibility and Frederic's skillful use of imagery to carry his themes, along with the more commonly noted traits of the novel, contribute to the achievement of and the continued interest in *The Damnation of Theron Ware.*

Source: Thomas LeClair, "The Ascendant Eye: A Reading of *The Damnation of Theron Ware*," in *Studies in American Fiction*, Vol. 3, No. 1, Spring 1975, pp. 95–102.

Sources

Carter, Everett, "Introduction," in *The Damnation of Theron Ware*, Harvard University Press/Belknap Press, 1960, pp. vii–xxiv.

Donaldson, Scott, "Introduction," in *The Damnation of Theron Ware*, Penguin, 1986, pp. vii–xxx.

———, "The Seduction of Theron Ware," in *Nineteenth-Century Fiction*, Vol. 29, 1975, pp. 441–52.

Garner, Stanton, *Harold Frederic*, University of Minnesota Press, 1969, pp. 33–38.

Howells, William Dean, "My Favorite Novelist and His Best Book," in *W. D. Howells as Critic*, edited by Edwin H. Cady,

Routledge & Kegan Paul, 1973, pp. 268–80; originally published in *Munsey's Magazine*, Vol. 17, April 1897.

O'Donnell, Thomas F., and Hoyt Franchere, *Harold Frederic*, Twayne, 1971, pp. 108–17.

Review of *The Damnation of Theron Ware*, in the *Atlantic*, Vol. 78, August 1896, pp. 269–76.

Further Reading

Briggs, Austin, *The Novels of Harold Frederic*, Cornell University Press, 1969, pp. 97–139.

> Briggs argues that Ware does not really undergo a fall from grace, similar to Adam and Eve, since he has changed little at the end from what he was at the beginning: an ambitious "climber" and a "snob" who has contempt for his flock.

Crowley, John W., "The Nude and the Madonna in *The Damnation of Theron Ware*," in *American Literature*, Vol. 45, No. 3, November 1973, pp. 379–89.

> Crowley argues that Ware is torn by an unresolved oedipal obsession between the sensual and the maternal aspects of the female, and this distorts his relations with Alice, Celia Madden, and Sister Soulsby.

MacFarlane, Lisa Watt, "Resurrecting Man: Desire and *The Damnation of Theron Ware*," in *Studies in American Fiction*, Vol. 20, No. 2, 1992, pp. 127–43.

> This feminist analysis argues that Ware occupies an ambiguous position in terms of gender. This is because the cultural role of a minister is to exhibit male and female characteristics, and sometimes Ware takes on the role of the female. His gender identity shifts often during the course of the novel.

Myers, Robert M., *Reluctant Expatriate: The Life of Harold Frederic*, Greenwood Press, pp. 115–34.

> Myers examines how the circumstances of Harold Frederic's life contributed to the novel. For example, the fact that Frederic kept two households, one of which had to be completely private, may have contributed to his presentation of how Ware tries to separate his inner self from his public persona as a minister.

Dandelion Wine

Ray Bradbury

1957

Dandelion Wine, first published in the United States in 1957, is the story of twelve-year-old Douglas Spaulding as he approaches manhood in the mythical city of Green Town, Illinois. As Douglas moves from a childlike state of ignorance toward the full knowledge of his own existence, he learns to value family, friends, and time. Moreover, as Douglas becomes increasingly aware that all life ends in death, he also must confront his own mortality and that fact that he, too, will someday die. This confrontation erupts in a mysterious summer illness that almost costs Douglas his life; his awakening from the fever coma signifies Douglas's mature acceptance and valuing of human life.

Dandelion Wine is different from most of the canon of Bradbury's work. Although he rejects the label of science fiction writer, it is true that most of his work could be classified as fantasy or science fiction. *Dandelion Wine*, on the other hand, grows out of Bradbury's own childhood in Waukegan, Illinois, in the golden years before the Great Depression. Bradbury himself frequently comments on the autobiographical qualities of the novel. He writes in his 1975 introduction to the book, "*Dandelion Wine* is nothing if it is not the boy-hid-in-the-man playing in the fields of the Lord on the green grass of other Augusts in the midst of starting to grow up, grow old, and sense darkness waiting under the trees to seed the blood." This, then, is a glimpse into the childhood and formative years of one of America's major writers, and a coming-of-age-story for readers of all ages.

Author Biography

Ray Bradbury was born to Leonard Spaulding and Esther Moberg Bradbury on August 22, 1920, in Waukegan, Illinois. He spent his formative childhood years in Waukegan, the town that became the basis for "Green Town," and the setting for several of his stories and novels.

In 1926, the family moved to Tucson, Arizona, where Bradbury's younger sister was born. She died of pneumonia in 1927, and the family returned to Waukegan. The family again moved to Tucson in 1932, only to return in 1933; their last move, however, was to Los Angeles in 1934, where Bradbury has lived ever since.

Bradbury fell in love with Hollywood during his teenage years, and spent much of his time trying to get a glimpse of his favorite screen and radio stars at their studios. He handed George Burns a script for his show every week until finally Burns used a small bit to close his show.

After graduation from high school, Bradbury pursued his writing, selling newspapers on street corners to support himself through 1942. His first professional publication, "Pendulum," appeared in *Super Science Stories* in 1941, the same year that he attended renowned science fiction writer Robert Heinlein's writing classes. By 1945, Bradbury was writing full time and placing stories in both science fiction "pulp" magazines as well as such mainstream publications as *McCall's*. During the late 1940s, he also began earning the kind of critical acclaim that would continue throughout his career. His stories regularly appeared in *The Best American Short Stories*, and he won an O. Henry award in 1947.

In the 1950s, Bradbury became a major American writer. In addition to publishing collections of short stories including *The Martian Chronicles* in 1950 and *The Illustrated Man* in 1951, he also brought his novel *Fahrenheit 451* to print in 1953. During this time, Bradbury continued to work as a dramatic writer as well, composing radio adaptations of his stories, television dramas, and the screenplay for John Huston's *Moby Dick*. In 1957, Bradbury finally published a novel he had been working on for nearly a decade, *Dandelion Wine*, a book that was later adapted as a full-length musical drama. The book drew heavily on Bradbury's own childhood in Waukegan, Illinois.

Over the next four decades, Bradbury continued to work prolifically, producing many collections of stories, screenplays, teleplays, voiceover narrations

Ray Bradbury   The Library of Congress

for documentaries and movies, essays, nonfiction books, speeches, lyrics, and poems. For his effort, he won awards, including (among many others) the Aviation Space Writers Association Award (1968, 1979); the Lifetime Achievement Award from the World Fantasy Association (1977); the Jules Verne Award (1984); Body of Work Award from PEN (1985); National Book Foundation's 2000 Medal for Distinguished Contribution to American Letters; and the National Medal of the Arts (2004). The Science Fiction and Fantasy Writers of America named him a Grand Master. Bradbury also has a star on the Hollywood Walk of Fame.

Although Bradbury suffered a stroke in 1999, he continued to write and publish work, including *One More for the Road* (2002), a collection of short stories; several collections of poetry; and the 2003 novel, *Let's All Kill Constance*.

Plot Summary

Sections 1–10

Because *Dandelion Wine* is what is sometimes called a composite novel or short story cycle, the plot does not follow the kind of development one

Media Adaptations

- Bradbury adapted *Dandelion Wine* as a musical several times, most notably in the 1967 Lincoln Center production. While reviews of the performance are available, there are no films of the production.

- *Dandelion Wine* was released on tape by Books on Tape on August 1, 1987.

would expect from a novel although the same characters continue to interact throughout the book.

Nevertheless, it is possible to break the book up into sections for discussion. In this first section, Douglas Spaulding opens the book by standing in the cupola of his grandparent's home and willing Green Town to life: "He folded his arms and smiled a magician's smile. Yes, sir, he thought, everyone jumps, everyone runs when I yell. It'll be a fine season. He gave the town a last snap of his fingers. Doors slammed open; people stepped out. Summer 1928 began."

In the next chapter, Mr. Spaulding takes his sons Tom and Douglas to the forest to gather wild berries. While there, Doug knows that something big is about to happen. Suddenly, he is overwhelmed by the sense of being alive and of being part of all that is alive. Later that day, the boys help their grandfather make the first batch of dandelion wine for the summer, the first ritual of summer.

In the second ritual of the summer, Doug obtains his new tennis shoes, shoes that he is convinced will allow him to run faster and farther than any shoes he has ever had before. He then opens a tablet and writes in it with his Ticonderoga pencil the first entry of his diary of the summer. He tells Tom that he intends to divide the diary into two parts: Rites and Ceremonies, listing things that they do every summer; and Discoveries and Revelations, a place where he will record what he thinks about the rites and ceremonies. Doug's writing in the notebook becomes an important structural device for the novel.

Sections 11–19

The story then turns to Leo Auffman, who decides to invent a Happiness Machine. However, although the machine shows everyone wonderful things, it brings pain and sadness to anyone who tries it. It eventually goes up in flames; but Leo finally understands that his family is the real Happiness Machine.

Next, the children visit old Mrs. Bentley. They refuse to believe that she was ever young, even when she shows them items from her youth. Eventually the children persuade her that they are right and that she has always been old. Doug later writes about this, and he and Tom decide that old people never were children.

Charlie Woodman then tells the boys that he has found a Time Machine in the person of Colonel Freeleigh, an old man who tells the boys many, many stories about the past. Doug, writing about this later, calls it "far traveling." Later, Doug returns to talk to Colonel Freeleigh and finds him dead.

Sections 20–30

Things begin changing for Doug and Green Town about section 20. Mr. Tridden, the trolley driver, tells everyone that the trolley is being decommissioned. He takes everyone for one last ride. In addition, Doug learns that his best friend, John Huff, is moving to Milwaukee. Doug wants Tom to promise never to leave. He is worried about God, and the future. Doug has learned the difference between playing dead and being dead, and it frightens him.

In section 28, Bill Forrester and Doug meet Miss Helen Loomis at the ice cream parlor. Bill Forrester accepts an invitation to go to the old woman's house for tea, and consequently begins spending everyday with her. It is clear that the two love each other very much; but for their ages, there would have been a romance. Helen dies later in August; however, there is an indication that perhaps during the next go around of life, the two might be in the right place at the right time and not miss each other.

Around this time, the Lonely One is reintroduced into the story. A frightening, mysterious figure who haunts the ravine, the Lonely One has been killing women all summer. In section 29, Lavinia Nebbs and her friends cut through the ravine on their way to the theater and stumble on the body of another woman. Doug is in the ravine with them, and is badly shaken. Lavinia insists on going to the theater anyway. Walking home alone through the ravine, she is frightened by footsteps behind her. She races to her home, locks the door behind her, and breathes a sigh of relief. It is then that she realizes that the Lonely One is in the house with her.

The next day the boys tell the story of Lavinia killing the man with her sewing scissors. They decide that this cannot really be the Lonely One. Doug remains shaken, and suddenly realizes that he, too, will die.

Sections 31–40

Doug and Tom next visit the arcade only to discover that the Tarot Witch, a wax figure who tells fortunes, is not working. Doug becomes convinced that she is being held captive and needs to be freed so that she can tell them the truth about the future. He steals her with the help of Tom and Father, but she does not reveal anything but a blank card. Shortly after this, the town is caught in an extreme heat wave, and Doug falls deathly ill. All are afraid that they will lose Doug.

Late one night, the junkman, Mr. Jonas, visits Doug while he is sleeping under the apple tree in the yard where his family has left him in the hope that it will cool him off. Mr. Jonas gives Doug magic cool air to breathe, and this cures him. The next day, rain falls on the town and Doug begins to write again.

In a final story, Aunt Rose visits Grandma and Grandfather's boarding house. She decides to set Grandma's kitchen straight, and in so doing, destroys Grandma's ability to cook. Doug sneaks into the kitchen late at night and undoes the damage. The boarders send Aunt Rose away.

In the final section, summer is over, and the porch furniture comes back into the house. Doug, standing in the cupola once more, commands the town to go to sleep.

Characters

Lena Auffmann

Lena Auffmann is married to Leo Auffmann and is the mother of their six children. She attempts to stop her husband from building the Happiness Machine and continues to be the voice of reason throughout the stories about the Machine. She tells Leo that he has made two mistakes with the machine: "You made quick things go slow and stay around. You brought things faraway to our backyard, where they don't belong. . . ."

Leo Auffmann

Leo Auffmann is the Green Town inventor. One evening when Douglas casually tells him to build a Happiness Machine, Auffmann undertakes what he believes will be his greatest invention. He works many long hours on the Machine, nearly destroying his health, his marriage, and his family in the process. After his son and his wife use the Machine to ill effect, he tries it himself, and is nearly killed in the ensuing fire. He realizes later that the real Happiness Machine is right in front of him, sitting on his own front porch: his family.

Mrs. Bentley

Mrs. Bentley is an elderly resident of Green Town, visited by children who refuse to believe that she was ever young. Under the constant pressure from the children, eventually Mrs. Bentley herself believes that she has never been young, that she has been seventy-two years old forever, that she does not have a first name, and that she has always lived in the same house.

Elmira Brown

Elmira Brown is a thirty-two year old woman married to the town postman. She is clumsy and often hurts herself; at the same time, she often blames others for her own problems. When she hears that her rival, Clara Goodwater, has received instruction manuals for becoming a witch, she believes that all of her tribulations have been caused by Clara casting spells. Although it appears that this is ridiculous, the ending of the story is ambiguous. How a reader ultimately receives Elmira largely depends on the reader's reception of Clara as well.

Miss Fern

Miss Fern is an elderly, unmarried woman who, along with Miss Roberta, owns the Green Machine.

Bill Forrester

Bill Forrester is one of the boarders at Grandfather and Grandma's house who finds a special relationship with Helen Loomis.

Colonel Freeleigh

Colonel Freeleigh is an elderly resident of Green Town who has lived all over the world. Charley Woodman discovers him and says that he is a Time Machine. Freeleigh shares his adventures with the boys in such a way that they feel transported to the time and place he describes.

Clara Goodwater

Clara Goodwater is a young matron of Green Town and the President of the Honeysuckle Ladies' Lodge. She has mail ordered books on witchcraft and magic, ostensibly for her cousin Raoul. She says that she is not a witch, in spite of Elmira Brown's accusation. However, by the end of the story, it is not clear whether she is admitting to witchcraft, or humoring Elmira in a fit of guilt over the latter woman's fall down the stairs.

Grandfather

Douglas and Tom's Grandfather owns the boarding house where many of the characters of *Dandelion Wine* live. He is especially important to the story as the maker of dandelion wine. He pays the boys a dime a bag for the flowers, then he processes them through the press in his basement, making one bottle of the elixir for each day of the summer. Grandfather is also the character who decides when summer begins and ends by choosing the day on which to hang the porch swing, and then take it back in the house for the fall.

Grandma

Douglas and Tom's Grandma's major role in *Dandelion Wine* is that of cook. Her meals are magical and unlike anything anyone has ever had. Each day she prepares large quantities of strange, delicious food for her family and for her boarders.

Great-grandma

Great-grandma lives at the boarding house. Her role in *Dandelion Wine* is that of an elder wise woman who knows when it is time to leave this life. She is the character who explains to Douglas just what death is, and who offers him solace from his contemplations of the process.

John Huff

John Huff is Douglas's closest friend. When his father gets a job in Milwaukee, John tells Doug that he will be leaving Green Town. John's importance in the book is that he serves to demonstrate to Doug the impermanence of life. As much as Doug wants things to stay the way they are, the characters continue to change and, in the case of John, leave Green Town.

Mr. Jonas

Mr. Jonas is the Green Town junkman. There is a magical quality about the man; the children can hear him coming long before adults know he is anywhere near. In addition, he is also a healer. During the night hours, he wanders the roads, dispensing aspirin or delivering babies. When Doug nearly dies, it is Mr. Jonas's bottle air that revives him.

The Lonely One

The Lonely One is the name given to a man who terrorizes the nights of Green Town. Women who find themselves in the Ravine after dark have a way of finding themselves murdered. Eventually, the town believes that the Lonely One has been killed by Lavinia Nebbs in her house. The boys, however, do not believe that the man was really the Lonely One; in their need to have a boogieman on which to focus their fears, they convince themselves that the Lonely One survives. More than a physical character, the Lonely One is also the specter of death. Like the Grim Reaper, he represents the end of time, the end of the world, and the end of life for Douglas.

Helen Loomis

Helen Loomis is a ninety-five-year-old resident of Green Town. A beautiful, wild woman in her youth, she passed up the chance for love. Now she develops a special relationship with Bill Forrester.

Lavinia Nebbs

Lavinia Nebbs is considered to be the "prettiest maiden lady in town." Lavinia demonstrates both her courage and her resourcefulness by killing the Lonely One with a pair of scissors.

Miss Roberta

Miss Roberta is Miss Fern's sister, and co-owner of the Green Machine.

Douglas Spaulding

Douglas Spaulding is the twelve-year-old main character of *Dandelion Wine*. The book begins with his awakening into life and closes with his near death. Doug is a writer. In his notebook with his Ticonderoga pencil, he attempts to make sense of the events of the summer as well as of life and death. It is almost as if he tries to capture each of the days in the same way his grandfather bottles the summer in the dandelion wine. In many cultures, reaching the age of twelve is the traditional coming-of-age time. For Doug, the summer of 1928 is just that. He becomes aware of the rituals and practices that structure Green Town just as he attempts to understand what these rituals embody. For Doug, this is the summer when he understands what it means to be alive; but it is also the summer when he knows in the very core of his being that all creatures die, including himself. This knowledge nearly kills him, and it is only through the intervention of Mr. Jonas with his magical air that he is revived. Doug stands in for Bradbury in this novel; not only is the role autobiographical, it is also a comment on the role of the writer, the one who gets everything moving, and who ultimately decides when the story is concluded.

Mr. Spaulding

Mr. Spaulding, Doug and Tom's father, is an important figure in the book, although his role is small. In the opening sequence of stories, it is Mr. Spaulding who takes the boys into the forest to gather wild berries. He seems to have a special connection to both the boys and nature, something that most adults in *Dandelion Wine* seem to have forgotten. Doug believes that his father has planned the outing specifically to initiate his son into the wonder of being alive.

Mrs. Spaulding

Doug and Tom's mother has only a minor role in the book. Her most important scene is when she and Tom go to look for Doug when he does not return home at the expected time. Her fear demonstrates to Tom that not even adults can control their environment.

Tom Spaulding

Tom Spaulding is Doug's ten-year-old brother. Not yet initiated into the mysteries of life, Tom is both confidant and enumerator for Doug. He keeps track of how many times they have done each of the rituals of summer. In addition, he listens as Doug tries to work through the puzzles of life. While he is not old enough to fully understand Doug's struggles, his listening and companionship allow Doug to accomplish what he must. It is clear that Tom's time will come as well and that in the future, he will have to face some of the same demons that have hounded Doug during the summer of 1928. For now, however, Tom is content and full in the moment.

Mr. Tridden

Mr. Tridden is the trolley driver of Green Town. When the trolley is scheduled for decommissioning, he gives all of the residents one final, free ride on the wonderful machine.

Charlie Woodman

Charlie Woodman is Doug's friend.

Themes

Time

As in many of his other works, Bradbury explores time in *Dandelion Wine*. The book begins on the first day of summer, 1928, and continues on chronologically until the last day of summer of the same year. This is calendar time, the day-by-day progression throughout the year. Bradbury underscores this progression through the scenes where the boys and Grandfather make dandelion wine, each bottle labeled for each day in the summer. As the number of bottles increases, the days of the summer dwindle. Calendars and clocks, however, only represent the kind of time that is measurable; these devices divide time up into ever smaller, equal divisions. Yet anyone who has ever thought about it knows that sometimes time passes more quickly or more slowly than at other times. Thus, while the calendar or the clock mark a linear, chronological progression, there is much that these devices do not reveal about time.

Bradbury introduces another notion of time through Colonel Freeleigh, a man who is able to travel freely through his memories, so much so that the children call him a Time Machine. When he tells the children his stories, he is able to transport them into a different kind of time, one that is cyclic, or circular. This is the time of stories and memory, moments that can be revisited again and again. Likewise, through the rituals of summer, those things the children do again and again, they are able to create a kind of sacred space that exists out of time.

Bradbury also uses clocks and calendars metaphorically in this novel to represent the time allotted to a person for a life. When Doug discovers he is alive, he suddenly realizes that he himself is a timepiece: "Twelve years old and only now! Now discovering this rare timepiece, this clock gold-bright and guaranteed to run three score and ten . . ." Thus, the passage of time through the summer in *Dandelion Wine* also serves to remind the reader that each human being has a metaphoric spring, and autumn in his or her life.

In *Dandelion Wine*, Doug experiences both kinds of time, chronological as well as ritual. In the tension between the two, Doug finds himself facing the most important questions of human existence.

Technology

Bradbury is often accused of finding technology distasteful or negative. In an article in *English*

Topics For Further Study

- *Fahrenheit 451* (1953) is a disturbing look at the future when books are burned by firemen. Read this book, and consider the importance of reading and writing in both *Fahrenheit 451* and *Dandelion Wine*.

- Bradbury is often classified as a science fiction writer. Research what is meant by the term "science fiction." Does Bradbury fit into this classification? Why or why not? Is *Dandelion Wine* a work of science fiction?

- Read Bradbury's *Zen and the Art of Writing*. What are some of Bradbury's major ideas about writing? Does Douglas use the same techniques in his writing that Bradbury describes? Practice some of the techniques he describes, and develop a portfolio of writings based on his ideas.

- Bradbury wrote many screenplays in addition to his novels, short stories, and plays. Perhaps his most famous is his 1956 screenplay for director John Huston's *Moby Dick*. Watch this version of the movie. Can you identify some of Bradbury's themes and ideas present in the film? Are there any points of connection between *Moby Dick* and *Dandelion Wine*?

Journal, Marvin E. Mengeling notes that Bradbury's "distrust of too much technology and mechanization" is a major theme in *Dandelion Wine*. In this novel, Green Town seems poised on the brink of a new age, one in which technology threatens to change human existence. Bradbury's attitude toward technology seems to be that people need to remember what is important in life. Leo Auffmann's attempt to build a machine that will give people happiness, for example, does just the opposite. People who use the machine find that because they see things they never knew they missed, they are now much more unhappy than they have ever been. In this case, then, Bradbury seems to be criticizing the way technology leads people into the desire for things, and for more technology. The real source of happiness, however, is not more things, but rather family. Indeed, Bradbury's concern with technology is also tied to his concern with time. He seems to be telling the reader that time with family and with friends is the way time ought to be spent, rather than monkeying around with new machines.

Death

Just as Douglas discovers early in the book that he is alive, and that he is part of a larger world in which everyone and everything is alive, he also discovers later in the book that he will eventually die, just as everyone and everything will eventually die.

This is a difficult concept for Douglas; however, the realization follows logically from not only what Doug can reason, but also from what he observes. In the space of a few short weeks, Doug loses his Great-grandma, Colonel Freeleigh, and Helen Loomis. In addition, he finds the corpse of the Lonely One's murder victim. The realization is overwhelming for Doug, and he falls into a strange illness, one that threatens to kill him. Only through the intervention of Mr. Jonas, and through his own decision that living is preferable to death does he recover. But the introduction of death as a theme in *Dandelion Wine* shifts the book away from a sentimental recollection of the perfect boyhood and toward a darker understanding of human existence.

Style

Setting

In *Dandelion Wine*, the setting of Green Town becomes almost another character. On the one hand, Bradbury has been very clear that he modeled Green Town after his own childhood home of Waukegan, Illinois. According to Bradbury, there were tree-lined streets, people sitting on porches on a summer evening, and even a frightening dark ravine. However, Green Town becomes mythic in its significance to *Dandelion Wine*. The town is isolated, surrounded by a deep forest, with no connection to the outside world. Symbolically, the town is a kind of Garden of Eden for Doug, the place where one day he realizes he is alive. Likewise, the Lonely One, skulking about in the ravine is akin to the serpent in Eden, the serpent who brings death to humankind. Doug's growing awareness of life and death is paralleled by Green Town's gradual change from an isolated city where no one new arrives and no one ever leaves to a town where people die, and people go away. For Doug, this new knowledge of his city is dangerous; it is after witnessing the murdered corpse in the ravine that he falls into the coma that nearly wins him for death. Thus, while Green Town is simply the setting, it provides the mythological grounding for the novel.

Archetypes

The Swiss psychologist Carl Jung theorized that there are particular, images, character types, settings and stories that operate across cultures, and that these archetypes are embedded deep within the human subconscious. Bradbury, who writes frequently in books such as *Zen and the Art of Writing* about tapping his own subconscious mind for material, makes use of the idea of the archetype in *Dandelion Wine*. Douglas is the archetypal young hero and his story is the archetypal quest story. In this type of story, the hero is nearly always a young person about to enter adulthood who receives a calling that starts him or her on his journey. For Douglas, the quest is metaphoric as he moves through a series of initiatory rites designed to bring him from childhood into adulthood. He first is aware of this on the day his father takes him to pick grapes. He realizes that his father and his grandfather "live on riddles;" that is, they have knowledge that is outside of his understanding as a child. However, when he is in the forest, he receives the archetypal call when he realizes that this is the day when everything will change. He is aware of some presence outside himself ready to pounce. When this "something" finally makes itself known, "the world, like a great iris of an even more gigantic eye which has also just opened and stretched out to encompass everything, stared back at him." From this moment on, with the utter certainty that he is alive, Douglas begins his journey to adulthood, encountering loss through both death and change, and his own near death.

Other archetypes that Doug encounters in *Dandelion Wine* include wise, older helpers such as his Grandfather and Colonel Freeleigh. He also

encounters evil in the form of The Lonely One. In an archetypal subplot, through his dream, he wanders in the "other world" where he sees John Huff, the Happiness Machine, the trolley, Colonel Freeleigh, and his great-grandma, all people and things that have passed out of his life. Mr. Jonas, then, plays the role of spiritual guide, the archetypal character who brings Douglas home from the otherworld. Douglas's awakening from his fever dream signifies a rebirth, and the end of his metaphoric journey. He is no longer a child, having earned his adulthood.

Historical Context

The Great Depression

Bradbury was born in 1920, and so was just nine years old when the Great Depression began, throwing his father out of work and forcing the family's move from Waukegan, Illinois. This event had a lasting effect on the writer. In his choice of his novel's setting, Green Town during the summer of 1928, Bradbury attempted to recreate a time and place that no longer existed, a place where the economic, political, and technological upheavals of the twentieth century had not yet touched. For Bradbury, the pre-Depression Midwestern town represented a kind of Eden, a place isolated from the rest of the world where people sat out on their porches at night and were truly neighborly. The social chaos brought on by the downward economic spiral of the Depression followed closely by the horrors of World War II made the final years before the Depression look particularly innocent and golden by comparison. This contrast, between the world of 1928, and the world of 1957, the year of the book's publication is stark, and renders Douglas's experiences all the more bittersweet.

The Cold War and the Nuclear Arms Race

During the years that Bradbury worked on *Dandelion Wine*, the United States was engaged in both World War II and the Korean War. Even when these wars ended, the struggle for world power between the Soviet Union and the United States continued in the cold war. At stake was the survival of the entire world, for as the cold war continued, both the United States and the Soviet Union (along with a number of other nations of the world including France, England, India, and China) began stockpiling stores of nuclear weapons to be used as a last

Compare
&
Contrast

- **1920s:** In the aftermath of World War I, the United States enters an isolationist phase, concerning itself with its own economy and politics, an isolationism that continues until the American entry into World War II in 1941.

  1950s: In the aftermath of World War II, the United States engages in the cold war with the Soviet Union, as the country attempts to stop the spread of communism throughout the world.

  Today: The Soviet Union no longer exists, and the cold war is now over.

- **1920s:** The stock market booms, and many invest in the stock market, often on credit, undermining the economic stability of the country. In 1929, the good times come to a halt with the stock market crash of October, ushering in the ten long years of the Great Depression that follows.

  1950s: As soldiers return home first from World War II and then the Korean War, unemployment rises and the country experiences another economic slow down, although not nearly as serious as in the Depression-era 1930s.

  Today: The bombing of the World Trade Center towers in 2001 leads to a substantial drop in the stock market, pushing up the unemployment rate and causing economic hardships for many Americans.

- **1920s:** The automotive and aviation industries are in their infancy, although it is clear that increased technology will lead the way to ever-greater productivity in both fields.

  1950s: Americans purchase cars in record quantities, made affordable by the growth of technology. The newly born aerospace industry races to develop technology to compete with the Soviet Union's launching of spacecraft.

  Today: Growth in technology has taken Americans to the moon and back, and now makes possible communication satellites and further exploration of space. The world grows ever more accessible because of cell phones, jet aircraft, computers, and television, all products of the rapid technological growth.

resort against the other nations in the event of full-scale war. Such use, however, would mean the end of the world, as the nuclear arsenal grew to such a size that scientists estimated that nations could blow up the planet seven times over.

Bradbury clearly hoped to return to a gentler, more naive time in his creation of Green Town. His thinly veiled distrust of technology had its roots in the 1950s, as he saw his nation rushing frantically toward some gigantic conflagration. The launching of the unmanned satellite Sputnik in 1957 by the Soviet Union, the first human object in orbit around the earth, only served to confirm both the promise and the dangers of technology for Bradbury, ground he had explored earlier in his 1950 collection, *The Martian Chronicles*. Although *Dandelion Wine* might seem to have little to do with the world at large, the novel, through its idealization of small town America in the years before the Depression, marked a rejection of the political and technological dangers of mid-twentieth century America.

Critical Overview

Dandelion Wine is a popular book that has never been out of print since its first publication in 1957. Often assigned to students in junior and senior high schools, *Dandelion Wine* is a book much-loved by readers and critics alike. Nevertheless, the book did not receive as much early attention as it might have. As George Slusser in his article "Ray Bradbury" in the *Dictionary of Literary Biography* notes in 1978, although Bradbury is an important writer, he has "unjustly suffered from critical neglect." Likewise, Marvin E. Mengeling, in his 1971 article "Ray

City street with a streetcar in the foreground in Westlake Shopping Area, Seattle, 1907. The trolley or streetcar in Green Town is a significant part of Doug Spaulding's boyhood experience in Ray Bradbury's Dandelion Wine © PEMCO-Webster and Stevens Collection; Museum of History and Industry, Seattle/Corbis

Bradbury's *Dandelion Wine*: Themes Sources, and Style," in *English Journal*, argues that although "Ray Bradbury happens to be one of America's major prose writers. . . . his works have been abysmally neglected by critics."

Like a number of later critics, Mengeling addresses this need in both the *English Journal* article, published in 1971, and much later in his book *Red Planet, Flaming Phoenix, Green Town: Some Early Bradbury Revisited*, published in 2002. Mengeling reads *Dandelion Wine* from an archetypal perspective in both sources, noting in the latter that "*Dandelion Wine*. . . is Ray Bradbury's first major imaginative attempt at reconciliation with his past and family. More specifically, it is Bradbury's first tentative step toward reconciliation with the Father."

In addition to Mengeling, many other critics note the archetypal patterns Bradbury uses in *Dandelion Wine*. For example, John B. Rosenman in the *South Atlantic Bulletin* looks specifically at the heaven and hell archetype in both Faulkner's "That Evening Sun" and Bradbury's *Dandelion Wine*. He argues that the ravine is "mysterious and malignantly alive." Further, the ravine "exert[s] a primal terrifying force and exude[s] an ominous menace

that pervades the work with an air of expectancy and suspense."

In one of the only readings that accounts for gender in *Dandelion Wine*, Robin Anne Reid argues that the book "focuses on the masculine world." Further, while Reid writes positively about *Dandelion Wine*, she also notes that the novel "does an excellent job of showing the initiation and maturation of a man in a traditional patriarchal culture, but its theme is not universally applicable to everyone, especially to women."

Finally, another approach that critics often take is a consideration of Bradbury's theme of childhood in his work. Damon Knight, in a much reprinted critique, offers a negative view of this treatment in *Dandelion Wine*: "Childhood is Bradbury's one subject, but you will not find real childhood here. . . ." He further accuses *Dandelion Wine* of being a "glutinous pool of sentimentality." Lahna Diskin, however, takes a much deeper look into Bradbury's children in an important essay, also reprinted in several volumes. She examines all of Bradbury's children, focusing particularly on Doug and Tom from *Dandelion Wine* and the boys of *Something Wicked This Way Comes*. She writes of the children, "Their most outrageous actions are instinctive ploys against the inevitable doomsday of exile from childhood. Thus, in both books, the boys live at the quick of life, marauding each moment. They are afire with ecstatic temporality, resplendent immediacy."

Criticism

Diane Andrews Henningfeld

Henningfeld is a professor of English at Adrian College who writes widely on literary topics for academic and educational publications. In this essay, Henningfeld analyzes Dandelion Wine *as an example of magical realism.*

Magical realism (sometimes called magic realism) is one of the most interesting literary trends to emerge worldwide during the second half of the twentieth century and the early twenty-first century. Generally associated with South American writers such as Jorge Luis Borges, Isabel Allende and Gabriel García Márquez, recent critics have also included North American writers such as William Faulkner and Toni Morrison within the genre. *Dandelion Wine*, written in the 1950s as a mainstream autographical novel, however, has not generally been read as a magical realist text; nevertheless, Bradbury as a self-admitted fantasist, leaves himself open for just such a reading. Indeed, an accounting of the magical elements in *Dandelion Wine* not only deepens the reader's understanding of the novel, it also revitalizes the text, making *Dandelion Wine* a surprisingly contemporary vintage. The purpose of this essay, then, is threefold: first, to provide a working definition of magical realism; second, to identify the elements in *Dandelion Wine* that can be classified as magical realism; and third; to consider how this approach opens the text to the twenty-first century reader.

Magical realism, in simplest terms, is the mixture of realistic elements along with fantastic elements. Further, the characters treat elements that might seem fantastic to the reader matter-of-factly. Likewise, everyday realistic elements for the reader may be treated as something magical by the characters. For example, in García Márquez's *One Hundred Years of Solitude*, the characters scarcely notice the flying carpets that gypsies ride into town, yet they are utterly astounded by ice. William Harmon and C. Hugh Holman, in *A Handbook to Literature*, write that in a magical realist work, "[t]he

frame or the surface of the work may be conventionally realistic, but contrasting elements—such as the supernatural, myth, dream, fantasy—invade the realism and change the whole basis of the art."

Dandelion Wine clearly offers examples of these elements. Its setting (or surface) is early twentieth-century, small-town America, its characters the men, women, and children of this town, all engaged in everyday, daily activities. Yet magic erupts from the first moment that Douglas climbs into his grandparents' cupola and wills the town into existence. Even in the most quotidian circumstance, an election for the presidency of a ladies club, there is an implication that witchcraft might be involved. Likewise, the main character, Douglas, is saved from death by a magical healer.

In their classic book *Magical Realism: Theory, History, Community*, Lois Parkinson Zamora and Wendy B. Faris argue that "magical realism is a mode suited to exploring—and transgressing—boundaries, whether the boundaries are ontological, political, geographical, or generic. Magical realism often facilitates the fusion, or coexistence, of possible worlds. . . ." Further, magical realist texts "often situate themselves on liminal territory between or among worlds—in phenomenal and spiritual regions where transformation, metamorphosis, dissolution are common. . . ." In other words, magical realist texts often include many different ways of interpreting the world, interpretations that often exist side by side. "Liminal territory" is something like a borderland, or the space between two places, ideas, or worlds. In boundary spaces, characters and locations can find themselves transformed, changed, or even dissolved. Focusing on these elements of magical realism offers a particularly rich reading of *Dandelion Wine* because it is in the geographical, temporal, mythological, and spiritual boundaries that magic most often erupts in the novel.

As Zamora and Faris describe above, Green Town coexists in two separate worlds. In the first, it is the real city of Waukegan, Illinois, the place where writer Bradbury was born. Readers know this from Bradbury's 1975 introduction to the book. At the same time, however, Green Town is a mythical location, a place that is not really anywhere or anytime. This is largely because Bradbury isolates the town; there is no one coming into the town from the outside, so it functions much as a Brigadoon or a Shangri La, or, for that matter, an Eden. At an even deeper level, however, Green Town is not anywhere or anytime because in the final analysis, it only exists in Bradbury's memory and imagination. Bradbury's description of the town imbues it with mythical qualities, and leads readers to understand that Green Town itself is a liminal space, a place where boys are transformed into men: "And here the paths, made or yet unmade, that told of the need of boys traveling, always traveling, to be men."

Likewise, the ravine serves multiple functions in the novel. Just as Waukegan is a real city, there is a real ravine in Waukegan, according to Bradbury. It is a place where the river cuts through the city to Lake Michigan. In *Dandelion Wine*, however, the ravine is not just a gully, but an opening into another mythic space not bound by the order or structure of the town. The ravine divides the town in two, and Douglas senses the primeval struggle between life and death in the space: "Panting, he stopped by the rim of the ravine, at the edge of the softly blowing abyss. . . . Here the town, divided, fell away in halves. Here civilization ceased. Here was only growing earth and a million deaths and rebirths every hour."

The ravine indicates the "coexistence of possible worlds." Whereas Green Town itself is ordered and ultimately knowable for Douglas, the ravine is not. It functions under a different reality from town, and the contrast opens the uncomfortable gap between order and chaos, between the knowable and unknowable. The ravine is the space where anything can happen: a young woman can be transformed into a corpse, or a young man into a hero. There is just no telling in such a magical place.

Dandelion Wine also suggests another pair of alternative realities coexisting in the same space. Bradbury clearly sets up two worlds, the world of the children and the world of the adults. When the children visit Mrs. Bentley, they are able to convince her that she never was a child herself. Indeed, Tom reports to Douglas who writes it down in his table, "Old people never *were* children!"

Tom, throughout the novel, is clearly within the realm of the children. When Douglas falls ill, for example, Tom tells Mr. Jonas "It's been a tough summer . . . Lots of things have happened to Doug." What he lists are the concerns of a child: Doug has lost his best aggie, someone stole Doug's catcher's mitt, Doug dropped his Tarzan statue, and it broke. Because he is a child, Tom fails to recognize that the summer has been hard on Doug not because he has lost his toys, but because he has lost his boyhood. Further, although Tom senses that Doug has had difficulties over the summer, there is no way that he can understand that the metamorphosis from child to adult has been exquisitely painful for Doug.

> " Readers can find on the streets of Green Town front porches, families, furniture—a perfect place to spend a long summer evening. At the same time, however, readers also find the spaces where the unpredictable and chaotic seep through."

As Doug wanders in the liminal territory between childhood and adulthood, he becomes obsessed with the Tarot Witch, a wax arcade fortuneteller. This obsession is a manifestation of Doug's fear of the future. Doug wants the Witch to reassure him that the future can be known, because if it can be known, then it can be controlled. When she issues a blank card, the blank card of the future, Douglas falls into a state of serious, and life-threatening, melancholy.

This is the final, and ultimate, liminal space of *Dandelion Wine*, the boundary between life and death that Doug travels as he falls ill. His is a disease of the spirit; the extraordinary transformation and metamorphosis that he has experienced over the summer threatens him with utter dissolution. In magical realist texts, these are the moments when magic is most likely to erupt, and so it does. Mr. Jonas, who is both junkman and spiritual healer in the coexistent worlds of Green Town, offers Doug a magic elixir: "GREEN DUSK FOR DREAMING BRAND PURE NORTHERN AIR. . . . derived from the atmosphere of the white Arctic in the spring of 1900, and mixed with the wind from the upper Hudson Valley in the month of April, 1910, and containing particles of dust seen shining in the sunset of one day in the meadows around Grinnell, Iowa. . . ." Doug, in a coma and dreaming under an apple tree in his back yard, breathes in the magic air and is healed.

It is clear in the final chapters that Doug has been transformed in the borderlands between life and death, and has become a healer himself, restoring his grandmother to her magical self after his Aunt Rose attempts to organize her kitchen. When

What Do I Read Next?

- *The Martian Chronicles* (1950) is a collection of intertwined short stories about a series of attempts to colonize Mars. Many critics consider this to be Bradbury's best book.

- *Conversations with Ray Bradbury* (2004), edited by Steven L. Aggelis, is an important collection of many interviews with Bradbury, who talks about his life and his writing.

- Jonathan R. Eller and William F. Toupance's *Ray Bradbury: The Life of Fiction* (2004) is the definitive critical biography of Bradbury and his work.

- *Bradbury: An Illustrated Life: A Journey to Far Metaphor* (2002), by Jerry Weist and Ray Bradbury, is a coffee table book with wonderful illustrations, copies of posters, photographs, scenes from films, and more.

- *Fahrenheit 451* (1953) is perhaps Bradbury's most famous book, set in the not-so-distant future when reading is a crime.

Doug, in the final section, climbs once again to his grandparents' cupola to put the town to sleep at the end of the summer, he does so as a young man, not as a child.

Some earlier critics have found *Dandelion Wine* to be a cloyingly sweet and overly sentimental bit of autobiographical and nostalgic fluff. These readers seem to have wanted Bradbury to create a "realistic" vision of childhood. However, a more contemporary consideration of magical realism suggests that Bradbury has created multiple worlds in his simple tales. Readers can find on the streets of Green Town front porches, families, furniture—a perfect place to spend a long summer evening. At the same time, however, readers also find the spaces where the unpredictable and chaotic seep through. Indeed, a reading that takes into account magical realism opens the door to the boundary lands where reader, writer, and text are utterly transformed by acts of co-creation. Like Grandfather in the cellar,

like Douglas in the cupola, and like Bradbury at his typewriter, readers create *Dandelion Wine* for themselves, the liminal space of the novel welcoming them in for just another sip.

Source: Diane Andrews Henningfeld, Critical Essay on *Dandelion Wine*, in *Novels for Students*, Thomson Gale, 2006.

Robin Anne Reid

In the following essay excerpt, Reid argues that Dandelion Wine *depicts a journey "toward masculine maturity" and "its theme is not universally applicable to everyone, especially to women."*

Alternative Perspective: A Gender Reading

Gender criticism is an approach to literary analysis that builds on the earlier work of feminist critics and draws on later work by gay and lesbian critics and by scholars in the newly developing field of men's studies. The basic assumption of gender studies is that while some aspects of maleness and femaleness may be biologically determined, social gender roles—masculinity and femininity—are learned and reflect specific cultural beliefs and specific social or historical contexts (Bressler 270).

Bringing the ideas of gender analysis to Bradbury's *Dandelion Wine* complicates any idea that this novel describes a universal theme of initiation or maturation and leads the reader to question how the novel presents the issues of what it means to be a preadolescent boy in a Mid-western town in the 1920s.

The family in *Dandelion Wine* is an extended family: several generations live, if not in the same house, close to each other. Doug, his brother Tom, and his father and mother live together, but close by is the boarding house where Doug's great-grandmother, grandmother, and grandfather live with various boarders. Other family members apparently live close by.

From the start, the novel makes clear that its central journey is one toward masculine maturity: Doug and Tom go with their father into the woods. This male journey into the woods, or wilderness, is a traditional theme in American literature. The woods, or the wilderness, around "civilization" are a domain inhabited by wild or untamed animals. The Ravine in the novel is another kind of wilderness, a more threatening place that only the "older boys" go to. Doug's mother is not a part of this journey, nor is she described as knowing what results. Later, Doug and his male friends Charlie and John run through the Ravine, while Tom stays at home with their mother. The mother and the young boy go to the Ravine when she worries about her son, but Tom's perception of the danger in the Ravine is removed when Doug returns. Neither mothers, girls, nor younger boys go into the Ravine. Women who go into the Ravine are menaced by a monster-killer called the Lonely One; one woman is killed, and her body is found in the Ravine.

The family and social structures of Green Town reflect the traditional model of sharply defined gender roles. Chores are designated as either for women or for men: women, like Doug's grandmother, do the cooking, while the grandfather, helped by the boys, makes dandelion wine. The sexes often separate for social gatherings: men smoke cigars, while ladies go to the movies together. The wives and mothers tend to stay at home, but all family members mingle on the porches in the evenings.

Women characters are always identified by their martial status. While there are a few bachelor characters, they are not identified as such, just called by their names. The children, with the exception of Tom, a younger boy, tend to play in groups segregated by sex.

Women who step out of traditional roles may suffer negative consequences. When Miss Fern and Miss Roberta run over Mr. Quartermain in their electric car, they retreat quickly to the attic of their house, but Doug saves them from public humiliation. Women like Miss Lavinia Nebbs or Miss Elizabeth Ramsell (the woman whose body Lavinia finds in the Ravine), who insist on going outside despite rumors of the Lonely One, risk death.

In terms of narrative time and the importance of the male characters, the novel focuses on the masculine world. That focus is shown most strongly in the portrayal of the Lonely One. When Tom and his mother go to the Ravine to search for Doug, she mentions that the Lonely One is around and that nobody is safe, although the Lonely One apparently kills only women. Lavinia Nebbs rejects the idea that the threat of the Lonely One should stop her from attending the movies, but she soon finds the body of his latest victim and is menaced herself. She kills an intruder in her house, but the boys' reaction to her act is disappointment. In one of the few times Tom joins Doug and Charlie, the three boys mourn the disappearance of the Lonely One, whose absence will turn their town into "vanilla junket." Only when Tom convinces them that the man killed is just a tramp, on the grounds that the real Lonely One wouldn't look like a normal man, do the boys return to their gleeful excitement over a serial killer menacing their town.

In a novel so concerned with the idea of death and its effect on human beings, a serial killer is thought of and enjoyed like a scary but thrilling movie. While the boys say they don't really wish Lavinia Nebbs had died in her house, the deaths of the women the Lonely One killed do not seem to be as real as the other deaths in the book, although Doug is affected by his near exposure to the Lonely One (he was in the Ravine at about the same time Elizabeth Ramsell was killed). In the terms of a gender reading, *Dandelion Wine* does an excellent job of showing the initiation and maturation of a man in a traditional patriarchal culture, but its theme is not universally applicable to everyone, especially to women.

Source: Robin Anne Reid, "*Dandelion Wine* (1957)," in *Ray Bradbury: A Critical Companion*, Greenwood Press, 2000, pp. 63–72.

Marvin E. Mengeling

In the following essay, Mengeling describes Dandelion Wine *as a novel about a "decisive type of initiation" of a young man into adulthood using three winemaking scenes as a structural device to "measure the growth of certain major characters."*

Ray Bradbury happens to be one of America's major prose writers. Yet his works have been abysmally neglected by critics. In the "Introduction" to *The Vintage Bradbury* (Vintage Books, 1965), Gilbert Highet writes: "He [Bradbury] has been misunderstood. He has been underestimated. He will gain a wider and more thoughtful public than he had at first; and his work will last." Certain to last are his two best books, *The Martian Chronicles,* interrelated stories about man's colonization of Mars, and *Dandelion Wine,* the story of one boy's summer growth toward self-knowledge and maturity in the Midwest of 1928. Of *Dandelion Wine,* Robert O. Bowen wrote in *The Saturday Review* (September 7, 1957): "No other writer since Mark Twain has caught the vitality and innocence of small-town American youth with as fine and mature a perception as Ray Bradbury's." This high praise is justified. Yet, there is practically no serious criticism of Bradbury's work, especially of *Dandelion Wine.* Truly, as Gilbert Highet remarked, Ray Bradbury has been underestimated. It is hoped that this introduction to one of his best books will begin to make Bradbury more understood, and perhaps through better understanding will come the higher estimation his work so much deserves.

> The general structure of the book seems influenced by both Whitman and Hawthorne. As is often the case in Whitman's poetry, Bradbury is singing the journey of spiritual discovery; the discovery of the 'miraculous' and 'mysterious' nature of even the most common people, objects, and events."

First, I will discuss the major themes and ideas in *Dandelion Wine*. Second, I will consider misconception or two which have plagued Bradbury and which have led to his works being both misunderstood and underestimated. Third, I will discuss the matter of sources, and finally, there will be some analysis of Bradbury's style and literary techniques.

In intricately tracing out the first main steps of initiation for twelve-year-old Douglas Spaulding, Ray Bradbury joins *Dandelion Wine* to a long and proud tradition in American literature. From the *Autobiography* of Benjamin Franklin down through works by Charles Brockden Brown, Richard Henry Dana, Herman Melville, Nathaniel Hawthorne, Walt Whitman, Mark Twain, Henry James, Stephen Crane, Theodore Dreiser, F. Scott Fitzgerald, Ernest Hemingway, Thomas Wolfe, John Steinbeck, Ralph Ellison, and John Knowles, the theme of initiation has been one of the very strongest currents in American literature. Mordecai Marcus, in his article "What Is an Initiation Story" (*Journal of Aesthetics and Art Criticism*, Winter 1960), states that there are basically three types of stories of youthful initiation: the tentative, the uncompleted, and the decisive. The "tentative" initiations lead "only to the threshold of maturity and understanding but do not definitely cross it." Such stories emphasize the shocks involved in maturing and the initiates are usually quite young. "Uncompleted" initiations take the protagonist over the threshold of maturity, but leave him struggling uncertainly with the many problems involved in such

a process. The "decisive" rites of passage are largely concerned with "self-discovery" and end with the main character fully mature and fully understanding of himself and his role in the world. *Dandelion Wine,* we will see, involves a decisive type of initiation to the extent that Douglas Spaulding, by book's end, is firmly embarked toward maturity and had made some important discoveries about himself.

The year is 1928, the last golden vintage year before the coming of the Great Crash, and the place is Green Town, Illinois, Bradbury's fictionalized version of Waukegan, Illinois. The tale begins as Doug awakens in the Victorian tower of his grandparents' house on the morning or the first day of summer, and it ends exactly three months later with Doug falling asleep in the same tower of the same house on the evening of summer's final day. The metaphor changes from a magician's fairy tale tower in the book's beginning to a more realistic tower at the end, for in three short months much of Douglas Spaulding has ceased to be a boy. And like Huck Finn and Nick Adams before him, he almost learns too much too quickly.

In the first half of the book, Doug discovers the "revelations" of life; what life is, the fact that he is alive, and how his life relates to the world around. The second half of the book largely concerns Doug's learning the balancing "revelations" of death; what death is, how it affects the world around him, and his coming to grips with the harsh realization that he too will one day die. Most important, though, he learns that all things, life and death, nature and man, move in cycles to which there is no foreseeable end.

Doug's primary initiation experience into a conscious sense of life takes place on summer's first day, "the first real time of freedom and living." His father takes Doug and Doug's brother Tom to the woods—"the very center of the quiet forest"—and Doug knew that somehow "this day was going to be different." Ostensibly, they have come to pick the first ripe fruits, the grapes and berries of the woods. Doug and Tom move in the "shadow" of a father who seems "very tall." That Bradbury is using the forest allegorically here, signifying the forest of life through which each of us must find his way, comes clear later in the story when Doug thinks, "Whatever you want . . . you got to make your own way. During the night now, let's find the path through the forest." Also, here in the forest scene, as in the scenes of wine making, Bradbury uses religious images to suggest the profound seriousness of these "rites of passage," as well as their ritualistic nature. Douglas is being initiated into some of the adult mysteries; a secular type of confirmation is taking place. Doug, awaiting a kind of mystic visitation or Pentecost which will bring a new knowledge and sense of life, participates in a quasi blood rite involving fox grapes: "Douglas, lost and empty, fell to his knees. He saw his fingers sink through green shadow and come forth stained with such color that it seemed he had somehow cut the forest and delved his hand in the open wound." Soon Douglas is ready for visitation: "Now, with the great Thing rushing near, falling down in the clear air above him, he could only nod, eyes shut." And then it hits. Douglas Spaulding awakens to a new world; he begins to see into the spiritual essence of things in a way reminiscent of the younger Emerson's *Nature:* "Douglas opened one eye. And everything, absolutely everything, was there. The world, like a great iris of an even more gigantic eye, which has also just opened and stretched out to encompass everything, stared back at him. . . . *I'm alive*, he thought." The journey of new discoveries and revelations is now begun. The forest scene ends with Doug appropriately leading his father and brother out of the woods.

But balancing off the life revelations, the exhilarating sense of being a part of some greater whole, are the revelations of fear, loneliness, and death. The major metaphor of death in *Dandelion Wine* is the ravine, which splits Green Town in two. It is on the edge of the ravine, the edge of the dark wilderness, that Tom Spaulding comes to realize "life's loneliness," that he "must accept being alone and work on from there." But Doug, as yet, shows no fear, and runs giggling and laughing through the nighttime ravine with his friends. Fear does not begin for Doug until section 21 when he learns that a little part of the world he thought so permanent is starting to fall away. Life's perfect "roundness" is beginning to shatter. He had thought that things "were at hand and would remain"; that things "would go on this way forever"; that life was "complete." But then he learns that his best friend, the admired and seemingly nonpareil John Huff is moving away, and for the first time Doug sees fear and uncertainty in one he had not thought capable of it; and for the first time real fear also comes to Douglas Spaulding. That evening, his desire to play "statues," his insistence on being "it," shows his still childish intuition to stop time, to achieve a stasis and thereby keep all things as they are now in his present. But all games have an end.

In section 16 Doug and Tom refuse to believe that old people were really ever young, but in section 18, after having met Colonel Freeleigh, Doug realizes that young people do grow old. He is not quite ready to admit that growing old is inevitably followed by death, but then, in section 25 Doug finds the heart-stopped body of the old Colonel. The short section 26 acts as postscript and gives Doug's reactions to having found his first corpse. The scene playfully begins with Doug pretending to have been shot by Tom; he clutches his heart and melodramatically keels over. But he soon gets up and walks away because Colonel Freeleigh has shown him that real death is not a game from which one can easily rise up. Doug is starting to lose his taste for childhood make-believe.

In section 28 ancient Miss Loomis dies a natural death, but Doug gets most of the Loomis story secondhand from his older friend, Bill Forester, and so the impact on him is not as great. Still, section 29 finds Doug pondering ever more about death and concluding that "happy endings" are only in the movies. In section 30 we have a scene involving the ravine and a periodic, psychopathic killer known only as The Lonely One. In this section Doug has his first real experience with violent death, seeing the body of Elizabeth Ramsell, in all its strangled grotesqueness, just as it was left by The Lonely One in the ravine. Doug is only capable of a "bleating sound" as he runs wildly off into the darkness. Doug is beginning to react to the death and violence all about him in much the same way Huck Finn once reacted; death and violence are starting to bother him, soon they will make him sick, and eventually they will almost take from him his will to live.

The death of Elizabeth Ramsell is quickly followed in this avalanche of obituaries by the natural death, in section 32, of Great Grandmother. As Doug sees the first death to touch his immediate family, he is forced to the difficult realization that he too one day will have to die. Transience, decay, death, he now realizes all apply, not simply to others, but to himself. It is more than difficult for him to put this down in writing in his "Journal of Rites and Revelations," but the truth cannot now be escaped. He must make his "summing up," and the total arrived at is this: "IF TROLLEYS AND RUNABOUTS AND FRIENDS AND NEAR FRIENDS CAN GO AWAY FOR A WHILE OR GO AWAY FOR EVER, OR RUST, OR FALL APART OR DIE, AND IF PEOPLE CAN BE MURDERED, AND IF SOMEONE LIKE GREAT GRANDMA, WHO WAS GOING TO LIVE FOR EVER, CAN DIE . . . IF ALL OF THIS IS TRUE . . . THEN . . . I DOUGLAS SPAULDING, SOME DAY . . .

MUST . . . But he cannot yet record the inevitable final word.

It is in section 37 that Doug loses his desire to live, for apparently he has seen too much real death, and it raises problems in his mind that he is still too young to resolve alone. In an archetypal sense it is his necessary descent into the underworld of death before the ultimate rebirth. "It's been a tough summer," Tom tells the junkman, Mr. Jonas, "Lots of things have happened to Doug." Tom is too young to recognize the real roots of Doug's troubles, but he has enough brotherly empathy to know that Doug has troubles for sure. Doug seemingly has decided to die, and what he needs now is someone to give him the desire to live. Mr. Jonas is a junkman who has had much experience in redeeming the world's throwaways, and whose name is reminiscent of Jonah, a Biblical personage who had much experience in solving large problems of the spirit. Truly, here is "no ordinary junkman." Mr. Jonas is a "rabbi in the wilderness" who "could not stand waste" and who has a "tendency toward preaching and descanting knowledge." As Doug slips into a mysterious sickness, he is visited by a phantasmagoric fever dream. And as the cyclical cicadas scream out time's quick passage in the background he sees a passing caravan of those summer people and things that for him have already come and gone: the trolley, John Huff, the Green Machine, Colonel Freeleigh, Mr. Auffmann, Great Grandma. It is a fever dream of transience, of time's eternal river moving, and now it is Doug's decision whether or not he will join the troupe and pass away.

It is Mr. Jonas who comes at night to Doug where he sleeps beneath the apple tree of knowledge, and leaves for his friend a bottle of "Green Dusk for Dreaming Brand Pure Northern Air." It is a symbolic bottle, a catalyst which helps pull together, and balance out all the pieces of new knowledge Doug has been picking up. In dreamstate Doug breathes in the will to live. The fever breaks and the pure rains come, and Doug, Bradbury writes in section 39, "had decided to live." He is happy now, but in a more mature way, for he has found at last his place in what Hawthorne once called "the magnetic chain of humanity," that is, his necessary relationship to others, and how they can live through him and he through them. Mr. Jonas had provided the catalyst to an ultimate answer; what one does with the knowledge, the "revelations," once they have been found: "Pass it on somehow, he thought, pass it on to someone else. Keep the chain moving. Look around, find someone, and pass it on. That was the only way."

It becomes rather clear at this point that Mr. Jonas, above all else, has been parading in the symbolic and archetypal guise of the Wise Old Man of fairy tales and dreams. In his essay "The Phenomenology of the Spirit in Fairy Tales," Carl Jung writes that "the frequency with which the spirit type appears as an old man is about the same in fairy tries as in dreams. The old man always appears when the hero is in a hopeless situation from which only profound reflection or a lucky idea—in other words, a spiritual function or an endopsychic automatism ot some kind—can extricate him. But since, for internal and external reasons, the hero cannot accomplish this himself, the knowledge needed to compensate the deficiency comes in the form of a personified thought, i.e., in the shape of this sagacious and helpful old man." Jung goes on to say that "often the old man in fairy tales . . . gives the necessary magical talisman, the unexpected and improbable power to succeed, which is one of the peculiarities of the unified personality in good or bad alike" (Jung, pp. 75–76). It is the "Green Dusk for Dreaming" that acts in *Dandelion Wine* as a magical talisman, and because Mr. Jonas comes to Doug while he is sleeping (Jonas says, "Sometimes the things you hear in your sleep are more important, you listen better, it gets through"), it is necessary to quote one more bit from Jung: "The old man thus represents knowledge, reflection, insight, wisdom, cleverness, and intuition on the one hand, and on the other, moral qualities such as goodwill and readiness to help, which makes his 'spiritual' character sufficiently plain. Since the archetype is an autonomous content of the unconscious, the fairy tale, which usually makes concrete the archetypes, can cause the old man to appear in a dream in much the same way as happens in modern dreams" (Jung, p. 77). All this is not to suggest that Bradbury has been writing a fairy tale, but rather to acknowledge that he recognizes many of the psychic problems connected with growth toward a unified Self, and that in *Dandelion Wine* he artistically makes use of the archetypal figures connected with such problems and such growth.

In section 39 Doug shows his new knowledge and passes on help to someone in need. Grandmother has made the error of voluntarily giving in to the foolish ways and notions of busybody Aunt Rose. Aunt Rose is the snake in Grandma's happy kitchen whispering sweet discontents into Grandma's ear: "There you are, Grandma, now you got everything where you can find it. Now you can *see!*" But instead, Grandma is "bewildered" and "stunned." She had not been satisfied with all her happiness, she had been led to covet more, and ends by almost losing all: "She got up and wandered out into her neatly-ordered, labelled kitchen, her hands moving futilely before her." It is now that Doug, knowing the problem, "began to move." He restores the kitchen to its unique pre-Rose state, its old unorganized state, and burns Grandma's new cookbook and hides her new rose-colored glasses for "seeing." And Grandma, after Douglas has shown her a course of action all the new glasses and Aunt Rose could not, "cried happily." "Junkman," Doug thinks, "Mr. Jonas, wherever you are, you're thanked, you're paid back. I passed it on, I sure did, I think I passed it on."

The climatic kitchen scene involving Doug, Grandma, and Aunt Rose, leads to consideration of another of Bradbury's major themes in *Dandelion Wine*, his distrust of too much technology and mechanization, coupled closely with a distrust of planned, modern life styles which leave little room for individuality, and perhaps no room for greatness. Time after time this long summer Doug has seen person after person fail who attempted to gain happiness out of mere mechanization or over-organization, rather than from love, human relationships, and respect for individual differences. He saw Mr. Auffmann's happiness machine bring sorrow. He saw the electric trolley of Mr. Tridden give way to a carbon-monoxide bus in the name of progress. He saw Miss Fern and Miss Roberta try to buy happiness in their Green Machine, and he saw them fail. And he saw that the Tarot Witch in the town Arcade was really only wheels and cogs after all. He has learned that it is people that matter, just as Leo Auffmann at last realized this: "You want to see the *real* Happiness Machine? The one they patented a couple thousand years ago, it still runs, not good all the time, no! but it runs. It's been here all along." And as Doug, Tom, and Grandpa look into Leo Auffman's front window they see the "real" happiness machine, Leo's wife and children. Things, hybrids, inanimate objects, can give small, transient joys, but the great and lasting happiness can only come from love between people. The machines stop, break down, rust out; but in their codes and rituals and descendants, people do live on.

It would be wrong to think, though, that Ray Bradbury is simply indicting machines, technology, and organization. He is not. Gilbert Highet comes close to Bradbury's true feelings concerning men and machines when he writes, "Technology he scarcely admires and scarcely uses. If it occupies his mind at all, it is not as a convenience or a source of extra muscle-power, but as a possible extension

of the abilities of the human spirit." The major error of many of the characters in *Dandelion Wine* is that they look wrongly to the machine to replace human values rather than to help preserve and extend them. Inherently, machines are neither good nor bad. Simply, we must run the machines, and we must force them to be leading tools in helping us to realize and extend the horizons of the human spirit.

There is a misconception that many readers have after finishing this book: the belief that Ray Bradbury is a sentimentalist about the past. This misconception most probably stems from the fact that Bradbury, mainly through his rich imagery, can so powerfully create a sense of the past. He so expertly gives us the "feel" of those times—the moon-colored ice cream, the straw hats, the porch swings, and the electric trolley of lemon color and orange—that many think any past which can be so deeply felt must be a past about which one is sentimental. But Bradbury has said, "A man cannot possibly speak futures unless he has a strong sense of the past. . . . Our exciting, awesome voyage into space, to the moon and Mars beyond, makes this the greatest age in all of man's history." Ray Bradbury, then, does not advocate a return trip down memory lane for reasons of sentiment, to moon over the loss of some imagined golden age, but so that we have a firmer perspective for our necessary move into a golden future, in a step by often agonizing step toward maturity. It is Grandpa in *Dandelion Wine* who makes the point most emphatically. At book's end he explains to the boys the real beauty of dandelion wine: "Better than putting things in the attic you never use again. This way, you get to live the summer over for a minute or two here or there along the way through the winter, and when the bottles are empty the summer's gone for good and no regrets and no sentimental trash lying about for you to stumble over forty years from now. Clean, smokeless, efficient, that's dandelion wine."

Dandelion Wine contains allusions to many authors. Among others, there are references to Plato, Shakespeare, Melville, Dickens, Whittier, and Poe. Of these, Melville (especially *Moby Dick*) is the most pervasive in terms of influencing Bradbury's imagery and philosophy. Also of seeming influence, though there are no direct allusions to them, are Walt Whitman (especially the pre-Civil War Whitman), Mark Twain, and possibly Nathaniel Hawthorne.

The general structure of the book seems influenced by both Whitman and Hawthorne. As is often the case in Whitman's poetry, Bradbury is singing the journey of spiritual discovery; the discovery of the "miraculous" and "mysterious" nature of even the most common people, objects, and events. His poetic prose attempts to reawaken our sense of wonder, attempts to open our senses to both ourselves and the universe about us. In "Song of Myself" Whitman chooses "leaves of grass" as his controlling metaphor to represent the essential spiritual and mysterious nature of even the most common, natural thing. Bradbury uses as his controlling metaphor the common but "noble" dandelion, whose natural and pure wine can lead one to the "miracle" of "renewal." As does "Song of Myself," *Dandelion Wine* moves through cycles or life and death, from innocence toward maturity, and ends by poetically singing of them all and with knowledge that all the seemingly chaotic portions of life and history are really part of some grand plan, some master pattern. As Douglas Spaulding comes to the end of his summer journey, Bradbury writes:

> June dawns, July noons, August evenings over, finished, done, and gone forever with only the sense of it all left here in his head. Now, a whole autumn, a white winter, a cool and greening spring to figure sums and totals of summer past. And if he should forget, the dandelion wine stood in the cellar, numbered huge for each and every day. He would go there often, stare straight into the sun until he could stare no more, then close his eyes and consider the burned spots, the fleeting scars left dancing on his warm eyelids; arranging, rearranging each fire and reflection until the pattern was clear.

And pattern there has been; the new knowledge of life always balanced against and made sweeter by death, the knowledge, as this quotation makes clear, of the cyclical essence of all things; that out of winter death there will always come "greening spring."

Bradbury, however, uses a structural device in addition to the Whitmanesque journey motif, a device to give balance and symmetry to what might otherwise seem a rather loose-leafed jaunt indeed. Just as Nathaniel Hawthorne used three scaffold scenes in *The Scarlet Letter* to give balance and symmetry to the whole, Bradbury uses his three scenes of wine making to impose an additional structural element. Grandpa and the two boys make dandelion wine at the beginning, middle, and end of the book; the June, July, and August crops. Also, as do the Hawthorne scaffold scenes, the three wine scenes allow us to better measure the growth of certain major characters.

In terms of philosophy, two of the book's sections are strongly reminiscent of chapters in Melville's *Moby Dick*. For example, section 32 has echoes of "Queequeg in His Coffin." In this section

Great Grandma decides that it is time for her to die, and so she does. Calmly she prepares her death—"such a simple act." In explaining to Tom why she has chosen this time to die, she draws us closely to the reasons of Queequeg: "Tom . . . in the Southern Seas there's a day in each man's life when he knows it's time to shake hands with all his friends and say good-by and sail away, and he does, and it's natural—it's just his time. That's how it is today. . . . I'm leaving while I'm still happy and still entertained." The fancy of both Melville and Bradbury seems to be that people can will to live and will to die. Great Grandma decides to die, and does. Queequeg and Doug Spaulding, after first deciding to die, decide finally to live instead. If it were possible for Queequeg to have known Doug's Great Grandma he surely would have approved of her death preparations, "for it was not unlike the custom of his own race, who, after embalming a dead warrior, stretched him out in his canoe, and so left him to be floated away to the starry archipelagoes; for not only do they believe that the stars are isles, but that far beyond all visible horizons, their own mild, uncontinented seas, interflow with the blue heavens; and so form the white breakers of the milky way."

Section 14 in *Dandelion Wine* is quite suggestive of "The Mat-Maker" chapter in *Moby Dick*, and strongly suggests that Bradbury agrees with Melville-Ishmael's ideas about the relative places of necessity, freewill, and chance in this complicated world of ours. It also suggests possible agreement with the Melvillian vision of the light and dark, the good and the evil, in the fabric of all things.

I will not end my discussion of possible sources without mentioning that there is a distinct sense of Mark Twain permeating this book. But *Dandelion Wine* has much more of *Adventures of Huckleberry Finn* in it than it does *The Adventures of Tom Sawyer*. The world of Green Town, Illinois, perhaps seems idyllic and romanticized at first, as does the Hannibal, Missouri, of *Tom Sawyer*, and yet, peering a bit closer, we find in Green Town a great deal of suffering, loneliness, and death, so much so, in fact, that close to the book's end Doug Spaulding, just as Huck before him, loses his desire to live. Here is the same ambivalence of *memory*—both the good and bad recalled—that makes *Huckleberry Finn* a more mature and realistic statement than *Tom Sawyer*. Also, both *Huck Finn* and *Dandelion Wine* are concerned with the strangely sexless initiations of boys about the same age who learn so much about life and death in the short space of a few months that they threaten to drop out of the game, but who finally regain health and approach psychological maturity by achieving a strong sense of human sympathy and responsibility.

It is Ray Bradbury's style that remains his most distinguishing characteristic. It is the Bradbury style which is unmistakable which is his alone. Gilbert Highet writes that his style is "a curious mixture of poetry and colloquialism." Robert O. Bowen talks of his "clean colloquial rhythms and rich metaphor." Undoubtedly it is his images and metaphors, and the way they are combined, which function as the outstanding single feature of his style. Bradbury is already famous for those stylized, concentrated passages of images which often appeal to the reader both concretely and abstractly. A passage from the first page of *Dandelion Wine* is typical: "A whole summer ahead to cross off the calendar, day by day. Like the goddess Siva in the travel books, he saw his hands jump everywhere, pluck sour apples, peaches, and midnight plums. He would be clothed in trees and bushes and rivers. He would freeze, gladly, in the hoar-frosted ice-house door. He would bake happily, with ten thousand chickens, in Grandma's kitchen." In a short space Bradbury has appealed rather distinctly to our senses of sight, taste, and touch; and unless it is possible to imagine thousands of baking chickens without imagining the delicious smell of them, then Bradbury has also appealed to a fourth sense as well. But notice too, the concrete-abstract nature of two of these images, a combination which tends to place an aura of the "miraculous" and "uncommon" around what we ordinarily think of as rather unmiraculous and ordinary objects; the "midnight plums" and the "clothing" of trees, rivers, and bushes. It is the concrete-abstract combination and the exceptional concentration that is the chief mark of Bradbury's imagistic style. But Bradbury's style is a curious mixture in other respects too. For example, although the book is narrated from the third person omniscient point of view, and although the imagery is generally of a brilliant and stylized nature, there is inter-spliced within its fabric the youthful hyperboles and emphatic repetitions that one would expect if the story were coming from the first person point of view of an unsophisticated, twelve-year-old boy. The reference to "ten thousand chickens" in the quote above is a typical example of much hyperbole that appears in the book. And to describe a night as "dark dark dark," or the ravine as "black and black, black," is typical of the kind or repetition for emphasis that we ordinarily hear from children, or from adults with much of their childhood still in them. This mixture of the youthful and the highly artful, the innocent

and the experienced, fits well in a book that emphasizes the cyclical nature of life; that every child is the father of man, that the young man can learn from the old, and the old can learn from the young. Here, style contributes much to meaning.

Finally to be noted is that Bradbury mixes both minor and major metaphors. For example, there is the major metaphor of the ravine as some deadly, evilly ravenous jungle beast. There is the metaphor of Colonel Freeleigh as a human time machine. Another of the book's major metaphors, carried throughout, is that of the town as ship and the northern Illinois prairie as ocean—probably more of the Melville influence. Melville, who once made a trip across northern Illinois to Galena, often wrote of the vast ocean as a kind of gigantic prairie. Bradbury reverses this metaphor; he talks about the gigantic prairie as a kind of ocean, and of the towns and cities as microcosm boats and ship: "The town was . . . only a large ship," he writes. At times he is afraid the "town would capsize, go down and leave not a stir in the clover and weeds." Grandpa stands on the "porch like a captain surveying the vast unmotioned calms of a season dead ahead." And sometimes the "winds dived and passed in the green depths, like ghost whales, unseen." In Melville's works, the ship as microcosm is one of the most basic archetypal symbols used, as is the journey to sea, to the primal beginnings, to discover the essential secrets of life and death. So it is with *Dandelion Wine*. Ship archetypes and metaphors of the sea quite significantly underscore the spiritual and psychological journey of Doug Spaulding, even though in concrete fact he sets foot on no real gangplank and breathes a thousand miles from the sea.

The last major metaphor of any importance, actually an archetype, is that of the river, which flows through most sections of the book. Considering the initiation aspects of the story, the river archetype is especially appropriate in *Dandelion Wine* due to its universal symbolic meanings of death and rebirth, of the transition of the life cycle from one phase to another, and of the steady flowing of time into an eternal future. There is, for example, section 7 in which Douglas listens to the twilight voices of the grown-ups on the porch and after supper: "Douglas sprawled back on the dry porch planks, completely contented and reassured by these voices, which would speak on through eternity, flow in a stream of murmurings over his body, over his closed eyelids, into his drowsy ears, for all time . . . the voices chanted . . . and moved on into the coming years." And then there is section 20, in which Doug and his friends take the final ride on the trolley of Mr. Tridden: "He ricocheted the brass handle, the trolley groaned and swung round an endless green curve, and all the time in the world held still, as if only the children and Mr. Tridden and his miraculous machine were riding an endless river, away." And there is section 37, in which Doug, during his fever dream hears the "frail but hearty voice" of now dead Great Grandma singing: "Yes, we'll gather at the river . . . river . . . river . . . Yes, we'll gather at the river. . . . That flows by the throne of God." Yes, even as in *Huck Finn*, the river archetype flows through the background to remind us constantly of the process taking place, the process of growth, the process of initiation, a process which has no foreseeable end as the spirit of man expands.

Source: Marvin E. Mengeling, "Ray Bradbury's *Dandelion Wine*: Themes, Sources, and Style," in *English Journal*, Vol. 60, No. 7, October 1971, pp. 877–87.

Sources

Bradbury, Ray, *Dandelion Wine*, William Morrow, 2001.

———, "Just This Side of Byzantium: An Introduction," in *Dandelion Wine*, William Morrow, 2001, pp. vii–xiv.

Diskin, Lahna, "Bradbury on Children," in *Ray Bradbury*, edited by Harold Bloom, Modern Critical Views series, Chelsea House Publishers, 2001, p. 76, originally published in *Ray Bradbury*, edited by Martin Henry Greenberg and Joseph D. Olander, Taplinger Publishing, 1980, pp. 127–55.

Harmon, William, and C. Hugh Holman, *A Handbook to Literature*, 7th ed., Prentice Hall, 1996, p. 304.

Knight, Damon, "When I Was in Kneepants: Ray Bradbury," in *In Search of Wonder: Essays on Modern Science Fiction*, Advent Publishers, 1956, pp. 108–13.

Mengeling, Marvin E., "Ray Bradbury's *Dandelion Wine*: Themes, Sources, and Style," in *English Journal*, Vol. 60, No. 7, October 1971, pp. 877, 882.

———, *Red Planet, Flaming Phoenix, Green Town: Some Early Bradbury Revisited*, Authorhouse, 2002, p. 154.

Reid, Robin Anne, *Ray Bradbury: A Critical Companion*, Greenwood Press, 2000, p. 72.

Rosenman, John B., "The Heaven and Hell Archetype in Faulkner's 'That Evening Sun' and Bradbury's *Dandelion Wine*," in *South Atlantic Bulletin*, Vol. 43, No. 2, 1978, p. 12.

Slusser, George Edgar, "Ray Bradbury," in *Dictionary of Literary Biography*, Vol. 2, *American Novelists Since World War II, First Series*, edited by Jeffrey Helterman, Gale Research, 1978, pp. 60–65.

Zamora, Lois, "Magical Romance/Magical Realism: Ghosts in U.S. and Latin American Fiction," in *Magical Realism: Theory, History, Community*, edited by Lois Parkinson Zamora and Wendy B. Faris, Duke University Press, 1995, pp. 499–501.

Further Reading

Bloom, Harold, ed., *Ray Bradbury*, Modern Critical Views series, Chelsea House Publishers, 2001.
    While most of the essays included in this collection are reprints, the collection as a whole gives students a broad survey of Bradbury criticism.

Bradbury, Ray, "Memories Shape the Voice," in *The Voice of the Narrator in Children's Literature: Insights from Writers and Critics*, edited by Charlotte F. Otten and Cary D. Schmidt, Greenwood Press, 1989, pp. 132–38.
    In this essential article, Bradbury discusses how he wrote *Dandelion Wine* using his own memories. This essay, titled "Just This Side of Byzantium: An Introduction," also appears in the 2001 William Morrow edition of *Dandelion Wine*.

Johnson, Wayne L., *Ray Bradbury*, Frederick Ungar, 1980.
    Johnson provides an interesting chapter on Bradbury's Green Town stories.

Mogen, David, *Ray Bradbury*, Twayne, 1986.
    Mogen's book offers both a thorough introduction to Bradbury and a work-by-work analysis of Bradbury's major fiction.

A Death in the Family

James Agee
1957

James Agee's novel *A Death in the Family* is a classic American story, chronicling just a few days in 1915 during which a husband and father is called out of town to be with his own father, who has had a heart attack, and while returning is killed in a car accident. Agee patterned the story closely after his own life, focusing on a boy who is the same age that he was when his father died. The narrative shifts from one perspective to another, including the young widow and her two children and her atheistic father and the dead man's alcoholic brother, to name just a few, in an attempt to capture the ways in which one person's loss immediately and powerfully affects everyone around.

The book was published in 1957 by McDowell, Obolensky, two years after Agee's death from heart failure at the age of 46, and was awarded the 1958 Pulitzer Prize for Fiction. Although Agee had worked on it for almost a decade, he had not produced a definitive final draft, and so his publishers had to put the book together in a way that they believed would make the most sense. They have indicated places where they added materials that come from outside of the flow of the story, such as the opening section "Knoxville: Summer, 1915," which was first published in the 1940s. Critics agree that the end product is a consistent novel, one of the most moving works ever written about one of the most traumatic experiences a child could ever face.

James Agee   The Library of Congress

Author Biography

James Rufus Agee was born on November 27, 1909, in Knoxville, Tennessee. As a boy, he was always called by his middle name, the name given to the main character in *A Death in the Family*. When he was six, Agee's father died in an automobile accident. Agee was sent to boarding school in his childhood, then to Philips Exeter Academy, which was to become a strong influence throughout his life. He then went to Harvard University, where he received an associate's degree in 1932. He married the first of his three wives the following year and went to work at *Fortune*, one of the country's preeminent business magazines. Though Agee's left-leaning politics disagreed with the magazine's focus on finance, his work there gave him the opportunity to work on his poetry.

In 1936, *Fortune* sent Agee and photographer Walker Evans to Alabama to report on the lives of tenant farmers. It was the middle of the Great Depression, and the suffering and dignity that Evans and Agee saw in their poor uneducated subjects impressed them so much that, when the magazine rejected their subsequent article, they expanded it to book length. The book, titled *Let Us Now Praise Famous Men* (1941), was ignored by a reading public that was focused on America's coming involvement

in World War II. Today, the book is considered to be one of the most important and moving documents available of that time.

While still working on the book, Agee branched out into another field of writing, that of movie reviewing. His reviews for *Time* and later for the *Nation* would in themselves have secured his place in the country's literary heritage, bringing an intellectual approach to reviewing just as film was gaining respect as an art form. His reviews, collected after his death in the two-volume collection *Agee on Film*, are as enjoyable as they are instructive.

In 1951, Agee published *The Morning Watch*, which gained only lukewarm critical response. He then combined his storytelling skills with his understanding of film and began writing screenplays. His first script was for *The African Queen*, starring Humphrey Bogart and Katherine Hepburn. It won Academy Award nominations for Agee and its director, John Huston. That same year, Agee suffered his first heart attack. Over the next few years, as he worked on *A Death in the Family* and his screenplay for the film *Night of the Hunter*, he suffered a series of heart attacks, eventually dying of heart failure on May 16, 1955.

Plot Summary

Knoxville: Summer, 1915

The segment titled "Knoxville: Summer, 1915" was originally published independently of *A Death in the Family*. In it, the speaker identifies himself as a grownup looking back on his childhood. He does not mention the characters who appear in the book: still, the quiet neighborhood evenings that Agee remembers in this section resemble ones experienced by young Rufus in the story that follows it.

Chapter 1

The first chapter focuses on the perspective of Rufus Follett, a six-year-old boy in Knoxville, Tennessee. Rufus and his father go to a Charlie Chaplin motion picture. On the way home, the father stops at a tavern, bragging about his son to the other people there. He tells Rufus to not tell his mother they stopped. In bed and falling asleep, Rufus hears his parents talking in the next room, vaguely understanding that his father is going somewhere.

Chapter 2

Jay Follet, the father of Rufus, receives a call late, around two in the morning, from his younger brother, Ralph. Ralph is drunk and explains, unclearly, that their father has had a heart attack. Jay is not able to tell just how serious it is but agrees to drive miles to the town where they live immediately.

He tells his wife, Mary, to stay in bed, that he can stop at a diner for something to eat, but she insists on making him a breakfast before his journey. In exchange, he makes the bed, as a surprise for her after he is gone. He tells her to think about something that she wants for her birthday that is coming up, and they share a happy, loving moment as he leaves into the darkness in the middle of the night.

Chapter 3

To cross the Powell river in his overnight car ride, Jay has to waken a man asleep at a ferry crossing. The man has Jay drive onto his boat, warning him that he will have to pay double fare to cover the boat's round-trip voyage, even though Jay himself is only going one way. When they reach the other side, though, they find a family in a horse-drawn wagon, waiting to take their produce to market. The ferryman says that he cannot fairly charge Jay the nighttime rate for a "dark crossing" since there is someone to pay for the boat's return trip.

Chapter 4

Before rising that morning, Mary lies in bed and thinks about her relationship with Jay. Though they have had difficult times, and his family has not been good to her, she prays to God that their future together will be peaceful.

Chapter 5

Mary explains to her children, Rufus and Catherine, that their father was called away and that he hopes to be home by the time they go to bed. In telling them that their grandfather might be dying, she discusses God and God's mysterious ways with them.

Chapter 6

Jay arrives at the family's house in LaFollette and finds that his father is not really in mortal danger. The narrative describes the events of the evening before from Ralph's point of view. Their father had suffered a worse heart attack than any he had suffered before, and the handyman called family and friends together. Distraught, Ralph had brought a bottle of liquor to the house with him and, as he drank through the night, had become increasingly angry and paranoid. He phoned Jay to make himself feel important.

Media Adaptations

- *A Death in the Family* was adapted to the stage as the play *All the Way Home* in 1960; a film version of the play was made in 1963.

- On March 25, 2002, PBS broadcast an adaptation of *A Death in the Family* directed by Gil Cates and starring Annabeth Gish and James Cromwell, as part of its *Masterpiece Theatre* series. It was written by Robert W. Lenski. The series was later released on VHS from Public Broadcasting System.

Chapter 7

While Rufus's father is away, Hannah Lynch, Mary's aunt, stops by to take the boy shopping. They have a strong relationship and enjoy shopping together. At the end of the expedition, Aunt Hannah buys him a cap, which is something that he wanted but his parents refused him.

Chapter 7 finishes Part I of the book with an extended scene, from the young boy's point of view, of being frightened in the darkness of night and of being comforted by his father with songs and with a stuffed doll that he had lost when he was younger. He then remembers the mystery surrounding his mother's pregnancy with his sister and the process of finding out about it.

Chapter 8

Part II starts with Mary receiving a phone call saying that Jay has been in an accident. She calls her brother Andrew, who has his friend Walter Starr drive him to the site. While they are gone, Mary discusses her fears with Aunt Hannah, as she tries to hope that it might not be a very bad accident, although each passing minute makes it clear that something is terribly wrong.

Chapter 9

Mary's parents, Catherine and Joel, who stayed home when Andrew received the call, wait for word about Jay.

Chapter 10

Andrew returns and confirms Mary's fear that Jay is dead. In shock, Mary asks for all of the details, but he leaves them until their parents can arrive.

Chapter 11

With Mary's parents in the house, Andrew gives the details of how Jay died: a cotter pin fell out, and he was unable to control the car, hitting his chin on the steering wheel and dying instantly.

Chapter 12

All of the people in the house feel a strange presence, and they become convinced that it is Jay's spirit, come home one last time. Only Joel Lynch, Mary's father, is skeptical about whether they have experienced a true supernatural event. In the end, Andrew takes his parents home, leaving Aunt Hannah to stay with Mary and to care for the children when they awake.

Chapter 13

Mary's parents and brother walk home, and Mary and Hannah go to bed. The focus shifts to Rufus's memories. This section begins with his encounters with the older boys on the block who took interest in him, having him dance and sing, though he could tell that they were laughing at him. It ends with a long story about a trip that the family once took out into the country to visit the oldest Follet, Rufus's great-great grandmother, who was born in 1802. Though she could hardly talk, she recognized people and hugged Rufus.

Chapter 14

Rufus and Catherine wake in the morning, and their mother tells them that their father will not be coming home.

Chapter 15

Aunt Hannah tries to explain death to Rufus and Catherine, telling them that it is God's will. Catherine still asks when their father is coming home.

Chapter 16

After breakfast, Rufus wanders outside, amazed that he does not have to go to school. He encounters the children who have bullied him. Some mock his father, calling him a drunk, or the car for being cheap, but most are sympathetic and a little in awe of Rufus.

Chapter 17

Father Jackson comes to the house. He is stern with the children, lecturing them about manners.

The children are visited by Walter Starr, who treats them well and expresses his respect for Jay.

Chapter 18

They go to the house of Mary's parents, where the body is laid out for viewing, and see Jay's corpse.

Chapter 19

Walter takes the children away, but he breaks the family's wishes and lets them watch the funeral procession from a hidden place because he thinks it is important for them.

Chapter 20

They return to their grandparents' house that evening. Feeling ignored, Catherine hides under the bed. Mary's brother Andrew takes Rufus for a walk and tells him an uplifting story about a butterfly that landed on the casket as it was lowered in the grave. His spiritual amazement gives way, however, to anger at Father Jackson, who has refused to give the full funeral prayer because Jay was never baptized. Rufus assumes that this anti-religious stance means that his uncle hates Mary.

Characters

George Bailey

George Bailey is the husband of Jay's sister Jessie.

Jessie Bailey

Jessie Bailey is the sister of Jay and Ralph.

The Ferryman

When he is traveling to LaFollette in the middle of the night, Jay Follet has to wake a Ferryman, whose job is to ride cars across the river on his flat ferryboat. The Ferryman is prepared to charge Jay a double rate but, finding a horse-drawn wagon of people going toward town and paying for the boat's return trip, can only fairly charge the single rate.

Catherine Follet

The young daughter of the Follet family, Catherine is frequently unaware of what is going on around her. She does not understand the full implications of her father's death and expects him to return to the family later. In the last chapter, as she moves around the house unnoticed, Catherine begins to understand the seriousness of what has happened.

James Follet

See Jay Follet

Jay Follet

Jay, also known as James Follet, is the man who dies in the novel. He is stable and reliable. He is shown to have been a favorite of his mother and his great-grandmother. Walter Starr, a family friend, is near tears as he tries to express to Jay's children his great admiration for Jay, who worked himself up from humble roots.

There are indications that Jay has not always been stable and reliable. After he leaves for his parents' house, his wife Mary reflects on the difficult times they have had as a couple, and on a "gulf" between them. His great aunt Sadie mentions sending a postcard to Jay and Mary in Panama, indicating that Jay has been a wanderer. Agee hints that Jay has had problems with alcohol in the past. Near the end of the first section, recalling his childhood, Rufus remembers fights between his parents concerning whiskey, an idea supported by the facts that Jay asks Rufus to keep their visit to a tavern a secret and that the neighbor children assume that he died from driving drunk.

Mary Follet

Mary is the wife of Jay, and the mother of Rufus and Catherine. She is a devout Catholic, praying for her husband's safety when he leaves the house in the middle of the night to go to his ailing father, praying even more that God's will is merciful when she hears that he has been in an accident, and relying most heavily on her faith when she hears that he has died. Throughout the night of her sudden widowhood, Mary drinks more whiskey than she ever would have thought possible, feeling no effect from it. She is constantly surprised that she is able to cope with the whole ordeal as well as she is, though, when it comes time to leave for the funeral, her legs give out under her.

Ralph Follet

Ralph, Jay's brother, is an undertaker. He lives near his parents' house and is summoned over when his father has a heart attack. While relatives wait for the doctor to determine just how serious the danger is, Ralph, an alcoholic, sneaks outside to drink. His weak attempt to hide the fact that he is drinking fails, especially when he hits his head on the door, pretending to go to the outhouse, and returns bleeding. He is alternately humiliated and self-righteous, and both moods drive him to drink more. When he calls in the middle of the night, Jay can tell he is drunk, and his trouble obtaining reliable information is the reason he leaves Knoxville to drive to the family house. Ralph's alcoholism is so well-known that Mary refuses to talk to him when the news comes out that Jay is dead; her brother Andrew, who has had to tell Ralph that they are using an in-town undertaker, comes away explaining "Talking to that fool is like trying to put socks on an octopus."

Rufus Follet

The book is focused on six-year-old Rufus, particularly during the autobiographical sections that the publishers have added at the end of Parts I and II. In these sections, which take place before the death of his father, Rufus is becoming aware of his place in society. He observes the social patterns of his neighborhood in Knoxville, five generations of his father's family, and the behaviors of his peers. His family showers him with love and his father affords him protection from his childhood fears in these flashbacks. When dealing with other children, however, Rufus finds that he is for some reason ostracized. He believes their interest in them is honest, at first, but the suspicion that they are mocking him grows when he hears them repeating things he has said and laughing.

Before his father's death, Rufus is anxious to grow up and be treated like an adult. He feels that his parents treat him like a child, and so he makes a point of giving orders to his sister Catherine, who is younger than he. The death pushes him into adulthood in ways that he could not anticipate.

Rufus's response to his father's death is less emotional than one might expect. He understands the idea of death and is blunt about stating it. He is saddened, but he also is mystified by the social customs surrounding death: the people coming to the house; the fact that he is kept home from school; the genuine interest and even respect of the children who had made fun of him.

At the end of the book, Rufus is just starting to show anger over the situation. When his uncle Andrew curses about the priest's refusal to say certain prayers over Jay Follet, who was not baptized, Rufus does not agree with Andrew but instead silently accuses his uncle of hating his devout Christian mother, indicating that, in the future, Rufus might be less accepting, less curious, and more defensive.

Sally Follet

Sally is Ralph's wife. She is ashamed of Ralph's drinking, a fact that he is well aware of. In his mind, Ralph accuses Sally of wanting other men but then remembers that he is unfaithful himself.

Granmaw

The grandmother of Jay's father, Granmaw is roughly 103 years old when the family travels out into the unoccupied hills to visit her in a memory that Rufus has at the end of Part II. She does not seem to be aware of the people who have come before her, but she responds favorably when Rufus is sent forward to kiss her and talk to her.

Father Jackson

Father Jackson is a Catholic priest who has come from Chattanooga to officiate at the funeral of Jay Follet. He is a stern man who, when left alone with the children, does not console them but instead corrects them on their manners. Hannah is resentful that Father Jackson does not leave the room when Mary is preparing for the funeral and her knees falter. Mary's brother Andrew is livid with anger that Father Jackson refuses to read the complete funeral service for Jay because Jay was not baptized.

Aunt Kate

In the memory that Rufus has of staying with his father's family when he was young, Aunt Kate and her husband, Uncle Ted, come from Michigan to visit. Aunt Kate is the daughter of Rufus's grandmother's half sister.

Andrew Lynch

When a man from out of town phones Mary and asks her to send a male family member to the accident scene, she phones her brother Andrew. Andrew takes the situation in hand, making arrangements for the body when he finds Jay dead, instead of calling Mary. He holds the information about Jay's death until he can show up and tell Mary about it in person.

For most of the novel, Andrew is on the periphery of the action, waiting for ways that he can be helpful to his sister. At the end he takes his nephew Rufus for a walk to talk with him individually. He tells him about a butterfly that landed on the casket as it was lowered into the grave, an event so spiritually uplifting that Andrew feels that Rufus ought to know about it. His wonderment is quickly followed, though, with hatred for Father Jackson, who has refused to read the full funeral service over Jay because he was not baptized. Andrew's hatred for the Catholic church at that time makes Rufus assume that Andrew hates Mary, too.

Catherine Lynch

Catherine, Mary's mother, is hard of hearing. As a result, she and her husband Joel are asked to stay home while Mary waits for news of the crash in the middle of the night, because conversation with Catherine would mean shouting into the ear trumpet she uses to magnify sounds. When they do go to the house in the middle of the night, Catherine is often left out of conversations because family members are speaking in hushed tones. This isolation, though, supports the idea that Jay's spirit has come through the house: while the fact that the others talk about it might be dismissed as just a collective mood, the fact that Catherine had the same sensation independently makes the experience much more real.

Hannah Lynch

Hannah, Mary's maiden aunt, makes herself available to help around the household during the crisis. She enters the novel before Jay Follet's death, when he is just away to his parents' house. She takes Rufus shopping, showing a bond with the boy when she buys him a cap that he has wanted but that his parents would not allow him to have. When news comes that Jay has been in an accident, Mary asks Aunt Hannah to come to her house and wait with her; after it has been determined that Jay is dead, she asks Hannah to stay the night. Hannah watches over the children while Mary is rendered incapable by grief.

Joel Lynch

Mary's father Joel works with Jay, though the novel does not specify what their business is. When the family is gathered together on the night of Jay's death and talking about spiritual matters, Joel is respectful, but he is open and honest about the fact that he cannot believe in God.

Thomas Oaks

Oaks is a handyman on the grandparents' ranch up in LaFollette.

Great Aunt Sadie

The sister of Jay's grandfather, she lives in a house out in the hills and tends to her own mother, who is referred to as "Granmaw." Sadie is an exacting woman, greatly angry with herself when she finds that she forgot Jay's family had sent her a notice of their new address. She feels that, with her aged mother to look after, she cannot afford to have any slips in her memory.

Walter Starr

Walter is a friend of the family who is glad to make himself available during the family's time of need. He has a car, and drives Andrew out to the accident site in the middle of the night. Later, he takes the children to his house during the funeral, but he breaks the family's wishes and lets them watch the funeral procession from a hidden place because he thinks it is important for them. He talks to them in a positive, uplifting way.

When he is left alone with the children at the funeral, Walter tells them of the tremendous respect that he had for their father: "Well, I thought the world of him, Rufus and Catherine. My own wife and son couldn't mean more to me I think." He goes on to describe himself as an ordinary man, noting that he thought Jay was one of the finest men who ever lived.

Uncle Ted

Rufus remembers Uncle Ted and his wife, Aunt Kate, visiting and going for a train ride into the Smoky Mountains with his family. Uncle Ted buys him a toy and is funny, but then he jokes that Rufus can make the cheese plate come to him by whistling for it. Rufus is too young to understand this as a joke, and his mother chastises Uncle Ted for taking advantage of the boy's trusting nature.

Victoria

Victoria is a midwife who helped Mary through her pregnancy with Rufus and, in Rufus's memory, returns to help deliver his sister Catherine. She is the first black person that Rufus has ever met, and his parents insist that he treat her with respect, which is not a problem because he has a genuine fondness for her.

Themes

Vulnerability

In a way, *A Death in the Family* stands as an extended meditation on human vulnerability. The story's figure of strength is the father, Jay Follet, a man who, it is revealed, has lived a hard life, raised himself up from humble beginnings in a log cabin, overcome problems with alcohol and marital instability and come out better for them all. When they find out that he is dead, his children

Topics for Further Study

- Research various funerary rites of different cultures and report on what each would have to offer the Follet family in a situation like the one presented in the book.

- The cabin that Rufus's Great Great Grandmother and his Great Aunt Sadie live in is back in the woods, away from civilization. Write a narrative describing what you think a day in the lives of these old women might be like.

- In the first chapter, Mary Follet refers to the actor Charlie Chaplin as "that horrid little man." Read a description of Chaplin from one of the film historians who think that he was one of the great geniuses of film comedy; then, watch a Chaplin silent movie from 1915 or before. Stage a debate between a Chaplin supporter and an opponent.

- Recall a death in your own family and describe how specific family members behaved; then, explain which members of the Follet or Lynch families you think those people you described were most like, and why.

immediately wonder how anybody could hurt him. Jay's death in a car accident could have been rendered as a bloody and violent, but Agee makes a point of noting frequently in the story that it actually takes very little to kill him: it is not the car careening up an embankment and flipping over on its back that does Jay in, but a mild little bump on the chin, causing a nearly imperceptible mark. Agee's point seems to be that, despite the sturdiness of the human body and its capacity to withstand a lifetime of pain and suffering, life can be cut short by just about any unexpected action.

Similarly, the family organism is vulnerable to unexpected loss. At the moment when Jay is torn away, his relationship with Mary is on the verge of a new beginning that she finds surprising. Their relationship up to then had been colder: his thoughtfulness about her coming birthday and the sweet gesture of his preparing her bed come as pleasant surprises to Mary. By putting Jay's death at a point where their love is growing, not fading or staying the same, Agee emphasizes the fact that life is fragile, and that not even love matters to death's approach.

The most vulnerable character, though, is Rufus, who is six years old when his father dies. Several factors make this loss particularly powerful to him. His sister Catherine, though younger, cannot fully understand the situation the way Rufus can, as Agee shows clearly when their mother first tells them about the accident: Catherine still waits for her father to return, but Rufus cuts through the delicate language about God calling Jay home to ask, "Is daddy *dead?*" Another reason that Rufus is particularly vulnerable is that, as a son, he has had a strong bond with his male parent, which Agee stresses by opening the novel with father and son attending a movie and walking home together. Although the book looks at the situation from various perspectives, most readers and critics remember it as Rufus's story, because he is the most vulnerable character, most sorely affected by Jay Follet's death.

Consolation and Comfort

Although this story is about human vulnerability, it is also about the ways that humans bond together to help make that vulnerability bearable. Part II, in particular, focuses on Mary's relatives coming together at her house on the night of the death, doing what they can to ease her suffering. For her brother Andrew and family friend Walter Starr, this means action: they are the ones who go to the scene of the accident, so that Mary will not have to face the gruesome details of Jay's death. For Mary's Aunt Hannah, the best way to comfort Mary, as she thinks several times throughout the night, is suppressing her own ideas, so that Mary can discover the things that she needs to experience about grief as she is ready for them. Her father waits until they are alone to quietly tell Mary that he will take care of the financial details so she need not bother herself with worldly concerns, and her mother, isolated by her own deafness, allows the conversation to go on around her, despite her frustration, rather than ask people to repeat things that Mary might find upsetting. Collectively, they bend their own values to the situation, as indicated by the fact that they allow Mary to drink too much if that is what she feels like doing, knowing that her comfort is more important than their own skepticism about alcohol.

In general, the adults in this story do little to comfort the children. Mary, when she is with them,

tries to make their burden more bearable, but her own grief is so overwhelming that she is kept too busy just trying to convince herself that she is going to cope. When she does talk with them, it is in terms of abstract Catholic theology that is meaningless to them. Aunt Hannah, also, is too busy with practical considerations to be much consolation, despite the fact that Agee establishes a strong personal bond between her and Rufus. The figures most comforting to Rufus are the two male figures closest in age to his departed father, Walter Starr and Andrew. Walter, who is himself a father, speaks directly to Rufus and Catherine about what a good man Jay was, which is just the sort of thing they need to hear; later, he lets them view the funeral procession because he decides that it is what they need. Andrew takes Rufus into his confidence, conferring on him the adulthood that he has been struggling with. This has positive implications, when he talks of the butterfly at the gravesite and Rufus realizes that this is something Andrew would tell to no one but him, but it also brings the burden of responsibility when Andrew rails against religion, detracting from what might have been one possible source of consolation for the boy.

Catholicism

It would be difficult to discuss *A Death in the Family* without looking at the role religion and particularly Catholicism plays in this traumatic episode in the characters' lives. There is no denying that the novel has a distinct spiritual vein, and that a belief in the supernatural helps to make Jay Follet's death bearable. In Chapter 12, the assembled members of Mary's family feel a presence that they cannot explain in any other way except to say that it is Jay's spirit walking among them, and Andrew, in the end, observes a butterfly at the casket that he feels sure is a sign of Jay's continuing on in the afterlife.

Agee is less clear in his portrayal of organized religion. On the one hand, it is shown to be a force for good, in that prayer gives Mary a way of coping with her life, which she feels is being torn apart by a "gulf" and a "widening" even before she suffers her devastating loss. On the other hand, Catholicism is represented in this novel by Father Jackson, a cold man who is shown first badgering the children at the time of their loss because of his focus on "manners" and then denying Mary the full prayer service because Jay, who was not baptized, is not strictly eligible. Father Jackson may carry the weight of the Catholic church, but he is clearly the least admirable character in the novel.

Agee's own religious belief is reflected best in the skepticism of Mary's father. When surrounded by the faith of others, Joel Lynch is respectful, and even a little jealous, because he cannot find within himself the faith that supports them. He is not opposed to faith—he says that it would not hurt him to have some, and in fact might do him some good—but he finds himself without any understanding of anything beyond the experience of his senses.

Style

Point of View

Some novels maintain a consistent point of view, that is, they tell their story from the perspective of one character. In *A Death in the Family*, however, Agee has chosen to alternate points of view. The novel is told at different times from the perspectives of each of the members of the main family discussed (Rufus, Jay, Mary and Catherine), as well as from the viewpoints of such secondary characters as Aunt Hannah, Ralph, Andrew, and Mary's mother and father. With this approach to the material, Agee is able to make this the story of a *whole* family, and not just the story of any one particular character.

Symbolism

In literature, a symbol is something that has both specific and general meaning: it fits into the story, but also indicates a meaning beyond its own place. Agee uses symbols in *A Death in the Family* that have personal, cultural, and spiritual meanings.

The cap that Rufus receives from his Aunt Hannah, for instance, has a symbolic meaning for him that other characters in the story do not recognize. To his parents, the cap is a foolish desire, a frivolous and unnecessary expense. To Rufus, though, the cap symbolizes a level of maturity that others do not yet see in him. Its symbolic meaning is so strong to him that he focuses on it throughout the night, anxious to show it to his father as a mark of achievement.

Readers might not think much of the Ferryman who carries Jay across the river in Chapter 3, unless they are aware of classical Greek literature. In Greek myth, the souls of the dead are ferried across the river Styx by Charon, the silent old boatman in charge of bringing new souls from the world of the living into Hades. While the Ferryman fits comfortably into the book, and would not be out of place in Tennessee in 1915, the use of a figure from

antiquity foreshadows, for those familiar with the myth, the fact that Jay will never return from the far bank of the river.

The most poignant symbol, however, is the butterfly in the story that Andrew tells Rufus about his father's burial. The reader does not need any outside understanding of what the butterfly symbolizes because Andrew explains its significance to his nephew, telling him that he thinks it is as much a miracle as anything he has ever seen. He makes the event miraculous for Rufus by sharing the story with Rufus when he would not share it with anyone else in the family. In this way, the meaning Andrew sees in the butterfly, Jay's soul being released, becomes real precisely because he has found meaning in it.

Historical Context

One aspect of the novel that is notably different than the way life is in contemporary America is the closeness of extended families, with adult children frequently living with or near their parents. When Jay's father is stricken with a heart attack, his son Ralph and daughter Jessie and their spouses are available to be at his bedside; when Jay dies, his wife's brother, her aunt, and her parents are within walking distance; and Great Aunt Sadie, a woman who is herself in her eighties, has responsibility for the well-being of her mother. In rural societies, as Tennessee was in the early part of the twentieth century, it is more common to find extended families supporting each other than it is in urban areas. Traditionally, populations of rural areas have been determined by the need for help: before industrialization, parents on family farms tended to have more children based on their need for helping hands.

By the time the book was written, though, there had been several dramatic shifts in the American population that weakened the family structure. For one thing, the country became overwhelmingly city-oriented during the first half of the century. In 1910, there had been 46 million people counted as rural residents and only two thirds that, or 30 million, were rural. By 1950, the percentages were more than reversed: 54 million people were rural, and 96 million were urban. This population shift is seen even more dramatically when it is realized that, a decade later, the rural population had stayed constant at 54 million, but the urban population had jumped to 125 million. In part, this population shift

Compare
&
Contrast

- **1915:** The Ford Model T, or "Tin Lizzy," revolutionizes transportation by offering affordable, mass-produced transportation to middle-class families.

  1950s: The automobile is an icon of the age, as materials and products that were unavailable during the Great Depression and World War II allow car makers to build their products bigger and faster.

  Today: Many drivers insist on sport utility vehicles because they want to feel safe, while others find the big, fortress-like vehicles to be a waste of fossil fuels.

- **1915:** It is not unusual for a family like the Follets to have a black nurse like Victoria, though southern states like Tennessee are strictly segregated.

  1950s: The Civil Rights movement is on the rise to destroy institutional racism.

  Today: Legal penalties are in place to punish racism, but blacks and whites in America still have vastly different outlooks and viewpoints.

- **1915:** The "ear trumpet" used by Mary's mother to augment her hearing is a relic, dating back to the 1800s. Electronic hearing aids are available, though not common.

  1950s: Transistor technology has made possible hearing aids that are small enough to be carried in a shirt pocket.

  Today: Hearing aids are powerful and small enough to be worn unnoticed within the ear canal.

- **1915:** Funeral parlors are in existence, but are only popular in urban areas. In a relatively small town like Knoxville, it is still common to hold wakes and funerals in the house of the deceased or a loved one.

  1950s: Americans are accustomed to their last viewing of deceased loved ones happening at a local funeral parlor owned by a member of the community.

  Today: Like much else in society, the funeral business is increasingly run by corporations, while consumers have an expanding variety of methods of self-expression in funerary arrangements that have become commonly accepted.

- **1915:** Long distance telephone service makes it possible to place a cross-continent call between New York and San Francisco.

  1950s: Telephone usage is common—there are about 55 million phones in the United States—but still expensive. Long distance calls are often placed through an operator.

  Today: Wireless phones have made it possible and affordable to call to anywhere, from anywhere.

---

was caused by younger people leaving rural areas and going to the cities in search of work, especially during the Great Depression, which spanned from the stock market crash of 1929 until America's entry into World War II in 1941.

City life was, almost by definition, less oriented around the family than the rural life that had dominated American culture in earlier centuries. Without the family structure to support them, millions of citizens, especially those who were older and less able to work, were faced with poverty. In 1935, during the height of the Depression, President Franklin Roosevelt signed the Social Security Act, to provide financial support for citizens who otherwise would be destitute. The support that this Act gave to elderly citizens who were on their own made older relatives less dependent on their younger relatives for simple subsistence.

Charlie Chaplin, still from the 1925 film The Gold Rush. *One of Rufus Follet's last memories of his father alive in James Agee's* A Death in the Family *is going to see a Charlie Chaplin motion picture with him* © Bettmann/Corbis

When Agee was working on this book in the 1950s, the family was also being weakened by the distractions that come from a leisure-oriented society. Television, in particular, became a mass-medium in the fifties, bringing the outside world into homes more vividly than radio ever could. The world that Agee describes in "Knoxville: Summer, 1915," a world of families gathering together on front lawns, playing with each other and mingling with the neighbors, was fragmented, as television offered a reason to stay isolated. Family discussion, once a focal point in households, became viewed

as a distraction. As the family drifted apart, the fifties bred a youth culture, with teenagers seeking to develop identities distinct from those of their parents and of earlier generations.

Critical Overview

Assessments of *A Death in the Family* at the time of its publication indicate that reviewers were not just out to honor the memory of a good writer who had died, but that they saw the qualities of the novel that have made it an American classic. Dwight MacDonald, writing in *The New Yorker*, noted that even though Agee died before final editing, the book "reads like a finished work—brilliant, moving, and written with an objectivity and a control he had not achieved before." Most reviews, like that written by Melvin Maddocks in *The Christian Science Monitor*, were generally pleased with the book while still recognizing its weaknesses. Examining how difficult it is to write convincingly from a child's perspective, Maddocks notes that "James Agee's posthumous novel is proof that the job can sometimes be managed accurately as well as fondly, vividly as well as indulgently." Maddocks goes on to list faults: "It can be merely rhetorical as well as eloquent. The words that click and shuttle to weave a vivid sensory pattern can also produce cotton wool. . . . Furthermore, it is doubtful that the novel was as completely finished as its publishers indicate." The fact that it was awarded the Pulitzer Prize for Fiction is an indication of the esteem held for this novel by critics of its time.

As the years have passed, *A Death in the Family* has come to be seen as James Agee's legacy, the lasting achievement of a writer who was mostly known in his day for his transitory magazine writing. Though it is uneven and very personal, the novel approaches one of life's most moving experiences with a poetic sensibility that speaks to readers across the generations. As Victor A. Kramer, a critic who has written extensively about Agee's life and career, wrote it in his essay "Urban and Rural Balance in *A Death in the Family*,"

> The text for Agee's unfinished *A Death in the Family* is . . . a book that functions on several levels at once: it is Agee's memorial; it is his examination of self; it is a picture of a particular era when urban and rural were blended; it is an archetypal rendering of what all persons learn, live, and love.

Criticism

David Kelly

Kelly is an instructor of literature and creative writing at two colleges in Illinois. In this essay, Kelly looks at Agee's use of geographical space.

James Agee's novel *A Death in the Family* is primarily, as its straightforward title indicates, about an emotional moment in a closed family unit including its surrounding relations. Agee's narrative travels from one point-of-view to another, giving his readers a range of perspectives, all used to show the void the death of Jay Follet, husband and father, creates. The book also travels through time, though that might not be a mark of Agee's artistry as much as it is the work of the editors who, after his death, wove outside material into the book. The story of Jay's death takes place across the span of just a few days, ranging from the night before it to a few days after, at his funeral; the included material, though, goes back to a time when Jay's son Rufus, a major character, was barely old enough to understand his surroundings. Adding these out-of-sequence episodes to the ends of Part I and Part II, plus the multi-page prose poem "Knoxville: Summer, 1915" rounds out young Rufus's experience in a way that a strictly chronological telling would miss.

It is the story's geographical breadth, even more so than its chronological depth, however, that adds the most to its effectiveness. This is a story about emotions, but the way that those emotions are most strongly presented is through Agee's use of places. He shows where people are in relation to one another in the world, as well as in their hearts. Any story has to take place somewhere, but the movement across physical space in this particular novel shows more about the inner lives of its characters, and in particular young Rufus, than the story conveys through just dialog and action alone.

Though every location in the book is important, it helps, for the sake of understanding their significance, to divide locations into three general categories. One of these categories is homes: since "family" is such an important part of the social dynamic that Agee is examining, it makes sense that this book would be dominated by variations on what family members call home. Another category would be locations that are passed in transition, by characters on the move from one place to another. Throughout the book, Rufus takes several walks with older relatives that radiate significance about what his life has been and what it is going to be, and Jay's fatal trip across the Tennessee countryside is certainly significant. Symbolically, these two ideas, home and beyond, meet at the corner of the block where the Follets live, which is where the boy becomes a part of the world outside of his family.

The one setting where most of the book takes place is, appropriately, the Follet house. This is a story about a family, after all, and it makes sense that the book should center around the place where the family gathers. Readers do not see this house as a place of comfort, though. Most of the time, it is the middle of the night, and the house is dark and quiet. Readers get to know Jay when he is preparing to leave for his parents' ranch out in the country in the dark. The bulk of the novel, the whole middle third, follows Mary's reactions from the time she is woken by the call to tell her of Jay's accident to her attempt to go to sleep at first light. There are other scenes in the house, but they are themselves shaded, either by actual night (as when Rufus, as an infant, has trouble sleeping because he fears the shadows in his room) or by the knowledge of Jay's death. The house is important to the family identity, but Agee does not allow readers to see it in happy times.

There are also homes of other family members presented. One of them, the house of Jay's parents, is a mirror image of the way his house is presented in Part II of the novel, with family and friends sitting the night out, offering comfort in the face of death (though in this case they are braced against a death that never comes). Readers' view of this home is obscured by the fact that this scene is told through the eyes of Jay's brother Ralph, who, due to alcohol and insecurity, renders a view of those around him that is skewed at best. Ralph is so self-absorbed, so focused on hiding his drinking problem that readers get little sense of Jay's mother, Jessie and George Bailey, Thomas Oaks or Sally Follet, who are there with him. As with the other house, this one is the focus of family solidarity, but it is shown in the novel as a dark and foreboding place.

The home that does seem comforting, even inviting, is the "great, square-logged gray cabin" where Jay's 103-year-old relative lives. Agee describes the house in mythical terms (for instance, the word "great" is used several times in the short descriptive passage, conveying a sense of grandeur). Everything about this ancestral home is shrouded in myth, from the trip there, which is guided by half-forgotten memories, to the unimaginable details of the old woman's life (born before Abraham Lincoln) to the woman herself, who seems incapable of understanding what is happening until young Rufus kisses her, at which point she reaches out to him, as if waking from an ancient sleep. Agee clearly wants to emphasize this cabin as a trip back in time for Rufus and for Jay, who is later said to have been born in a log cabin. It is a return home for Jay's father, too, and for his brother. This obscure cabin out in the sunshine is home to all of them, a home that they have traveled from in the varied courses of their lives.

Although homes as places of comfort is a theme in this novel, the next most frequent place

> While the novel is mainly about the way family members come together at a time of tragedy, the street corner represents the beginning of the natural growth process of splintering off from the family. The journey of life begins."

for staging events in this novel is in transit, with characters who are passing through the space they inhabit. Three times throughout the novel, Rufus goes walking with adult family members. The first is in the opening chapter, when he and his father walk home from the movies. During this walk there are signs of Jay's unrooted nature and his looking backward, from his searching in the tavern for people from "back home" in the Powell River Valley (which in itself foreshadows "Powell Station," the place a man calls from to tell Mary of Jay's accident) to the comfort he derives from in the big rock they stop by, which offers him a piece of nature in the middle of the city. Jay takes Rufus into his confidence on the way home, telling him to not mention the saloon to his mother, making this walk a rite of passage for the boy as he is treated, in one thing at least, as his father's peer.

The walk that begins the novel is counterbalanced with the walk that Rufus takes at the end, with his uncle Andrew. Their man-to-man talk reflects the way Jay and his son shared a secret, as Andrew tells Rufus about the butterfly at the grave, which, Agee makes clear, he would not tell anyone else. This walk ends with Rufus saddled with even more adult responsibility as he witnesses Andrew, enraged about Father Jackson, losing his temper, giving him the unusual sight of an adult out of control of his emotions.

Within the story, before Jay's death, Rufus walks downtown with his mother's aunt Hannah to go shopping. This trip, like the other, presents Rufus away from home but safely under the guardianship of an adult relative. His trip with Hannah is particularly significant because their comfortable relationship is to become an important element of

What Do I Read Next?

- Agee's only other novel, *The Morning Watch* (1950), is about a boy at a boarding school in the mountains of Tennessee who has a religious reaction to the natural world that surrounds him.

- Agee was sent away to school at age nine to St. Andrew's, a small Episcopalian school. While there, he began a lifelong relationship with Father James Harold Flye. Agee's correspondences with Flye over the next thirty years, concerning his innermost considerations of moral and spiritual matters, his thoughts on art and alcoholism, and the trials of living, are collected in *Letters of James Agee to Father Flye* (1962).

- *A Death in the Family* is concerned with the process of coping with death, which is the subject of Elisabeth Kubler-Ross's groundbreaking psychology text *On Death and Dying* (1969). Kubler-Ross was the person who first charted the five stages of grief: denial, anger, bargaining, depression, and acceptance.

- One of the great achievements of this novel is the way it evokes the mood of death and mourning throughout. James Joyce, one of the masters of English literature, was expert at evoking the feeling of life burdened by the knowledge of mortality, especially in the short story "The Dead," which is considered one of the greatest stories ever written. It is a part of Joyce's collection *Dubliners* (1914).

- Because of his intense poetic sensibilities and early death, Agee has been treated as a cult figure by some readers. His life is examined in minute detail in Laurence Bergreen's biography *James Agee: A Life* (1984), which captures Agee's magnetic allure while not failing to examine the less admirable aspects of the writer's life.

Rufus's life, as Hannah will undoubtedly have a central role in helping Mary raise her children.

The one other significant location in the novel is the corner of the block where the Follet family lives. This is the place where Rufus is seen without adult supervision. It is here that he grows up socially and develops his own unique personality.

The corner is first introduced into the story as the place where Rufus, when he was younger, watched daily as his father "waved for the last time and disappeared," and where he watched each afternoon for his father's return. Gradually, Rufus went to the corner on his own, and there encountered children who were not as nurturing as his family members had been, mocking him and confusing him with their ill-natured hostility. In full view of his house, waiting while his father is in transit between the outside world and home, he does whatever he can to join that world of outsiders, even though he knows that he is making a fool of himself.

After his father's death, he is accepted by a few of the other children, at least by the those who pity him and those who defer to his status as a boy who has gone through the unimaginable, magic process of orphan hood. While the novel is mainly about the way family members come together at a time of tragedy, the street corner represents the beginning of the natural growth process of splintering off from the family. The journey of life begins.

The street corner is also where Walter Starr stops his car to let the Rufus and his sister watch Jay's casket loaded into the hearse and taken away. It shows a tremendous measure of respect on Walter's part, trusting them to be cope with the sight that no other adults in their lives trusts them to see. Their view from the corner represents both of the main themes present in this novel's geography: home, and going away from it.

The event that disrupts the Follet family in *A Death in the Family* is traumatic in itself, especially to a boy Rufus's age. Still, Agee showed good artistic sense when he avoided telling the story through action and dialog, which could easily tilt the writing toward over-sentimentality. People in this novel behave as if in a daze, shrouded by the dark still of the night or by the sheer weight of sorrow. The significance of this situation is not shown entirely through character interaction, so Agee fills in the missing elements about Jay and Rufus and their personalities by implying a great deal with the setting of each scene. This story is centered around home, in its many various forms, but when there is a death in the family, home is only the beginning.

Source: David Kelly, Critical Essay on *A Death in the Family*, in *Novels for Students*, Thomson Gale, 2006.

George Toles

In the following essay excerpt, Toles explores Agee's reunion with self and family in A Death in the Family.

The work of nostalgic vision in both Wilder and Agee is to accommodate the writer's self within an idealized family or community setting, where an absent parent's presumed intention for one's life and the self's own confused image of what it wants, are magically reconciled. The self must find a way to breathe and stretch out full length in its parent's presence but be persuaded at the same time that the parent is happy or appeased. James Agee's "nostalgia" is an attempt to close up the hollow spaces in the "family rooms" he describes, since beyond these rooms, he is convinced, "none can care . . . and none can be cared for." It is the child's still uninhibited and unaggressive tenderness (rather than Wilder's courteous formality and well-bred "neighborliness") that serves as Agee's language of accommodation. The violently disruptive image of the "taloned" mother (in the catalogue passage), sucking her child dry in the guise of nurturing him, was formed, almost without Agee's conscious assent, in a different emotional country. It is a country that Agee does not dare to let his writer's voice visit too often. Such images are torn, as he sees it, from the ignominy and desolate solitude of maturity. Nothing inside him matured, Agee believes, at the rate of his sense of failure. Every source of adult pleasure—friendship, sex, drink, even conversation—had somehow to be accelerated in compensation for that. He therefore pursued them all, throughout his adult life, with a near-demonic, self-squandering compulsiveness.

Agee regarded his adult self as the doomed antithesis of the kind of forbearing love that his prose everywhere celebrates. As I previously suggested, he generally identifies this adult self with acquisitiveness and naked want: it is tormented, insatiable, constantly giving pain. (How does one "make do" with an abandoned "locust shell" for an identity?)

> " *Agee regarded his adult self as the doomed antithesis of the kind of forbearing love that his prose everywhere celebrates.*"

The half-completed wish in Agee's central fantasy is to get himself "all the way home." The "hitch" in this fantasy is that most of what he "knows" himself to be would be inadmissible there: not only in the sight of his family but, crucially, in his own sight as well. The tenant family experience has such immense private significance for Agee because in the Gudger dwelling he almost achieves the sense that he can go back home as a whole person. In the presence of these appallingly harmed individuals who have next to nothing that anyone would desire to take from them (what have they not already lost?), Agee's own clamorous needs are gradually stilled within him, and his ordinarily acutein him, and his ordinarily acute consciousness of isolation abates. In the magnificent dinner scene that is the emotional and moral climax of *Let Us Now Praise Famous Men,* Agee "discovers" himself seated at his own family's table once again after a long and bewildering absence, and allows himself—gently, gratefully—to be fed:

> To say, then, how as I sat between the close walls of this hallway, which opened upon wide night at either end, between these two somberly sleepy people in the soft smile of the light, eating from unsorted plates with tin-tasting implements the heavy, plain, traditional food which was spread before me, the feeling increased itself upon me that at the end of a wandering and seeking, so long it had begun before I was born, I had apprehended and now sat at rest in my own home, between two who were my brother and sister, yet less that than something else; these, the wife my age exactly, the husband four years older, seemed not other than my own parents, in whose patience I was so different, so diverged, so strange as I was; and all that surrounded me, that silently strove in through my senses and stretched me full, was familiar and dear to me as nothing else on earth, and as if well known in a deep past and long years lost; so that I could wish that all my chance life was in truth the betrayal, the curable delusion, that it seemed, and that this was my right home, right earth, right blood, to which I would never have true right.

It is with the hope of resuming this self-preserving family meal that Agee drafted his unfinished (and perhaps, given the impossible nature of its task, unfinishable) novel about his early childhood, *A Death in the Family*. The main subject of this book—his father's death by automobile accident when Agee was a child of six—taxes Agee's powers of accommodation to the limit at every point of its treatment. He is attempting to relive without rage, and on an imaginative plane of yielding acceptance and forgiveness, the most agonizing and insupportable event of his life. The loss of his father stands, in relation to the life-history that follows it, as the black page that has "marred all the rest." Mark Doty, in a valuable study of Agee's quest for selfhood, *Tell Me Who I Am* cites the following passage from Thomas Wolfe in order to establish, in the widest possible context, the meaning of Agee's search for his "lost father":

> the deepest search in life, it seemed to me, that thing that in one way or another was central to all living, was man's search to find a father, not merely the father of his flesh, not merely the lost father of his youth, but the image of strength and wisdom external to his need and superior to his hunger, to which the belief and power of his own life could be united.

The myriad tiny and large gaps of sympathy and understanding dividing the members of Agee's family during the various stages of the tragedy in *A Death in the Family* Agee endeavors to bridge or seal over by means of an incandescently empathetic language. These gaps, however, all pass into insignificance when set against the gaping chasm of the father's removal; the available sum of remembered or borrowed tenderness Agee draws upon cannot be made sufficient to cover that.

As I noted at the beginning of this discussion, Agee's language typically generates outsize images which the self tries to burrow into and inhabit bodily. When Agee feels himself received by the thing his words are imaging, he loses, if only fleetingly, all sense of inner impoverishment. One cannot be filled by what one sees and still be vacant. For Agee then there is a decisive difference between being in one's language and being in oneself. He regards the former as the condition of endless "entering in"; the latter is an involuntary exile, what Italo Svevo calls "one long shivering." Language, however, can be a reliable refuge and safeguard only if some part of it issues from a source outside the self—a purer region than anything the self knows in its own person and that does not partake of its contamination. As in the case of the "right home" he describes in *Let Us Now Praise Famous Men,* Agee "would never have true right" to his highest verbal gifts. Before he could proceed with a project as psychologically fraught with

danger as *A Death in the Family,* I would argue, it was essential for him to invoke an imaginative presence stronger in all ways than himself to be his language advocate. The ghost of Jay Follett (Agee's father), which is literally called into being in the novel to re-visit its former home in the early morning hours after Jay's death, beautifully fulfills this function. The language of memory in *A Death in the Family* is underwritten by the ghostly father, as though everything belonging to this book has been held in trust for his child until he was old enough to make honorable use of it. The peace and acceptance that the words of the novel try to release from the interstices of blank tragedy are emotions the father's spirit might wish to be found there, and it is by his light alone, Agee implies, that they can become visible to others.

The narrative perspective throughout the novel remains fixed in the space briefly occupied by the paternal apparition on its farewell visit to the Folletts: the space of a boundless, sympathetic hope, lacking all foreknowledge. Agee tries to reconstruct his childhood home as his father would like it to be remembered and attempts, as far as he able (without resorting to deliberate falsehood), to respect his father's parting wish that "all be well there" in his absence. Agee assigns no impressions or perceptions to his own surrogate (the child Rufus) that would prove a barrier to his father's immediate recognition of him.

"This is exactly where our conversation and shared activity broke off," Agee is implicitly saying. The self that he resurrects is well acquainted with solitude but not yet walled in by it. A fearful gentleness is still his instinctive response to things; his confusions do not breed cruelty, and they live at no great distance from his goodness. No act that the child Rufus has performed or contemplated as yet exceeds his father's capacity to understand and forgive. Agee struggles to rehabilitate an image of himself identical to that fixed in the still unbetrayed gaze his father turned toward him during their final evening walk home together—a gaze that "sealed their contract."

The almost unearthly purity and vulnerability Agee's language aspires to in *A Death in the Family* are meant to prevent father and son from breaking faith with each other a second time, even when death intervenes. "As long as I am able to write in this way about my father's life," Agee seems to be saying, "I have not totally abandoned my father in the place where death divided us. The part of me that knew you directly, father, and possessed your love (because of what I then was) is still there where you left it. Using the words that belong to both of us—formed, as they are, out of your generosity and my great need—we can go back and seek out the spot where we sat together in the dark for the last time, and it will be the same as it was on both sides."

After Jay's ghost leaves his house, one family member who sensed his presence surmised that he had come in grieving protest over the fact that "he had no time to adjust his mind and feelings" for his separation from his family. His life had been wrested away from him somehow, and he returns home in the vain, restless hope of being able to do something about it. He can do nothing for himself, of course, but he manages to bring his wife the assurance that he is no longer joined to the accident that killed him but rather "calm" and mysteriously "taken care of," and he blesses the lives of his sleeping children. The creation of Agee's book is best approached, I think, as an exactly parallel return visit; Agee, no less exiled than his father is, seeks to come back home for a timeless interval and reach out of his personal darkness to touch once more the lighted rooms where his family dwells. The few points of perfect family intersection can be brought so close together in this interval that "moments of solitude," as Sharon Cameron puts it, seem almost "the exception rather than the rule." Though powerless to save himself or to shift events from their appointed course, Agee magically weaves out of his own fear and sorrow an assurance for others in which a growing calm and love are powerfully visible.

There is a quietly building tension, however, in the child's attempts to fuse his purposes and sensibility with those of the departed father. At various points the desire for fusion moves disturbingly close to a desire for death. The atmosphere of gentleness and striving tenderness that mantles so much of the book's action is frequently strained, in ways the reader can feel, from being pressed so fiercely against the darkness it means to hold at bay. When the child Rufus listens to his mother singing "Go Tell Aunt Rhoda," he finds one phrase that he doesn't understand vaguely troubling, but he prefers not to ask what it means, "because although it sounded so gentle he was also sure that somewhere inside it there was something terrible to be afraid of *exactly because it sounded so gentle* (emphasis mine). The same paradox informs the image of the window in Jay's bedroom, where death softly implants its features: "He only saw the window, tenderly alight within, and the infinite dark leaning like water against its outer surface." Finally, in the central scene I have alluded to several times, where father and son sit together in contented silence midway through their walk home,

there is a root-acknowledgment of the kind of inner chasm that love's best effort can neither reduce nor succor: "although his father loved their home and loved all of them, he was more lonely than the contentment of this family love could help; that it even increased his loneliness, and made it hard for him not to be lonely."

One cannot easily avoid the suspicion that all of the book's rescued moments of calm and serenity have this at their base. The novel's calm is the painfully deceptive calm of the father's composed features as he lies in his coffin. Agee's habitual reluctance to relinquish things from his gaze is nowhere more in evidence than in his obsessive scrutiny of his father's face in death. A minute scar on his chin, whose presence the eye can barely detect, is the only mark of the accident that claimed his life. Agee (child and adult) traces the line of this scar countless times, as though in its hideous capacity to reassure, and in its innocence about its own dread meaning, it was like a word of warning forming inaudibly on his father's lips. The scar is all that divides the living from the dead, the father's warm, enveloping presence from the rigid but serene nullity of his absence. The young, open face that even in its last repose declares its connectedness to everything vital is somehow in permanent retreat from the child that comes to it, as always, for answers. It has withdrawn to where the eye can't follow, leaving behind the secure, seemingly protected bulk of the man's strength. It is this latter ground of vacated strength, this solid, formidable absence that Agee endeavors to occupy for the writing of *A Death in the Family*. Perhaps the incomplete wish secretly plotted in this book is the desire to exchange places with the dead father.

As the father stands, apparitionally, at death's tightening border and peers back longingly toward his missed life, the child Agee positions himself in the shadowy rooms of the living and gazes fixedly toward death. It is as though a terrible and unintelligible error has been committed in destroying the father rather than the son. The former's tremendous energy, strength, and joyful exuberance, after all, had nothing whatever to do with death, just as the child's ever increasing isolation and estrangement make a very small claim to life. In one of the lengthy insert sections of the narrative, Rufus, well in advance of his father's passing, is lovingly wooed by the "darkness" in his bedroom:

> Beneath his prostrate head, eternity opened. . . . And darkness, smiling, leaned ever more intimately inward upon him, laid open the huge, ragged mouth—
> [The boy screams for his father]

Child, child [says the voice of darkness] why do you betray me so?. . . . You know that you can never get away: you don't even want to get away.

But with that, the child was torn into two creatures, of whom one cried out for his father.

The "creature" who cried for his father is soon comforted by him. "The room opened full of gold, his father stepped through the door and closed it quietly." The "prostrate head" that had been pillowed by the gentle, hollow shadows of night feels its father's "strong" hand beneath it. The other "creature" of the passage, who remained silent, would presumably have been content to be devoured. Agee's father never knew this creature existed, but in fact, it was the part of his son that "grew" (all deformed) to manhood. The dream-logic of this episode, within the larger narrative context, is that Jay Follett, by rescuing his son from the darkness for which this son was fated (and already half-reconciled), somehow took the burden of the darkness upon himself and surrendered his life to it. Given the choice, his father would have done everything in his power to protect him. Can one be sure that he didn't go so far as to make a secret arrangement with an ironic god: his life to be sacrificed in place of his unworthy son's?

The passionate will to undo such an exchange lies behind the astonishing dream-sequence, which the editors of Agee's posthumously published manuscript could find no place for in the version of the novel that they assembled (Doty 106–110). The dream begins with an unnamed man (clearly Rufus as an adult) returning to Knoxville, where he sees a crowd of individuals (grown-up versions of the schoolboys who sadistically taunted Rufus en route to school?) "doing some terrible piece of violence" to a man lying upon the ground. (Initially he is referred to as John the Baptist but he quickly turns into Jay Follett.) "The pit of his (the Agee surrogate's) stomach went cold, yet now he felt really at home." He fully expects the hostile crowd to cease punishing the man on the ground and direct its fury against him instead: "—that's all right to(o). Not just exactly, but the way it was meant to be . . . it was not his business to try to alter fate." Instead of attacking him, however, the crowd disperses. Agee's surrogate, who is filled with compassion at the sight of this "brave," stricken man, first cradles him "like a baby," then lifts him on his back and proceeds to carry him through the city streets. The destination for this walk, eerily, is the corner where Agee and his father sat together during their final walk—a large rock "under a stray tree." In the course of the journey, the body

proceeds to decompose and stink. It finally proves such an unendurable weight that the son can no longer carry it properly: "He is filled with shame. He found the body had sagged clumsily during his carelessness, and he readjusted his hold, to carry it more decently." At last he is obliged to drag the body along the pavement like a sled. "It's a hell of a way to treat anyone, but it'll have to do." When he arrives at his destination, he feels a flinching deep within him compounded equally of "tenderness, melancholy, and joy" at the realization that the place is exactly as he remembered it: ". . . the same tree even, and the tree had not even grown an inch. So shabby and sad; it had been waiting there all this time, and it had never changed, not a bit." Agee's persona imagines that the tree "aloofly" welcomes him: "Well. So you came back?" The completion of the trip, however, does not revive the dead father. By his manner of jerking the body over the curb, the son causes his father's head to be severed from its body, and as the dream concludes, the head inwardly contracts "like a jellyfish or an armadillo."

In this most extreme version of the half-completed wish, Agee is allowed both to go back home as a man and to carry his father with him, but there is no release from his psychic burden upon his arrival. Father and son clearly achieve a monstrous partial fusion here; at every stage of the dream Agee appears to be both inside and outside himself simultaneously, and one has the continual sense of a dizzying interpenetration of identities. The boundary lines firmly separating "what is his" from "what is mine" have completely collapsed, so even the landscape is empowered to take on aspects of both free-floating selves. The tree at the corner, for example, is not only the father and son's shared image of the past, perfectly preserved, but also the betrayed father reproving his son for having abandoned him ("Well. So you came back"), as well as the starveling child, who has never entered maturity ("the tree had not even grown an inch. So shabby and sad"). The rotting body that the son tries so "carefully" to preserve as he carries and pulls it through the streets is at once the weight of his father's life, which the son must carry in his absence, and the horribly befouled remains of his father's "hopes" for his son's own life. (Whenever you dishonor yourself, you dishonor me.) The body is principally identified with Agee's private shame and disgrace by the time he gives it the violent yank that decapitates it. Yet there is also a helpless, guilty anger brought on by the son's uncertainty about what his father expects of him. The father is

Oxford-Bellevue Ferry carrying cars across the Tred Avon River on Maryland's eastern shore

© Paul A. Souders/Corbis

looking for things in his son that the son could never be after the father abandoned him. (All personal strength—perhaps the very idea of strength—died with Jay Follett.)

The arduous journey home is, of course, an attempt to stave off a catastrophe that has already happened, that even now crushes the weak son under its weight. If his father is still miraculously waiting for him at their secret meeting place, he will not have to die this time. The son's thoroughly disintegrated, inwardly festering life can be buried in his father's place. This suppressed emotional core of *A Death in the Family* is engendered out of the same impossible confinement in familial love that produced Emily's cry of anguish during her failed return to earth in *Our Town*. The innumerable imaginative concessions that Agee makes to his father's vision of family reality—the channelling of all his rage and grief into a vocabulary of love-drenched sympathy—cannot entirely subdue the terrible ache of protest forming within. In the sudden, overwhelming bareness of the stage in *Our Town,* or on the equally bare stage of Agee's nightmare (his memory drained for once of those shimmering images where it is usually possible for him to take cover), we enter a condition of utter

exposure to each writer's family solitude. Here the compensating force and aspiration of nostalgic desire ("finding ourselves not in the world we love, but knowing how deeply we love it, enjoying some conviction that we will return, or discover it, or discover the way to it") yields no shelter or protection (Cheever 158). "The pit of his stomach went cold," Agee tells us, "yet now he felt really at home."

Source: George Toles, "'Practically an American Home': James Agee's Family Solitudes," in *Southern Literary Journal*, Vol. XXV, No. 2, Spring 1993, pp. 39–56.

Victor A. Kramer

In the following essay excerpt, Kramer discusses Agee's recollection of a simpler more rural past being encroached upon by an urban future in A Death in the Family.

II

As Agee was first planning *A Death* it appears that he wanted to rely upon a technique similar to that employed in *Famous Men*. That is, he would write only what he could remember. This is especially true of the opening and closing sections of the book and the interchapter materials, which fall outside the main chronological sequence. But this

> The central theme of Agee's book is domestic love—a subject that seems particularly unpromising for a novelist in the middle part of the twentieth century."

novel also developed out of a larger conflict; in a fundamental way it was Agee's mode of simultaneously remembering the past and getting away from the horrors of the present. He wrote much of the text that became this novel in the late 1940s, a time when he was especially disturbed by the use of the atomic bomb as well as the problem of how individuals can survive in a mass society. Both "Dedication Day" and "Scientists and Tramps" are from this period. In "1928 Story," written at approximately the same time as *A Death* was begun, Agee begins by outlining the disappointment and frustration his speaker feels in not having written as much, or as well, as he might have. In "1928 Story" such statements flow into a remembrance of earlier times, and the speaker is able to catch the beauty (and awkwardness) of earlier moments.

In *A Death in the Family* Agee also took very simple events from his childhood and then allowed his imagination to play over them. Some parts of his remembrance are therefore chronologically months or years in advance of the father's death. With such reference points it was possible for him to reconstruct the domestic love that enveloped the young Rufus, a love that combined country and city attitudes.

Agee was only six years old when his father died; thus while his book is definitely written to honor his father, it is also an attempt to catch a moment then three decades in the past. As Agee matured, he came to realize that particular events and places in his childhood neighborhood had been experienced both by him and his father. For instance, the railroad viaduct, which today still bridges the valley between the business center of Knoxville and residential areas, was a specific place that Agee associated with his father. The bridge is very carefully described in the fictional account of Rufus and Jay, and the description reveals the method of the

entire book. Details about the remembered past are evoked through careful attention to the "dignity of actuality." Rufus recalls how "Whenever they walked downtown and walked back home, in the evenings, they always began to walk more slowly, from about the middle of the viaduct, and as they came near [their] corner they walked more slowly still, but with purpose. . . ." Through this specific attention to details of place, such a passage suggests how Rufus intuitively sensed the homesickness of his father.

Readers of this novel, usually first recall the sketch "Knoxville: Summer of 1915," which was chosen by David McDowell as an opening for the book. Its dominant tone is one of nostalgia for an earlier quiet time; and it, as already suggested, is one of several autobiographical or reminiscent pieces about Tennessee that were written in the 1930s. Another is an experimental poem, entitled In Memory of My Father, in which some of the same imagery employed in the novel is used; the poetic remembrance of a small child, going to sleep and comforted by the parent, is an image suggesting all children in similar circumstances. Agee's 1936 sketch, "Knoxville: Summer of 1915," similarly does an economical job of evoking an atmosphere like that which Rufus and his father enjoy, such as at the beginning of the novel when they go to the movies and later walk home together. In the "Knoxville" sketch, inserted as an introduction, a time of harmony with nature is imagined: the cities' noises are blended with natural ones. But the mood that actually generated the novel is evident in an excluded passage that I have edited and entitled "Dream Sequence." This is the real introduction to the novel. In it the tension between country and city is clearly evident. Edited nine years after the novel's publication, Agee's "Dream" begins as nightmare and suggests that only through a work of art can any lasting harmony be achieved. It is necessary for the artist first to exorcise the nightmare of urban life if the peacefulness of a remembrance like *A Death in the Family* is to be created.

"Dream Sequence" is a sketch recording the nightmare of a narrator (very much like Agee) who recalls how he found himself on a crowded city street—perhaps New York, perhaps Chattanooga—but then obviously Knoxville: "The town had certainly changed. It wasn't as he remembered it from childhood, nor did he like its looks as well as his memories of it . . . Even the heat and sunlight of the weather was different, it was the weather of a bigger, worse, more proud and foolish city . . . " The narrator then relates how he saw a group of people doing something horrible to someone, and upon approaching that crowd he knew the figure was John the Baptist and that he was being stoned. The narrator decided a proper burial was in order, and he began that chore. He began pulling the corpse down the sweltering and then freezing streets—symbolism that suggests the passing of years. And as time passed, the terrain became more and more familiar. In both this "Dream" and in the opening section of the novel, Agee recalls the outcroppings of limestone common to the landscape of Knoxville. A visitor to Agee's old neighborhood in Knoxville would notice the same outcroppings today.

Two things become clearer to Agee's dreamer. First, he was getting closer to his old childhood neighborhood, and this was the atmosphere he and his father used to enjoy in their privacy late at night: "The corner was where he used to sit with his father and it was there of all times and places that he had known his father loved him . . . and his father had come out of the wilderness." And secondly, if the man was John the Baptist, he was somehow also the narrator's father, and he, the Christ, had failed his father. The question is how that failure could be (at least partially) rectified. The answer is to go back into those years, by way of a work of art, and to do honor to the memory of the father by evoking as much of those times as possible. This became the basic method, and accomplishment, of Agee's novel. To remember, or to infer, as much as possible, and thereby through art to impose order upon the chaos of life, its disruptions and its memories.

The last pages of the "Dream Sequence" possess a calmness similar to the opening of the book. Agee's return to the calmness of his childhood, interrupted by the father's death, is made, therefore, by way of the horrors of contemporary life, an urban life symbolized by a maddened crowd. Agee's homage to this father, then, seems to be both a recapitulation of what he remembered and a symbolic statement about all who are drawn to the city.

There is both terror and a large amount of nostalgia in what Agee decided to write about, yet it is only through nostalgia that it is possible for a writer of fiction to achieve a perspective adequate for such a vision of how rural and urban forces were once in conjunction to form particular moments of domestic love. Agee wanted to do honor to that earlier time. To do so, his memory became as important as his imagination. It is significant to observe that throughout the manuscript for this novel the names of real persons are consistently used. The same is true of much of the manuscript for *The Morning Watch* and *Let Us Now Praise Famous Men.*

Agee wrote in one of the working notes for *A Death in the Family* that Jay, the father, was a "victim of progress." One of the variant sections for the book is a discussion between the parents about the dangers of purchasing an automobile. What better symbol, we might ask, is there for the fragmentation of family? A particular marriage and its love provided an atmosphere for Rufus; and the inference is clearly suggested that the child drew upon the earlier time when rural forces, and the presence of the father, were being blended with city life. Agee and modern American culture and modern Americans, however, seem largely to have lost the strength to be gained from such a blending.

Clearly there is the possibility that, had Agee lived to complete his novel, he would have written more sections stressing his autobiographical remembrances of both country and city. One such excluded section is a two-page sequence in which Rufus recalls how his father used to spit in the fireplace—much to the horror of the mother. After she had instructed Jay not to do such a thing in front of Rufus, Rufus continued to observe Jay doing it, but only when the mother was absent.

When Rufus is in the presence of either of his parents, or when he thinks about them, Agee stresses the contrast between them, yet also their contribution of qualities that make the child's world secure. One section of the novel is, appropriately, a stream-of-consciousness monologue in which the child muses about the differences he senses between his parents: "She wore dresses, his father wore pants. Pants were what he wore too, but they were short and soft." Similar passages are incorporated throughout the text.

It is the combination of mother and father, with their differing attitudes, that allows Rufus to feel at ease. Rufus remembers a motoring trip to visit the father's relatives: *"After the dinner the babies and all the children except Rufus were laid out on the beds to take their naps, and his mother thought that he ought to lie down too, but his father said no, why did he need to, so he was allowed to stay up."* Similarly, when Rufus is first introduced to his great-great-grandmother, and he kisses her, the mother voices concern and his father says "Let her be." Jay will have Rufus experience as much of the diverse world as possible, and he tries not to be overly protective. In another episode Aunt Hannah senses that the cap Rufus wants is correct for a boy who wants to be grown up. A year earlier Rufus had asked his mother for a cap but suffered a rebuff when she refused. We can understand with Rufus that, if Jay took him shopping, "his father wouldn't mind" if he had such a cap, even though his mother "wouldn't want him to have a cap, yet." Hannah reflects that "Mary would have conniption fits" over Rufus's choice, but "Jay wouldn't mind."

In a related way, during the opening pages of the novel when Jay and Rufus are getting ready to go see a Chaplin movie, Jay enjoys asking "What's wrong with [Charlie]?" "not because he didn't know what she would say, but so she would say it." And then when Rufus and his father go, ritualistically, to the movies they feel all the more enclosed in each others' presence. This fictional father is somewhat rough, a bit coarse, and country. But the boy's mother seems overly genteel; and going to the movies is an escape from her for both father and son. On the walk home Jay stops off at a saloon looking for friends from his home area in the mountains. This is, perhaps, one of the most poignant scenes in the novel because the saloon is both a meeting place and a reminder of the inevitability that the rural connections of the past are impossible to maintain. The many hints throughout this text about Jay's alcoholism (by inference a commentary on Agee's own drinking problems) are another way of commenting on the difficulty of adulthood and change.

Rufus senses that he needs and will need both parents, but he is without such abstract knowledge. Agee, looking back over his own life and his remembrance of those years, also saw the need for the balance provided by both parents and their traditions. Therefore, the picture we are given of Rufus's parents frequently combines their best qualities. Where this is most apparent is the contrast in the scenes where Jay and Mary, separately, sing to Rufus. Jay loved to sing the old country songs that he remembered from childhood. Rufus also realized that sometimes his father joked by talking like a "darky," and "*the way he sang was like a darky too, only when he sang he wasn't joking*." Rufus also remembered how his parents sang together and how beautifully his mother's clear voice combined with Jay's, yet he also sensed that when she tried to sound like a country singer she could not do it. Rufus "liked both ways very much and best of all when they sang together and he was there with them, . . ." yet he is suddenly separated from such experience when his father is killed and the boy is thus doomed to his mother's dominant influence.

Throughout the novel it is implied that Jay has accommodated himself to living in the city. The passage describing his journey to his own father's sick bed, the very trip that ironically leads to his death, points up how he must have often felt about aspects of the city. "The city thinned out," Agee wrote, and for a few minutes Jay drove through

the darkened evidences of that kind of flea-bitten semi-rurality which always peculiarly depressed him: mean little homes, and others inexplicably new and substantial, set too close together for any satisfying rural privacy or use, too far, too shapelessly apart to have adherence ["coherence" in pencil manuscript] as any kind of community; mean little pieces of ill-cultivated land behind them, and alongside the road, between them, trash and slash and broken sheds and rained-out billboards. . . .

This is the same kind of feeling almost everyone experiences (unconsciously perhaps) as movement from urban to rural is experienced. Such a feeling would have been all the more acute if a rural background were one's origin. Then, it might seem, material progress and faith in institutions—whether governmental or religious—might be increasingly difficult to accept. Seventy years ago, when Agee's father was in his middle thirties, it would have clearly been an even more poignant feeling, and this is what Agee seeks to evoke.

It is also made clear that Agee's fictional family was in the habit of going into the country for Sunday drives. The ferryman who takes Jay across the river recognizes him: "You generally always come o' Sunday's, year womurn, couple o'young-guns," and Jay answers with a monosyllabic reply reflecting his country ties: "Yeahp." Jay's wife also clearly senses that Jay feels most comfortable in the country; and when she prepares Jay's breakfast in the early morning of his departure, she does it the way she imagines a mountain woman might.

Another revealing interchange between spouses about family and change occurs in the novel during one of the family trips to visit relatives. On that particular Sunday the parents attempt to figure out how old the great-great-grandmother might be, and Mary comments "*—why she's almost as old as the country, Jay*." Jay's reply suggests an enormous amount about how the parents think. He immediately meditates on the natural world—the geological fact of the mountains; but the mother thinks of the nation's government. Dealing in abstract concepts is not Jay's ordinary mode of thought. He deals more immediately with the concrete, and it is for such reasons that he enjoys being with Rufus and singing old songs. There are many manuscript variants from the section about singing that demonstrate Agee's fascination and interest in this subject. During one of his evenings of song Jay recalls how his own mother used to sing to him (and how those times are gone), yet how through one's children they can be repeated, at least a little bit: "Just one way, you do get back home. You have a boy or a girl of your own and now and then you remember, and you know how they feel. . . ."

III

There is yet another way to "get back home," and that is the artist's. In one of the working notes for the novel Agee recalled that on one of the mornings surrounding his father's funeral he and his sister were taught how to read the comics—arms just so, legs up, and bellies on the floor, and he added a comment that such actions implied archetypal actions performed by those unaware of what they were doing. Agee's entire fictionalization is archetypal in this manner. Thus various parts of this book work similarly to suggest either the fragmentation of family or the loss of rural virtues. A motif buried in this text, yet referred to regularly in the working notes, is Agee's fascination with Rufus's inability to fight and Jay's subsequent embarrassment about this lack. The scene about the child's wandering the Knoxville streets the morning after his father's death symbolically enacts what all must feel in such situations. In this sense Agee's concerns are archetypal. His novel is a meditation about a wider pattern of all fathers absorbed by the city, then senselessly killed, with their families then accordingly destined to be formed in their absence.

The central theme of Agee's book is domestic love—a subject that seems particularly unpromising for a novelist in the middle part of the twentieth century. But delicate domestic love, which has been experienced by millions and millions of families, is what holds Agee's remembrance together. The family has always provided comfort and nurture, but in a society like today's, the family seems best described by Henry Adams in his delineation of the centrifugal forces generated by the society. Family members spin away from each other as external activities become more pronounced. However, each action and gesture of love is unique, and as these, individual acts are performed, they have value within a unique framework. It was such a realization, along with the conviction that city forces were becoming stronger, that must have prompted Agee to "go back into those years."

Source: Victor A. Kramer, "Urban and Rural Balance in *A Death in the Family*," in *James Agee: Reconsiderations*, edited by Michael A. Lofaro, University of Tennessee Press, 1992, pp. 104–18.

Eugene T. Carroll

In the following essay excerpt, Carroll describes the poetic landscapes and symphonic structures Agee creates in A Death in the Family.

A Death in the Family, by and large, demonstrates Agee's strong and gifted sense of symphonic form, not only in the poetic and imagistic movements of each of the parts but in the interplay between sets of characters who, as Concannon points out, "move together and apart in a dance-like rhythm of dialogue and introspection." In Part 1, Rufus is not always sure of his father in their duet of men's night out, i.e., the Chaplin film; the bar scene (where there is no music), and the nightscape of Knoxville. Agee's landscape at night details in duet the innocence of memory, Rufus in concert with his father, every sound recorded: "Deep in the valley an engine coughed and browsed; couplings settled their long chains, and the empty cars sounded like broken drums" or "Sometimes on these evenings his father would hum a little and the humming would break open into a word or two, but he never finished a part of a tune, for silence was even more pleasurable. . . ." The warm dark night is interrupted only twice for quick glimpses of Agee's perennial memory, momentary flashes of "the odd, shaky light of Market Square," and incongruity of life and picture: "A dark-faced man leaned against the white brick wall, gnawing a turnip; he looked at them with sad, pale eyes, . . . and Rufus, turning, saw how he looked sorrowfully, somewhat dangerously, after them." A moment later, Jay and Rufus pass a wagon with a large sleeping family and a woman wearing a sunbonnet: "Rufus's father averted his eyes and touched his straw hat slightly; and Rufus, looking back, saw how her dead eyes kept looking gently ahead of her." Even later, the father and the son, the duet of love and contentment, sit on a rock above North Knoxville: "Where were no words, or even ideas, or formed emotions, of the kind that have been suggested here, no more in the man than in the boy child." Agee builds image upon image of "dark night," interlocking the time frames of his father's last evening of life and Rufus's own feelings of security and trust despite the sadness of the "dark-faced" man and the "dead eyes" of the woman near the wagon. The first chapter ends, Rewak points out, as the father and the son walk in silence, "the rest of the way home," and the last chapter will end as Rufus and Andrew walk "all the way home." "Between these two events," Rewak concludes, "Agee has built around the word, 'home,' the connotations of peace and strength but also death and fear."

" As theme and counter-theme, life and death move slowly or rapidly through the sensibilities of these characters or their responses to their day and to each other."

In the second chapter of Part 1, Agee shifts, with poetic and musical skill, to the relationship between husband and wife, Jay and Mary, as the former prepares to leave in the middle of the night to visit his ailing father. Their "domestic particulars" are both comedic and serious; Mary is prudish and overly religious while Jay, not always successful in the "verities" of home and family, tries to remember what to do outwardly, "Bring your *shoes*—to the kitchen," and inwardly, so as not to awaken the children. Mary, the wife and mother, the epitome of domesticity, symbolizes a part of the Follet family's strong belief in warmth and strength. Jay prepares to leave the bedroom when he turns to look at the unmade bed: "Well, he thought, I can do something for her. . . . He drew the covers up to keep the warmth, then laid them open a few inches, so it would look inviting to get into." His movement is nostalgic, remembering sensitive and husbandly details: things, little things that mean so much. Mary's breakfast for Jay is large today: eggs, bacon, pancakes, and coffee. Jay returns the favor by heating warm milk, an image to be repeated in later chapters: "She poured the white, softly steaming milk into a thick, white cup and sat down with it. . . . Because of the strangeness of the hour and the abrupt destruction of sleep, the necessity for action and its interruptive minutiae, the gravity of his errand and a kind of weary exhilaration, both of them found it peculiarly hard to talk, though both particularly wanted to." Now as Jay prepares to leave, Mary "remembers" a new clean pocket handkerchief; the couple walks to the edge of the porch, where "deep in the end of the back yard, the blossoming peach tree shone like a celestial sentinel," and they struggle with departure in their goodbyes. Even the customary morning rhyme is "remembered" but not sung: "Goodby, John, don't stay long / I'll be back in a week or two."

Agee, in the next several chapters, enlarges on the fundamental character and personalities of Jay, Ralph (his brother), and Mary as they react to their own particularly interior landscapes, a blending of picture and tone. Jay drives from the warmth of his hearth to the black unknown ahead of him as he leaves Knoxville behind: "Along his right were dark vacant lots, pale billboards, the darker blocks of small sleeping buildings, an occasional light," to "that kind of flea-bitten rurality" with "mean little homes . . . mean little pieces of ill-cultivated land behind them," and a "late, late streetcar, no passengers aboard, far out near the end of its run." After his encounter with the ferryman, who, like Charon, gives him a final ride across the river, he finds that the land becomes more familiar, "real, old, deep country now. Home country." The simplicity of life, the landscape of "place" is here at home, "where he felt much more deeply at leisure as he watched the flowing, freshly lighted country; and quite consciously he drove a little faster than before."

Mary's landscape, on the other hand, is one of guilt or religiosity, symbolized by the "white" sleep. Her concern centers not so much on her husband's leaving but on her unspoken and sometimes unconscious feelings about her father-in-law because "everyone forgave him so much and liked him so well in spite of his shortcomings . . . a kind of weakness which took advantage and heaped disadvantage and burden on others." If the call in the night concerned her mother-in-law, Mary would have felt differently. She turns to prayer, when "I almost *wished* for his death!" and she immediately reverts to her religious scruples, praying for help and understanding for herself, her father-in-law, and her husband. Her landscape, unsettled at times, is peopled, though, with the intimate and loving associates of family, Jay, Rufus, her daughter Catherine, and Aunt Hannah: "I must just: trust in God. . . . Just do His will, and put all my trust in Him." The "stream of whiteness" breaks as she awakens to another day: "A streetcar passed: Catherine cried."

Ralph's landscape is one of self-pity and the bottle, and while Agee paints a dismal picture of a man incapable of giving or even feeling love, he never condemns him, only letting the color and odor of irresponsibility, self-destruction and helplessness strongly stand out. When Ralph approached his mother to show his affection for her, she turned away, knowing that "he was beseeching comfort rather than bringing it." Agee's Ralph is a pathetic character, reeking of booze and self-pity, a slobbering figure of a man, fat, disgusting, and uninteresting to all, including his wife. A one-dimensional human, Ralph contrasts sharply with Jay and almost any other man in his narrow frame of reference; even the house hand, Tom Oaks, can ask the mother if he is needed and to call if she wants anything. Ralph's shame borders on self-hatred, and his landscape, like a wild, erratic storm, defeats him constantly. When one of life's strongest and most inevitable tests come to his family, "one of the times in a man's life when he is needed and can be some good, just by being a man," Ralph fails and ends up as a weakling.

In the fifth, sixth, and seventh chapters of Part 1, Agee begins to escalate the whole thematic structure of the novel into small, delicate, comedic or serious moments, exquisite scenes of "standing time." Moods become like movements of a symphonic piece—some slow, some fast, some moderate in tone with flowing, endless themes and counterthemes. Some of the scenes bring the human spirit back into focus; others show grim turns of grief and loss, and still others extend more understanding and peace. In the fifth chapter, for example, Rufus, when told by his mother of the possibility that his grandfather might die, comes to grips, momentarily, with what a loss is all about and equates the possible passing of his grandfather with the death of his cat: "Mama," Rufus said, "when Oliver went to sleep, did he wake up in heaven too"? Mary, startled but always straitlaced, and always relying on what the church teaches about death, fends Rufus off with meaningless adult answers that center, first, upon the anxiety that the children should finish breakfast and prepare for school, and second, with the repetitious "I don't know." Within the purest realm of child-like reasoning, Rufus satisfied himself about who gets into heaven in the case of the rabbits who were bloodied to death by the dogs: "Why did God let the dogs in"? Mary, agitated but resigned, replies, "We mustn't trouble ourselves with these things we can't understand. We just have to be sure that God knows best." Rufus plays the comedic and unexpected role: "I bet they sneaked in when He wasn't looking. . . . Cause He sure wouldn't have let them in if He'd been there. Didn't they Mama? Didn't they"? Mary once again retreats to the church's stand, this time speaking theologically of good or evil and God or the devil, playing a rapid-fire but unwieldy exchange with Rufus, whose only repeated words are "what" or "why." She opens with the word "tempts"; he seizes onto that word and asks: "What's tempt?" She hesitates and says: "the Devil tempts us when there is something we want to do, but we know it is bad." Rufus continues the momentum: "Why does God let us do bad things?" Mary: "Because He wants us to make up

our own minds." "Why" is the continually drumming word for Rufus, but finally the dialogue ends with Mary's carefully spaced words, which are intended to be emphatic: "God—doesn't—believe—in—the—easy—way." Catherine, innocent and wide-eyed through the exchange, injects another comedic touch: "Like hide-and-go-seek." Rufus, agitated and angry, blusters at her: "God doesn't fool around playing games, does He, Mama! Does He! Does He!" Rufus, unbowed by his mother's defense of his sister but aware that he must apologize for unbecoming behavior, says unwittingly: "I *am* sorry, Catherine. . . . Honest to goodness I am. Because you're a little, *little* girl. . . ." Not realizing what he had just said and how it affected Catherine, Rufus is sent "brusquely" off to school.

Agee's women, like Mary and little Catherine, symbolize a sense of gentility, the love and respect for home and "place," but more than any other characteristic, they instinctively and successfully balance the need for the virtues of faith, hope, love, and even reserve, to be alive and vibrant. Mary, for example, is patient and giving, and unlike Jay, she demonstrates an interior of self-restraint. Those attributes become more apparent in another scene, when Rufus (Agee) accepts an invitaton to go shopping with Mary's Aunt Hannah, whom Rewak calls "the strongest character in the book." Mary and Hannah are much alike, at this point, and although the aunt is older and wiser, her feelings toward her niece are from a completely interior point of view and never spoken. When Hannah asks Mary if Rufus would like to go shopping with her, Mary's tone in return is reserved and hesitant. Hannah is "tempted to tell her not to make up children's minds for them but held onto herself. . . ."

In the afternoon, when the two leave for the shopping tour, the streetcar carries them to Gay Street and the stores. Once inside, Rufus pays little attention to what his great-aunt is doing or saying; he focuses instead on "the clashing, banging wire baskets which hastened along on little trolleys, high above them all, bearing to and fro wrapped and unwrapped merchandise, and hard leather cylinders full of money." The contrast between the two sharpens vividly when Hannah asks Rufus if he would like a new cap; as they move to men's furnishings, Hannah's eyes fall on "a genteel dark serge with the all but invisible visor, which she was sure would please Mary, . . ." but Rufus's senses were "set on a thunderous fleecy check in jade green, canary yellow, black and white, which stuck out inches to either side above his ears and had a great scoop of visor beneath which his face was all but lost." Aunt

Hannah thinks of the reaction from Mary, perhaps even Jay, and certainly the boys on the block, but she refrains from comment; Rufus likes the cap and she buys it. Agee's treatment of Aunt Hannah is one of respect for age, wisdom, and strength of character. She personifies a two-tiered dimension of womanhood: first, in elegance, graciousness, beauty, and a love of "remembrance," and second, in the awareness of the youth and vigor of the generations behind her. Agee's keen wit about Hannah is apparent with a reference to her "pouring gravely through an issue of 'The Nations.'"

As theme and counter-theme, life and death move slowly or rapidly through the sensibilities of these characters or their responses to their day and to each other. The interpolated prose-poems after chapter 7 support a different tonality, the overwhelming memories of Rufus as a child with loving parents nearby. Ohlin, writing of these memories, argues: "The long lyrical section describing Rufus's fear of the dark goes so far beyond anything that could possibly be characterized as the child's awareness that it becomes, in effect, expressive of Agee's effort to move inside the experience rather than of the experience itself." Rufus fears the blackness and the premonition of the death that will shortly take place; in this nightmare of time, unlike the peace and tranquility of "Knoxville," Rufus, as an infant in a crib, can see and hear "a serpent shape" on the wallpaper or voices like locusts that "cared nothing for him" before Jay came in to quiet him. Rufus "remembers" Jackie, the cloth dog, and remembers his father singing familiar songs, some old, some popular: "Frog he would a wooin' go un-hooooo," "I got a gallon on a sugarbabe too," or "Google Eyes," and the old and loving spiritual, "Git on board, little children." Mary also sang softer and more maternal songs to Rufus, perhaps because she was pregnant with Catherine. He liked "Sleep, baby sleep," "Go tell Aunt Rhoda," but especially, "Swing low, sweet cherryut," sung either by his father or mother; the reflection is on home, the meaning of home, the journey of life to death, and is summed up in "Comin' for to care me home." Agee's mood and tone, like that of Thomas Wolfe, his sonorities of sound in music, of distance and nearness, of simplicity and complexity, reverberate in: "How far we all come. How far we all come away from ourselves . . . you can never go home again. You can go home, it's good to go home, but you never really get all the way home again in your life."

Agee's sensitive perceptions of his father reflect the strongest kinds of images of Jay (100–101), with detailed precision of what he wore—for example, "hard" pants, "hard" coats, "hard" celluloid collars, and "hard" buttons on a vest; or of the smells associated with maleness—i.e., "dry grass, leather and tobacco"; or of the case of a big mustache, not particularly enjoyed by Mary. When Jay was talking about the "mush'tash," "he was joking, talking like a darky. He liked to talk darky talk and the way he sang was like a darky too, only when he sang he wasn't joking." Rufus, too, becomes reacquainted with a "darky" or "colored" in a scene with Victoria, black Victoria, who had taken care of him when he was born; now that Mary is about to give birth to Catherine, she reemerges to take him to his "Granma's." Mary cautions Rufus not to refer to her color or her "smell"; Rufus, throwing caution to the wind, asks directly: "Why is your skin so dark," and Victoria answers: "Just because that was the way God made me." Against the background of a "yellow streetcar," Victoria reminds Rufus that he should be more careful about asking a "colored" why her skin is dark, but adds lovingly: "You make me feel happy . . . I missed you terribly, honey." Agee's finely tuned senses, like the mechanics of the streetcar, move the experiential memories beyond the darkness and the light and signal life as is was in another time and death as it is to be.

In Part 2, the daily lives of Mary, Andrew (her brother), and Aunt Hannah, in particular, and others in general, come to an abrupt halt as Jay's death becomes a part of their sensibilities. Mary sends her brother to find out if Jay is injured or dead, and in the meantime she prepares the downstairs bedroom for what may be a long convalescence, brings "clean sheets and pillowcases" to the bed, plumping and smoothing the pillows, bringing out the bedpan and the thermometer, replacing the guest towels, every action designed to relieve the tension, and finally, falling down on her knees, to utter the words of the Cross she knows so well: "O God if it be Thy will." With Hannah at her side, Mary begins her long vigil of faith and hope, small talk, and tea as the symbol of warmth. Time, as a measure of day and night, disappears; conversation becomes inactive, and silence pervades as the two women wait and wait and wait. "Mary did not speak, and Hannah could not think of a word to say. It was absurd, she realized, but along with everything else, she felt almost of a kind of social embarrassment about her speechlessness." Hannah, thirty years ago, lost and grieved as Mary would tonight. The women pray an alternate litany for God's forgiveness and quietly say the "Our Father." The rhythms of life have closed down, and with every tick of the clock and Andrew's absence or lack of a phone call, death is no longer a possibility but a truth.

Finally, after long hours of waiting, Andrew brings the fatal news to the waiting women, and Mary, alone now as a widow, says in a small voice: "I want whiskey," to preserve a closeness, a last bond with Jay: "I want it just as strong as I can stand it." Andrew, in concert with Mary, plays his double role as loving brother and uneasy messenger with honesty and devotion. The other members quickly come to the house, Mary's father offering philosophical words for her sorrow and loss: "Just spunk won't be enough; you've got to have gumption." The family hears details of the accident and death for their needs and knowledge. Andrew—as Rewak writes, "perhaps the most likeable person in the book, for he is always entirely honest with his feelings"—calls Ralph to inform him of Jay's death. With significant irony, Ralph's conversation is never heard and barely reported; Andrew's comments afterwards, though, are clear: "Talking to that fool is like trying to put socks on an octopus."

In the middle of their grieving process, the family members become very much aware of a "presence" in the house, each one coming to a feeling of someone "never for an instant in one place. It was in the next room, it was in the kitchen, it was in the dining room." In guarded seconds with Andrew, Mary shows her intensity about his death: "it simply felt like Jay . . . I just mean it felt like his presence." Later, as they listen for additional sounds, Mary remarks that Jay has gone to see the children in their bedroom for the last time. She feels his "presence" in the room, "of his strength, of virility, of helplessness, and of pure calm." He leaves, as he came, quietly and with his duty done, and Mary accepts her loss: "God help me to *realize* it." The family members resume their grief individually and collectively and then leave; Andrew, the family poet, reflects on God's order of life, Jay's death, and his own personal sense of loss. In the early morning hours, walking home, he "remembers" the words of the hymn, *above thy deep and dreamless sleep, the silent stars go by.* In past years, those words were ones of comfort, but now death interrupts, and his belief in people, in his own continuity, in the justice and mercy of God and in his own hard wish to know God, are shattered. In the house, meantime, Mary and Hannah go to bed, and latter's heart and mind empty and heavy, the former accepting the finality of Jay's death and her own faith in God: "Thy will be done."

In the last three interludes before Part 3, Agee's mirror to the past illuminates, in the first scene, the powerful struggle of Rufus to accommodate other boys from the street and the neighborhood, some young, some older, as friends in his life. He sees these boys, either "cocksure" of themselves or attentive, smiling, and curious, as companions growing up. At times they show contempt and amusement as they use his name in a chorus ditty: "Uh-Rufus, Uh-Rastus, Uh-Johnson, Uh-Brown / uh-What ya gonna do when the rent comes round?" Bewildered and hurt, he asks his parents about his name, and Mary replies that, while the "colored" people use the name, "it was your great-grandfather Lynch's and it's a name to be proud of." Rufus is not convinced altogether, but his identity and position with the boys is partially solved when he sings for them in his own childlike fashion: "I'm a little busy bee, busy bee, busy bee, / I'm a little busy bee, singing in the clover." As he dances and sings he watches the faces of the boys, the older ones "restrained and smiling," the middle-sized boys with faces of "contempt." In the second scene, more in association with Agee's sensibilities, the countryside provides pastoral beauty. The family is driving into the back country, the deep, hill country, a timeless place with its history but very little present. The central figure is Rufus's great-great-grandmother, whose longevity, as Coles writes, "is beyond any meaning of age most of us know. . . ." Agee's description is a composite of mood, picture, tone, color, and rhythm of words, "white bone and black vein . . . brown-splotched skin, the wrinkled knuckles . . . a red rubber guard ahead of her wedding ring . . . her eyes . . . as impersonally bright as two perfectly shaped eyes of glass." The family talk has been on the events of history she has lived through: the Civil War, President Lincoln, and even the age and time before and after. Now Rufus, the oldest of her great-great-grandchildren stands before her to close the generational gap; when he kisses her, the bonding is complete. In the third and final scene of the interludes, Rufus rides on a train through the Smokies with Jay, Catherine, and Uncle Ted and Aunt Kate, the latter relatives of a nonentity status from Michigan. The scene has little do with the physical journey but much to do with growing up and the interplay between parents and children and other adults. Ted wants Rufus to whistle at a meal for more cheese, and when he cannot, Mary protests Ted's continuing tease: "I think it's a perfect shame, deceiving a little child like that who's been brought up to trust people. . . ;" Jay, Ted, and Kay disagree, and Mary—again on the defensive—concludes: "But he's been brought up to trust older people when they tell him something." Agee's unusual picture of childhood innocence, loneliness, and the preparatory moments of experience in life points out not only fears and hopes and a child's naïveté but, more than anything else, Agee's search, a longing and pleading search for an answer to "tell me who I am."

Source: Eugene T. Carroll, "Mood and Music: Landscape and Artistry in *A Death in the Family*," in *James Agee: Reconsiderations*, edited by Michael A. Lofaro, University of Tennessee Press, 1992, pp. 82–103.

Sources

Kramer, Victor A., "Urban and Rural Balance in *A Death in the Family*," in *James Agee: Reconsiderations*, edited by Michael A. Lofaro, University of Tennessee Press, 1992, pp. 104–18.

MacDonald, Dwight, Review of *A Death in the Family*, in the *New Yorker*, November 16, 1957, p. 224.

Maddocks, Melvin, Review of *A Death in the Family*, in the *Christian Science Monitor*, November 14, 1957, p. 7.

Further Reading

Doty, Mark, *Tell Me Who I Am: James Agee's Search for Selfhood*, Louisiana State University Press, 1981.

One of the most psychologically intensive studies of Agee's life, this book draws heavily off his letters and the writings of those who knew him.

Kramer, Victor A., "Remembrance of Childhood," in *James Agee*, Twayne's United States Authors Series, No. 252, Twayne Publishers, 1975, pp. 142–55.

This section of a standard overview of Agee's life and work focuses on *A Death in the Family* and how it joined the end of Agee's life with his first memories.

Lowe, James, *The Creative Process of James Agee*, Louisiana State University Press, 1994.

Lowe's general theme is "disparateness" throughout Agee's works: the ways in which his writings in different genres tended to draw in different directions.

Madden, David, ed., *Remembering James Agee*, Louisiana State University Press, 1974.

Madden provides a collection of essays by people who knew Agee, including Father James H. Flye, Robert Fitzgerald, Dwight Macdonald, and Whittaker Chambers.

Moreau, Geneviève, *The Restless Journey of James Agee*, William Morrow, 1977.

This book gives equal attention to Agee's life and his work, claiming not to be a biography but a literary examination of the ways he drew from the familiar for his writing.

Spiegel, Alan, *James Agee and the Legend of Himself*, University of Mississippi Press, 1998.

Spiegel organizes his book around ancient mythic motifs, examining how Agee's writings built a mythic personality for the author.

Elmer Gantry

Sinclair Lewis
1927

Sinclair Lewis's *Elmer Gantry* (New York, 1927) is a ferocious satire against Protestant fundamentalist religion in the American Midwest. It tells the story of a hypocritical, corrupt, but very successful preacher named Elmer Gantry. Elmer starts his career as a Baptist and then joins up with a charismatic but equally unprincipled female revivalist preacher. After her death, he joins the Methodist Church. Amoral and relentlessly ambitious, Elmer builds a statewide and national reputation as a fiery preacher who never tires of denouncing vice, while at the same time feeling no need to curb his own vices, particularly adultery.

Besides being an effective satire targeted against religious hypocrisy, *Elmer Gantry* provides insight into the clash of cultural forces in America in the 1920s. During this period, traditional religious believers were deeply disturbed by the encroachments made on faith by science and secularism. They also decried the growth within the church of the "higher criticism," that sought to understand the Bible based on modern methods of scholarship.

On publication, *Elmer Gantry* had a sensational reception. So scandalous was Lewis's portrayal of religion that the novel was banned in several cities and denounced from pulpits across the nation. The famous evangelist Billy Sunday called Lewis "Satan's cohort."

Over seventy-five years after it first appeared, *Elmer Gantry* still has power to shock as well as amuse.

Sinclair Lewis The Library of Congress

Author Biography

Harry Sinclair Lewis, best known as Sinclair Lewis, was born on February 7, 1885, in Sauk Centre, Minnesota. His father was a physician. In 1903, Lewis went to Yale University, where he served as editor of the *Yale Literary Magazine*. During his Yale career Lewis also traveled widely, including a trip to England working on a cattle boat, and he also lived in the Utopian colony at Englewood, New Jersey, which was founded by the novelist Upton Sinclair. He graduated from Yale in 1908 and worked in various jobs in the publishing industry, including editor, reporter, manuscript reader, and reviewer. While working for the *Daily Courier* in Waterloo, Iowa, in 1908, he wrote an editorial about fraudulent evangelists, which suggests that the seeds of *Elmer Gantry* were already being sown.

Lewis married Grace Livingston Hegger in 1914, and they had one son, Wells, in 1917. Pursuing a career as a freelance writer, Lewis began to produce fiction with ease and ingenuity, and he published five novels from 1912 to 1919. However, these were exercises in popular, rather than literary, fiction. Lewis's first real success came with *Main Street* (1920), the book that made him famous. It was both a popular and critical success, selling 295,000 copies in the first year. Lewis's reputation as a satirist of American life continued to develop in the 1920s with the novels *Babbitt* (1922), *Arrowsmith* (1925), *Elmer Gantry* (1927), and *Dodsworth* (1929). In 1926, Lewis refused the Pulitzer Prize for *Arrowsmith*, because he believed it would compromise his artistic independence.

Lewis divorced his wife in 1928, and married Dorothy Thompson. They had a son, Michael, in 1930, the same year that Lewis became the first American to win the Nobel Prize for Literature.

During the 1930s and 1940s, Lewis published a further nine novels, as well as plays and short stories. But he did not achieve the heights of success he had enjoyed during the 1920s. Only the novels *It Can't Happen Here* (1935) and *Kingsblood Royal* (1947) have stood the test of time.

Lewis's personal life was troubled, and he and his second wife were divorced in 1942. In 1944, his son Lieutenant Wells Lewis was killed in action in France during World War II.

Lewis died of heart disease in Rome, Italy, in 1951.

Plot Summary

Chapters 1–8

Elmer Gantry begins in 1902. Elmer Gantry and his roommate, Jim Lefferts, have traveled from their college in Kansas to Cato, Missouri, to see their girlfriends. After dinner, the drunken Elmer picks a fight with a man who is heckling Eddie Fislinger, a fellow Terwillinger College student, as he preaches to an outdoor crowd. Eddie spreads the word that Elmer, who has never shown any zeal for religion, has been converted. Jim tries to persuade Elmer not to go along with it, but when Elmer attends the Annual Prayer Week he cannot resist the emotionalism of the service. Everyone congratulates him on his conversion. That night he has doubts, but he is persuaded to speak the following night at the Y.M.C.A. He cribs some passages from a book and then gives a rousing sermon. The college president declares that he is a born preacher, and everyone urges him to become a minister. Liking the idea of having power over an audience, Elmer convinces himself he has been called to the ministry.

Elmer attends Mizpah Theological Seminary, a Baptist institution in Babylon, in the Midwest. In 1905, after two years' study, he is ordained. During his final year he is restless and bored, but he is given a Sunday appointment at a country church in

Schoenheim, eleven miles away, with Frank Shallard as his assistant. At the church, Elmer tries to seduce Lulu Bains, the daughter of one of the deacons, while Shallard warns him against even the appearance of evil.

Chapters 9–16

Under pressure from Elmer, Shallard resigns. Lulu becomes devoted to Elmer but he gets bored with her. Lloyd Naylor, who is in love with Lulu, complains to Lulu's father about Elmer's amorous conduct towards her. Bains and Naylor confront Elmer at the Seminary and tell him he must marry Lulu. Elmer is forced to agree, but promises himself he will find a way out of the engagement. He behaves cruelly to Lulu, and when Floyd comforts her with a kiss, Elmer, who has planned the whole incident, bursts in on them with Lulu's father. Bains promises Elmer that he will make Lulu marry Floyd. Pretending to be outraged, Elmer resigns his position.

Elmer's next position is at a church in Monarch. On the train he meets a traveling salesman who invites him for a drink, which results in Elmer failing to keep his appointment at the church. Fired from the Seminary, he is hired as a traveling salesman of farm implements.

After two years as a salesman, Elmer meets Eddie Fislinger at his church in Kansas, and he decides he wants to be a preacher again. In Nebraska, he attends a meeting of the evangelist Sharon Falconer. He falls for her on sight, and follows her to Lincoln, Nebraska, for her next revival meeting. In Lincoln, he persuades her to let him speak at the meeting about how he, a businessman, was converted. The speech is a roaring success.

Elmer is so infatuated with Sharon that he gives up smoking and drinking for her. Sharon soon fires her assistant, Cecil Alyston, and appoints Elmer as his replacement. For two years, he helps her lead revival meetings in large cities, mastering the art of press advertising and fundraising. But it all comes to an end one night in Clontar, on the New Jersey coast, where Sharon has purchased a pier. During the opening service, with a crowd of more than four thousand, fire breaks out. Elmer escapes by knocking other people out of the way, but Sharon is burned to death.

Elmer tries but fails to continue as an independent evangelist. He joins up with Mrs. Evans Riddle, who teaches New Thought, a Westernized version of Indian religion. But he is caught stealing from the collection and is fired. He starts to

teach Prosperity classes on his own but cannot make a living from them.

Chapters 17–24

Elmer borrows a hundred dollars from Shallard, who is now a minister and is married with three children. In Zenith, Elmer meets Bishop Toomis, a prominent figure in the Methodist Church. Elmer joins the Methodists and is sent to the small town of Banjo Crossing, where he falls in love with Cleo Benham, the daughter of a church trustee. His flamboyant preaching style makes a big impression on the small town. He marries Cleo but gets bored with her and resents her lack of sexual passion.

Elmer works diligently and is rewarded at the Methodists' Annual Conference by being sent to a bigger church, at Rudd Center. He spends a year there, and three years in Vulcan, where Cleo gives birth to two children. Then from 1918 to 1920 he is in Sparta, where the population is 129,000. At Sparta, Elmer gains statewide fame for his sensational sermons denouncing drinking and other sins. He is rewarded by being appointed minister of the Wellspring Methodist Church in the large city of Zenith, where the worldly trustee, T. J. Rigg, advises him to bring in the crowds with a rousing sermon denouncing vice. Elmer is soon preaching to crowds larger than almost all the churches in Zenith. His ambition knows no bounds.

Chapters 25–33

Elmer meets up again with Lulu, now married to Floyd Naylor, and they resume their flirtation. At his Lively Sunday Evenings, Elmer gets up to many publicity-generating stunts. He also forms a Committee on Public Morals, persuades the police to make him a temporary lieutenant, and personally leads raids on the red-light districts. He denounces other churches for their laxity in condemning sin. Elmer moves in ever-higher social circles and goes on a three-month speaking tour aimed at the youth of America. He raises money to build a new church.

Elmer denounces his old classmate Shallard, who now preaches at a Congregational church in Zenith, calling him practically an atheist. Shallard is forced to resign. Some while later Shallard goes on a lecture tour to speak against fundamentalism. In a southwestern city, he falls into the hands of violent fanatics who beat him so badly he is blinded.

The new Wellspring Church has been built, and Elmer is awarded an honorary doctorate from Abernathy College. He becomes one of the first clergymen in the country to have his services broadcast by radio, and in 1924, he travels to Europe with Cleo. On his return, Elmer meets J. B. North, who is in charge of the National Association for the Purification of Art and the Press, known as Napap. After North invites him to lecture for Napap, Elmer is filled with ambition to combine all the moral organizations in America, with himself as the leader. He speaks in many big cities and acquires a new secretary, Hettie Bowler, with whom he has an affair. He successfully schemes to become pastor of the prestigious Yorkville Methodist Church in New York and the new executive secretary of Napap. Meanwhile, Hettie turns out to be a married woman who, with her husband, tries to blackmail Elmer. Elmer, with the help of T. J. Rigg, turns the tables on her and preserves his career.

Characters

Cecil Aylston

Cecil Aylston is Sharon Falconer's assistant. He is a well-educated Englishman in his early thirties with a colorful past. He fell in love with Sharon when he first met her, and is devoted to her. After Sharon dismisses him in favor of Elmer, Cecil tries to conduct a rescue mission in Buffalo. He dies in a gambling den.

Barney Bains

Barney Bains is a deacon at the Baptist church in Schoenheim and the father of Lulu. Bains initially forces Elmer to agree to marry Lulu, but later, after Elmer shows him Lulu kissing Floyd Naylor, he orders Lulu to marry Floyd.

Lulu Bains

Lulu Bains is the daughter of Barney Bains. Elmer tries to seduce her, but once she has become devoted to him he gets bored with her and treats her cruelly. She is forced by her father to marry Lloyd Naylor. Lulu later meets Elmer again many years later in Zenith, where they resume their clandestine affair. After Elmer dumps her for Hettie, Lulu loses interest in life.

Cleo Benham

Cleo Benham is the high-minded daughter of Nathaniel Benham. She engages in worthy activities at the church in Banjo Crossing, and falls in love with Elmer. Elmer at first returns her affection, and they get married. Elmer starts to detest her when he finds out that she is cold, sexually.

Nathaniel Benham

Nathaniel Benham is a trustee of the Methodist church in Banjo Crossing and the father of Cleo.

Nellie Benton

Nellie Benton is Jim Leffert's girlfriend when he is a student.

Dr. Howard Bancock Binch

Dr. Howard Bancock Binch is a prominent Baptist who defends the literal interpretation of the Bible in his writings.

Chester Brown

Chester Brown is a prominent Methodist preacher in Zenith and one of Elmer's rivals.

Horace Carp

Horace Carp is a student at Mizpah Theological Seminary. He ends up as a minister in the Episcopal church.

Hettie Dowler

Hettie Dowler becomes Elmer's secretary at Zenith when Elmer is already famous. She and Elmer have an affair, which later turns out to be a trick on the part of Hettie and her husband Oscar to blackmail Elmer. Elmer's lawyer outwits Hettie's lawyer, and she is forced to withdraw the charges she made against him and state that she was part of a plot by the liquor interests to ensnare him.

Sharon Falconer

Sharon Falconer is a charismatic evangelist who travels around the country holding spectacular revival meetings. She dresses in exotic outfits such as Grecian robes, and uses a gold and white pyramidal altar. These help her to put on a dramatic show that wins many converts. Sharon believes she is above sin and that she can do anything she wants to because she is God's messenger. She even tells Elmer (who falls for her the instant he sees her) that she is the reincarnation of Joan of Arc, although she later admits that she does not really believe this. "I'm a very ignorant young woman with a lot of misdirected energy and some tiny idealism," she explains to Elmer. Elmer wants to marry her but she says she is too old for marriage (she is thirty-two, three or four years older than Elmer) and she must also remain free to devote herself to her missionary work. Sharon's real name is Katie Jonas; she picked out the name Sharon Falconer when she was working as a stenographer.

Eddie Fislinger

Eddie Fislinger is a student at Terwillinger College and the president of the Y.M.C.A. Initially, he is an enemy of Elmer and tries to prevent him from becoming president of the student body for the second time. Eddie is an enthusiastic Christian who becomes a student at Mizpah Theological Seminary and later a minister in western Kansas. Elmer despises him.

Elmer Gantry

Elmer Gantry was raised by his mother, a staunch Baptist, in the small town of Paris, Kansas. At Terwillinger College, Elmer captains the football team. He is friendly but self-important; everyone thinks he is popular, but in fact he has almost no friends. He hates piety and prefers drunkenness, profanity, and seducing women. Elmer gets converted to Christianity only because he cannot resist the pressures put on him to do so. He enters the ministry because he cannot think of anything else to do in life. He soon discovers he has a gift for preaching, and he loves the feeling of power he gets when his sermons move his congregation. As a preacher, he shamelessly plays on people's emotions and their fear of Hell. He is not a deep thinker and does not really care whether the Baptist doctrines he preaches are true or false. He thinks they might, for all he knows, be true, and that is enough for him. Elmer loves to preach against immorality but feels no need to be moral himself. Fired from the ministry after going drinking rather than contacting his new church, he works for two years as a traveling salesman. He is drawn back to preaching when he falls in love with Sharon Falconer, and he hones his publicity and fundraising skills with

her for several years until her death. After a brief interlude with Mrs. Evans Riddle's New Thought movement, and teaching Prosperity classes on his own, Elmer joins the Methodist Church. Driven by ambition to become a bishop, he is hugely successful, and is given bigger and bigger churches. His specialty is in denouncing vice, and in Zenith he even leads a police raid on the local dens of iniquity. Now famous, Elmer's ambitions know no bounds, especially when he starts to work with the National Association for the Purification of Art and the Press. He has an affair with his secretary, who then tries to blackmail him, and only escapes ruin because he has a clever lawyer. At the end he is still eyeing the women in the congregation even as he calls for a crusade to make America a moral nation.

Mrs. Gantry

Mrs. Gantry is Elmer's mother. She is a widow who owns a millinery and dressmaking shop. She is also a pious churchgoer who has always wanted Elmer to become a preacher.

Dr. Otto Hickenlooper

Dr. Otto Hickenlooper is a prominent Methodist minister in Zenith, and one of Elmer's rivals.

Juanita Klauzel

Juanita Klauzel is Elmer's girlfriend in Cato, Missouri, when he is a student at Terwillinger College.

Jim Lefferts

Jim Lefferts is Elmer's roommate and his only friend at Terwillinger College. Jim is the college freethinker and the only person who has any influence on Elmer. Jim doubts the literal truth of the Bible and has contempt for the church. When Elmer is converted, Jim moves out of his room in disgust. He later becomes a lawyer.

Ad Locust

Ad Locust is a traveling salesman for the Pequot Farm Implement Company who befriends Elmer on the train to Monarch.

Philip McGarry

Philip McGarry is the minister of the Arbor Methodist Church in Zenith. He has a Ph.D. from the University of Chicago who espouses a very liberal theology. Known as the *enfant terrible* of the Methodist church, he is ruthlessly critical of others. Elmer loathes him but Frank Shallard regards him as a friend.

Floyd Naylor

Floyd Naylor is a large and rather stupid farmer in Schoenheim who is in love with Lulu Bains, whom he eventually marries.

Bess Needham

Bess Needham marries Frank Shallard and bears him three children.

J. E. North

J. E. North is the executive secretary of the National Association for the Purification of Art and the Press (Napap). He meets Elmer on a steamer home from Europe and invites him to lecture on behalf of Napap.

Reverend Andrew Pengilly

Reverend Andrew Pengilly is the old pastor of the Catawba Methodist Church. He is a simple, decent, pious man who is loved by his congregation. He befriends Frank Shallard.

Don Pickens

Don Pickens is Frank Shallard's roommate at Mizpah Theological Seminary.

Mahlon Potts

Mahlon Potts is the influential minister of the First Methodist Church in Zenith. Elmer thinks he is fat and pompous, but respects him nonetheless.

Reverend Dr. Willoughby Quarles

Reverend Dr. Willoughby Quarles is president of Terwillinger College. He urges Elmer to become a minister.

Mrs. Evans Riddle

Mrs. Evans Riddle is the proprietor of the Victory Thought Power Headquarters in New York. She teaches classes in Concentration, Prosperity, Love, Metaphysics and Oriental Mysticism, and invites Elmer to join her.

T. J. Rigg

T. J. Rigg is a famous criminal lawyer and a trustee of Wellspring Methodist Church in Zenith. He is a worldly man and gives Elmer some shrewd advice about how to build up the church.

Judson Roberts

Judson Roberts is an evangelist who is the state secretary of the Y.M.C.A. He preaches at the service that gets Elmer converted. However, Roberts doubts the truth of the doctrines he preaches so convincingly.

Frank Shallard

Frank Shallard is a student at Mizpah Theological Seminary, but he doubts the literal truth of the Bible. He is influenced by the atheistic Dr. Zechlin who lends him theological works by liberals and skeptics. Despite his doubts, and following Zechlin's advice, Shallard decides to remain in the church. He is ordained despite the examiners' doubts about his orthodoxy, and he takes charge of a small church in Catawba. But throughout his career he wonders whether there is any value in his work. He is encouraged to stay in the church by the Reverend Andrew Pengilly, and he ends up as a minister of a Congregational church in Zenith. Elmer forces him to resign by questioning his religious beliefs, after which Shallard gets a job with the Charity Organization Society. He is invited by a group of scholars to go on a lecture tour to oppose religious fundamentalism, but his first lecture, in a city in the southwest, he is interrupted by local toughs. Shallard is then attacked by religious fanatics and blinded.

William Donninger Styles

William Donninger Styles is a rich businessman in Zenith. He is treasurer of the Congregational church, but Elmer succeeds in getting him to support the Methodists instead.

Bishop Wesley R. Toomis

Bishop Wesley R. Toomis is a bishop in the Methodist Church who has a great reputation as an orator and thinker. He welcomes Elmer into the Methodist church.

Reverend Jacob Trosper

Reverend Jacob Trosper is the dean and chief executive of Mizpah Theological Seminary. He looks stern and Elmer is afraid of him.

Wallace Umstead

Wallace Umstead is a student Mizpah Theological Seminary who becomes the secretary of the Zenith Y.M.C.A.

Dr. Bruno Zechlin

Dr. Bruno Zechlin is Professor of Greek, Hebrew, and Old Testament Exegesis at Mizpah Theological Seminary. He long ago lost his faith in the literal truth of the Bible and has become an atheist.

After Elmer writes a critical comment about him on a blackboard, Zechlin, who is suspected of heresy, is forced into retirement by the Seminary. He goes to live with his niece and dies within two years.

Harry Zenz

Harry Zenz is a student at the Mizpah Theological Seminary. He is known in his church for his piety, but in fact he is an atheist. He ends up as minister of a large church in a West Virginia mining town.

Themes

Anti-clericalism

Throughout the novel, clergymen and the church are presented in an extremely unflattering light. For the most part they are hypocrites, not even believing the doctrines they preach to their congregations every week. Judson Roberts, the enthusiastic, apparently confident evangelist who converts Elmer, admits to himself that his preaching is dishonest. He plans to quit the church and get a good job selling real estate.

The attack on the hypocrisy of Protestant ministers continues throughout the novel. At Mizpah Theological Seminary, Elmer and his fellow students all smoke in their dormitory, even though smoking is practically forbidden. When the pious Eddie leaves the room, all they want to talk about is sex. Harry Zenz does not believe a word of what he is taught at the seminary. He also thinks that Baptist leaders are "word-splitting, text-twisting, applause-hungry, job-hunting, medieval-minded second-raters. . . ." Horace Carp hates the Baptists and wants to switch to the more upscale Episcopalians as soon as possible because this will give him a better social position in which he will ". . . be able to marry a nice rich girl." Brother Karkis only wants his divinity degree so he can get a better paying job.

The evangelist Sharon Falconer, although she is not attached to any particular church, is no exception to the anti-religion theme. She turns to healing the sick not because she has a gift or a calling for it but because it is more profitable than mere evangelizing: ". . . the whole evangelist business was limited, since even the most ardent were not likely to be saved more than three or four times. But they could be healed constantly, and of the same disease."

In Zenith, when a group of local clergymen meet as the Committee on Public Morals, they

Topics for Further Study

- Discuss the issue of creationism and evolution. Should creationism be taught in public schools? Is there really a conflict between science and religion, between reason and faith, or can the two live in harmony?

- Watch the 1960 film version of *Elmer Gantry*. Is Elmer the same in the movie as he is in the novel, or have the filmmakers altered his character? What are the major differences between the film and the novel?

- Write a brief character sketch of Frank Shallard and describe his role in the novel. Why does Lewis include him in the book?

- Consider the character of Jim Lefferts, as revealed in the first three chapters. What sort of a man is Jim? What are his leading characteristics? Then read chapter 30, section 5, where Jim reappears. How would you describe his demeanor? Is he successful? Which man seems to have the more vitality? This short scene is written from Elmer's point of view. Rewrite it from Jim's point of view. Think about how Jim would view Elmer, and how he might react to what Elmer says.

reveal a distinct lack of brotherly love amongst themselves:

> They all detested one another. Every one knew of some case in which each of the others had stolen, or was said to have tried to steal, some parishioner, to have corrupted his faith and appropriated his contributions.

In many ways, of course, Elmer is the worst of them all. He possesses none of the cardinal virtues and many of the cardinal sins. He uses the church to further his own ambitions for power and fame. He is a social climber and a publicity seeker. He feels little desire to practice what he preaches. He does not really hate sin, because it is useful to him: the more vice he can discover and denounce, the more his reputation as a man of God grows.

Liberalism versus Literalism

Within the Protestant church, a battle rages between the traditionalists, or fundamentalists, who believe in the literal truth of the Bible, and the liberals, who believe that some parts of the Bible may be understood in a symbolic sense. The fundamentalists also have to deal with outright skeptics, like Jim Lefferts, and covert atheists like Dr. Zechlin.

Terwillinger College and Mizpah Theological Seminary are both fundamentalist institutions. When Lefferts asks Reverend Quarles, the college president, an awkward question about some passages in the Bible, Quarles tells him not to question the ways of the Lord. Quarles has no time for ". . . vain arguments that lead nowhere!" Quarles is hostile to the kind of free intellectual inquiry that the liberals advocate, and he relies instead on prayer and faith.

The fundamentalists believe that if even one thing in the Bible is questioned it is only a matter of time before faith is undermined completely. This is indeed what happened to Dr. Bruno Zechlin, one of the faculty at Mizpah, who lost his fundamentalist faith even before he received his theological doctorate. He survived for a while by interpreting some of the Biblical stories as symbols that revealed the glory of God and the leadership of Christ. But not long after that he lost his faith in God altogether and became an atheist.

The debate between fundamentalists and liberals is conducted amongst the students at Mizpah. The pious but stupid Eddie complains that ". . . [E]verything we Baptists stand for is threatened by those darn so-called liberals. . . ." He is referring to the practice of open communion, which is favored by liberals, as opposed to the closed communion of the fundamentalists, according to which only Baptists are allowed to participate in the rite. Harry Zenz vehemently disagrees with Eddie.

Of the other characters, Frank Shallard and Dr. Philip McGarry are examples of the liberal tendency in the church. McGarry is accused by the fundamentalists of heresy, and he does not seem to accept the traditional dogmas of the Methodist Church: ". . . [T]he only dogma he was known to give out positively was the leadership of Jesus—as to whose divinity he was indefinite."

The clash between fundamentalists and liberals comes to a dramatic and violent climax in the final incident involving Shallard. When he at last finds the courage, now that he is out of the church, to speak his mind, he is viciously attacked and blinded by fundamentalist fanatics.

Style

Picaresque

Elmer Gantry is a picaresque novel. A typical picaresque narrative chronicles the exploits of a rogue, an immoral but not criminal character who lives by his wits. There is no character development, and so Elmer, after his character is first established, does not change during the course of the novel. The main purpose of the picaresque novel (a modern example of which is Saul Bellow's *The Adventures of Augie March*), is satire. Satire ridicules its subject, with the intention of arousing contempt or scorn in the reader. A satire can be aimed at an individual or a group. In *Elmer Gantry*, the object of Lewis's satire is not only Elmer himself—who after the tabernacle fire ". . . rescued at least thirty people who had already rescued themselves. . . ."—but the entire clerical profession and the fundamentalist Protestant dogmas they represent. For example, the division between Northern and Southern Baptists is explained in this way: ". . . [B]efore the Civil War the Northern Baptists proved by the Bible, unanswerably, that slavery was wrong; and the Southern Baptists proved by the Bible, irrefutably, that slavery was the will of God." Later in the novel, Frank Shallard realizes how threatened conservative clergymen are by scientific knowledge and how inadequate they are to preside over educational institutions. According to such people:

> A proper school should teach nothing but bookkeeping, agriculture, geometry, dead languages made deader by leaving out all the amusing literature, and the Hebrew Bible as interpreted by men superbly trained to ignore contradictions, men technically called 'Fundamentalists.'

Christian beliefs about the proper observance of Sundays also comes under heavy satirical fire in this passage: ". . . [T]he Maker of a universe with stars a hundred thousand light-years apart was interested, furious, and very personal about it if a small boy played baseball on Sunday afternoon."

Historical Context

Fundamentalism

Protestant fundamentalism was in part a reaction in the early twentieth century to the development of the "higher criticism" in Biblical scholarship. Higher criticism was a method of Biblical criticism that originated in Germany. It applied the methods of historical and literary analysis in order to determine the

Compare & Contrast

- **1920s:** From 1920 to 1933, the sale of alcohol is prohibited in the United States. The aim is to reduce crime and other social problems and improve health. However, although alcohol consumption does decrease, crime and corruption around alcohol increase. Public officials are bribed by gangsters to overlook illegal brewing and selling of alcohol.

  Today: Advocates for the legalization of marijuana use arguments drawn from the experience of Prohibition. They claim that banning marijuana leads to drug trafficking which benefits organized crime; that the illegal sale of marijuana is linked to violence and terrorism; and that it presents huge costs to the taxpayer for law enforcement.

- **1920s:** In Tennessee in 1925, a law known as the Butler Law is passed banning the teaching of the theory of evolution in public schools. In the so-called Scopes Monkey Trial in 1925, the state,

aided by fundamentalist and Bible expert William Jennings Bryan, wins the case brought against J. T. Scopes, a biology teacher. Scopes is defended by well-known lawyer Clarence Darrow.

  Today: Many fundamentalist Christians still favor the teaching of creationism (the biblical account of creation) alongside, or in place of, the teaching of evolution in public schools.

- **1920s:** The growth of the automobile industry marks the emergence of the consumer society. In 1929, there are more than 27 million cars in America, which amounts to nearly one per household.

  Today: According to the Bureau of Transportation Statistics, the average American household has 1.9 cars, trucks, or sport utility vehicles and 1.8 drivers. Since there are 107 million U.S. households, that equals 204 million vehicles and 191 million drivers.

---

authorship, date and place of composition of the books of the Bible. Higher criticism also showed that some elements in the Bible were also found in other religions and mythologies (the virgin birth, for example). This tended to undermine the uniqueness of Christianity and the literal interpretation of the Bible. Traditionalists, therefore, rejected the new approach of liberal theology. In the novel, when Elmer takes up his first appointment in a small-town Methodist church, one of the first questions the fundamentalist trustees asks him is, "Do any monkeying with this higher criticism?" Against the tide of modernist thought that included science and secularism, fundamentalists insisted on the truth of their core doctrines, including the virgin birth, the physical resurrection of Jesus, the atonement, the infallibility of the Scriptures, and the second coming of Christ.

Revivalism

During the late nineteenth and early twentieth centuries, there were many evangelists, like Elmer

and Sharon Falconer in the novel, who traveled around the country conducting revival campaigns for large audiences. One famous evangelist was Gipsy Smith (1860–1947), an Englishman who made twenty-six trips to the United States. On his first visit in 1889, he held campaigns in cities from Boston to San Francisco. In 1928, he preached in a tent in Long Beach, California to more than 5,000 people, and on his return to America the following year, when he was nearly seventy years old, he attracted even larger crowds, including 15,000 in Winston-Salem, North Carolina. In the novel, people in Nebraska say that Sharon Falconer compares with the great evangelists of the past, naming Gipsy Smith as one of them. They also name Billy Sunday. Billy Sunday (1862–1935) was a professional baseball player who quit baseball a few years after he had a religious conversion. He became a Presbyterian preacher, and was famous for his energetic, fiery sermons in which he denounced liberalism, the theory of evolution, and the evils of drinking.

Burt Lancaster as Elmer Gantry, preaching before a microphone, still from the 1960 film version of Elmer Gantry © United Artists/The Kobal Collection. Reproduced by permission

He also raised large amounts of money at his meetings, and like Elmer Gantry, he was one of he first evangelists to spread his message through the new technology of radio.

Another famous name was Aimee Semple McPherson (1890–1944), a female evangelist who clearly resembled the fictional Sharon Falconer. McPherson preached in southern California from 1918 to the 1940s. Like Sharon, she drew huge crowds and practiced faith healing. She wore expensive clothes and jewelry and put on a spectacular show. McPherson was involved in a scandal in 1926. She was reported missing after swimming off Venice Beach, California, turning up five weeks later in Mexico, claiming she had been kidnapped. But a grand jury investigation found that McPherson had spent a pleasant month in Mexico with a married man from her church. This was not the last of McPherson's affairs; one of her lovers described the homemade altar in her apartment, in front of which they would make love—which is strikingly similar to the scene in Chapter 12 of *Elmer Gantry*, in which Elmer and Sharon also make love before an altar in her house in Virginia.

Critical Overview

On publication in 1927, *Elmer Gantry* created a public furor. According to Mark Schorer, in his introduction to *Sinclair Lewis: A Collection of Critical Essays*, "No novel in the history of American literature outraged its audience so completely, and very few novels in American literature had a larger immediate audience." The book was banned in Boston and other cities and denounced from hundreds of pulpits. One cleric suggested that Lewis should be imprisoned for five years, and there were also threats of physical violence against the author. The adverse publicity helped sales, and 175,000 copies were sold in less than six weeks.

Reviewers were divided on the merits of the novel. Some found it repugnant and accused Lewis of grossly distorting his subject matter. Others praised its accurate reporting and its denunciation of hypocrisy, comparing Lewis to great satirists such as Voltaire and Swift. Charles W. Ferguson, in the *Bookman*, described *Elmer Gantry* as a "glorious lampoon," although he also commented that the novel was a ". . . social commentary and not a work of fictional art. As a character, Dr. Gantry lacks verisimilitude, and he lacks it more the longer he lives."

Later judgments have also been mixed. For Sheldon Norman Grebstein, writing in 1962, the novel ". . . has snap, flavor, a strong narrative line, a good deal of authenticity . . . But it is distorted, even too much for satire; it lacks conflict and contrast." In a generally favorable assessment, James Lundquist, in *Sinclair Lewis*, brings attention to Lewis's mastery of irony, but he also comments on a weakness in the plot, arguing that the final crisis Elmer faces is unconvincing in its details.

Criticism

Bryan Aubrey

Aubrey holds a Ph.D. in English and has published many articles on twentieth century literature. In this essay, Aubrey discusses how Lewis's characterization in Elmer Gantry *serves his satiric purpose.*

Institutionalized religion has attracted its fair share of satirical assaults in its time, but *Elmer Gantry* must surely rank as the most savage in American literature. Lewis is like a ruthless hunter who spares nothing and still has ammunition left at the end of the day. It is a fairly narrow assault, since Lewis's targets are confined to Protestant churches and revival campaigns, but within that range, Lewis's fire is deadly and continuous. For the most part, he does not create complex human portraits but caricatures. Those who believe in the doctrines of the church are presented as fools or morons, and are easy targets for malicious fun. One such incident (chapter 2, section 3) is when the pious but not very bright Eddie Fislinger is outwitted by Jim Lefferts's atheist father for the amusement of Jim and Elmer. The incident is not strictly necessary for the plot, and Lefferts's father never appears in the novel again.

There are several other minor characters who are introduced with no apparent purpose other than to serve as victims of the author's anti-religious inclination. One such character is the dean of Terwillinger College, who makes a brief appearance in chapter 4, section 3, in which he wonders, in conversation with his wife, whether he has sacrificed too much by going into the ministry. He wonders whether he might have become a great chemist, which would surely have been better (and more profitable) than "year after year again of standing in the pulpit and knowing your congregation don't remember what you've said seven minutes after you've said it." From discontented dean, who never appears again, the narrative moves immediately to the aged parents of the dean's wife. The wife is full of complaints about the life she has had to lead, married to a preacher, criticized by the church women if they thought her clothes weren't suitable, sick of "having to pretend to be so good when we were just common folks all the time!" Her tirade at her husband, who only wants to be allowed to go to sleep, includes the following passage:

> Oh, dear. Fifty years since I married a preacher! And if I could still only be sure about the virgin birth! Now don't you go explaining! Laws, the number of times you've explained! I know it's true—it's in the Bible. If I could only *believe* it!

Another minor character who serves as one small brick in the vast anti-clerical edifice that is *Elmer Gantry* is Dr. Howard Bancock Binch, a renowned defender of the literal truth of the Bible. Binch is brought on for one five-page section of chapter 14, when Elmer and Sharon happen to meet him in Joliet and lunch with him. Binch is a dreadful character who leers at Sharon and has an excessive interest in church fundraising. He advises Elmer not to denounce vice directly, by naming names and giving addresses of illegal drinking places, because the owners of such buildings—who

> **"** Elmer of course towers above everyone else in the novel. He is a gigantic, larger-than-life character. He is also too bad to be true."

of course have no knowledge of any illegal activities—are often leading church contributors and attacking them would jeopardize their support for the church. This is tantamount to an admission that the church is happy to receive money that is tainted by the very practices it denounces so vehemently.

Binch is also a snob who has contempt for other preachers. At a revival meeting he does not like to include all the preachers in town. If all of them are there, he says,

> . . . you have to deal with a lot of these two-by-four hick preachers with churches about the size of woodsheds and getting maybe eleven hundred a year, and yet they think they have the right to make suggestions!

Even the physical description of Binch is calculated to evoke disgust: "Dr. Binch stopped gulping his fried pork chops and held out a flabby, white, holy hand."

Having ridiculed the unfortunate Dr. Binch, Lewis removes him from the scene and never mentions him again.

In creating the evangelist Sharon Falconer, the author presents himself with a bigger, although more complex, target. Sharon is a woman of many selves: she is imperious and efficient, but also vulnerable. She is flirtatious, and able to get men to do her bidding. She is volatile, self-dramatizing, self-deceiving, self-promoting, cunning, playful, cynical, ambitious, and ruthless—a Cleopatra of the revivalist circuit. She is certainly not the saintly evangelist she presents herself to be, and she maintains a smug sense of superiority over the common folk she seeks to save. After she admits to Elmer that she loves to dance, she says, "Oh, of course I roast dancing in my sermons, but I mean—when it's with people like us, that understand, it's not like with worldly people, where it would lead to evil." It is not hard to see how she and Elmer are a perfect match.

What Do I Read Next?

- Lewis's *Arrowsmith* (1925) is one of his most admired novels. It portrays the career of Martin Arrowsmith, a dedicated, idealistic physician and truth-seeker who is severely tested by the cynicism he encounters in the medical profession.

- *The Damnation of Theron Ware* (1896), by Harold Frederic, has many similarities to *Elmer Gantry*. The Reverend Theron Ware is a young, ambitious Methodist minister whose encounter with the new intellectual ideas of "higher criticism" and Darwinism destroys his simple faith in Methodism and ruins his career.

- Thornton Wilder's novel *Heaven Is My Destination* (1934), which is both comic and sad, follows the adventures of George Brush, a traveling salesman who unlike Elmer Gantry is a sincere convert to religious faith. He travels across America during the Depression, determined to live a good life, but he is frequently misunderstood by people he encounters.

- *Summer for the Gods: The Scopes Trial and America's Continuing Debate over Science and Religion* (1997), by Edward J. Larson, is an account of the 1925 Scopes Monkey Trial in Tennessee. Larson provides an excellent cultural history of an issue—the teaching of religion and science in public schools—that remains relevant today.

The steady accumulation of damning portraits of those whose spiritual home is the Protestant church, and the lack of any serious counterweight to them, led Rebecca West, in a hostile review of *Elmer Gantry* that first appeared in 1927, to write that Lewis lacked the necessary requirement of the satirist, which was to "fully possess, at least in the world of the imagination, the quality the lack of which he is deriding in others." West's point was that Lewis effectively exposes the charlatans and the way they misuse their power, but fails to show how that religious power might better be used.

West's point is a telling one. The relentless, unrelieved exposure of religious hypocrisy, while amusingly presented in parts, tends to become wearying. It is a pity that Lewis did not choose to develop more fully the few exceptions to the prevailing mendacity, including the lightly sketched figure of Reverend Andrew Pengilly. Pengilly is an old Methodist pastor who is something of a saintly figure. He befriends Shallard and tries to answer Shallard's doubts about the truth of the Christian faith. Disappointingly though, Pengilly's arguments do not rise above the commonplace. For all his wisdom, he speaks in platitudes, although Lewis does give him one searing moment of insight. It comes when Elmer regales Pengilly with a self-congratulatory story about the success of Elmer's ministry in Zenith. Pengilly sees through him with the spiritual eye of an eagle, and asks, "Mr. Gantry, why don't you believe in God?"

Indeed, why doesn't he? Elmer would probably not be able to answer this question. It is not so much that he does not believe in God. He is no Harry Zenz or Bruno Zechlin, who have both thought deeply about theology and have emerged as atheists. Elmer's mind is shallow; he simply does not have the capacity for serious thought about such issues. One might say that on matters of truth, he is neutral; he is not a believer or a nonbeliever. One thing he is aware of is that professing belief serves his purposes very well, and for all he knows, every word of Baptist or Methodist dogma might be true.

Elmer of course towers above everyone else in the novel. He is a gigantic, larger-than-life character. He is also too bad to be true. Can there ever have lived a clergyman with Elmer's astonishing range of vices: his chronic insincerity, his hypocrisy, his lust, his overweening ambition, his cynicism, his appalling behavior to his family? Elmer cheats, he boasts, he lies, he deceives. He is an opportunist, a rogue, a charlatan. And yet

Lewis's attitude to his character is a little more complex than this long list of his faults might suggest. Mark Schorer, in his biography of Lewis, records a remark that Lewis made to his friend Richards Brooks in 1946. According to Brooks, "He [Lewis] confessed that he really loved Elmer, the big bum, and hated only what he stood for; but halfway through the novel he had been carried away, and turned on his character and demolished him."

Based on the evidence in the novel, there is some truth in this comment. Although Elmer is clearly a self-centered individual from the beginning, Lewis presents him, up to and including his conversion, as being swept along by sociological and psychological forces over which he has no control.

The sociological factor that works against Elmer is the entire small-town Protestant environment in which he was raised. As a boy, the Baptist church was all he knew. He was saturated with it—the sermons, hymns, Bible stories, funerals, weddings, Sunday schools. The church filled him with awe, frightened him, became the center of all his emotions. As Lewis so devastatingly wrote, Elmer "got everything from the church and Sunday School, except, perhaps, any longing whatever for decency and kindness and reason." The implication is that those three qualities were not present in the Baptist church of Paris, Kansas. For such a high-spirited boy as Elmer, this was such a limited, stifling environment to grow up in that it effectively steered him away from the kind of occupation that would have suited him much better: "It was lamentable to see this broad young man, who would have been so happy in the prize-ring, the fish-market, or the stock exchange, poking through the cobwebbed corridors of Terwillinger."

The psychological factor that works against Elmer is the mechanics of the conversion experience. Lewis attacked it as no more than mass hysteria. "They hypnotize themselves," says Jim Lefferts to Elmer, trying to persuade him not to go along with it. Lewis's description of the service at which Elmer succumbs is compelling in its evocation of the rampant emotion of the occasion. Elmer is subjected to a kind of collective emotional manipulation. Everything conspires to overwhelm him and break down his defenses; he does not really have a chance. Later, Lewis will show Elmer no mercy, but at this stage his target is not so much the soon-to-be preacher but the social and psychological context in which he is formed.

Lewis seems to have had a particular loathing of the conversion experience that is so central to Protestant spirituality. He returns to it in the context of Sharon's revival meetings. He takes care to point out that people return again and again to get converted, which would seem to negate the idea that they are "saved" in a once in a lifetime experience. He also notes that the more bizarre and irrational the experience, the more the evangelists value it, but he leaves the reader in no doubt about the contempt with which he views such phenomena: ". . . once occurred what connoisseurs regard as the highest example of religious inspiration. Four men and two women crawled about a pillar, barking like dogs, 'barking the devil out of the tree.'"

For the evangelists, the irrational is valued more highly than the rational, but for the novelist, the reverse holds true.

Source: Bryan Aubrey, Critical Essay on *Elmer Gantry*, in *Novels for Students*, Thomson Gale, 2006.

Martin Light

In the following essay excerpt, Light examines quixotic elements in Elmer Gantry.

The angriest of Lewis's novels, *Elmer Gantry* seems to arise from impulses that invert the quixotic. Elmer, after all, is not an idealist; though he ventures forth, he does not do so in the name of chivalry; and, finally, he does not practice the transmuting powers of fancy. Nevertheless, it is possible to recognize the working of quixotic elements throughout the novel, especially in the fancifully conceived Sharon Falconer and in the character who is a foil for Elmer, Frank Shallard. The novel is absorbing, and I should like to say a few words about it.

What has educated Elmer (a few books, oratory, sermons, tracts, hymns, and a smattering of a college education) must be ridiculed in order to purge it from the land. Lewis's attack upon the villages—nowhere so embittered as in *Elmer Gantry*—occurs through exposure of the cultural opportunities which the village provides, and these are thin indeed. Most literary materials found in the village are reflections of American popular culture before the turn of the century. They were intended to feed the American dream, but instead fashioned the nightmare—out of books!

Elmer seems a demonic figure. He is out for money and pleasure and power—and the ministry is the career which gives him all three. He is a complete hypocrite and a complete opportunist. As Mark Schorer has pointed out, Elmer is rarely aware of himself as a hypocrite and achieves neither insight nor growth. Nevertheless, Lewis

> *Elmer seems a demonic figure. He is out for money and pleasure and power—and the ministry is the career which gives him all three."*

supplies sufficient background to account for Elmer's going into the ministry.

Elmer himself had owned "two volumes of Conan Doyle, one of E. P. Roe, and a priceless copy of 'Only a Boy.'" His literary inspirations were McGuffey's Readers, Nick Carter, Bible stories, and such stock characters as "Little Lame Tom who shamed the wicked rich man that owned the handsome team of grays and the pot hat and led him to Jesus. The ship's captain who in the storm took counsel with the orphaned but righteous child of missionaries in Zomballa. The Faithful Dog who saved his master during a terrific conflagration. . . ." (Later Elmer runs from a conflagration, saving no one but himself.)

Elmer's friend Jim Lefferts, a freethinker, has a somewhat wider list than Elmer: an encyclopedia, *Pickwick,* Swinburne, Ingersoll, and Paine. But in the house of Elmer's mistress, Lulu Bains, they sing and read "Seeing Nelly Home," "Old Black Joe," "Beulah Land," *Farm and Fireside,* and *Modern Priscilla.* When Elmer joins evangelist Sharon Falconer, he supplies poetry for her sermons, using Ella Wheeler Wilcox, James Whitcomb Riley, and Thomas Moore, with philosophy from Ralph Waldo Trine. Bishop Toomis possesses a complete Dickens, a complete Walter Scott, Tennyson, Macaulay, Ruskin, Mrs. Humphrey Ward, Winston Churchill, Elizabeth of the German Garden, and books on travel and nature study: *How to Study the Birds, My Summer in the Rockies,* and *Pansies for Thoughts.* His mind was shaped most of all by his souvenirs of his travel-adventures. Some characters from Lewis even read Sinclair Lewis himself; the Reverend Philip McGarry asks his friend Frank Shallard to "forget that you have to make a new world, better'n the Creator's, right away tonight—you and Bernard Shaw and H. G. Wells and H. L. Mencken and Sinclair Lewis (Lord, how that book of Lewis', 'Main Street,' did bore me . . .)."

Lewis indicates the shaping of minds and values in such a village as Elmer's:

The church and Sunday School at Elmer's village, Paris, Kansas, a settlement of nine hundred evangelical Germans and Vermonters . . . had been the center of all his emotions, aside from hell-raising, hunger, sleepiness, and love. And even these emotions were represented in the House of the Lord, in the way of tacks in pew-cushions, Missionary Suppers with chicken pie and angel's-food cake, soporific sermons, and the proximity of flexible little girls in thin muslin. But the arts and the sentiments and the sentimentalities—they were for Elmer perpetually associated only with the church.

The church provided all the music he ever heard, his only oratory except for campaign speeches by politicians, all his painting and sculpture, and all his philosophic ideas. "In Bible stories, in the words of the great hymns, in the anecdotes which the various preachers, quoted, he had his only knowledge of literature." Lewis exercises his bitterness against the failures of the church by making the church itself accountable for Elmer's being no better educated. His widowed mother was "owned by the church," we are told, and the fact that the boy was fatherless is less important than that the church could not provide Elmer with principles.

In his preparation for the ministry, it is ironic that Elmer plagiarizes his first (and most frequently useful) sermon from the social reformer Robert G. Ingersoll: "Love is the only bow on life's dark cloud. It is the Morning and the Evening Star. It shines upon the cradle of the babe, and sheds its radiance upon the quiet tomb . . ." As Elmer's career begins its ascent, we learn something more of the images which fill his mind:

For all his slang, his cursing, his mauled plurals and singulars, Elmer had been compelled in college to read certain books, to hear certain lectures, all filled with flushed, florid polysyllables, with juicy sentiments about God, sunsets, the moral improvement inherent in a daily view of mountain scenery, angels, fishing for souls, fishing for fish, ideals, patriotism, democracy. . . . These blossoming words, these organ-like phrases, these profound notions, had been rammed home till they stuck in his brain, ready for use.

Thus equipped, Elmer advances to conquer the world. Later he was to learn "that references to Dickens, Victor Hugo, James Whitcomb Riley, Josh Billings, and Michelangelo give a sermon a very toney Chicago air." Though he does not have quixotic benignity, helpfulness, or idealism, he does have visions of how the ministry can be useful to him; he sees "thousands listening to him—invited to banquets and everything . . .," and he dreams of "hundreds of beautiful women [who weep] with conviction and rush down to clasp his hand."

In addition to his hypocrisy and his ignorance, Elmer is a liar, a sinner, and a coward. Though the bulldog of the football team in college, Elmer shows his cowardice during the fire in Sharon Falconer's tabernacle (which is built out over the water): "In howling panic, Elmer sprang among them, knocked them aside, struck down a girl who stood in his way, yanked open the door, and got through it . . . the last, the only one, to get through it." He then ran out a little into the surf and dragged in a woman who had already safely touched bottom, and then at least thirty more who had already rescued themselves. "A hundred and eleven people died that night, including all the gospel-crew save Elmer."

After the fire and Sharon's death, Elmer is conscience-stricken. He searches for his better nature: he will start again, never lie or cheat or boast. He will begin as a preacher in a small town, will enliven it and lift it. "Life opened before him, clean, joyous, full of the superb chances of a Christian knighthood. Some day he would be a bishop, yes, but even that was nothing compared with the fact that he had won a victory over his lower nature." He kneels in prayer, but in that instant he sees Cleo and at once thinks of seducing her.

Elmer, like other Lewis protagonists, fears marriage. After his wedding to Cleo, he gasps to himself, "Oh, good God, I've gone and tied myself up, and I never can have any fun again!" His treatment of her on the wedding night is reminiscent of Eddie Schwirtz's treatment of Una Golden. The bell-boy is scarcely out of the room when Elmer grabs Cleo. She cries out, "Oh, don't! Not now! I'm afraid!" He replies, "That's damned nonsense!" Later he says, "Come on now, Clee, show some spunk!" Making fun of her, he thinks, "Fellow *ought* to be brutal, for her own sake." Brute, fake, or philanderer, Elmer Gantry seems nevertheless destined for a successful career. As he gains experience, Elmer attempts to broaden his mind. He begins a course of home study, in a brief episode which must play ironically against Benjamin Franklin's self-education. Elmer reads Browning, Tennyson, Dickens. To increase his vocabulary he begins a word list: incinerate, Merovingian, Golgotha, Leigh Hunt, defeasance, chanson—romantic-sounding words.

Lewis's ingenuity was not exhausted on Elmer. Sharon Falconer is an equally striking example of his satiric power. She is a monstrous creation who seems to grow in size with each revelation of her craziness. She appears to Elmer as a saint, arms outstretched, stately, slender and tall, passionate.

Her voice was warm, a little husky, desperately alive.

"Oh, my dear people, my dear people, I am not going to preach tonight—we are all so weary of nagging sermons about being nice and good! I am not going to tell you that you're sinners, for which of us is not a sinner? I am not going to explain the Scriptures. We are all bored by tired old men explaining the Bible through their noses! No! We are going to find the golden Scriptures written in our own hearts, we are going to sing together, laugh together, rejoice together like a gathering of April brooks, rejoice that in us is living the veritable spirit of the Everlasting and Redeeming Christ Jesus!"

Declining from this spirituality, she gives her gospel-crew a pep talk: let's hit people hard for money-pledges. Like ordinary mortals, she is often weary. She is also an insane perversion of the sanctity of the elect, for she declares to Elmer, "I can't sin! I am above sin! I am really and truly sanctified! Whatever I may choose to do, though it might be sin in one unsanctified, with me God will turn it to his glory. I can kiss you like this—" Quickly she touches his cheek, "Yes, or passionately, terribly passionately, and it would only symbolize my complete union with Jesus! I have told you a mystery." She is the supreme fantasist. She has created an enchanted image of herself, and she has convinced her audience of that image, so that they see her as she wants to be seen, and only we, given glimpses of another self when she reveals herself to Elmer, come to know how complete and insane is her transformation. She is of the occult; she is a witch. She tells Elmer that she has visions; God talks to her. But shifting moods again, she can acknowledge that she is just an ignorant young woman with a lot of misdirected energy—and even an evil one: "Oh, I hate the little vices—smoking, swearing, scandal, drinking just enough to be silly. I love the big ones—murder, lust, cruelty, ambition!" She invites Elmer to visit the old Falconer place in Virginia, but when they arrive, she confesses that she is really just Katie Jonas, born in Utica, whose father worked in a brickyard. She had bought the plantation just two years before. "And yet I'm not a liar! I'm not! I *am* Sharon Falconer now! I've made her—by prayer and by having a right to be her!"

That night she seduces him. "Come! It is the call!" He follows her to her bedroom where he sees "a couch high on carven ivory posts, covered with a mandarin coat; unlighted brass lamps in the likeness of mosques and pagodas; gilt papier-mâché armor on the walls; a wide dressing-table with a score of cosmetics in odd Parisian bottles; tall candlesticks, the twisted and flowered candles lighted; and over everything a hint of incense." She gives him a robe for the service of the altar. Like a priestess she takes him to the chapel, a shrine with hangings, a crucifix, statues of the Virgin, and heathen idols, including a naked Venus. Here she kneels. "It is the hour! Blessed Virgin, Mother Hera, Mother Frigga, Mother Ishtar, Mother Isis, dread Mother Astarte of the weaving arms, it is thy priestess. . . ." They read from the Song of Solomon. She sinks into Elmer's arms.

Yet at the fire, it is Sharon who is heroic. "He could hear her wailing, 'Don't be afraid! Go out slowly! . . . Don't be afraid! We're in the temple of the Lord! He won't harm you! I believe! Have faith! I'll lead you safely through the flames!'" When Elmer tries to make her escape, she pushes him away. "He looked back and saw her, quite alone, holding up the white wooden cross which had stood by the pulpit, marching steadily forward, a tall figure pale against the screen of flames."

One admirable character, Frank Shallard, makes an essentially quixotic response to Elmer and his deceits. He has been educated by Roger Williams, Adoniram Judson, Luther, Calvin, Jonathan Edwards, George Washington, Lincoln, Robert Ingersoll, William James, and Fraser's *Golden Bough.* "He had learned to assemble Jewish texts, Greek philosophy, and Middle-Western evangelistic anecdotes into a sermon." Frank's mentor has been Father Pengilly, a fanciful figure whom we have already discussed.

Frank finds some shame in being a preacher and longs to prove that he is nevertheless a "real man." "Not only had he been swathed in theology, but all his experience had been in books instead of the speech of toiling men. He had been a solitary in college, generous but fastidious, jarred by his classmates' belching and sudden laughter." Like Carol Kennicott, he suffers a betrayal by books, for his reasoning had been turned from an examination of men as mammals to the mystic theories of souls and their salvation. Shortly Frank meets more of real life than he is prepared for. In a notable passage Lewis tells us sympathetically of the problems of the rebel, of the preacher or the writer who suffers from sensitivity and innocence:

> He was supposed to cure an affliction called vice. But he had never encountered vice. . . . How long would a drunkard listen to the counsel of one who had never been inside a saloon?
>
> He was supposed to bring peace to mankind. But what did he know of the forces which cause wars, personal or class or national; what of drugs, passion, criminal desire; of capitalism, banking, labor, wages, taxes; international struggles for trade, munition trusts, ambitious soldiers?

Frank suffers from self-consciousness about his occupation; it is the same sense of doubt which Lewis has expressed about the writing career: "Frank still resented it that, as a parson, he was considered not quite virile; that even clever people felt they must treat him with a special manner; that he was barred from knowing the real thoughts and sharing the real desires of normal humanity."

The Reverend McGarry tells Frank simply to accept the church with all its imperfections—with its Gantrys—and turn to giving hope and comfort to the piteous human beings who come to the church for help. But Frank rages on at the inconsistencies in doctrine, the contradictions in the Bible, the evil men who are ministers, and the fools and dullards who work about him in Zenith: Gantry, Bishop Toomis, Chester Brown, Hickenlooper, and Potts—Potts especially, who "gets his idea of human motives out of George Eliot and Margaret Deland, and his ideas of economics out of editorials in the *Advocate,* and his idea as to what he really is accomplishing out of the flattery of his Ladies' Aid!" Frank adds that he doesn't find Jesus an especially admirable character—Jesus was more vain and furious than a leader should be. What of Jesus's teachings? "Did he come to bring peace or more war? He says both. Did he approve earthly monarchies or rebel against them? He says both." Most distressing of all, says Frank, the sermons of the preachers are "agonizingly dull." So Frank leaves the church temporarily to enter the army where he learns to be "common with common men"; he schools himself further with *Ethan Frome, Père Goriot, Tono-Bungay,* and Renan's *Jesus.* Later Frank is thrown from the church and he ventures forth as a worker in a charity organization. Traveling in the Southwest, he is beaten and blinded. He calls out to God for help. Afterward, he must resign himself to helplessness for the rest of his life.

Elmer Gantry has been called the "purest Lewis" by Schorer. Form in the novel, he contends, requires that there be an opposition between the individual and society; yet in this book there are "no impediments to Elmer's barbarous rise from country boob to influential preacher." *Elmer Gantry* is a loosely episodic chronicle, he continues, "which suggests at once that there will be no sustained pressure of plot, no primary conflict about which all the action is organized and in which value will achieve a complex definition." At each of the three climaxes in the book, Lewis retreats into melodrama. Thus,

Schorer concludes, there is no pressure upon Elmer to be forced into a position of new self-awareness. D. J. Dooley remarks that to Lewis "Christianity is not only untrue, but inconceivable." Dooley feels that *Elmer Gantry* is flawed "because it is neither a realistic portrayal of the state of religion in America nor a caricature whose manifest unfairness can be forgiven because of the wit and humor which have gone into it." True, unless, taking our cue from Sharon Falconer and the multitude of fraudulent evangelistic minor characters in the book, we begin to see *Elmer Gantry* as Lewis's triumphant depiction of a land of demons and grotesques of all sizes and shapes, created from the extremes of human impulse and incapable of self-awareness because they are already beyond it, Elmer included.

Nothing reveals Lewis's isolation from an overview of life more clearly than the way he dismisses religion. His quest for God is a secular quest. In "A Letter on Religion" published in 1932, Lewis declared: "It is, I think, an error to believe that there is any need of religion to make life seem worth living." He said that he had known several young people who had been reared entirely without thought of churches or of formal theology, and they seemed happy. "Their satisfaction comes from functioning healthily, from physical and mental exercise, whether it be playing tennis or tackling an astronomical problem." While this notion of religious rites on the tennis court is rather curious, Lewis seems nevertheless to acknowledge a religious impulse, even if he would eliminate God and organized churches. Thus Rebecca West could write incisively about the religious and historical perspectives of *Elmer Gantry:* "The passages in the book which present to one what Mr. Lewis regards as the proper attitude to religion are disconcertingly jejune." Miss West goes on to say that like Mark Twain, who in *Connecticut Yankee* looked at medieval Europe and said, "My, weren't they dumb?" Lewis has no sense of the struggle of the human mind to evolve from chaos to the achievements of his age. Miss West points to Frank Shallard's accusation against Jesus: "Did He ever suggest sanitation, which would have saved millions from plagues?" She comments, "As for the suggestion that Christ should have halted on the way to the Cross to recommend the American bathroom, . . . it ought to go into the Americana section of the *American Mercury.*" She concludes her essay as follows: "If [Lewis] would sit still so that life could make any deep impression on him, if he would attach himself to the human tradition by occasionally reading a book which would set him a standard of profundity, he could give his genius a

Shirley Jones as Lulu Bains with Burt Lancaster as Elmer Gantry, still from the 1960 film version of Elmer Gantry © United Artists/The Kobal Collection.

Reproduced by permission

chance." Miss West expresses a prevailing attitude toward Lewis, but she does not, I think, understand what his best books accomplished. It may be that the essential lesson which Lewis's experience of America taught him was that the barriers to education, self-discovery, and fulfillment were formidably guarded by exploiters and cranks: thus his anger; thus his satire. His genius took its chance in mockery, parody, grotesquerie, and excessive performance.

Elmer Gantry, then, is notable as the book in which Lewis moved religion to the center of his critique of American values and declared it to have failed. He thereby makes a defiant gesture, nonetheless, somewhat apart from his customary preoccupation with quixotic heroes whom he could admire for their protests, rebellion, and search for freedom.

Source: Martin Light, "*Mantrap* and *Elmer Gantry,*" in *The Quixotic Vision of Sinclair Lewis*, Purdue University Press, 1975, pp. 98–107.

James Lundquist

In the following essay excerpt, Lundquist suggests that Lewis portrays religion as stifling, as a manifestation of the pioneer mentality that characterized the old American and has become a threat to the new American.

Sacrilege is a word that was used often in the violent arguments that accompanied the publication in 1927 of *Elmer Gantry*. Lewis's version of what passed for religion in the United States of the 1920s brought him threats against his life and gave his name the same rhetorical function in Protestant fundamentalist sermons as that of Clarence Darrow, Darwin, and the devil himself. *Elmer Gantry*, like *Arrowsmith*, is an account of career development. At the start of the novel Elmer is a college football player so little given to piety that he is known as "Hell-cat." At the end of the book he is Dr. Gantry, minister of the large Wellspring Methodist Church in Zenith, with hopes of becoming the head of a national moral-rearmament organization, the National Association for the Purification of the Arts and the Press (Napap). But unlike Arrowsmith, Elmer Gantry's rise is depicted negatively. His decision to enter the ministry is dishonest and contrary to his own nature, and it costs him the respect and friendship of his agnostic college roommate, Jim Lefferts. Every decision Elmer makes thereafter is one of compromise. Early in his preaching career he jilts a country girl who loves him and whom he has seduced. He has an affair with female evangelist Sharon Falconer, which ends with her death in a flaming tabernacle. He marries a woman he does not love. And he has involvements with several of his church secretaries. Yet through it all, he is awarded ecclesiastical advancement, even though he barely escapes ruin at the conclusion of the novel when one of his secretaries, Hettie Dowler, tries to blackmail him. But while Elmer's career ascends, that of the honest Frank Shallard, who goes to the seminary with Elmer, descends to the point where Frank is beaten up by members of the Ku Klux Klan for preaching what he believes to be the truth.

Elmer Gantry, like all of Lewis's big novels, is part of one program. In it he established ties with *Main Street*, *Babbitt*, and *Arrowsmith*. He dealt with the connection between small-town provinciality and the religious proclivities of the time, the relationship between the gospel of Christianity and the gospel of business; and, because the novel was written out of the atmosphere surrounding the Scopes Monkey Trial, he dealt with the conflict between science and religion. But what perhaps made *Elmer Gantry* seem like such an act of outrage to so many readers is that Lewis did not simply treat religion in relation to other aspects of American

life; he saw it instead as the molder of basic attitudes, most of which were, in his opinion, bad.

Lewis made the point that Protestantism has nurtured America in the same way it has nurtured Elmer. It has provided much of his and America's taste in architecture, clothing, music, literature, philosophy; it has provided everything but "any longing whatever for decency and kindness and reason."

In *Elmer Gantry* Lewis suggested that what is wrong with the small town, what is wrong with business practices, and even what is wrong with the intellectual attitudes that make it difficult for the scientist to go about his research honestly are all due to the hold Protestantism has on American consciousness. The one completely positive character in the book, Frank Shallard, wants to make Christianity an active force for social good; as it is, it is a negative force, a threat to freedom. Like Matthew Arnold, whose thinking Lewis often paralleled, Lewis maintained that Hebraism has too much prevailed over Hellenism and that what is needed is more sweetness and light (Elmer, with his black hair and black eyes, is, of course, the enemy of light). Lewis said, flatly enough, that religion in the United States has become stifling; that, like the pioneer economy and the pioneer mentality of which it is a manifestation, it has become a threat instead of a benefit.

The impact of religion on Elmer Gantry symbolizes what it has done to the American spirit. At the beginning of the novel, Elmer is drunk, but he is drunk only in the fashion of a hell-raising college boy who talks a little like Huck Finn (his companion, perhaps significantly, is named Jim). But soon the church tightens its grip on him; and for Elmer, there is no possibility of lighting out for the territory. He is coerced into becoming a minister because his family, his town, and his college are so tightly structured around the church. Elmer is beset on all sides; his mother, the YMCA, the president of the college, even a visiting evangelist—all single him out in their prayers and exhortations. He relents and the dark fabric of the preacher's suit is draped over a body that is full of blind, yet healthy and normal impulses. The result is as discouraging, as horrifying, as it would have been if Huck had been converted by Miss Watson's Bible stories.

Elmer Gantry, like the big Lewis novels that preceded it, is centrally concerned with the struggle between the old and the new. In a sense it is more centrally concerned because the pull between the old American and the new American was so apparent in the religious controversies of the time.

A modernist movement, led by such preachers as Harry Emerson Fosdick and reinforced by the essays that appeared in *The Christian Century*, was concerned with making the church more of a live option for the intellectual and the sophisticated city dweller. Opposition to the movement was vicious; Fosdick was ousted from his New York pulpit, and in the Bible Belt and the deep south, fundamentalism cranked itself up into a powerful machine that found expression through anti-evolution measures volumes of blue laws, and the Ku Klux Klan. As the years went on, however, compromises were reached, and these can be seen in the career of Elmer, who begins as a fundamentalist and winds up as the pastor of a large, urban church. He retains his theological naïveté, however, and it is clear that his modernism is not sufficient.

But Elmer does have a program in Napap, which he hopes will make him something of a moral dictator. The purpose of Napap is "to make life conform to the ideals agreed upon by the principal Christian Protestant denominations." This would be accomplished by combining into one association all the moral organizations in America—the Anti-Saloon League, the Lord's Day Alliance, the Watch and Ward Society, and the Methodist Board of Temperance, Prohibition, and Public Morals—and then lobbying for legislated morality. Napap would bring about nationwide censorship of novels, plays, paintings, and movies. It would end Sunday entertainment, curtail freedom of speech, and put restrictions on the rights of Catholics. The result would be the fascist state against which *Babbitt,* in anticipation of *1984,* warns. At the end of the novel, Elmer is on bended knee, praying, "We shall yet make these United States moral nation!" The irony in Elmer's last statement underscores the immorality of the kind of enforced morality Elmer has in mind. It also underscores what Lewis saw as one of the greatest dangers in American society—the tendency toward excess not only in religion but also in production, consumption, patriotism, and the proliferation of institutions. . . .

Source: James Lundquist, "Moralities for a New Time," in *Sinclair Lewis,* Frederick Ungar Publishing, 1973, pp. 33–60.

David J. Dooley

In the following essay excerpt, Dooley calls Elmer Gantry *a picaresque novel that "begins as a satire of revivalism."*

Elmer Gantry is a picaresque novel. Its hero makes his way, with the help of native cunning and

> A more elaborate kind of fantasy arises out of Lewis's belief that formal religion is based on the self-interest of its leaders."

oratorical ability, through almost the whole domain of religion in the United States. One device after another is employed to introduce him to new denominations and round out the picture. However, Lewis does not seem to have had such an intention at first; once again, half the novel is concerned with one theme and half with a related but different one. It begins as a satire of revivalism: Elmer is thrown out of a Baptist seminary, becomes a farm implement salesman, and then finds his niche—or pedestal—as a Billy Sunday partnered with an Aimee Semple McPherson. But though this satire is perhaps the best part of the book, revivalism is not the only target. The Baptist influences to which Elmer is subjected in his youth, particularly at Terwillinger College and Mizpah Theological Seminary, are handled very roughly. And when his hero joins the Methodist Church, Lewis takes full advantage of the opportunity to satirize another sect. Other Protestant groups also get their share of abuse, as do the Jews and the Catholics. Lewis seems determined to avoid religious discrimination: all sects appear in equally bad light.

It is not merely a case of the good priest versus the bad priest. Elmer is, obviously enough, an example of the latter. But the only good ministers of the Gospel seem to be those who, like Dr. Bruno Zechlin, the Old Testament scholar at Mizpah, have given up their religious beliefs. Philip McGarry, Ph.D. in economics and philosophy, is made to show that no educated person can believe in Christianity except in a very vague way: "the only dogma he was known to give out positively was the leadership of Jesus—as to whose divinity he was indefinite." The good pastor, the Reverend Andrew Pengilly, finds God in nature, feels religion rather than reasons about it, and doesn't give a hang for doctrinal differences.

There is a good priest whose career runs counter to that of the bad priest Gantry, but he ceases to be a priest. Frank Shallard has doubts while he is still at the Seminary. They are encouraged by Dr. Zechlin, who tells him that no reasonable person can be a believing Christian; nevertheless, he ought to stay in the church to liberalize it from within—in effect, to destroy it. Eventually pressure from Gantry and his own conscience force Frank to resign from the ministry and turn to social work. But the honest man who dares to live according to his convictions, and to speak about them in public, has no place in a superstitious society; when he gives an antifundamentalist lecture, Frank is beaten and blinded.

Undoubtedly many of the excesses Lewis describes, especially those connected with revivalism, deserve the treatment they get. Nevertheless, it is soon apparent that he has gone too far; to him, Christianity is not only untrue, but inconceivable. All those who profess to be religious in the novel are shown as hypocrites or morons; the best we can expect, apparently, is a nominal profession of belief for the sake of convenience: the good shepherd is the one who sees that his lambs are fed with material food, not stale spiritual claptrap. If a satirist depicts the object of his satire as based on humbug, advocated by humbug, and defended by humbug, he must employ a great deal of wit and fantasy to prevent his attack from seeming cross-grained and peevish. *Elmer Gantry* fails because it is neither a realistic portrayal of the state of religion in America nor a caricature whose manifest unfairness can be forgiven because of the wit and humor which have gone into it.

There is a great deal of fantasy in the novel, but it is weird and crude and goes badly with the realism. An example is the bizarre marriage ceremony which takes place between Elmer and evangelist Sharon Falconer before her grotesque shrine. A more elaborate kind of fantasy arises out of Lewis's belief that formal religion is based on the self-interest of its leaders. As in *Babbitt* and *Arrowsmith*, we are made aware that there are sinister forces combining to strike at the very foundations of American liberties. Here, they are the sinister forces of righteousness.

> It was on the steamer home that he met and became intimate with J. E. North, the renowned vice-slayer, executive secretary of the National Association for the Purification of Art and the Press—affectionately known through all the evangelical world as "the Napap." Mr. North was not a clergyman (though he was a warm Presbyterian layman), but no clergyman in the country had more furiously pursued wickedness, more craftily forced congressmen, through threats in their home districts, to see legislation in the same

reasonable manner as himself. For several sessions of congress he had backed a bill for a federal censorship of all fiction, plays, and moving pictures, with a penitentiary sentence for any author mentioning adultery even by implication, ridiculing prohibition, or making light of any Christian sect or minister.

> The bill had always been defeated, but it was gaining more votes in every session . . . [407–408].

It is Elmer's Napoleonic ambition to combine all such organizations to the greater glory of himself:

> He would combine in one association all the moral organizations in America—perhaps, later, in the entire world. He would be the executive of that combination; he would be the super-president of the United States, and some day the dictator of the world [409].

We are back in the land of wizards and ogres once more.

In fact, the question of whether Elmer is a human being or an ogre in the novel is a relevant one. At times he is almost satanic, a compendium of all the vices; they are too many and too flagrant for him to be real. But occasionally Lewis tries to endow him with a soul, as in the incident of his conversion at Terwillinger College. Elmer is the great man steadily making his way upward in the world—the man of immoderate personal ambition—and the great man hasn't time for scruples. Since he is ordinarily only a caricature, we cannot consider him a believeable human being; and when Lewis tells us that he has a conscience, we refuse to believe it.

After he had become a celebrity, Lewis usually managed to avoid controversy over his books by being out of the United States when they appeared. The publication day of *Elmer Gantry* found him wandering through Europe with Ramon Guthrie; from Dubrovnik, Yugoslavia, he commented in the most innocent tones on the stir he had caused: "The violent Kansas City blokes have been asinine. I'm grateful to them for proving the book." Very few observers, however, thought that he had been as fair and dispassionate as he pretended; one comparatively balanced review of the novel was entitled "'Red' Lewis in a Red Rage," and his former professor William Lyon Phelps declared in an interview that the book must have been written when Lewis was "literally foaming at the mouth. . . ." Edwin Muir was one of the few critics who found some complexity in Lewis's attitude toward his central character; he thought this complexity was due to the division of intentions which was evident in other Lewis novels—Lewis wanted to write both a satire and a novel, to indict his hero and to sympathize with him at the same time. It might seem that the last thing in the world Lewis wanted was sympathy for Elmer Gantry, whom he regarded, he told Allen Austin years later, as "a hypocrite through and through." Yet he wrote in the *Nation* in 1928, "Actually, I like the Babbitts, the Dr. Pickerbaughs, the Will Kennicotts, and even the Elmer Gantrys rather better than anyone else on earth." Furthermore, he told Betty Stevens that the Babbitts "were my children and I wanted to reform them. Gantry, too. Even Gantry wouldn't have been such a bad fellow if he'd been, say, a salesman." Only a very curious moral outlook could have permitted the creator of such a monster as Elmer Gantry to say that his character's lack of a sense of decency would not have been objectionable if he had changed his profession. . . .

Source: David J. Dooley, "Aspiration and Enslavement," in *The Art of Sinclair Lewis*, University of Nebraska Press, 1967, pp. 126–31.

Sources

Ferguson, Charles W., Review of *Elmer Gantry*, in *Critical Essays on Sinclair Lewis*, edited by Martin Bucco, G. K. Hall, 1986, pp. 47–48; originally published in the *Bookman*, March 1927.

Grebstein, Sheldon Norman, *Sinclair Lewis*, Twayne United States Authors Series, No. 14, Twayne, 1962, pp. 99–107.

Lundquist, James, *Sinclair Lewis*, Frederick Ungar Publishing, 1973, pp. 49–53.

Schorer, Mark, "Introduction," in *Sinclair Lewis: A Collection of Critical Essays*, edited by Mark Schorer, Prentice-Hall, 1962, p. 4.

———, *Sinclair Lewis: An American Life*, McGraw Hill, 1961, pp. 737–38.

West, Rebecca, Review of *Elmer Gantry*, in *Sinclair Lewis: A Collection of Critical Essays*, edited by Mark Schorer, Prentice-Hall, 1962, pp. 39–45; originally published in *New York Herald Tribune Books*, March 13, 1927.

Further Reading

Dooley, D. J., *The Art of Sinclair Lewis*, University of Nebraska Press, 1967, pp. 126–30.
> Dooley argues that the novel fails because it is not a realistic portrayal of religion, and it lacks sufficient wit and humor to compensate for its unfairness.

Light, Martin, *The Quixotic Vision of Sinclair Lewis*, Purdue University Press, 1975, pp. 99–107.
> Light examines what he sees as quixotic elements in the novel, especially in the characters Sharon Falconer and Frank Shallard.

Schorer, Mark, "Afterword," in *Elmer Gantry*, Signet Classics edition, New American Library, 1967, pp. 419–30.
> Schorer discusses Lewis's research for the novel, including the clergyman he met in Kansas City. He also analyzes the characterization and structure of the novel and Lewis's occasional failure to integrate his story-telling with the social facts he presents.

———, "Sinclair Lewis and the Method of Half-Truths," in *Society and Self in the Novel*, Columbia University Press, 1956, pp. 117–44.
> Schorer analyzes the novel's lack of conflict and dramatic counterpoint; there are no obstacles to Elmer's success, since the good characters are weak and play only peripheral roles and there are no competing orders of value, since everything is corrupt.

The God of Small Things

Arundhati Roy

1997

Arundhati Roy's debut novel *The God of Small Things* rapidly became a world-renowned literary sensation after it was published in New Delhi in 1997. Immediately recognized as a passionate, sophisticated, and lushly descriptive work, it won Britain's prestigious Booker Prize and launched its author to international fame. The novel tells the story of the Kochammas, a wealthy Christian family in a small village in the southern Indian state of Kerala. Based loosely from the perspective of Rahel Kochamma, who has returned to her hometown to see her twin brother, it pieces together the story of the dramatic events of Rahel's childhood that drastically changed the lives of everyone in the family.

The God of Small Things is an ambitious work that addresses universal themes ranging from religion to biology. Roy stresses throughout the novel that great and small themes are interconnected, and that historical events and seemingly unrelated details have far-reaching consequences throughout a community and country. The novel is therefore able to comment simultaneously on universal, abstract themes, and a wide variety of ideas relating to the personal and family history of the members of the Kochamma family as well as the wider concerns of the Kerala region of India. Some of the novel's most thoroughly developed themes are forbidden love, Indian history, and politics. It is in love and politics that Roy's carefully constructed, multifaceted narrative tends to dwell, and it is when love, politics, and history combine that Roy is able to communicate her most profound authorial insights.

Author Biography

Born circa 1960, Roy grew up in Aymanam, a village in the state of Kerala, in southern India. Her father, a Hindu tea planter from Bengal, was divorced from her Syrian Christian mother when Roy was very young, and Roy was raised by her mother, who ran an informal school. Roy left home when she was sixteen and lived in a squatter's colony in New Delhi, selling empty beer bottles for a living. She eventually went to architectural school and married a fellow student, Gerard Da Cunha. Both quit their studies and moved to Goa, which is in Southwestern India. Roy eventually left Da Cunha and moved back to New Delhi where she found a job at the National Institute of Urban Affairs.

While living in New Delhi, Roy met the film director Pradeep Krishen (whom she later married) and accepted a small acting role that he offered. Soon afterwards, she traveled to Italy on a scholarship to study monument restoration. Roy began to write screenplays while she was in Italy, and she and Krishen later collaborated on a television series that was cancelled after they had shot several episodes. She then wrote two screenplays that became films, and she began to write prose until her critical essay of the celebrated film *Bandit Queen* caused considerable controversy. Roy withdrew to private life to work on her debut novel, which took her nearly five years to complete.

The God of Small Things rapidly became an international sensation, winning Britain's Booker Prize. After its publication, Roy began to work as a political activist, writing essays and giving speeches on a variety of issues, including capitalist globalization, the rights of oppressed groups, and the negative influence of United States culture and governmental policy on the rest of the world. She has been imprisoned for her positions and activism, but she continues to fight for a variety of liberal causes. Roy received the Sydney Peace Prize in November of 2004.

Arundhati Roy © Robert van der Hilst/Corbis

narrator describes the funeral of Sophie Mol, Rahel and Estha's cousin, and the point after the funeral when Ammu went to the police station to say that a terrible mistake had been made. Two weeks after this point, Estha was returned to his father.

The narrator briefly describes the twins' adult lives before they return to Ayemenem. In the present, Baby Kochamma gloats that Estha does not speak to Rahel just as he does not speak to anyone else, and then the narrator gives an overview of Baby Kochamma's life. Rahel looks out the window at the building that used to contain the family business, Paradise Pickles and Preserves, and flashes back to the circumstances surrounding Sophie Mol's death.

Chapters 2–4

The second chapter describes the trip in which Rahel, Estha, Ammu, Chacko, and Baby Kochamma travel to the town of Cochin in order to pick up Margaret Kochamma and Sophie Mol from the airport. They are on the way to see *The Sound of Music*, but they are delayed at a train crossing by a Marxist demonstration in which Rahel sees her friend Velutha, who is a Paravan, or Untouchable Hindu, employed by the Kochamma family. When she yells to him out the window, Ammu scolds her furiously.

Plot Summary

Chapter 1

The God of Small Things begins with Rahel returning to her childhood home in Ayemenem, India, to see her twin brother Estha, who has been sent to Ayemenem by their father. Events flash back to Rahel and Estha's birth and the period before their mother Ammu divorced their father. Then the

A flashback describes Velutha and his relations with the Kochamma family, and then one of the protesters opens Rahel's door and makes Baby Kochamma wave a Marxist flag. Before they drive away, Chacko says that Ammu, Estha, and Rahel are "millstones around his neck." In chapter 3, which takes place in the present day, the narrator describes the filthiness of the Ayemenem House. Estha comes home, goes upstairs, and takes off his clothes to wash them while Rahel watches.

Chapter 4 continues the story of the family trip at the point when they arrive at the movie theater. Ammu makes Estha go to the lobby because he cannot resist singing along, and the Orangedrink Lemondrink Man at the refreshments counter forces Estha to masturbate him. The family leaves early because Ammu sees that Estha will be sick, and on the way out she comments on the sweetness of the Orangedrink Lemondrink Man. Rahel says "why don't you marry him, then?" Ammu tells her that comments like these make people love you a little less. Rahel worries that Ammu will love Sophie Mol more than her. The twins fall asleep next to each other in Chacko's room.

Chapters 5–7

Back in the present day, the narrator describes the filthiness of the river, just a stream now because of a saltwater barrage, and the five-star hotel that has taken over the "History House," which was formerly the home of an Englishman who took on traditional Indian customs. Rahel then answers Comrade Pillai's invasive questions and remembers his son Lenin.

In chapter 6, the family picks up Margaret and Sophie Mol from the Cochin Airport. Baby Kochamma tells the twins they are the ambassadors of India. Chacko happily introduces everyone, but Estha does not say "How do YOU do?" as Ammu requests, and Rahel hides behind a curtain. Ammu later scolds them angrily, and the twins talk with Sophie Mol.

Chapter 7 is in the present day, when Rahel finds her and Estha's *Wisdom Exercise Notebooks* and reads the corrections that Ammu made in them. She remembers Ammu's last visit before she died and the lonely circumstances of her mother's death.

Chapters 8–11

When the family arrives at the Ayemenem House with Margaret and Sophie Mol, the narrator compares the situation to a play. Rahel escapes from the distribution of Sophie Mol's cake to play with Velutha, and Ammu exchanges a meaningful glance with Velutha.

In chapter 9, Rahel remembers her and Estha becoming friends with Sophie Mol, and, in the present day, she walks into the abandoned factory. Chapter 10 describes Estha's thoughts while he wandered from Sophie Mol's reception at the house and into the pickle factory. He and Rahel decide to take a stockpile of things to the History House. The twins find a boat by the river and Velutha helps them repair it. In chapter 11, Ammu dreams of a one-armed man until the twins wake her, and she realizes that Velutha is the man of whom she dreamed, the God of Small Things.

Chapters 12–15

In the present day, Rahel goes to see the traditional kathakali dancing in the Ayemenem temple and Estha shows up as well. Chapter 13 recalls the story of Margaret and Chacko's relationship and then describes the circumstances leading up to Sophie Mol's drowning, beginning with Vellya Paapen's visit to the Ayemenem House. Vellya Paapen tells Mammachi of Velutha's affair with Ammu and offers to kill his son, and Mammachi shouts, spits at him, and pushes him to the ground. Mammachi and Baby Kochamma then manage to lock Ammu in her room, and the next morning they receive the news that a white child was found drowned in the river.

At the police station, Baby Kochamma lies to Inspector Thomas Mathew that Velutha threatened them and tried to force himself on Ammu. The inspector then interviews Comrade Pillai about whether Velutha has any political support and, discovering that he does not, instructs his men to attack Velutha.

In chapter 14, Chacko visits Comrade Pillai and asks him about Velutha. Comrade Pillai, because of his own ambitions in the Communist Party, tells Chacko that Velutha is a dangerous party member who should be fired. Velutha comes to see Comrade Pillai, after Mammachi screams at him and fires him, and Comrade Pillai tells Velutha that he has no support from the party. In chapter 15, Velutha swims across the river to the History House.

Chapters 16–20

The twins and Sophie Mol run away from home in chapter 16, and Sophie Mol drowns after their boat tips over on the way to the History House. Chapter 17, in the present day, describes Rahel and Estha lying in bed, remembering their childhood. In chapter 18, the Kottayam police find Velutha sleeping next to Rahel and Estha at the History House, they and beat him until he is nearly dead.

Inspector Mathew interviews the twins in chapter 19 and discovers that Velutha is innocent. He tells Baby Kochamma that if the children do not identify Velutha as their abductor, he will accuse Baby Kochamma of filing a false report. Baby Kochamma tells the twins that they and Ammu will go to jail unless they accuse Velutha, and Estha goes into Velutha's cell to condemn him. It is not until the next morning, after Velutha has died, that Ammu goes to the police station to set the record straight.

Chapter 20 describes the scene at the train station when Estha is leaving for Calcutta, and then changes to the present tense, when Estha and Rahel begin to make love. Chapter 21 flashes back to the point at which Ammu finds Velutha at the river and she and Velutha make love for the first time.

Characters

Aleyooty Ammachi

Aleyooty Ammachi is Rahel and Estha's great-grandmother. Her portrait hangs prominently beside that of Reverend Ipe in the Ayemenem House.

Baba

Baba is Estha and Rahel's father. Ammu divorces him when the children are very young. He was a violent alcoholic who not only beat his wife and children, but attempted to prostitute his wife to his English employer. Baba has remarried, resigned from his job on a tea plantation, and "more or less" stopped drinking when, after Sophie Mol's death, Estha moves in with him in Calcutta. When Estha is an adult, Baba sends him back to Ayemenem and emigrates to Australia.

Reverend E. John Ipe

Estha and Rahel's great-grandfather, Reverend Ipe had been known as Punnyan Kunju, or "Little Blessed One," since he was blessed by the Syrian Christian Patriarch at age seven.

Joe

Joe is Margaret Kochamma's second husband, who dies in a car accident shortly before Margaret and Sophie Mol travel to Ayemenem.

The Kathakali Men

Karna and Kunti, the Kathakali Men, perform the traditional Hindu dancing that Rahel and Estha go to see.

Ammu Kochamma

Ammu is Rahel and Estha's mother. She is a beautiful and sardonic woman who has been victimized first by her father and then her husband. While raising her children, she has become tense and repressed. Ammu grew up in Delhi but, because her father said that college was an unnecessary expense for a girl, was forced to live with her parents when they moved to Ayemenem. She met her future husband at a wedding reception. She later divorces him and returns to the Ayemenem House when he starts to abuse the twins.

Ammu's latent "Unsafe Edge," full of desire and "reckless rage," emerges during Sophie Mol's visit and draws her to Velutha. After the horrific climax to the affair, Ammu sends Estha to live with his father and leaves Rahel in the Ayemenem House while Ammu looks for work; but Ammu loses a succession of jobs because she is ill. Ammu dies alone in a cheap hotel at the age of thirty-one. Chacko has her cremated because the Syrian Christian Church will not bury her.

Baby Kochamma

Nicknamed "Baby," Mammachi's sister, Navomi Ipe Kochamma, is a judgmental old maid with tiny feet. Rahel thinks, "She's living her life backwards," because Baby Kochamma renounces the material world when she is young, but becomes very materialistic when she is old. Throughout her life, Baby Kochamma is an insecure, selfish, and vindictive person.

When she was a girl, Baby Kochamma fell in love with a handsome Irish monk named Father Mulligan who made weekly visits to her father. Although they did nothing more than flirt while talking about the Bible, when he moved to Madras she became a Roman Catholic and entered a convent in Madras in the hopes of being with him. After her hopes were crushed, she left the convent and traveled to the United States to study, returning to India obese and devoted to gardening. During the time of Sophie Mol's visit, Baby Kochamma is a nuisance who pesters the twins because she dislikes them and Ammu. She is later revealed to be cruel and insidious, because she is the one that convinces the twins to condemn Velutha; and it was due to her manipulations of Chacko that Ammu is forced to leave the house and Estha is returned to his father. In her old age, Baby Kochamma becomes a bitter and lonely woman addicted to television, after having locked herself inside the family house.

Chacko Kochamma

Chacko is Ammu's intellectual and self-absorbed older brother. He was a charming but very unclean Rhodes Scholar at Oxford, and he met Margaret while she was working in an Oxford café. Deeply in love with Margaret, in part because she never depended on him or adored him like a mother, he marries her without telling his family. She grows tired of his squalor within a year, however, and divorces him around the time that their daughter is born.

Between his divorce and Sophie Mol's death, Chacko grew fatter and became obsessed with balsawood airplanes, which he unsuccessfully attempted to fly. He was also unsuccessful at running the pickle factory, which started to lose money as soon as he attempted to expand the operation. A "self-proclaimed Marxist," Chacko attempts to be a benevolent employer and even plans to organize a union among his own workers. However, he is insistent that he is the sole owner of his factory, his house, and other possessions that he actually shares with women. Sophie Mol's death is completely devastating for him. After her death, he emigrates to Canada.

Estha Kochamma

Estha, which is short for Esthappen Yako, is Rahel's twin brother. He is a serious, intelligent, and somewhat nervous child who wears "beige and pointy shoes" and has an "Elvis puff." His experience of the circumstances surrounding Sophie Mol's visit is somewhat more traumatic than Rahel's, beginning when he is sexually abused by the Orangedrink Lemondrink Man at the Abhilash Talkies theater. The narrator stresses that Estha's "Two Thoughts" in the pickle factory, which stem from this experience (that *Anything can happen to Anyone* and *It's best to be prepared*) are critical in leading to his cousin's death.

Estha is the twin chosen by Baby Kochamma, because he is more "practical" and "responsible," to go into Velutha's cell and condemn him as their abductor. This trauma, in addition to being shipped to Calcutta to live with his father, contributes to Estha becoming mute at some point in his childhood. Estha never went to college and acquired a number of habits, such as wandering on very long walks and obsessively cleaning his clothes. He is so close to his sister that the narrator describes them as one person, despite having been separated for most of their lives.

Mammachi Kochamma

An elegant woman in her old age although she is nearly blind, Mammachi is Rahel and Estha's grandmother. Brutally beaten by her husband, she nevertheless cries at his funeral and shares many of his values, including an extremely rigid view of the caste system. She began the pickle factory and ran it successfully, and she was an "exceptionally talented" violinist, although Pappachi disallowed her to take further lessons when he heard this. Mammachi loves Chacko with blind admiration and deeply dislikes Margaret Kochamma. Nevertheless, she tolerates and even facilitates Chacko's affairs with factory workers, although she is so horrified when she hears of Ammu's affair with Velutha that she attacks both Velutha and his father, and locks Ammu in her room.

Margaret Kochamma

Margaret is Sophie Mol's mother and Chacko's ex-wife. She is from a strict, working-class London family and was working as a waitress in Oxford when she met Chacko. Marrying him because of his uncontrolled personality that made her feel free, Margaret soon realized that she did not need him to accept herself, and she divorced him. When her second husband Joe dies, Margaret accepts Chacko's invitation to Ayemenem for Christmas, and she is haunted by this decision for the rest of her life. When Margaret sees her daughter's body, she feels an irrational rage towards the twins and seeks out Estha several times to slap him.

Pappachi Kochamma

Shri Benaan John Ipe, known in the family as Pappachi, is Rahel and Estha's grandfather. He was an "Imperial Entomologist" under British rule and an Anglophile whose greatest setback was not having named a moth that he discovered because government scientists failed to recognize it as a new species until later. Seventeen years older than his wife, he was extremely resentful of her and beat her regularly with a brass vase until Chacko ordered him never to do it again. Pappachi Kochamma also beat his daughter and smashed furniture, although in public he convinced everyone that he was compassionate and neglected by his wife. In his old age, he rode around in his blue Plymouth that he kept entirely to himself.

Rahel Kochamma

Rahel is Ammu's daughter and Estha's younger sister by eighteen minutes. An intelligent and honest person who has never felt socially comfortable, she is something of a drifter, and several times the narrator refers to her as the quality "Emptiness." When she is a girl, her hair sits "on top of her head like a fountain" and she always wears red-tinted plastic sunglasses with yellow rims.

Although Ammu often chastises Rahel for being dirty and unsafe, she loves her very deeply, and Rahel is equally devoted to her mother. Rahel also loves Velutha and her brother, with whom she shares a "single Siamese soul." She is traumatized by Sophie Mol's drowning, Velutha's death, and Ammu's death. Although these events do not seem to deprive her of her quirkiness or brightness, they contribute to her sense of sadness and lack of direction in later life. After Ammu dies, Rahel drifts between schools, receiving little attention from Mammachi or Chacko. Rahel then enters an architecture school but never finishes the course, marries an American named Larry McCaslin, and lives with him in Boston until they are divorced. She moves to Washington, D.C. and spends several years as a night clerk at a gas station before returning to Ayemenem to see Estha.

Kochu Maria

Kochu Maria is the Kochamma family's "vinegar-hearted, short-tempered, midget cook." She does not speak any English and, although she has always "noticed everything," she eventually stops caring about how the house looks and becomes addicted to television.

Kochu Thomban

Kochu Thomban is the Ayemenem temple elephant. When Rahel sees him in the present day, he is no longer "Kochu Thomban" ("Little Tusker") but "Vellya Thomban" ("Big Tusker").

Kuttappen

Velutha's older brother, Kuttappen is paralyzed from the chest down and confined to his house, which he shares with his brother and father.

Inspector Thomas Mathew

The Kottayam police chief is a practical, cynical, and brutal man who deals carefully with the scandal of Sophie Mol's death and Ammu's affair with Velutha. He taps on Ammu's breasts and insults her when she comes to make a statement about Velutha because the police chief strongly believes in the conventional caste system.

Larry McCaslin

Larry is Rahel's American husband, whom she met at the college of architecture in Delhi while he was working on a doctoral thesis, and with whom she moves to Boston. He holds her "as though she was a gift" and notices a hollowness in Rahel's eyes

that seems to contribute to their lack of understanding and eventual divorce.

Miss Mitten

Rahel and Estha's tutor whom they dislike, Miss Mitten is a Born Again Christian who scolds the twins for reading backwards. She is killed by a milk van.

Father Mulligan

Father Mulligan was Baby Kochamma's would-be lover. An Irish monk who came to Kerala to study Hindu scriptures "in order to be able to denounce them intelligently," he flirted with Baby Kochamma while ostensibly talking about the Bible. Eventually, he converts to Hinduism, staying in touch with Baby Kochamma, and dies of viral hepatitis.

Murlidharan

Perched on the milestone of an intersection, Murlidharan is the "level-crossing lunatic" the family encounters on their way to Cochin.

Comrade E. M. S. Namboodiripad

Chacko's hero and the leader of Kerala's democratically elected Communist government, Comrade Namboodiripad is a moderate, particularly during his second term.

Orangedrink Lemondrink Man

The man who works behind the refreshments counter at the Abhilash Talkies movie theater forces Estha to masturbate him. He looks like an "unfriendly jeweled bear" and deeply traumatizes Estha, who believes the Orangedrink Lemondrink Man will find him in Ayemenem.

Comrade K. N. M. Pillai

Comrade Pillai is "essentially a political man" who plots to become the leader of the Communist Party in Ayemenem. With many connections and building influence, he is involved in a number of business ventures, including making signs for the pickle factory. After he betrays Velutha because he wants to rid himself of any competition in the party ranks, Comrade Pillai lays the seeds for dissatisfaction among the workers of Paradise Pickles and organizes the unionization that contributes to the factory's collapse. This does not help him rise to power in the party, however.

Kalyani Pillai

Kalyani is Comrade Pillai's quiet wife.

Latha Pillai

Comrade Pillai's niece, Latha, recites a poem by Sir Walter Scott for Chacko.

Lenin Pillai

Lenin is Comrade Pillai's son. He is a slightly awkward boy who grows up to be a secretary in Delhi.

Kari Saipu

Kari Saipu is the "Black Sahib," the Englishman who took on traditional Indian customs. The twins know his house, which was unoccupied after Kari Saipu shot himself, as "the History House." This house is the location of Ammu and Velutha's meetings.

Sophie Mol

Sophie Mol is Chacko and Margaret's daughter. She is a frank and spirited English girl characterized by her bellbottoms and her go-go bag. Although the twins are prejudiced against her because they have been so insistently instructed about how to behave when she arrives, she manages to win them over. This is partly because she is charming and outgoing, and partly because she rejected the advances of Chacko, Mammachi, and Baby Kochamma in favor of befriending Rahel and Estha.

One reason Sophie Mol's death is so important to the book's main themes is that she represents a combination of Indian and British identities. The narrator is careful to call her "Sophie," her English name, combined with "Mol," the phrase for "girl" in the local language of Malayalam. Although Sophie Mol never takes to Indian culture, she does make a great effort with the twins before she accidentally falls into the river and drowns.

Vellya Paapen

Velutha's father, Vellya is an "Old-World Paravan" who feels he is indebted to Mammachi for paying for his glass eye. He is tortured about his son's affair with Ammu and tells Mammachi about it.

Velutha

An Untouchable worker at the pickle factory and a close friend to Rahel and Estha, Velutha is blamed for killing Sophie Mol and raping Ammu. In fact, he has nothing to do with Sophie Mol's death, and he carries on a brief and voluntary affair with Ammu until Inspector Thomas Mathew's police officers beat Velutha until he is nearly dead.

Velutha's name means "White" in Malayalam, so-called because he has such dark skin. Mammachi noticed his prodigious talents in making and fixing things when he was young and convinced his father to send him to the Untouchables' School founded by her father-in-law. Velutha became an accomplished carpenter and mechanic, and acquired an assurance that scared his father because it was unacceptable among Untouchables. Velutha disappeared for four years and was hired by Mammachi upon his return to Ayemenem. A member of the Communist Party, he never quite fits into his role as an Untouchable, and he begins an extremely passionate affair with Ammu when Sophie Mol arrives in Ayemenem. After Comrade Pillai refuses to help him, the police officers beat him, and Estha identifies him as their abductor. Velutha dies in jail.

Themes

Indian History and Politics

Indian history and politics shape the plot and meaning of *The God of Small Things* in a variety of ways. Some of Roy's commentary is on the surface, with jokes and snippets of wisdom about political realities in India. However, the novel also examines the historical roots of these realities and develops profound insights into the ways in which human desperation and desire emerge from the confines of a firmly entrenched caste society. Roy reveals a complex and longstanding class conflict in the state of Kerala, India, and she comments on its various competing forces.

For example, Roy's novel attacks the brutal, entrenched, and systematic oppression at work in Kerala, exemplified by figures of power such as Inspector Thomas Mathew. Roy is also highly critical of the hypocrisy and ruthlessness of the conventional, traditional moral code of Pappachi and Mammachi. On the opposite side of the political fence, the Kerala Communist Party, at least the faction represented by Comrade Pillai, is revealed to be much more concerned with personal ambition than with any notions of social justice.

Class Relations and Cultural Tensions

In addition to her commentary on Indian history and politics, Roy evaluates the Indian postcolonial complex, or the cultural attitudes of many Indians towards their former British rulers. After Ammu calls her father a "[sh——t]-wiper" in Hindi for his blind devotion to the British, Chacko explains to the twins that they come from a family of Anglophiles, or lovers of British culture, "trapped

Topics For Further Study

- Roy has published a great deal of political writing, has worked as an activist, and has been imprisoned for her political beliefs. Research her political views and activities, and read some of her political writings. How would you characterize Roy's position on issues such as globalization and terrorism? What have been the results of her activism in India and around the world?

- As an Indian novel written in English, *The God of Small Things* is part of a genre of literature stretching back to the days of the British Raj. Research the ways in which Roy's novel relates to this tradition, which includes authors such as R. K. Narayan and Salman Rushdie. In what ways docs Roy's novel fit into this tradition, and in what ways does it belong outside of it? What innovations does Roy bring to Indian literature in English, and why are they important? How does Roy's novel relate to Indian politics, and how is this similar or different to the ways in which the novels of her predecessors have related to Indian politics?

- Some readers and critics have found elements of *The God of Small Things* offensive or controversial. Research the nature of the outcry against the novel, particularly in India and in Britain. Which aspects of the work were controversial, and why? What were the results of the controversy? Describe your reaction to moments of the novel such as when Estha is forced to masturbate the Orangedrink Lemondrink Man, when Ammu and Velutha make love, and when Rahel and Estha make love. Discuss how elements of the forbidden and the taboo relate to the central themes of the novel.

- Communism has been a uniquely prominent force in the state of Kerala, India. Research the activities of the various factions of the Communist Party in Kerala. How did communism develop and spread in the region? What are the key ways in which communist thought has affected Kerala's history? How does the history of the communist parties in Kerala relate to the history of communism throughout South Asia? Discuss the state of communism in Kerala today.

---

outside their own history and unable to retrace their steps," and he goes on to say that they despise themselves because of this.

A related inferiority complex is evident in the interactions between Untouchables and Touchables in Ayemenem. Vellya Paapen is an example of an Untouchable so grateful to the Touchable class that he is willing to kill his son when he discovers that his son has broken the most important rule of class segregation—that there be no inter-class sexual relations. Nearly all of the relationships in the novel are somehow colored by cultural and class tension, including the twins' relationship with Sophie Mol, Chacko's relationship with Margaret, Pappachi's relationship with his family, and Ammu's relationship with Velutha. Characters such as Baby Kochamma and Pappachi are the most rigid and vicious in their attempts to uphold that social code,

while Ammu and Velutha are the most unconventional and daring in unraveling it. Roy implies that this is why they are punished so severely for their transgression.

Forbidden Love

The many types of love in Roy's novel, whether they are described as erotic, familial, incestuous, biological, or hopeless, are important to the novel's meaning. However, Roy focuses her authorial commentary on forbidden and taboo types of love, including Ammu's love for Velutha and Rahel's love for Estha. Both relationships are rigidly forbidden by what Roy calls the "Love Laws," or "The laws that lay down who should be loved, and how. / And how much." Although breaking these laws is the worst of taboos, and those who break them are brutally punished, desire and desperation overcome the Love Laws at the key moments of Roy's novel.

One interpretation of Roy's theme of forbidden love is that love is such a powerful and uncontrollable force that it cannot be contained by any conventional social code. Another is that conventional society somehow seeks to destroy real love, which is why love in the novel is consistently connected to loss, death, and sadness. Also, because all romantic love in the novel relates closely to politics and history, it is possible that Roy is stressing the interconnectedness of personal desire to larger themes of history and social circumstances. Love would therefore be an emotion that can be explained only in terms of two peoples' cultural backgrounds and political identities.

Style

Non-sequential Narrative

The God of Small Things is not written in a sequential narrative style in which events unfold chronologically. Instead, the novel is a patchwork of flashbacks and lengthy sidetracks that weave together to tell the story of the Kochamma family. The main events of the novel are traced back through the complex history of their causes, and memories are revealed as they relate to each other thematically and as they might appear in Rahel's mind. Although the narrative voice is omniscient, or all-knowing, it is loosely grounded in Rahel's perspective, and all of the episodes of the novel progress towards the key moments in Rahel's life.

This non-sequential narrative style, which determines the form of the novel, is an extremely useful authorial tool. It allows Roy a great deal of flexibility as she chooses which themes and events are most important to pursue. The author is able to structure her book so as to build up to the ideas and events at the root of the Kochamma family's experience.

Foreshadowing

Throughout Roy's novel, the narrative voice emphasizes that it is building towards a mysterious, cataclysmic, and all-important event. Roy even provides details and glimpses of the event, which she refers to as "The Loss of Sophie Mol," and quotes characters remembering it and referring to it vaguely far before the reader discovers what has happened. Because of this technique, called foreshadowing, Roy builds considerable tension and

intrigue into *The God of Small Things*, and she is able to play with the expectation and anticipation that the reader feels.

Historical Context

Because of the efforts of the political and religious leader Mohandas Gandhi, India became independent on August 15, 1947 at the stroke of midnight, after more than three hundred years of a British colonial presence. The British partitioned the former colony into the nations of India and Pakistan (comprised of East and West regions), but this was unsuccessful in quelling agitations between Hindus and Muslims. The borders were only rough designations of religious majorities, and millions died as Hindus in Pakistan moved to majority-Hindu India, and Muslims in India moved to majority-Muslim Pakistan. Ammu was five years old in 1947, living with her family in the Indian capital of New Delhi.

Jawaharlal Nehru, the Prime Minister of India from Independence until his death in 1964, struggled to foster economic growth and became involved in various territorial disputes. In Kerala, the Communist Party of India (CPI) was elected to power in a state government led by E. M. S. Namboodiripad in 1957, but Nehru dissolved it in 1959. In 1962, the year Rahel and Estha were born, India fought a limited war over a border dispute with China. As a result of the Chinese conflict, the CPI split between a pro-Russian faction, still called the CPI, and a faction that grew to be less influenced by foreign governments, called the Communist Party of India (Marxist). In the mid-1960s, a further split in the Indian communist parties formed the Naxalites, who advocated an immediate communist revolution, while tensions between Pakistan and India flared into war in 1965.

After Prime Minister Lal Bahadur Shastri died of a heart attack in 1966, Nehru's daughter Indira Gandhi (no relation to Mohandas Gandhi) assumed the post amidst a severe draught and growing unemployment. These conditions contributed to the major losses that Gandhi's Indian National Congress Party suffered in the 1967 elections. As Gandhi's intentions for the Congress Party became clear, tensions arose between liberal and conservative members of the party, and in 1969, the year of Sophie Mol's visit to Ayemenem, the Congress Party split. Although Indira Gandhi remained in control of the larger, liberal faction, she was forced to forge alliances with left-wing parties in order to maintain control of the government.

Compare & Contrast

- **1969:** E. M. S. Namboodiripad's communist government of Kerala falls for the second time, and the Indian National Congress Party dissolves into two groups.

1990s: Indian Prime Minister Rajiv Gandhi is assassinated in 1991 and is succeeded by P. V. Narasimha Rao. A series of leadership struggles begins in 1996, when Rao is forced out of power.

Today: Manmohan Singh is appointed prime minister of India in May of 2004, after the Congress Party unexpectedly wins the election and its leader Sonia Gandhi, widow of Rajiv Gandhi, declines the post in order to appease Hindu nationalists. Communism remains a powerful force in Kerala politics.

- **1969:** Kerala is a lush and warm region of southern India with a uniquely high literacy rate. Public welfare systems have become much more substantial since independence, but the agricultural economy remains similar to the economy in the days of the British Raj.

1990s: Kerala's economy is still based on rubber, coconut, and spice production, but economic reforms are placing much more emphasis on large private corporations, and India is opening up to foreign investment.

Today: India has one of the largest and fastest-growing economies in the world, and the trend towards privatization continues. Kerala has a literacy rate near ninety percent, which is the highest of any state in India.

- **1969:** Post-colonial Indian literature written in English is becoming a popular genre of its own, developed by writers such as R. K. Narayan.

1990s: Salman Rushdie has been a dominant force in the Indo-British literary scene since he published *Midnight's Children* in 1981.

Today: Indian writing in English is a wide and diverse genre of literature, and Roy is one of its most successful stars, even though she has published only one novel.

Further tensions with Pakistan led to India's involvement in a conflict between East Pakistan and West Pakistan in 1971, which led to the independence of Bangladesh (formerly East Pakistan). Indira Gandhi was convicted of minor election law violations in 1975, but she declared a state of emergency in order to stay in power. Widely unpopular, this move allowed her to arrest opposition leaders and censor the press, and she was defeated in the 1977 elections. Gandhi was elected once again in 1980, however, and began to meet with foreign leaders while dealing with several insurgencies in India. In 1984, she sent Indian troops to storm a Sikh temple, killing the Sikh guerillas inside, and this event led to her assassination by two of her Sikh bodyguards. Gandhi's son, Rajiv, succeeded her to the leadership of the Congress Party and was elected prime minister in 1985. Rajiv Gandhi sponsored economic reforms, but he was criticized as an indecisive leader and lost the 1989 election.

Roy wrote her novel in the early 1990s, during a period in which Rajiv Gandhi was assassinated by a Sri Lankan Tamil in 1991 while campaigning for an election that political analysts believe he would have won. The present-day events in *The God of Small Things* occur in 1992, when Congress/I (formerly the Congress Party) leader P. V. Narasimha Rao was prime minister. Rao became known for his sensitive handling of Hindu-Muslim tensions, his economic reforms, and his progressive foreign policy in response to the collapse of the Soviet Union. He lost power in 1996 amidst charges of corruption, however, and this began a series of leadership struggles that continued through India's announcement in 1998 that it was a nuclear power; Pakistan made a similar announcement shortly thereafter.

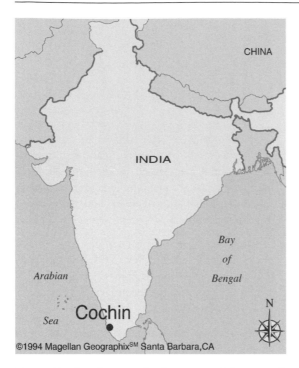

Map of India showing the location of the city of Cochin in sourthern India © MAPS.com/Corbis

Critical Overview

The God of Small Things was an unprecedented international success for a first-time author. It won a publishing advance reputed to be near one million dollars, and it won Britain's most prestigious writing award, the Booker Prize, in 1997. Reviews in the United States were very positive, often including high praise such as that of Ritu Menon in her review for *Women's Review of Books*: "*The God of Small Things* is a seduction from start to finish." Although the novel was generally well-reviewed in Britain, there was some controversy about its success, and a minority of critics, including the previous Booker Prize Committee Chairperson Carmen Callil, said on television that it did not deserve the prize. The novel has also caused some controversy in India, where it was first published. Communists, including E. M. S. Namboodiripad, took exception to Roy's portrayal of communist characters, and the lawyer Sabu Thomas filed a public interest petition claiming that the novel was obscene.

Critics generally group the novel into the genre of post-colonial Indian literature that takes Indian politics and history as its subject. For example, the anonymous reviewer in the March 15, 1997 edition of *Kirkus Reviews* characterizes Roy's style as "reminiscent of Salman Rushdie's early work." Like the novels of the influential Indian-British author Salman Rushdie, *The God of Small Things* is written in English, for a Western readership as much as an Indian readership, and it takes on a variety of historical and political themes.

Criticism

Scott Trudell

Trudell is an independent scholar with a bachelor's degree in English literature. In the following essay, Trudell discusses the significance of the sexual encounters between Rahel and Estha, and Ammu and Velutha.

The God of Small Things builds an incredible amount of anticipation and expectation for the definitive moment of the story. With all of its foreshadowing, its emphasis on tracing one's steps, and its insistent suggestion that everything, from politics to erotic desire, is intimately connected, Roy's novel places a great deal of emphasis on the central event of the twins' childhood that caused the momentous changes in the Kochamma family. The reader comes to expect, because of the narrator's many references to "the Loss of Sophie Mol," that everything will boil down to one key moment, and that this moment will involve Sophie Mol's death.

It eventually becomes clear, however, that Sophie Mol's actual drowning is an accident, an understated tragedy in which she simply vanishes in the river. Like all of the characters' lives and the events of the plot, Sophie Mol's death is intimately tied to many other elements, including Estha's sexual abuse, Sophie Mol's relationship to the twins, and the host of factors that led to the tragedy. But the actual loss of Sophie Mol does not reveal much about the deep historical forces at work in Ayemenem, and it does not explain what truly causes or defines the Kochamma family's experience.

Instead, Roy's trajectory of foreshadowing and anticipation leads to the two forbidden, taboo erotic relationships of the novel—between Ammu and Velutha, and Estha and Rahel. These are the episodes at the core of the unraveling plot and the crux of the book's meaning. All of the tension, desire, and desperation beneath the surface of the narrative converges into these expressions of love, which are examples of perhaps the greatest, most unthinkable taboos of all. This essay will discuss why the two forbidden sexual episodes in the final two chapters of *The God of Small Things* are so crucial to the history of the Kochamma family and the emblematic of the meaning of the novel.

Before discussing the significance of these episodes, however, it will help to establish how and why they are so closely connected. It is immediately clear that they have much in common as doomed, forbidden love trysts, and it is no coincidence that they are revealed and described next to each other, at the end of the narrative. However, there are other, less obvious connections. During Estha and Rahel's erotic encounter, for example, there are repeated references to Ammu such as calling Rahel's mouth "Their beautiful mother's mouth" and there is the statement that the twins are at the "viable die-able age" of thirty, Ammu's age between her affair with Velutha and her death. Equally important is the phrase, "They were strangers who had met in a chance encounter," because it is more applicable to Velutha and Ammu than to the twins. Also key at this point, late in chapter 20, is the narrator's statement about Rahel and Estha that "once again they broke the Love Laws," which uses the term that had previously been applied to Ammu and Velutha and implies that the twins' situation is a reoccurrence of the affair of 1969.

By closely connecting Rahel and Estha's sexual relationship to Ammu and Velutha's, Roy suggests that present-day events converge with the events surrounding Sophie Mol's death, and that each strain of the plot has the same thematic resolution. The two instances of breaking of the Love Laws form a key to understanding the rest of the book; they are both the result and the cause of the novel's action. This is why the narrator writes that the story "really began in the days when the Love Laws were made," back through the colonial and pre-colonial history of Kerala. The Love Laws represent the strict confines on human behavior—the caste systems, social pressures, and political restrictions that horrify people beyond expression when they are broken. The central action of the novel is about breaking them, and the tragedy that results from breaking them.

For one thing, therefore, the forbidden love affairs at the end of the novel are crucial because they reveal the disgust and horror with the lovers that is at the root of the violence and tragedy directed against them. Present-day Western readers probably do not consider inter-caste romance repulsive, but they are quite likely to be shocked and offended by incest. Incest is as taboo in twenty-first-century Western society as an inter-caste sexual affair would

> "The twins' love-making is a metaphor for their search for this fractured and traumatized joint identity in their adulthood, and it is a real, physical and emotional expression of their grief and longing."

have been in the 1960s, and probably still is, in Kerala. The reader's reaction to such violations of the Love Laws allows him/her to understand how and why such drastic social and political consequences could have resulted from the transgressions at the end of *The God of Small Things*. Roy allows the reader an insight into the emotional basis behind the careful, planned brutality of those dedicated to Kerala's social code, such as the Touchable Policemen who believe that in beating Velutha to death they are enforcing the Love Laws and "inoculating a community against an outbreak."

However, the love affairs also allow the reader to identify with the transgressor, and they inspire a sympathetic reaction for four people who are abused, tortured, and betrayed by their society's most fundamental rules. The reasons for Ammu's turn to Velutha are sharply drawn and inspire a great deal of sympathy when she studies her body, the body of an "inexperienced lover," in the mirror and peers "down the road to Age and Death through its parted strands." Ammu's love affair is, in a sense, the cause of the novel's tragedy because it shatters her family, condemns Velutha to a brutal death, traumatizes Rahel and Estha for the rest of their lives, and results in her own decay and death. It is also, however, the result of an entire lifetime of abuse, confinement, and imprisonment in a stinting social code. This code not only fails to protect Ammu against her father beating her with a brass vase, her father imprisoning her in the house even when she is an adult, and her husband beating her; it actually leads to these consequences. When she recognizes that Kerala's social code is in the process of forcing her down Baby Kochamma's path of bitter, joyless confinement to the house until death, she acts in perfectly understandable desperation and attempts to find some brief joy with Velutha.

What Do I Read Next?

- *The Guide* (1958) is R. K. Narayan's popular tale of Raju, a former convict who is mistaken for a holy man upon his arrival in Narayan's fictional universe of Malgudi.

- Salman Rushdie's *Midnight's Children* (1981) is a multifaceted and ambitious work about India's history since its independence from Britain. Focusing on the story of Saleem Sinai, who was born at the stroke of midnight marking Independence, it includes elements of magic and fantasy, and it is highly allusive to classic texts including the Bible and *Arabian Nights*.

- Roy's third volume of nonfiction, *War Talk* (2003), is composed of fluent and engaging arguments about the negative impacts of globalization, the danger of nuclear proliferation, and the devastating impact of the Bush administration's foreign policy on the Third World.

- E. M. Forster's *A Passage to India* (1924) is the classic modernist text about the clash of British and Indian cultures during the British Raj. The plot centers around the Indian Dr. Aziz, who is accused of raping an English woman.

Similarly, Rahel's affair with Estha can be interpreted as the result of a social code, both in Kerala and in the United States, that has traumatized her and deprived her of her childhood. The "Quietness and Emptiness" that characterize Estha and Rahel stems from Velutha's death and their parents' difficulties in raising them, but also stems from a society that is cruel, harassing, and violent towards a single mother and her children. From Baby Kochamma to Chacko to the Orangedrink Lemondrink Man, people are prejudiced towards Ammu and her children, and take advantage of them. Rahel and Estha's incestuous contact is their attempt to find comfort in each other, although, unlike Ammu and Velutha, they are not even able to reach a joyful release from their problems, and "what they shared that night was not happiness but hideous grief."

In addition to what they reveal about the cultural and political content of Roy's novel, the two affairs communicate a great deal about the novel's psychological subtext. In the course of the book, both Ammu and Rahel experience identity crises whose primary goals are, in a sense, discovering who and what they are in relation to their culture and family. Rahel travels back to Ayemenem to see her brother, but her journey is perhaps better described as a quest, through her memories, to discover herself and the roots of her history. The third-person narrator of *The God of Small Things* is omniscient, and not strictly confined to any particular perspective, but the narrative voice is grounded in Rahel's memories. Events and remembrances weave into the story as they might appear in Rahel's mind, and the novel is structured around her search to understand herself and her past.

Rahel's incestuous contact with Estha is so crucial and definitive in this identity search because, as the narrator stresses insistently, her brother is herself. In opening passages of the novel, the narrator relates that, during their childhood, "Esthappen and Rahel thought of themselves together as Me, and separately, individually, as We or Us. As though they were a rare breed of Siamese twins, physically separate, but with joint identities." The twins' love-making is a metaphor for their search for this fractured and traumatized joint identity in their adulthood, and it is a real, physical and emotional expression of their grief and longing.

Ammu's affair with Velutha is also, in a sense, a search for herself; this is clear from the lengthy passages in which the narrator describes the desperation in Ammu's strictly confined life and her need to live and experience joy. When Ammu studies herself in the mirror and tests whether a toothbrush will stay on her breast, she reveals that she understands herself through her body and her sexual identity, and she seeks out Velutha in order to discover the beautiful part of herself.

The forbidden love affairs that come at the end of Roy's novel, therefore, work together to provide a single metaphor for the key struggles and meanings of the novel. The twins' incestuous contact and Ammu's affair with Velutha are metaphors for, and physical enactments of, the psychological identity struggles of the novel's protagonists. These struggles extend, by implication and because they are so closely connected to the political subtext of the novel, to the wider political and psychological identity struggles of all those afflicted by the oppressive social code of southern Indian culture.

Source: Scott Trudell, Critical Essay on *The God of Small Things*, in *Novels for Students*, Thomson Gale, 2006.

Joyce Hart

Hart is a freelance writer and author of several books. In the following essay, Hart goes behind the story contained in The God of Small Things *to study Roy's poetic language and unique writing style.*

Arundhati Roy's novel *The God of Small Things* has many excellent qualities. The setting is exotic; the voice is unique; the characters are complex; and the plot line is mysterious. Any one of these, done as well as Roy's skills have provided, might have been enough for the author to win the Booker Prize, one of the most distinguished literary awards; but with one more distinctive characteristic added to the mix—Roy's poetic and imaginative writing style—there is no question that this book will long remain one of the most fascinating novels of the twentieth century.

Upon the first read of *The God of Small Things*, one cannot help but be drawn into the story that Roy has created, wondering, with each succeeding chapter, what could possibly happen next. There are questions about who these characters are; where the plot line is going; and what the missing details are that the author has purposefully left out, taunting the reader to hurriedly move forward. Even the setting of the story is alluring with its freshly conceived scenery, unusual town names, striking tropical flora and fauna, as well as the strange social customs. The storyline twists around unsuspecting corners, as the narrator takes readers into the dark depths of the characters' souls. And even though, after reading this book, one might sense the quality of writing of this gifted novelist, it might take a second, and maybe even a third, reading before one can actually pay attention to the underlying style that makes this novel so invigorating to read. The purpose of this essay is to do just that: to examine not the story but Roy's unique writing technique; and to point out the poetic qualities of her writing.

One of the first elements of the author's writing that readers confront as they begin this novel is Roy's creative vocabulary—creative in the sense that she makes up new words. In the first pages, for example, Roy uses the words "dustgreen trees" and later portrays a smell as "sicksweet." Two things happen when she puts two words together like this (which she consistently does throughout

Men loading sulfur into baskets in the port of Cochin, India © Enzo and Paolo Ragazzini/Corbis

the novel). First, she captures the attention of the reader. There are no such words as "dustgreen" and "sicksweet," which her audience will immediately realize, and yet readers will know exactly what the author has intended by using such new words. Secondly, the words not only make sense, they describe the objects they are referring to with much greater depth than most single adjectives and metaphors could possibly do, and the author accomplishes this with minimum verbiage. "Dustgreen," for instance, is used to describe both a color and a condition, and with this one inventive word, Roy gives her readers a fully sensual image. Dust is gritty and dry, like the weather she is trying to depict. So in using a word such as "dustgreen," Roy helps readers not only to visualize the setting but also to feel it. A similar double sense is created with the word "sicksweet." Readers not only can taste and smell it, they can feel it in the pit of their stomachs, just as Rahel and Estha feel when they think about the world that Roy has created for them in her novel. The sweetness of the odor has attracted these characters to explore their world; but the consequences and the reactions of their world have made them sick. Thus, these "double words" are more than the sum of their parts. They are not just two words haphazardly added together, but rather they are almost

> Roy knows that sometimes words that children hear are creepy, furry insects. Other times they are slimy wells that threaten to swallow all who hear them."

like short poems. They offer the reader vivid images through short expressive words.

Other examples of combining words appear when the narrator pulls readers into the funeral of Sophie Mol, a flashback that occurs at the beginning of the novel. When a baby bat climbs up Baby Kochamma's sari, making the woman scream, Roy provides her readers with a sample of the noises of confusion in the congregation, which she represents with the words: "Whatisit? Whathappened?" and "a Furrywhirring and a Sariflapping." With these new words, readers are given a complex picture of the bewilderment that is occurring inside the church. Not only do these words refer to sounds, they also provoke a sense of movement. People are turning their heads back and forth, searching for the source of the yelling and its cause as they try to figure out what is happening ("Whatisit? Whathappened?"); bats are beating their wings, trying to escape ("Furrywhirring"); and women are flapping the material of their costumes to make sure that there are no bats climbing on them ("Sariflapping"). Once again, Roy has created vibrant descriptions in using her newly conceived words. It is as if she has captured a whole movie scene, filled with motion and sound, with just a minimum use of syllables.

There is another form of creative vocabulary that Roy makes up. This one reflects children trying to make sense of the adult world through little bits of information that they receive. For instance, again at Sophie Mol's funeral, the protagonist Rahel attempts to repeat words that she has heard during the religious ceremony. But in a child's world, not only is it hard to grasp the full meaning of language; it is also sometimes difficult to take hold of the full word. So in repeating the Biblical quote that refers to the body decomposing and returning to the dust from whence it came, Rahel tries to mimic the priests. But instead of saying "dust to

dust," she says: "*Dus to dus to dus to dus to dus.*" This is what the words sound like to her. And by Roy using this phrase (as well as other similar, child interpretations throughout the novel), she places her readers inside the mind of the very young. Readers thus are provided with a different view of reality, one that is seen through the eyes of her young characters, children who must face some very tragic circumstances very early in their lives. Rahel, in this instance, cannot fully comprehend death, so she repeats the priests' words as best she can, twisting her tongue around them, attempting to make a kind of song out of them, hoping that eventually the phrase might help her understand. "Sophie Mol died because she couldn't breathe," Rahel believes. "Her funeral killed her." And it is Roy's creative use of language that makes readers not only mentally visualize what is happening inside Rahel's mind but to feel the confusion, the struggle with her conflicts, and the great challenges that confront her.

In the middle of the story, the narrator shines more light on Roy's understanding of how children perceive the world through language that they do not fully understand. While the family is awaiting the arrival of Sophie Mol and her family at the airport, Estha and Rahel are misbehaving. Their uncle suggests that their mother deal with them "later," a word that plays with Rahel's mind. "And Later became a horrible, menacing, goose-bumpy word. Lay. Ter. Like a deep-sounding bell in a mossy well. Shivery, and furred. Like moth's feet." This passage sums up the foundation upon which Roy has built her literary vocabulary, her creative construction of language for this story. It explains why she is so focused on language, especially when dealing with her youngest of characters. Roy is sensitive to the distorted world that children must plow through, hoping to find their way. She remembers how difficult language was to understand and yet at the same time how powerful words could be for children. Even when words are not fully comprehended, or at least not identified with proper dictionary meanings, they are felt. Words for children have more than sound; they have lives of their own. And the tone of them can be frightening. Roy knows that sometimes words that children hear are creepy, furry insects. Other times they are slimy wells that threaten to swallow all who hear them.

One more way that Roy adorns her story is through the use of poetic images which are as colorful as the tropical paintings of Paul Gauguin. The author obviously does not paint with oils to do so but rather with vibrant words, such as when she is

A Dalit (Untouchable) shouts anti-government slogans in New Delhi © Reuters/Corbis

describing the first raindrops of the monsoon season when she writes: "Slanting silver ropes slammed into loose earth, plowing it up like gunfire." The first component that makes this sentence so beautiful is the alliteration with the letter *s*, which sounds slippery just like the rain she is portraying. Then there is the overall image of hard raindrops falling on the dry earth. The rain is so hard and the earth is so dry that when the water first hits the dirt, dust flies up into the air as if the earth is being shot at. This sentence is poetically powerful on many different levels. But besides creating an image, it also provides a psychological reference. Rahel has just returned in Ayemenem as the narrator describes this scene. Change is in the air as the edge of the monsoon season pushes the dry weather away. But there is also a sense of danger presented here. The author uses the word *gunfire* in her metaphor, as if a warning is being given. The timeframe of this novel is contorted, moving from the present to the past and back again, over and over again. So when the above sentence appears in the story, the damage to Rahel has already happened; but the reader is still in the dark because the story has just begun. So the warning is not given for Rahel's sake but for the reader's. It is as if the author is alerting the reader that this is not going to be an easy, entertaining story. There are many events that will be hard to take, and Rahel's return is but one of the markers for these difficult changes.

There is another passage that serves a dual purpose. It appears on the first page of the novel. The narrator is describing the landscape as the monsoon season begins. "Boundaries blur as tapioca fences take root and bloom." Here there is another reference to great change, as dried out branches that once looked like a fence are now blossoming and thus fading into the rest of the vegetation around it. Whereas fences normally standout as rigid boundaries, in this instance the boundary itself becomes part of the garden. Besides creating a poetic image, Roy foreshadows a theme that will prevail throughout the story, one in which boundaries between sex, race, social status, and rational and irrational reality will cease to exist. As a matter of fact, the whole first chapter provides a foreshadowing of the rest of the novel. Roy either cleverly hints at events that will come, or else she completely throws her readers into very specific events but only gives readers quick, short glimpses, teasing them forward.

Examples of how Roy gives hints and glimpses into the future of the novel include her reference to the "Orangedrink Lemondrink Man" and her mentioning that he did something to Estha; but she does not say what that was. And Roy describes Rahel as being "brittle with exhaustion from her battle against Real Life," although readers have no idea what this battle entailed. Then later in the first chapter, Inspector Thomas Mathew toys with Rahel's mother, Ammu, when the woman goes to the police station: "He tapped her breasts with his baton. Gently. Tap tap. As though he was choosing mangoes from a basket." There is a lot suggested in this phrase. First there is the superior stance of the inspector. There is also the sexual overtone. And then there is the reader's curiosity, which is aroused by questions such as why has Ammu gone to see the policeman? And why is he intimidating her? Then shortly after this encounter, Ammu says: "He's dead." Readers do not know who has died nor what all these passages mean. Roy is fully aware of keeping her readers in the dark, but she does not worry about the confusion. The author does not rush to fill in all the gaps. This is because she is a profoundly confident and creative writer. Roy tells her story the way she wants to relate it. And she does it in a language that suits her characters' minds. And it is her confidence, creativity, and poetic style that make Roy's writing so refreshing, make her story so enticing to read over and over again.

Source: Joyce Hart, Critical Essay on *The God of Small Things*, in *Novels for Students*, Thomson Gale, 2006.

Laura Carter

Carter is currently employed as a freelance writer. In this essay, Carter considers the social malaise present in Roy's version of contemporary Indian society as a function of Western influence.

Permeating Arundahti Roy's *The God of Small Things* is an India devoid of a sense of history, one that has laid waste to the Western world. It is a desolation foreshadowing what lies, even eats away at, the core of the novel—when a people, in this case, the people of India, lose their sense of history, the results are devastating to all. In the opening chapter of her work, Roy introduces the reader to world of what was. Relationships are broken, gardens go asunder, homes lay waste, victims of abject filth fueled by apathy and neglect. It is a circumstance Roy paints aptly and repeatedly from the opening pages until Sophie Mol's tragic end.

The British influence of the Indian culture insidiously lurks at the heart of the novel. Baby Kochamma appears at the beginning of the novel to Rahel to be a caricature of her former self, defined by her dyed jet-black hair along with its by-product, a pale gray stain imprinted on her forehead. She has also begun to wear makeup, that when applied in the dark confines of her home, appears to be slightly off, "her lipstick mouth having shifted slightly off her real mouth." The silence between Baby Kochamma and Rahel when they are reunited, both now as adults, mirrors this strangeness, described as sitting "between grandniece and baby grandaunt like a third person. A stranger. Swollen. Noxious." Conversation is stilted, and the two struggle to find words. But the reader soon learns that circumstances were once different. The narrative recalls a past featuring a different Baby Kochamma, one who had previously spent her afternoons in a sari and gumboots, where she tended to an ornamental garden fantastic enough to attract attention from neighboring towns.

But much has changed. The garden is as toxic as the reunion between relatives, abandoned, having "grown knotted and wild, like a circus whose animals have forgotten their tricks. The reason for Baby Kochamma's neglect, stems from her "new love," a satellite dish antenna. This event generates "impossible excitement" in Baby Kochamma literally overnight, hypnotic in its intrusion into her existence. She abandons her love for gardening for the sake of the WWF and other televised amusements. "In Ayemenem," says the narrator, "where once the loudest sound had been a musical bus horn, now whole wars, famines, picturesque massacres and Bill Clinton could be summoned up like servants." This newfound attraction, the reader also discovers, is the catalyst for Baby Kochamma's absurd new look, defined by badly dyed, brittle hair and painted lips, influenced by television programming the likes of *The Bold and the Beautiful* and *Santa Barbara*.

The social malaise framing the events of the novel is aptly described by Chacko, an India-born, Oxford educated man who sees, yet cannot transcend, the hypocrisies of his westernized culture. It is Chacko who is quick to point out that the family's desire to see *The Sound of Music* is "an extended exercise in Anglophilia." He tells the twins that they are all Anglophiles, "pointed in the wrong direction, trapped outside their own history and unable to retrace their steps because their footprints had been swept away." He explains to them that history is "like an old house at night. With all the lamps lit. And ancestors whispering inside." To understand one's history is to enter this house, to understand and hear the whispers, to see the books, pictures and smell the smells that linger within its walls. Yet in the next breath, he is apt to express himself in what is characterized as his "reading aloud voice," an affectation developed during his studies at Oxford. His fondness for his Oxford days culminates not only in his affinity for literature, but for the reverence he holds for both his American-born ex-wife and their daughter.

No one character seems to escape the tentacles of Western culture. An element of violence punctures the novel, first, in Baby Kochamma's husband, Pappachi, who beat her regularly yet fancied himself to be a proper English gentleman within the context of his own arrogance and exceedingly destructive nature. Then there is Ammu, his daughter, mother of Rahel and Estha, who returns home after surviving a violent attack from her drunken husband. The cause for the assault, the reader learns, stems from a request by her husband's British employer to sleep with Ammu as a way to preserve his position with the company. Ammu's refusal to comply spurns the attack from her spouse. When she decides to leave her husband, her family's response is surprisingly negative, according to the narrator. In the Kochamma family, Ammu's integrity takes a backseat to preconceived notions of British values. "Pappachi would not believe her story—not because he thought well of her husband, but simply because he didn't believe that an Englishman, any Englishman, would covet another man's wife." It is this Western influence that further polarizes the family. As a result of this influence, Ammu is osterisized by her own people, as are her innocent children, predicated or based on a sort of high-flying, false perception of English decorum as having transcended Indian culture.

Velutha is in a similar, if not worse position in modern Indian society. When the British came to his town, his, among other Paravans, Pelayas and Pulayas, wanted to avoid "Untouchability" by Christian conversion and membership in the Anglican church. Rather than escape persecution, these groups found that they had instead relinquished any claims to government benefits, their Christianity rendering them "casteless" outcasts in their own society. Recalling Chacko's own lesson in histrionics, Roy says of the fate of Velutha's people, "It was a little like having to sweep away your footprints without a broom. Or worse, not being allowed to leave footprints at all." In so much as Velutha is loved, and even admired by Baby Kochamma, he remains a social outcast. Because of this imposed status and its perceived impact on the Kochamma family, i.e., the affair between Velutha and Ammu, Velutha is eventually betrayed by Baby Kochamma to preserve the family name. In the end, authorities misuse this information to their

> It is Chacko who is quick to point out that the family's desire to see *The Sound of Music* is 'an extended exercise in Anglophilia.'"

advantage to subdue the Indian community. A brutal beating meant to send a message to quiet rebellious rumblings results in Velutha's death.

Sophie Mol's death remains at the heart of the story, and weighs heavily on Estha and Rahel. It functions as a leveling force for all concerned. It is the pivotal point at which familial bonds are permanently severed. Her life is symbolic and central to the novel. She epitomizes all that is British, described upon her arrival: "She walked down the runway, the smell of London in her hair." Her father, Indian, her mother, American, Sophie Mol is a product of a biracial marriage. Ironically, despite these familial ties, she has little or no connection with India. She has instead been raised in England by her American-born mother, well-removed from the influences of the India people. Ironically, Sophie Mol's British affectations have elevated her status, somehow overshadowing her Indian origins. Her cousins, Estha and Rahel, stand in her shadow. Rather than being elevated or embraced for their Indianness, they are overlooked in Baby Kochamma's home. And when Sophie Mol tragically dies, the event tears apart core relationships in the Kochamma household. The family puts all of their energy into Sophie Mol, and her death, even though their history with the child suggests she is more or less a stranger, admired more for her golden hair, western mannerisms and dress. Instead of accepting responsibility for their part in the accident, tragically, both Chacko and Baby Kochamma blame Rahel and Estha, and begin to treat them as outcasts.

Roy speaks of India's history as if it were creeping in the shadows, represented by "History House" looming in the "Heart of Darkness" at the other side of the river. History House is haunted by an Englishman who had gone native, the "Black Sahib" who it was intimated had committed suicide after his family was permanently separated by his young lover's parents, presumably Indian and perhaps, ironically so, bent on the child's Anglicization. Driven by their need to escape from a hostile family life, the twins look to History House as a way to escape the constraints of their own world. What happens when they decide to cross the river, to be with Velutha, the man they "weren't supposed to love" on that fateful day on the back veranda changes the course of their lives, and their affinity to the world forever. Adds Roy, "While other children of their age learned other things, Estha and Rahel learned how history negotiates its terms and collects its dues from those who break its laws." Both of the twins hear history's "sickening thud," they in fact "smell its smell and never forget," a smell described as "old roses on a breeze."

Estha and Rahel's lost innocence culminates in the tragic events on the veranda at history house. It is there that Velutha's blood is spilled. He is violently beaten in front of the children as the result of lies Baby Kochamma has told merely out of vanity, to protect her "good name" and reputation. His death is also a function of the social climate in the area. Velutha is used as an example by the authorities of those who remain out of step with the new regime or the British way of life. He is beaten and killed, so preaches Roy, in an account as seen through Rahel's and Estha's eyes. What they witnessed in History House, the author contends, was "a clinical demonstration in controlled conditions" of "human nature's pursuit of ascendancy." She goes on to explain, "Structure. Order. Complete monopoly. It was human history, masquerading as God's Purpose, revealing herself to an under-age audience." Ultimately, it is the influence of outside political and social forces that kill Velutha both spiritually and physically, as well as permanently scar Estha and Rahel's psyches.

The author, when asked just what the god of small things is, simply stated that it is "the inversion of God," a "not accepting of what we think of as adult boundaries." Roy asserts that throughout the course of the narrative, "all sorts of boundaries are transgressed upon." It is, according to Roy, small events and ordinary things "smashed and re-constituted, imbued with new meaning to become the bleached bones of the story." Subsequently, it is these small events and ordinary things that form a pattern for her narrative. "A pattern," says Roy, "of how in these small events and in these small lives the world intrudes." She believes that because of these patterns, and what they imply, that people go virtually unprotected, "the world and the social machine intrudes into the smallest, deepest core of their being and changes their life."

Returning to the story, it is easy to identify the psychological undercurrent Roy speaks of. All of the events in the story are a by-product of Western influence in what has become, more or less, a British colony. Tepid river waters bloated with dead finish mirror the encroachment of the industrial machine, as does the hypnotic quality of the satellite dish holding the Kochamma house hostage. Throughout the novel, the twins are encouraged to speak English rather than their native language, to covet whiteness instead of their Indian heritage, yet they cannot transcend who they are and fail miserably. Compounding their failure is Sophie Mol, their English cousin, who manages to capture Baby Kochamma and Chacko's attention immediately with her Western affectations. And when Ammu's affair fails miserably, she expresses her sorrow by directing her rage towards her own children, as did her husband and parents towards her. Like dominoes, these circumstances and others stack up, then collapse, setting into motion a tragic chain of events that cannot be controlled.

By the author's own admission, she does not attempt to define what modern day India is or what it means to be Indian. What she does do so aptly, is to weave a subtle tale of circumstances that collectively, permanently shape and form the lives of her characters, leaving an indelible mark that no doubt will be transferred, one generation to the next. Remarks the narrator of Arundhati Roy's *The God of Small Things*,

> Perhaps it's true that things can change in a day. That a few dozen hours, like the salvaged remains of a burned house—the charred clock, the singed photograph, the scorched furniture—must be resurrected from the ruins and examined. Preserved. Accounted for.

Source: Laura Carter, Critical Essay on *The God of Small Things*, in *Novels for Students*, Thomson Gale, 2006.

Douglas Dupler

Dupler is a writer and has taught college English courses. In this essay, Dupler explores the relationship between individuals and the cultural forces acting upon them within the novel.

Arundhati Roy's novel *The God of Small Things* reveals a complex relationship between individuals and the historical and cultural forces that shape them and their society. In Roy's novel, a so-called Big God presides over the large happenings of the world, the "vast, violent, circling, driving, ridiculous, insane, unfeasible, public turmoil of a nation." In contrast, it is a Small God that resides over the individual lives caught up in forces too powerful and large for these individuals to understand and to change. This Small God is "cozy and contained, private and limited," residing over people for whom "worse things" are always happening. Individuals ruled by the symbolic Small God adopt resignation and "inconsequence" in the face of mass movements, while at the same time their oppression makes them "resilient and truly indifferent."

The novel takes place in modern India, in the state of Kerala, during a time of social change and upheaval and as television is just beginning to broadcast "television-enforced democracy" into an insular world. The characters in Roy's novel exist in a culture of strict rules. There is a caste system and a class system that exert much force upon the characters. Conflict is created for the individuals who can't adhere to these systems of social organization and control. Indeed, the greatest conflict in the story, a love affair between Ammu and Velutha, is the result of individuals rebelling against the historical and cultural structures of caste and class; this is an affair between a Touchable and an Untouchable. In the beginning of the novel, the tragedy is foreshadowed and explained when the narrative states, "They all broke the rules. . . . They all tampered with the laws that lay down who should be loved and how." As an entire culture strains against ancient laws and customs, Roy's novel brings this struggle down to the level of individuals, in a "time when the unthinkable became thinkable." That is, individuals have begun to question and act against the laws that had rigidly remained for so long.

The novel ranges in scope from the epic to the minute. The narrative gives lush detail of the everyday life in India, and contains colors, textures, and many characters. At the same time, the narrative also shifts to expose the larger forces that drive the characters. For instance, the narrative gives broad details about the trajectory of the lives of some of the characters, including Rahel, Ammu, Chacko, Margaret, and others. The novel also gives details about some of the political movements of the days, as when it describes the workings of Communism within the state of Kerala. The novel weaves several layers of perspective of the social order, including the simplicities of individuals in their everyday lives; broad views of character's lives and how they arrived at their places in the story; and larger events that provide glimpses of the historical and cultural forces at play in the world. The relationship between these levels of existence is complex and subtle, and the narrative states that

> " The characters in Roy's novel exist in a culture of strict rules. There is a caste system and a class system that exert much force upon the characters. Conflict is created for the individuals who can't adhere to these systems of social organization and control."

this relationship is tenuous and that "things can change in a day" for any of the characters.

The narrative shows in several instances how casual comments and decisions can have deep repercussions, showing the power of choice that individuals have within their social lives. For instance, when Ammu angrily scolds Rahel by telling her, "When you hurt people they begin to love you less," this moment has far-reaching effects in the lives of the characters. This off-hand remark is instrumental in making Rahel run away from the family, an event that also brings about the death of Sophie Mol and then Velutha. In another example, when Margaret Kochamma decides to return to India after the death of her husband, this decision leads to the death of her daughter Sophie and will haunt her "for as long as she lived."

The narrative utilizes shifts in time to illustrate how the world for the characters has changed. The present moment of the novel occurs as Rahel returns to Ayemenem at the age of thirty-one. The narrative uses broad flashbacks to show the world that Rahel remembers as a young child, when the tragedy occurred that changed her life forever. When Rahel meets Comrade Pillai as an adult, there is an underlying tension in the meeting, because Pillai had played a role in the death of Velutha. This history will not go away and pervades the moment. This is recognized when the narrative states, "she and he knew that there are things that can be forgotten. And things that cannot."

One of the historical forces that shaped modern India is its colonial past under British rule. For the characters in the novel, this past is still alive.

Chacko, who received his education in England, educates the twins Estha and Rahel on the ways of the world. He tells them that their family is "all Anglophiles. . . . Pointed in the wrong direction, trapped outside their own history and unable to retrace their steps because their footprints had been swept away." This allusion to their footprints relates to the caste system in India. The narrative mentions a time, within memory, when Untouchables, or the lowest caste of people, were required to sweep away their footprints in public for higher caste members. When the British ruled, yet another form of class structure was imposed upon the society. This structure, according to Chacko, "locked out" Indians from their world, because of a war that made them "adore [their] conquerors and despise [themselves]." From Chacko, the twins "learned how history negotiates its terms and collects its dues from those who break its laws." For Chacko, Indians in relation to the English will always be "Prisoners of War."

Colonialism affects other characters in the novel as well. Baby Kochamma, in her youth, had defied her family's wishes and converted to a Roman Catholic, mainly due to her infatuation with a priest named Father Mulligan. Throughout the story, Baby Kochamma's bitterness and treachery plays a role in the tragedy, as though she is unwittingly making other people suffer for her own unrequited longings and heartache. There is also tension between Mammachi and Margaret Kochamma. Margaret is a British woman who married and then divorced Chacko. Mammachi "despised" her and refers to Margaret as the "shopkeeper's daughter," an insult containing the ring of class snobbery. Another telling collision of the two cultures occurs subtly during the scene in which Estha is molested, when the family had gone to see the film *The Sound of Music.*

The narrative states that the story being told, including the tragedy, began "thousands of years ago. . . . Before the British . . . the Dutch . . . [and] Christianity." The story actually "began in the days when the Love Laws were made." Indeed, the story, and the tragedy therein, show that it is human passion that cannot be controlled and contained by cultural rules. In their love affair, Ammu and Velutha are well aware of the dangers and taboos of their relationship, and yet they are powerless to stop their desire. Desire, or the force of life, overpowers the cultural forces that would deny it; the narrative declares that "biology designed the dance." One day, as Ammu is watching Velutha play with Rahel, she begins to feel her desire for him. In this scene, "centuries telescoped into one evanescent moment."

Likewise, when Velutha notices that "Rahel's mother was a woman," in a brief moment he notices things that "had been out of bounds." In their attraction, the "cost of living climbed to unaffordable heights," and Velutha was about to "enter a tunnel" that would lead to his "annihilation." In the end, cultural forces would have their say over the individual's breaking the rules.

The relationship between Velutha and Ammu is symbolic of the conflicts in the culture. Velutha is from the Untouchable caste, but his many positive qualities cause Ammu to fall in love with him, while the twins Rahel and Estha adore him and play with him often. Velutha's excellence as a person illuminates the unfairness of the caste laws. When Velutha is seen marching in a Communist parade, it illustrates the changing structure of political power in the culture. Velutha's grandfather had converted to Christianity, but even the new religion could not overcome the entrenched caste laws of the society, and the churches became segregated for the Untouchables.

Velutha is hardly an obsequious slave. He is described as a handsome, kind, intelligent, and clever man. He has an "unwarranted assurance" about him and he bothers people because of the "way in which he disregarded suggestions without appearing to rebel." Velutha's qualities, the narrative states, might be desirable in Touchables, but in an Untouchable they could be "construed as insolence." With Velutha, the cultural laws are seen as restricting excellence. There is something about Velutha that represents escape for Ammu, who is from a higher caste. When she sees him, he represents something other that the "smug, ordered world that she so raged against."

The individual freedom represented by the love between Velutha and Ammu is short-lived, and other characters in the story act their parts in continuing the cultural constraint of such displays of rule-breaking. Baby Kochamma lies and betrays Velutha, as does the Communist Pillai, which leads to the murder, by official forces, of Velutha. Indeed, it is betrayal by individuals that sends Velutha on his "blind date with history," in which he is murdered unjustly for breaking the Love Laws. Estha gets caught up in the situation as well, when he is manipulated by Baby Kochamma into lying against Velutha. For Estha, this event has long-reaching effects in his life, as he loses his voice and lives numbly thereafter.

In the end, the novel shifts and the cultural forces begin to exert their power over the individuals.

Baby Kochamma performs her machinations "not for Ammu," but to "contain the scandal" that has occurred when the Love Laws were broken. When the narrative notes that the characters are living in "an era imprinting itself on those who lived in it," it shows that the God of Big Things is again residing over the God of Small Things. When the cultural powers decide that Velutha must be held responsible for breaking the rules, the story provides a glimpse of the men in power, Comrade Pillai and Inspector Mathew. These men are "without curiosity" and are "terrifyingly adult" in the way they operate. So controlled are they by the rules of their culture, they have become "mechanics who serviced different parts of the same machine." When the police beat Velutha to death, it is an impersonal event, as the caste laws had severed "any connection between themselves and him . . . long ago." Later, many years after the incident, the culture protects the men who uphold its prejudices and injustices. When Rahel meets Comrade Pillai, she notices that he "didn't hold himself in any way personally responsible for what had happened. He dismissed the whole business as the Inevitable Consequence of Necessary Politics."

Source: Douglas Dupler, Critical Essay on *The God of Small Things*, in *Novels for Students*, Thomson Gale, 2006.

Ritu Menon

In the following review, Menon declares that The God of Small Things *"is about childhood and the loss of innocence."*

The God of Small Things is a seduction from start to finish. The cover photo, a grey-green lily pool with three luminously pink waterlilies, compels you to pick up the book almost as you would pick a flower; the paper's texture and shade evoke clotted cream; a satisfying weight and pleasing typeface make its physical crafting as elegant as its literary craft is inspired. Arundhati Roy's loving and meticulous attention to detail is evident in both. (At the launch of the book in Delhi, Roy explained that she had insisted on complete design control over the book.)

It almost makes you wish Roy hadn't issued so many disclaimers in the interviews she has given to the media: I don't read, she insists, so I don't know what my literary influences are; I don't know the rules of writing so I can't say I've broken them; I don't ever rewrite because writing for me is like breathing how can you rebreathe a breath?

Yet, effortless as it might appear, it is clear that heart, soul and intellect have gone into the making of this book, and any writer worth her salt knows

> Ammu's death is quite gratuitous, and Estha's silence a ploy to allow Rahel the sole privilege of speech. By the end of the novel, Rahel has transmuted into Roy; Velutha, Ammu and Sophie are dead; Estha is speechless. Of the five main characters only Rahel, quite literally, lives to tell the tale."

how much work, and reworking, that entails. When Roy is excavating her own past and ransacking memory, how to tell the story, more than the story itself, is the real challenge. In this she has succeeded splendidly and spectacularly.

The God of Small Things is about childhood and the loss of innocence. The fear of it, the terror and love of it, the deep scars it leaves. Estha and Rahel, seven-year-old twins in south India's Kerala, grow up in their grandmother's home with their divorced mother and an odd assortment of relatives. Mammachi, the grandmother, has a way with pickles; after her husband's death, she sets up a prosperous pickle factory. With Mammachi, the twins and their mother, Ammu, live uncle Chacko, once a Rhodes scholar, and Baby Kochamma, their maiden great-aunt. Ammu is trying to manage her life and children, Baby Kochamma is trying to manage her single state (by living her life backwards, Rahel says) and Chacko manages the pickle factory. This factory is the focus of a subplot which takes in the Communist politics of Kerala, trade unionism, and the illicit relationship between Ammu and Velutha, a low-caste employee in the factory—whom Estha and Rahel love with the unconditional love that only children can have.

Into this world of slow, meandering rivers and thick foliage, heavy furniture in dark rooms decorated with stuffed animals who peer down benignly, enters Sophie Mol, the twins' half-English cousin, Chacko's daughter. Sophie drowns while the children are out alone on the river. This is death number one. Her dying is the unexpected trigger that turns Estha's and Rahel's world upside-down and insideout, and is more or less directly responsible for the deaths of Velutha and their mother. Deaths apart, there are pederasty, a hint of incest, the tempestuous and utterly transgressive affair between Ammu and Velutha, the kind of violation of Love Laws that can only bring doom. In a sense, this is a chronicle of deaths foretold; the only problem is, they're the wrong deaths. But I'll return to this later.

The novel itself covers one day in the life of the children, the day that opens with Sophie Mol's funeral. The very first chapter tells the whole "story," as it were. It is a mark of Roy's brilliant structuring of the book that the story then unfolds, and crosses over, and flashes back, and weaves in and out of the minds and hearts of its two protagonists with breathtaking virtuosity. Roy has said in more than one interview that the architecture of the book is plain to see: she "drew" the book as a series of graphics and "saw" its pattern emerging. After that, it "revealed itself sentence by sentence." What it revealed is what forms the "deep substance" of her story—the really real story, that is, of a fragile world under threat, of the impossibility of ever again knowing the security of absolute trust. Long before the end of the book, long before the deaths have taken place, you know that Rahel and Estha will never be the same again.

The gradual contamination of relationships by the perfidy of the adult world is exquisitely presented through a series of vignettes and revelations: the trip to meet Sophie at the airport; the drive to Abhilash Talkies to see *The Sound of Music*, and What Happened There to Estha; the [reason] why Baby Kochamma can only live in the past and why Estha withdraws into silence; why Pappachi's moth hovers with such menace at the edge of Rahel's consciousness; why Uncle Chacko and Ammu are at daggers drawn. . . .

Roy's portrayal of Kerala and the Syrian Christian community she herself grew up in are evocative and telling; her ability to climb into a child's skin is remarkable. Listen to Rahel, for example, after Ammu has told her that she "loves her a little less" for having said something she shouldn't have.

> "But what about my punishment," Rahel said. "You haven't given me my punishment?" "Some things come with their own punishments," Baby Kochamma said. . . .
>
> Some things come with their own punishments. Like bedrooms with built-in cupboards. They would all learn more about punishments soon. That they came in different sizes. That some were so big they were like cupboards with built-in bedrooms. You could

spend your whole life in them, wandering through dark shelving.

> . . . "Goodnight Godbless," Ammu said. But she said it with her back. She was already gone. . .
>
> Rahel Alone watched them walk down the hotel corridor like silent but substantial ghosts. . . . The red carpet took away their feet sounds.
>
> Rahel stood in the hotel room doorway, full of sadness.
>
> She had in her the sadness of Sophie Mol coming. The sadness of Ammu's loving her a little less. And the sadness of whatever the Orangedrink Lemondrink Man had done to Estha. . . . (pp. 109–110)

But as one reads on, the deceptively simple style, the mannerisms—stand-up capital letters, words run into each other or broken apart—make one a little uneasy. A bit too self-indulgent? Perhaps. And perhaps, too, a reluctance to outgrow the child and inhabit the body of an adult.

The novel proceeds along two timetracks: the time of the child, Rahel, and of the Rahel who returns to Ayemenem 23 years later, at 31, the age at which her mother died. The deadly accuracy and unself-consciousness of the child give way to opacity, a dissembling, almost an inability to relate to the family of her childhood. The triadic relationship between Ammu, Estha and Rahel is so full of ambiguity that it cries out for development. Yet it remains at best static, at worst silent or simply absent. The novel doesn't end; it just peters out.

The other thing which makes me uneasy is the overlap between autobiography and fiction. Much fictional writing proceeds from autobiography, and Roy's adoption of this tactic is not unusual. What it does to the novel, however, particularly to those bits that feature the adult Rahel, is to blur the distinction between Roy and Rahel almost completely, down to the diamond in the nose and the feathery collar-bones. In itself this can be quite disarming, making for unexpected transparency. But it does have other consequences, because gradually the reader realizes that Rahel's real twin is not her brother Estha, but Roy herself.

This unacknowledged twinning first pushes Estha to the edge of the frame and then silences him altogether; it also, I suspect, lies behind the death of Ammu. Neither plot development seems warranted, even though Roy provides some ostensible reasons for both. Ammu's death is quite gratuitous, and Estha's silence a ploy to allow Rahel the sole privilege of speech. By the end of the novel, Rahel has transmuted into Roy; Velutha, Ammu and Sophie are dead; Estha is speechless. Of the five main characters only Rahel, quite literally, lives to tell the tale.

Of course, one can argue that there is nothing reasonable or orderly about dying and that any death is arbitrary. Nevertheless, in a story that has been so carefully and intelligently "constructed" in every sense of the word; it does seem as though the narcissistic impulse triumphs over what would have been a logical, brilliant and profoundly tragic conclusion—the death of Rahel herself. In the absence of that denouement, *The God of Small Things* remains a dazzling first novel of rare accomplishment, but it is not one of the Great Stories that Roy herself refers to in the book, even though it has been written with her life.

Source: Ritu Menon, "The Age of Innocence," in *Women's Review of Books*, Vol. 14, No. 12, September 1997, pp. 1–3.

Laura Shapiro

In the following review, Shapiro describes The God of Small Things *as "a banquet for all the senses we bring to reading."*

Something else for Salman Rushdie to worry about: a new writer with a magical first novel about India

After you turn the last page and start thinking back on *The God of Small Things*, Arundhati Roy's glowing first novel, you find you're still deep inside it. You can feel against your skin the lush vines and grasses, smell the pickled mangoes and sweet banana jam, hear the children singing as their uncle's car carries them home to disaster. Disaster was waiting from the start, for the novel begins with a little girl's funeral. Sophie Mol, almost 9, has drowned; and her twin cousins and their mother are mysteriously, horribly implicated. The details don't fall into place until the end of the book. But making our way there, we move through a landscape of sensory imagery so richly evocative that, like the 7-year-old twins, we seem to have lived the tragedy long before we can understand it.

Roy, 37, grew up in Kerala, the state in southwest India where her novel is set. She's been through architecture school and written the screenplays for two highly regarded Indian films; and now she proves herself to be an extraordinary novelist. Inevitably she will be compared with Salman Rushdie, whose novels ("Midnight's Children," "The Satanic Verses") were the first to carve out a definitive place in English fiction for books about India by Indians. Indeed, hardly a season seems to go by now without a talented young writer emerging from the Subcontinent with a new book and a bid for Rushdie's mantle. It's true that like Rushdie, Roy plays often and delightedly with language, loves songs and

jingles and doggerel, and scatters capital letters where they're bound to startle. Some of her characters, too, are very much in his vein, off-beat and emotionally gnarled. The twins, for instance: forcibly separated after the tragedy, they grow up with jagged edges that never heal. Eventually the boy, Estha, stops speaking and the girl, Rahel, stops feeling.

But Roy is no disciple of anyone: a distinctive voice and vision rule this book. Her sentences, though drenched in unforgettable metaphor, are perfectly chiseled. "Once the quietness arrived, it stayed and spread in Estha," she writes. "It sent its stealthy, suckered tentacles inching along the insides of his skull, hoovering the knolls and dells of his memory, dislodging old sentences, whisking them off the tip of his tongue . . . He grew accustomed to the uneasy octopus that lived inside him and squirted its inky tranquilizer on his past."

Sophie Mol's death is only one of the disasters spawned by history, love and human cruelty here, yet *The God of Small Things* is never grim. It's way too full of life for that. Much of the narrative is filtered through Rahel's perspective, and the girl's imagination gives a wonderfully magic buoyancy to the page. At an airport where she's behaved so badly her only allies are the cement kangaroos that serve as trash receptacles, Rahel glances at them as the family leaves. "Cement kisses whirred through the air like small helicopters," writes Roy, and the pleasure she takes in such imagery is contagious. This outstanding novel is a banquet for all the senses we bring to reading.

Source: Laura Shapiro, "Disaster in a Lush Land," in *Newsweek*, Vol. 129, No. 21, May 26, 1997, pp. 76–77.

Sources

Menon, Ritu, "The Age of Innocence," in *Women's Review of Books*, Vol. 14, No. 12, September 1997, pp. 1–3.

National University of Singapore, *Postcolonial and Post Imperial Literature online*, www.postcolonialweb.org, March 29, 2005.

Review of *The God of Small Things*, in *Kirkus Reviews*, March 15, 1997, p. 412.

Roy, Arundhati, *The God of Small Things*, Random House, 1997.

Further Reading

Dodiya, Jaydipsinh, and Joya Chakravarty, *The Critical Studies of Arundhati Roy's "The God of Small Things,"* Atlantic Publishers & Distributors, 1999.

This collection, published in New Delhi, is the earliest book-length volume of criticism on Roy's novel.

Eder, Richard, "As the World Turns," in *Los Angeles Times Book Review*, June 1, 1997, p. 2.
Eder provides a mixed review of Roy's novel, praising her evocative depiction of the story and characters but arguing that she loses control over the narrative.

Thornmann, Janet, "The Ethical Subject of *The God of Small Things*," in *Journal for the Psychoanalysis of Culture and Society*, Vol. 8, No. 2, Fall 2003, pp. 299–307.

Thornmann's psychoanalytical interpretation of Roy's novel includes an argument about the applicability of the Oedipal complex to the work.

Truax, Alice, "A Silver Thimble in Her Fist," in the *New York Times Book Review*, May 25, 1997, p. 5.
Truax's descriptive review of *The God of Small Things* is an example of the very positive response to Roy's work in the United States.

The Name of the Rose

Umberto Eco
1980

First published in Italy in 1980 as *Il nome della rosa*, William Weaver's English translation of author Umberto Eco's *The Name of the Rose* appeared in the United States in 1983, and in England in 1984. The novel, with its labyrinthine plot, deep philosophical discussions, and medieval setting, seemed an unlikely candidate for worldwide success. Yet by 2004, the book had sold more than nine million copies and had never been out of print. Critics and readers alike enthusiastically received *The Name of the Rose*, and the 1986 Jean-Jacques Annaud film, starring Sean Connery and Christian Slater, only fueled interest in the novel.

If *The Name of the Rose* seems an odd choice for such critical and popular acclaim, Eco's elevation into literary superstardom seems just as surprising. A scholarly university professor, Eco's main fields of interest include semiotics, aesthetics, and medieval philosophy. Before *The Name of the Rose*, Eco was well-known among academicians as the writer of many scholarly books, particularly in the field of semiotics. No one could have predicted the furor caused by his debut novel; yet the well-drawn characters, the mysterious setting, and the detective-fiction plot continue to attract a diverse audience for the book. In addition, new critical studies of *The Name of the Rose* appear frequently, and there seems to be no slowing of critical interest. Rich, complicated, and multi-layered, *The Name of the Rose* promises to be an important novel for study for years to come.

Umberto Eco © Peter Turnley/Corbis

Author Biography

Umberto Eco was born on January 5, 1932, in Alessandria, Italy, to Guilo and Givovanna Eco. He attended the University of Turin, where he studied medieval philosophy and aesthetics. He published his doctoral thesis, *Il Problema estetic in Tommaso d'Aquino* (*The Aesthetics of Thomas Aquinas*) in 1956. In that same year, he began his academic career as a lecturer at the University of Turin. Eco's familiarity with and attraction to popular culture was manifested early; he began writing a monthly column called "Diario minimo" in 1959, and has continued to comment actively on current affairs and culture since that time. Eco has continued to teach at a variety of worldwide universities, and he served as the chair of the semiotics department at the University of Bologna in Italy for many years. Beginning in 1999, he served as the President of the Scuola Superiore di Studi Umanistici at the University of Bologna.

For most of Eco's early career, he was well known as an academic writer and teacher of semiotics and philosophy. Most scholars considered his work to be brilliant. However, in 1980, the publication of *Il nome della rosa* (*The Name of the Rose*) in Italy, followed by the 1983 publication of the English translation, shifted Eco from the relative obscurity of a well-published academic to the public limelight as a literary super star with a best-selling novel. In 1984, Eco published an English translation of an essay on the composition of *The Name of the Rose* called "Postscript to *The Name of the Rose*." This essay is included in the Harcourt 1994 edition of the novel.

Eco has won many awards for his fiction, including the Prix Medicis Etranger, 1982, for *The Name of the Rose*; France's Commandeur de l'Ordre des Arts et des Lettres, 1985; the Marshal McLuhan Award from UNESCO Canada and Teleglobe, 1985; the Chevalier de la Legion d'Honneur, France, 1993; Golden Cross of the Dodecannese, Greece, 1995; and the Cavaliere di Gran Croce al Merito della Repubblica Italiana, 1996.

Eco followed the successful *The Name of the Rose* with several more novels, all translated into English by William Weaver. These include *Foucault's Pendulum* (1989); *The Island of the Day Before* (1995); and *Baudolino* (2002). In addition, Eco has produced an astounding number of books in Italian, as well as English, on a variety of philosophical topics, as well as countless interviews, articles, and essays.

Plot Summary

Naturally, A Manuscript

The novel *The Name of the Rose* begins with what appears to be a preface to the book itself. In the opening pages, a narrator who seems to be Eco describes finding a book in 1968 that reproduced a fourteenth-century narration by the monk, Adso of Melk. The preface continues to describe how the narrator then lost the book, only to find it again under strange circumstances. He also describes his choice to publish his edition of the manuscript as well as the editorial choices he has made.

Prologue; First Day; Second Day; Third Day

Next, readers find a prologue provided by Adso of Melk, written as an old man. The events he is about to relate are in the distant past and took place when he was a young Benedictine novice in the service of a Franciscan monk, William of Baskerville.

Adso shifts to the past, specifically to the year 1327, dividing his story into seven days with each day structured by the canonical hours, those hours when the monks engage in formal prayer. On the first day, William and Adso approach the abbey, an abbey that contains the greatest library in all Christendom. They come as emissaries from the emperor to participate in a debate with a papal legation over the poverty of Christ as well as the status of the Franciscan order. They are greeted by the abbey cellarer, Remigio, who is astounded by William's knowledge about the abbot's lost horse.

Later, in their room, the abbot Abo visits William and Adso. He tells them the story of Adelmo of Otranto, a young illuminator who has fallen (or was pushed) to his death. He asks William to investigate. The two enter into a discussion about the library, and the abbot explains that only the librarian and his assistant may enter the library.

William and Adso then meet Ubertino, an elderly Franciscan taking refuge at the abbey, as well as Severinus, the herbalist; and Nicholas, the glazier. They also meet Jorge of Borgos, an elderly blind monk who is angry about laughter.

The morning prayers are interrupted early the next day because villagers have found a dead monk in a vat of pig's blood. It is Venantius, a translator and friend of Adelmo's. Severinus and William examine the body for evidence. Throughout the day, William and Adso continue to learn more about the library and the abbey. It is clear that the monks are hiding something. In addition, throughout the day, there are a number of learned conversations about laughter and heresy. Eventually, William learns about a secret entrance to the library, and he decides to investigate. He first goes to the Scriptorium, looking for a particular book that he believes both Adelmo and Venantius were reading. While there, William and Adso are disturbed, and someone steals both the book and William's glasses.

Next, William and Adso enter the labyrinth of the library. William believes that he has figured out the architecture, but he is wrong, and the two have great difficulty leaving the library before eventually finding their way out.

On the third day, Berengar, the assistant librarian, goes missing and a blood stained cloth is found in his cell. William continues his investigation and is successful in deciphering a code left by Venantius that William believes will guide them in further searches of the library for the lost book. Later that night, Adso finds himself alone in the kitchen and encounters a young peasant girl who seduces him. This is his first sexual experience. He falls deeply in love with her, although he does not now or ever learn her name. Confused and guilty, he confesses to William, who offers him absolution.

Media Adaptations

- *The Name of the Rose* was made into a film in 1986, directed by Jean-Jacques Annaud and starring Sean Connery as William of Baskerville, Christian Slater as Adso of Melk, and F. Murray Abraham as Bernard Gui. The film was released on DVD in 2004 and is available from Warner Home Video.

As the day draws to a close, the pair find Berengar dead in a tub of water.

Fourth Day; Fifth Day; Sixth Day

On the fourth day, the Franciscan legation arrives, as does Cardinal del Pogetto and Bernard Gui, sent from the Pope. Again, there is a good deal of discussion about heresy, and both sides prepare for the meeting. The reader learns that Bernard Gui is an Inquisitor, a position formerly held by William, who has given up his judgeship because of the difficulty of knowing the truth. Late in the evening, William and Adso again try to find their way to the "finis Africae," the room in the library where they believe the lost book is located. They are still unable to access this room because they do not know the codes. Meanwhile, Salvatore, who procures women for the cellarer, is captured by Bernard Gui, as is the girl Adso loves. She is accused of witchcraft, and Salvatore and Remigio are placed under arrest.

On the fifth day, a heated debate between the Franciscans and the Pope's envoys takes place. Meanwhile, Severinus is found murdered, and the book that William has entrusted to him has been stolen. William believes that Malachi has the book. Bernard holds court, questioning the cellarer who eventually confesses to all of the murders as well as to heresy. It is clear, however, that it is the inquisitorial methods that have elicited the confessions rather than the truth.

On the sixth day, Malachi keels over dead during prayer. William continues to investigate the murders and is convinced that there is a pattern that connects all of the murders as well as the mystery of the library. Just as it appears that William will solve the case, the abbot tells William that he no longer wants him to investigate. Remigio has confessed, and the abbot is worried more about the good name of the abbey than the truth. Undaunted, William and Adso return to the library. They discover that the abbot is in a secret stairway and will soon suffocate if they are unable to find their way to the top of the labyrinth and enter the finis Africae. Late that night, the two finally enter the finis Africae.

Seventh Day; Last Page

In the finis Africae, William and Adso find Jorge. He is the mastermind behind the murders, although neither the pattern nor the motive is as William had surmised: Adelmo's death was a suicide; Venantius, Berengar, and Malachi died from reading the lost book whose pages had been poisoned by Jorge; Malachi killed Severinus; and Jorge refuses to save the abbot who suffocates in the secret stairway. William correctly surmises that the book they have been seeking is Aristotle's treatise on comedy. Jorge refuses to let anyone read it and instead chooses to eat the poisoned pages. He also knocks over Adso's lamp and sets the entire library ablaze. William and Adso barely escape with their lives, and the library is lost.

In the chapter called "Last Page," Adso returns to his present and tells of how William later died of the plague mid-century. He also tells of returning to the charred remains of the library and sifting through the remains, trying to find something that made sense. He ends his manuscript not knowing for whom he writes and no longer knowing what it is about.

Characters

Abo

Abo is the abbot of the Benedictine abbey who asks William to investigate the murders of several monks. Abo is more interested in the good name of the abbey than he is in the truth. At the end of the novel, Abo has died, the victim of murder himself.

Adelmo of Otranto

Adelmo is a young illustrator of manuscripts. Before the book opens, he has engaged in a homosexual affair with Berengar, perhaps in order to gain access to an important, yet sequestered, book. As a result, he has committed suicide just before William and Adso's arrival at the abbey.

Adso of Melk

Adso of Melk is an elderly Benedictine monk who writes of his experiences as a young novitiate who accompanies William of Baskervilles on his trip to a northern Italian abbey in 1327 where they encounter a series of murders. Adso thus plays two roles in the novel: in the first place, his is an older voice, one that has had time to consider and reflect on the events of which he writes. In the second, he is young, innocent and naïve, the younger son of a wealthy nobleman, pledged to the church. *The Name of the Rose* is very much the story of Adso's coming of age; he loses his virginity to a young peasant girl, and he grows from ignorance to knowledge. He encounters the most pressing theological debates of his day at the abbey, as well as a thirst for knowledge that leads several other young monks to their deaths. He also plays "Watson" to William's "Sherlock" in the investigation of the murders. Eco's intention that readers connect Adso to Watson is clear: "Adso" in Italian and French is pronounced nearly identically to Watson in those languages. Adso's simple questions allow William to expound on his hypotheses and methodology in solving the crimes, mirroring the relationship between Dr. Watson and Sherlock Holmes in the stories by Sir Arthur Conan Doyle. Ironically, chance comments from Adso provide the key clues for William.

Benno of Uppsala

Benno is a rhetorican, someone who studies the figures of language. He dies by rushing into the library to save books and becomes engulfed in flames.

Berengar of Arundel

Berengar is the assistant librarian at the abbey and is thus privy to many of the secrets of the place. He is also a homosexual who has engaged in affairs with both Malachi, the chief librarian, and Adelmo. Berengar is murdered (by being poisoned with a poisoned book).

Bernard of Gui

Bernard is a real historical figure who was an important judge in the Inquisition, sentencing many heretics to their deaths by fire. In this novel, Eco portrays Bernard as an inquisitor who, in his obsessive pursuit of the Truth, subjects suspects to torture and the threat of horrible death. His inquisitorial techniques lead to confessions; yet it seems clear that, while he arrives at confessions, he fails to arrive at the truth of the murders. His chief role in the novel is as a mirror for William, whose ideas about truth, orthodoxy, and heresy stand in direct contrast to Bernard's.

Jorge of Burgos

Jorge is a blind, elderly monk who knows a great deal about books and the library. (Late in the book, William deduces that he was even the head librarian for a time.) In one of the most important passages in the novel, he and William enter into a heated debate over laughter. This debate reveals William's position as an early humanist and liberal theologian, while Jorge is both conservative and strongly opposed to anything but a strict interpretation of the Bible. Toward the end of the novel, it is revealed that Jorge is the real power in the abbey. He has worked diligently across the years to prevent access to Aristotle's lost book on comedy, even to the extent of poisoning the pages so that anyone who reads the book will die. Jorge believes that the book could cause the complete destruction of Christianity, and so feels that he is doing the will of God by first destroying those who would read the book and finally destroying the book itself.

In a mostly playful tribute, Eco models Jorge after Jorge Luis Borges, the influential Argentine writer. As Eco writes in his "Postscript to *The Name of the Rose*," "I wanted a blind man who guarded a library. . . . and library plus blind man can only equal Borges, also because debts must be paid."

Malachi of Hildesheim

Malachi is the chief librarian of the abbey. As such, he alone knows the exact location of every book stored in the library and all of the entrances and exits to the building. He has unrestricted access to the library and to the books, but can prevent others from entering or from reading books that he deems dangerous. Malachi serves a gatekeeper role, both to the library and to knowledge. He dies from reading the poisoned book.

Nicholas of Morimundo

Nicholas is the abbey's glazier. That is, he is the monk in charge of glass in the abbey. He is fascinated by William's glasses and learns to construct a new pair when William's are stolen.

Remigio of Varagine

Remigio is the cellarer of the abbey. His job is to supply the abbey with food and to care for the storing of food. He is short, stout, and jolly, someone who clearly partakes of his position to supply himself well. He also satisfies his carnal appetites on peasant women with whom he trades provisions for sex. He was formerly a member of a heretical sect, and under Bernard's inquiry ends up confessing to all of the murders and to heresy. As a result, he is condemned to burn.

Salvatore

Salvatore is an oddly-shaped and animal-like monk who speaks a pastiche of all the European languages. He procures women for Remigio and was also a member of a heretical cult.

Severinus of Sankt Wendel

Severinus is the herbalist at the abbey, and as such has both knowledge of and access to herbs of all sorts, including poisonous ones. He supplies Malachi with the herbs needed to create visions in anyone who attempts to enter the library, and he also unwittingly supplies Jorge with the poison that contaminates Aristotle's book on comedy. Severinus is killed by Malachi, who steals Aristotle's book from him.

Ubertino of Casale

Ubertino is an elderly Franciscan who has taken refuge at the abbey for many years. Many of those who followed him or his fellows bordered on heresy, according to the orthodox church, and thus Ubertino's life is in danger as a result of the debate between the papal legation and the Franciscan brothers. Ubertino's role in the novel is to provide a statement of the Franciscan position on love and poverty. His attachment to Adso, however, is not unproblematic. In several scenes, it is clear that Ubertino feels an unseemly attachment to the young man.

Venantius of Salvermec

Venantius is a young translator of manuscripts who recognizes Aristotle's book on comedy for what it is because of his knowledge of Greek. He dies, poisoned by the book.

William of Baskervilles

William is a Franciscan monk sent by the emperor to mediate the debate between the papal legation and the Franciscan order on the question of Christ's poverty. William is a former inquisitor; however, he has given up this role as he realizes that the line between heresy and orthodoxy is very thin. He is heavily influenced by the teachings of Roger Bacon, a rational empiricist. This means that William uses his observations to test his hypotheses rather than appealing to either pure reason or authoritative text. Like his teacher, William of

Topics For Further Study

- *The Name of the Rose* is filled with literary, historical, and philosophical allusions. Use "An Annotated Guide to the Historical and Literary References in *The Name of the Rose*" in *The Key to "The Name of the Rose"* (1999) by Adele J. Haft, Jane G. White, and Robert J. White, to select one or more significant historical figures to research. How does Eco draw on this figure in his novel?

- Most critics agree that Edgar Allan Poe is the father of the detective story. Read "Murders in the Rue Morgue," "The Purloined Letter," and "The Mystery of Marie Roget" by Poe, stories that all feature his detective, C. Auguste Dupin. Identify the most striking conventions of the detective story. What do readers expect to find when they read a mystery? How does Eco meet or subvert these expectations? How does reading Poe change or influence your reading of *The Name of the Rose*?

- Write out a time line of the major historical events in Western Europe in the fourteenth century. How do these events play a role in *The Name of the Rose*? How does having a background in medieval history affect your reading of *The Name of the Rose*?

- Examine as many copies of medieval manuscripts as you can find. (Good places to look include art history books or on line medieval history sites, such as the University of Oxford's Bodleian Library Western Manuscripts webpages, or the British Library's Lindisfarne Gospels webpage.) If possible, visit a museum and view a real medieval manuscript. At the same time, research the writing of medieval manuscripts. Write an essay in which you consider the techniques, strategies, problems, and challenges faced by medieval scribes in their efforts to produce texts.

Occam, William of Baskervilles is a nominalist and rejects the notion of universals. That is, he believes that only individual things exist, and that abstract general concepts only exist in the mind and nowhere else. For example, a nominalist would say that while there are many individual chairs, there does not exist in reality a universal chair from which all individual chairs are copied.

William is a wonderfully complicated character. In some ways, he is clearly modeled after Sherlock Holmes in his name, his appearance, and his method. In other ways, he seems to be modeled after Eco himself. William often seems to be a modern semiotician who finds himself struggling within the confines of medieval debate. He is remarkably intelligent, and yet he arrives at his final solution to the mystery of the murders purely by chance and not by his investigative method. William struggles with his own arrogance and his own thirst for knowledge, the very attributes which lead others in the book to their deaths. Ultimately, it is William's interference in the case that leads to the destruction of Aristotle's book on comedy, which is the very thing William seeks.

Themes

Language

Semiotics is Eco's academic field of study, and greatly influences the ideas on which he builds his novel. Semiotics refers to the study of signs, sign systems and the way meaning is derived. Signs can be nearly anything in a given culture that conveys information. Signs are generally conventional; that is, signs are meaningful to those who understand the unwritten codes that underpin them. A good example of this might be the way that people greet each other from culture to culture. In American culture, kissing someone on arrival is a sign designating a close and intimate relationship between the two people. Men, however, rarely kiss each other, although they might hug and slap each other on the back. In France, however, the sign is subtly different, and strangers meeting for the first time might kiss each other on each cheek. For those who understand such signs, the communication is clear.

The Name of the Rose is nothing if not a story of signs, including religious, political, and social signs, among many others. William prides himself as a savvy reader of signs; yet his mistake—in assuming that the system underpinning the series of murders was following the pattern of the Apocalypse—demonstrates how a faulty initial assumption can lead to a complete misunderstanding of a situation. In such a case, while the signs are still there, they have no meaning because there is no underpinning system. Likewise, the novel's title is ambiguous and mysterious because it is impossible to assign one meaning to the sign "rose." As Eco writes in the "Postscript," "the rose is a symbolic figure so rich in meaning that by now it hardly has any meaning left. . . . The title rightly disoriented the reader, who was unable to choose just one interpretation."

Nominalism

Nominalism is also an important topic or theme in *The Name of the Rose* closely related to language. During the Middle Ages, there was heated debate over the nature of reality. Realists, such as Jorge in the novel, argued that there were such things as universals. Realists support the supposition that to every name and term there corresponds a positive reality that is outside of the mind. Thus, there would be a universal "rose" that exists in reality outside of the mind, and that individual roses only differ accidentally one from another rather than in substance. Nominalists, such as William of Ockham and William of Baskerville, would argue, however, that there are only individuals. Universals are only categories the mind uses to make sense of the world rather than having any extra-mental reality. While this argument seems abstract, it is pertinent to the novel. The closing Latin words, translated into English, demonstrate this: "yesterday's rose endures in its name, we hold empty names." Thus, *The Name of the Rose* is a book about an empty sign, about the *name* of the rose, rather than the rose itself.

Style

Detective Fiction

Detective fiction is one of the most popular genres of novels in contemporary culture. Yet it seems an unlikely choice of format for such an erudite writer and book. Eco chooses detective fiction very deliberately, however, and not only to make his book more of a commercial success. Detective fiction offers a series of conventions and rules that attract a particular kind of reader, one who knows what ought to happen next. In addition, the reader of detective fiction is not taken in by what people say; rather, they have learned to look carefully at evidence and to make guesses about what might be the reality of the case. Some of the conventions of detective fiction found in *The Name of the Rose* include the ultra-intelligent detective; his faithful if obtuse young companion; a series of murders; a series of witnesses and interviews; villains who try to foil the investigation; and a final assembly of those involved where the detective reveals the murderer, the motive, and the means of the murder. In *The Name of the Rose*, Eco plays with his readers' expectations, creating a tension between what his audience believes will happen and what really happens, calling attention to the novel as a text, not reality. Furthermore, such playing with generic conventions undermines all such conventions, and reminds reader that what they are reading is a novel, not life.

Intertextuality

Another device that Eco employs magnificently is intertextuality. Ross Murfin and Supryia M. Ray in *The Bedford Glossary of Critical and Literary Terms* define it as "the condition of interconnectedness among texts, or the concept that any text is an amalgam of others, either because it exhibits signs of influence or because its language inevitably contains common points of reference with other texts through such things as allusion, quotation, genre, style, and even revisions." For postmodernists, the notion of intertextuality is an important one; it suggests that all literature, and for that matter, all writing, is comprised of writing that has already and always been written. Thus, text leads always to more text, rather than to some transcendental truth. *The Name of the Rose* draws on vast numbers of other texts in its constructions as evidenced by *The Key to "The Name of the Rose,"* by Adele J. Haft, Jane G. White, and Robert J. White, a whole book dedicated to identifying the medieval historical and literary allusions, and translating passages from Latin and other languages into English. Indeed, some critics have called *The Name of the Rose* a pastiche, or collage of many other sources, pasted together into something like a novel. By creating such a text, Eco opens the door to many interpretations.

Compare
&
Contrast

- **1300s:** Religious philosophers argue over the proper interpretation of the written text of the Bible. Those who find themselves on the wrong side of the debate are often burned for heresy.

  1970s: Philosophers of language for the past decades have argued that reality is created by text rather than the reverse. Jacques Derrida, the father of deconstruction, writes that text is no more than the play of signifiers.

  Today: Debate over the meaning (or lack of meaning) of language continues, although deconstruction has less influence in academic debates.

- **1300s:** The Black Death rages across Europe mid-century, leading people to believe that it could be a punishment from God and a sign of the Apocalypse.

  1970s: At the height of the cold war, the entire world fears nuclear holocaust and the post-Apocalyptic vision. Movies such as *Planet of the Apes* graphically provide images of such a future.

Today: While the ending of the cold war eases nuclear fears, the destruction of the World Trade Center Towers in 2001 raises renewed fears of destabilization and chaos at the hands of terrorists. Further, it raises fears of another worldwide plague precipitated by terrorists.

- **1300s:** Scribes work long hours copying manuscripts in the attempt to recover and preserve knowledge that was lost during the fall of the Roman Empire but finally makes its way back to Europe through the growing trade with the East.

  1970s: Libraries and books exist worldwide and are easily accessible. Technology such as typewriters and copy machines, as well as radio and television, make information quickly and readily available.

  Today: The explosion of computer technology puts entire encyclopedias on one small disk. There is sometimes the experience of "information overload," as well as the confidence that anything that needs to be known can be accessed on the Internet.

Historical Context

Italy in the 1970s

While *The Name of the Rose* is set in the fourteenth century in an unnamed Italian abbey, it may also be read as allegory of Western culture in general, and Italy in the 1970s, specifically. David Richter in his essay, "The Mirrored World: Form and Ideology in Umberto Eco's *The Name of the Rose*" argues that whether the reader associates Emperor Louis with the USSR and Pope John XXII with the United States or the reverse, Eco seems to be concerned "with the impact of their struggle on the three billion people elsewhere in nations that might have preferred to remain unaligned . . ." The cold war, reaching its height during the years that Eco wrote the novel, deeply influenced the writer, and it is little wonder that the confrontation between the papal legation and the Franciscans is so heated.

Perhaps even more relevant to the novel, however, is the kidnapping of Aldo Moro by the Red Brigade. The kidnapping took place on March 16, 1978, the month Eco reports he began writing the novel. Moro was the President of the Christian Democratic Party and had been Prime Minister of Italy three times. A series of convoluted negotiations ensued as different parties tried to secure Moro's release. Much of what happened is ambiguous; however, Moro was eventually murdered. Eco and other Italian intellectuals were deeply shocked by this assassination, and his outrage seems to make it into the pages of *The Name of the Rose*.

Europe in the 1300s

The fourteenth century was a watershed period in medieval history, and there is little question of why Eco chooses to situate his novel in this troubled time. In the first place, philosophers and theologians were deeply immersed in a number of debates, including not only the question of Christ's poverty, but also the nature of language and truth. If language cannot be connected to a transcendent reality outside of the words themselves, then it undermines the entire Christian project. While this concern seems more postmodern than medieval, any close reading of medieval philosophers demonstrates the anxiety caused by new ways of thinking. In addition, Eco deliberately chooses to have Adso write about the events of 1327 from the vantage point of the middle of the century, at a time after the ravages of the Black Death. The spread of the plague in the years between 1348 and 1350 was cataclysmic; Europe lost nearly one-third of its total population, sending social, political, and religious institutions into chaos. For Adso, the plague must have seemed Apocalyptic. He mentions the death of William in the plague, and his own existence in an "aged world." The contemplation of death and of the world grown old is a common medieval motif; yet the images that Eco provides of Adso sifting through the ashes of the burned Scriptorium could just as easily apply to some cold war vision of nuclear holocaust. Thus, the connection between the twentieth century and the fourteenth century seems closer than might otherwise be thought.

Christian Slater as Adso of Melk with Valentina Vargas as the Girl, still from the 1986 film version of The Name of the Rose © Neue Constantin/ZDF/The Kobal Collection. Reproduced by permission

Critical Overview

The Name of the Rose, first published in Italian in 1980 and in English in 1983, was both a critical and popular success, staying at the top of the best-seller lists for weeks, and eventually selling more than a million copies in hard cover and more in paper back. The novel has remained in print for more than two decades, and continues to generate a large body of critical commentary. While academic interest might have been predicted, given Eco's reputation as a scholar, the popular response to the book took all by surprise. Who could have imagined that a long, complicated, multi-layered novel, set in the fourteenth century and with long passages of untranslated Latin, German, and French would appeal to the world-wide reading public?

Contemporary reviews find a variety of reasons for its appeal. Masolino D'Amico, in a review for the *Times Literary Supplement*, for example, says that *The Name of the Rose* "is no mere detective story; rather, its framework serves as a vehicle for nothing less than a *summa* of all the author knows about the Middle Ages … Eco's rare gift for

epitome has a chance to shine forth in this book and his own delight in his task is often infectious." D'Amico argues that the main point of the book is "to vindicate humour." Likewise, Gian-Paolo Biasin in *World Literature Today* writes that "Play is at the core of the plot." Michael Dirda, in *The Washington Post* review of the novel credits "Gothic hugger-mugger" with lightening "Eco's operatic gravity." He also, however, notes the vast scope of the novel: "In its range, *The Name of the Rose* suggests an imaginative *summa*, an alchemical marriage of murder mystery and Christian mystery."

In the years since the book's publication, scholars have written volumes dedicated to unpacking the novel. Many note the influence of Jorge Luis Borges, the great Argentine writer, on Eco. Eco himself makes it clear in the "Postscript to *The Name of the Rose*" that he deliberately invokes Borges in his character Jorge of Borgos, the blind librarian. Other critics note the connections between *The Name of the Rose*, Sherlock Holmes, and other detective stories. Jorge Hernández Martín, for example, devotes five chapters of his book *Readers and Labyrinths: Detective Fiction in Borges, Bustos*

Domecq, and Eco to this project. He writes, "The name of Eco's detective, William of Baskerville, evokes in turn the renowned sleuth of Baker Street and Holmes's best known case, *The Hound of the Baskervilles.*"

Still other critics concentrate on the intertexuality of the novel. Teresa De Lauretis in her chapter "Gaudy Rose: Eco and Narcissism," suggests that *The Name of the Rose* is "made up almost entirely of other texts." Likewise, Peter Bonandello in *Umberto Eco and the Open Text: Semiotics, Fiction, Popular Culture* argues that Eco's "work represents a pastiche and a parody of a number of other traditions—some obvious, others less so—that enable the novel to appeal to all his intended audiences simultaneously."

Other readings include Jonathan Key's "Maps and Territories: Eco Crossing the Boundary," in which he carefully examines the role that the abbey map and the library map play in the reading of the novel. He argues that "the library as map of the world stands as a metonym for the frequently expressed formulation of the novel as a device for mapping the world."

Indeed, there seem to be as many readings as there are critics of this novel. All are universal in their praise for the richness of the text, and for the possibilities for continued study.

Criticism

Diane Andrews Henningfeld

Henningfeld is a professor of English at Adrian College who writes widely on literary topics for academic and educational publications. In this essay, Henningfeld discusses the concept of the labyrinth, the encyclopedia, and model reader for The Name of the Rose.

Entering a book as wonderfully rich and complicated as *The Name of the Rose* is both exhilarating and frightening. Where to begin? How to read? What ought a reader do with the vast quantities of information Eco spills out on every page? One helpful way of entering the text is to first consider two of Eco's controlling metaphors—the labyrinth and the encyclopedia—then to examine the idea of the model reader, and finally to imagine a number of possible (but by no means exhaustive) entry points.

That Eco wants readers to consider the idea of the labyrinth is clear. Early in the book, Abo tells

William to beware of the library: "The library defends itself, immeasurable as the truth it houses, deceitful as the falsehood it preserves. A spiritual labyrinth, it is also a terrestrial labyrinth. You might enter and you might not emerge." In addition, Eco has written extensively on the idea of the labyrinth in his essays on semiotics. Rochelle Sibley, in her chapter "Aspects of the Labyrinth in *The Name of the Rose*: Chaos and Order in the Abbey Library," both reviews and comments on Eco's use of labyrinths. According to Sibley, Eco classifies labyrinths in three ways: the "classical;" the "Mannerist maze;" and the "rhizome," or net. The classical labyrinth has just one path in and out, and no decisions are required of the labyrinth walker. The maze, on the other hand, has several entrances, and many dead ends, cross roads, and mis-directions. The abbot's statement to William seems to refer to this kind of labyrinth; there is always the danger that those entering a maze may become so hopelessly lost that they will never find their way out. Indeed, it is this notion of the labyrinth that may intimidate readers of *The Name of the Rose*. For readers accustomed to thinking about the labyrinth as a maze where one must choose the right path to reach the center, or heart of the maze, choosing the "right" path into *The Name of the Rose* is nothing if not daunting. What if the reader makes a mistake and finds him or herself in a blind alley? Further, given the sheer number of entry points the novel offers, choosing just one may prove an impossibility.

However, Eco posits a third kind of labyrinth which he calls the rhizome or net. Sibley quotes Eco's definition of a net from *Semiotics and the Philosophy of Language* (1984):

> The main feature of a net is that every point can be connected with every other point, and, where connections are not yet designed, they are, however, conceivable and designable. A net is an unlimited territory. . . . the abstract model of a net has neither a center nor an outside.

Thus, in a rhizome, a labyrinth walker may move from point to point because all points are connected. Moreover, the pathways between the points are not yet fully defined; connections may still be made. Considering the labyrinth in this sense provides the reader with nearly endless possibilities for interpretation. Indeed, wandering in a rhizome ought not elicit fear, but rather laughter, as the reader moves from node to node, recognizing that walking in circles in this kind of maze is not necessarily a bad thing, as new connections might reveal themselves at any moment. As Jorge Hernández Martín writes in his book *Readers and*

Labyrinths: Detective Fiction in Borges, Bustos Domecq and Eco, "The possibilities for reading *The Name of the Rose* are as varied as the many individuals who appropriate the text by their readings."

An additional metaphor employed by Eco that is helpful in reading *The Name of the Rose* is the encyclopedia. Again, this term surfaces primarily in Eco's semiotic work, and it has technical meanings beyond the scope of this essay. Nonetheless, the reader of *The Name of the Rose* can think of an encyclopedia in the more common usage of the term: a collection of knowledge, comprised of many sources, categorized and organized so that that a reader can move from topic to topic. Not surprisingly, delving into an encyclopedia often pushes a reader to make new connections. The encyclopedia is a particularly apt metaphor for a novel set in the Middle Ages, which was a time of great encyclopedists. As Christina Farronato observes in her book *Eco's Chaosmos: From the Middle Ages to Postmodernity*, "The medieval thinkers had an encyclopaedic approach to the reality of the universe. They elaborated a series of encyclopaedias that served to catalogue every object or event in the universe." Moreover, the fourteenth century in particular was a time of great social, religious, and political upheaval. Consequently, the medieval encyclopedists felt great pressure to recover and preserve the treasure troves of knowledge endangered by the fall of Rome and the crises of their own time.

Eco uses the notion of encyclopedia on a personal level. Each person is like a continually growing encyclopedia. Thus, for Eco, *The Name of the Rose* is not merely a novel, but also a cataloguing of his own encyclopedia. It is this encyclopedia that creates the labyrinth and the world of the novel. Why is this important for the reader to know? Because the way a reader brings his or her own encyclopedia to bear on *The Name of the Rose* will deeply impact the text the reader and the author collaboratively create. As Eco writes in the "Postscript," "What model reader did I want as I was writing? An accomplice, to be sure, one who would play my game."

Consequently, because Eco's encyclopedia is vast, there are many *The Name of the Rose* novels. It is in format a detective novel. Thus, readers who are aficionados of this genre will have no difficulty recognizing William of Baskerville and Adso of Melk as Sherlock Holmes and Doctor Watson. In addition, these readers know from their own experience that there will be murders to be solved

> Eco welcomes readers into the murmuring labyrinth he has created in *The Name of the Rose*, and eagerly shares his encyclopedia with those readers who dare to play his game."

and evidence to observe. However, because Eco is also playing a game with the reader, most reader expectations of how the crime will be solved are undermined, not because the crimes go unsolved, but because William turns out to be utterly wrong in his assessment of the situation. He tells Adso, "I have never doubted the truth of signs, Adso; they are the only things man has with which to orient himself in the world. What I did not understand was the relation among signs. I arrived at Jorge through an apocalyptic pattern that seemed to underlie all the crimes, and yet it was accidental." For the reader of detective novels, such an admission is unheard of; although the detective might follow several blind leads, he or she ought to always find the truth in the end. In *The Name of the Rose*, however, William simply finds accident, not order, and chaos, not truth.

Readers who hold the literature of Argentine writer Jorge Luis Borges in their personal encyclopedias, likewise, will have no difficulty recognizing other structural influences. Eco uses several of Borges's stories; he also creates the character of Jorge of Borgos as a blind librarian. Any reader of Borges knows that Borges himself was both a librarian, and blind. Specifically, Eco borrows both style and content from Borges's "Tlön, Uqbar, Orbis Tertius," a story that opens with these lines: "I owe the discovery of Uqbar to the conjunction of a mirror and an encyclopedia." Borges goes on to write about the loss of an article in an encyclopedia and his search to recover it. The story is remarkably similar to the opening of *The Name of the Rose*, called by Eco, "Naturally, a Manuscript." The insertion of a labyrinth in *The Name of the Rose* also has its roots in another short story by Borges, "The Garden of Forking Paths." In this story, Borges creates a labyrinth that is not a physical labyrinth, but is instead a book. Finally, in

What Do I Read Next?

- *A Distant Mirror: The Calamitous 14th Century* (1978), by Barbara Tuchman, is a fascinating and readable study of Europe in the 1300s.

- In 1993, noted historian of philosophy Frederick C. Copleston published the second volume of his *History of Philosophy*, which covers the philosophy of the Middle Ages, including discussions of both Roger Bacon and William of Ockham.

- *Sherlock Holmes: The Complete Novels and Stories* (1986) provides an excellent introduction into Sir Arthur Conan Doyle's legendary sleuth.

- Eco's *Foucault's Pendulum*, translated into English by William Weaver in 1989, is another philosophical novel, investigating the secrets of the Knights Templar.

- Jorge Luis Borges's *Labyrinths: Selected Stories and Other Writings* (1962), edited by Donald A. Yates and James E. Irby, contains some of Borges's most influential stories, including "Death and the Compass," "The Garden of Forking Paths," "Pierre Menard, Author of the *Quixote*," and "Tlön, Uqbar, Orbis Tertius."

Borges's famous detective story, "Death and the Compass," the detective follows a series of clues that seem to point to a particular pattern. He fails to apply Ockham's razor, "the principle that one should not postulate the existence of a greater number of entities or factors when fewer will suffice," according to Frederick C. Copleston's *Medieval Philosophy*. Instead, the detective chooses an elaborate pattern based on the Cabbala to explain a series of murders. Like William, this detective finally finds the answers he seeks, but only accidentally.

Finally, readers who bring to the novel an encyclopedia that includes knowledge of medieval history, literature, philosophy, aesthetics, and religion will find a very different kind of reading and will find evidence of Eco's use of Roger Bacon, William of Ockham, and Thomas Aquinas, among many others. Such a reader will understand the intricacies of the debate between the papal legation and the Franciscans, and will delight in the finer points of orthodoxy and heresy. It is also likely that such a reader will have at least a rudimentary knowledge of Latin, and perhaps German, and so, will find the text less opaque than readers who do not know these languages.

There are countless entries into the labyrinth that is *The Name of the Rose*, some of them not even yet discovered. This is because, according to Teresa De Lauretis in her essay "Gaudy Rose: Eco and Narcissism," *The Name of the Rose* "is a novel made up almost entirely of other texts, of tales already told, of names either well known or sounding as if they should be known to us from literary and cultural history; a medley of famous passages and obscure quotations, specialized lexicons and subcodes . . . and characters cut out in strips from a generic World Encyclopedia." Lauretis here echoes Adso's epiphany:

> Until then I had thought each book spoke of the things, human or divine, that lie outside books. Now I realized that not infrequently books speak of books: it is as if they spoke among themselves. In the light of this reflection, the library seemed all the more disturbing to me. It was then the place of long, centuries-old murmuring, an imperceptible dialogue between one parchment and another, a living thing, a receptacle of powers not to ruled by a human mind, a treasure of secrets emanated by many minds, surviving the death of those who had produced them or had been their conveyors."

Eco welcomes readers into the murmuring labyrinth he has created in *The Name of the Rose*, and eagerly shares his encyclopedia with those readers who dare to play his game. He invites readers to move quickly from node to node, seeking knowledge, building connections, seemingly finding a pattern in the novel, and in the world. In the end, however, *The Name of the Rose* does not offer a glimpse of the truth at all, but rather provides only Adso's "lesser library . . . a library made up

Jean Mielot at work in a fifteenth century scriptorium © Bettmann/Corbis

of fragments, quotations, unfinished sentences, amputated stumps of books."

Source: Diane Andrews Henningfeld, Critical Essay on *The Name of the Rose*, in *Novels for Students*, Thomson Gale, 2006.

John J. Burke Jr.

In the following essay excerpt, Burke contrasts the postmodern depiction of medieval times found in Eco's The Name of the Rose *with Sir Walter Scott's medieval novels.*

When we turn to Umberto Eco's *The Name of the Rose* we turn to a postmodern story set in medieval times; in 1327, to be precise. Eco's novel begins with prefatory material that resembles the beginnings of Scott's novels with their prefatory material from Jedediah Cleishbotham, Laurence Templeton, the Wardour manuscript, and Dr Dryasdust. The point of both is to explain how a story about long ago should only now be surfacing in modern times, but the explanations never really explain anything. It is all very much tongue in cheek.

Instead of the onmiscient narrator who tells the story in a Scott novel, Eco prefers to have his story told through the eyes of Adso of Melk, who at the time of the events in the story was a novice Benedictine. However, Adso is also telling us this story as a monk looking back over the very early part of his life. The story he tells us begins as he and his companion, a Franciscan friar archly named William of Baskerville, approach a Benedictine monastery high in the Appenines in northwest Italy, a place remarkably close to the village where Umberto Eco himself was born and raised. William, a former inquisitor, with Adso as his assistant, has come to the monastery to work out a settlement in the dispute between the Pope and the Emperor, one that touches on the emergence of radical groups within the Franciscan order. The views of those radical Franciscans sound much like the liberation theology that has caused such a stir in our own times. But the Franciscans of the fourteenth century, instead of challenging the entire social order, were primarily challenging a wealthy and worldly church.

Whatever the historical currents, though, Adso's story almost immediately turns into a murder mystery. Shortly after the two arrive at the monastery they learn that the body of a young monk named Adelmo of Otranto had been found at the foot of some high windows at the entrance to the monastery's famed library. The mystery thickens when the deaths of other monks by foul play seem to point toward the existence of a serial killer. There are hints that the bloody deeds have something to

> The difference between knights and monks may reveal that Eco does not share Scott's interest in the soldier or warrior as a cultural ideal. Eco clearly prefers men of learning, people suspiciously like modern-day university professors such as himself. Most of the characters are involved in the world of books."

do with the monastery's library which we learn was deliberately constructed as a labyrinth. There are further hints that seem to tie the murders to prophecies in the Bible, especially to the final book of the Bible, the fevered, frenzied, obscure Book of the Apocalypse. Among other things the Book of the Apocalypse enumerates seven danger signs that are to precede the coming end. The sequence of the murders continues to follow the pattern spelled out in the Book of the Apocalypse, and before the story comes to an end there are indeed seven murders to correspond to the seven signs. The end of the world would seem to be upon us.

Nevertheless, what we learn at the end is that the seven murders are actually unconnected with one another. After all, there can be no real answers in a poststructural world: logic, order, structure are merely fictions we impose on the world. The human mind compulsively constructs explanations for why things happen, but in the end all is random and accidental. The initial murder was actually a suicide that resulted from a suffocating guilt over homosexual conduct. Another was caused by curiosity about what was forbidden or off limits, or we might say censored, and so on until eventually we come face to face with the distorted face of fanaticism in the person of the blind Jorge of Burgos. Jorge is completely convinced that he is right, and he would willingly become a martyr rather than give up on his view of what the world should be. His real aim, as we see it, is mind control. Jorge wants to keep Aristotle's lost treatise on comedy out of the hands

of future generations because he believes they would interpret it as a licence for laughter. Jorge objects to laughter because it is a sign of our refusal to take things seriously. Therefore, laughter is unseemly and irreligious. Jorge is the man who would rather burn books than allow anyone else access to their secrets. He does in fact set a fire which spreads throughout the monastery, eventually reducing all of its treasures to ashes except for a few scattered remains and fragments. It is out of such fragments that Adso has constructed or reconstructed the narrative we have been reading.

The medieval world we see in Eco's *The Name of the Rose* provides an instructive contrast with the medieval world we see in Scott's novels. It may be tempting to think that the difference between them is not so much the difference between the romantic and the postmodern as it is the difference between a Protestant and a Catholic view of the Middle Ages. Though there is certainly some truth to that observation, it would not be sufficient for explaining the nature of the difference. For one thing, it is not at all clear that they differ much about faith. There is no more emphasis on honest religious faith in *The Name of the Rose* than there is in the Waverley novels. There is fanaticism, to be sure, but the fanaticism of Jorge of Burgos is of the same kind and perhaps of the same degree as that which is portrayed in novel after novel by Scott.

Still, there are differences, and the differences are quite revealing. Eco chooses a monastery as his setting, an institution thought of as typifying the Middle Ages. But his is a most unusual medieval monastery: Eco's monks don't much bother with the practice of monastic silence; nor, curiously enough, do any of them seem to spend much time in prayer; more peculiar yet, there are no communal celebrations of the Catholic liturgy, or if there are they are nowhere in sight. Eco's monastery, in short, seems conceived of less as a testimony or tribute to religious faith of any type than as an experiment in international communal living. The debates over poverty among the various factions within the Franciscan movement remind us further of various medieval experiments with communal property and/or ownership. It would be hard to believe that Eco when writing this was not thinking about the ideological debates between the capitalist West and the communist East. Eco's fable has even proved prophetic, perhaps unexpectedly so, but it has to be a gloomy tale for those who share Eco's Leftist sympathies. For his story acknowledges the predictable failure of all such high-minded social experiments. It will be, as we well know, the wealth of nations, not their poverty, that becomes the master political ideal. Monasticism was doomed to fade away because it was unable to contain the individualistic impulses it sought to harness or repress.

Not only is the religious basis of medieval life nowhere in sight, neither is chivalry. That may be in part because for Eco even the possibility that people could or would act from entirely noble motives is not even worth conceiving, or perhaps that the very act of conceiving it would be harmful because it would nourish dangerous illusions. The conception of character in this book proceeds clearly enough from the proposition that all human behaviour operates according to mixed motives. William of Baskerville may be the book's nominal hero, but he is not as pure as we may want him to be. His knowledge of the consciousness-raising qualities of herbs and plants is a subject of wonder to those about him, but there is also speculation that his cool detachment from the swirl of passions about him can be attributed to his habit of chewing on something that has a narcotic effect on him. That aside, we are asked to admire William for his tolerance, for his open-mindedness, and for his sparkling intelligence. Nevertheless, the story does undercut its obvious hero, though not because he is a pothead. William fails in the end at all his assignments. Perhaps Eco is suggesting that reason will prove unequal to the task before it. In any event, William is unable to solve the mystery surrounding the murders until it is too late and catastrophe is inevitable. He also fails to bring about peace between the Pope and the Emperor. There is no confidence in the value of good intentions or even of well-meaning actions in this postmodern fable.

The difference between knights and monks may reveal that Eco does not share Scott's interest in the soldier or warrior as a cultural ideal. Eco clearly prefers men of learning, people suspiciously like modern-day university professors such as himself. Most of the characters are involved in the world of books. Books are represented as powerful and influential, and they are spoken of respectfully. The library, not the chapel, is the most important part of this monastery. Moreover, this library is constructed as a labyrinth, which contains its own allegory of learning. Books inhabit a place where those who succeed in finding their way in may easily get lost, and never find their way out. To emphasise this meaning of his fable Eco has gone on in his Postscript to *The Name of the Rose* to speak of different kinds of labyrinths, and to suggest that a rhizome labyrinth is the proper model for his own narrative. With other types of labyrinths there is a beginning and an end, but in a rhizome there is no beginning and no end. There can only be constant but purposeless motion in a rhizome labyrinth as people try to find their way out of their predicaments. But there can never be any success because there is no solution, no way out. The point then of this medieval fable about the postmodern world is that it is not to be understood. What joins us to those who have preceded us is a sense of muddle. Nothing really means anything. The only certainty is death. The only defence we have in the face of such absurdity is laughter, and we may even lose that grace because the grim-eyed fanatics would like to steal that away from us too.

The clearest contrast between the medievalisms of Scott and Eco comes, it seems to me, in the theory of history that is projected by their narratives. For Scott the pull of the Middle Ages was undeniably a potent one, but however powerful the enchantment Scott's feet were firmly planted in the present, as David Daiches and so many others have pointed out to us time and again. History for Scott represented progress, and in that sense his basic allegiance was to the ongoing legacy of the Enlightenment. His stories are not intended to be at the service of escapism. They function rather to confirm the superiority or betterness, if you will, of the present while allowing their pictures of past realities to criticise our sense of the present, thereby enlarging our possibilities for the future.

History in Eco is quite another matter. History represents decline for Adso. Adso's text winds into other texts, but into none so clearly and so insistently as into the Book of the Apocalypse. Not only does the Book of the Apocalypse provide the false pattern that was supposed to make sense out of the murders in the monastery: it is embedded in the consciousness of characters, most of whom—Friar William being a singular and important exception—are expecting the end of the world at any moment. Eco's story does indeed teach a kind of apocalyptic end when a great fire actually does consume the great monastery and its magnificent library. The fire and its mushroom cloud of smoke inevitably lead us to think of a possible nuclear conflagration, and thus of the threat of apocalyptic doom that hangs over our own times. That may be the firmest link Eco sees between our own time and the world of the Middle Ages. The story in *The Name of the Rose* presents itself as a window into the Middle Ages. It tells of conflict between the Pope and the Emperor, heresy and inquisition, monks and monasticism, factions within the Franciscans. But it eventually becomes clear that what

Sean Connery as William of Baskerville and Christian Slater as Adso of Melk, still from the 1986 film version of The Name of the Rose

© Neue Constantin/ZDF/The Kobal Collection. Reproduced by permission

appears to be a window is really a mirror. We may think we are looking back at them, but actually we are only looking at ourselves, and that is how Umberto Eco intended it to be. He seems to have discovered that the best way to make comments on our own times in a telling fashion is to make them teasingly. Thus he distances himself as much as possible from the present, selecting a setting so strange that at least initially there would be no confusion between ourselves and them. This is a highly useful narrative strategy. The medievalness of his narrative allows Eco to eliminate or filter out all the superficial trappings what we consider essential to modern life—the ringing of our phones, the buzz of our TV sets—to focus on those things that are more interesting about us, and probably more important. What we can see in Eco's mirror includes: a gnawing sense that we are not up to the intellectual challenges we face, either individually or collectively; social and political discontent that comes with an unequal distribution of the world's goods; a pervading sense of doom because the wizardry of modern science has left us perched on the edge of the abyss, waiting for an end that can come at any time. Laughter is the best weapon we have

against all this, and possibly the only one. History for Scott was hope. History for Eco is a struggle against despair.

Source: John J. Burke Jr., "The Romantic Window and the Postmodern Mirror: The Medieval Worlds of Sir Walter Scott and Umberto Eco," in *Scott in Carnival*, edited by J. H. Alexander and David Hewitt, Association for Scottish Literary Studies, 1993, pp. 556–68.

Benjamin A. Fairbank Jr.

In the following essay, Fairbank notes connections between The Name of the Rose *and the Sherlock Holmes detective stories.*

> "It seemed to me, as I read this page, that I had read some of these words before, and some phrases that are almost the same, which I have seen elsewhere, return to my mind?" —William of Baskerville to Adso of Melk

In Umberto Eco's novel *The Name of the Rose,* the protagonist, the detective—monk, the intellectual ascetic from England who unravels the murder mystery in the fourteenth-century Italian monastery, is named William of Baskerville. Of all good English names, why William of *Baskerville?* It is, of course, to suggest the presence of the spirit of Sherlock Holmes bringing light of reason to the monastery—Eco is broadly insinuating that the preeminent detective of recent history is at hand. It may be possible to write a review or an article about *The Name of the Rose* without mentioning Sherlock Holmes, but we have yet to see one; no one overlooks the hint of the Baskerville.

As Sherlockians read *The Name of the Rose* they will surely resonate to a sense of the familiar as the story begins and unfolds—a sense that goes far beyond the name of Baskerville. Although Adso of Melk, a Benedictine novice who is the narrator, is writing of his relationship with William of Baskerville when he says

> During our time together we did not have occasion to lead a very regular life: even at the abbey we remained up at night and collapsed wearily during the day, nor did we take part regularly in the holy offices,

it is plain that the same passage could apply to another detective, as seen by his biographer-assistant. And that assistant, give or take a consonant or two, was very nearly also named Adso. The similarity between Adso and Watson extends further than their names. Both are removed from the main action of the story by literary devices, and both use their bafflement in the methods of their associates to heighten the suspense before the resolution of the mystery.

In the case of Watson, he stands apart from the direct action in the early stories because of his semi-invalid status caused by the aftereffects of his bullet wound in his shoulder that caused his leg to ache, later because of his removal from Holmes due to his marriage and his increasing medical practice, and throughout the stories because of the intellectual gulf between them. Adso cannot participate as an equal with William of Baskerville because of his youth and inexperience, as well as because of his intellectual inferiority.

Holmes's well-known remark from *The Second Stain,* "Now, Watson, the fair sex is your department," suggests another similarity between Watson and Adso. Adso in *The Name of the Rose* does indeed make the fair sex his department, although the incident is not a major part of his narrative. Is this in part an artful reference to Watson's proclivity for womanizing?

Holmes and William of Baskerville share other similarities and abilities. Both enjoy impressing a client with the magnitude of their abilities—not only is that evident throughout the Canon, Holmes admits as much himself in one of the two stories told in the Holmesian first person when he says, in *The Blanched Soldier,* "I have found it wise to impress clients with a sense of power, and so I gave him some of my conclusions." William of Baskerville greets a searching party from the monastery with as Holmesian a demonstration of off-the-cuff deductions as one is likely to find anywhere outside the Canon when he gives a full description of a horse he has never seen. Later, William explains his deductions to Adso, just as Holmes typically does to his clients and to Watson.

Yet many of these similarities between Holmes and William could be drawn between Holmes and almost any fictional detective. Sherlock Holmes was, after all, the prototype detective of literature, second only, perhaps, to Dr. Joseph Bell. Is there more direct evidence that Sherlock Holmes and William of Baskerville are equivalent? Indeed there is. Eco lets his readers know early on that the game is afoot. Truly, as Rosenberg quotes from Congreve in his discussion of Sherlock Holmes, "Naked is the best disguise." Eco nakedly puts into the account of Adso of Melk the following:

> On those occasions a vacant, absent expression appeared in his eyes, and I would have suspected he was in the power of some vegetal substance capable of producing visions if the obvious temperance of his life had not led me to reject this thought.

What? What was that? Have Sherlockians not heard those words before? Do they not arouse a

" Is his use of Holmes as his detective a cagey device to titillate Sherlockians? Or is there a deeper meaning in the choice, a meaning perhaps related to Eco's field of semiotics, the study and theory of symbols, signs, and their meaning?"

sense of recognition, even déjà vu, a description of another man in another time? One described by Watson in *A Study in Scarlet* as he said:

> On these occasions I have noticed such a dreamy, vacant expression in his eyes, that I might have suspected him of being addicted to the use of some narcotic, had not the temperance and cleanliness of his whole life forbidden such a notion.

And that, if you please, is in a book translated from Italian into English so that any of Watson's words from Adso's pen have been twice translated, once from English to Italian and then back again! The similarities do not end there. Close by we find Watson saying of Holmes

> . . . he was possessed of extraordinary delicacy of touch, as I frequently had occasion to observe when I watched him manipulating his fragile philosophical instruments.

Adso makes a remarkably similar observation: "He possessed, it seemed to me, an extraordinary delicate touch, the same that he used in handling his machines." Moreover, Adso says, "During our period at the abbey his hands were always covered with the dust of books, the gold of still-fresh illumination, or with yellowish substances he touched in Severinus's infirmary."

May we hear from Dr. Watson, please, still in *A Study in Scarlet?* "His hands were invariably blotted with ink and stained with chemicals. . . ."

William of Baskerville's temperament and moodiness also bear distinct similarities to those of Sherlock Holmes. Adso offers:

> His energy seemed inexhaustible when a burst of activity overwhelmed him. But from time to time, as if his vital spirit had something of the crayfish, he

moved backward in moments of inertia, and I watched him lie for hours on my pallet in my cell, uttering barely a few monosyllables, without contracting a single muscle of his face.

Watson, not to be outdone, observes of Holmes, in the same story cited,

Nothing could exceed his energy when the working fit was upon him; but now and again a reaction would seize him, and for days on end he would lie upon the sofa in the sitting-room, hardly uttering a word or moving a muscle from morning to night.

Not even William's appearance escapes implicit comparison with that of Holmes. We find Adso saying of William of Baskerville:

Brother William's physical appearance was at that time such as to attract the attention of the most inattentive observer. His height surpassed that of a normal man, and he was so thin that he seemed still taller. His eyes were sharp and penetrating; his thin and slightly beaky nose gave his countenance the expression of a man on the lookout, save in certain moments of sluggishness of which I shall speak. His chin also denoted a firm will. . . .

And as for Holmes? Again in *A Study in Scarlet* the good doctor observes:

His very person and appearance were such as to strike the attention of the most casual observer. In height he was rather over six feet, and so excessively lean that he seemed to be considerably taller. His eyes were sharp and piercing, save during those intervals of torpor to which I have alluded; and his thin, hawk-like nose gave his whole expression an air of alertness and decision. His chin, too, had the prominence and squareness which mark the man of determination.

Come, Messrs. Conan Doyle/Watson and Eco/Adso, have you been speaking of two men or of one?

Other reminders of Holmes's methods and idiosyncrasies reflected in William's activities abound in the book—a few more here will illustrate their presence. William, in tutoring Adso in his method, instructs: "My good Adso, during our whole journey I have been teaching you to recognize the evidence through which the world speaks to us like a great book." Let it be remembered that one of Holmes's early articles, in which he set out the fundamentals of his system of observation and deduction (which Watson read with indignant skepticism), was titled, according to Watson in *A Study in Scarlet,* "The Book of Life."

William's disquisition on the solving of mysteries could have been spoken by Holmes himself, and his invitation to Adso to join him in a burglary has a distinctly Holmes-and-Watson ring to it:

". . . You provide the lamp. Linger in the kitchen at dinner hour, take one. . . ."

"A theft?"

"A loan, to the greater glory of the Lord."

"Then count on me."

The exchange recalls Holmes's and Watson's dialogue as Holmes solicits Watson's cooperation in his deception of Irene Adler in *A Scandal in Bohemia* or Holmes's recruitment of the reluctant Watson for the burglary of 13 Caulfield Gardens, the residence of Hugo Oberstein in *The Bruce-Partington Plans.*

Williams and Holmes's difficulties in unraveling the tales told by footprints run along similar lines. First let us hear from Adso:

"A fine mess," William said, nodding toward the complex pattern of footprints left all around by the monks and the servants. "Snow, dear Adso, is an admirable parchment on which men's bodies leave very legible writing. But this palimpsest is badly scraped, and perhaps we will read nothing interesting on it."

Watson had a similar story to tell in repeating Holmes's remarks about the effects of weather on footprints in this dialogue between Holmes and Stanley Hopkins in *The Golden Pince-Nez:*

"Tut-tut! Well, then, these tracks upon the grass—were they coming or going!"

"It was impossible to say. There was never any outline."

"A large foot or a small?"

"You could not distinguish."

Holmes gave an ejaculation of impatience, "It has been pouring rain and blowing a hurricane ever since," said he. "It will be harder to read than that palimpsest."

Similarly, both Holmes and William of Baskerville include among their talents the breaking of secret codes. Holmes easily breaks the secret writing which was designed to resemble a child's playful drawing (*The Dancing Men*), while William, using similar methods, breaks a more complex code. Even their respective comments on code-breaking are analogous—"What one man can invent another can discover," says Holmes, while William paraphrases ". . . remember this—there is no secret writing that can not be deciphered with a bit of patience."

The two share a certain vanity or need for appreciation regarding their work. Watson tells us that, at the climax of *The Six Napoleons,*

A flush of colour sprang to Holmes's pale cheeks, and he bowed to us like the master dramatist who receives the homage of his audience. It was at such moments that for an instant he ceased to be a reasoning machine and betrayed his human love for admiration and applause.

There is much the same spirit in the observation of Adso: "I had already realized that my master, in every respect a man of the highest virtue, succumbed to the vice of vanity when it was a matter of demonstrating his acumen. . . ."

What, then, is the reader to make of all of this? Why this virtual "Case of Identity" between Sherlock Holmes and William of Baskerville? In part, Eco may be slyly nudging fellow Sherlockians in the ribs, as if to say, "Here, along with everything I have worked into the story for artists, for theologians, for medievalists, for antiquarians, and for everyone else, I have included a few tidbits for you—see what you can find." (That Eco is an accomplished Sherlockian scholar can be seen from a perusal of the book *The Sign of Three: Dupin, Holmes, Peirce,* which he edited with Thomas A. Sebeok, and to which he contributed a chapter titled "Horns, Hooves, Insteps: Some Hypotheses on Three Types of Abductions.") Although that may be part of the truth, such an interpretation is insufficient—it trivializes an important aspect of a book that is far too significant to treat as trivial.

While others have noted the general Holmes/Baskerville similarity, as when Rodin and Key say "In sum, there is little doubt that the main character of *The Name of the Rose* possesses some Sherlockian characteristics," the virtual identity of the key descriptive passages goes beyond mere general similarity. The question of why Eco draws the parallel so strongly with Holmes remains an intriguing one. Clearly it is not a plagiarism in the sense of lifting something from Doyle which makes his story more valuable than it would otherwise be—he has taken no plot, no action, no locale from Doyle to use as his own. The characters, however, are more than similar; they are identical: in appearance, habits, methods, and manners, William of Baskerville *is* Sherlock Holmes.

In his *Postscript to THE NAME OF THE ROSE,* in which he comments on many different aspects of *The Name of the Rose,* Eco gives a clue as to what he had in mind in drawing the Holmes/William parallel when he says: "I needed an investigator, English, if possible (intertextual quotation), with a great gift of observation and a special sensitivity in interpreting evidence." He never mentions the Holmes/William parallel more explicitly, although he does state, in the *Postscript,* that the detective aspect of the story was never intended to be paramount. Is his use of Holmes as his detective a cagey device to titillate Sherlockians? Or is there a deeper meaning in the choice, a meaning perhaps related to Eco's field of semiotics, the study and theory of symbols, signs, and their meaning?

If the use of Holmes as William is intended as a sign, rather than as a quiet jest, what can Holmes stand for? At a minimum, he stands for the most eminent, successful, and widely known detective of fact or fiction. Other figures in *The Name of the Rose* are said to be patterned after similarly monumental models. Critics and commentators have seen Pope John Paul II, Jorge Louis Borges, Stalin, and Che Guevara, among others, disguised on Eco's pages. Eco may be matching giant against giant in his narrative. Many another novelist has used the surface of a narrative to convey other, deeper, ideas—Thomas Mann's *The Magic Mountain* comes to mind as a book about which historians and critics have suggested that the individual characters, their conduct and personalities, represent the countries from which they came, and their interactions in the book mirror the attitudes and actions of the same countries prior to World War I.

Other writers have not hesitated to smuggle hidden characters into their work, sometimes in the most unexpected or original ways. Alan Heimert found parallels to contemporary historical issues and figures hidden in *Moby Dick,* including even parallels between the appearance and political characteristics of John C. Calhoun and Captain Ahab, and between Moby Dick himself and Daniel Webster. In that work Heimert quotes Emerson as saying "The artist must employ the symbols in use in his day and nation to convey his enlarged sense to his fellow men." Many of the symbols, most especially including Sherlock Holmes, chosen by Eco for use to convey his ideas transcend day and nation and speak to readers of many nations and modern times, though some be symbols current in the fourteenth century. Writing of a lighter work, Diana Butler has pointed out that Lolita was a butterfly; that Nabakov used fragments of scientific descriptions of a butterfly in creating his word picture of Lolita.

It would be a mistake to try to read too much into the Holmes-Baskerville identity. The identity is just one thread of the tangled skein that makes up *The Name of the Rose.* To Sherlockians, that thread may seem to dominate, but taken as a whole, *The Name of the Rose* seems well described by Holmes's remark in *The Speckled Band,* "These are very deep waters," or perhaps better yet by his remark in *The Reigate Squires,* "These are much deeper waters than I had thought." *The Name of the*

Rose has something for almost everyone. The hints and quotations alluded to here are for Sherlockians; other relevant disciplines will have their own guides to the work.

Finally, note that in the preface Eco implies that books can be lost, quoted, found, hidden, intertwined into other books, and generally mixed up in mysterious ways. He may be telling us that such mixings up of books are part of what we are to look for in *The Name of the Rose,* an idea which is supported by the quotation which prefaces this article, and by several ideas from the *Postscript:*

> Thus I rediscovered what writers have always known (and have told us again and again): books always speak of other books, and every story tells a story that has already been told . . . books are made only from other books and around other books. . . . Moral: there exist obsessive ideas, they are never personal; books talk among themselvcs, and any true detection should prove that we are the guilty party.

The Sherlockian passages presumably are only one group of hidden quotations among many. If so, who is to say how much more gold, how many more hidden books, are to be mined from the same source? Such mining, if it is to be successful, may have to resemble the process of finding a wax vesta buried in the mud, the topic of a conversation between Holmes and Inspector Gregory during the investigation of thc murdcr of John Straker in *Silver Blaze:*

Source: Benjamin A. Fairbank Jr., "William of Baskerville and Sherlock Holmes: A Study in Identity," in *Baker Street Journal,* Vol. 40, No. 2, June 1990, pp. 83–90.

Brendan O'Mahony

In the following essay, O'Mahony, in an attempt to arrive at the hidden moral of The Name of the Rose, *explores the dialectical thread running from fanaticism to humor in the story.*

I no longer know what it is about.

The reaction of many people to this monumental, labyrinthine novel written in the form of a fourteenth-century manuscript by the world renowned semiotician, Umberto Eco, has been a certain frustration or puzzlement, especially at what the brief Epilogue on the last page seems to suggest: "I leave this manuscript, I do not know for whom; I no longer know what it is about: *stat rosa pristina nomine, nomina nuda tenemus* [the primal rose remains in name, we retain only pure names]." The final phrase echoes the mysterious title of the book.

It is frustrating to read a bulky, sophisticated, indeed encyclopaedic novel, only to find at the end

an admission by the chronicler that he no longer knows what it is about. But I refuse to accept such an admission at face value, and consider that Eco *means* something quite different from what the text *says.* I do not exclude the possibility that Eco wrote the novel in a spirit of playfulness; but he brought all his erudition as a historian, philosopher, aesthetician, literary scholar and first-class linguistician to bear on perfecting it. He researched the early fourteenth century thoroughly and attended to extraordinary detail. Despite the violence, general turmoil and complexity, the novel has a message—benign, but serious, perhaps even uncomfortable.

To attempt an interpretation of the novel may be hazardous, in that it may give the impression of trying to say how the book *should* be interpreted, in a normative fashion. In that regard I am forewarned by what Eco says elsewhere, namely, that the novel is a vehicle for generating interpretations, and by his own refusal to supply a particular interpretation. As a reader, however, one is entitled to attempt *an* interpretation, conscious that it is not the only one.

My first reaction to the novel was that it was an elaborate joke, a prank in which Eco the linguistician amused himself by reconstructing a typical medieval manuscript, but not baulking at the inclusion of twentieth-century elements, from Joyce and Borges to Wittgenstein; and that he unleashed it on an unsuspecting popular readership (who apparently—and conveniently—found it entertaining) in the form of a detective story. As I read on, however, I began to feel that the work was laced through with serious intent. This was confirmed when William announced that "in this story things greater and more important than the battle between John [the Pope] and Louis [the Emperor] may be at stake." The story always seemed to be going in two directions at once: while playful, it was serious; despite its historical setting, it spoke of and to our times; it was part factual, part fictional; "behind a veil of mirth it concealed secret moral lessons." Eco was recreating the fourteenth-century world, but *ironically*—using actual historical events (e.g. the Inquisition, the disputes about poverty) and identifiable personalities of that period (such as the Franciscans William of Ockham and Roger Bacon of Oxford, Pope John XXII at Avignon, King Philip of France, *et al.*), but also fictitious characters and a fictitious chronicler of the epoch. He had given the story a historical setting, but it was *his* story. So it was only quasi-historical, in the style of Manzoni's *I promessi sposi.* And like Manzoni's masterpiece (and so many classic medieval comic stories), it appeared to contain a serious moral. My question thus became one about the content of the book, not about its literary form: "what is this moral lesson?"

After a second reading, I wondered if the *pot-pourri* of "marketable" ingredients that is *The Name of the Rose* (with its murders, tortures, executions, sex, money, religion, witchcraft, magic, and so on) could be unified in terms of one overall theme, a single Ariadne's thread which would lead us through the labyrinth of the novel. Eventually I decided that it could, and that the thread took the shape of a single dialectical movement, which Eco had orchestrated in an enormously diversified range of conflicts. I wanted to call the work a "Tractatus contra zelotes", or an "Apologia for Humour", or perhaps "A Feast of Fools" (an expression used in the novel).

The negative pole of the dialectical movement in the novel is fanaticism. Eco's work is full of fanatics and of obsessions of all kinds. Some of the monks are fanatics for learning, for example Benno, who has a "lust for knowledge . . . knowledge for its own sake," "an insatiable curiosity" for secular or profane as well as religious scholarship, for science and exegesis. The monks in the monastery would do anything, literally take any means, including murder, to acquire knowledge. It is even suggested that young Adelmo might have surrendered his comely body to the lusts of the passionate Berengar in exchange for secret knowledge. Some monks have an obsession for interpretations of the *Apocalypse,* and there are those who are obsessed with the Abbey Library, which looms so large in the plot: old Jorge of Burgos, for instance, the Library's blind guardian turned assassin. There are some who are fanatically against homosexuals, as was common at the time. There are fanatical religious, notably the Spirituals or Fraticelli, who were fanatics for the simple life and poverty; while the Flagellantes were fanatics for flogging, for self-inflicted penance. There are reformers, who were so fanatical that they burnt down the houses and belongings of others, only to be branded, in their turn, for heresy and burnt at the stake, going to their death with *their* truth intact. Remigio, we are told, has a "lust for death." On the other hand, there is the fanaticism of those who crave for power and wealth, in both Church and State—"our holy and no longer Roman Pontiff lusts for riches"—and the fanaticism of the ecclesiastical and civil authorities, carrying out bloody massacres on any band of dissidents, be they Waldensians, Cathars, Fraticelli or Dolcinians. Both were tyrannical institutions,

> " It is we, the readers, with our obsessive ideas, who are the villains of the piece. We are the culprits who have and spread those attitudes of fear, intolerance, guilt, shame, narrow-mindedness, bias, hatred, fanaticism and repression, which prevent truth from emerging— that truth which would set us free."

which demanded conformity. Their power lay not only in wealth and force, but in surrounding themselves with secrecy (creating the division of those-who-know and the outsiders-who-do-not-know through the myths of élitism and gnosticism) and in instilling fear (by reprisals on opposition, official sanction, excommunication leading to execution, and an elaborate spy system). And the Church, of course, could add the power of guilt.

The novel portrays all these fanaticisms in action, coming into conflict with one another, because people take themselves too seriously. But while the powerful and fanatical guardians of tradition ban other fanatics to the margins of society, they themselves live in fear of something—of a knowledge that would lead to freedom.

Almost from the beginning of the novel, Eco cleverly introduces one weapon which, if released, would undermine the fact that each side is taking itself too seriously; which would combat the loss of freedom and break down fanaticism and fear. That weapon is humour. Humour enables people to set up a distance between themselves and their attitudes so that they might get a healthy perspective on their "truth". And so we are presented with a spiral of comic deflations. This is the antithesis in the dialectical movement.

Dramatically, this focal concern for interjecting humour takes the most unexpected form of a hunt for a missing Greek manuscript, the missing second book of Aristotle's *Poetics* dealing with comedy, elaborately hidden in the labyrinth of the enormous library. This is the forbidden book. It is shielded by Jorge, the eighty-year-old, stern traditionalist, whose sight is turned inward (he is blind) and for whom laughter is demonic.

There is a scene in which Friar William is involved in a serious discussion with the monks about the licitness of laughter. He argues that comedy and laughter can be good medicine and instructive, and that it is a typically human (as opposed to animal) characteristic. Jorge argues, on the contrary, that the fact that "laughter is proper to man is a sign of our limitation," that Scripture never refers to the man Jesus as laughing. His refrain, "that Christ did not laugh," is the revered position of the Gospel and the Fathers of the Church. That is *the* truth, the tradition that must be preserved. He points out that only corrupt, sacrilegious parodies of Scripture, like the *Coena Cypriani* (an ironic account of the Last Supper attributed to St Cyprian) extol comedy, in the tradition of the *ioca monachorum,* forbidden reading for novices and young monks, in which everything is described as real but upside down. Only in works like these do you find stories about Jesus joking with the Apostles. William retorts that St Francis of Assisi too "taught people to look at things from another direction."

Another manuscript in the library among the banned books, the work of a third-century Egyptian alchemist, attributes the creation of the world to divine laughter. But William is curious as to why Jorge wants to shield the second book of Aristotle's *Poetics* from everyone, more so than any of the other works which praise laughter. Jorge's reply is instructive: "Because it was by the Philosopher [i.e. Aristotle]. Every book by that man has destroyed a part of the learning that Christianity had accumulated over the centuries ... Every word of the Philosopher, by whom even saints [e.g. Aquinas] ... swear, has overturned the image of the world. But he had not succeeded in overturning the image of God. If this book ... had become an object for open interpretation, we would have crossed the last boundary." But Jorge has another reason, which Aristotle understood only too well when he argued that the seriousness of opponents must be deflated with laughter. Jorge says: "Law is imposed by fear. This book would define laughter as the new art ... for cancelling fear." Aristotle's philosophy would provide a rational justification for what Jorge calls "the marginal jests of the debauched imagination," whereas Christian tradition "favoured the restraint and intimidation of the effects of laughter by sternness." Elevated to an art by Aristotle, this comic

deflation could be turned on the noble and praiseworthy. Aristotle considered comedy to be a great antidote to fear, but Jorge is afraid of our redemption from fear.

William argues emphatically for the defusion by means of humour or comedy of the lust for the preservation of truth so sternly upheld by Jorge, of this fanaticism for tradition. "Perhaps," he says, "the mission of those who love mankind is to make people laugh at the truth, *to make truth laugh,* because the only truth lies in learning to free ourselves from insane passion for the truth." This alone, he maintains, can save us from becoming "slaves of our ghosts."

We have thus moved from fanaticism as the negative pole or thesis, to a unique means for breaking it down, namely *humour,* which becomes the antithesis. The question remains: "what is the positive pole, the synthesis, to which the dialectic now aspires?" I think it can be summed up in the following terms: tolerance, and the celebration of true freedom from the tyranny of absolutes and the fear of repression.

Tolerance is sought on different levels in the novel, one of which concerns the outcast. There are several poignant pleas for bringing the outcast, the marginals of society, heretics and homosexuals, symbolized by the lepers, back into the flock so that they are integrated. William remarks: "The people of God cannot be changed until the outcasts are restored to its body." There is a further appeal when William and Adso discuss alleged heresies, how they originate and how to distinguish between orthodoxy and heresy. Heretics, according to William, are those who are excluded from the closed circle of the so-called faithful: "The recovery of the outcasts demanded the reduction of the privileges of the powerful, so the excluded who became aware of their exclusion had to be branded as heretics. ... All heresies are the banner of a reality, an exclusion. Scratch the heresy and you will find the leper. Every battle against heresy wants only this: to keep the leper as he is." Adso had been surprised that William, a Franciscan, should not consider that St Francis had succeeded in integrating the outcast. Had he not been the first to go among the lepers? William had replied: "Francis wanted to call the outcast ... to be part of the people of God. If the flock was to be gathered again, the outcasts had to be found again. Francis didn't succeed, and I say it with great bitterness. To recover the outcasts he had to act within the Church, he had to obtain the recognition of his Rule, from which an Order would emerge, and this Order, as it emerged, would recompose the image of a circle, at whose margin the outcasts remain."

The theme recurs in a different context, when William is debating with the Pope's legation from Avignon. He attacks the tyranny of both Church and State, outlining his concept of a democratically elected government, with legislative power in the hands of the citizens who could express their will by means of "an elective general assembly." Then he rounds on the exercise of authority in the Church, condemning its involvement in civil administration; and, quoting the example of Christ, who came on earth to serve, not to be served, he adds: ". . . Christ . . . did not come into this world to command, but to be subject to the conditions he found in the world . . . He did not want the apostles to have command and dominion." From this William draws the conclusion that it seems wise that "the successors of the apostles should be relieved of any worldly or coercive power." Religion is an area of freedom. One cannot be coerced to believe either by torture or threat of execution. If coercive measures have to be taken against a herctic whose action harms the community of the faithful, then having warned him, one should hand him over to the secular arm. If Christ had willed that his Church have coercive powers, then, "Christianity would no longer be a law of freedom, but one of intolerable slavery."

This, then, is one level on which the story pleads for tolerance and a restoration of the freedom of the children of God.

Eco approaches the same theme of tolerance and freedom from the point of view of the thirst for truth and certainty in knowledge. This is a typical *motif* of the detective story ("How do I know I know?", "How can I be so sure?"), and it anticipates a certain reply: that there *is* some way I can be sure. It is also an ideological question, and a problem with a long and chequered history in philosophy. Eco makes it clear what has influenced him on this point: two fourteenth-century Franciscan philosophers from Oxford University, the Nominalist William of Ockham and Roger Bacon. The classical realist notion of truth as *adaequatio intellectus ad rem*—"the adjustment between the thing and the intellect," or the conformity of our mind with what is (i.e. the given order in the universe)—was already on the decline with philosophers like Ockham; and it is Ockham whom our William echoes when he claims that there is no order in the universe. This scandalizes Adso, who has a nostalgia for order. But order is now seen to derive partly at least from one's

mind's capacity to regulate and introduce order, so that one's *perspective* on the universe becomes increasingly important. The middle-aged William is constantly in doubt, not sure of himself any more, as he had been when, as a young Inquisitor, he handed down judgements of life and death. As if regretting the passing of his early devotion to certainty and truth, based on an independent world-order, he says: "at a time when as a philosopher I doubt the world has an order, I am consoled to discover, if not an order, at least a series of connections in small areas of the world's affairs." This is a reference to William of Ockham's undermining of the classical principle of causality (according to which everything that begins to be must have a cause) and of the power of reason to justify a necessary connection in this principle, reducing it to a simple connection between cause and effect to which we grow accustomed by constant "association".

If Ockham sowed the seeds of the scepticism so typical of the modern period in philosophy (which begins with Descartes's methodological doubt in the seventeenth century), Roger Bacon is the late-medieval precursor of the New Science, with its emphasis on methods of observation and experiment. He drew up Categories which were laws of the mind, telling us how we perceive reality. He developed Optics so as to improve on Nature, to correct "the errors of nature," like William's eye-glasses. In science there is a definite method, parameters are drawn and one works within a certain framework. Truth is known within that framework, provided one moves coherently, becoming a matter of "coherence" within a given system. This puts paid to the classical view of absolute truth, universally valid for all men at all times and all places, or to so-called eternal verities.

Adso notices William's reluctance to give a single answer, but does not understand. He is still too young to have acquired that stage of learned ignorance (*ignorantia docta*) in which "I know that I do not know—any longer." "I understood at that moment my master's method of reasoning and it seemed to me quite alien to that of the philosopher who reasons by first principles, so that his intellect almost assumes the ways of the divine intellect." The innocent Adso then plucks up the courage to say to William: "Therefore you don't have a single answer?" William replies:

"Adso, if I did, I would teach theology in Paris."

"In Paris do they always have the true answer?"

"Never," William said, "but they are very sure of their errors."

"And you, . . . never commit errors?"

"Often. . . . But instead of conceiving only one, I imagine many, so I become a slave to none."

William plays with many possibilities of meaning, following clues and trying to see connections, which makes Adso despair of his master, for he himself is on the side of "that thirst for truth" that inspires the Inquisitors.

The point Eco is making here is that, if one is sure that one possesses absolute truth or eternal verity, then one cannot easily tolerate another possibility of truth; and if one does not agree, then the other must be wrong. In that age, the operative axiomatic principle was that *Error has no rights*. This is a formula for intolerance and it justified the atrocities of the Inquisition and the Crusades. Non-conformists had to be excluded or eliminated. If, however, the subjects of rights are neither truth nor error, but persons, then, although people may differ, they have a right to their beliefs. They have a right even to be wrong. If each side claims absolute truth, there is an inevitable clash of contradictory opposites, and no dialectic is possible. Progress can be made only by the elimination of one side or the other.

The question of truth, therefore, is not only one of knowledge ("How do I know that I know?"), but a moral one ("How do I know I am right?", and correspondingly, "How do I know you are wrong?"). Here, the dividing line is even more blurred. Grey areas increase. All now depends on my system of values, whence it is derived, and how I apply it in my situation, as well as your set of values and your situation. If I, or rather, any institution considers itself to be in possession of indubitable truth about right and wrong on the basis of revelation; and further, if it considers that there is no room for change or progress, one cannot argue with it. It becomes fanatical in ensuring that error, which has no rights, is stamped out. In the novel, William admits that, as he matures, he can no longer clearly distinguish between right and wrong, the sinner and the mystic. He is taking his cue from both Aristotle and Scripture. It is a central tenet of Aristotle's moral philosophy that only the virtuous man can recognize what is right; and Scripture says: "Judge not and you shall not be judged" (*Luke* 6:37). Here again we find an intimation that absolute rights and wrongs are hard to come by, which reads as a further plea for tolerance.

The question also raises the matter of religious beliefs and practices, of orthodoxy and heresy. William suggests that the lust for orthodoxy can be transformed into heresy, and that heresy brought under control becomes orthodoxy. The clash between orthodoxy and heresy is typified for us by a conflict over the *Koran* between the traditionalist Adso, who calls the *Koran* "the Bible of the infidels, a perverse book"—the librarians had classified it, along with books of natural science, under "books of falsehood"—and William, who replies by referring to the *Koran* as "a book containing a wisdom different from ours." William's plea is for religious tolerance, not in a negative sense, but meaning respect for another's path, i.e. religious freedom.

Many modern thinkers, since Nietzsche in the nineteenth century, have had a horror of absolutes. For them, there is no single, over-arching metaphysical or religious truth in the light of which a person can say: "I know that I know." They argue that there are different systems, different perspectives, and that one must not be a slave to any one of them and intolerant of the rest. No one has a monopoly of truth. Whoever claims he does, does not allow truth to emerge in history. He wants, like Jorge, to "preserve" the truth already possessed. And so, the conflict goes on, as the suppression of truth is unabated; and the dialectical movement of the novel passes into the present and stretches indefinitely into the future.

Having followed the dialectical movement of *The Name of the Rose,* we are now in a position to discern something or Eco's serious intent, the "moral" of his story, and to interpret what he means when he says at the end: "I no longer know what it [the manuscript] is about." Just as Beckett might ask: "what does it matter who speaks?", Eco is saying: "what does it matter who the author is, or what his authority might be to speak?" It is we, the readers, with our obsessive ideas, who are the villains of the piece. We are the culprits who have and spread those attitudes of fear, intolerance, guilt, shame, narrow-mindedness, bias, hatred, fanaticism and repression, which prevent truth from emerging—that truth which would set us free. We imagine that we are innocent, but we all stand accused, like the community and guests of the monastery, on whom Jorge, in his final sermon, passes sentence. "All of you no doubt believe that . . . these sad events [murders] have not involved your soul," and that all but *one* are innocent. "Madmen and presumptuous fools you are!" "The Antichrist, when he comes, comes in all and for all, and each one is a part of him."

Eco seems to be saying that no one can claim to stand innocent, with unsullied hands, in a blood-stained world: "Pilate wandered around the refectory like a lost soul asking for water to wash his hands." Like Pilate, we cannot wash our hands clean, we are all guilty. There is no particular culprit; we, the readers, are the assassins. That is the final irony.

Source: Brendan O'Mahony, "*The Name of the Rose*: 'Tractatus Contra Zelotes,'" in *Italian Storytellers: Essays on Italian Narrative Literature*, edited by Eric Haywood and Cormac O'Cuilleanain, Foundation for Italian Studies, 1989, pp. 229–42.

Sources

Biasin, Gian-Paolo, Review of *Il nome della rosa*, in *World Literature Today*, Vol. 55, No. 3, Summer 1981, pp. 449–50.

Bondanella, Peter, "'To Make Truth Laugh': Postmodern Theory and Practice in *The Name of the Rose*," in *Umberto Eco and the Open Text: Semiotics, Fiction, Popular Culture*, Cambridge University Press, 1997, pp. 93–125.

Borges, Jorge Luis, *Labyrinths: Selected Stories & Other Writings*, New Directions, 1964, p. 3.

Copleston, Frederick C., *Medieval Philosophy*, Harper Torchbooks, 1961, p. 121.

D'Amico, Masolino, "Medieval Mirth," in the *Times Literary Supplement*, January 9, 1981, p. 29.

De Lauretis, Teresa, "Gaudy Rose: Eco and Narcissism," in *Reading Eco: An Anthology*, edited by Rocco Capozzi, Indiana University Press, 1997, p. 243.

Dirda, Michael, "The Letter Killeth and the Spirit Giveth Life," in *Book World–The Washington Post*, June 19, 1983, pp. 5, 14.

Eco, Umberto, *The Name of the Rose*, translated by William Weaver, with Author's Postscript, Harcourt, 1994.

Farronato, Cristina, *Eco's Chaosmos: From the Middle Ages to Postmodernity*, University of Toronto Press, 2003, p. 13.

Haft, Adele J., Jane G. White, and Robert J. White, *The Key to "The Name of the Rose,"* University of Michigan Press, 1999, p. 175.

Key, Jonathan, "Maps and Territories: Eco Crossing the Boundary," in *Illuminating Eco: On the Boundaries of Interpretation*, edited by Charlotte Ross and Rochelle Sibley, Ashgate, 2004, p. 16.

Martín, Jorge Hernández, *Readers and Labyrinths: Detective Fiction in Borges, Bustos Domecq, and Eco*, Garland Publishing, 1995, pp. 150–51.

Murfin, Ross, and Supryia M. Ray, *The Bedford Glossary of Critical and Literary Terms*, Bedford/St. Martin's, 2003, p. 219.

Richter, David, "The Mirrored World: Form and Ideology in Umberto Eco's *The Name of the Rose*," in *Reading Eco: An Anthology*, edited by Rocco Capozzi, Indiana University Press, 1997, pp. 256–75.

Sibley, Rochelle, "Aspects of the Labyrinth in *The Name of the Rose*: Chaos and Order in the Abbey Library," in *Illuminating Eco: On the Boundaries of Interpretation*, edited by Charlotte Ross and Rochelle Sibley, Ashgate, 2004, pp. 28–29.

Further Reading

Eco, Umberto, "How and Why I Write," in *Umberto Eco's Alternative: The Politics of Culture and the Ambiguities of Interpretation*, edited by Norma Bouchard and Veronica Pravadelli, Peter Lang Publishers, 1998, pp. 282–302.
> Eco offers an excellent first person account of his writing process, describing how he first builds a world for his novels.

Eco, Umberto, and Thomas A. Sebeok, *The Sign of Three: Dupin, Holmes, Peirce*, Indiana University Press, 1983.
> Eco and Sebeok have assembled a collection of ten essays examining the method of abduction in the works of Poe's detective Auguste Dupin, Sir Arthur Conan Doyle's detective Sherlock Holmes, and American semiotician Charles S. Peirce.

Inge, M. Thomas, ed., *Naming the Rose: Essays on Eco's "The Name of the Rose,"* University Press of Mississippi, 1988.
> Inge has collected ten essays by noted scholars as well as a preliminary checklist of Eco criticism in English, current to 1988.

Radford, Gary P., *On Eco*, Thomson/Wadsworth, 2003.
> Radford provides a cogent and comprehensive introduction to the thinking of Umberto Eco.

The Prime of Miss Jean Brodie

Muriel Spark
1961

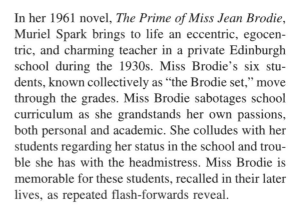

In her 1961 novel, *The Prime of Miss Jean Brodie*, Muriel Spark brings to life an eccentric, egocentric, and charming teacher in a private Edinburgh school during the 1930s. Miss Brodie's six students, known collectively as "the Brodie set," move through the grades. Miss Brodie sabotages school curriculum as she grandstands her own passions, both personal and academic. She colludes with her students regarding her status in the school and trouble she has with the headmistress. Miss Brodie is memorable for these students, recalled in their later lives, as repeated flash-forwards reveal.

Indeed, it is in putting this 1930s story in personal and historical perspective that some of its darker meaning emerges. In the pre–World War II days, autocratic, orderly, and foolish Miss Brodie is infatuated with Mussolini and Hitler. Inclined to think of herself as European, Miss Brodie praises fascism, her very taste for it a sign of her cultivation. Deluded by the appeal of absolute domination, with its apparent order and efficiency, Miss Brodie forgets that each person, however low and powerless, is a human being with rights. In her ridicule of Mary Macgregor, in her irresponsible direction to Joyce Emily Hammond to go off and fight for Franco, and in her attempt to sexually manipulate Rose Stanley, Miss Brodie sets morality aside and denies the humanity of her students. Mary's death in a fire in 1943 connects this denial to the greater obscenity occurring at the same time on the Continent in the death camps. In sum, readers are at first charmed and amused, and then jolted

into pondering the serious, indeed dangerous, side of this nostalgic portrait of the 1930s and pubescent childhood.

Author Biography

Muriel Spark was born February 1, 1918, in Edinburgh, Scotland. She wrote poetry and worked at various editing jobs during the late 1930s and through the 1940s. In the mid-1950s, Spark became interested in Cardinal Newman's writings on Catholicism. With an English Presbyterian mother and a Jewish father, Spark felt somehow at a theological loss; Catholicism seemed to offer her a specific location or frame of reference, and she converted in 1954.

During the 1950s, Spark edited letters of the Brontës and co-edited letters of Mary Shelley and John Henry Newman. Her first novel, *The Comforters* appeared in 1957. Along with collections of short stories and poems, Spark published four more novels before she brought out her most famous novel, *The Prime of Miss Jean Brodie*, which first appeared in the *New Yorker*. This novel was published in England in 1961 and in the United States in 1962. Later, it was made into a play and then into a movie. Spark continued writing novels into the 1980s, often dealing with themes connected to religious conversion. Her 1981 novel, *Loitering with Intent*, deals with problems connected to autobiography and biography.

Muriel Spark lived in Central Africa during the years leading up to World War II. During that war, she resided in England and worked for the Foreign Office. Ultimately she settled in Italy. She was married and divorced and had one child, a son.

Plot Summary

Chapter 1

Boys on bikes talk to five sixteen-year-old, fourth-form school girls, who are distinguished from one another by the way they wear their panama hats. These girls, along with one other, form "the Brodie set," a select group formed six years before when they were Miss Brodie's elementary-level pupils.

In their conservative 1930s Edinburgh school, Miss Brodie is known for teaching unconventional subjects. Her students have heard of "Mussolini,

Muriel Spark © Hulton-Deutsch Collection/Corbis

the Italian Renaissance painters . . . and the word 'menarche.'" They count on their fingers, albeit quite accurately. Miss Brodie's set has by now adapted to the more orthodox curriculum of the upper grades, but they continue to be connected to each other through their friendship to their former teacher, whom the headmistress and others find highly suspicious. Miss Brodie boasts that she is "putting old heads on [their] young shoulders," and she affirms, "all [her] pupils are the crème de la crème."

Miss Brodie's set bears the imprint of their teacher and, like her, are famous, ostracized, and suspected of disloyalty. The set comprises Monica Douglas, a prefect and math expert; Rose Stanley, "famous for sex"; Eunice Gardiner, a "glamorous" swimmer and "spritely" gymnastics student; Sandy Stranger, "notorious for her small, almost nonexistent, eyes"; Sandy's best friend, Jenny Gray, known for her elocution and plans to become an actress; and finally, Mary Macgregor, the "silent lump, a nobody whom everybody could blame." The rich but delinquent Joyce Emily Hammond, a transfer student, tags along hoping in vain to become a member of the set.

Miss Brodie invites the set to dinner, revealing that there is "a new plot . . . to force [her] to resign." These students are in her confidence, while other staff members are not. Some members of the

Media Adaptations

- Adapted from the novel and based on a screenplay by Jay Presson, the film of *The Prime of Miss Jean Brodie*, starring Maggie Smith in the lead role, was released in 1968. In 1988, the novel was made available on audiocassette, and the film was reissued on VHS during the 1990s.

faculty think Miss Brodie's style would fit a more progressive school, but Miss Brodie, who is in her "prime," is intent on remaining at Blaine, where she works as "a leaven in the lump." Like Julius Caesar, Spark writes, Miss Brodie can only be removed from her post by assassination.

The chapter concludes with a history lesson that Miss Brodie gives this set six years earlier, when they are ten, she is forty, and the year is 1930. She tells them the story of her lover, Hugh, who was at that time twenty-two years of age (six years younger than Miss Brodie). Hugh was killed the week before Armistice in 1918. Hugh, a countryman, had proposed to Miss Brodie, anticipating that they would have a quiet life together. It is an autumn day when Miss Brodie tells the girls this story; sitting outside, the girls brush leaves from their hair. Hugh "fell like an autumn leaf," Miss Brodie says, making the girls cry. When the headmistress, Miss Mackay, approaches, the girls are silent. Later, Miss Brodie commends them for that, saying, "Speech is silver but silence is golden." The chapter ends with the poignant information that Mary Macgregor is to die at age twenty-three in a hotel fire.

Chapter 2

Mary Macgregor, right after the outbreak of World War II, joins the Wrens. She continues to be clumsy and blamed. When she is deserted quickly by a new boyfriend, she looks back on her days in Miss Brodie's class as the only time when she was really happy. The poignant description of her death in a 1943 Cumberland hotel fire juxtaposes a moment in class when, as a ten-year-old, she is faulted for having spilled ink.

Sandy Stranger, on her tenth birthday, asks Jenny Gray to tea. Over pineapple and cream they discuss "the happiest days of [their] lives." Unlike Miss Brodie who has her prime, their parents got married and had sexual intercourse. The girls ponder the fact that the art teacher, Mr. Lloyd, "must have committed sex with his wife" because "he" has had a baby. Delighted to be left alone, the girls review their short story about Hugh Carruthers, Miss Brodie's fiancé, who was killed near the end of World War I. Sandy gets ink on her blouse and gets to go to the science room and have it removed by the beautiful Miss Lockhart.

Twenty-eight years later, in 1958, when Eunice is thirty-nine, she plans a return to Edinburgh and resolves to put flowers on Miss Brodie's grave. In conversation with her husband, Eunice reports that Miss Brodie was forced to retire, having been "betrayed by one of her own girls," and right after World War II she died. Eunice says Miss Brodie was "sane as anything" and "full of culture."

In 1931, Miss Brodie leads her eleven-year-old students on a long walk through the "reeking network of slums" called Old Town. Sandy has a fantasy about Alan Breck from *Kidnapped*. She realizes that the school group constitutes the body of which Miss Brodie is the head; like a divine injunction they stick together. If Sandy were nice to the always-criticized Mary, then Sandy would break apart this united group. It reminds her of Miss Brodie's admiration for Mussolini's troops. Lecturing about John Knox and Mary Queen of Scots, Miss Brodie seems oblivious to the signs of poverty in the street, to the street fight, and the obscene language directed toward the students. Sandy, who grows up to be the nun Sister Helena of the Transfiguration, always remembers the insight that "there were other people's Edinburgh quite different from hers."

Miss Brodie defines education: "*ex*, out, and *duco*, I lead. . . . To [her] education is a leading out of what is already there in the pupil's soul." She insists that she draws out what is in her students and does not put ideas in their heads. She has an appointment with the headmistress but is not worried. She affirms that her "methods cannot be condemned" because they are not "improper or subversive." After the walk, the girls are treated to tea at Miss Brodie's flat.

Chapter 3

The "most sexual year" for the Brodie set is 1931, their last year with Miss Brodie before moving into the senior level. During this year, Miss

Brodie becomes the focus of the two male faculty members, Mr. Lloyd and Mr. Lowther. Monica Douglas catches Miss Brodie kissing the married art teacher, Mr. Lloyd, and Miss Brodie and Mr. Lowther are absent from school for two weeks during which time they become lovers. Jumping ahead to 1946, Miss Brodie tells Sandy over lunch about her attachment to these men.

In 1931, a man exposes himself to Jenny, who is later questioned by a female police officer. This woman, whom Sandy names Anne Grey, becomes the protagonist in one of Sandy's daydream fictions. Miss Brodie takes more interest in the music classes, and when she needs art books from Mr. Lloyd's room, she sends Rose for them. Sandy and Jenny notice that Rose is changed, that perhaps she has entered puberty. Later Miss Brodie speaks about her World War I lover, Hugh, who is now described as artistic. Jenny and Sandy amuse themselves by writing the correspondence between Mr. Lowther and Miss Brodie.

Chapter 4

The following school year (1932–1933) Miss Brodie's set advances to the senior level, all of them taking the classical curriculum except for Mary, who takes the modern. The girls perform Miss Lockhart's science experiments, and five of them study Greek while Mary studies German and Spanish. The headmistress divides the Brodie set and separately questions the girls, hoping to obtain incriminating information about Miss Brodie. One by one Miss Mackay's schemes fail. In the senior school, Sandy remarks that "There's not much time for sex research," and Jenny for one believes she is "past . . . her early sense of erotic wonder."

In late spring 1933, Mr. Lowther begins receiving the housekeeping services of the sewing teachers, Ellen and Alison Kerr; Miss Brodie takes a special interest in the job they do and intervenes in the kitchen. Miss Brodie attends church weekly, then goes to Mr. Lowther's house. The Brodie set visit her there, two at a time. During these visits, Miss Brodie questions the girls about Mr. Lloyd. She is glad to learn that Rose is sitting for Mr. Lloyd. In the summer, Ellen Kerr and Miss Gaunt inform the headmistress, Miss Mackay, about the night-dress under the pillow on Mr. Lowther's bed.

Miss Brodie vacations in Germany this year instead of Italy and returns to happily pronounce that Hitler is "a prophet-figure like Thomas Carlyle, and more reliable than Mussolini."

Chapter 5

Sandy examines Mr. Lloyd's paintings of Rose and thinks they all look like Miss Brodie. In one, Mr. Lloyd has overemphasized Rose's breast. Sandy sees paintings of Eunice and Monica, also. Paintings of Mr. Lloyd's wife and children do not look like Miss Brodie, but his paintings of the schoolgirls capture something of their teacher. Sandy insists with "near-blackmailing insolence" that Mr. Lloyd's paintings reveal his fixation on Miss Brodie. Her attitude angers him, and he kisses Sandy intensely and then insults her.

As the girls become fourteen and fifteen, Miss Brodie confides in them about Mr. Lowther's devotion to her, along with his simultaneous consideration of one of the Kerr sisters as a possible mate. Miss Brodie wants to confide more completely in one of the girls, and she selects Sandy for her confidante. By the summer of 1935, Miss Brodie can remark that all of her ambitions are fixed on Sandy and on Rose, who continues to sit for Mr. Lloyd. Miss Brodie says Sandy has insight and Rose has instinct.

Sandy feels deprived of the religion of John Calvin, which shapes the worldviews of Miss Gaunt and the Kerr sisters, and she says Miss Brodie "had elected herself to grace . . . with . . . suicidal enchantment." She also concludes that Miss Brodie wants Rose to become Mr. Lloyd's lover and for Sandy "to act as informant on the affair." However, as it turns out, Rose only models for Mr. Lloyd, and Rose is the one who carries the information back when Sandy has sex with him. Miss Brodie focuses more on her aspirations for Rose and ignores Mr. Lowther. After several months, Mr. Lowther's engagement to Miss Lockwood is announced in the paper.

Chapter 6

At seventeen in 1937, the girls are still quizzed by the headmistress about Miss Brodie. They see Miss Brodie as an "exciting woman." Though Mr. Lowther is happy with his wife, he continues to look at Miss Brodie with admiration. The new girl, Joyce Emily Hammond, also admires her. Taking Miss Brodie's political views to heart, Joyce Emily disappears from school, and six weeks later students learn that she has run away to Spain and died in a train accident.

In the final year, only four of the original six girls are still enrolled at Blaine School. Mary has left to study shorthand and Jenny has transferred to a drama school. The academic and professional futures of the four are described.

Speaking explicitly to Sandy, Miss Brodie predicts that "Rose and Teddy Lloyd will soon be lovers." Sandy, so full of fictions, realizes that this fantasy is not a game, not "unreal talk," but real manipulation. Sandy realizes Miss Brodie "was obsessed by the need for Rose to sleep with the man she herself was in love with." Sandy understands now that in truth Miss Brodie's dramatic posturing masks a real intention to play God in the lives of her students: "She thinks she is Providence . . . she thinks she is the God of Calvin." Rose is not manipulated into becoming Mr. Lloyd's lover, however; she shakes "off Miss Brodie's influence as a dog shakes pond-water from its coat."

During the summer of 1938, Miss Brodie visits Austria and Germany and returns to announce the countries are "now magnificently organised." Sandy becomes Mr. Lloyd's lover, but from that relationship she values most his religion, Catholicism; subsequently Sandy becomes a nun. In that senior year, when quizzed by Miss Mackay, Sandy directs the headmistress to shift from scrutinizing Miss Brodie's sex life to looking at her politics. Sandy says, "She's a born Fascist." Once revealed, this political position forces Miss Brodie to resign at the end of that school year. Ironically, as she wonders which of the students betrayed her, Miss Brodie tells Sandy that Sandy alone is "exempt from suspicion." To which Sandy replies: "If you did not betray us it is impossible that you could have been betrayed by us."

As a nun, Sandy publishes a book on psychology entitled *The Transfiguration of the Commonplace*. She is visited by people who admire the book and by other members of Miss Brodie's set. To a young man who visits, Sandy admits being influenced by her childhood teacher. Eunice lays flowers on Miss Brodie's grave. Monica asks Sandy about the betrayal, and Sandy asserts, "It's only possible to betray where loyalty is due."

Characters

Miss Jean Brodie

Miss Jean Brodie is an eccentric, egotistical, and idealistic lower-level teacher at the Marcia Blaine School for Girls in Edinburgh, Scotland. In the years leading up to World War II, Miss Brodie teaches in a theatrical manner and makes an impression on her prepubescent students, with whom she colludes in sabotaging the academic curriculum. Having lost her fiancé, Hugh Carruthers, in World War I, Miss Brodie becomes attached to the married art teacher, Mr. Lloyd, and because of his marital status, she diverts her sexual attention to the bachelor music teacher, Mr. Lowther. Miss Brodie loses her job at the school when one of her favorite group of students betrays her fascist political sentiments to the headmistress, Miss Mackay.

Hugh Carruthers

Hugh Carruthers, age twenty-two, is killed one week before Armistice in 1918. He was the fiancé of Miss Brodie. Sandy Stranger and Jenny Gray coauthor a romantic story about Hugh and Miss Brodie. After Miss Brodie develops attachments for the art teacher, Mr. Lloyd, and for the music teacher, Mr. Lowther, her stories about Hugh infuse his character with traits transparently borrowed from the other two men.

Monica Douglas

Good at math, likely to be angry, and with a red nose and fat legs, Monica Douglas is one of the Brodie set. Monica sees Miss Brodie kissing Mr. Lloyd in the art room and tells the other members of the set about it.

Eunice Gardiner

Small, neat Eunice Gardiner belongs to the Brodie set. She is well known for her skills in swimming and gymnastics. On a tiring day, Miss Brodie would ask Eunice to do a somersault in class to provide "comic relief." Later in life, in conversation with her husband, Eunice reports that Miss Brodie was "full of culture" and decides to locate the teacher's grave and lay flowers on it.

Miss Gaunt

Miss Gaunt, sister of a minister and not a fan of Miss Brodie, teaches the Brodie set while Miss Brodie is off, apparently ill for two weeks. Since Mr. Lowther is absent during the same period, Miss Gaunt theorizes that "Miss Brodie has the same complaint as Mr. Lowther."

Jenny Gray

Jenny Gray, one of the Brodie set, has excellent elocution and plans to be an actress. While in the lower grades, Jenny is the best friend of Sandy Stranger. During the school year 1931–1932, Jenny is shocked when a man exposes himself to her. Later, she and Sandy Stranger make up stories about the female detective who comes to interview Jenny, and they amuse themselves by writing a correspondence between Miss Brodie and Mr. Lowther.

Joyce Emily Hammond

Joyce Emily Hammond is a rich outsider, a newcomer to the school. She hopes, perhaps by virtue of having two first names, to become a member of Miss Brodie's set. Later, Joyce Emily takes up Miss Brodie's suggestion to go to Spain to support Franco. Joyce Emily dies in a train wreck en route.

Alison Kerr

With her sister, Ellen, Allison Kerr teaches sewing at the Blaine School. The Kerr sisters volunteer to keep house for Mr. Lowther after school on weekdays and on Saturday mornings. The Kerrs are animated by their new role in serving Mr. Lowther, but Miss Brodie establishes her turf in his life by overseeing their cooking on Saturday morning and then spending the rest of the weekend with him, fattening him up.

Ellen Kerr

Miss Ellen Kerr is the older sister of Alison Kerr. When changing Mr. Lowther's bed linens, Ellen discovers a nightdress folded neatly under one of the pillows. She and Miss Gaunt take this information to the schoolmistress, Miss Mackay.

Mr. Theodore Lloyd

One-armed Teddy Lloyd is the senior girls' art teacher at the Blaine School. He and his wife have another child while Miss Brodie's set are ten years old. Thus, the girls know he "has committed sex." When the set are eleven, Monica Douglas claims she has seen Mr. Lloyd kissing Miss Brodie. Later, Mr. Lloyd paints several portraits of Rose Stanley, which Sandy Stranger says all look like Miss Brodie, and he has a sexual relationship with Sandy.

Miss Lockhart

Miss Lockhart is the Blaine School science teacher. She has short gray hair and a golfer's tan. She cleans ink out of the girls' blouses. When the ten-year-old girls get to visit the science room, they catch a glimpse of the chesty senior girls and the beautiful Miss Lockhart. After Miss Brodie loses interest in Mr. Lowther, he marries Miss Lockhart.

Mr. Gordon Lowther

Mr. Lowther is the music teacher for all grades at the Blaine School. With Mr. Lloyd, Mr. Lowther is attracted sexually to Miss Brodie and is considered one of her allies. Mr. Lowther lives alone in his parents' home, receives housekeeping services from the Kerr sisters, and has a sexual relationship with Miss Brodie. When she loses interest in him, he marries Miss Lockhart.

Mary Macgregor

Mary Macgregor is "the last member of the [Brodie] set" for good reason. She is known as "a silent lump, a nobody whom everybody could blame." In the first chapter, a flash-forward informs readers that Mary dies in a hotel fire at the age of twenty-three. Later, when others know of her death, they look back on being cruel to Mary in school and wish they had been kinder.

Miss Mackay

Miss Mackay is headmistress of Marcia Blaine School for Girls. She "believes in the slogan 'Safety First,'" which is proven from Miss Brodie's point of view, by the picture of Stanley Baldwin, once prime minister, on Miss Mackay's office wall. A conservative educator, Miss Mackay suspects Miss Brodie's teaching methods divert from school policy and wishes Jean Brodie would resign.

Rose Stanley

Rose Stanley, one of the Brodie set, is "famous for sex." She models for Mr. Lloyd, even in the nude. As Rose goes through puberty, her transformation makes a hit with schoolboys but she does not have the sexual relationship with Mr. Lloyd, the anticipation of which gives Miss Brodie vicarious pleasure.

Sandy Stranger

One of the Brodie set, Sandy Stranger is "notorious for her small, almost nonexistent, eyes" and "famous for her vowel sounds" which "in the Junior school, had enraptured Miss Brodie." Sandy would recite passages from Tennyson's "The Lady of Shalott," causing Miss Brodie to affirm: "Where there is no vision . . . the people perish." Sandy has the vision Miss Brodie lacks and, with her insight about Miss Brodie's effects on the girls, decides to stop Miss Brodie. Sandy reports to the headmistress that Miss Brodie is "a born Fascist." When she grows up, Sandy becomes a nun—Sister Helena of the Transfiguration—and publishes a well-received book on psychology.

Themes

Private School Education

The Prime of Miss Jean Brodie is set in a 1930s private school in Edinburgh. The interaction

Topics
For Further
Study

- Research current law on the rights of students to disagree with their teacher or to protest school policy. Write an essay in which you evaluate those rights in light of the way your school handles dissent from students.

- Write a characterization of a teacher you had who left an impression on you. Specify what lessons you learned from this teacher and how your view and evaluation of the teacher has changed over the time since you were in the that class.

- Do some research about school clubs and the rules that determine membership. Write a paper

in which you explore ways schools can be more democratic in their policies regarding groups.

- Write an essay on victimization, beginning with what it is and how it often occurs with prejudice and racism. Research people who fought against the Third Reich during World War II. You might investigate the Polish resistance movement in Warsaw, efforts by the Jews in the Warsaw ghetto to accumulate arms and fight back, and efforts at Auschwitz—for example, the successful detonation of one of the crematoria by camp prisoners.

---

between the small staff, the personality of the head-mistress, and the way teachers deal with students provide the framework for this novel's action. The kinds of social behavior and classroom decorum typical of this privileged class and setting are dramatized. While Miss Brodie insists on the girls walking with their heads up and keeping their sleeves neatly cuffed, she colludes with them to circumvent the curriculum and subvert the head-mistress's authority. Pretending to teach the regular subjects of history and math, Miss Brodie instead elaborates on various unrelated topics, all of which are of great interest to her—her World War I fiancé, her vacations in Italy and Germany, her favorite Renaissance artists, along with information about cold cream treatment for skin and details about puberty. Her classroom is her stage, and Miss Brodie maintains that she is devoting her prime to her girls and that her girls are "the crème de la crème."

Sexual Maturation

At ten and eleven, the prepubescent girls are curious and shy about sexual matters. They have a sketchy idea about sexual intercourse and make up scenarios about how it occurs. They conclude that since Mr. Lloyd's wife has had another baby, Mr. Lloyd "has committed sex" with her. Sandy Stranger sublimates her sexual interest into daydreams

about fictional characters from *Kidnapped* and *Jane Eyre*. A man exposes himself to Jenny. Rose goes through puberty first and later becomes known among schoolboys for being sexy.

In the following couple of years, the girls begin to intuit Miss Brodie's sexual attachment for the art teacher, Mr. Lloyd, and her pursuit of the music teacher as a way of "working it off on Mr. Lowther."

Flash-forward passages describe the women these girls become. For example, Eunice speaks to her husband about her intention on their upcoming trip back to Edinburgh to locate and decorate Miss Brodie's grave, and in another instance Jenny, now married many years, suddenly feels erotic energy for a stranger in Italy.

Rose models nude for Mr. Lloyd and Sandy becomes his lover. In all, the novel economically maps out the movement through adolescence to sexual awareness and sexual roles.

Betrayal

Miss Brodie repeatedly affirms her commitment to her girls, the proof of which is that she is devoting the prime of her life to their education. She makes an impression on them, attaching them to her by taking them into her confidence. She attaches personally and inappropriately to a chosen group of six students, whom she treats to outings at the theater and invites to her home for tea. Yet, Miss Brodie is verbally abusive to Mary Macgregor; every time she berates Mary as a "stupid lump," Miss Brodie both betrays her responsibility as a teacher and denies Mary's humanity.

While espousing loyalty to her students, Miss Brodie habitually sabotages school policy and Miss Mackay's authority. Miss Brodie is also quick to sense plots to get her to resign. Thus she "teaches" betrayal and distrust. When her chosen set of students are in their senior year, Miss Brodie is sufficiently obsessed with her frustrated attachment to Mr. Lloyd that she attempts to manipulate Rose into becoming his lover. That she is thus willing to treat a student like a surrogate object of vicarious sexual expression constitutes a serious breach of ethics. When Sandy "betrays" her teacher, she is only acting out what she has observed for years in Miss Brodie herself.

Victimization

Mary Macgregor is victimized at the Blaine School. She is ridiculed and scorned by Miss Brodie, and the other students follow suit, valuing their status with their teacher over being kind to Mary. Miss Brodie pushes innocent Mary out of art class, accusing her for instigating the misconduct begun by others. Miss Brodie and the students see Mary as a "stupid lump," a thing to be kicked around with impunity. Only knowledge of her untimely death at twenty-three causes her persecutors momentarily to regret the way they treated her. Mary Macgregor's victimization is a cue about the reality of fascist and Nazi racism and oppression. She dies in a fire in 1943, at the same time when millions of people are being reduced to ash in Nazi death camps. Thus, Mary's role and fate in the novel are poignant testimony to the effects of domination and subjugation. In another way, Joyce Emily Hammond is also a victim. A rebel seeking a cause, Joyce Emily takes up Miss Brodie's irresponsible recommendation that she go off to Spain and fight for Franco. Joyce Emily dies in a train wreck en route.

is "notorious for her small, almost nonexistent, eyes," and Mary Macgregor is famous for "being a silent lump, a nobody whom everybody could blame." When the character reappears in the text, the famous trait is repeated, like a tag or code for identification. This pattern has a humorous effect, but it also reduces the characters to two-dimensional figures like those in comic strips. As the story develops the traits become significant in other ways. Rose may be famous for sex, but she does not become sexually involved with Mr. Lloyd as Miss Brodie anticipates. Sandy may have nonexistent eyes, but she has insight enough to understand the dynamic at work between Miss Brodie and Mr. Lloyd and to see evidence of it in Mr. Lloyd's paintings. And Mary, though taken for a lump and victimized as a thing, is nonetheless a human being whose humanity is underscored by the description of her silent death. The image of her running back and forth in the hotel hallway, trapped in the fire and choked by smoke elicits compassion and undermines the comedy that works at her expense.

Treatment of Time

The story is told in chronological order covering the period from the fall of 1930 to the summer of 1939, yet at certain points the story suddenly leaps into the distant future, revealing important information that, in a more traditional story structure, would be withheld until it occurs in chronological order. In this way, the present of the novel is seen in contrast to the future, through the lens of retrospect it is reframed and can be reinterpreted. One example of how this technique works is in the several passages which show the students' later assessment of Miss Brodie: Mary Macgregor, at twenty-three and recently dropped by a boyfriend, looks back on her school years as her happiest time. Eunice tells her husband of twenty years that she intends on their return to Edinburgh to lay flowers on the grave of Miss Brodie because she was "full of culture." And Sandy, who betrays Miss Brodie and thus contributes to her being forced to resign, later admits that her career in psychology and success as an author results from the impression Miss Brodie made on her.

Style

Repetition

Characterization of the Brodie set is achieved in part by repetition of the girls' famous traits. For example, Rose is "famous for sex," Sandy Stranger

Historical Context

The Great Depression

The late 1920s and the decade of the 1930s witnessed a global economic depression. Prices

Compare
&
Contrast

- **1930s–1940s:** By 1933, when Germany passes its own mandatory sterilization law for "defectives," the United States is the world leader in mandatory sterilization of institutionalized people. In the United States some 30,000 are sterilized, all in institutions. In Germany during the 1930s, some 300,000 are sterilized in the attempt to ensure that traits like feeblemindedness (low IQ), pauperism (being poor), sexual promiscuity, and criminality are not passed on to the next generation.

  Today: People with inherited diseases such as Huntington's disease and Alzheimer's disease may choose not to have children in order to avoid passing on this inheritable trait. However, in most cases, the state position is that this decision is a personal one.

- **1930s–1940s:** The science of eugenics in Europe and the United States theorizes that many ills besetting the human race can be eliminated. The trials at Nuremberg reveal the Nazi atrocities performed in the name of eugenics research and the manner in which sterilization evolved to euthanasia during Hitler's pursuit of the Final Solution.

Today: Genetically modified organisms (GMOs) and cloning offer benefits and dangers to food production in the United States and elsewhere in the world. Stem cell research is a contested issue and, as of 1999, the growing of human embryos for the purpose of using stem cells is illegal in the United States.

- **1930s–1940s:** In 1944, Raphael Lemkin publishes *Axis Rule in Occupied Europe*, which documents mass extermination and coins the word genocide. In one definition, genocide refers to the attempt to eradicate ethnic or cultural identity through mass murder. The Third Reich systematically murders at least 5.6 million European Jews, along with millions of other "undesirables" during World War II.

Today: Human Rights Watch, Amnesty International, and Genocide Watch work to broaden the definition of genocide in order to include, for example, the mass murder of civilians by Stalin. These organizations also support an international tribunal where those accused of crimes against humanity can be brought to justice. In 1994, genocide occurs in Rwanda when extremist Hutus murder 500,000–1,000,000 people, mostly members of the Tutsi ethnic group.

---

inflated, currency lost its buying power, and millions of people lost their jobs. The New York Stock Market crash in late 1929 announced financial calamity to stockholders. Post–World War I Germany struggled to pay back its war debt from World War I, and unemployment in that country rose to almost 40 percent. The United Kingdom was less harshly hit by the depression. It witnessed unemployment increases during the 1920s but had in place government aid to address the problem. In *The Prime of Miss Jean Brodie*, Miss Brodie leads her students through the Old Town of Edinburgh where the streets are full of unemployed men, and where anger flares out at the sight of these privileged schoolgirls and their arrogant teacher.

The Rise of Fascism

Benito Mussolini (1883–1945) came to power in Italy in 1922 during a time of economic trouble and a pervasive sense that Italy had won World War I but had lost the peace. During the late 1920s, the fascist government intervened to save industries and increase employment. Gradually, Mussolini took more control of his government. At first he hesitated to support the election of Hitler in Germany, but by late 1936 cooperation was forming between Italy and Germany.

The Rise of National Socialism (Nazism)

Desperate for economic reprieve, humiliated by the outcome of World War I, and seeking easy

Former prime minister of Italy Benito Mussolini is one of the fascist dictators Miss Brodie admires and emulates in Muriel Spark's The Prime of Miss Jean Brodie   © Bettmann/Corbis

answers, many Germans listened to the angry tirades of Adolf Hitler (1889–1945) who blamed the depression on the Jews and the Communists. Defying the Treaty of Versailles that prohibited Germany from building a military again, Hitler promised a stronger Germany through military power. The National Socialist Party, of which he was the head, was elected in the early 1930s. By 1933, Hitler was named chancellor, and soon afterward that he dissolved the government that elected him and became an absolute dictator. Nazism idealized the so-called Aryan race, while subjugating Jews and other unacceptable groups. Germany's grandeur was

predicated on the extermination of European Jewry and the absolute domination of other European countries. With Mussolini's support, Hitler annexed Austria in 1938. World War II began when Germany invaded Poland in 1939; France and Great Britain then declared war on Germany.

Critical Overview

To say *The Prime of Miss Jean Brodie* was well received is an understatement. One of the finest works by the already well-established novelist Muriel Spark, this novel was heralded for its economic style, its charm and humor, and for its exploration of the dark side of idealism and commitment. Samuel Hynes, writing in *Commonweal*, stresses that the novel "is as good as anything Mrs. Spark has done. . . . It is intelligent, witty, and beautifully constructed." In describing the protagonist and her students, a reviewer for *Library Journal* remarks: "Miss Spark's account of the awakening and maturing of adolescent girls is realistic and at times amusing. Though the idol of their teens had feet of clay, she left an indelible mark on their lives." Finally, Granville Hicks, writing in *Saturday Review* affirms that Spark "proved herself to be highly talented and remarkably versatile." Compared to the likes of Evelyn Waugh and Iris Murdock, Spark is, according to Hicks, a writer who "goes her own way, and a fascinating way it is." The novel he concludes is "admirably written . . . extremely amusing, and deeply serious."

Criticism

Melodie Monahan

Monahan has a Ph.D. in English. She teaches at Wayne State University and also operates an editing service, The Inkwell Works. In the following essay, Monahan examines how autocracy subverts education and delivers different lessons in The Prime of Miss Jean Brodie.

In Muriel Spark's 1962 novel, *The Prime of Miss Jean Brodie*, the outside of the in-group, "the Brodie set," is defined by the peripheral "silent lump" Mary Macgregor and the excluded newcomer Joyce Emily Hammond. It is 1936, and this clique of sixteen-year-old girls was formed six years earlier when, as newcomers to Miss Brodie's class, they were drawn into her orbit. In the first pages readers are charmed by the witty caricatures and the funny portrait of this privileged girls' school in Edinburgh, in which an eccentric spinster teacher directs her class to prop up their books and remember the subject of the moment just in case they are intruded upon by the headmistress. The classroom is a stage for Miss Brodie, who begins her performance with what *she* did on her "summer holiday." Self-centered Miss Brodie *is* the real subject of the class. The impressionable and powerless ten-year-olds are swept up by their teacher's bravura, by her explicit sabotage of school curriculum, and by her promise that, if they pay close attention to her, they can become "the crème de la crème."

At the end of the first chapter, as Miss Brodie discovers Mary is not listening, readers learn that "Mary Macgregor, lumpy, with merely two eyes, a nose and a mouth like a snowman, who was later famous for being stupid and always to blame . . . at the age of twenty-three, lost her life in a hotel fire." This information, with its telling simile, shifts the lens through which readers view the subject of this novel. On the one hand, the subject of privilege, academic hierarchy, even the childhood competition for insider status and the angst of not quite belonging, all have a nostalgic, autumn yellow sweetness. The story comes across as innocent and benign. On the other hand, foreknowledge and retrospect transform the view: suddenly the objectified "lump" Mary Macgregor, the class reject, is a human being, vulnerable, fated to suffer, and mortal; readers are reminded of other denigrated people who in 1943 disappeared in the fire of the Holocaust.

Readers in 1962 and afterward look with retrospect on this story of the 1930s: they know what was really brewing in that decade, and they know the Holocaust that blackened the decade that followed it. But in the 1930s and without the advantage of foreknowledge, Miss Brodie is naively infatuated with the orderliness of fascism, the tidy brown shirts, and the "magnificently organised" Nazi Germany and Austria. Back from vacations on the Continent, she praises Mussolini's efficiency and Hitler's reliability. She teaches her students to march with their heads up, and one of them, Sandy Stranger, understands that "the Brodie set was Miss Brodie's fascisti." Indeed, Miss Brodie's political posture nicely complements her self-concept as a European in her prime; it mirrors her arrogant egocentric teaching style. But the case of Mary Macgregor cautions readers to consider the humanity of the underdog and the oppressed. The characters Mary and Joyce Emily urge readers to consider the sequence of events that spool out from a given childhood moment as well as the destructiveness that results from elitism, however it is defined. Hierarchy causes underlings to vie for position and get in step; they in turn push away those below them. The elitism that enthralls Miss Brodie, both on a national and personal scale, requires victimization.

Mary Macgregor is a scapegoat and victim. In art class, when the students snicker at the way Mr. Lloyd uses his pointer to trace the buttocks of Botticelli's gauzy female figures, Mary laughs without understanding why, her "giggles . . . caused by contagion." Miss Brodie sees her laughing, "openly like a dirty-minded child of an uncultured home," and jerks Mary out of her seat, pushing her from the room. This action judges Mary the "ringleader" and since she is "apprehended," the other girls "were no longer in the wrong." Mary is guilty because she is perceived to be acting like a person from a lower class family and that assumption reasserts the privileged status of the other students who incited her laughter in the first place.

When Miss Brodie leads her students into the Old Town, she ignores or does not see the poverty. She does not appear to hear the insults hurled at her and her lineup of little rich girls. She does not see the fight in the street. Sandy is uncomfortable and has an urge to be nice to Mary; Sandy even imagines "the possibilities of feeling nice from being nice to Mary instead of blaming her." But Miss Brodie's voice arrests the urge. Sandy views her companions as "a body with Miss Brodie for the head;" this insight leads Sandy to understand that she would separate herself from this single body if she were nice to Mary. The scene in Old Town demonstrates how privilege can turn a blind eye to the lack of it, and how group membership exists by virtue of its exclusivity. Mary walks behind the group, crying silently so Miss Brodie will not hear her. It is true that Miss Brodie and her chosen set of students are not directly responsible for the hotel fire in which Mary dies. But the manner of Mary's death graphically depicts how trapped Mary is in her circumstances and how unheard she is in her pain. The point of describing her death is to emphasize that Mary is a human being, a person who is worthy of fair treatment and compassion—even if she is not as bright as other people. The scene in Old Town suggests how fascism spreads through the troops it enlists.

Miss Brodie assumes that her teaching "methods cannot be condemned unless they can be proved to be in any part improper or subversive." Proving them so on both counts is easy. Joyce Emily Hammond, a rebel without a cause, hears Miss Brodie's applause for Franco and takes to heart her teacher's improper suggestion that she "go to Spain to fight for Franco." Later, knowing full well that Joyce Emily dies en route in a train wreck, Miss Brodie foolishly insists, "she would have done admirably for him, a girl with instinct." Miss Brodie does not value the girl's life, nor does she see her own complicity in the girl's death.

Moreover, in the manipulative, highly unethical triangulation in which Miss Brodie fancies the

> " Hierarchy causes underlings to vie for position and get in step; they in turn push away those below them. The elitism that enthralls Miss Brodie, both on a national and personal scale, requires victimization."

idea of her student, Rose Stanley, having sexual intercourse with the art teacher Mr. Lloyd, Sandy realizes that Miss Brodie's toying with her students' lives is not a game and not theoretical. Sandy sees that Miss Brodie "was obsessed by the need for Rose to sleep with the man she herself was in love with." Enraged, Sandy condemns Miss Brodie: "She thinks she is Providence . . . she thinks she is the God of Calvin, she sees the beginning and the end." Sandy intends to stop Miss Brodie, and she does it by telling the headmistress, "[Miss Brodie]'s a born Fascist." This information leads to Miss Brodie's forced resignation in the summer of 1939. Daring to speak this truth is what Miss Brodie later calls betrayal. Years later, when Miss Brodie and the girls know how Mary died, they sometimes regret their treatment of her. Years later Miss Brodie concedes that "Hitler *was* rather naughty."

Arrogant, myopic, irresponsible, and unethical, Miss Brodie deludes herself that she is committed to her girls' education. In fact, her false sense of superiority feeds their elitist attitudes, and her blind favoritism dismisses those who do not measure up. Sandy says Miss Brodie plays God. In a literal sense, Miss Brodie does not cause the train wreck that kills Joyce Emily Hammond, but the ideas Miss Brodie espouses contribute to that outcome. Moreover, the belief that Mary Macgregor is a "lump" and "always to blame" makes her akin to the nameless millions who became ash in the Nazi furnaces. What then is the end of autocracy, especially in the classroom, and what is the end of fascism? Both autocracy and fascism indoctrinate and charm; they inebriate the chosen with self-importance and require its adherents to climb up on the heads of others and then crush those underneath.

What Do I Read Next?

- In the novel *The Abbess of Crewe* (1974), Spark seems to parody the Watergate scandal, using an abbey instead of the White House and Abbess Alexander instead of former President Richard Nixon.

- In *The Girls of Slender Means* (1963), Spark writes about poor young women living in a boarding house during the summer of 1945 and their interaction with a cynical poet.

- In *Symposium* (1990), Spark tells the story of a dinner party. The butler gives the guest list to thieves who rob the guests' houses while they are away. During the dinner party, flashbacks reveal information regarding the guests' lives.

- Award-winning, twentieth-century playwright Lillian Hellman's longest-running play, *The Children's Hour* (1934), follows two women who run a private boarding school. When a delinquent pupil from an affluent, well-regarded family starts a rumor about the two headmistresses, tragedy ensues and the two women's lives are forever changed.

- In Rebecca Goldstein's *The Late-Summer Passion of a Woman of Mind* (1989), forty-six-year-old philosophy professor Eva Mueller is fixated on a twenty-year-old college student of hers. The relationship helps Eva confront her father's involvement with the Third Reich.

- Set in the Middle Ages, Sherryl Jordan's *The Raging Quiet* (1999) tells the story of Marnie, a woman who befriends the village outcast, Raven, a man people believe is insane but whom Marnie discovers is only deaf. Through a system of hand gestures, she is able to communicate with him. Then she is threatened with being ostracized, too. The novel explores the dangers in targeting people because they are different.

- In Theodore Weesner's *Novemberfest* (1994), a fifty-two-year-old professor of German at a New Hampshire college finds himself in a professional and personal crisis that causes him to relive a love relationship he had when he was stationed in Germany during the 1950s.

To lead autocratically requires great and myopic egocentrism. The individual on top sees the world from her own perspective; everything in the world gets interpreted in terms of the self and what the self wants. Theoretically, education expands awareness beyond immediate microcosmic knowledge toward the diverse worlds of others. It invites one to see humanity amid great diversity. In Old Town, Sandy realizes that "there were other people's Edinburghs quite different from hers." Miss Brodie remains blind to them.

Source: Melodie Monahan, Critical Essay on *The Prime of Miss Jean Brodie*, in *Novels for Students*, Thomson Gale, 2006.

David Kelly

Kelly is an instructor of literature and creative writing at two colleges in Illinois. In this essay, Kelly looks at how Miss Brodie's romantic idealism may have been the best response to the changes that were taking place in the world of the novel.

One of the roles of grammar school can be considered to be sheltering growing, developing minds from the complexities of the outside world, and teachers are considered to be guides, to help young people cross the bridge into adult life. These expectations fail, however, when schooling takes place under stressful circumstances, or when an instructor is disdainful about adult life, warning students against it rather than teaching them coping skills. Something like this happens in Muriel Spark's novel *The Prime of Miss Jean Brodie*. The story takes place in a unique social situation: not the extremes of wartime, but rather the uncomfortable lull between the two World Wars during the first half of the twentieth century. The extraordinary instructor, Miss Brodie, is not set on subverting the education system out of simple spite, but because she has higher goals for her students than the usual school curriculum offers. To inspire their artistic and spiritual sensibilities, she stirs up their sense of romantic possibility. Miss Brodie's methods are not always undertaken with her students in mind; one might wonder, in fact, whether she really thinks of her students at all, or if she is lost in her own romantic fantasies.

Readers of the book encounter a postwar world where everyone is familiar with entitlement and with loss. It was published in the 1960s, when a generation of Britons was old enough to look back at the class system that had stood in place for centuries before the war, and remember pieces of it without really understanding its nuances. The book shows children of privilege, in a respected private school, comfortable with their lives and critical of each other in ways that only cliquish children can be. They interact with instructors who have learned that life can be considerably difficult.

The adults of the book are all broken by the ravages of time, damaged by the First World War, or oppressed by the burdens of religion. Preeminent among them is Jean Brodie herself, who purposefully disconnects from her surroundings but is astoundingly able to cope with the same problems that crush the spirits of those around her. Spark has loaded the novel with characters who might each have been contemptible if they were not written carefully enough to be recognizably real, and they draw from readers more pity than scorn. The question in the end is whether Miss Brodie herself is contemptible, pathetic, or even, given the times and the situation she lived in, triumphant.

At first, the situation at the Marcia Blaine School reeks of romantic possibility, which supersedes any sense of loss or tragedy that the students could derive from the world around them. In the book's opening scene, for instance, the girls of "the Brodie set" flirt with a crowd of boys so undistinguished that three of the five of them have the same name. Even if the girls do realize that they are smarter and more all-around worthy than these boys, their egos are still held in check by their growing interest in the opposite sex. The chance that they, or for that matter any of the adults in the novel, might lose hope in the face of the squalor of Edinburgh in the 1930s is counterbalanced by the possibility for romance onto which they all hold.

The grimmest daily reminder of the First World War is the empty sleeve of their art instructor, Teddy Lloyd, who lost his arm in battle.

> " Miss Brodie's romantic ambitions slide toward the commonplace, from the mythical Hugh Carruthers to the dashing Teddy Lloyd to the commonplace Gordon Lowther, and she cannot even secure that final, least-appealing suitor for her own."

These girls, who would have been born just after the war, have no personal connection to what life during wartime was like. To them, Lloyd could easily be seen as a broken, pathetic figure. That he is an art teacher, rather than an instructor in a more theoretical field such as literature or history, makes his infirmity just that much more poignant, because painting and sculpting are physical activities that rely on delicate control. Poignant though it is, Lloyd's loss is never construed as horrible, because it gives Teddy Lloyd a romantic mystique.

Lloyd is a handsome man. That is more important to his students than his missing limb, indicating to modern readers the extent to which children of the post-war years must have been used to seeing amputees throughout their lives. Furthermore, Teddy Lloyd is not shy about using his good looks and romantic bearing to his own advantage: he is so self-assured, in fact, that he deals with Sandy Stranger's implied threat when she points out his infatuation with Miss Brodie by kissing the teenaged girl and calling her ugly, rightly confident that she will be too enraptured by his charm to take any action against him (they later become lovers). More than his good looks and confidence, though, Lloyd is a romantic figure for the Brodie simply because their leader, Miss Brodie, romanticizes him.

It is clear that Miss Brodie has cast Lloyd into the same romantic role played by Hugh Carruthers, her dead fiancé, lionized in the stories that she tells her girls. Both men were victims of the First World War, and both have been made unavailable to Miss Brodie. In the case of Hugh, the separation is irreversible, due to his heroic death. As to Lloyd, Miss Brodie renounces her passion for him because of his Catholicism. Although she is not willing to admit to anything like respect for the Catholic Church, she still is not willing to cross the Church by having an affair with a married man who has several children. Miss Brodie's image of herself as free from conventional morality is put to the test and bested by her relationship with Teddy Lloyd: He shows no hesitancy for taking her as his mistress, just as, later, he proves willing to have an affair with a student. Still, she refuses to become involved with a married man. The girls who look up to Miss Brodie, having limited experience with death (until later, when the Second World War would acquaint them with all of the sense of tragedy they observed in their elders), watch as the physical impediment of death changes to a moral hindrance that separates Miss Brodie from her happiness.

The short life and pathetic death of Mary Macgregor, often noted as the fool of the Brodie set, shows the maturation process that grief takes the girls through, a process that Miss Brodie herself misses. Spark lets her readers know from the second chapter that Mary is to die at age twenty-three, pointlessly and ingloriously, running up and down the hall during a fire in a hotel. This pathetic end shades her life with a dingy hue: readers are not allowed the fantasy of believing that she will come through the taunts of her classmates and of her instructor better for the experience. Spark points out that she was to remember her years with the Brodie set, who treated her as nothing more than an idiot, as the happiest years of her life. Still, Sandy and Rose later remember her as someone who they mistreated, and so they have their own lesson in how to think of the dead. Their response is much more stable than Miss Brodie's exaggerated memories of Hugh, who will forever be a legend in her mind.

After excluding Teddy Lloyd as a lover, Miss Brodie turns her attention to Gordon Lowther, a bachelor music teacher who is stable but not exciting. Lowther lacks imagination, and so it would seem that he would be grateful for the opportunity to spend time with an artistic soul like Miss Brodie—or so she sees this case. While her youthful affair with Hugh was cut down by gunfire and her affair with Teddy Lloyd halted by her sense of honor, there is nothing to stop her from loving Lowther except for the fact that she finds him uninteresting. She clearly finds him to be "commonplace," a word that she uses throughout the novel to describe things that she feels lack the appropriate artistic temperament. Her affair with him is presented as an act of pity and it reeks of desperation, dragging Miss Brodie down to the level of two spinster seamstresses, the Misses Kerr. When Miss

Brodie defends her struggle for Lowther's attentions in terms of her ancestor who was a desperate gambler and thief, the Brodie girls can see that she is willing to do whatever she can to win Lowther, just as long as it does not require feigning interest in him. Still, emotionally cold as she is, her loss of such an undistinguished man is a harsh blow to Miss Brodie's general belief that romance is hers for the asking.

The battle for the heart of Gordon Lowther is lost while Miss Brodie has been on vacation to Germany, to observe Hitler's Third Reich. Here, Miss Brodie's romantic life parallels the rise of a new, dangerous social order that developed during the 1930s. The Kerr sisters, who at first seem the greatest threat to her conquest of Lowther, represent a previous, genteel generation, concerned with sewing and keeping house; in an earlier day they would have easily earned their place at Lowther's house at Cremond. Having decided to compete against the Kerrs, Miss Brodie clumsily tries to outshine them at their own domesticity by feeding Lowther until he is unable to stuff any more food in his mouth. To their position she adds her own modern posture, becoming sexually involved with Lowther while refusing to marry him. Her fierce independence only holds his attention for a short time, though, before Miss Lockhart, an athletic (she golfs with Lowther) and competent (she handles explosives casually) woman, presents an even stronger version of femininity. Over all, Miss Brodie's romantic ambitions slide toward the commonplace, from the mythical Hugh Carruthers to the dashing Teddy Lloyd to the commonplace Gordon Lowther, and she cannot even secure that final, least-appealing suitor for her own.

It is easy to see the appeal that an independent woman like Miss Brodie would have for the young girls who come into her class at age eleven, having lived in the sheltered world of school all of their lives. It is just as easy to see how, when they are in their upper teens and have experienced the world a bit more, they could see her as a desperate and unhinged woman, aligning herself with repressive political ideologies and declaring her pity for a man who up and marries someone else. In the end, she has lost her position and her lovers, and she could seem pathetic, if not for the fact that she never loses her self-assurance. Sandy, the student who makes it her mission to betray Miss Brodie, ends up struggling with her moral issues by becoming a nun, wearing her hands down by grasping at the grille of her cell, always a prisoner. Spark's message appears to be that, in dealing with an increasingly harsh world, Miss Brodie's self-delusion triumphs over cold realism.

Source: David Kelly, Critical Essay on *The Prime of Miss Jean Brodie*, in *Novels for Students*, Thomson Gale, 2006.

Laura Carter

Carter is currently employed as a freelance writer. In this essay, Carter considers Spark's discussion of free will as it relates to the novel's protagonist, Miss Jean Brodie.

In *The Prime of Miss Jean Brodie*, Muriel Spark tackles the subject of personal freedom. In her novel, Miss Brodie's free, independent spirit fares poorly under the weight of contemporary social dictates. Her need to openly express her own autonomy is overshadowed by decorum, shattering any illusions of personal choice and freedom. In the tradition of many novelists preceding her, Sparks raises important questions about the struggle for feminine autonomy in a restrictive society.

Miss Jean Brodie was a character inspired by Spark's own childhood and adolescence in the center of Scottish culture. Hal Hager in a supplemental chapter of Spark's work describes at the heart of the novel "a deliberately restricted, firmly grounded, localized group of characters whose lives are shaped by a single exceptional personality." The exceptional personality he mentions is, of course, Jean Brodie, who he describes as one bent on breaking free of restrictive modes of thinking, feeling, and being. And all of the characters are limited in many ways. Readers are well acquainted with Miss Brodie's flair for independence. She is a colorful creation—strong willed, forceful with her students yet acutely aware of the unorthodox, even unacceptable nature of her teaching methods in the context of her teaching environment. The practices she employs to instruct and shape "her set," or the Brodie girls, encourage them to think beyond the confines of traditional female roles.

Spark's work mirrors a rich history of female characters in literature who attempt to go beyond the boundaries of polite society to gain a sense of autonomy. Emily Brontë's Kathy, heroine of *Wuthering Heights*, for instance, is transformed from a vibrant, beautiful young woman to a sickly, bed ridden, frail semblance of her former self whose stubborn love affair with a rogue or rough character leads to her ultimate demise or death. Charlotte Perkins Gilman's *The Yellow Wallpaper* considers the phenomenon of women's nervous disorders at the turn of the century and how the collective stifling of the feminine intellect leads to

> Spark's novel is a philosophical model for determinism, a belief that every physical event, including human cognition and action, is causally determined by an unbroken chain of prior occurrences."

complete insanity, as the protagonist of the story begins to mingle with other poor female souls trapped behind the wallpaper. Finally, it is in Kate Chopin's novel *The Awakening* that Edna challenges conventional nineteenth-century mores, weighing love, marriage and her own independence, only to turn to suicide as an avenue to her own freedom.

In all of these examples, female protagonists venture too far from their understood social roles resulting in their own peril. In none of the narratives do the characters openly pursue their true desires; rather, they suppress the urge towards self-expression. They are confined by the criticism of their contemporaries, unable by self-will and determination to live fulfilled lives. Freedom for them is an illusion, as is the power to choose one's own path. They exist, rather, in the privacy of their own minds, and this is where the struggle arises. There has, for instance, been much debate about the end of Chopin's novel. In a sea of choices, how could suicide surface as a viable option? A closer look reveals how limited Edna's choices really were. She could choose to be with her lover, she could be married, or she could live alone. The thought of impropriety with a lover or the chance to marry, in other words, become another man's possession, are unappealing. But to abandon her family for a solitary existence is equally unacceptable to her when she is expected to do otherwise.

Spark's character makes for a fair comparison to Chopin's Edna. Miss Brodie, it is revealed, rather than accepting any students, selects her "special girls" on their ability to keep her teaching philosophy, along with her life, a secret. She deems herself their protector, coping with any troubles she may have working on their behalf. For their sake, rather than follow the traditional school curriculum, Miss Brodie sets aside standard texts in favor of what is already there "in the pupil's soul." In order to protect herself in the classroom, she asks her students to conceal what she is doing, telling them at one point to prop up their history books as if they are reading them, in the event that she is discovered. And her solution to the end-of-term examinations is a simple instruction to her students: "I trust you girls to work hard and try and scrape through, even if you learn up the stuff and forget it the next day." What drives Miss Brodie? "It is for the sake of you girls," she claims, "my influence, now, in the years of my prime." Her power comes from the loyalty of this carefully chosen, close-knit circle of young women. Wielding her influence over them, she anticipates any crisis that might arise with her employer by preparing her students for any probing and incriminating questions the headmistress might ask of them.

The reader also learns of her affairs with several teachers at the school. First, there is her unrequited love, Mr. Teddy Lloyd. An insistence on decorum or good behavior forces her away from Lloyd, and she is driven, she claims, to enter into a love affair with Gordon Lowther, another teacher at the school. In the 1930s this would have been publicly viewed as extremely bad behavior. The affair became one of Miss Brodie's secrets, to be concealed by members of her set. Casual sexual relations with a man outside of marriage were an unspeakable offense for a woman. And, she resorts to equally unorthodox methods when Lowther marries another woman. Without the distraction of her lover, Miss Brodie redoubles her efforts with Lloyd, using two of her students to act as lover and informant, respectively, in an effort to maintain her hold on Lloyd. Misconduct, she claims, is an appropriate outlet for her, because she is "in her Prime." A few of her students look beyond the powerful figure, recognizing the need for diversion that compels Miss Brodie, admiring her method of "making patterns with facts," her "excessive lack of guilt" and her entitlement to a lifestyle "outside the context of right and wrong."

In the tradition of those that have come before her, Spark's character perishes by moving outside social mores or rules. Despite her attempts at maintaining secrecy, Miss Brodie's improprieties result in her forced retirement from her beloved teaching position. Like those female characters that stray too far from the norm, her covert or secretive manipulations of her students, as well as her peers, leave her closed to any outside influence or criticism

from anyone, constructive or otherwise. Any kind of objectivity regarding her activities is forsaken for the desire to enjoy her prime. And the results are even dangerous to Miss Brodie. Like Chopin's Edna, Miss Brodie lives within the realm of her own desires amongst her students, but she is never truly free to share her teaching methodologies or personal life with those outside of the classroom. Rather than engage in an affair with Lloyd, she uses her young, impressionable students to fulfill her romantic fantasies. Her behavior as a teacher moves from admirable to reckless as she sinks deeper and deeper into her deluded state. Sandy contemplates this madness as her affections change for her teacher, suggesting that her teacher "thinks she is Providence," or "the God of Calvin," and that there were "many theories from the books of psychology categorized Miss Brodie."

Historically, similar novels challenge philosophical notions of freedom. Spark's novel is a philosophical model for determinism, a belief that every physical event, including human cognition and action, is causally determined by an unbroken chain of prior occurrences. In physics, for example, the events of the universe operate within a set of fixed, knowable laws. Determinists believe that because of such laws, people are fundamentally incapable of independent choice, leaving no basis for morality. Spark's text raises similar questions of culpability or blameworthiness. Could Miss Brodie have made different choices? Could she have risen above the dictates of her own environment and realized true freedom? Resoundingly the answer is no. The social restrictions of Miss Brodie's time render her character powerless to change her destiny, resulting in her mental decline and subsequent retirement. It is Sandy who describes her teacher's predicament aptly, claiming Miss Brodie "had elected herself to grace in so particular a way and with more exotic suicidal enchantment than if she had simply taken to drink like other spinsters who couldn't stand it anymore."

The structure of the novel also lends itself to this philosophical interpretation. Unlike the traditional novel, the fate of the characters in Spark's novel is understood from the beginning. The information is relayed either via flashback or as the Brodie narrative unfolds. For example, it is in a flashback that the audience learns that Sandy has devoted the greater part of her life to a nunnery, after writing a psychological study inspired by Miss Brodie. Eunice reveals in another flashback that Miss Brodie was betrayed by one of her own girls and forced to retire early. There are also repeated statements made throughout the narrative concerning the fate of several characters. In the case of Mary McGregor, the reader is continually reminded of her tragic death by house fire. Statements concerning Mary appear throughout the narrative, reminding the reader that Mary was not only "stupid and always to blame," but who, "at the age of twenty-three, lost her life in a hotel fire."

Spark's technique of repeating select phrases about the fates of those characters central to the novel throughout the work establish a framework by which the reader can piece together or more clearly realize or identify the actions of the character that contribute to specific outcomes. Mary's fate is mirrored in one frantic reaction in the science lab, similar to the day she frantically runs "hither and thither" in the hall of a hotel, until she dies. Repeated phrases as well as the reiteration of specific character traits are a way to reinforce the notion that the characters' reactions are part of their persona, just part of who they inherently are. Like determinism, this mode of character development seems to suggest that they are not acting as a matter of free will, but as a matter of course, the outcomes of their future lives have been determined and their fates, a matter of time.

Muriel Spark's *The Prime of Miss Jean Brodie* weaves in several elements, in terms of both plot and character, to demonstrate the limits to which Miss Brodie and her students can dictate the course of their own lives. Compared to authors the likes of Emily Brontë, Spark's works from a traditional genre of literature of which female characters attempt to move past social and cultural restrictions to define themselves. Her novel is a rich exploration of the anatomy, not only of a character, but of the society that drives individual behavior. Spark's study leaves the reader to grapple with questions not so easily resolved. In a broader sense, it mirrors the internal struggles inherent in contemporary society—the timeless struggle to be unique, to be autonomous, in a world that demands conformity.

Source: Laura Carter, Critical Essay on *The Prime of Miss Jean Brodie*, in *Novels for Students*, Thomson Gale, 2006.

Benilde Montgomery

In the following essay, Montgomery explains how the character Sandy's conversion is motivated by the Catholic philosophies of Cardinal Newman, perhaps referencing Spark's own conversion to Catholicism.

In her recent autobiography, *Curriculum Vitae* (1993), Muriel Spark confirms that the theological

> " If Brodie began her prime mindful of her students' welfare, she ends it, like all other political and religious fascists, obsessed with imposing a myth about a fabulous past on a vulnerable present."

writings of Cardinal Newman played an important role in her conversion to Catholicism. Indeed, she has made this claim before ("Conversion"), as has her former friend and coeditor, Derek Stanford, who suggests that Newman's and Spark's conversions were similar. Newman, he says, "had been a Catholic without recognizing it. In going over to Rome, he found what he was looking for—what, indeed, he was—though without liking it when he got there." Although in *Curriculum Vitae* Spark comes to repudiate many other of Stanford's claims about her, she does not deny this similarity and, in fact, uses Newman's own point that conversion is "not a thing one could propound 'between the soup and the fish' at a dinner party" to defend her cutting short a discussion of her own. Nonetheless, while Spark avoids discussing the particular and difficult process of religious conversion in her autobiography, it is the frequent subject of her fiction, and at the center of her most famous fiction, *The Prime of Miss Jean Brodie*, where the process of Sandy's conversion follows, not surprisingly, the outlines drawn by Newman and, as *Curriculum Vitae* suggests, imitated by Spark herself.

In Newman's scheme, conversion is not a static business but a slow and continuing process. Therefore, conversion, for him, neither concludes nor leads to simple peace or repose. Restating ideas implicit throughout his work, but never more explicitly so than in *An Essay on the Development of Christian Doctrine*, Cardinal Newman speaks in his *Apologia* of Catholic Christianity as an "arena" wherein "Authority" and "Private Judgement" are "combatants in [an] awful, never-ending duel." Newman further insists that "it is necessary for the very life of religion, viewed in its large operations and its history, that [this] warfare should be incessantly carried on." It should be said that this understanding of Catholicism is not unique to Newman. The Austrian Catholic historian, Friedrich Heer, for example, sees the history of Catholicism advancing dialectically between the poles of orthodoxy and heresy. And Thomas J. J. Altizer, commenting on both Newman and Heer, sees Catholicism as an "evolving faith" whose identity at any one time is "a consequence of its internal struggle with heresy," apart from which "the Church would not and could not evolve." So conceived—that is, as an "arena," an "incessant warfare," and "internal struggle"—Catholicism defeats the expectations of those who come to it seeking equanimity and calm, and indeed gives a positive and necessary value to their opposites, that is, to tension and conflict. Even Newman's own boast that since his conversion he has "been in perfect peace and contentment" (*Apologia*) explodes in the face of facts. Newman's biography shows that his later life was dominated not by repose but by warfare, and not with the established church from which he had withdrawn but with many inside the church he had joined: suspicious fellow Catholics, particularly the "orthodox" Manning and other ultramontanists who imagined Catholicism not as Newman's dynamic arena of concrete history and struggle but as something static, aloof from its own history and therefore beyond change.

Interestingly, before reading Newman, Spark considered herself primarily a poet and wrote no fiction at all. This fact prompts Alan Kennedy to pinpoint Newman as the common denominator of both Spark's religious conversion and her later literary career. Spark, indeed, had postponed her conversion to Catholicism wondering, "If I become a Catholic, will I grow like them?" ("Conversion") She came to see, however, that "the Roman Catholic faith corresponded to what I had always felt and known and believed" (*Curriculum*), and consistent with this, she claims that she speaks "far more in my own voice as a Catholic" ("Conversion"). Moreover, Spark seems to agree with her character in *Loitering with Intent* (1981) who defends Newman's *Apologia* as "among the best" of spiritual autobiographies so thoroughly that she uses it as the model for her own. Even the title Spark chose for her autobiography, *Curriculum Vitae* (1993), echoes her spiritual mentor's. So, too, does her choice of an intertextual style: Letters are reprinted, critical reviews are recalled and corrected, poems are reproduced, all, in Newman's words, "to prevent misconception" (*Apologia* 35), and in Spark's, "to put the record straight"

(*Curriculum*). Although not so speculative and defensive as the *Apologia*, *Curriculum Vitae* ends like it: with its subject's conversion to Catholicism but with no mention of the later tensions that conversion to Catholicism necessarily includes.

Because Spark believes that "the existential quality of a religious experience cannot be simply summed up in general terms" (*Curriculum*), she has left speculation on the tensions that accompany conversion to her fiction where, like Newman, her convert-protagonists find in their new Catholicism "incessant warfare" and "internal struggle." For example, Caroline Rose of *The Comforters* keeps running into "spiritual risks" and, in the confusion of voices that she begins to hear, must constantly struggle to distinguish the natural from the supernatural. Barbara Vaughan of *The Mandelbaum Gate* is a "private judging Catholic" caught in a world where all religious and national identities converge, and where she must struggle to balance her sexuality and the demands of Catholic law. In *The Girls of Slender Means*, Spark explicitly associates Selina's desire for "equanimity of body and soul, complete composure whatever the social scene," with the very opposite of Catholicism. Her commitment to equanimity, even in the face of her own death, is the very "vision of evil" that Nicholas Farrington rejects to effect his own conversion, a conversion that brings him not peace but bloody martyrdom as a missionary Brother in Haiti. No less troubled by the discomfort of conversion is Spark's most well-known Catholic, Sandy Stranger, the ill-at-ease cloistered nun in *The Prime of Miss Jean Brodie* whose conversion, like Nicholas Farrington's, includes the rejection of a vision of evil. Here Sandy rejects the vision offered her by the charismatic Miss Brodie, who, both crypto-Catholic and crypto-fascist, desires not only that her girls achieve Selina's equanimity ("You girls must learn to cultivate an expression of composure. . . . Walk with your heads up, up like Sybil Thorndike, a woman of noble mien") but also that they assume for her the risks of actual and concrete history that she, aloof and composed like the ultramontanist Catholics of Newman's later years, dare not take.

Nonetheless, most critics, like Sandy herself, become obsessed only with the character of Jean Brodie and thereby misread the novel as only a character sketch of her. They thereby relegate Sandy to secondary status, paying little heed to the tension between the two characters at the center of the novel and to Sandy's primary role as witness, judge, and "assassin." After all, Sandy's notoriously "small, almost non-existent eyes" observe most, if not all, the action, and more than any of the other Brodie girls, Sandy carries the weight and impact of Brodie's philosophy, confiding to her inquisitor that above literature, politics, and theology, the most profound influence on her development was Miss Brodie. While the others remember Brodie sentimentally, she is at the very core of both Sandy's vocation and of her book on the "nature of moral perception," even as that book reacts against Brodie's teachings. Placing the inquisitor both at the end and toward the beginning of the novel, Spark also suggests that much of the novel is Sandy's reminiscence, a suggestion that provides Jay Presson Allen's dramatization of the novel with its structure.

Further, in *Curriculum Vitae* Spark makes such clear links between her own life and Sandy's that one suspects that one of the records Spark wishes to set straight is the importance of Sandy not only as a figure in her most popular novel but also as a key to understanding her own life. For example, in the novel Spark writes of Sandy Stranger that she

was sometimes embarrassed by her mother being English and calling her "darling," not like mothers of Edinburgh who said "dear." Sandy's mother had a flashy winter coat trimmed with fluffy fox fur like the Duchess of York's while the other mothers wore tweed or, at the most, musquash that would do them all their days.

In *Curriculum Vitae*, Spark writes of herself that

My mother, who was English, used to come and fetch me from school. It was my daily dread that she should open her mouth and thus betray her suspect origins. "Foreigners" were fairly tolerated but "the English" were something quite different. It was not only the accent that betrayed Englishness. It was also turns of phrase and idiomatic usage. . . . My mother also wore a winter coat trimmed with beige fox fur in the style of the then Duchess of York. . . . This was entirely out of place. My mother ought to have worn tweed or, in very cold weather, musquash.

Also, at a tea party in the novel, Sandy feels "offended and belittled" when Jenny's mother remarks, "My word . . . they've [Sandy and Jenny] been tucking in!" At a similar tea party with her schoolfriend, Frances Niven, Spark records in *Curriculum Vitae* that one of Frances's aunts said, "'Look at them tucking in!' I seemed to be the only child who heard this, and although I didn't make any fuss, I was ridiculously affected." These and numerous other verbal linkages invite readers to reappraise Sandy's function in the novel and, through the specific terms demanded by fiction, to reconsider the nature of Spark's own religious conversion.

Needless to say, not all critics have avoided Sandy and her conversion to Catholicism, but those who do speculate on it tend to read as negative both its dynamism and its accompanying tensions. In spite of what William Lynch, S. J., would call Sandy's courageous "descent into the finite"—her willing embrace of those concrete particulars that for Brodie remain ill-conceived wishes—Sandy's critics call her, among other things, "unpleasant" (Kennedy 185), "malicious" and an "aesthete" (Laffin 215, 221). She is said to be "disgusted with humanity" (Friedman 103); her conversion is seen by one critic only as "a retreat from everyday reality" (Bold 71), and by another as "unexplained and unfathomable" (Adler 599). Yet another critic sees the novel's end dominated by a "justified Miss Brodie presiding calmly over a lost innocence" (Kermode 271). These readings, moreover, often suggest a sympathetic Miss Brodie as Sandy's victim. Indeed, Allen's screenplay not only ignores any reference to the religious context in which Spark so carefully sets her novel, it also draws Sandy as a jealous, spiteful teenager who ultimately joins the philistine assault on an otherwise charming spinster. Although Allen's earlier playscript (about which Spark writes that she had the "distinct impression that my views, as author of the book, were not really welcome" [*Curriculum*]) at least acknowledges the fact of Sandy's conversion, it places Sandy in a placid convent garden, an image more consistent with Miss Brodie's pre-Raphaelite longings than with the realism of Spark's novel and the dynamic "arena" and "never-ending duel" of Spark's and Newman's vision of Catholicism. Ironically, Ray Shaw's review of a 1994 London revival of the play dismisses this convent scene as a weakness in the play which "does not add anything to it."

The story of Newman's conversion in the *Apologia* follows the theoretical foundations he laid down earlier in *The Development of Christian Doctrine*. There he defines "development" as "the germination and maturation of some truth or apparent truth on a large mental field" that "cannot progress at all without cutting across and thereby destroying or modifying and incorporating within itself existing modes of thinking and operating," throwing off "whatever in them it cannot assimilate." (*Development*) Indeed, Newman's movement away from the established church toward Roman Catholicism imitates, at least intellectually, this pattern. Although the "great revolution of mind" that occurred during the Long Vacation of 1839 led him to conclude that the established church was in the same relationship with Rome as were the Christian heretical movements of the fifth century (*Apologia*), he did not seek formal admission to "the one Fold of Christ," until October 1845, striving during the intervening years to modify, incorporate, assimilate, and, in some instances, throw off those "corruptions" within the established church he found inconsistent with the evolving Apostolic tradition. As Altizer points out, such a theory of doctrinal development (and in the case of the *Apologia* Newman's personal, intellectual development) gives Christian heresy "a fully positive identity," making it one of the necessary and historical poles of the dialectic that grounds and thereby names "integral Catholicism."

Indeed, Nick Farrington's "vision of evil," a vision that for Spark "may be as effective to conversion as a vision of good" (Slender 118), has a similar, positive identity, as do the "barbarians" of the Cavafy poem Spark quotes in the novel: "And now what will become of us without the Barbarians? / Those people were some sort of a solution." In *Slender Means*, these "barbarians" are associated with the defeated Nazis. In *Jean Brodie*, Miss Brodie is associated with fascism and has a similar and necessary function in Sandy's conversion. Brodie's presence in the novel is positive insofar as she is, like the "barbarians" of Cavafy's poem and heresy within Newman's scheme, something to negate, transcend, and leave behind as the "inevitable" counterpart and foil of orthodoxy (Altizer 184). Imbued with Calvinism and already having put on the mind of her Roman Catholic lover, Sandy eventually uses "the economy" (a concept Spark borrows from Newman's *Apologia*) of Teddy Lloyd's method not only to put a stop to the evil Miss Brodie but also to recognize that Miss Brodie's notable defects "had not been without [their] beneficent and enlarging effects."

Within the walls of the Marcia Blaine School, a school that Spark describes as having an "ordinary rule," an "authorized curriculum," and an "orthodox regime," Miss Brodie is a self-proclaimed heretic. She declines to participate in the "never-ending duel" that Newman finds "necessary for the very life of religion" by declaring a separate peace in favor of "private judgement." Creating a schismatic sect with herself as a rival Pope, she is not so much a "parody of the Christian Church" (Lodge 136) as she is the type of all Christian heresy: gnostic, disembodied, exclusive, discontinuous with a catholic and universal tradition, and immune to history. Specifically, in her "contempt for the Modern side," Jean Brodie resembles most those late-nineteenth-century Protestants, Tractarians, and ultramontanist Catholics who, in Newman's words, are "ever hunting for a fabulous primitive simplicity"

(*Essays*). Disillusioned at every turn by the concrete messiness of actual history and the primal reflexes of the body, these despairing, sectarian heretics, of whom Brodie is the specific instance, triumphed for a time in the production of, among other things, a "Syllabus of Errors," parodied by Spark in Brodie's list of do's and don't's: A window opened 6 inches "is perfectly adequate. More is vulgar," roll down your sleeves "at once, we are civilized beings." Horrible to say, in their own prime, many of these antimodernist, ultramontanist Catholics fell, like Brodie, too easily into the arms of twentieth-century fascism.

Although the exceptional martyr may prove the rule, fascism flourished first in those parts of the world most self-consciously "Catholic." Dare we remember that as the von Trapps escaped across the Alps, their coreligionist archbishop in Vienna, Cardinal Innitzer, was rushing to salute Adolf Hitler on his balcony and to support the Anschluss in a pastoral letter that ended with a carefully hand-written "Heil Hitler!"? Spark's fictional counterpart of Innitzer is, of course, Miss Brodie, who, "by temperament suited only to the Roman Catholic Church," stands "in her brown dress like a gladiator with raised arm," shouting "Hail Caesar! . . . radiantly to the window light." In that image and others like it (Mary MacGregor, Brodie's Jew, swallowed up in flames; Joyce Emily killed as she rushes toward Franco's army), Spark lifts the novel out of the idiosyncratic and beyond the "isolated communities" (Parrinder 28) about which she is sometimes accused of writing. If readers and critics, too, succumb easily to Miss Brodie's charms, we are in the company of those midcentury Scottish schoolgirls and those millions of other Europeans similarly seduced. In *The Girls of Slender Means,* evil wears an alluring Schiaparelli dress. In *Jean Brodie*, the heretical Miss Brodie ignores the boring history lessons of the "authorized curriculum" in favor of properly pronounced versions of aesthetic verse or frequently revised stories out of her own sentimentalized past, stories that have nothing to do with "the ordinary world."

Nonetheless, Sandy's movement toward Catholic orthodoxy could not have begun without the positive allure of this kind of heresy, even as that "beneficent and enlarging" encounter with Jean Brodie's "Catholic temperament" provides her ultimately with "something to react against." But, as with Newman's reaction to the established church, Sandy's rejection of that heresy is never absolute, but rather evolves as part of a continuous and "developmental" process. The seeds of Brodie's heresy once planted in Sandy unexpectedly take root. Nurtured by Sandy's unique imagination, they develop into the Catholic vision of Sister Helena of the Transfiguration, a name that evokes not only the conversion of Constantine but also his mother's discovery of the True Cross. If Jean Brodie represents "completely unrealized potentialities," as Spark maintains ("Keeping It Short"), these potentialities are realized fully in Sandy, for the novel inseparably fuses the rise and fall of Sandy Stranger and Jean Brodie, as well as the progress of Western history. In September 1939, as the war against Hitler begins, Sandy converts to Catholicism and Brodie is discharged from Marcia Blaine. In "the year after the war," Brodie dies, and Sandy, like Brodie reborn and transfigured, enters the convent as Sister Helena and writes a famous book on moral perception.

As a child, Sandy Stranger is drawn to Miss Brodie out of loneliness and fear: Sandy is not a stranger (or herself, if you will) so long as she remains part of Brodie's isolated sect. Although Brodie's clashes with Miss Mackay teach Sandy an important truth, that "people glued together in grown-up authority differ," "group-fright" seizes Sandy whenever she wishes to differ with Miss Brodie and be kind to Mary MacGregor, for "by this action she would separate herself, and be lonely." Sandy's instinct for goodness, however, eventually triumphs, because she leads what she calls "a double life." This "double life" allows her to live both in quotidian reality and, at the same time, in the world of her own imagination. Fed by this imagination, whose rich quality Brodie's lacks (Brodie, after all, expects the beautiful Rose to flower, not "pig-eyed" Sandy), she sees, even as a child, a clear, if innocent, analogy between Brodie's "set" and Mussolini's fascisti. Moreover, when, "chin up, up, up," Brodie marches her girls through the Edinburgh slums and urges them all only to "pray for the Unemployed," Sandy is "very frightened." Apprehending the evil of economic deprivation in the analogy of a serpent, she sees the destitute move like "one dragon's body," a "snaky creature" shivering in the cold. Like Spark who reports on a similar trip to the slums of Edinburgh (*Curriculum*), Sandy learns here another less innocent, but more crucial, truth: Primal evil is not abstract but concrete and tangible, a reality Miss Brodie's first history lesson in a snakeless "garden . . . underneath the secure shade of the elm" failed to include.

Because Brodie's imagination never progresses beyond the "aesthetic," she is incapable of considering "the moral" in any form. Although Spark describes Edinburgh's Old Town as a "reeking network of slums," Brodie regards it only as a curious artifact, a place where once "history had been lived" [emphasis mine]. She points out that "architecturally speaking, there is no finer sight in Europe." Sure that Hitler's social reorganization would "save the world," Brodie can admit, at tea after the war, only that Hitler was "rather naughty." Sandy's imagination, on the other hand, develops beyond the aesthetic and, ultimately, to the religious. During her last semester with Miss Brodie, she becomes fascinated with the demonstrable facts of concrete and present history: with the details of Miss Brodie's assignation in the art room; and, urging Jenny not to tell Miss Brodie, with the investigative work of "Detective Sergeant Anne Grey," for whom she "quite deserted Alan Breck and Mr. Rochester and all the heroes of fiction" that Brodie has urged upon her. Lacking Sandy's instinct and insight, Miss Brodie uses her imagination only as a distraction, a device either to relieve her boredom or to defend herself from the present and the actual. Unlike Sandy, she cannot resist the allure of more surface; and, consequently, in spite of her protests that art and religion come first, she is, outside Marcia Blaine, a common dilettante who understands neither very well. Incapable or unwilling to confront the reality of evil, and therefore unwilling to engage herself seriously with any objective norm, she would undoubtedly dismiss Newman's saying that the very "essence of all religion is authority and obedience" (*Development*) with the same irony she uses to criticize Teddy Lloyd: "He's a Roman Catholic and I don't see how you can have to do with a man who can't think for himself."

Brodie, of course, does not stand still while Sandy develops. The growth of the one so interpenetrates the growth of the other that Sandy wonders "to what extent it was Miss Brodie who had developed complications throughout the years, and to what extent it was her own conception of Miss Brodie that had changed." Spark tells us that "it was not a static Miss Brodie who told her girls, 'These are the years of my prime . . .' but one whose nature was growing under their eyes, as the girls themselves were under formation." She is quick to add, however, "that the principles governing the end of her prime would have astonished herself at the beginning of it." To use Newman's language, Sandy's movement toward orthodoxy is a "genuine development," while Miss Brodie's growth can only be called a "corruption," the kind of corruption that in the natural world follows upon "prime." Specifically, Newman says that corruption is "the breaking up of life, preparatory to its termination [which] begins when life has reached its perfection, [it] being at the same time the reversal and undoing of what went before" (*Development*). He adds that "one cause of corruption in religion is the refusal to follow the course of doctrine as it moves on, and an obstinacy in the notions of the past" (177). If Brodie began her prime mindful of her students' welfare, she ends it, like all other political and religious fascists, obsessed with imposing a myth about a fabulous past on a vulnerable present. So variable are Brodie's stories about her youthful beloved, Hugh Carruthers, the Fallen Leaf of Flanders Fields, that even the girls notice that Brodie easily accommodates past facts to serve fancy's present end. Nonetheless, she is determined to fulfill her private fantasy with wounded Teddy Lloyd, even if she must play pander to her favorite girls and send another to a horrible and ironic death.

Yet, as Newman puts it, "the same philosophical elements, received into a certain sensibility or insensibility to sin and its consequences, leads one mind to the Church of Rome; another to what, for want of a better word, may be called Germanism" (*Development*). Having learned from Miss Brodie the aesthetics of Catholicism—Giotto, Dante, the Pope, the frighteningly well-ordered Italian and Bavarian "scenes"—Sandy receives these facts through a sensibility alive to the reality of evil and sin, a sensibility that Miss Brodie lacks. Not unlike St. Helena discovering the True Cross, Sandy returns alone not to Jerusalem but to the Old Town where she had had her original vision of primal evil. Here she begins to learn lessons that the heretical curriculum of Miss Brodie omitted: that sin and guilt are real, that God is the ultimate authority, and that the sin of presumption is a "suicidal enchantment" more potent than drink for spinsters, like Miss Brodie, "who could not stand it anymore."

If Sandy ultimately finds the despair of Calvinism "something definite to reject," and the presumption of Miss Brodie "something to react against," she finds a middle way in Teddy Lloyd with whose mind Sandy becomes "deeply absorbed" and from whom she extracts his Roman Catholic religion "as a pith from a husk." Because Brodie dismisses the body in favor of "higher things," she not only persists in her insensitivity to sin, she also confuses respectability with morality: "We must keep our good name." Like her other false prophecies, the "magnificently elevated above the ordinary" affair with Teddy that she engineers for the barely pubescent Rose explodes into a

triumph for body and fact. The maimed and adulterous body of Teddy Lloyd that Brodie dared not touch becomes, however, the particular means through which Sandy finally recognizes the Catholicism that has been growing inside her. Wounded and sinful like the church itself, Teddy, quite tellingly, also sees as the church has seen since medieval times, interpreting his world in the terms of likeness and difference, those terms that undergird the Scholastics' *analogia entis* itself. Rendering the invisible visible, Teddy's transfiguring art captures both the realistic likeness of the Brodie girls and at the same time the face of Jean Brodie, that absent presence beneath and beyond them that makes them one. In doing so, he shows Sandy another kind of "double life," not the isolating and imaginary life of her childhood but the kind of imagination through which Catholic Christianity understands itself. In it she recognizes a counterpart for her childhood's instinctive longings. Like Spark, she too finds her own authentic voice. Unlike Brodie's, Sandy's development is, therefore, genuine and real. As Newman asserts, "There is no corruption if [a development] retains one and the same type . . . if its beginnings anticipate its subsequent phases . . . if it has a power of assimilation and survival and a vigorous action from first to last" (*Development*). Miss Brodie's ancestor Willy died on a gibbet of his own devising; "betrayed" by her student Sandy, Jean Brodie ultimately dies of an "internal growth."

So Sandy enters a cloister, writes a famous book, and we leave her, come to her own prime, clutching "the bars of her grille more desperately than ever." Fully conscious of Miss Brodie and of how easily "corruption" follows upon prime, Sandy anticipates, I suspect, the difficulties of developing into her own future. To say, as Friedman does, that "conversion itself may not 'save' us" suggests that conversion is an isolated, static event rather than the dynamic process that Newman and this novel have described. Moreover, as "retaining one and the same type" is indicative of genuine development, Sandy Stranger's conversion has up to this point satisfied Newman's criteria: Unlike her youthful escapism, Sandy Stranger's development has not left her less a stranger than she was before. Rather it has contextualized the existential reality of exile itself, putting Sandy Stranger in the company of people like Newman who years after his own conversion can say, no less despairingly than Sandy, "Were it not for this voice, speaking so clearly in my conscience and my heart, I should be an atheist, or a pantheist, or a polytheist when I looked into the world" (*Apologia*). Reacting against and rejecting the authoritarianism of Miss Brodie's fascism, Sandy Stranger enters the Catholic Church and thereby embraces another kind of authority, an authority grounded not in personal power but in a dynamic tradition that, Newman contends, does not tyrannize but rather provokes, in its "never-ending duel" with "private judgement," the warfare that is the necessary condition for the very life of religion. As this same provocative authority once received Sandy into the secure and sectarian life of a convent, so now the same church, in the form of Sandy's religious superiors, requires that she take a further step: to look beyond the shadows of the visiting parlor into the face of the world she was tempted to ignore. As in its own process of continuous conversion, the authority of the Roman Church, hearing the voice of Newman in its Second Vatican Council, rejected as internal heresy the sectarian and antimodern posture of Vatican I, Sandy too is asked by that authority to examine her own temptation to sectarianism that accompanies her own prime. Like her youthful membership in Brodie's crème de la crème, the isolation of the cloister has provided her only a temporary shelter, one that she must now reconsider so that the positive and necessary warfare at the heart of genuine conversion may continue. If Sandy has found in the church "quite a number of Fascists much less agreeable than Miss Brodie," Sandy's development up to this point assures us that it is not she who will die of an internal growth, but rather those others who refuse to come to the window, and who like Spark's Salina, have cultivated an "expression of composure," and sit "when they received their rare visitors, well back in the darkness with folded hands."

Source: Benilde Montgomery, "Spark and Newman: Jean Brodie Reconsidered," in *Twentieth Century Literature*, Vol. 43, Spring 1997, pp. 94–106.

Sources

Hicks, Granville, "Treachery and the Teacher," in *Saturday Review*, January 20, 1962, p. 18.

Hynes, Samuel, Review of *The Prime of Miss Jean Brodie*, in *Commonweal*, February 23, 1962, p. 567.

Review of *The Prime of Miss Jean Brodie*, in *Library Journal*, January 1, 1962, p. 114.

Spark, Muriel, *The Prime of Miss Jean Brodie*, Harper-Collins, 1999.

Further Reading

Bottner, Barbara, *Let Me Tell You Everything*, Harper Collins, 1989.

> The main character in this story, Brogan, is a bright high school student, full of feminist ideas, when she develops a crush on her social studies teacher. The protagonist confronts the imminent divorce of her parents, and her trip through teenage angst is both humorous and thought-provoking.

Drabble, Margaret, *The Radiant Way*, Knopf, 1987.

> The ironic title of this novel comes from a children's primer that depicts life as peaceful and cooperative, which is not quite the experience of the novel's Cambridge University school chums from the 1950s who reconnect in London in the 1980s.

Newman, John Henry, *Apologia pro Vita Sua*, edited by Ian Ker, Penguin Books, 1994; new edition of work originally published by Longman, Green, Longman, Roberts, and Green, 1864.

> Newman accounts for his spiritual growth from youth through adulthood. A one-time Anglican, Newman converted to Catholicism in 1845, an event he discusses in this work.

Spark, Muriel, *Curriculum Vitae: An Autobiography*, Houghton Mifflin, 1993.

> Spark credits the writings of Cardinal John Henry Newman with playing a significant role in her conversion to Catholicism, which plays an important role in her fiction.

The Satanic Verses

Salman Rushdie

1988

Salman Rushdie's *The Satanic Verses* rapidly became one of the most widely known and controversial books in the world when it was published in 1988. Reviled by much of the international Muslim community, the novel was banned in India and protested across the world for its portrayal of certain sensitive topics such as the wives of the chief Islamic prophet Muhammad and the infallibility of the Islamic holy book, the Qur'an. After the Iranian Ayatollah Khomeini issued a "fatwa," or Islamic judicial decree, that Rushdie and those involved in the publication of the book be killed, the novel made headline news across the globe and inspired a diplomatic crisis between countries, including Britain and Iran.

Although *The Satanic Verses* does address the religious beliefs and practices of Islam, this is only one aspect of a complex and highly allusive novel that produces a broad and ambitious commentary about the philosophical and religious problem of good and evil. In fact, Rushdie's novel is steeped in commentary about British and South Asian politics and culture; it takes on a diverse variety of themes involving cultural and racial identities (particularly Asian and African immigrant identities), and it is concerned with literary aesthetics and the nature of truth. All of these ideas are incorporated into an eventful storyline involving Gibreel Farishta and Saladin Chamcha, two characters with complex British/Indian identities caught in an epic battle that takes place between London and Bombay in the 1980s. Both of the main characters

begin to take on supernatural qualities and visit alternate worlds, such as that of Gibreel's extended dreams about the Islamic prophet Muhammad. *The Satanic Verses* has been widely misunderstood and defamed, but it has also fascinated its readers, opened up an international debate about censorship and the function of literature, and confirmed Rushdie's status as one of the most important contemporary writers in the English language.

Author Biography

Rushdie was born on June 19, 1947 to a prosperous family in Bombay, India. Although his background was Muslim, Rushdie was not brought up as a believer. He was sent away when he was thirteen to a private education in England, where he was harassed by his peers, and Rushdie's family joined him in Kensington, London, between 1962 and 1964 before moving to Pakistan. Rushdie attended King's College, Cambridge, graduating in 1968 with a master's degree in history. After living briefly in Pakistan, Rushdie moved back to England and worked in advertising, publishing, and television.

Rushdie wrote one novel that was rejected and abandoned two others before publishing his first novel, *Grimus* (1975). This debut was unsuccessful, and Rushdie began to work for the Camden Committee for Community Relations assisting Bangladeshi immigrants. *Midnight's Children*, his second novel, was published in 1981 and won Britain's prestigious Booker Prize, launching Rushdie to fame in Britain and South Asia. While this novel takes India and Indo-British relations as its main subject, *Shame* (1983) focuses on Pakistan. During the 1980s, Rushdie also wrote a travelogue about Nicaragua and pursued his interest in film, producing two documentaries.

The infamous series of events that followed the publication of *The Satanic Verses* in 1988 began when, immediately after its publication, Muslims across the world began to protest. The novel was banned in India, copies of it were burned publicly, and a number of demonstrators were killed or injured when protests turned violent in India and Pakistan. In February of 1989, the Ayatollah Khomeini, who was the Muslim religious and political leader of Iran, issued a fatwa that the author and all those involved with the publication of the book were sentenced to death. Rushdie went into hiding, not to emerge until 1995, while three people involved

Salman Rushdie   AP/Wide World Photos. Reproduced by permission

with the book were attacked, including the Japanese translator, who was killed. Since then, Rushdie has continued to publish short stories and novels including *The Moor's Last Sigh* (1995). He splits his time between London, New York, and India, where he was granted a visa to return in 1999 after years of exile.

Plot Summary

The Angel Gibreel

The Satanic Verses begins with a description of Gibreel Farishta and Saladin Chamcha falling from a plane into the English Channel and surviving. Gibreel is flying to London to find his lover, Alleluia Cone, while Saladin is coming home from an acting gig in Bombay. Before blowing up the plane, terrorists hijack their jumbo jet and hold them captive for one hundred and ten days, during which time Gibreel fights against the sleep that brings him vivid religious dreams.

Mahound

Chapter 2 dramatizes Gibreel's dream about the experience of the chief Islamic prophet Muhammad, whom the narrator calls Mahound, in the city of Jahilia. It refers to Muhammad's period of persecution in Mecca and the episode in which several "satanic verses" were alleged to have been told to Muhammad and later expunged from the Qur'an. After several confrontations with the Grandee of Jahilia, his wife, and the poet Baal, Mahound flees the city.

Ellowen Deeowen

An old Englishwoman named Rosa Diamond finds Gibreel and Saladin washed up on the seashore and nurses them back to health. Saladin has begun to take on the features of the devil while Gibreel appears to have a halo around his head. Saladin calls home, but quickly hangs up after a man answers, and then the police come to arrest him and beat him brutally. A physiotherapist named Hyacinth nurses Saladin back to health and then escapes with him; Saladin returns home to find his wife in bed with his friend, Jumpy Joshi. Meanwhile, Gibreel escapes from Rosa Diamond, who had been immersing him in the secret love story of her past. Gibreel wanders through London until he finds Allie Cone.

Ayesha

Chapter 4 is another of Gibreel's dream visions, beginning with the Imam of Desh, who is an exile in London until he forces Gibreel to accompany him to witness the revolution in his home country. This episode refers to the 1979 Islamic fundamentalist revolution in Iran. Gibreel then dreams of Mirza Saeed Akhtar's passion for Ayesha, who claims to be a prophet, and informs Mirza Saeed that his wife Mishal has cancer. Ayesha convinces the entire village to go on a pilgrimage by foot to Mecca, announcing that God will part the Arabian Sea for them.

A City Visible but Unseen

Jumpy takes Saladin—who is becoming more and more like the conventional image of the devil—to the Shaandaar Bed & Breakfast, where Saladin discovers that he has lost his job, that his wife has become pregnant by Jumpy, and that Gibreel is going to make his dreams into movies. Enraged, Saladin becomes larger and is taken to the Hot Wax nightclub, where he loses his supernatural qualities and swears revenge on Gibreel. Gibreel, meanwhile, lives passionately with Allie but becomes consumed by jealousy and leaves her apartment to wander London believing that he is an archangel. He fails in his quest to announce the message of God and finds his way back to Allie's doorstep.

Return to Jahilia

The next section of Gibreel's dream narrative—which many Muslims consider offensive and blasphemous—describe Mahound's conquest of Jahilia. Salman the Persian complains to Baal of the problems and absurdities of Mahound's sacred verses, particularly their treatment of women. Mahound spares the lives of all of his former enemies in Jahilia, except Baal, who hides in a brothel and marries its twelve prostitutes that have taken the names of Mahound's wives in order to attract clients. Baal is eventually found and executed, but Hind, who pretended to convert to Islam, has been practicing black magic and manages to summon the devil Al-Lat to kill Mahound.

The Angel Azraeel

Saladin goes home and informs Pamela that he will live in the house for the time being, despite her continued affair with Jumpy. Jumpy is deferential to Saladin and invites him to partake in their protests against the incarceration of Uhuru Simba for the series of "Granny Ripper Murders" that have shaken London. Saladin then meets Gibreel again at a party hosted by S. S. Sisodia and begins to take his revenge by arousing Gibreel's mad jealousy. Soon, Saladin drives Gibreel to smash Allie's precious possessions and leave her, which Allie will not forgive. Gibreel comes to believe that he is the angel of destruction, Azraeel, while riots involving Asians and Blacks break out after Uhuru Simba is killed in prison and revealed not to have been the murderer. Jumpy and Pamela die in a fire related to the riots, and Saladin attempts to save the Sufyan family from a fire in the Shaandaar Café but he collapses and is saved instead by Gibreel.

The Parting of the Arabian Sea

In the hospital with Saladin, Gibreel dreams the conclusion of the narrative involving the pilgrimage of Ayesha and the villagers of Titlipur. Mirza Saeed follows the pilgrims in his station wagon, urging them to turn back, but they follow Ayesha despite a number of calamities and walk into the sea. Some say they walked directly into heaven, but the episode is based on the real events of 1983 in which thirty-eight Muslim pilgrims drowned in the Arabian Sea believing that the waters would open for them. Mirza Saeed returns home, where he starves to death.

A Wonderful Lamp

Eighteen months after the fires, Saladin flies home because his father is dying of cancer, and they are reconciled. Saladin inherits his father's fortune and takes up with Reeny Vakil. Meanwhile, Gibreel has begun an unsuccessful comeback tour, making movies of his dreams; he is haunted by his jealousy and Allie's refusal to be reconciled with him. After killing Sisodia and throwing Allie from Everest Vilas, Gibreel shows up in Saladin's father's home, takes a revolver out of Chamcha's magic lamp, and shoots himself.

Characters

Mirza Saeed Akhtar

A zamindar, or land-owner, Mirza Saeed is the descendent of an ancient family who desperately attempts to convince his beloved wife and the other villagers to turn back from her pilgrimage with Ayesha. He feels great lust as well as hate for Ayesha.

Mishal Qureishi Akhtar

Mirza Saeed's wife, Mishal is terminally ill with cancer and convinced that Ayesha is a holy prophet.

Ayesha

Ayesha is the name of four characters. The first mentioned is the empress whom the Imam forces Gibreel to help him destroy in Gibreel's dream. The second is the butterfly-eating would-be prophet from another of Gibreel's dreams. This Ayesha is characterized by her great beauty and the complete and uncompromising certainty of her visions from the angel Gibreel, and she leads her entire town of pilgrims over hundreds of miles and into the Arabian Sea. The third Ayesha is Mahound's young and beautiful wife, who (Salman the Persian implies) was unfaithful to Mahound, and the fourth is the prostitute (and Baal's favorite wife) who takes the name in order to attract customers.

Baal

Baal is the greatest satirist of Jahilia. "A sharp narrow youth" during chapter 2, he writes jeering verses about Mahound at Abu Simbel's command. In chapter 6, however, at fifty years old, Baal experiences "a thickening of the tongue as well as the body" and, after hiding in a brothel and marrying twelve prostitutes who pose as Mahound's wives, he is discovered and executed. His name is associated with a variety of pagan gods in the Hebrew Bible.

Billy Battuta

A "whiz-kid tycoon" who Saladin describes as a "Playboy Pakistani" and a "con-man" who exploits women, Billy invests in re-launching Gibreel's career and gets into trouble with the police in the United States and Britain.

Bilal

Bilal is an "enormous black" slave whom Mahound frees and makes his disciple. Bilal (or Bilal X) is also the name of the American singer and convert to Islam (a parody of the folk star and convert Cat Stevens) who is close to the Imam of Gibreel's dream.

Pimple Billimoria

"The latest chilli-and-spices bombshell," Pimple is Gibreel's co-star before he vanishes from Bombay and during his unsuccessful comeback.

Pamela Lovelace Chamcha

Saladin's wife, Pamela falls out of love with him when he leaves for India, and she takes Jumpy Joshi as a lover when she believes that Saladin has died. Saladin describes her as "frail as porcelain, graceful as gazelles." She has an aristocratic English voice, but she is not actually a stereotypical upper-class English woman at all, having been abandoned by her parents when they committed suicide. She works in community activism and dies along with Jumpy, whose baby she is carrying, in a fire in the Brickhall Community Relations Council building.

Saladin Chamcha

One of the two main characters of Rushdie's novel, Saladin is defined throughout much of the novel by his desire to become entirely English and his association with evil. Called Salahuddin Chamchawala when he was born, Saladin dreams of escaping from his father and their Bombay home throughout his childhood, and he associates all that he dislikes about India with an incident in which an old man forces Saladin to masturbate him. He goes to England to study, resolves to become completely English largely out of resentment towards his father, becomes an actor with an amazing capability for vocal impersonations, and assimilates completely (or so he thinks) into British culture.

Saladin begins to experience an identity crisis, however, during his extramarital affair with Reeny Vakil, and this is one of the explanations behind his estrangement from his English identity and his transformation into the devil. He begins associating with the oppressed groups of Asian and African immigrants to England who are living in London during a time of racial strife. Despite all of his bitterness and anger, Saladin rarely does anything truly evil or demonic, and he grows to have a much more mature understanding of his bifurcated Indian and British identity.

Saladin's relationship with Gibreel is quite complex, despite the fact that it is often referred to as a fight between evil and good. Saladin resents Gibreel because of his effortless luck and because Gibreel abandoned Saladin to the police after their fall from the plane. Eventually, Saladin takes revenge on Gibreel by placing a series of phone calls in which he pretends to be Allie Cone's lovers. Saladin's abbreviated last name, Chamcha, means "spoon" in Hindi, which is why Gibreel calls him "Spoono."

Changez Chamchawala

Saladin's father, Changez is a brilliant and mischievous man who also has a tyrannical and domineering side. Changez's relationship with his son is extremely important to Saladin's development, and it disturbs Saladin deeply that Changez remarries another woman named Nasreen less than a year after his first wife's death, then takes his former maid as a kind of concubine who dresses up as his first wife. Saladin is estranged from his father for much of his adult life, but they are reconciled as Changez is dying of cancer.

Nasreen Chamchawala

"The slightest, most fragile of women" who dresses with "excessive verve," Nasreen is Saladin's mother and Changez's first wife.

Alicja Cone

Alicja is Allie's spirited mother, who frowns upon her relationship with Gibreel and moves to California to marry a professor.

Allie Cone

Allie, short for Alleluia, is a "climber of mountains, vanquisher of Everest, blonde yahudan [Jew], ice queen," and lover of Gibreel. She feels silenced after climbing Everest, as though everything else in her life will be downhill, and she is plagued by painful flat-footedness that will make it impossible to be a mountain climber any longer. Although she loves Gibreel and takes care of him, she cannot stand his extreme jealousy and eventually leaves him. Eventually, Gibreel goes insane and murders her, pushing her to her death from Everest Vilas in Bombay.

Elena Cone

Allie's sister, Elena, is a model and a drug addict who drowns in her bathtub at twenty-one.

Otto Cone

Allie's father is a Polish émigré to England and a survivor of a Nazi death camp. He is a captivating and somewhat quirky art historian who attempts to assimilate entirely into English culture.

Martín de la Cruz

The Argentine Martín is Rosa Diamond's would-be lover.

Henry Diamond

Known as "Don Enrique of Los Alamos" in Argentina, Henry is Rosa's husband.

Rosa Diamond

Rosa is the old woman who finds Gibreel and Saladin after their fall into the English Channel. She sees visions of English history and draws Gibreel into the secret story of her past in Argentina.

Sarpanch Muhammad Din

Sarpanch is the pilgrim of Titlipur who takes Mirza Saeed's side in the station wagon after his wife dies early in the voyage.

Eugene Dumsday

Dumsday is the anti-Darwin creationist who sits next to Saladin on the *Bostan.*

Gibreel Farishta

Born "Ismail Najmuddin" in British Poona, Gibreel moves to Bombay when he is thirteen to work with his father as a food carrier. Babaseheb Mhatre takes Gibreel in after his parents die and arranges for him to work in the movies. Eventually becoming a star in theological movies, Gibreel begins to sleep with many different women, including Rekha Merchant, and rises to enormous fame. He is nearly killed by a bout of seemingly inexplicable internal bleeding, during which he loses his religious faith. After meeting and falling in love with Allie Cone while eating a great deal of pork at a famous Bombay hotel, Gibreel flies to London to find her.

One of Gibreel's definitive characteristics is that he gets away with everything and is entirely effortless in his approach to life, but this is contradicted by his severe episodes of supernatural visions and insanity in the course of the novel. He dislikes England and English culture and has a vicious jealous streak that eventually drives him to insanity and murder. Since Gibreel leaves Bombay within a week of his fortieth birthday, the new life he attempts to start with Allie Cone can be seen as a mid-life crisis of sorts. Gibreel is associated with the Biblical archangel Gabriel and seems to represent the forces of good for much of the novel, but this changes at certain key points, which reveals that good and evil are not clear-cut categories.

Salman Farsi

Salman the Persian is Mahound's disciple until he becomes disillusioned with the prophet and falsely transcribes some of the verses of the Qur'an. He flees from Mahound, but the prophet finds him in Jahilia and allows him to travel to Persia.

Bhupen Gandhi

Bhupen is a sensitive poet and journalist who, along with his friends George Miranda and Reeny Vakil, is an example of a Bombay intellectual.

Girls of the Curtain

The twelve prostitutes of the Curtain brothel take the names of Mahound's wives and marry Baal the poet.

Hamza

Mahound's uncle, Hamza is a renowned warrior who fights for Mahound. Hind butchers him and eats his heart.

Hind

Hind is the "ferocious, beautiful" wife of Abu Simbel of Jahilia. She remains everlastingly young and powerful, devouring men literally as well as sexually. She survives Mahound's conquest of Jahilia.

Imam

The Imam, or Muslim religious leader, from Gibreel's dream narrative is an exile who despises London but is forced to live there until he returns in triumph to a revolution in his homeland. His character is based on the Iranian fundamentalist leader, the Ayatollah Khomeini, who sentenced Rushdie to death.

Hanif Johnson

A "smart lawyer and a local boy made good" who is generally disliked, Hanif maintains an office above the Shaandaar Café. When he learns that he is involved with Mishal, Hind furiously kicks him.

Jumpy Joshi

Jumpy is Saladin's friend who feels extremely guilty about his ongoing affair with Saladin's wife. Although his real name is Jamshed, he is known as Jumpy because of his "enormous capacity for nervous agitation," his thinning hair, and his unique giggle. He is a martial arts instructor.

Kasturba

Saladin's caretaker when he was young, Kasturba begins to act and dress as Changez Chamchawala's late wife Nasreen at some point after Changez's remarriage.

Khalid

Water-carrier of Jahilia and disciple of Mahound, Khalid becomes a general in Mahound's armies.

Inspector Stephen Kinch

Inspector Kinch is a corrupt police officer involved in the death of Uhuru Simba.

Madam of the Curtain

A nameless madam who runs the brothel in Jahilia.

Mahound

Mahound is a long-disused European term for Mahomet or Muhammad, the founder of Islam and the final, most important prophet of God in the Islamic faith. Said to be a merchant who was born in Mecca, Muhammad claimed to have been visited by the Archangel Gabriel and told to memorize the verses that became the Islamic Qur'an. In 622, he was forced to flee from Mecca to Medina, both cities in Northern Arabia, but eventually his armies conquered Mecca and the other pagan tribes of Arabia.

Mahound appears in chapters 2 and 6 of Rushdie's novel, which are versions of the religious history of Mecca, known in the book as Jahilia, which is an Islamic term for the ignorance of God's message. The novel implies (very controversially) that Mahound manufactures the messages of Gibreel to suit his temperament and desires, and that Mahound was a jealous man who disliked women.

Mimi Mamoulian

Saladin's Jewish costar on British television and radio, Mimi has a wide range of impersonations. She becomes involved with Billy Battuta despite Saladin's warning that he will exploit her, and she spends some time in jail for participating in one of his con-artist schemes.

John Maslama

Owner of the Hot Wax nightclub, Mr. Maslama meets Gibreel on the train to London and believes that Gibreel is the archangel of God.

Rekha Merchant

Gibreel's most serious lover in Bombay, Rekha appears to him after her suicide as a vision on a flying rug. Gibreel continually returns to her because, unlike his other lovers, she both abuses him and consoles him, which Gibreel cannot resist. She is married to a man summed up by the narrator as "a mouse with money and a good squash wrist," and she has three children whom she throws to their deaths, along with herself, as a result of Gibreel's departure to London. Gibreel finally makes her apparition disappear by telling her that there is no God but God.

Babasaheb Mhatre

Grand Secretary of the Bombay Tiffin Carriers' Association, the Babasaheb takes the orphaned Gibreel into his home and arranges for him to be in the movies.

George Miranda

A fat, "young Marxist film-maker" with a waxed mustache, George is Reeny's friend. He hates the "disembodied, invisible" power of America and knows all of the Bombay film gossip.

Nasreen II

Changez's second wife has the same name as his first, as well as the same "birdlike" body type.

Ooparvala

Ooparvala (God), who may also be Neechayvala (Satan), appears to Gibreel and tells him to get back to work as an angel.

Osman

A Hindu convert to Islam, Osman earns his living as a clown and is in love with Ayesha.

Sherpa Pemba

Pemba is Allie's friend and fellow-climber. They climbed Everest together and reached the peak without oxygen tanks.

Hyacinth Phillips

Hyacinth is Saladin's physiotherapist in the hospital. She escapes with him and the other monsters but then changes shape inside a church and attacks him along with a number of similar creatures.

Pinkwalla

Pinkwalla is the D. J. at the Hot Wax nightclub.

Mr. Qureishi

Mishal Akhtar's father, Mr. Qureishi is a rich banker who finds his daughter and wife on their pilgrimage and tells them to abandon it.

Mrs. Qureishi

Mishal's mother, Mrs. Qureishi undertakes the pilgrimage, but eventually comes to Mirza Saeed's side and attempts to dissuade her daughter from continuing.

Dr. Uhuru Simba

Formerly Sylvester Roberts, Uhuru is the black activist leader who is falsely accused of committing the serial "Granny Ripper Murders." He is murdered in jail, presumably by the police.

Karim Abu Simbel

Abu Simbel is the Grandee of Jahilia until he surrenders his city to Mahound. A tall man in white robes whose "gait contains the lilt, the deadly elegance of power," he forces Mahound to flee the city. The crisis in Jahilia strips Abu Simbel of his grandiloquence and, in chapter 6, he has grown into a "soft and pursy old age."

S. S. Sisodia

Sisodia is the rich and enigmatic Indian film producer who speaks with a stutter.

Aurora del Sol

Aurora is Martín de la Cruz's jealous fiancé.

Sri Srinivas

Srinivas is the Brahmin toy-maker who accompanies Ayesha and Mirza Saeed on the pilgrimage.

Anahita Sufyan

Anahita is Mishal Sufyan's slightly jealous younger sister.

Hind Sufyan

Sufyan's bitter wife, Hind despises England and blames her husband for all of her problems. She is the cook and money-maker at the Shaandaar Café and Bed & Breakfast.

Mishal Sufyan

Mishal is the Sufyans' attractive teenage daughter who falls out with her mother and marries Hanif Johnson. She is the best student in Jumpy's martial arts class.

Muhammad Sufyan

The mild and kind-tempered owner of the Shaandaar Café, Sufyan is devastated when he discovers that his wife has been overcharging the immigrants he thought he was helping.

Tavleen

Tavleen is the chief hijacker of the *Bostan*. She speaks with a Canadian accent and blows up the plane.

Zeeny Vakil

Zeeny is the exciting and attractive dark-skinned Indian woman involved with Saladin. They met when they were teenagers, when Zeeny was a "rash, bad girl," and she retains a streak of craziness in her adult life. She is a doctor who works in a hospital and with the homeless as well as an art critic and Bombay socialite, and she has made it her project to return Saladin to his Indian roots.

Hal Valance

Hal is Saladin's bigoted, rude, and greedy producer who cuts him out of *The Aliens Show* because he believes the market for ethnic actors is shrinking.

Vallabh

Vallabh is Changez Chamchawala's old and faithful servant.

Maurice Wilson

The ghost who haunts Allie, Maurice Wilson is the yogi (practitioner of yoga) who died on Mount Everest while attempting a solo ascent.

Themes

Good and Evil

The Satanic Verses touches on a great variety of political, cultural, abstract, and theoretical themes. Many of its most central ideas relate to philosophical and religious notions of good and evil. The narrator tends to view the plot as an epic battle between Gibreel, the angel of good, and Saladin, the devil of evil. Rushdie reinforces this framework by giving these characters their supernatural qualities.

Good and evil in the epic battle between Gibreel and Saladin often refer to two main areas:

national/ethnic identity and religious faith. Gibreel's status as an angel is closely related to his crisis of faith, and his transformation begins shortly after he develops the conviction that God does not exist. Meanwhile, Saladin's metamorphosis into the devil is inextricable from his quest to assimilate entirely into British culture and his association with oppressed Asian and African immigrants in England. Like the other magically deformed creatures who escape from the hospital, Saladin assumes his devilish shape because English racism has transformed him with its "power of description." Why exactly Gibreel embodies good, while Saladin embodies evil, is never made entirely or explicitly clear, and as the reader rapidly becomes aware, notions of good and evil are hopelessly jumbled by the end of the first chapter.

Countless other situations also take the form of a fight, or confrontation, between good and evil ideas, labeled as such for a variety of reasons including religious faith, political persuasions, racial identities, and positions of power. In Gibreel's dream world (where prophets battle non-believers, pagans and poets), in the volatile political context of 1980s London (where immigrants are demonized, oppressed, and harassed), and in the lives of the many supporting characters (in which, for example, lovers such as Allie and Pamela are variously idealized and degraded), there is often an interplay and battle between notions of good and evil, or of the demonic and the angelic. In all of these situations, the novel strongly suggests that good and evil are rather confusing and shifting categories. At various points, Rushdie seems to be implying that good and evil are nothing more than man-made notions defined and based on what is most convenient for the group or person in the position to judge.

Racial and Cultural Identity

Rushdie's exploration of race, culture, history, ethnicity, and nationality takes many forms. One of the ways in which this commentary is most apparent is in the identity crises of several of the novel's main characters. Before the plane crash, Saladin is initially defined by his desire to assimilate entirely into British culture. Gibreel, on the other hand, seems to feel entirely comfortable and complete in his Indian identity and persona, while disliking and insulting British culture and identity. Both characters change markedly in the course of the novel as they find that their identities are split between two worlds and cultures. Gibreel's ultimate madness and death can be attributed in large part to his

Topics For Further Study

- Research the events following the publication of *The Satanic Verses*. Then, discuss some of the things the episode reveals about the various communities involved (such as fundamentalist Islamic groups, the Western and Indian governments, the news media, and the international community of authors) and the attitudes of each of these groups towards literature.

- Examine the many magical and fantastical elements of Rushdie's novel. Why do Gibreel and Saladin assume supernatural qualities? How does the magic in the novel relate to its main themes? Choose one magical motif in particular, such as Gibreel's angelic qualities or the appearance of God/Satan in the novel, and discuss how this motif is important to the meaning of the work as a whole.

- *The Satanic Verses* contains numerous allusions to political and cultural events and situations in England. In what ways is Rushdie a political novelist? How does he approach political themes, and what angle does he take? How does he go about evoking the cultural atmosphere of London, and what is his perspective? Examine his treatment of the condition of immigrants to the United Kingdom, and discuss the main points he is trying to make about English culture and politics.

- Research why sections of the novel were offensive to Muslims, namely the chapters "Mahound" and "Return to Jahilia." What aspects of these chapters were particularly offensive? Why are they considered blasphemous? Discuss the function of these chapters within the meaning of the novel and why you think Rushdie included them.

---

inability to reconcile his love for Allie (characterized by paleness, whiteness, and Englishness) with his Indian race, nationality, history, and culture.

Rushdie is particularly concerned with the situation of immigrants to Great Britain, and many of the major characters go through a difficult process of acceptance and assimilation into English society. In fact, the plot of the novel can be seen as a metaphor for the British immigration experience, as though each immigrant, particularly those that are Indian, must endure a journey like that of Gibreel and Saladin. Rushdie considers how the experience of voice- and personality-shifting immigrants like Saladin is different from that of somewhat more uncompromising and unchanging immigrants like Gibreel.

Both types of immigrants find themselves confronting a brutal and oppressive system of authority in Britain. Racism is rampant among white English characters, particularly the police, who are extremely violent and unjust towards Asians and Africans. Rushdie, therefore, comments not just on abstract and philosophical questions about identity; he considers in depth the actual situation of groups

of people trying to negotiate their place in a difficult and racist society. He also offers a glimpse of the ways in which identity is also complex and difficult to negotiate amongst Bombay intellectuals such as Reeny and her friends, who find that foreign cultures strongly impact their beliefs and their understandings of themselves.

Islam

The aspects of the novel that some consider inflammatory and controversial are all related to its allusions to, and commentary about, the religion of Islam. Rushdie implies that the Qur'an, like many human achievements, was formed as a result of human history and human fallibility. He also refers to elements of Muslim history, such as Muhammad's multiple wives, in a manner that criticizes the conventional treatment of women in Muslim society, and can be construed as satirical of the prophet. Rushdie's treatment of Islam is an important theme that is not as simple as a condemnation or satire, however. He makes lengthy allusions to Islamic beliefs and traditions not simply to convey his opinions about the negative, hypocritical, or absurd aspects about the religion, but to explore, for example, his commentary on good and evil in another context.

it relates to Rushdie's commentary on religion, and good and evil.

Style

Magic Realism

The literary device of "magic realism," or the use of supernatural elements within an otherwise realistic narrative, is one of the most important stylistic aspects of *The Satanic Verses*. Gibreel's transformation into an angel, and Saladin's into a goat-man/devil, are examples of this device, as are other impossible or magical events such as Rekha's appearance on a flying carpet and Gibreel's trumpet of fire.

Magic realism, which is popular among Latin American postmodern writers such as Gabriel García Márquez, is useful in several main ways. First, it allows the author great flexibility in elaborating on the meaning of the story; by imbuing Gibreel and Saladin with magical characteristics, for example, Rushdie is able to emphasize much more directly and physically how and why they are connected to ideas of good and evil. Also, magic realism is a useful authorial technique for challenging the reader's assumptions and encouraging him/her to think about the themes of the work in a new and different way. Finally, the use of supernatural occurrences can make a work appear to take the form of an epic tale, since classic and religious epics often include supernatural events and deities. Because it challenges its readers' understandings of conventional reality, and because it seems to read like a classic or religious text, *The Satanic Verses* is able to more convincingly address ambitious themes such as human truth, religion, and history.

Narrative Voice

The majority of *The Satanic Verses* is written from an omniscient, third-person narrative perspective, which means that the narrator describes the events of the novel from an all-knowing, external standpoint. In chapter 7, over four hundred pages into the novel, the narrator makes a first, mysterious appearance in the first person. Asking the reader not to ask him/her to "clear things up," the narrator says that he/she previously appeared to Gibreel, meaning that the narrator is Ooparvala (God), Neechayvala (the devil), or both. This mysterious and interesting detail (and joke) implies that God has control over the narrative of the novel, and

Historical Context

Britain in the 1980s

Rushdie was living in London when he wrote *The Satanic Verses*, and 1980s London is also the main historical context of the novel. Throughout the 1980s, the conservative Margaret Thatcher was prime minister of England. Known for her policies of reducing government spending on everything except defense, as well as privatizing government-controlled industries, Thatcher was ideologically akin to the American President Ronald Reagan.

The early 1980s in England were marked by rising unemployment, but Thatcher's government remained popular and won the 1983 election largely because of Britain's involvement in the Falklands War. Argentina, which had long claimed ownership over the British territorial islands on its shores, sent forces to the island in 1982, and Thatcher responded by sending a British naval task force that defeated the Argentines.

After the 1983 election, Thatcher presided uncompromisingly over a series of domestic disturbances beginning with the Miner's Strike of 1984–85. Because the government announced that it was closing twenty large mines, and because unions were concerned about Thatcher's actions to reduce their power, the unsuccessful strike began and went on for nearly a year amidst police violence and intimidation. Meanwhile, in the fall of 1985, a series of confrontations between white police officers and predominantly black youths began in London and Birmingham. Two possible causes of these violent confrontations were the difficult economic circumstances, and the conservatism and intolerance of the British government.

India in the 1980s

The party of Prime Minister Indira Gandhi, daughter of Jawaharlal Nehru (the first prime minister of independent India), was elected back into power in 1980. Gandhi had a series of key meetings with foreign leaders, while dealing with several insurgencies in India. She was assassinated by her own Sikh bodyguards in 1984 because of her previous decision to storm a sacred Sikh temple in Punjab that was being held by insurgents. Also in 1984, the infamous industrial disaster occurred in Bhopal, India, when the Union Carbide pesticide

Compare
&
Contrast

- **1980s:** Margaret Thatcher, known for her inflexible, conservative beliefs, is prime minister of Britain.

  Today: Tony Blair, the leader of the Labor Party who pioneered the "New Labor" movement, embracing a degree of privatization, has been the British prime minister since 1997.

- **1980s:** Militant Islamic fundamentalism is gathering force in the Arab world. The United States government is providing arms and training to Osama bin Laden and his group of Muslim fighters in the Afghan War against the Union of Soviet Socialist Republics.

  Today: Since the terrorist attacks of September 11, 2001, Western countries have adopted new attitudes towards foreign policy, partly to attempt to address Islamic fundamentalist terrorist organizations.

- **1980s:** Jim Henson's Muppets, which satirize politicians and celebrities, are trendy and popular in the Western entertainment world. Bombay's "Bollywood" film scene has an enormous number of devoted viewers in India.

  Today: Animated satires like *The Simpsons* are one of the most popular forms of television entertainment in Britain and the United States. Although Western entertainment is more accessible in India than it was twenty years ago, Bollywood continues to be extremely popular.

- **1980s:** Salman Rushdie goes into hiding after the Iranian fatwa condemns him to death.

  Today: Publicly "pardoned" by the Iranian government, Rushdie lives openly and attends many public events, although he does continue to employ bodyguards.

plant located near the city leaked toxic gas that killed thousands of people and injured hundreds of thousands.

The Satanic Verses

Rushdie's novel is brimming with allusions to historical and contemporary events, philosophies, and people, but perhaps the most important extended reference in the novel is to several verses that Satan allegedly tricked Muhammad into including in the Qur'an, and which Muhammed later expunged from the Islamic holy text. The main source for the controversial story, which is rejected by nearly all major Muslim scholars, is the biography of Muhammad by the Arabian historian Ibn Ishaq, written 120–130 years after the prophet's death. Now available only in a heavily revised version, the biography claims that Muhammad included verses of revelation that accepted the divinity of three pagan goddesses of Mecca. Gratified, Meccans ceased their persecution of the prophet until the Angel Gabriel appeared to Muhammad and instructed him that the verses were

profane. Muhammad took back his words, claiming they were inspired by Satan, and instructed his scribes (Muhammad is said to have been unable to read or write) to remove the verses from the Qur'an. The incident is so sensitive amongst Muslims because the belief that the Qur'an is an infallible transcription of God's word is at the heart of the religion.

Critical Overview

An enormous amount has been written about Rushdie's extremely controversial novel, although only a segment of the reaction to *The Satanic Verses* and its effects around the world involves any literary analysis of the work. Writings about the novel can be roughly separated into several main categories, the first being its prominent place in the news media. Newspapers such as the *Los Angeles Times* carried the story of the controversy on the front page and quoted Khomeini's original fatwa (in "Khomeini Says Author of '*Satanic Verses*' Should Be Killed," by Charles P. Wallace and Dan Fisher): "I inform the proud Muslim people of the world that the author of '*The Satanic Verses*,' a book which is against Islam, the prophet and the Koran, and all those involved in its publication who were aware of its content, are hereby sentenced to death."

Rushdie's novel has been widely denounced and condemned by Muslims who consider it blasphemous. The most influential of these condemnations was that of Khomeini, but numerous other Muslim scholars and leaders condemned the novel and its author. In their 1989 anthology *The Rushdie File*, Lisa Appignanesi and Sara Maitland collect the most important writings and speeches by both sides of the debate about *The Satanic Verses*. Another category of writings about the novel is that of the historians and cultural theorists that have taken Rushdie's novel as their subject, using the events surrounding its publication to explore relations between Islam and the West, and to explore as well postcolonial politics and intercultural attitudes.

The final category of writings about *The Satanic Verses* involves critical analysis of the literary content of the novel, although this style of writing was initially overshadowed by the furor following the book's publication. In the fall of 1988, the novel received the Whitbread Prize for the best novel in England that year, and some critics lauded the book's literary merits. In his 1988 review for *London Review of Books*, Patrick Parrinder writes that the book is "damnably entertaining, and fiendishly ingenious." American newspapers and magazines such as *The New York Times* printed mixed reviews, however, and some critics criticized Rushdie for his indirectness and incomprehensibility. However, *The Satanic Verses* is generally considered a key novel in Rushdie's oeuvre, and many literary critics have written at length about its theological, philosophical, political, and cultural meanings.

Criticism

Scott Trudell

Trudell is an independent scholar with a bachelor's degree in English literature. In the following essay, Trudell discusses Rushdie's commentary on Islam in The Satanic Verses.

The fatwa ordering Muslims around the world to murder Rushdie and his collaborators has

Ayatollah Khomeini, leader of the Islamic Revolution in Iran, greets followers in Tehran in February 1979 © Bettmann/Corbis

irrevocably affected how Western readers approach the novel. Because of the dangerous and sensitive political context, many Western critics have downplayed the work's direct engagement with the Islamic religion so as not to seem to be giving credence to the Islamic fundamentalist outcry against it. Rushdie himself, in a series of understandable attempts to save his own life, claimed to the press that his novel should not be seen as insulting Islam. At one point, he even went so far as to embrace the central tenets of the religion, although he later rescinded this position.

The fact is that the novel's commentary on Islam is at the center of its thematic agenda. *The Satanic Verses* is, first and foremost, about how humans develop and practice notions of good and evil, and, specifically, how these notions are determined by religion. Islam is the religion that Rushdie uses to explore these universal themes and, in the process, he makes a number of specific and satirical criticisms about common Muslim practices, including the typical treatment of Muslim women, the connection between Islamic fundamentalism and violence, and the persecution of writers in the name of Islam. Tracing all of these topical themes back to their historical and ideological origins, Rushdie

"

To Rushdie, therefore, the moral system of Islam is nothing more than an extremely effective method by which individuals and groups gain absolute power and authority without the need to justify themselves rationally."

provides a substantial criticism of the tenets and contemporary practices of the religion.

This commentary begins explicitly, as "The Angel Gibreel" and Saladin fall from the heavens "To be born again," a clear and common metaphor for spiritual rebirth. Rushdie's references to religion then remain explicit and evident throughout the novel, as Gibreel transforms physically into an angel and experiences extended dreams about Muslim prophets, while Saladin becomes a goat man imbued with the features of the devil. Their epic battle, which eventually comes in the form of Saladin haunting Gibreel with the "satanic verses" of prank phone calls that make him, like the prophet Mahound, fiercely jealous, is portrayed in terms of a fight between good and evil.

What good and evil actually entail, and whether Saladin and Gibreel can be said to conform to these notions has become indistinguishably complex by the time of final confrontations. Gibreel is depressed, schizophrenic, plagued by doubt, and when he does believe he is the angel of God his actions are often not just insane but destructive, as when he blows fire on London through his magic trumpet. Saladin, meanwhile, is revealed to be not so much an evil monster as a sympathetic victim of an identity crisis whose career, wife, and respectability are suddenly taken from him. His only act that can be considered "evil" is his revenge on Gibreel, and the terrible results of the prank phone calls are mainly a result of Gibreel's own consuming jealousy.

In fact, nowhere in the novel is the meaning of good and evil entirely clear, and the sacred is very often closely associated with or mistaken for the profane. Gibreel becomes the angel of God immediately after he has lost his faith and stuffed himself with pork, Ayesha the prophet stones a baby and then leads her followers to a watery death, Mahound's wives are doubled in the brothel of Jahilia, and holy Imam of Desh, a parody of the Ayatollah Khomeini of Iran, is a bitter and "monstrous" figure fueled by hate and shown swallowing his people whole. Rushdie establishes with examples such as these that holy is by no means good and profane is by no means evil. The chapters about Mahound suggest explicitly that the Qur'an is by no means the infallible word of God and that good and evil are, in fact, entirely human constructions.

A skeptic who dismisses the idea that the sacred and religious are morally good, Rushdie suggests that the chief prophet of Islam is much like a poet, which is perhaps why Mahound feels so threatened by Baal. *The Satanic Verses* suggests that the monotheistic, absolutist text of Islam is a fiction of verses just like that of Baal's. Its only essential difference is paraphrased early in the novel by the Islamic terrorist Tavleen: "History asks us: what manner of cause are we? Are we uncompromising, absolute, strong, or will we show ourselves to be timeservers, who compromise, trim and yield?" In other words, the difference between the cause of art and literature and cause of the Islamic faith is not that one was inspired by God via the Angel Gabriel. Rather, the Qur'an is different from the words of a shape-shifting, multi-voiced and flexible poet only in that it claims to rigidly pin down exactly what is good and evil, for all time.

Indeed, the narratives from Gibreel's dream cycle establish that religious "good" and "evil" are simply categories that Mahound, Ayesha, and the Imam of Desh define based on what is most expedient for their personal desires. Since Gibreel has no answers from God, who appears as a combination God/Satan figure to clarify that there is no distinction between Al-la and Al-lat, it is clear that these devout figures have produced their certainties for themselves. Mahound (like Ayesha and the Imam of Desh) manufactures his timeless transcription of the will of God entirely from his own head, and he does so in order to impose his own ideas of authority and uncompromising power upon the world.

It is because of this absolutism that Islam, to Rushdie, produces so many evils. Inflexible ideology is responsible for most of the evils in the novel, from the destructive religious impulses of Mahound, Ayesha, and the Imam, to the brutal and inflexible immigration policies of Margaret "the Iron Lady" Thatcher's Britain. The inability of the British police to understand or accept diversity, as well as the harshly bigoted ideology of Britons like Hal Valance, is the true cause of the violence and mayhem in London, as well as the fact that immigrants are transformed into monsters by the "power of description."

Rushdie's most fluent and specific condemnation of absolutism, however, remains in the context of Islam. One of the most important explications of the author's attitude towards the religion comes during Salman Farsi's conversations with Baal in which he condemns Mahound and the Qur'an. Salman (it is no coincidence that he shares his name with Rushdie) begins by ridiculing the many extremely specific and businesslike aspects of the Qur'an that make him suspect that Mahound is simply conjuring up the verses himself. He then traces the fact that the Qur'an gives men the right to have multiple wives back to Mahound's desire to convert the widows of Jahilia, and the common Islamic practice for men to dominate women, to Mahound's bitterness at the women of Yahtrib (Medina).

This section is not merely a criticism of certain specific Islamic traditions; it is an attack at the entire premise of the moral authority of a religious text such as the Qur'an. Rushdie's implicit argument is that uncompromising, faith-based morality is extremely dangerous because it does not need to answer to any rational critique and is easily crafted to suit one all-powerful authority. This criticism could apply, by extension, to religions such as Christianity and Judaism, but the analogy is less perfect because the belief that the holy text is a direct transcription of God's will is uniquely important to Islam.

To Rushdie, therefore, the moral system of Islam is nothing more than an extremely effective method by which individuals and groups gain absolute power and authority without the need to justify themselves rationally. Poets, scribes, and shape-shifting actors like Baal, Salman Farsi, and Saladin are contemptible to Islam, and therefore demonized, because they are constantly quibbling, satirizing, and questioning this moral tyranny. They are flexible and adaptable, and their ideas are similar to the "Satanic Verses" that Mahound originally included in the Qur'an because they make space for a variety of authority figures and power systems. Absolutism, both in politics and in morality, is the antithesis of their value system.

Similarly, Rushdie's *The Satanic Verses* is in direct confrontation with the moral foundation of

What Do I Read Next?

- *Midnight's Children* (1981) is Rushdie's compelling novel about Indian history and identity. Focusing on the story of Saleem Sinai, who was born at the moment of Indian independence, the work includes elements of magic realism and alludes to classic texts, including the Christian Bible and *Arabian Nights*.

- Nicholas Mosley's *Hopeful Monsters* (1990), winner of the Whitbread Prize in 1991, is the story of two European intellectuals and their journey around the world as they become involved in the scientific, political, and religious controversies of the era.

- Rushdie's *Imaginary Homelands: Essays and Criticism, 1981–1991* (1992) is a collection of seventy-five articles ranging from political to religious to artistic subjects, and it includes two of Rushdie's key articles in response to the circumstances following his publication of *The Satanic Verses*.

- Rudyard Kipling's *Kim* (1901) is the classic colonial British novel about the orphaned Kim O'Hara and his experience growing up in India.

the Islamic religion, and is so offensive to it, because it questions, satirizes, and ridicules Islam's absolutist moral code. In a way, the extreme and fanatical reaction to the novel on the part of many Muslims including the Ayatollah Khomeini, an extremely powerful and influential religious leader with great authority, proves that a strong current of absolutism continues in many interpretations of the Islamic tradition. Indeed, Khomeini and the other Muslim fundamentalists who denounced the novel and demanded Rushdie's death, proved not just that their moral systems are tyrannical and absolutist, but that an author, whether or not he/she claims to be a prophet of God, has the power to shake the world with a pen.

Source: Scott Trudell, Critical Essay on *The Satanic Verses*, in *Novels for Students*, Thomson Gale, 2006.

Jacqueline Bardolph

In the following essay excerpt, Bardolph explores how The Satanic Verses *"in its depiction of the characters as they grapple with language—conception, speech, writing—embodies a form of courage."*

To name the unnamable, point at frauds, to take sides, start arguments, shape the world and stop it from going to sleep." This passage from *The Satanic Verses* has been quoted as a defence of the right and duty of the artist. But the context takes it away from this romantic and irresponsible attitude. It goes on: "And if rivers of blood flow from the cuts his verses inflict, then they will nourish him." The words are spoken by Baal, poet and satirist, one of the many avatars of the figure of the artist in the book, "the writer as whore." This can be used as a preliminary warning before any study of this polyphonic novel: not one sentence out of the multiplicity of voices or statements can be used in isolation, extracted from the whole. "Language is courage: the ability to conceive a thought, to speak it, and by doing so to make it true." Like the preceding statement this is both true and false within the text, being the vision of Jumpi Joshi, a little-known poet and martial arts instructor who may suffer from another type of delusion: the writer as *guerrillero,* writing from "the barrel of a pen."

Yet, given the novel itself and the unforeseen consequences of its publication, as it came to the attention of people who in the normal course of things would never have been its readers, this proud pronouncement will help to give an outline of one of the possible approaches to this major book.

"The ability to conceive a thought, to speak it," says Joshi, who is a poet; I would add a third element—"to write it." Like Rushdie's previous novels, *The Satanic Verses* has among its major topics language and artistic creation, in a way that connects modern metafictional themes with the condition of the exile and immigrant (Rushdie, who has three countries, like his hero Omar Khayyam's three mothers, has given *Midnight's Children* to India, *Shame* to Pakistan, and this third book in the trilogy to the Britain of the immigrant). Among the many avatars of the writer or artist in *The Satanic Verses*—in fact, it can be claimed that most of the male characters are so many facets of his vision, like the myriad facets of a fly's eyes—a coherent team takes prominent place: the central figure is the prophet, the one who "proffers," the voice in the desert, or his profane negative, Mahound. Before the voice must come inspiration: this is Gibreel, the angel Gabriel, creating visions of an uncertain nature—are they, for instance, the truth about the one God, or satanically inspired visions about three unholy goddesses? And modestly, at the end of the production-line, sits Salman the Persian, the "myopic scrivener," an essential cog in the wheel transferring the voice to the Book, not wholly responsible for its content, maybe even guilty of transforming a sacred vision into a "Book of Rules" (when and how to eat, wash, marry, defecate . . .).

I shall explore briefly how the book, in its depiction of the characters as they grapple with language—conception, speech, writing—embodies a form of courage.

The most obvious one is also central: the ability to speak. Particularly in societies, past or present, with a strong oral culture, the act of utterance has always had something sacred about it, and is potentially fraught with danger—to which can be added linguistic uncertainty. Like most writers from the Commonwealth who write outside an implicit language-norm, Rushdie is aware of the richness and perils of this *métis* situation. In *Midnight's Children,* he could represent the head-on collision of different cultures in the two language-marches which clash in Bombay and start a language-war. Other writers, in Africa for instance, have tried in various ways to come to terms with the representation and expression of linguistic plurality when dealing with well-defined cultures. *The Satanic Verses* chooses to speak from the point of view of the immigrant in Britain, or anywhere, where it is no longer possible to set up clear-cut identities in opposition. "This approach enables Rushdie to enter into and tease out with great clarity and vividness the structure and inner dynamics of the immigrant's everyday life, including racism, self-alienation, the joys and tortures of harbouring several selves, and the fantasized reality in which he is forced to live." Rushdie has now joined other writers who grope for expression as they give voice in a single work to a whole range of varieties of English: one thinks of Selvon, of Desani's *H. Hatterr,* or of Wendt's narrative personae, all with an attentive ear to a wide range of spoken idioms, none of which claims to be a norm.

The Satanic Verses, like a radio play, provides a varied collection of modern British usages, each with its distinctive flavour and rhythm. Brought up in a tradition of oral storytelling, Rushdie recalls the pleasure of mimicry, born of variety, but also shows a new language taking shape. For the novel is not a collection of documents centred on a central "RP" voice: the whole narrative shares this chaotic multiplicity, more so than *Midnight's Children* or *Shame,* where, after all, other languages were represented through the medium of English. Here is the true challenge of the immigrant: he has no mother-tongue left, "'An Indian translated into English-medium. When I attempt Hindustani these days, people look polite.'" He will have to make do with the unstable forms born of multicultural contact, and make them work for him. The dialogue and the narrative are extremely varied in scope: suburban Indian English, Bombay's mixture of Colonial and Americanese, London West Indian or African, new-generation Asian English, mid-Atlantic show-biz jargon—they all coexist in the pages and merge with the narrative voice.

The primary risk in being so close to specific dialectal variations in their own time and space is the loss of universal relevance. Babylondon is alive in these pages, for those of us who have heard at least some of these varieties; but what of other readers, elsewhere, in years to come? What about translation? This irritating factor is one way of stating the predicament of the exile. It is embodied in Saladin, one of the two major characters, a radio actor with chameleon voices, "the Man of a Thousand Voices and a Voice." He is the image of the artist as impersonator, or liar, a mere trickster, taken over by his text.

But artist and migrant are one in their plight: they have so many voices that they have lost their own. Where is the central identity connected with the physical memory of the first cry, breathing, the mother tongue? Saladin in mid-flight between India and England can feel his vocal chords readjusting to a new accent, a new rhythm. If language is identity, the simple shaping of the mouth and throat around a consonant can make of you an alien, a potential traitor, as Nuruddin Farah has shown in *Maps* in the case of Misra. *Grimus,* Rushdie's first novel, was already expressing the circular torture represented by this protean gift, this "polyglot frenzy":

A man rehearsing voices on a cliff top: high whining voices, low gravelly voices, subtle insinuating voices, raucous strident voices, voices honeyed with pain, voices glinting with laughter, the voices of the birds and of the fishes. He asked the man what he was doing (as he sailed by). The man called back—and each word was the word of a different being:—I am looking for a suitable voice to speak in. As he called, he leaned forward, lost his balance and fell. The cry was in a single voice; but the rocks on the shore cut it and shredded it for him again.

> *The Satanic Verses,* like a radio play, provides a varied collection of modern British usages, each with its distinctive flavour and rhythm."

Is pain the only possible unifying factor? The comfort of nostalgia or return is not available to the exile, who can no longer idealize the tolerant pluralism of the Bombay of his youth: it cannot be retrieved from the past before Independence or Partition. The babble of voices of the seven hundred children of midnight is at first an exhilarating sound, their very diversity a promise. As the child hero grows, "the miracles inside his head," when the Midnight's Children Conference took place in his brain through telepathy, turn into a nightmare. After the paranoid over-confidence of the child, Saleem finds it impossible to control the discordant voices. Multiplicity in that novel is at first a source of wonder but turns at the end into a threat, the menace of annihilation. "only a broken creature spilling pieces of itself into the street, because I have been so-many too-many persons." It demands courage to go on speaking in a polyphonic manner, while looking for the one voice: the suffering involved is well represented in *Grimus,* with its reference to the mystical Sufi quest for the One, based on 'Attâr's *Conference of the Birds.*

Maybe the voice which fears fragmentation, the biblical curse of division, as it strives to speak for Babylondon can trace its trouble to the source. The voice of the prophet singles him out and makes him an obvious target; but is he really the originary utterer of the message? Isn't he merely the messenger, who exposes himself by clamouring what God's go-between, the angel Gabriel, has whispered in his ear or shown to him in a dream? Gibreel Farishta, an Indian film-actor who can no longer impersonate Hindu deities on Bombay screens, is afraid to sleep because in his dreams he is Gabriel and as such participates in three long stories which are the major subplots of the novel, the best-known one being connected with the dictation of Satanic verses to Mahound. The three parables explore the same question: is inspiration good or evil—to be trusted, dismissed, or examined in the sceptical light of reason? Are the protagonists of the three stories—Ayesha the prophetess, Mahound, Desh the Imam—receiving a divine message or projecting their own dreams and desires in the reading of the dreams? And what if Gabriel himself is delivering messages after he has lost his faith?

All of the elements which revolve around this central question represent another way in which language is courage: the courage to conceive certain thoughts, the courage of the imagination. Daniel Sibony, a psychoanalyst writing about the Rushdie affair, claims for the artist the right to fantasize, "le droit au fantasme." It is a right which has its own dangers, even before public utterance and writing. The artist who explores such areas on the border of the unconscious runs risks. If he must feel free, he is bound to transgress even against his own norms merely by conceiving certain topics and giving them shape. Rushdie is once more handling dangerous material: in previous books he dealt with the brother-sister bond and the dark mother; here he explores the various figures of the mother as whore, the connection with Islam, sex, death, and the sacred. The awesome links are forged in an intrepid manner—which has hurt many, as it has hurt him. A fantasy, given free rein, knows no respect or reverence. What is most sacred can become burlesque; mundane characters can be inflated to mythic proportions. God can be equated with the photo on the back cover (*Verses* 318). In such a family romance, the affectionate and querulous invective of the son against his father can be voiced to Abraham in plain English "[Ibraham,] the bastard. . . ."

The novel has the courage to keep to the logic of the oneiric vision, bringing to light raw materials which have the coherence of dreams, in which characters merge into one another, in a chain of metamorphosis to which the key is not always provided. The punning language of the unconscious establishes a connection between Allah, the dark goddess Al-Lat, and the blond Allelluiah Cone or Allie, who is close to Ayesha (prophetess, or wife, of the Prophet; or empress; or chief whore). And Allah/Al-Lat connects with the problem of evil—Atallah, Othello, the mystery of "motiveless malignity." There is a risk in exposing in words a vision so highly charged with explosive material, without being sure whether they are god-sent revelations or inane trifles. The reader can identify with the puzzlement of "the dreamer who knows he dreams," and yet is deeply disturbed by the emotional impact of such mental images. When can one be sure the cosmic vision is not just a narcissistic projection? Or even the projection of other people's

dreams and desires, which the angel-poet, sponge-like, has absorbed? (It is here we find the relevance of the introductory fable about Rosa Diamond.)

Having gone "au fond de l'inconnu pour trouver du nouveau," the artist can discover very dark visions. They may refuse to fit nicely with the rational political views of the writer—as, for instance, in the scene in the Hot Wax Night Club, when Maggie Torture is burnt in effigy and melts to a puddle: the images of racial or class hatred clash with the sane proposals for racial harmony in explicit statements. *The Satanic Verses* lends great significance to a dark figure which recurs from book to book—obtrusive, ambivalent, difficult to account for: in *Grimus,* the madam of the brothel called "The House of the Rising Son" is a dark threatening woman called Liv; in *Midnight's Children,* Kali the black goddess of fertility and death vies with the Widow, the castrating mother of India; in *The Satanic Verses,* one has the pagan goddess Al-Lat, cruel and alluring, who keeps reasserting herself to Mahound in spite of his will to believe in the one God. Is the dark vision satanically inspired or part of an important truth?

This is where the book connects up with ancient moral and theological debates. But the problem remains the same for prophet and poet: dreams are dangerous stuff. Are they good and loaded with meaning, or self-indulgent and private? The novel states that there are two kinds of ideas. Saladin, the rational, worldly aspect of the artist and exile, has "soft ideas" of the kind that compromise, accept the contours of the world, and live through "selected discontinuities." Gibreel, the erratic self-centered actor given to inspiration, has "hard ideas" which come in two kinds: the dangerous, rigid ones that do harm to society—see how the Imam Desh has followed him—or, less often, the "hard idea" that will act as a lever to move the world. How is one to know which vision, which god-sent words, have this power? The prophetic nature of the visions which have thus surfaced in the mind is far from certain. But the prophet has no chance in his wrestling with the angel, as witness the oft-cited parable of the conscious mind struggling with the creative force.

Dangerous thoughts have been conceived, then voiced aloud, as Jumpi Joshi's statement acknowledges. Now comes the third phase, when "language is courage" applies to the process of writing itself, when Salman the Persian, "the scum," sits modestly like a slow-witted, unreliable scribe with diminished responsibility.

For Rushdie does not create poetry, or plays, or short fiction, but uses the Western genre of the novel. He has not chosen the relative freedom allowed to the *Arabian Nights* or to allusive traditional poetry, nor, at the other extreme, the comfortable "objectivity" of the chronicler or journalist. He works in a contemporary format, linked in the West to a certain function, a certain aesthetic code, and he attempts to shape it to his needs, which extend beyond the scope of most modern novels.

Source: Jacqueline Bardolph, "Language Is Courage: *The Satanic Verses*," in *Reading Rushdie: Perspectives on the Fiction of Salman Rushdie*, edited by M. D. Fletcher, Rodopi, 1994, pp. 209–20.

Janet Mason Ellerby

In the following essay, Ellerby explores the "mutability and immutability of the female subject" in The Satanic Verses.

As a Western reader, *The Satanic Verses* matters to me not because of its irreverence for the prophet Muhammed, but because of what it tells me and shows me about what it means to be female in this final decade of the twentieth century. The novel warns me of the dangers of "the achievement of femininity" and of the mutability of the female subject when she "falls in love" or becomes the desiring subject as well as the object of male desire.

First, however, the novel makes very real the charismatic sexual power of the male to illustrate the force of heterosexual desire and the consequent psychological and physical dangers to women. Gibreel Farishta is the beloved of Allie and Rekha Merchant, but he has had a promiscuous sexual history before meeting them. He thought of women as vessels that he would fill temporarily and then move on. It was their nature, he believed, to understand him and to forgive him. Because he is irresistibly attractive to women, they have spoiled him with their generosity. Their willingness to forgive him, says the narrator, was that which corrupted him, for he lived without knowing that he was doing anything wrong at all.

Gibreel's corrupt belief in his innocence is significant, for it is generous women who have allowed him to believe that he can simply move solipsistically through the bodies of desiring women without regard for their well-being. His blindness allows him callously to announce to Rekha Merchant that he has fallen in love with Allelulia Cone without even a glimmer of understanding of the desperate pain his rejection will cause her. Yet this inability of the man to empathize

> **First, however, the novel makes very real the charismatic sexual power of the male to illustrate the force of heterosexual desire and the consequent psychological and physical dangers to women."**

with a woman has been caused, says the narrator, by women. Because women have allowed Gibreel to treat them irresponsibly, he can abruptly leave Rekha, weeping, face-down on the floor of her apartment without realizing the mortal danger his rejection places her in. She takes her two daughters and one son to the roof of her high rise and falls. There are no survivors—only rumors that Gibreel is to blame. Her suicide note reads, "Many years ago . . . I married out of cowardice. Now finally, I'm doing something brave." Nevertheless, her ghost tells Gibreel: "It was you who left me, her voice reminded his ear, seeming to nibble at the lobe. It was you, O moon of my delight, who hid behind a cloud. And I in darkness, blinded, lost, for love."

Before her death, Rekha sees her suicide (and the murder of her children) as an act of bravery. Desire has led her to take action, to become the agent of change. As the desiring subject, she is mutable; her desire for Gibreel has reversed her basic instincts from wishing to protect her children from harm and to live, to wishing for death. However, after her death, she understands that, in fact, she was lost in darkness, blinded by desire. She knows that to forgive Gibreel his insensitivity was wrong; now she desires revenge. She places a curse on him:

> Now that I am dead I have forgotten how to forgive. I curse you, my Gibreel, may your life be hell. Hell, because that's where you sent me, damn you, where you came from, devil, where you're going, sucker, enjoy the bloody dip.

In fact, Rekha's curse is amazingly effective. Gibreel falls in love with Allie, but it is not a love that brings him the understanding and sensitivity that he lacked. He knows that she could bring to him "the best thing . . . the deepest thing, the has-to-be-it," but he cannot find it within himself to trust her her, perhaps because he himself moved without concern for the objects of this desire—from woman to woman—for so long. Instead of finding peace and renewal with Allie, he is tormented by obsessive jealousy. he raves at her as he gives in to recreating her past as a series of lovers. He imagines them waiting for her still. Thus it is very simple for Saladin Chamcha, Rushdie's version Iago, to set the trap—to create the satanic verses—for as a mediocre actor and a cuckolded husband, he wants to avenge himself on Gibreel out of envy for Gibreel's successes (as an actor, as a well-loved citizen of India, and as the man with whom women fall in love). Allie has no idea that Saladin finds her desirable, nor does she sense his envy. But because he cannot hope to possess Allie, she comes to represent the entirety of his loss, and he sets out to destroy both her and Gibreel. Allie and Gibreel, each in a vulnerable position of desire for one another, easily become pawns of his manipulations. Disguising his voice, Saladin calls Gibreel on the phone over and over again and delivers verses that reveal his knowledge of Allie as a lover (details Gibreel himself has confided in Saladin). These are the satanic verses of the novel's title, which return again and again to torment Gibreel. Saladin can mimic voices both deep or squeaky, slow or quick, sad or cheerful, aggressive or timid. He slowly releases them to invade Gibreel's already precarious world, weakening his defenses between what is real and what is not. Gibreel is irresistibly drawn into Saladin's manipulative web of deceit:

> Little by little their [the verses'] obscene, invented women began to coat the real woman like a viscous, green film, and in spite of his protestations to the contrary he started slipping away from her; and then it was time for the return of the little satanic verses that made him mad:

> *Roses are red, violets are blue,*
> *Sugar never tasted sweet as you.*

The voices change Gibreel's concept of Allie, and she becomes both the desirable and detestable. Jealousy, however, is triumphant; Gibreel comes to treat her cruelly and without remorse.

And Allie—how has she allowed herself to become this pawn of men? Is she to be blamed for being too forgiving? Is she to be held responsible for the debacle of her love affair because of her generosity? Before Gibreel, Allie had been a powerful woman, having successfully climbed Mount Everest. Upon tenaciously reaching the seemingly insurmountable summit of ice and rock, she had experienced a miraculous transcedence. Afterwards, she chose to remain alone in the world, turning away

from her sexuality that it might not absorb her. Gibreel is the first man she has slept with in five years. Before him, she had resisted the Freudian quest for femininity. She knew that were she to participate in this heterosexual love narrative, she could lose her autonomy and its accompanying power of self-direction. But Gibreel diminishes even her transcendence of Everest: she becomes subsumed by him and consumed by her sexual desire. During their first weeks together, they spend almost all their time in bed, making love six or seven times a day, their hunger for one another inexhaustible. "You opened me up." Allie told him. Her comment is important. It appears that Gibreel has motioned her toward the fulfillment of her sexuality, and this fulfillment becomes more important to her than any of her other accomplishments, past and future.

Allie has changed. She, herself, is surprised by her new, accommodating personality. Because Gabreel is so sulky when she asks him to do his share of the household chores, she finds herself not only doing these tasks herself but also taking on the responsibility of cajoling him back to good humor. He is, of course, being driven mad by Saladin's satanic verses and by his own psychotic belief in himself as the archangel who has come to save if not the entire world, at least London. He begins a cycle of leaving her, and when he does she falls to the floor weeping, much as Rekha Merchant did the day Gibreel left her for the last time. Allie cannot believe that she is playing this part, "like . . . a character in a story of a kind in which she could never have imagined she belonged." But she does now belong to the master narrative of the heterosexual romance, in which male desire still dominates, and she becomes fiercely "written" by that narrative to the point of becoming its victim.

Because Gibreel is mad, Allie takes it upon herself to care for him with the same tenacity with which she climbed Everest. She begins to think of saving him as she had thought of conquering the mountain, determined to help him back to sanity and not to allow her devotion to him to subside. She is conflating the two narratives of love and individual conquest that have nothing in common and this only works to increase her own fragility and jeopardy, and losses that telling feeling of being caught in the wrong kind of love story. Instead she has become the one who will heal him so that they might resume their great love; hence, she becomes bound to him as healer, redeemer, and lover.

Nevertheless, she does begin to see the hopelessness of his position (of her and by his madness), his irrationality, and his out-of-control suspiciousness. She even sees intellectually that her more "real" life is being suspended or buried at Gibreel's expense. She begins to ask questions, to think agin about her needs and her right to also set terms for their relationship. But she is also firmly ensnared in the Freudian master narrative—now even her biology is controlling her conduct. Though she wants to leave him, she can't because now not only does she want him, she also wants his child. Finally, when she discovers that Gibreel is having her follower, she is able to make the break. The notes she leaves him is telling: "This is killing me." Although this is often a cliché of exaggeration, I think we should take Allie's declaration seriously. The change brought by her sexual entanglement with Gibreel is, in fact, killing off the autonomous, healthy, ambitious Allie. As object of his desire, she has taken on a submissive subject position that is in conflict with her other "selves" and, in fact, requires that she act against them.

On her departure, Gibreel leaves her apartment in another fit of jealous rage at having the object of his desire taken from him. Yet Allie helplessly takes the responsibility for his rage, saying, "I feel in some obscure way to blame . . . it's my fault." Thus the master narrative remains intact despite her temporary departure, which is followed soon after by her return. Her quest is now not that *her* life work out, but that *theirs* does. I would argue that it is, in fact, not even *their* for which she takes responsibility, but Gibreel's exclusively. His greatest need is to maintain the narrative that has made her exclusively the object of his desire, and she will maintain it as long as she can. Gibreel complains to Saladin that it is her beauty that is driving him mad because he has witnessed how men, slobbering and groping, are drawn to her no matter what. He feels that he has every right to be her protector from male lust.

Speaking of women, de Lauretis says, "And so her story, like any other story, is a question of his desire." Allie has arrived at the end of her quest by effacing herself because of her desire for Gibreel. She is not really a private person, as Gibreel insists; but she is the private property of Gibreel. She confirms her capitulation when she confesses to Saladin that she no longer hopes that her life could count as important, as taking first place. Her life has now become their life; she can no longer think of herself in the first person "I."

Still the satanic verses continue over the phone, goading Gibreel, infuriating him, making more and more precarious his tenuous hold on sanity until he flees Allie again, but not before demolishing her apartment. And Allie responds, repeating Rekha Merchant's curse: "Die slowly! Burn in hell!" However, Allie meets Gibreel again. We are told nothing of this meeting; we do not know why she goes with Gibreel to his apartment, why she follows him to the top of his apartment, Everest. We have only the newspaper account: she falls to her death as did Rekha Merchant before her. Our only other account is the mad Gibreel's:

> . . . she changed in front of my eyes I called
> her names whore . . .
> [b——] cool as ice
> stood and waited. . . .
> Rekha was there. . . .
> It was Rekha's idea take her upstairs summit of
> Everest once you've been there the only way is
>   down
> I pointed my finger at her we went up
> I didn't push her
> Rekha pushed her
> I wouldn't have pushed her. . . .
> I loved that girl.

Allies death remains obscured by the cloudy memories of a madman intent on committing suicide. Such narrative irony is a fit emblem for Allie's final and complete surrender of all of her realized and potential subject positions to Gibreel's control.

Still, according to Rushdie, the novel ends happily. Saladin, the perpetrator of the satanic verses that drive Gibreel mad and lead Allie ultimately to her death, is reborn on his return to India and reclaims his true Indian name, Salahuddin, and his more authentic identity. Despite all the wrong he has done, it is he who has the good fortune of getting another chance for which, the narrator remarks, there is no accounting. So there is a change in the master narrative. Rushdie's Iago is redeemed, or rather, he gets another chance. But there is a reason for his good fortune and Allie's bad fortune. The Narrative has swerved in order to save Salahuddin, but not to extricate Allie from the entanglements of the most imperialistic of all narratives—that story that leads a woman to identify herself no longer as a self-directed, self-critical agent, but instead as receptive to the thoughts and volitions of a man's dominating impulsiveness.

For Freud, Allie achieves her femininity as she succumbs to the subject position of the feminine in the heterosexual dyad—the object of male desire. Again this narrative prevails over all others. Because Gibreel is lost to madness and suicide, so must Allie, who the narrator insists is entirely blameless and unjustly injured, be enigmatically sacrificed. On the margin of the dyad is Salahuddin, who tried to drive a man to complete paranoia, knowing that the way to do so would be to exploit Allie and choosing her because he had no way of gratifying his own voyeuristic desire for her. Salahuddin also took the subject position of the male who desired Allie as object, and was, like Gibreel, able to claim agency and act upon the vulnerable pair. Thus both Gibreel and Salahuddin can act as agents when they make Allie the object of their desire; however, Allie is disempowered and left finally at the mercy of their manipulations.

As an initial reader of *The Satanic Verses,* I refused Rushdie's ending and created my own out of my narrative desires. But this was not a tenable position. On confronting again the concreteness of the text, I have had to revise my first reading. I cannot bring Allelulia Cone back to any sort of textual life. However, through a more self-conscious reading, I can write beyond the ending by critiquing the master narrative that leads women to give up their agency and power when they adopt the position of woman within the heterosexual romantic dyad. As a postmodern feminist critic, I can persistently engage in dialogues with already written narratives in ways that can increase our self-consciousness. Only by interrogating the constitution of femininity can women take more forceful positions within dyads of reciprocal desire in which they will be subjects and agents rather than objects to be acted upon.

Source: Janet Mason Ellerby, "Narrative Imperialism in *The Satanic Verses,*" in *Multicultural Literatures through Feminist/Poststructuralist Lenses,* edited by Barbara Frey Waxman, University of Tennessee Press, 1993, pp. 173–89.

Simona Sawhney

In the following essay excerpt, Sawhney explores the theme of metamorphosis, particularly how it relates to migrancy, in The Satanic Verses.

Inhabitations

But if you are in doubt as to what We sent down to Our slave, then produce a Sura the like thereof, and summon witnesses of yours other than, God, if you are truthful. —*The Bounteous Koran* 6

The composition of the Qur'an is not a miracle. Human beings are capable of the same, and of better. —Nazzam the Mu'tazilite, qtd. in Adonis 41

We remember that Gibreel's sequential dreams about the life of Muhammad/Mahound begin after he recovers from a long illness and that the recovery itself begins exactly at the moment when he confronts his own loss of faith. The illness has been for him a period of constant prayer and pleading—the plea for recovery slowly changing to the more

desperate plea for an interlocutor. From questioning the nature of God ("Are you vengeance or are you love"), he now begins to question the very existence of God: "Ya Allah, just be there, damn it, just be." It is at that terrible moment of isolation, when he realizes "that there was nobody there at all," that his illness gives way to recovery. The narrator calls this a "day of metamorphosis," and thus records this as one among the several scenes of metamorphosis that occur in a text that, on one level, is constituted as a conversation between Ovid and Lucretius.

Metamorphosis thus becomes a guiding trope of the novel: a metaphor that responds at once to the lives of migrants, the transformations of tales, and even to the sly slippage between desire and intention, the hidden and the acknowledged, that becomes crucial to Mahound's story. The connection between migrancy and metamorphosis is fairly obvious. It surfaces in the novel's distinction between exile and migrant: the exile guards against change, stubbornly holding on to the dream of return, "frozen in time"; the migrant becomes invaded, transformed, metamorphosed. Thus on a thematic level, the drama of metamorphosis is enacted in the stories of various migrants whose lives (and bodies) are transfigured in postcolonial cities, while on a formal plane, this drama is played out in the mutations of literary traditions and genres that produce the gargantuan and wildly allusive body of the cosmopolitan text.

After Saladin's ordeal at the hands of the British police, when he finds himself suddenly transformed into a bestial creature, the change is explained in terms of a loss of identity that has left him vulnerable to the power of description vested in his captors, the police, and more generally, in the entire state apparatus. The text suggests that Saladin's transformation is partly the result of his having succumbed to that power of description, and also that he was particularly vulnerable to it because he had already lost a refuge or home that a more stable sense of identity would have provided. Saladin himself ruminates on a version of this explanation when he reflects on the two theses on metamorphosis that his friend Sufyan recounts to him: Lucretius's idea that change necessarily entails a kind of death—the death of the old self—and Ovid's belief that souls themselves remain constant even as they "adopt in their migrations ever-varying forms." Saladin chooses Lucretius over Ovid: "A being going through life can become so other to himself as to *be another,* discrete, severed from history." His transformation thus becomes a sign of both a prior and a future homelessness: now that he has become an other, he has been splintered from history itself. The novel does not quite endorse his reading of his own situation, for by the end of the book, not only has Saladin regained his human appearance but he has also returned to a life and a land that he thought he had entirely forsaken.

In some ways, Gibreel's metamorphosis appears to be more violent, especially in terms of its final consequences. Perhaps the violence of the change—from believer to skeptic—registers more deeply with Gibreel because he is someone who wishes to remain the person he always was: "continuous—that is, joined to and arising from his past . . . at bottom an untranslated man," as the narrator says much later. Despite his avowed renunciation of faith, he finds that he cannot dissociate himself quite so easily from the passion that has hitherto sustained his life and now manifests itself in the extravagance of his dreams. Through the final implicit victory of Saladin, the novel suggests that Gibreel's greatest error might well lie in his overriding desire for continuity and authenticity.

The thematic resemblances among all the different dream narratives are quite apparent. They are all narratives of departure and return, of lost homelands, and most obviously, of struggles with faith; and their connection to Gibreel's waking life is easily established. Gibreel's own appearance in the dreams as a confused and helpless Angel Gabriel, a nonknower or nonbeliever who finds himself forced to be a messenger of faith, is also clearly related to the roles he plays in theological movies, or more accurately to the roles he will play after his crisis of faith. What is perhaps more interesting is the way in which this crisis manifests itself in the dreams: a crisis of will that presents itself most strongly as a crisis of utterance. For it is his absolute inability to fathom the mystery of his own utterances in the dreams that causes him the greatest discomfort of all. The problem is not merely that he is perceived as a messenger of divine utterance, but that in some inexplicable way, he *becomes* such a messenger—he is, in fact, able to say exactly what his listeners wish to hear, although he does not know whence such speech appears:

> All around him, he thinks, as he half-dreams, half-wakes, are people hearing voices, being seduced by words. But not his: never his original material.— Then whose? Who is whispering in their ears, enabling them to move mountains, halt clocks, diagnose disease?

Gibreel, of course, is not the only one plagued by the confusion of voices: in what has now

 The thematic resemblances among all the different dream narratives are quite apparent. They are all narratives of departure and return, of lost homelands, and most obviously, of struggles with faith. . . ."

become the most notorious section of *The Satanic Verses,* it is Mahound who acknowledges an error of recognition and naming. Having first accepted as divine revelation the dictates of a voice that sanctions the worship of the old goddesses of Jahilia within the practice of Islam, Mahound later decides that the message he received came in fact from the devil and orders that it be expunged from the record of revelation. Rushdie's narration of the "satanic verses" incident becomes perhaps the text's most powerful strategy for questioning the authority and transmission of revealed words. The episode itself has been described by several Muslim historians and biographers, of whom the best known are the ninth-century historians Al-Tabari and Ibn Sa'd. Whether or not these accounts are true, they nevertheless suggest that an anxiety regarding the phenomenon of revelation was evident quite early in the history of Islam.

Ibn Sa'd relates that at a time when Muhammad strongly desired to establish better relations with his countrymen, he was once at the Ka'ba, reciting from the Koran.

> When he came to the passage: "Do you behold Allat and Al 'Uzza, and also Manat, the third idol?"—which now concludes: "What? shall ye have male progeny and Allah female? This were indeed an unfair partition!"—Satan suggested two lines to him: "These are the exalted females, and truly their intercession may be expected." (Andrae 19)

Muhammad then prostrated himself and prayed, and the whole tribe of Quraish followed him. Later that evening, when the prophet was meditating at home, the angel Gabriel appeared to him, and Muhammad recited the sura to the angel. "Have I taught you these two lines?" asked Gabriel (Andrae

19). Muhammad then realized his error and re-marked that he had attributed to Allah words that He had not revealed.

The story has evoked responses of several kinds. Tor Andrae claims that "the whole narrative is historically and psychologically contradictory" (19), but maintains that there is some element of accuracy in it: in one instance, Muhammad did in fact attempt a compromise between monotheism and pagan idolatry in order to reach an under-standing with his people. Providing ample justifi-cation for the resentment of later Muslim historians against orientalist biographers, he then declares that "parallels to such opportunism are by no means lacking in Mohammad's later conduct."

Montgomery Watt is more sympathetic in his treatment of the incident. He argues that even the cult of the goddesses might be considered a "vague monotheism" insofar as the enlightened Arabs re-garded the deities as manifestations of a single di-vine power. Thus the word *goddess* here suggests a sacred power associated with certain places, rather than a more elaborately anthropomorphized deity. The Semitic religion, Watt says, "has a less personal conception of the divine" than, for in-stance, Greek paganism. Thus, Muhammad and his followers might not have regarded the worship of the goddesses as being necessarily a violation of the monotheistic principle.

Orientalist scholars have always shown a par-ticularly strong interest in the story, often retelling it in ways that have angered Muslim historians. Many of the latter maintain that it is a fabrication, propagated by those who wished to attack the very basis of Islam: the idea of monotheism or *tawhid.* This is the view of Muhammad Husayn Haykal, one of the most respected biographers of the prophet, who writes:

> the forgers must have been extremely bold to have attempted their forgery in the most essential princi-ple of Islam as a whole: namely, in the principle of *tawhid* . . . in which [the prophet] never accepted any compromise.

Rafiq Zakaria has also dealt at length with the incident in his book *Mohammad and the Quran,* partly in order to expose the various prejudices that have always accompanied the narration of the in-cident and partly as a polemic against Rushdie. Zakaria charges that Rushdie "opened old wounds" by his "lurid picturization of this incident." Like Haykal, Zakaria reads the story as a negation of the central message of the Koran and a slur on Muham-mad's mission. He comments on various readings

of the incident and finally presents as conclusive the assessment of Sir Syed Ahmad Khan (1817–98), perhaps the most eminent Muslim intellectual of undivided India, and the work of Maulana Abul'ala Maudidi, the founder of the Jamaat-i-Islami, "the foremost [Muslim] fundamentalist or-ganization in South Asia" (Zakaria 16). Maudidi's version of the incident is particularly interesting in that it shifts the burden of error from the prophet to the listening congregation. While the prophet was reciting the sum "Al Najm," Maudidi says, the listeners were so elated by his eloquence and by the mention of the three goddesses that they did not hear what he actually said. They thought the god-desses were being praised when in fact their au-thority was being dismissed. Later, when the Quraish realized their mistake, they invented the story of satanic intervention as an expression of their displeasure with Muhammad. Thus it remains a story of mis-hearing and misjudgment, but in this version it is the pagan Arabs who allow their de-sire to obscure or redirect the course of revelation.

However, Zakaria's main argument has more extensive implications. It rests largely on a blanket repudiation of the traditions on which early Arab writers based their work. Various authorities are quoted to demonstrate that the works of the eighth-century writer Ibn Ishaq and the ninth-century writ-ers Tabari, Waqidi, and Ibn Sa'd have little basis in historical accuracy and instead rely largely on gos-sip and myth. According to Zakaria, not only are these writers themselves irresponsible and roman-tic in their approach to the material, but also the very tradition on which they base their work is sus-pect, for their accounts contradict each other in sev-eral instances and "none of them has produced any reliable evidence" for their work. Zakaria agrees with Maudidi's conclusion that perhaps with the best of intentions, they failed to see the "incongruity and contradictory nature" of this tradition.

Zakaria and other modern commentators judge the work of the early chroniclers, like that of Rushdie perhaps, by the standards of accuracy and inaccuracy, the demands for evidence and rational cogency, that are properly characteristic of the de-sire for a scientific, empirical history, even though in this case it is the history of a miracle or a faith that is under scrutiny. I am certainly in no position to read or analyze the original work of the early writers, but it does seem that in judging this work from the perspective of empirical historians, the modern commentators are making what one might call a generic error, where a history that has not yet emerged as distinct from legend or poetry is now judged by the alien standards of history as a social science. It might be instructive for us to note that for scholars like Zakaria, as for the Sikh terrorist Tavleen in the novel, it becomes a relatively easy matter to assimilate a certain version of history within the project of revelation: in the name of such a history, it is finally literature that must be silenced. What first appears, then, as a complaint directed against orientalist writers turns out to be an expression of discomfort with all work that cannot be relegated to the margins of Islamic historiography. Those who have charged Rushdie with joining ranks with imperialists, as well as those who have hailed him as a champion of Western values of freedom and democracy, would do well to remember that in fact, Rushdie has predecessors in the Arab tradition itself, and that the battle between gossip and truth, or literature and history, need not be waged at the boundary between East and West.

In Rushdie's text, the interest in the episode of the satanic verses shifts to some degree. Certainly the incident is still concerned with the tension between monotheism and polytheism, which acquires a specific resonance for Indian Islam, crowded by a pantheon of Hindu deities. But Rushdie focuses more explicitly on what has been a source of anxiety for the tradition as well as for modern Muslim scholars: the incident's skillful subversion of the very phenomenon of revelation. In *The Satanic Verses,* the episode's significance derives from Mahound's tacit acknowledgment of a failure of recognition—a failure that is mirrored in Gibreel's failure, later in the novel, to recognize the voice of Saladin in the telephonic verses that prove to be his undoing. The verses that Mahound proposes as true revelation to replace the earlier, heretical words seem to settle the question of monotheism quite definitively—even as they make use of a familiar misogynist detour—but they offer little help in laying to rest the anxiety about recognizing (and naming) the sources of belief. In Rushdie's text, the new verses read:

> Shall He have daughters and you sons? That would be a fine division!

> These are but names you have *dreamed of,* you and your fathers. Allah vests no authority in them. (emphasis added)

It is evident that Rushdie's translation consciously calls attention to the ambiguous status of dreaming, which can signify at once an idle fantasy and a profound vision. Most other English translations of the sura "Al Najm" of the Koran, to which Rushdie's text refers, do not use the word *dream* at all. Nevertheless, one may read the sura itself as

betraying an anxiety about revelation, at least in its overriding concern with establishing its own authority. The sura in the text of the Koran reads:

> By the star when it sinks down, your companion [Muhammad] neither strays nor is allured; neither does he speak out of whim. It is naught but a revelation inspired, taught him by one vigorous in power [Gabriel], prudent and in true nature, while poised on the uppermost horizon. Then he drew near and lower, until he was at two bow lengths distant or nearer. Then he revealed to His servant what He revealed. The heart did not falsify what he saw. Do you dispute over what he saw? . . . Indeed he saw his Lord's greatest signs. Have you seen al Lat and al 'Uzza, and Manat the third, besides? Have you [begotten] males and has He [begotten] females? That is indeed an unjust partition. They are nothing but names you yourselves and your fathers named them. God has sent no authority concerning them. They [the Pagans] but follow surmise and what the souls desire, when indeed there came to them guidance from their Lord. (*The Bounteous Koran* 700–01)

At least in light of what we already know about the sura, it is hard not to read the first few lines as responding to voiced or unvoiced allegations about the source of revelation. The text appears to be particularly concerned to establish the purity of the prophet's declarations. It states that they stem neither from whim nor desire—the desire, for instance, to either placate or defy the idolaters—but that they only record what was revealed to the prophet by the archangel.

For Rushdie's story, however, the archangel is not a transparent authority but only a figure of deference. Who really speaks, the novel asks, when the archangel speaks? Thus in the novel, the focus shifts to Gabriel; and in his dreams of doubt and despair, Gibreel Farishta, whose name literally means Gabriel Angel, appears to himself as an archangel forsaken by his faith. In these dreams Gibreel becomes the guarantor of revelation, except that the archangel himself does not know whose messages he transmits or how he transmits then. When Mahound decides that the earlier revelation about the goddesses was but a trick of the devil, Gibreel the messenger is more mystified than anyone:

> Gibreel, hovering-watching from his highest camera angle, knows one small detail, just one tiny thing that's a bit of a problem here, namely that *it was me both times, baba, me first and second also me.* From my mouth, both the statement and the repudiation, verses and converses, universes and reverses, the whole thing, and we all know how my mouth got worked.

Gibreel's mouth, as we know, gets "worked" by Mahound's will, as it does in other dreams by the imam's or Ayesha's will, so that Gibreel remains, in every scene, an actor reciting words that he neither chooses nor even understands.

How then are we to read such a version of the story of the satanic verses? As an allegory that dramatizes the relationship between politics and religion, the legislator and the angel of God, such that the legislator actually becomes a ventriloquist who turns the gods into his puppets, as in Hobbes's account of the early lawgivers? As a psychological reading of the mystery of revelation, which demonstrates that what is imagined as revelation is but the desire of the prophet? Or to go even further, as a suggestion that the sacrosanct voice of the heart—whether it be named instinct, desire, or revelation—is nothing but a ruse of power, its instrument and slave? The text itself corroborates all these readings, and possibly others as well. We may, indeed, keep in mind that since the story of the satanic verses, like several other episodes in the novel, is narrated as a dream, we should perhaps also allow our approach to be guided by the peculiar logic of the dream world. We could at least say that like a dream, the story is overdetermined, that the elements in the story are determined by several contexts, and that each of these contexts might be represented in the story by various elements.

Thus we find, condensed in Gibreel's dreams, images of the Bombay film world, the legends of Islamic hagiography, the backdrop of an India struggling to define itself as a socialist, secular state, and the dreamer's own struggles with his loss of faith. On a more overtly linguistic level, the dreams are also connected to the dreamer's names: the name he was given, Ismail Najmuddin (Star of the Faith), which perhaps guides his later preoccupation with the sura "Al Najm" (the Star) of the Koran; and the stage name he adopts, Gibreel Farishta (Gabriel Angel), in memory of his mother, who thought of him as her very own angel, "her personal angel, she called me, *farishta,* because apparently I was too damn sweet." We might also note here the ways in which the names of other characters circulate through the various episodes of the book—Hind, Bilal, Ayesha—appellations that proliferate like metaphors. As the plot moves from one landscape to another, from the real world to the dream world, we encounter familiar figures, names, references: memories both preserved and strangely transformed. Gibreel's dreams thus become the dreams of the novel itself, the text's own dreaming of its manifold contexts.

We might find here a way of understanding why the source of revelation, or indeed of utterance

itself, becomes such a persistent enigma in Rushdie's treatment of the satanic verses episode. If the text continually draws attention to its own inability to name the source of utterance, and if it explicitly focuses on the possibility of error whenever such an attempt at naming is made, then by this very gesture it points toward that which perhaps defines it as a text—that is, as a literary rather than a revealed text. In spite of a momentary error, Mahound can later definitively assert that his words bear the authority of divine law, but a story like that of the satanic verses can only circulate by veiling its sources: its power derives precisely from its lack of authorization. It has a history but no recognizable origin: as gossip, fable, indictment, or parable, it becomes the shadow play that mimics and mocks the drama of revelation. It inhabits the story of revelation, one might say, in a way that is just as disruptive or as uncanny as the way in which the novel inhabits the epic, or the secular inhabits the sacred. The text's preferred model for such inhabitation is the experience of the dream, perhaps because dreams represent to us at once the most intimate and the most alienating relationship we can have with ourselves.

Source: Simona Sawhney, "Satanic Choices: Poetry and Prophecy in Rushdie's Novel," in *Twentieth Century Literature*, Vol. 45, No. 3, Fall 1990, pp. 253–77.

Sources

Parrinder, Patrick, "Let's Get the Hell Out of Here," in *London Review of Books*, Vol. 10, No. 17, September 29, 1988, pp. 11–13.

Rushdie, Salman, *The Satanic Verses*, Viking, 1988.

Wallace, Charles P., and Dan Fisher, "Khomeini Says Author of *Satanic Verses* Should Be Killed," *Los Angeles Times*, February 15, 1989, p. 13.

Wood, Michael, "The Prophet Motive," in the *New Republic*, Vol. 200, No. 10, March 6, 1989, pp. 28–30.

Further Reading

Cavanaugh, Christine, "Auguries of Power: Prophecy and Violence in *The Satanic Verses*," in *Studies in the Novel*, Vol. 36, No. 3, Fall 2004, pp. 393–404.
  Cavanaugh's article discusses the theological context of Rushdie's novel and its commentary about how violence is related to prophecy.

Erickson, John, *Islam and Postcolonial Narrative*, Cambridge University Press, 1998, pp. 129–60.
  The chapter on Salman Rushdie in Erickson's scholarly work discusses *The Satanic Verses* in terms of its depiction of Islam's relationship with the West.

Pipes, Daniel, *The Rushdie Affair: The Novel, the Ayatollah, and the West*, Carol Publishing Group, 1990.

Pipes provides a study of the circumstances surrounding the publication of Rushdie's novel, including an analysis of Rushdie's intentions and reactions to the fatwa.

Rushdie, Salman, "In Good Faith," in *Newsweek*, Vol. 115, No. 7, February 12, 1990, pp. 52–56.

Rushdie's important article about *The Satanic Verses* defends his novel, argues why it should not be offensive to Muslims, and asks for the right to free expression.

Seminick, Hans, *A Novel Visible but Unseen: A Thematic Analysis of Salman Rushdie's "The Satanic Verses,"* Studia Germanica Gandensia, 1993.

Seminick's analytical approach to *The Satanic Verses* offers a useful deconstruction of the novel's themes.

Sophie's Choice

William Styron
1979

William Styron's 1979 novel *Sophie's Choice* consists of a story within a story. The first story is of the summer of 1947 when the narrator, then age twenty-two and using the nickname Stingo, loses his job at McGraw-Hill in New York City. He moves to a Brooklyn boarding house where he sets about writing what he hopes will be the next great American novel. While Stingo tries to write this book, using the recent suicide of a childhood friend as a catalyst, he becomes involved with two other residents, the co-dependent Sophie and the psychotic drug addict Nathan. The second story emerges piecemeal from Sophie, who tells Stingo about her life over the past decade: of living in Cracow, Poland, the daughter of a university professor; of her marriage to her father's protégé; of living with her two children in Warsaw after her father and husband are murdered; and of her imprisonment at Auschwitz. Because she survived, Sophie feels implicated in Nazi atrocities. She is ashamed of her father's fascist beliefs and guilt-ridden for having helped with his pamphlet advocating the extermination of the Jews, for failing to protect her children, and for using her father's views as an argument to wangle her freedom from the camp. Her abusive relationship with Nathan exacerbates these feelings. Alcohol abuse by all three characters makes matters worse.

The nature of evil and the widening circle of implicating others in its perpetuation constitutes the central subject in this novel. In addition to that subject, however, the novel takes itself as its subject.

In a surprisingly self-referential and reflexive way, the novel is about writing a novel. It describes Stingo's uncertainty and writer's block; it includes drafts from 1947 and criticizes them from the narrator's 1977 perspective.

The novel is also about the real world on which it is based. Like other works of historical fiction, it presents historical characters in fictional roles. It also breaks the illusion of that fictive world with digressions: on World War II; on the nature of evil; on recommended readings for public school children (although given its obscenity *Sophie's Choice* itself is probably not appropriate); and on Elie Wiesel's criticism of novels on the Holocaust. In sum, it may be safe to say that storytelling is both the method and the examined subject of *Sophie's Choice*.

Author Biography

William Styron was born June 11, 1925, in Newport News, Virginia. He attended a private Christian school and Davidson College in North Carolina before graduating with a bachelor's degree from Duke University in 1947. Like Stingo in *Sophie's Choice*, Styron experienced the death of his mother when he was a teenager, and after college, began his professional life as an assistant editor for McGraw-Hill in New York City. Styron later served in an editorial capacity for the journals *Paris Review* and *American Scholar*. He also served in the U.S. Marine Corps during World War II and the Korean War.

Often compared to Faulkner, William Styron writes in a literary tradition associated with the South. Several fathers in his fictions, including Stingo's father, are reminiscent of Styron's own liberal-thinking, gentlemanly father, William Clark Styron, a shipyard engineer who died in 1978. Styron's fictional fathers speak for equality and tolerance in a harsh twentieth-century world that does not hear them.

Styron wrote three novels, *Lie Down in Darkness* (1951), *The Long March* (1956), and *Set This House on Fire* (1960), before he won a Pulitzer Prize for *The Confessions of Nat Turner* (1967), a first-person narration that tells the story of the 1831 Virginia slave rebellion. Twelve years later, in 1979, Styron published *Sophie's Choice*, his study of human domination in Nazi-controlled Poland and in a sadomasochistic sexual relationship.

The author of five novels, a play, several essay collections, and an autobiography, Styron published *Darkness Visible: A Memoir of Madness*

William Styron   AP/Wide World Photos. Reproduced by permission

in 1990, a work that describes his 1980s descent into depression. Taking his title from Milton's *Paradise Lost* (the words come from Satan's description of Hell), Styron explores the depression he experienced which was brought on in part by four decades of alcohol abuse and the death of his father. In 1993, he published three autobiographical stories, *Tidewater Morning: Three Tales from Youth*, his first work since recovering from his mental illness.

William Styron and his wife, Rose Burgunder Styron, whom he married in the 1950s, have devoted their lives to literature and to human rights. Rose Styron was contributing poetry editor for *Paris Review* and a proponent of Amnesty International. William and Rose Styron have stood up repeatedly against oppression and prejudice worldwide. Styron's exploration of evil and its aftermath in *Sophie's Choice* is only one instance of decades of focus on, and resistance to, tyranny.

Plot Summary

Chapter 1

Set in New York in the summer of 1947 and told from the first person point of view, *Sophie's*

Media Adaptations

- *Sophie's Choice* was made into a film starring Meryl Streep as Sophie and Kevin Kline as Nathan. It is available on a 1992 video and a 1998 DVD.

Choice begins with Stingo, a McGraw-Hill assistant editor, ranting about the "clubfooted syntax" and "unrelenting mediocrity" of other people's manuscripts. But Stingo also admits he rejected the manuscript of *Kon-Tiki*, a work that later became a "great classic of modern adventure." As Stingo toys with the idea of becoming a writer, he copes with sexual frustration and the reality of being a virgin. To sublimate his sex drive, he plunges into "make-believe" fiction, avoiding his "homework . . . composing jacket blurbs." Stingo loses his job, and Mr. Farrell urges him to *write [his] guts out*."

The narrator reveals that it is now thirty years later; the year is 1977. He is looking back to that summer when he set out to be a writer, when he still went by his childhood nickname Stingo. Readers learn in the course of the novel that, at fifty-two, the narrator is a successful author of several novels, including one on Nat Turner. Stingo thus emerges as the simulacrum of William Styron.

Thus, the chapter is devoted to writing, publication, writers, editors, and editors who are would-be writers. It echoes the famous line from *Moby Dick* ("Call me Ishmael") in the narrator's comment, "Call me Stingo," and refers to famous American writers, such as Katherine Porter, John Hersey, and Thomas Wolfe.

Chapter 2

As the now-unemployed Stingo considers his next move, a letter providentially arrives from his father, explaining an inheritance Stingo is to receive. The legacy is proceeds from the sale of a named slave Artiste. The father explains that Stingo's great-grandfather sold Artiste, "an innocent boy of 16 into the grinding hell of the Georgia turpentine forests." The recently discovered and appraised eight hundred dollars in gold coin allots to Stingo a legacy of five hundred dollars. Ironically, profits from the slave trade will support Stingo, who is to write novels about racism.

Stingo moves to Yetta Zimmerman's "unrelievedly pink" boarding house in Brooklyn. There he faces the "simultaneously enfeebling and insulting . . . empty page." Frustrated with not writing and "a little goatish," he hears a creaking bed in the apartment overhead. He meets Morris Fink, who describes the lovers, Sophie and Nathan. Next, Stingo witnesses the couple fighting and after the verbally abusive Nathan leaves, Stingo meets Sophie, with whom he falls "fathomlessly in love." Seeing the tattooed number on her arm, he assumes she is Jewish.

Chapter 3

Stingo is amazed the next day by Sophie and Nathan's happy invitation to join them for a day at Coney Island. Nathan undergoes "a remarkable transformation," flipping from abuser to gentleman and back to abuser. Hungry for friendship, however, Stingo ignores the signs of something wrong. Nathan accuses Stingo as a Southerner of being complicit in the lynching of Bobby Weed. Nathan says: "The fate of Bobby Weed at the hands of white Southern Americans is as bottomlessly barbaric as any act performed by the Nazis during the rule of Adolf Hitler." Sixteen-year-old Weed was accused like the slave Artiste and died in the same Georgia forest where Artiste disappeared. Stingo remarks that he should have seen the signs, packed up, and left; had he done so there would be "no story at all to tell." Instead, he chooses to "plunge on toward Coney Island," assuming that the three of them will be " 'the best of friends.' "

Chapter 4

Sophie describes her childhood in Cracow. She explains that Nathan, when he is in one of his fits, accuses her of being anti-Semitic because she is Polish. She feels guilty about the fact that Poland was strongly anti-Semitic, and she equates this feeling with what Stingo must feel being from the racist South. The Germans arrived in Cracow in September 1939 and immediately executed all university faculty, including her father and husband. She says: "only a Jesus who had no pity and who no longer cared for me could permit the people I loved to be killed and let me live with such guilt." Stingo sums up more of Sophie's story, including her arrival in New York, her experience of "digital rape" on a train, her work for the chiropractor Dr. Blackstock, and her meeting Nathan Landau, who rescues her when she collapses at the Brooklyn Public Library. He also points out that Sophie lies about the past. For example, she claims here that Nathan is her second sexual partner. Later, she tells about Jozef, her lover in Warsaw. Stingo says that he "was fated to get ensnared, like some hapless June bug, in the incredible spider's nest of emotions that made up the relation between Sophie and Nathan."

Chapter 5

Stingo's father writes again, with news of another inheritance, this time a peanut farm allocated in the will of a friend, just the place for Stingo to live and write. Stingo languishes with his novel idea, thinks his idea "pathetically derivative" because in his novel about Maria Hunt, he wants to "do for a small Southern city what James Joyce" did for Dublin—"invent Dixieland replicas of Stephen Dedalus and the imperishable Blooms." (Instead, the mature narrator writes a novel about Stingo and the "perishable" Sophie and Nathan.) Enflaming Stingo's self-doubts, Nathan claims that Southern literature is over and Jewish literature's day has come. At Coney Island, Stingo meets the "Jewish Madonna" Leslie Lapidus, who invites Stingo to have sex with her. Stingo's writing on Leslie is quoted and then criticized for its lack of irony. The mature narrator then "rewrites" the scene between Stingo and Leslie, using curiously mock-romantic language. Stingo offers to elucidate Faulkner, whom Sophie is reading, because he has "practically memorized" the collection she is reading.

Chapter 6

Stingo relates how Nathan cared for Sophie after she collapsed in the library, preparing calf's liver for her because he suspects she suffers from anemia. Nathan is a well-read American Jew, obsessed with World War II atrocities. Sophie reveals she is Polish, not Danish as Nathan first thought. Then she tells Nathan some of her past, beginning with the fact that in April 1943 she was arrested and transported to Auschwitz-Birkenau. Because of her perfect German, Sophie is selected to serve as secretary for the Auschwitz commandant, but despite this favored position, she contracts scurvy and scarlet fever. Again, Stingo points out "that Sophie was not quite straightforward in her recital of past events." The mature narrator reflects that her "hideous sense of guilt" caused her repeatedly to reassess the past. The narrator quotes Simone Weil's explanation of survivor guilt: "Affliction stamps the soul to its very depths with the scorn,

the disgust and even the self-hatred and sense of guilt that crime logically should produce but actually does not." Sophie is secretive and reticent about the past, because she feels responsible for it. Nonetheless, she is able to tell Stingo things she cannot tell Nathan.

One part of her story reserved for Stingo pertains to Rudolf Franz Höss, SS Obersturmbannführer, Commandant of Auschwitz, for whom Sophie worked for ten days. (The historical Rudolf Franz Höss [1900–1947] was commandant of Auschwitz from May 1940 until December 1943. For war crimes, he was hanged on April 16, 1947, at Auschwitz.) Styron cites information about Höss here, saying that he illustrates "the true nature of evil." Styron asserts that everyone should read about Höss, even "our beloved children, those incipient American leaders at the eighth-grade level . . . should be required to study it along with *The Catcher in the Rye*."

Chapter 7

Making a huge jump from background on Höss to Stingo's sexual frustration, the narrator devotes this chapter to Stingo's failed attempt to have sexual intercourse with Leslie. Included is a long excerpt from his 1947 writing on the experience. He calls this inconsequential episode with Leslie "a nice counterpoint" to the larger narrative about Sophie.

Chapter 8

Nathan praises Stingo's writing. Thus coddled, Stingo is slow to see "seeping out of Nathan, almost like some visible poisonous exudate, his latent capacity for rage." Nathan enraged is as toxic as the gas chambers. Another huge fight occurs. Later, drinking with Stingo, Sophie tells him more. Nathan returns and accuses Sophie of infidelity. He suspects her employer, Dr. Blackstock, and he suspects Stingo. Though unwilling or unable to intervene, Stingo admits that Nathan "might be dangerously disturbed." Nathan attacks Stingo's writing, claiming that it amounts to the "first Southern comic book." Later Stingo discovers that Sophie and Nathan seem to have moved out, taken most of their things and headed off in different directions. Three days later Sophie returns, but readers do not learn that for another hundred pages.

Chapter 9

The mature narrator discusses research from the 1960 and 1970s: George Steiner's essays, collected in *Language and Silence* (1967) and Richard

Rubenstein's *The Cunning of History* (1975). In the years since 1947, the story of Sophie and Nathan continues to haunt the narrator. By 1967 he realized he would have to deal with their story, just as in 1947 he had successfully dealt with the story of "the doomed Maria Hunt."

Steiner's concept of "time relation" causes the narrator to feel "the shock of recognition." Steiner explores the implications in the fact that people have vastly different experiences at precisely the same moment: "The two orders of simultaneous experience are . . . a paradox—Treblinka *is* both because some men have built it and almost all other men let it be." Stingo was eating bananas in Raleigh, North Carolina, one "lovely spring morning," just at the moment that Sophie entered Auschwitz. On October 3, 1943, in training in the Marines and at Duke University, Stingo writes a letter to his father, the big news on his mind is the Rose Bowl. On that same day, 2,100 Greek Jews are gassed and cremated at Auschwitz. The fact that things co-occur suggests that events are linked, and that idea is developed in the narrator's quotations from Rubenstein, who argues that the Nazi state of domination derived from the institution of slavery. This chapter includes information about the fascist beliefs of Sophie's father and her husband, about her husband's abuse of her, and about how both father and husband were "sucked like . . . mere larva into the burial mound of KL Sachsenhausen." Her shame comes from being related to them and loving them.

Chapter 10

From the stairwell of the Höss house, Sophie can "peek" at the unloaded boxcars, watch the ash spew from the crematoria smokestacks, and hear the infernal prisoner band music. In this house, Sophie is sexually assaulted by Wilhelmine, the housekeeper. She vomits on the staircase and then soothes Höss when he gets a migraine. The construction of a new crematorium at Birkenau has been slowed, and he fears being found derelict in his duties. Sophie sees Höss as her only hope of escape. When she learns he is being transferred to Berlin, Sophie presents her father's pamphlet to him, hoping to convince him that she is a fascist too and should be freed from the camp. Höss talks about himself, and Sophie pleads for him to intervene on behalf of her son.

Chapter 11

Stingo's father visits New York and cautions Stingo about the differences between the North and the South. The father says the North will pay for

its racism. He notes the uneasiness brewing in Northern slums and anticipates the race riots that actually do occur twenty years later in 1967. Stingo's father has had a fight with a cabdriver and is appalled by his incivility. He contends that when people speak in uncivilized ways they degrade themselves. Stingo's father has excellent language skills, but he is quicker to see racism in the North than to recognize it in his own thinking.

Stingo thinks back to his mother who died when he was thirteen. He regrets that once he failed to come home and start the fire for her and as a result she was dangerously cold for hours. His father punished him by making him wait in the woodshed until he got as cold as his mother had gotten. Staying overnight in his father's hotel, Stingo dreams of Artiste, connecting him to Nat Turner, and in the morning he temporarily decides to return home with his father to Virginia. Had he followed out this plan, he would not have intervened in Sophie's affairs and that might have been better for her in the long run.

Lebensborn, "a product of the Nazis' phylogenetic delirium," is discussed next. This program placed Aryan-looking children, kidnapped from occupied countries, in pro-Nazi German families inside Germany. Ironically this program, which sickened Sophie when she was in Warsaw, became her hope at Auschwitz for Jan's "liberation" from the Children's Camp.

Sophie and Stingo get drunk. She tells him about a trip she and Nathan took to Connecticut, how he beat her up and obscenely denigrated her in a woods. The alcohol lubricates her narration: "whiskey transformed her speech into a spillway." She reveals that Nathan is addicted to Benzedrine and cocaine, that these drugs make him crazy. On that trip he lured her with the idea of committing suicide by taking sodium cyanide, which she calls one of his "morbid tricks." Sophie is fascinated by Nathan, turned on by him when he is high. The obscene descriptions of their sexuality in this chapter dramatize how sexism, racism, and domestic violence are interconnected by dominance. Caught in the delusional swirl of sexual arousal and alcoholism, Sophie loses herself; she claims, "Without Nathan I would be . . . nothing." Not coincidentally, she felt the same way in the Höss household.

Chapter 12

Hung over, Sophie and Stingo go to Jones Beach, along the way making anti-Semitic remarks. Sophie talks about her lover Jozef, the teenage resistance fighter in Warsaw. She tells about being arrested with her two children, the first mention of her daughter. She also gives a tender portrait of Eva's flute teacher, the arthritic Stefan Zaorski. Stefan is with Eva in the group at Auschwitz selected for immediate extermination. She describes how Jozef and his half-sister Wanda urged Sophie to assist in the resistance work. She admires their courage and is disturbed that she could not participate. She wanted to protect her children. Their arrest is described in greater detail.

The narrator gives statistics on Jewry in Warsaw and stops to think again about Sophie's father. They were all "helpless participants," but what would her father have thought had he realized the fate of his own grandchildren? Professor Bieganski was blinded by his fascist obsession and thus he failed to "foresee how sublime hatred could only gather into its destroying core, like metal splinters sucked toward some almighty magnet, countless thousands of victims who did not wear the yellow badge."

Chapter 13

Sophie describes the verbal abuse she received from her husband. She tells of meeting Walter Dürrfeld, director of IG Farbenindustrie, who visited her father before the War and flirted inappropriately with her. (The historical Walter Dürrfeld was head of the Farben rubber factory at Auschwitz from 1941 to 1944. He was tried at Nuremberg and sentenced to eight years in prison.) In the camp, Wanda visits Sophie, bringing news of Jan and urging Sophie to help the resistance prisoners by stealing a radio from Höss's house. On the last night in that house, Sophie had an erotic dream about Dürrfeld whom she had not seen in years, and the next day she saw him as he left Höss's office. Years later when Sophie tells Stingo about these memories, she confesses again "her 'badness.'" Having pondered her "misplaced guilt" for years, the narrator concludes that "absolute evil paralyzes absolutely."

Chapter 14

Nathan, Sophie, and Stingo plan a trip South after the lovers marry, and Stingo resolves to write a novel based on the life of Nat Turner. Stingo meets Nathan's brother, Larry, who explains Nathan's mental illness and asks Stingo to watch Nathan and report back to Larry if there are signs of danger. Then, inexplicably, Stingo takes a ten-day vacation to visit an old buddy from his Marine days, and while he is away, Nathan beats up Sophie and threatens her with a gun. When Stingo returns, Nathan

threatens him, accusing Stingo of having betrayed him with Sophie. Sophie and Stingo flee Brooklyn in fear of their lives.

Chapter 15

Stingo and Sophie head south on a train. Stingo contemplates how to end the novel he is writing about Maria Hunt; as Sophie sleeps, he thinks about the novels he will write in the future, perhaps a masterpiece about Nat Turner. Even Sophie gets into planning a book: "I want to write about Auschwitz. . . . I could write in Polish or German or maybe French," she remarks. She could write about the atrocities and how the Nazis drove people to do unthinkable things. In Warsaw, Wanda told her what was happening at Treblinka and Auschwitz. Sophie was ashamed to admit to Wanda that the "Fascist professor from Cracow," was in fact her father. Sophie talks about how Jozef and Wanda got guns to Feldshon, a Jew in Warsaw, how Wanda showed her photographs of dead children, "a great mass of sticks." The narrator describes in detail the trains Nazis used to transport people to the camps and the band music the prisoners could hear from the train platform.

Next, comes the story of Sophie's "choice," how she was coerced by a sadistic Nazi doctor, who first lusts after her, to choose between her children. This event, withheld until the penultimate chapter, holds the key to understanding Sophie's psychology and the nature of pure evil. Forced to engage in the "selection," Sophie breaks in two herself. She *is* her children and to choose between them is to cut in two her own identity, her own congruency. Thus, she incorporates in herself the antagonistic roles of victimizer and victim. The mature narrator describes the Nazi doctor as a Christian who, in his youth, wanted to go into the ministry. To meet "the demands of butchery," he must have been consuming "a great deal of alcohol." On the platform he acts like God, deciding who lives and who dies.

Stingo and Sophie get off the train in Washington, D.C., and posing as a minister with his wife, Stingo gets them a hotel room near the capitol.

Chapter 16

Sophie resists Stingo's proposal of marriage. She admits giving up the hope of finding Jan, thinks he may have died from exposure and pneumonia in the camp. She wonders, if she had chosen Jan instead of Eva, would it have made any difference? She concludes, "Nothing would have changed anything." That night in the hotel room, they have sexual intercourse. Stingo imagines Sophie's initiation of sex as the sign she agrees to marry him. But when he wakes up and finds her gone, he feels betrayed and angry about not being able to extricate her from Nathan's snare. Given the note she leaves and his sense that their intimacy was really an "orgiastic attempt to beat back death," Stingo returns to New York fearing the worse.

En route to New York on the train, Stingo is joined by an African American woman whom he calls the "dark priestess." Together they read scriptures of lamentation. "Plunging deathward," Stingo surrenders himself to a great grief, knowing that "something terrible was going to happen to [Sophie], and to Nathan, and that [Stingo's] desperate journey to Brooklyn could in no way alter the fate they embraced." Stingo arrives at the boarding house to hear Morris Fink's summary of events there, and to see Sophie and Nathan, a double suicide, encircled together like lovers in her bed. Next comes their funeral; Stingo reads over the adjacent graves a poem by Emily Dickinson, which begins, "Ample make this bed."

Heartsick with grief, Stingo goes to the beach at Coney Island. He remembers his trip to the park with Nathan and Sophie. He falls asleep on the beach and children bury him in the sand. When he wakes, he sits up as one newly risen from a shallow grave and sees the morning star.

Characters

Artiste

Stingo's ancestors were slave owners. The will of Stingo's grandmother alluded to some gold coins, "the proceeds of the sale of a 16-year-old negro boy named Artiste." The orphaned Artiste, along with his two younger sisters, was bought at auction by Stingo's great-grandfather in Petersburg, Virginia, in the late 1850s. It was alleged that Artiste made some kind of "advance" toward a white girl. It was assumed he was guilty, so Artiste was sold by Stingo's great-grandfather "into the grinding hell of the Georgia turpentine forests." When the white girl later confessed to having falsely accused Artiste, the great-grandfather felt both grief and guilt. He had committed what Stingo's father calls "one of the truly unpardonable acts of a slave-owner—broken up a family." To correct the matter, he inquired by mail and courier and was ready to buy Artiste back, but the slave boy was never located. Almost five hundred dollars, left from Artiste's sale price of eight hundred

dollars in gold coin, constitutes Stingo's inheritance. Ironically Stingo, who will write novels about racism and oppression, begins his career as a writer living off the proceeds of a slave sale.

Professor Zbigniew Bieganski

Professor Zbigniew Bieganski holds the title of Distinguished Professor of Jurisprudence at Jagiellonian University in Cracow, Poland, and Doctor of Law at other German universities. He is an anti-Semite fascist, a known extremist in the academic community and scoffed at as something of a dandy and a crackpot. He writes a pamphlet on the Jewish problem that Sophie is compelled to copyedit, duplicate, and distribute. Sophie later views her father as

> a man who had exercised over his household . . . a tyrannical domination so inflexible yet so cunningly subtle that she was a grown woman, fully come of age, before she realized that she loathed him past all telling.

The professor welcomes the Nazi occupation of Poland. However, he is rounded up with other faculty and murdered by soldiers inside the Third Reich.

Dark Priestess

In his final and futile pursuit of Sophie, Stingo is joined on the train by an African American woman. She tells him, "Sonny . . . dey is only *one* Good Book. And you got it right in yo' hand." Stingo is distraught because he fears he will be too late to save Sophie. He and the black woman read aloud from the Bible, beginning with Psalm 88. They read Ecclesiastes and Isaiah. Stingo finds the "grand old Hebrew woe . . . more cathartic," so they returned to Job. When the woman, whom Stingo calls "dark priestess," gets off at Newark, she predicts, "Ev'ything gone be all right." This woman affirms the importance of finding the necessary words for lamentation; a nonbeliever, Stingo is nonetheless comforted by her and the scriptures they read together.

Dr. Walter Dürrfeld

Based on a historical person, the character Dr. Walter Dürrfeld directs IG Farbenindustrie near Leipzig. He visits Professor Bieganski in Cracow in June 1937. During his visit, Dürrfeld criticizes the British, yet he wears a smart British suit and smokes British cigarettes. Sophie finds his elegance and cultivation attractive, and the married Dürrfeld, who is many years her senior, inappropriately flirts with her. By 1943, Dürrfeld is head of Farben's industrial complex at Auschwitz. Sophie sees him in the Höss house, but he does not recognize her; she is no longer the pretty girl he met in 1937. Sophie comments that, while on the first occasion, "one of Poland's most influential anti-Semites . . . uttered not a word about Jews. Six years later almost all she heard from Dürrfeld's lips concerned Jews and their consignment to oblivion."

Sophie's Choice is full of historically factual information. The Farben chemical company, precursor of BASF, used slave labor; it flourished during the war years on profits it made from manufacturing the cyanide pesticide, Zyklon-B, and selling it to the Third Reich. Starting at Auschwitz in 1941, this chemical was used in the gas chambers to exterminate millions.

Mr. Farrell

Mr. Farrell, Stingo's immediate supervisor at McGraw-Hill, once wanted to be a writer but "got sidetracked." He describes how editorial work made him deal "with other people's ideas . . . rather than [his] own" and that doing so is "hardly conducive to creative effort." Farrell's great grief is that his son, Edward, a promising writer who, at nineteen, had already been published in the *New Yorker*, was killed on Okinawa by sniper fire in 1945; he was probably "one of the last marines to die in the war." The narrator reveals that he, too, was a marine and had gone to Okinawa, arriving there perhaps just a little while after Eddie was mortally wounded. Eddie's story makes the narrator feel "foreshortened, shriveled." When they talk for the last time, Mr. Farrell tells Stingo, "Son, *write your guts out.*" Writing is a meaning-making process, one way to "fix" or frame loss. For Mr. Farrell, writing is a way to stay on track.

Morris Fink

Morris Fink rents a room at the Zimmerman boarding house and likes gossiping about the other residents. Fink calls Nathan a "golem" because he witnesses Nathan's physical and verbal abuse of Sophie. On the day of the double suicide, Fink grows suspicious when no one answers Sophie's door when he knocks on it. He contacts Nathan's brother, Larry, and together they discover the bodies of Sophie and Nathan in her bed. Afterward, Morris wonders if there was anything he could have done to prevent the suicides.

Rudolf Franz Höss

Based on the historical person, Rudolf Franz Höss, the SS Obersturmbann-Führer and commandant of Auschwitz concentration camp, is married and has five children. He lives with his family in a house that has views of the train platform and the smoke rising from the crematoria. Sophie is his secretary for ten days. Höss detests homosexuality and any deviation from rules of conduct. He struggles against his sexual attraction to Sophie, who has the Aryan features (blue eyes, blond hair, and white skin) favored by the Nazis. Also, he respects her bilingual and secretarial skills.

Höss is compulsive about accomplishing tasks on time and, during the ten days, is violently disturbed when progress slows on construction of a new crematorium at Birkenau. Höss suffers a migraine headache when confronted with this problem and fears he will be reprimanded for negligence by his superiors. He interprets his transfer to Berlin as a reprimand. Höss recognizes Sophie's manipulation of him with the story of her father's pamphlet.

Before Höss leaves Auschwitz, he promises Sophie that he will arrange for her to see her son, but then he reneges in fear that such an act of compassion might suggest, or indeed prove, his weakness.

Maria Hunt

Maria Hunt is first mentioned in a letter to Stingo from his father who sends news of her death. The twenty-two-year-old Hunt has just committed suicide by jumping out the window of a tall building quite close to where Stingo lives. Stingo remembers being attracted to her when they were in school together as children, and he wonders if he could have prevented her death. He decides to write his first novel using Maria Hunt's life as a starting place.

Jozef

The teenage Jozef, a Warsaw resistance fighter and Sophie's lover, lives with his half-sister Wanda in an apartment directly below Sophie and her children. Though Sophie refuses to help them in their work, she admires Jozef and Wanda for participating in the underground movement. Jozef's job is to murder Poles who betray the location of Jews in hiding to the Nazis. Jozef is an anarchist and an atheist. Nonetheless, he believes in a free Poland; every time he murders a Pole, he vomits in moral revulsion. Several days after Sophie is arrested in March 1943, Jozef is murdered by the Ukrainian guards whom the Nazis use to carry out assassinations.

Larry Landau

Larry Landau, the older brother of Nathan Landau, is a medical doctor who confirms Nathan's suspicion that Sophie is suffering from iron deficiency and is dangerously anemic. Larry prescribes medicine for her. He warns Stingo about Nathan's mental illness and urges Stingo and Morris Fink, another renter, to call him immediately if Nathan presents an extreme threat. Larry also asks them not to call the police. This restriction contributes to Fink's hesitation on the final day when he discovers Sophie has returned and suspects that Nathan will arrive with a gun. Too late, Fink calls Larry to come to the boarding house. They discover the bodies of Sophie and Nathan, lying together like lovers in Sophie's bed. Perhaps Larry's role suggests that, even when others are informed and alert, they still cannot control the outcome.

Nathan Landau

Nathan Landau, a twenty-nine-year-old manic-depressive schizophrenic, is a chemical and alcohol addict who controls others by being beguiling and sadistic by turns. Nathan claims to be a cellular biologist, but the truth is he works in the library of a chemical company. Though he does not have a college degree, Nathan is well-informed about physiology and can diagnose Sophie's anemia when he first sees her in the Brooklyn Public Library. Morris Fink calls Nathan a "golem," a Yiddish word taken from the Hebrew, meaning literally a shapeless mass.

Nathan's brother, Larry, a physician, informs Stingo about Nathan's mental illness. Nathan becomes obscenely abusive during the summer of 1947 and suggests the idea of suicide to Sophie. In October of that year, he convinces Sophie to commit suicide with him. They use the drug sodium cyanide, coincidentally the same chemical used to gas people in the Nazi death camps. Nathan and Sophie are buried side by side in a new cemetery on Long Island. Over their graves, Stingo reads Dickinson's poem that begins, "Ample make this bed."

Leslie Lapidus

Leslie Lapidus, the wealthy "Jewish Madonna," speaks in sexually explicit ways to Stingo when they meet at Coney Island, an amusement park and beach located in Brooklyn. Stingo incorrectly believes that Leslie welcomes sexual intercourse with him. She invites him to her home on the day her parents leave for a vacation, but when he attempts to have sex with her she backs off, admitting that she is a virgin. In truth, Leslie is only a tease—the "Jewish princess" her father takes her to be.

Thomas McGuire

Thomas McGuire, a New York taxicab driver, has a fight with Stingo's father, who is new to New York City and inadvertently offends McGuire by giving him too small a tip. McGuire pulls quickly out into traffic, and Stingo's father falls against a sign and hurts his head. Later, as the father reflects on the fight, he predicts race riots in the North that actually occur twenty years later. The tiny episode with McGuire illustrates how ignorance of a different culture can lead to conflict.

Wanda Muck-Horch van Kretschmann

The socialist Wanda Muck-Horch van Kretschmann, the half-sister of Jozef, shares his zeal for a free Poland. She is the offspring of a German father and a Polish mother, born in Lodz, a town much affected by German commerce, industry, and culture. Like Sophie, Wanda speaks excellent German and loves German culture, particularly the classical music of Bach and others. She came to Warsaw to study voice at the conservatory; however, the outbreak of World War II ends that aspiration. A beautiful woman with red hair and boyish ways, Wanda is a lesbian who is deeply attached to Sophie. Wanda is deported to Auschwitz with Sophie. In the camp Wanda courageously manages to get news to Sophie of Jan, Sophie's son. When her work with the resistance is revealed, Wanda is hung on hooks and suffers a slow, agonizing death. On the final page of the novel, Stingo groups Wanda among the "beaten . . . martyred children of the earth."

Stingo

Stingo is the youthful persona of the fifty-two-year-old narrator of *Sophie's Choice* who uses a childhood nickname and never reveals his actual name. Stingo was born and raised in Virginia. His mother died when he was a teen. At the beginning of the novel, in the summer of 1947, Stingo is employed as a copyeditor at McGraw-Hill in New York City.

Raised a Christian but referring to himself as an agnostic, Stingo rents a room in the Flatbush boarding house run by Yetta Zimmerman, in a mostly Jewish neighborhood in central Brooklyn. He meets several residents, including Sophie Zawistowska, Nathan Landau, and Morris Fink.

At twenty-two, Stingo is inexperienced sexually. He is naïve, insecure; he sometimes misinterprets others and has unrealistic ideas about his future love life. The mature narrator, who no longer uses the nickname Stingo, has the luxury of hindsight. He can see the youthful Stingo's foolishness and self-absorption. The older narrator mulls over the past and is able to place the summer's events in a larger historical context. The mature narrator has had excellent success with his novels and journal articles.

Stingo's Father

Stingo's father, a liberal Southerner from Virginia, briefly visits his son in New York City in the summer of 1947. The father inadvertently insults a taxicab driver with too small a tip. The cabby calls the father an obscene name, and the father's angry remarks cause Stingo to reflect on how language affects relationships. Stingo sees that according to his father, "people abrogated their equality when they were unable to speak to each other in human terms." In other words, the person who uses degrading language is himself degraded by it.

Stingo's father writes letters to his son about family history, including the great-grandfather's sale of the slave Artiste. Stingo's father also reports Maria Hunt's suicide in a letter. He sends Stingo an inheritance from the slave sale which supports Stingo after he loses his job at McGraw-Hill. Stingo's father later urges Stingo to leave New York and settle on a peanut farm in Southampton County, Virginia, which Stingo's father has unexpectedly inherited from a friend.

Stingo's father has a self-deluding view of race relations. He claims that the unpardonable sin of slavery was breaking up families, thus distancing himself from the greater sin of denying other people's humanity by treating them like objects. Stingo's father criticizes the North for not facing its own racism and race problems (thus assigning to Northerners the denial which he as a Southerner also engages in) and he anticipates the race riots of 1967.

Fritz Jemand von Niemand

Not based on an historical person, Hauptsturmführer Fritz Jemand von Niemand is Nazi officer and medical doctor. He forces Sophie to choose between her children upon their arrival at the concentration camp. He has Nordic good looks, "attractive in a thin-lipped, austere, unbending way" and a feminine face. Sophie reports, "If he had been a woman, he would have been a person I think I might have felt drawn to." As a younger man, Von Niemand was a devout churchgoer and had ambitions to enter the ministry. His father coerced him into becoming a doctor. As a Nazi, he is haunted by the role he has of playing God on the Auschwitz train platform, choosing who will live and who will die. He may also fear being identified as less than a fully masculine soldier, and this fear may contribute to his particularly sadistic treatment of Sophie.

Later Sophie believes she made a fatal error in arguing with von Niemand. She tells him she is Catholic and that her children "are racially pure." Her perfect German draws dangerous attention to her and perhaps contributes to von Niemand's sadistic decision to make her choose between Jan and Eva.

Stefan Zaorski

Stefan Zaorski, a young bachelor crippled with arthritis, is a flutist in the Warsaw Symphony Orchestra. Because he has a crush on Sophie, he agrees to give flute lessons to her daughter Eva. In a tender scene, Sophie observes Stefan hobbling to catch up with Eva and Jan after a flute lesson. He needs to refine his directions on fingering an arpeggio. He plays Eva's flute, but his music is drowned out by a squadron of Luftwaffe bombers. Stefan is murdered at Auschwitz along with Eva.

Music has an important role in this novel; it confirms the best in culture and soothes grief. However, the music from the prisoner band at Auschwitz is a bizarre control and torture device, signifying the barbarism that can result from blind nationalism.

Eva Zawistowska

Eva Zawistowsa, Sophie's daughter, is a precocious ten-year-old with exceptional talent in playing the flute. Sophie "could not consider raising Eva without giving her a knowledge of music. One might as well just say no to life itself." At Auschwitz Sophie chooses Eva to die and Jan to live, an act that plagues Sophie for the rest of her life.

In the moment of their separation, Sophie sees that, along with Eva, her crippled flute teacher Stefan Zaorski is "dispatched to the left and to Birkenau" to die in the gas chambers. Sophie believes she played a part in Eva's murder. Sophie's construction of this memory illustrates how as a survivor internalizes responsibility for the abuse perpetrated by someone else. Instead of blaming her tormentor, she blames herself. Thus, the victim continues to be victimized.

Jan Zawistowska

Jan Zawistowska, Sophie's son, chaperones his sister, Eva, to her flute lessons in Warsaw and comforts her when she is cold and hungry. When Sophie and the children arrive on the train platform at Auschwitz, Sophie chooses Jan to live. He is incarcerated in the Children's Camp and may have died there from exposure and pneumonia. His actual fate is unknown. Sophie is hounded by guilt over the selection she was forced to make upon arrival at Auschwitz. Thus, she is unable to see that everyone on the platform has been "chosen" by the Nazis to die and that she is unable to spare either of her children from this fate.

Kazik Zawistowska

Kazik Zawistowska is the protégé of Professor Bieganski and Sophie's abusive husband. With Sophie, he fathers two children, Jan and Eva. Kazik is at Jagiellonian University in Cracow, Poland, when the Nazis arrest all the faculty members. Along with Professor Bieganski, Kazik is executed by soldiers in the Third Reich at Sachsenhausen, a nearby labor camp. The irony is that both the professor and Kazik are anti-Semitic Nazi sympathizers. Nonetheless, as intellectuals, they are perceived to be enemies of the Third Reich, and are thus among those the Nazis believe must be murdered.

Sophie Zawistowska

The character referred to in the title of this novel is Sophie Bieganski, a gentile born and raised in Cracow, Poland. Her fascist, autocratic, father, a professor at the local university, teaches Sophie to speak perfect German along with excellent French. As a young woman, Sophie works as his secretary. She marries his protégé, Kazik Zawistowska, a similarly abusive man, whom she grows to hate. She has two children with Kazik: a son, Jan, and a daughter, Eva. She witnesses the arrest of her father and husband, who are later murdered at Sachsenhausen, a labor camp near Cracow.

Sophie moves with her children to Warsaw. In a group arrest of citizens, she is discovered to have illegally hidden meat under her dress; she hoped to deliver the meat to her sick mother. With her children and hundreds of other people, Sophie is transported to the Nazi concentration camp at Auschwitz. On arrival, Sophie is forced to choose between her children—an act that combines the role of victim and abuser in her mind. Sophie survives until the camp is liberated. After the War, she lives temporarily in a displaced persons' camp and then moves to New York City. In New York, she enters into an abusive, addictive relationship with Nathan Landau and is befriended by Stingo. In the autumn of 1947, Sophie and Nathan commit suicide together, using the same chemical that exterminated millions at Birkenau and in other death camps.

Zosia

See Sophie Zawistowska

Themes

Evil

This novel explores evil in many forms (racism, sexism, substance abuse, domestic violence, and wartime atrocities). It suggests that oppression is a source of evil—that the state of complete domination achieved by the Third Reich evolved from the institution of slavery. It illustrates how people try to save themselves from the widening vortex of hatred. For example, Sophie thinks she is safe as long as the Germans focus on destroying the Jews. She insists her children are "racially pure," exploiting Nazi racism in a futile attempt to protect her children. Later, Höss informs Sophie that Poles are "an enemy of the Reich." He says Poles living in Germany are being "marked with a *P*—an ominous sign." In a world of hate and domination, where everyone is potentially at risk, how is one to survive? And if one does survive, how is one to live with the memory?

One evil is connected to another and all people are implicated in the evil perpetrated by some. This connection is insisted upon by Richard L. Rubenstein's *The Cunning of History*, from which Styron quotes. Rubenstein states that the Nazi "'society of total domination,' evolv[ed] directly from the institution of chattel slavery as it was practiced by the great nations of the West." This thesis works to erode American self-righteousness in the face of German racism.

Domestic Abuse

Sophie has the symptoms of a battered woman. In a sexual relationship with an abusive partner, she tries to exert power indirectly by manipulating, placating, apologizing, and bargaining. Each time she is beaten up, she apologizes. Each time the partner returns, she assures herself the worst is over. Dealing with random and uncontrollable abuse, she is controlled by her learned helplessness. She confuses who is wrong and who is right. She clings to the abusive relationship because the only "love" she knows is abusive, and she believes the only treatment she deserves is abuse. She learns verbal abuse from her father and her husband; the Nazi doctor and Höss find her sexually attractive and are abusive to her; Nathan Landau is attracted to her Danish beauty and appalled by the fact that she is actually a Pole, which in his sick mind identifies her as an anti-Semite. Addicted to the erotics of violence, Sophie is unable to function in an equitable relationship. The relatively healthy relationship Stingo offers threatens to unhinge her from the

Topics For Further Study

- Imagine that you have only twenty-four hours to vacate your home, possibly for the last time. You have no idea where you are going or why you are being forced to leave. You have been told you can only take what fits in your backpack. Decide what you will carry with you. Then write an essay explaining your choices and how evaluating them in the light of this hypothetical scenario affected your assessment.

- Read Elie Wiesel's autobiographical book *Night*, and compare his memories of Auschwitz with what Sophie says about the concentration camp. Styron includes in *Sophie's Choice* an assertion by Wiesel that novels based on the Holocaust "cheapened" the subject because the topic had become "fashionable, guaranteed to gain attention and to achieve instant success." Write an essay in which you agree or disagree with Wiesel's position, contrasting his own book with Styron's novel.

- Research online either Rudolf Höss or Walter Dürrfeld and write a summary of the information you collect. Evaluate Styron's handling of the character in the novel, determining if the fictional role fits the historical person.

- Interview someone you know who has been an eyewitness to or lived through some historical event—for example, the Civil Rights movement or the antiwar movement of the 1950s and 1960s, the Vietnam War, the Gulf War of the early 1990s, or the September 11, 2001, terrorist attacks on the United States. Write a summary of the interview and then present the summary to the interviewee. Ask that person to evaluate your summary for its accuracy and to identify topics that have been distorted or omitted. Present to the class your findings regarding how accurate summaries from interviews are.

---

abuse she has come to believe she deserves. Battered woman syndrome requires professional intervention and therapy, but even with this kind of support, battered women frequently return to their abusive partners and many are killed by them.

Denial

Denial is an unconscious mechanism which helps people repress unwanted information about themselves or about the world. Americans who focus on Nazi war crimes may be less inclined to ponder the U.S. use of atomic bombs on two Japanese cities. Similarly, they may feel unconnected to the racist atrocities committed in the American South or the genocide of Native American tribes. Northerners may be appalled by Southern lynching and asleep to the racism that contributes to urban ghettos throughout the United States. So long as people locate evil away from the self, they postpone recognizing their own role in its perpetuation. Stingo's inheritance is a literal sign that he is the inheritor of his culture. Once people experience

what Styron calls "the shock of recognition," they can begin to feel compassion for the other, a feeling that erodes subject/object distinction and affirms the essential oneness of all humankind.

Style

Literary Allusion

A literary allusion is a reference to another work of literature. It places the work at hand in a literary context and draws meaning from the works to which it alludes. The novel is saturated with such allusions. It alludes, for example, to John Donne and to Dante's *Inferno* and the lovers Paolo and Francesca. It refers to James Joyce and compares this novel to his *Ulysses*. Readers who know these other books increase their understanding of the present work and its layered meaning. In many cases, Styron comes across as self-congratulatory, placing his work in the context of great works of

Compare & Contrast

- **1940s:** While suicide is often the result of emotional or mental illness, it is treated as a crime by the U.S. legal system.

  Today: Suicide bombers kill themselves to make political statements all over the world, and people who are terminally ill seek physician-assisted suicide to bring an end to their suffering.

- **1940s:** After World War II, high-ranking Nazi officers are tried at Nuremberg, Germany. Many of these men are hanged.

  Today: The U.S. Justice Department Office of Special Investigations continues to identify people in the United States who are guilty of Nazi war crimes. Identified persons are either deported or stripped of their citizenship. Between 1979 and 2002, 71 are stripped of their citizenship and 57 are deported.

- **1940s:** Drug research takes place in the hopes of helping people cope with mental illness. Drugs like Benzedrine are sometimes used illegally to help combat depression.

  Today: Risperdal, the leading drug used to combat schizophrenia, which is prescribed to more than 10 million people worldwide, is found to have potentially life-threatening side effects.

---

literature. Toward the end of the novel, the narrator praises his favorite sentence about love, calling the idea "the property of God," and including himself as its author in a list of prophets that includes Jesus and Buddha. While Styron accumulates meaning with some allusions, his ego sabotages the effectiveness of others.

Juxtaposition

The stories told in *Sophie's Choice* are not presented in chronological order. Meaning comes in some instances from the proximity of parts of the stories. George Steiner's idea of "time relation" draws attention to the idea of juxtaposition. For example, on the day Sophie arrives in Auschwitz, Stingo is bulking up his weight by gorging himself on bananas. He is intent on passing an exam for acceptance into the Marines, but he has as of yet not heard of Auschwitz. Another example occurs while Sophie looks at the picture album of Emmi Höss, the commandant's daughter. Sophie smells burning flesh from the crematoria; Emmi closes the window against the stink and then describes the heated swimming pool at Dachau. Putting the daughter's frame of reference next to the extermination of the Jews heightens the disconnect necessary for Nazis to carry out the Final Solution.

Historical Context

World War II

The Nazi system of human extermination during World War II (1941–1945) was publicized following the liberation of the concentration camps. Newsreels in American theaters showed the appalling details. By the summer of 1947, people were slowly waking up to the atrocities. Thirty years later, the narrator still ponders the heinous events, studies scholarship on the Third Reich, and tries to understand it as a spectacular instance of pure evil. Stingo has the opportunity to hear from an eyewitness, and thus his historical awareness is abruptly sharpened. This awareness of events in which he had such a peripheral military part leads to his reevaluation of his own cultural heritage.

Critical Overview

Mixed reviews came out in response to the publication of *Sophie's Choice*. It was found to be "affecting and thoroughly convincing" by a reviewer for the June 11, 1979, issue of *Time* magazine. But John W. Aldridge, writing in *Harper's* (September

Jewish women pulling hopper cars of quarried stone along "Industry Street," in Plaszow concentration camp, Krakow, Poland, 1944 Photograph by Raimund Tisch. USHMM Photo Archives

1979), regretted Styron's inability "to make his material meaningful." Another reviewer, writing for the *New Yorker* (June 18, 1979) summed up the novel as "an elaborate showcase of every variety of racial prejudice and guilt." This reviewer found Styron's prose "loaded with overwrought sentences . . . and with ponderous lectures that reduce Sophie's story to the stuff of theory."

Benjamin DeMott in the July 1979 *Atlantic Monthly* attempted to balance the centrality of Stingo, his family, and his past, with Sophie's "fearful and ponderable life." DeMott criticized the dissonance between chapters spent on Stingo's "bizarre and comic passage through the straits of virginity," and Sophie's "monologues," full of "events [that] are both hideous and unsurprising." DeMott also faulted Styron's inclusion of material that disengages the reader's feelings about the story, calling it "academic banality." He found disruptive the "treatises concerning the technology of despots of mass murder" and insisted that summaries of scholarship shatter the novel's fictive world. Nonetheless, DeMott commended Styron for his accomplishment in the portrait of Sophie that "reaches toward the full truth of human panic at the edge of oblivion." In all, reviews addressed the disparate parts of the novel. Some reviews were,

in some cases, compelled by the Holocaust story but at the same time put off by the discursions into lecture and pomposity.

Criticism

Melodie Monahan

Monahan has a Ph.D. in English. She teaches at Wayne State University and also operates an editing service, The Inkwell Works. In the following essay, Monahan explains how the two story lines in Sophie's Choice *blur the roles of abuser and victim.*

William Styron's book, *Sophie's Choice*, tells a story inside another story and, in the telling of these stories, the book reads like a novel. But, in other places in the text, the book does not read like a novel. There are excerpts from unpublished work (with editing comments on them), historical background information, and summaries of scholarship. If readers are to understand the meaning of *Sophie's Choice*, then they must be able to explain how these disparate parts work together.

The central content of *Sophie's Choice* is the story of Sophie Zawistowska, a Polish gentile who

> " The same evil at work in kidnapping human beings and reducing them to property (as in slavery) is at work in the domination and dehumanization that culminate in a machinery for extermination."

survives Auschwitz where she loses her children. And who then, having arrived in New York, is drawn into a self-destructive, abusive relationship with an American Jew—the psychotic drug addict, Nathan Landau. Paralleling Sophie's story is the story of Stingo during the summer of 1947, when he becomes friends with Sophie and Nathan. Stingo's story is mostly about his setting out to become a writer and about his sexual initiation. Stingo's story contains letters from his father and excerpts from writing Stingo does in 1947. In 1947, Sophie draws her story from her immediate memories of living in Poland before and during World War II; Stingo's story, full of his hopes for the future, is told across the span of thirty years, from the point of view of the successful author Stingo is to become.

In addition, the novel includes information about the real world on which this fiction of Sophie is based: population statistics for Jews in Warsaw; information about the IG Farben chemical conglomerate at Auschwitz; biographical information on Rudolf Höss, the Nazi commandant of Auschwitz from 1940 to 1943; and quotations from theoretical works by mid-twentieth century scholars and thinkers, such as Simone Weil, George Steiner, Richard Rubenstein, and Holocaust survivor, Elie Weisel. These parts of the book interrupt the "fiction" of the novel in order to discuss the Holocaust.

Why does Styron frame Sophie's story with Stingo's story? Why are these two stories freighted with historical, biographical, and theoretical writings? The answer to these questions lies in a connection drawn in some of the research material Styron quotes—namely, that the Nazi state of domination developed out of the institution of slavery.

The same evil at work in kidnapping human beings and reducing them to property (as in slavery) is at work in the domination and dehumanization that culminate in a machinery for extermination.

Disbelief in these connections derives, in part, from the fact that others remote from the events are unaware of them or deliberately disassociate themselves from them. Their tendency to disconnect is partly explained by George Steiner's theory about simultaneity: at the same moment hordes of people were being gassed in concentration camps, "the overwhelming plurality of human beings, two miles away on the Polish farms, five thousand miles away in New York, were sleeping or eating or going to a film or making love or worrying about the dentist.... Their coexistence is so hideous a paradox—Trebinka *is* both because some men have built it and almost all other men let it be." In other words, because people are separated across time or space, they can deny their connection to human events in which they are not immediately and directly involved.

In reading Steiner, the narrator feels a "shock of recognition." As Sophie stepped onto the train platform at Auschwitz, embracing her two children for what was to be the last time, Stingo was gorging himself on bananas. It was a lovely April day, rimmed with forsythia, but Sophie was slipping into "living damnation," to use Steiner's words, while Stingo was hoping to bulk up his weight in order to pass the physical examination for entrance into the Marines. Sophie was already starving and would continue to starve; Stingo was trying to increase his weight. He had not yet heard of Auschwitz.

Ironically, Stingo's first season as a writer, who will in time publish books about Nazism and racism, is financed by money he inherits from his great-grandfather's sale of the slave called Artiste. Does that make Stingo responsible for slavery? Styron would probably answer that it connects Stingo to a slave culture. Nathan taunts Stingo with Southern racism, with the fact that Southern whites lynch blacks, and Stingo winces in tracing parallels between the Georgia lynching of Bobby Weed and the fate of Artiste. As long as people disconnect from the evil, see it as true of others but not true of themselves, they separate themselves from others, assigning to others what they insist is not true of themselves. Thus, they affirm otherness and hierarchy. This action fuels oppression and all its attending ills. The collision of stories in the book brings about Stingo's awakening to the humanity of all people and to the implied responsibility all people, however remote, share in oppression. Thus, Styron establishes a connection between Stingo's past regarding slavery and Sophie's past regarding the Third Reich.

The book's title directs readers to another connection. Sophie makes two major "choices," one in the past, one in the present summer; arguably neither one is a deliberate and free choice. First, she is coerced to select between her two children when they first arrive at Auschwitz. Second, in Washington, D.C., Sophie leaves Stingo and returns to Nathan. In both cases, the choice expresses victimization and how, in the victim's mind, the distinction between perpetrator and victim can be blurred. Sophie is hounded by the guilt she feels regarding her children's fate, but the fact is she was the pawn of a Nazi sadist, completely powerless to protect her children. In the second case, now the victim of domestic abuse, Sophie acts like any abused woman may act; she returns to her abuser, plunging toward destruction because she believes she is nothing without her abuser. Thus, she embraces her own destruction, having been long taunted by claims that she is unworthy of living.

This confusion between abuser and victim is carried further in the characterization of the Nazi doctor, Fritz Jemand von Niemand, who forces Sophie to choose between her children. Von Niemand, the abuser, is characterized as a divided man, both dominant and vulnerable. He is attractive, young, and "silkily feminine." Sophie admits, "If he had been a woman, he would have been a person I think I might have felt drawn to." When the doctor meets Sophie he is "undergoing the crisis of his life: cracking apart like bamboo, disintegrating." Before the war he was a churchgoer, and aspired to the ministry, but a money-hungry father forced him into medicine; this point constitutes coercion. Now a doctor, von Niemand knows himself part of "a mammoth killing machine," as much a cog in the works as the slaves he chooses to labor for IG Farben. The hint of femininity suggests that perhaps he is a homosexual or has at least a tendency not to identify with the masculine military role—in either case, he may be terrified that he will be categorized among those hated groups selected for extermination. In this scene of unthinkable torture and pain, readers are asked to consider how the abuser may have himself been coerced, may himself be potentially a victim.

In the final scenes in which Stingo pursues Sophie, sees her and Nathan curled in death, attends

Memorial to workers who died at the Buchenwald concentration camp © Ira Nowinski/Corbis

their double funeral, and grieves for his friends, the narrator directs readers to texts of lamentation. Stingo reads the Old Testament on the train as he returns to Brooklyn, the poem by Dickinson over the graves, and finally, recalls the few worthy sentences from his 1947 summer writings. The narrator focuses in the final couple pages on one sentence from that summer: "*Let your love flow out on all living things.*" This idea, admittedly "the property of God," has "been intercepted—on the wing, so to speak—by such mediators as Lao-tzu, Jesus, Gautama Buddha and thousands of lesser prophets." To feel this all-encompassing, impersonal love is to be able to grieve for human suffering. Compassion, rooted in awareness that all beings are united, allows a person to feel the interconnectedness of all human life. Evil encompasses all humans; the suffering it causes is for all of people to acknowledge. In so far as Stingo can realize his cultural connections to evil and his membership in the human family, he identifies with the suffering. The rage and sorrow demand that he mourn all "the beaten and butchered and betrayed and martyred children of the earth." This mourning enacts resurrection: Stingo dreams of death and awakens to morning.

But is it enough to mourn for the effects of colossal evil? Sophie's story is interrupted twice by

Stingo's departure—once for a weekend date with Leslie, once for a ten-day vacation with an old Marine buddy. These anticlimactic sexual scenarios may work in the text to illustrate how people can be aware of evil only to a degree, and then their own immediate interests or drives take them away from attending to it. Perhaps, in trying to comes to terms with the Holocaust and with the post–World War II responses by Americans to it, Styron suggests that, because people are separated from the site of atrocity and self-absorbed in their immediate circumstances, they lose track of evil, thus falling asleep to their participation in it.

Source: Melodie Monahan, Critical Essay on *Sophie's Choice*, in *Novels for Students*, Thomson Gale, 2006.

Richard G. Law

In the following essay excerpt, Law explores how Styron incorporates various voices and narrative perspectives in order to inform the reader's "encounter with Auschwitz."

In *Sophie's Choice*, the telling of the tale is contrived to display the capacity of fiction to illuminate a subject that baffles ordinary inquiry and to test the claims of art against perhaps the extreme form of knowledge: the meaning of Auschwitz. The novel also makes imperious demands on the reader, who is lured into constructing a text of the Holocaust—a process which, while productive of insights that are perhaps available in no other way, comes at the cost of a painful imaginative involvement. An essential part of the "argument" of *Sophie's Choice*—and of the implied claims for fiction which are embodied in it—is that the direct and unmediated encounter with the heart of darkness is not only dangerous, but may, by its very nature, prevent comprehension. Given a subject which cannot be confronted without danger of engulfing the viewer, the controlled distancing of art may be a necessary component of understanding.

Accordingly, the novel alternates between intense glimpses of its subject and moments of great psychological distance and abstraction, drawing the reader into a rhythm of confrontation and evasion. One of the primary means by which the reader's encounter with Auschwitz is controlled and manipulated is through the alternation of complementary but quite different narrative perspectives. Stingo's point of view provides a direct though naive experience, approaching Auschwitz more or less accidentally and unwillingly. Through Stingo, the reader has a direct glimpse not of Auschwitz, but of the delayed *effects* of Auschwitz on another.

Stingo's experience is supplemented by the point of view of the mature authorial voice of the narrator, who offers a retrospective, frequently satirical reconstruction of his younger self's encounter with Sophie and her past. This retrospective view is informed by a broad scholarly rumination on the records of and commentary about the Holocaust, including extensive quotations from both victims and Nazi officials. In this way the book gives expression to many voices (no one of which can presume to capture "Auschwitz") even as it assimilates them to its own ends.

I

The subject of the Holocaust represents a test case for exploring the limits of what we conventionally call knowledge. It is hard to "know" Auschwitz. The experience of the camps exists so far outside normal human frames of references that the very facts of the case are, in a sense, unimaginable. As Styron himself has asserted, "Auschwitz can be compared to nothing"; "Auschwitz must remain the one place on earth most unyielding to meaning or definition." Moreover, the mind has defenses against such horror which are not easily overcome. It is no small task, then, to attempt to link the incommensurate with the familiar, to bring what lies at such an extremity within range of our ordinary powers of vision. What can be known of the phenomenon of industrialized mass murder is also complicated by the different senses by which we understand the word "knowledge." One kind of knowledge is the historian's, which is abstract and retrospective—its value deriving in part from its very distance from the events themselves and from the extent to which the events can be processed (interpreted) for general use. Quite another kind of knowledge is, of course, to have been there: "Only survivors of Auschwitz know what it meant to be in Auschwitz." Such knowledge is untranslatable and incommunicable; it not only transcends interpretation but defies attempts to make sense of it.

Between the former kind of knowledge and the latter, of course, lies an enormous distance which the novel invites us to contemplate. As Styron was aware, formidable commentators like Elie Wiesel have advised that fiction writers not even try to deal with the subject—that to make it a subject of fiction is somehow a desecration of the memory of the victims. Similarly, George Steiner has asserted that the only proper response is silence. Styron's novel, however, is directed squarely at the Steiner-Wiesel position that art can only trivialize an experience like the Holocaust. The "ultimately transcendental and important thing about art," Styron has claimed, "is its ability to do anything—that's the definition of art. It can deal with any experience—past, present, or future. . . ." In dramatizing the position that silence will not do as an answer to the camps, the novel has as much to say about the nature and capabilities of art as about Auschwitz. It is as if the novel accepts its subject as a challenge: if *Sophie's Choice* can provide a medium in which Auschwitz can, in some meaningful sense, become known, then literature can treat anything; no subjects are off-limits; no veils may be drawn across any area of human experience.

Styron's act of writing the novel, then, involves a monumental presumption and irreverence. He refuses to concede any privileged area to "insiders" or to bow to any form of proprietorship— a stance which had embroiled him earlier with some members of the black intelligentsia over *The Confessions of Nat Turner,* just as it has antagonized some Jewish readers of *Sophie's Choice.* But the novel embodies a kind of reverence as well, in that Styron's position, regardless of the components of personal arrogance or humility in it, implies that the imagination can function in a saving way at the very margins of human experience.

II

If *Sophie's Choice* is as preoccupied with the problem of knowledge as is *All the King's Men* or *As I Lay Dying,* it also attempts to overcome the obstacles to knowledge with techniques familiar from those precedents: it explores minutely a particular instance (Sophie's season in Hell) as a synecdoche of the Holocaust. The text draws a familiar distinction between abstract and concrete knowledge, the historian's knowledge vs. the victim's, and it relies heavily on the power of imagery to combine both, to fuse concepts and emotions, the general and the particular, in complex, highly charged dramatic actions. Like Faulkner's *The Sound and the Fury,* Styron's novel is constructed around a powerful germinal scene which the rest of the work may be said to gloss. Styron has referred to the genesis of the novel as a waking dream which imposed itself on him and became the controlling metaphor for the whole work. The image which troubled Styron involved a young woman on the platform at Auschwitz being forced to choose between her children. That image focused and contained several decades of his pondering on the meaning of the death camps: "I suddenly realized that this had to be the metaphor for the most horrible, tyrannical despotism in history, that this was

> **Styron's act of writing the novel, then, involves a monumental presumption and irreverence. He refuses to concede any privileged area to 'insiders' or to bow to any form of proprietorship. . . ."**

a new form of evil. . . ." This single scene defines the world the Nazis made; it explains the secret wellspring of Sophie's mystifying behavior and the source of the irrational guilt which destroys her. It also dramatizes—by a process this essay will explore—as much of the heart of the darkness as is possible to dramatize.

It is critical to note that the reader encounters the core scene of Sophie with her children on the platform at Auschwitz only on page 484 of a 515-page text, by which point the narrative, through the powerful spectacle of her suffering, has converted the reader's initial gossipy interest in Sophie into a profound sense of empathy. Knowledge of her "choice" is withheld until the reader is prepared for it, subtly, by sensing in her attempts to start a new life in New York the consequences of some unknown event—the shadow of some unspeakable experience in her past—which has left Sophie obscurely crippled. In the meantime, by becoming gradually acquainted with Sophie and her story, the reader has descended, step by step, through layer after layer of her psychic pain, each layer worse than the last—and each, in a sense, unimaginable, unevocable, except by the process and in the context of the tale in which we have become immersed.

Because of its literally almost unspeakable subject, the manner of the unfolding of the tale is an exercise in overcoming, or putting to sleep, reader resistance. To keep the reader's imagination from evading the nature of Sophie's experience, Styron employs a variety of stratagems, some simple and others Byzantine in their elaborateness. The unfolding of the narrative, then, is a kind of trick which simultaneously carries us toward and hides its destination. The whole narrative is skillfully crafted to get us in a frame of mind where we

What Do I Read Next?

- In the Pulitzer Prize–winning novel *The Confessions of Nat Turner* (1967), Styron tells the story of the 1831 Virginia slave rebellion. The novel explores the effects of the institution of slavery on American history.

- *Darkness Visible: A Memoir of Madness* (1990) is Styron's autobiographical essay about mental depression, which was brought on by the death of his father and many decades of alcohol abuse.

- In *Stones from the River*, Ursula Hegi tells the story of Trudy Montag, a dwarf who lives with her father in Burgdorf. Spanning the years from 1916 to the 1950s, the novel is about this little town of ordinary German citizens who carry on with their lives despite the horrific events occurring around them.

- Nobel laureate Elie Wiesel's *Night* is a work of creative nonfiction that follows the experience of a young Jewish boy through the oppression of Nazi occupation and the horrors of the Nazi concentration camps. This is a seminal work of Holocaust literature that explores religious faith, the bond between father and son, the survivor coming to terms with humanity, and the importance of learning from the terrible events of history.

---

cannot evade, or fail to imagine, the experience of genocide from the point of view of one of its victims.

Given the gruesome opportunities of the subject matter, there are very few actual scenes of Auschwitz, and few of them are particularly sensationalized or physically brutal. Although his portrayal of the camp is carefully based on surviving documents, Styron resists, for the most part, direct representation of its most sensational features. A careful reader of Emily Dickinson, Styron evidently holds with her that, because of its power to blind, "the Truth must dazzle gradually." Accordingly, most of the brutal realities of the camps are realized by suggestion, by brief direct glimpses, and by analogy. We acquire a sense of the degree to which Sophie has been brutalized in the camp from the way her father, an ardent fascist, treats her before the war and from the way her lover, Nathan Landau, treats her afterwards; we sense something of the camp's limitless oppression and dehumanizing impersonality from the anonymous digital rape of Sophie in the subway in New York. Similarly, from Stingo's haunted conscience about failing his cancer-stricken mother, we acquire the barest inklings of Sophie's sense of guilt—just the faintest sense of that open oven door of memory she encounters when she thinks of her children.

Such reserve and indirection are characteristic of the narrative stratagems generally in *Sophie's Choice*. The experience of direct, scalding pain is, of course, not the object of the narrative, but rather a sympathetic intuition of the dimensions of Sophie's agony. Styron uses very shrewdly his art form's ability to move toward insight by the "stairway of surprise." By careful preparation and frequent deception, the narrative takes us up to one threshold of revelation after another and then stops, the narrator seeming always just about to show us things or tell us things. By such means it manages to take us places we would refuse to go if we sensed the destination. The components of the victim's experience of Auschwitz are vividly suggested in the narrative, but the task of assembling and understanding them belongs to the reader.

Sophie's Choice is presented in the form of a *Bildungsroman* in which the organizing axis of the narrative is Stingo's quest for knowledge. All of the elaborate excursions and digressions contribute to that developing line. Stingo is presented as a characterization of Styron himself at 22: a lonely ex-Marine with both literary and amorous ambitions seeking his fortune in the city. Stingo's is a familiar tale of initiation in which a callow, superficial sense of self and world is demolished by his "education." Stingo's attainment of a more mature and adequate perspective is not dramatized, although his having arrived at it is implied in the presence of the mature authorial voice, who has somehow survived and come to terms with the knowledge that Sophie represents. In reminiscing about the summer of 1947, the mature narrator speaks to us out of a successful career as a writer—a success which has, by some means difficult to fathom, been engendered by the experience that overwhelms his younger self. In mediating between the reader and the traumatic experience which constitutes Stingo's education, the mature narrator plays an unobtrusive but significant role in assembling the tale and controlling reader responses. Using the guise of confessional autobiography, the mature narrator dramatizes his younger self's failure to comprehend and assimilate his education while simultaneously taking the reader on a torturous journey almost to the center of that experience.

The narrative he constructs of his early shortcomings is self-consciously intertextual; it casts Stingo as a twentieth-century version of Melville's Ishmael, setting out in Brooklyn on a "voyage of discovery": "my spirit had remained landlocked, unacquainted with love and all but a stranger to death." In a technique also reminiscent of *Moby-Dick,* the narrative has a double story line with dual protagonists and dual centers of interest, so that Stingo's own story emerges out of his telling us the story of the second figure, Sophie, whose name means "wisdom." The narrative is structured so that for Stingo to discover the answers to the riddle of Sophie, to know Sophie, as it were, would amount to a resolution of his quest. What Stingo acquires by way of an education is an experience of "evil," which is also the subject of the mature narrator's brooding enquiry.

Styron gives Stingo's initiation story important twists: his education involves gaining a perspective adequate for his ambition to become a writer. The narrative therefore recounts Stingo's discovery of both a subject and the resources within himself to treat it—the *knowledge,* presumably, to interpret it. Organized in this way, the fictive world which emerges in the narrative has a bearing on and provides a partial definition of the writer's craft and calling. However, Stingo's education consists largely of discoveries—in scenes such as the revelation of Nathan's madness—of the invalidity or unreliability of his knowledge.

Learning of Sophie's past and observing her eventual death constitute the chief means through which Stingo acquires an experience of evil. The two mysteries, Sophie and Auschwitz, are telescoped together, with Sophie serving as the focal point through which the mystery of Auschwitz can be glimpsed: "It have thought that it might be possible to make a stab at understanding Auschwitz by trying to understand Sophie. . . ." However, the youthful Stingo is too stunned to assimilate, even vicariously, Sophie's experience of evil. A product of a safe, white, middle class, Protestant Tidewater Virginia upbringing, Stingo appears an unlikely candidate for either mature understanding or Parnassus. He suffers from a peculiarly American innocence, epitomized by his "virginity," which not even a hitch in the Marine Corps in World War II could alter. Naive, frequently obtuse, and sexually obsessed, he is, for much of the narrative, essentially a comic figure, providing a kind of bizarre (but often welcome) relief from the unfolding horrors of Sophie's past.

But it is important to note that the mature narrator, even in his retrospective account, is not readily able to follow the track of Sophie's experience to her nightmare encounter on the platform either. One index to the difficulty the narrator has in assimilating the knowledge that Sophie represents is the manner of the telling of Sophie's tale, which is as circuitous in its own way as the telling of *Absalom, Absalom!* To an extent, the narrative technique dramatizes not just Stingo's repeated failures to comprehend, but the older narrator's cautious approach toward the death camps. Aspects of her past, or aspects of what is known of Auschwitz, are worried at length, as if no context could be large enough to encompass and no background sufficient to explain the impending revelation. Typically, key information is offered up piecemeal, in fragments which have to be assembled by the reader, or as generalization separate from context or details. Events and information come jumbled together in baffling counterpoint, sometimes juxtaposed as if to comment on one another, and at other times seemingly to retard the action, as if to postpone the platform encounter.

The gradual unfolding of Sophie's past is structured around a number of moments of revelation which require revisions of Stingo's previous estimates of her. These moments function as mileposts in the narrative's approach toward the secret of her life. The need for continual revision is partly a result of Sophie's reticence about things and partly of her active duplicity. She lies about her unhappy marriage and her relationship with her father, fabricating a parent who is a kindly paragon of virtue and learning, rather than a fanatical anti-Semite who had imagined and passionately advocated for others the kind of fate which overwhelms his daughter and grandchildren (237 ff.). She suppresses her wartime experiences in Warsaw and the fact that she had a son at Auschwitz and a daughter also. Last of all, the revelation that she was forced to choose between them comes only slowly, after many evasions, so that each revelation forces Stingo to construct a new interpretation of her past and therefore of her "present" character and situation. Also absent from early accounts of her past is the "fact" that, in the moral quagmire that was Auschwitz, Sophie was not simply a victim of the Nazis, but, in a complex and extremely tenuous way, an accomplice.

But the need for revision is also partly a result of the strangeness and enormity of what is to be understood. Preoccupied by his own sexual enterprises and blinded by his infatuation with her, Stingo is obviously not very astute in his reading of Sophie. He is taken in by her evasions and fails to comprehend her real needs for assistance. For example, after his comically disastrous attempts with Leslie and Alice, Stingo has his longed-for sexual encounter with Sophie, but the act is a grim parody of intimacy, and it fails to effect the magical changes in himself that he had hoped for. In fact, the loss of his "virginity" is largely ancillary to his education, and it certainly does nothing for his powers of observation. Stingo fails to realize that, for Sophie, the experience is merely a brief anodyne for her pain, which is intense enough to make death desirable. Stingo, the aspiring novelist, is not astute enough to recognize how little his offer of a Southern pastoral retreat, complete with matrimony and an on-looking Protestant community, could appeal to Sophie in these circumstances. He also fails utterly to grasp the dual roles Nathan has played in her life as healing savior and the pursuing demon of her conscience. By presenting himself in the role of yet another male savior, Stingo shows himself insensitive to the elements of her life of struggle for independence of male domination. Finally, he is oblivious to her dread of having more children. His catalog of missed signals is great enough to suggest that another, less tragic outcome might have been possible, had he truly *known* Sophie.

Stingo misunderstands Nathan as thoroughly as he does Sophie, oscillating until nearly the end between admiration and loathing of this older, mysterious figure. In one typical revelation, Sophie confides to Stingo that Nathan was addicted to drugs. "How blind I had been!" Stingo exclaims, in the throes of a complete reinterpretation of Nathan's past behavior. For a time, Nathan's demon acquires a specific shape and rationale in Stingo's mind, only to be expunged as an explanation by Larry Landau's further revelation of Nathan's madness a hundred pages later. But these failures of Stingo to comprehend critical issues throughout the narrative are not merely illustrative of his flaws of character. They dramatize the elusiveness of the understanding he seeks. And because the mature narrator does not share with the reader the benefits of his own hindsight, but withholds information and silently encourages false or incomplete appraisals, the reader is left equally at sea—therefore sharing with Stingo multiple experiences of disquieting misapprehension, revision, and reinterpretation. This technique involves the reader intimately in Stingo's experience, in Stingo's "voyage of discovery." By such means, as we shall see, the narrative encourages in the reader a sense of involved discovery which is closely akin emotionally to actual experience. Drawing the reader into constructing the text also has the function of bringing into consciousness the provisional nature of the kind of knowledge at issue here: the "truth" is invariably grimmer and more complex than the reader's first estimates of it. At the same time, the center of attention in the novel is subtly shifted from the events themselves to the process of interpreting experience *as* text and to the writer's act of reconstituting experience *in* the text. Thus, the technique also illustrates the arbitrary nature of the discourse in which knowledge is ordinarily framed.

III

Larry Landau's disclosure, "the truth is that my brother's quite mad," is one of the most significant expectation-shattering revelations in the novel. Like the revelation of Darl's insanity in *As I Lay Dying,* it has the effect of dramatically overturning the reader's previous estimates and forcing a fundamentally different reconstruction of the narrative. The revelation about Nathan's clinical history of insanity demolishes the most fundamental interpretative paradigm of the narrative as the reader had been led to conceive it—the novel as essay on the nature of evil. Nathan's violent abuse of Sophie had had the function throughout most of the narrative of embodying the principle of evil that has deformed Sophie's life and prospects. As Sophie's torturer in the New World, Nathan is presented, seemingly, as a "mirror" or extension of Auschwitz. By bringing atrocity on a mass industrial basis down to a recognizable human scale, Nathan had also served as one of the means by which the reader is empowered to

Jewish children in a concentration camp, still from a postwar Soviet film, Auschwitz, Poland   USHMM
Photo Archives

imagine the larger "absolute evil" of the camps. Consequently, Dr. Landau's description of his brother Nathan's diagnosis—"Paranoid schizophrenic, or so the diagnosis goes, although I'm not at all sure if those brain specialists really know what they're up to"—is a transforming event which wrenches the frame of reference onto an entirely different plane. The terms of explanation shift: "insanity" is suddenly substituted for "evil"; the language of morality is replaced by a discourse which is secular and scientific.

This discovery of the cause of Nathan's behavior—or rather, this definition of it—forces us to revise our understanding of the relationship between Sophie and Nathan and its role in Sophie's impending doom. Having been invited by the narrative to construct an indictment of Nathan as brute and torturer, the reader finds this indictment suddenly quashed. It is no longer clear, given this revelation, whether Nathan functions as a moral extension of the camps—or whether the camps, too, represent a manifestation of collective madness (an idea which is hinted at once, in a thought attributed to Nathan on page 323). The "fact" of Nathan's madness therefore leaves the reader unhooked from any certain set of terms or interpretive frame and unsure of how to judge what has happened. Schizophrenia,

that mysterious and tragic ailment, is an acid capable of dissolving even complex moral judgments—thus denying us the moral judgment of Nathan which we had been permitted to make and robbing us of the precious sense of comprehension that condemnation of Nathan had provided.

The operative definition of evil—the version of it which presents itself as an issue in the text—is domination: evil consists of exalting either self or some abstract value into the supreme or sole value and reducing all else, including others, to instruments. In the autobiographical testament of Commandant Höss, for example, "real evil" appears as a kind of twisted piety, joined with an egotism which directs all natural pity away from one's victims and toward one's self. Simone Weil and Hannah Arendt are quoted on the "true nature of evil," which is allegedly "gloomy, monotonous, and boring." Whether boring or flamboyant, evil appears to consist of one human being's ruthless use of another, with the Nazi concentration camps, with their total and utterly uninhibited domination of human beings, illustrating evil in its ultimate or "absolute" form. This definition allows the narrator to place American slavery, Professor Bieganski's treatment of Sophie, and Nathan's behavior as her lover in a moral continuum.

The paradigm of evil demands, as terms of discourse, some axiomatic concept of value (e.g. human life), a perversion of privation of that value, along with the concept of choice. The paradigm of mental illness, on the other hand, implies a determinative chain of causes and effects operating uniformly in a physiological system. In the latter kind of discourse, value and choice can scarcely enter into the operations of "indifferent nature"; thus, any supposed agency responsible for "evil" recedes into the recesses and obscure chemical transactions of Nathan's brain.

By a kind of Faulknerian irony, almost immediately after the revelation of Nathan's insanity, Nathan finally succeeds in seducing Sophie into suicide. Or at least they both die. Like Cash Bundren witnessing his brother Darl trussed up and carted off the Jackson, the reader is forced to confront the tenuousness of the connections between our language and the world which it organizes for us—particularly the arbitrariness of our collective definitions of "sane" and "insane," and of the terms of discourse which they evoke. Denied the explanation of evil, the reader must grope for some alternative interpretive map, for a language *past* the "sanity and insanity" of human doings but adequate to our "horror and astonishment" at both. Thus, this "epiphany" does not so much enlighten us as bring us up short against the limitations of our perceptual templates and the poverty of our explanations. This encounter with a paradigm-shattering event is especially significant in a narrative which identifies Auschwitz as a kind of ultimate object of knowledge, because it appears to problematize the narrator's meditations on the nature of the "evil" which Auschwitz represents in so ghastly a form.

Source: Richard G. Law, "The Reach of Fiction: Narrative Technique in Styron's *Sophie's Choice*," in *Southern Literary Journal*, Vol. 22, No. 1, Fall 1990, pp. 45–55.

Rhoda Sirlin

In the following introduction to her William Styron's "Sophie's Choice": Crime and Self-Punishment, *Sirlin examines Styron's background, his debt to European existential thought, and the critical reception of* Sophie's Choice.

With rebellion, awareness is born. This central theme of Albert Camus' famous philosophical essay *The Rebel* an exploration of an individual's passionate affirmation that underlies the act of rebellion, might well serve as a springboard for an understanding and appreciation of William Styron's fiction. According to Camus, the question raised by

rebellion today is whether or not it is possible to find a rule of conduct outside the realm of religion and its absolute values. The rebel demands order in the midst of chaos, unity in the heart of the ephemeral. Not merely self-indulgent or resentful, then, the true rebel is concerned with communal or ethical values. By rebelling, an individual defends the dignity common to all people. Suffering saves the rebel from solitude by immersing him in a collective experience. "I rebel—therefore we exist."

The twentieth-century rebel, in particular, rebels not only against the injustice of death and the wastefulness of evil but also against a divine authority, realizing the throne of God has been overturned with human beings inheriting the crown. Without a belief in destiny, we are left mired in the throes of chance, with no divine justice. For Camus, however, the answer is not to negate everything by embracing nihilism; that is mere servitude. Real freedom is submitting to values which defy history, is learning to be human by refusing to be a god. The philosophy of the rebel is, therefore, one of limits, of a life of moderation, but a life riddled with risks.

William Styron's fiction has been and will continue to be misunderstood without an awareness of his debt to European existentialist thought, to Camus' secular humanism in particular, and without an awareness of Styron's desperate need to combat stereotypes through his fiction, stereotypes which limit the felt life. Styron's own life bears witness to this. Although Southern by birth, he is not strictly a Southern novelist. He is a transplanted Virginian who lived in Paris, founded the *Paris Review*, and then settled in Connecticut. His roots are rural and Protestant, but his fiction is primarily urban and ethnic. Styron mercilessly reveals our spiritual morass, chaos, instability, and suffering. However, he leads a rather quiet, stable life; he has been married for over three decades to an accomplished Jewish poet and Amnesty International activist, and has four children. An ex-Marine, Styron clearly mistrusts the military mind. Now a Northern liberal Democrat, Styron's Virginia Tidewater background undoubtedly shaped his humanistic values and contributed to his libertarian attacks on injustice. He has spoken eloquently against capital punishment, has helped save the life of a subliterate black man, Benjamin Reid, and has refused to write an already-paid-for article for *The New York Times Magazine* on the New York Democratic Convention because he "didn't find enough interesting material."

Styron's activities since the late 1960s reveal growing political and international concerns. In

1968, he was a delegate to the Democratic National Convention. He was a witness at the trial of the "Chicago Seven" in 1969 and was the only American writer to attend a symposium in Soviet Asia at Tashkent, the Soviet Union. In 1977 he participated in a Moscow conference of American and Soviet writers. Styron was invited to the inauguration of François Mitterrand in 1981 and that same year opposed the establishment of the Nixon Library at Duke University. In 1982 he wrote the introduction to Mitterrand's autobiography, *The Wheat and the Chaff.* Styron lobbied in Congress in 1983 on behalf of a bill which would allow authors to make tax-deductible donations of their manuscripts to nonprofit institutions. In 1984 he attended an Amnesty International conference in Tokyo. In 1988 he protested the nomination of Judge Robert Bork to the Supreme Court. Most recently he and members of the Freedom-to-Write Committee of the American Center of PEN sent a letter to the Israeli government urging it "to cease its practice of censorship" of Palestinian writers and journalists in the West Bank and Gaza. This letter, drafted after months of heated discussion, has divided some of the leading writers in the United States. He has also protested the censoring of Salman Rushdie's *The Satanic Verses.* Styron, in short, has been able to wed literary and political interests, disproving the notion that only Europeans know how to mix literature and politics.

This biographical information is crucial insofar as it helps us to understand the criticism that has been levied against his writing. His first novel, *Lie Down in Darkness* (1951), although winning for Styron at age twenty-six the Prix de Rome of the American Academy of Arts and Letters, was thought "not Southern enough" by many critics, not the new *The Sound and the Fury;* Styron suffered because he chose not to be a mere recipient of a tradition which promotes and glorifies the Southern past. He then wrote *The Long March* (1953), an anti-war novella, unfashionable in the 1950s. In the book the Marines became a symbol of American totalitarianism, but in the television production of the novella, Styron's unorthodox stand was watered down to make it more palatable for the American audience. In 1960 Styron published his second novel, *Set This House on Fire*, again a disappointment to many critics partially because it veered even further from his Southern roots. Most of the action takes place in a small Italian village populated by self-indulgent, corrupt Americans who bring crassness and violence to the Italian villagers. Here Styron rejects the stereotype of the naive

> " Styron's work proves that the novel is still a plausible art form, that literature is still worthy of a kind of faith, one that can transform us by providing us with knowledge and order."

American corrupted by European wickedness. His fourth novel, *The Confessions of Nat Turner* (1967), although winning a Pulitzer Prize, generated bitter attacks because it was not pro-black enough. Some thought it an outrage that a Southern white man could pretend to understand the mind of a black slave, to speak with a black man's voice, this in the middle of the fiercely political black nationalist movement of the late 1960s. Styron urges us not to lump all slaves or slaveowners into one stereotyped category. His research led him to the conclusion that black insurrections were the exception and not the rule in pre-Civil War America, again an unpopular notion in the late 1960s.

His fifth and most recent novel, *Sophie's Choice* (1979), was on the hardcover bestseller list for forty-seven weeks and won the American Book Award for fiction. Despite this acclaim, the novel offended some who thought it in poor taste to create a non-Jewish heroine who survived the Nazi concentration camps—a Christian survivor of Nazi totalitarianism. Some thought it even more audacious for Styron to fuse Jewish and Southern literary traditions, two of America's richest literary heritages. Yet Styron links what are for him the two horrors of modern times—slavery and genocide in the American South, and slavery and genocide in Nazi Eastern Europe. One of the epigraphs to *Sophie's Choice* is a line from André Malraux's *Lazare:* "I seek that essential region of the soul where absolute evil confronts brotherhood." The absolute evil that Styron dramatizes in the novel is what became known on both the slave auction blocks and in the Nazi concentration camps as "selection," the separation of families and friends into those sent off to die and those sent off to be worked to death. The Old South's "final solution" was also

America's "absolute evil." Clearly, many critics will not let this parallel go unchallenged.

For Styron, if the Holocaust is the central horror of the twentieth century, it is not because it was anti-Semitic but because it was anti-life. Holding on to repressive traditions too is anti-life, as is any belief in absolute values. Styron's fiction provides no answers but urges us instead to question everything. Affirmations, then, are singular, personal; his optimism is provisional. Hope can often sap up of our needed strength to combat injustices on earth. Styron has been criticized for his supposed pessimism, yet out of despair artists create. Styron would argue that all great art has been born of a pessimistic view of life often brought out of perilous times and out of suffering. If we can overcome the need to stereotype, the need not to think, awareness is born, and with awareness comes action, and with action comes personal meaning. Here Styron echoes Camus' sentiments: in a world of unhappiness, we must create happiness.

Many of Styron's fictional characters, however, are unable to create happiness. Many seem afflicted with an acute case of emotional and intellectual arrest, stifled by Romantic and Puritan myths, unable to live in the present. Styron often uses interior monologues to portray our spiritual malaise; nostalgic reveries, however, cannot cure the illness. Some characters choose suicide, some murder, some prolong their agony by living a dead life. Many just hide behind outdated political, religious, or artistic abstractions. But for Styron and Camus, to be fully human is to doubt. One either chooses the creative present, this world, or one chooses death. Finding spiritual sustenance in our modern wasteland is the job of the living. Resisting nihilism, therefore, is one of Styron's most urgent themes. Human beings must demand meaning in a world that denies it; this is the true absurd position but, for Styron, the only liberating one. Since there is no absolute order, knowledge, or salvation, only humanistic values can combat the senselessness of violence, the purposelessness of most of our lives.

The first step towards this renewal is accepting our loss of innocence. The pervasive myth of the American Adam is stultifying, even treacherous, according to Styron. In this way, Styron is countering a dominant stream of American writers who yearn for an Edenic past, rebuking the prevailing American tendency towards nostalgia, a tendency which produces stunted individuals and often less-than-great fiction. Styron's vision, then, is closer to Melville's than to Emerson's or Whitman's. Evil is not merely the privation of good; it lies within us, not in abstract systems, for it is we who create divisive, destructive systems which serve to separate us. After visiting Auschwitz, Styron asked not where God was but where humanity was. The emergence of maturity and the ability to love require the purging of self-illusions and grandiose Puritan and Romantic myths. One must rebel to grow, and even failed rebellion is preferable to mere Faulknerian endurance. Suffering and struggle can indeed be purgative, creative; rebellion and struggle, therefore, dominate all of Styron's fiction.

Styron's work proves that the novel is still a plausible art form, that literature is still worthy of a kind of faith, one that can transform us by providing us with knowledge and order. Although Styron tampers with chronology and different points of view, he is basically a traditional novelist who worries about plot, character, and setting, and who concerns himself with the lofty themes of his literary forebears—goodness, evil, race, slavery, time, love, death, and redemption. The writers for whom he has a particular fondness are Tolstoy, Conrad, Flaubert, Melville, Faulkner, Fitzgerald, Thomas Wolfe, Walker Percy, and Philip Roth. Because Styron is a man firmly rooted in the present, he has been able to merge his literary and political passions. Yet he is no mere apologist defending or justifying particular political philosophies. His fiction urges us instead to resist propaganda, to resist stereotypes or easy solutions, to reject lies. It is not through hope but through revolt that human beings can establish justice on earth. With rebellion, awareness is born. It is this seemingly simple yet revolutionary ethic that will be explored here in Styron's fiction.

Americans have warmly embraced Camus' secular ethics, his atheistic humanism, despite our pretensions towards religious piety. Yet Camus was censured and even ostracized at home for his unorthodox truths. American writers like Poe, Hemingway, Faulkner, and Styron have found receptive audiences in Europe while meeting with criticism at home. The best American writers have always been able to give body and voice to the tragic elements that our society officially wishes to ignore but which exist in the unspoken consciousness of many. Styron has spoken out for those who keep silent, but in so doing he has run the heavy risk of being ostracized by American critics and readers.

Styron confesses at the outset of *Sophie's Choice,* through an epigraph by Rainer Maria

Rilke, that the whole of death is beyond description just as the act of love is, yet he attempts to describe both in this great novel. Auschwitz, Styron says, must remain the one place on earth most unyielding to meaning or definition. Auschwitz is an ever-present reminder that our fate will be sealed the day we forget how to love. Styron's fiction reminds us just how fragile love is, that the essential "choice" we all make is between death and the love of the living. Although Styron has not lived the life of a pariah, his works have been nonetheless revolutionary. Tacked to his studio wall is a famous line from Flaubert: "Be regular and orderly in your life like a Bourgeois so that you may be violent and original in your work."

Although *Sophie's Choice* won the American Book Award for fiction, it met with some very mixed reviews. Generally favorable reviews appeared in the *Christian Science Monitor, Commonweal, The Atlantic Monthly, Time, America, The New Statesman, The New York Times Book Review, Newsweek, Commentary, The Virginia Quarterly Review, The Yale Review, The Village Voice,* and *Vogue.* Critics such as Doris Grumbach, Paul Fussell, John Gardner, Gail Godwin, Peter Prescott, Jonathan Yardley, and Larzer Ziff regard *Sophie's Choice* as at least a major work if not a masterpiece.

Some critics, however, regard the novel as bombastic and melodramatic—in short, a colossal failure. Robert Towers in *The New York Review of Books* argues that the voice of Stingo and other deficiencies make it difficult to regard the novel as even a noble failure. Robert Alter in *Saturday Review* contends that the ties between the personal frame and historical subject do not quite hold. Julian Symons in the *Times Literary Supplement* also argues that the novel is divided into two parts that are not very closely stitched together, that the novel is a melodrama and not a tragedy. John Aldridge in *Harper's* asserts that the novel has no ideas to express, that Styron uses pyrotechnics. Jack Beatty in *The New Republic* calls the novel sluggish, self-indulgent, dull, wordy, and windy. *The New Yorker* calls the novel contrived, humorless, overwrought, and ponderous. And David Evanier in *National Review* calls *Sophie's Choice* not a novel but copious notes towards a novel, totally lacking in form, the bad writing of which is more memorable than the good.

For these and other reasons, *Sophie's Choice* has engendered almost as much controversy as *The Confessions of Nat Turner* did in 1967. This book will demonstrate, however, that *Sophie's Choice* is

Styron's most audacious, original, and artistically successful novel to date. First, this book will counter the many critics who have assailed the novel as anti-Semitic; *Sophie's Choice* does dramatize the madness of anti-Semitism without itself being anti-Semitic. In response to these critics who conclude that the novel tramples on sacred ground by fictionalizing the Holocaust, especially since Styron is neither a Jew nor a Holocaust survivor, this book will argue against silence in the face of the horror of the Holocaust. Fictionalizing this catastrophe does not necessarily trivialize the tragedy. A novel can, in fact, penetrate our consciousness more deeply than a historical account by affording some artistic distance—which diminishes the tendency towards numbing produced by a historical or strictly autobiographical account. Rather than trivializing the Holocaust, *Sophie's Choice* dramatizes the tragic dimensions of this unparalleled event and shows how the tragedy continues to manifest itself more than two generations after the fact, causing great anguish to its survivors and nonsurvivors, to their children and grandchildren, to Jews and Gentiles, to Europeans and Americans.

This book will also counter the argument that *Sophie's Choice* is a sexist novel, that Styron and his youthful alter ego, Stingo, are misogynists. It is true that *Sophie's Choice* explores the evils of sexism, but it is not sexist itself. Styron sets his novel in the "frozen sexual moonscape of the 1940s," a time following the Second World War of great sexual and moral confusion. Sex becomes the symbolic setting for the novel, "a nightmarish Sargasso Sea of guilts and apprehension." *Sophie's Choice* does dramatize the consequences of patriarchal cultures which make men and women victims and victimizers, that force us to behave according to stereotyped roles. For this Styron has been branded a sexist, when actually he is just demonstrating the disastrous effects of sexism on both sexes.

Finally, this book will explore the novel's powerful theme—absolute evil. The metaphor for this evil is Sophie's forced choice: she must choose which one of her two children to have murdered by the Nazis. Styron insists that evil is mysterious and inextinguishable, that Americans are not chosen people exempt from the world's demonism; American innocence is shown as potentially lethal. *Sophie's Choice* is then an American spiritual journey into the mystery of iniquity, a twentieth-century *Moby-Dick.* The many Melvillean overtones will be explored, linking Styron to the great nineteenth-century anti-Transcendental novelists such as Hawthorne, Melville, Twain, and James, a noble tradition which continues in twentieth-century writers like Faulkner and Styron who have a tragic view of the human condition. While insisting on the power and inextinguishability of evil in human beings and nature, Styron ultimately provides a compassionate vision of humanity struggling for meaning in an indifferent universe. The characters in *Sophie's Choice*, although limited by heredity and environment, are still capable of great love and loyalty despite their suffering, despite the obvious madness of the twentieth century. In this sense, although the evil that is the Holocaust pervades this novel, so too does brotherhood, and that is why the novel's epigraph, "I seek that essential region of the soul where absolute evil confronts brotherhood," is not only apposite to the theme but also reveals Styron's daring as a novelist—his ability to give voice to a few of the "beaten and butchered and betrayed and martyred children of the earth." In a world which permitted the black edifice of Auschwitz, *Sophie's Choice* asserts, albeit tentatively, that love may yet be possible, that loving must not be an absurdity after Auschwitz. *Sophie's Choice* urges us to conquer our grief through love and laughter, without which aggression against the self or others is the only alternative.

In an era of fashionable postmodern minimalism and nihilism, Styron has created characters who seek the high-minded solace that is available in self-knowledge, in the future, in love. Styron is one of the few contemporary novelists who create characters still struggling for transcendence, showing that life is serious, not just trivial and grim, that characters can make important though limited choices, that there are issues worth clarifying. By insisting on affirming the values the Nazis denied their victims, Styron makes the human face richer and more admirable.

Styron, therefore, must be appreciated as one of the most audacious and humane voices in contemporary literature. With tremendous sympathy for the casualties of history, he continues to be on the side of the humiliated, the persecuted, and the suffering. While all of his fiction has been concerned with human domination and with the pathos of victims of that domination, *Sophie's Choice* in particular dramatizes the horrific consequences of a victimizer's inability to identify with his victim. *Sophie's Choice* dares to try to understand and express compassion for victims and victimizers. It is to be hoped that Styron will continue to challenge the moral and intellectual complacency of his readers with fiction that demonstrates that there is no rational order in existence, that human beings are at risk of extinction, and that rebellion, therefore,

in a post-Holocaust world is critical to our survival as a species.

Source: Rhoda Sirlin, "Introduction," in *William Styron's "Sophie's Choice": Crime and Self-Punishment,* UMI Research Press, 1990, pp. 1–8.

Richard Pearce

In the following essay excerpt, Pearce examines Styron's "attempt to approach what is beyond the limits of human imagination" in Sophie's Choice.

Sophie Zawistowska, just beginning to recover from the horrors of Auschwitz, was returning home from work on the Brooklyn BMT. The subway was already hot and crowded when a group of youngsters dressed in baseball uniforms thrust aboard, shouting and pushing in all directions. Sophie was crushed between two sweating shapes as the train shuddered to a halt and the lights went out—and, in the darkness with the noise making a scream impossible, she felt a hand rising between her thighs and then a finger, neither random nor clumsy but "working with surgical skill and haste." Simple panic turned to shock and "horrified disbelief." She "heard herself gasp 'Please,' certain of the banality, the stupidity of the word even as she uttered it." Nor had the atrocities she witnessed or the outrages suffered "numbed her to this gross insult." "A straightforward . . . rape would have done less violation to her spirit and identity."

Sophie's Choice is filled with nightmares of both the daylight and nighttime worlds, but, except for the climactic incident which explains the title, no scene is more harrowing. The dark, crowded subway is a nightmare, where the threat derives not from some demonic power but the ordinary. Sophie is absolutely helpless and senselessly assaulted. Her assailant is anonymous; she can neither see his face nor sense his body. So she is isolated not only from the other passengers but from the assailant himself. She cannot make him know how she feels, "through a grimace or a hot level stare or even tears." She is even cut off from her self by the disembodied finger "working with surgical skill," thoroughly depersonalized.

In this singular rape—with its terrifying banality, senseless rationality, and impersonal threat that reaches from beyond the sightlines of the subway car—William Styron is leading toward the impossible subject of a novel that took him ten difficult years to write. True, Sophie is not a Jew, and the novel is designed to show how the Nazi threat extended beyond their primary victims. Moreover, it was surely Styron's purpose to show the

Holocaust resulting from the cruel logic of history, as well as one nation's attempt to murder the Jewish people. Nonetheless *Sophie's Choice* is about that particular crime—or, I should say, about an American writer's attempt to approach what is beyond the limits of the human imagination.

Styron was willing to take on the black critics in *The Confessions of Nat Turner* and the Jewish critics in *Sophie's Choice* because he is one of the few major contemporary writers who believes in the power of the novel to grapple with historical reality, awaken consciousness, and achieve a kind of redemption. But from *The Confessions of Nat Turner* he seems to have learned a lesson about how to approach a subject that is so threatening. Rather than stepping into the center and identifying with the victim, he has built a bridge—with two spans. First, he has created a narrator with whom he could easily identify, reviving a technique he employed in his first two novels, and who is frankly like the aspiring writer he was when, living in Brooklyn, he began *Lie Down in Darkness*. Second, he has chosen as his narrator's link a woman who, though violated by the Nazis, was not a Jew, and who was indeed implicated in the Nazi crime. Sophie leads Stingo, and with him the reader, toward the novel's actual subject: the ultimate nightmare of history. But the novel never reaches its subject. By focusing on Sophie—who takes us no closer to "the heart of darkness" than did Conrad's Marlowe—he leaves the Holocaust unimaginable and unutterable. By identifying with Stingo, and limiting the reader to his point of view, he compels us to recognize the limitations of our imagination and language in dealing with the historical event we must nonetheless confront.

Stingo's postadolescent obsessions are embarrassing and incongruous. But they dramatize his innocence as well as the distance between his world and ours. The sexual revolution of the sixties, the decline of the novel, the neglect of history, and the displacement of crisis theology have made it hard to imagine a young man in his twenties who still sees sex as a mystery, models himself after Thomas Wolfe, and seeks redemption for his grandfather's sin as a slaveowner. Even more important, Stingo's obsessions exemplify what he learned from reading George Steiner: the problem of "time relation," or the impossibility of reconciling the Holocaust with any other order of simultaneous experience. Steiner describes two brutal deaths at the Treblinka extermination camp, and then points out, "Precisely at the same hour in which Mehring and Langner were being done to death, the overwhelming plurality of human beings, two miles away on the Polish farms,

> "Sophie leads Stingo, and with him the reader, toward the novel's actual subject: the ultimate nightmare of history. But the novel never reaches its subject."

five thousand miles away in New York, were sleeping or eating or going to a film or making love or worrying about the dentist. This is where my imagination balks." And so does Stingo's when he thinks that at the same moment Sophie was boarding the train to Auschwitz, he was gorging himself on bananas. Though he was stuffing himself to pass the physical exam for the Marine Corps, it was not to fight the Nazis (for, like millions of Americans, he had never even heard of the concentration camps); his racist imagination had focused all its animosity on the "Oriental foe." Stingo's initiation, while not simultaneous with Sophie's experience at Auschwitz, is simultaneous with his discovery of her experience. Indeed, it is simultaneous with her first fully conscious confrontation with it. As her experience becomes part of his initiation, we come to understand their absolute irreconcilability.

Stingo begins with the normal fantasies of a young man his age in a period of sexual repression. Alone in New York, looking out of his apartment window onto the garden below, he imagines making love to a Mrs. Winston Hunnicutt on an Abercrombie & Fitch hammock, only to be interrupted by the arrival of Thornton Wilder, or E. E. Cummings, or Katherine Anne Porter, or John Hersey, or Malcolm Cowley, or John P. Marquand. But when he moves to the pink apartment in Flatbush, just below Nathan and Sophie, his dreaming takes on a darker side. He has just heard that Maria Hunt, whom he had "passionately but chastely adored" as a fifteen-year-old, had committed suicide (like Peyton Loftis) by leaping out of a window in New York. And he dreams of her standing before him "with the abandon of a strumpet stripping down to the flesh." While this dream is partly comic—"she who had never removed in my presence so much as her bobbysocks"—it is more morbid and threatening. And when he awakes in "dire distress," the "primeval groan . . . wrenched from the nethermost dungeons of my soul" comes less from the frustrations of celibacy than deep feelings of guilt. Moreover, when the thumping of the mattress upstairs causes him to feel "another nail amplify my crucifixion," the language is only in part the hyperbole of an energetic youth drawn to gothic romance. Stingo tells us that his most memorable dreams have dealt with either sex or death; we see how the two are related. His dream of Maria has produced an impression only matched by one eight years before, when he saw his mother's "shrunken, cancer-ravaged face twist toward me in the satin vault." He later recalls the cold winter day she was dying, and he selfishly forgot to bring wood for her fire.

Stingo's "crucifixion" ironically foreshadows the relationship into which he will soon be drawn. And this is reinforced by Sophie's distant resemblance to Maria, or, even more, by the look of despair like that "Maria surely must have worn . . . along with the pre-monitory, grieving shadows of someone hurtling headlong toward death." Nonetheless, his dreams, as well as his self-absorption and self-dramatization, are incongruous with Sophie's living nightmares. They make her actual dream—which also connects sex and death—stand out in sharp relief.

Sophie is at Auschwitz, fortunate to be working as a secretary for the commandant, Rudolf Höss. She has just failed in a clumsy attempt to steal his daughter's radio, her first and only act in support of the Resistance. Exhausted, she falls asleep and dreams of walking on a beach, clothed in a transparent skirt, and followed by an attractive German she cannot quite recognize. "He smiled at her with clean white teeth, stroked her on the buttocks, uttered a few words that were at once barely comprehensible and flagrantly lewd, then disappeared." Soon she finds herself in a chapel, standing before a primitive altar, unclothed and giggling when the chapel is "suddenly suffused by the grief of a single contralto voice and the strains of [a] tragic cantata." The man from the beach reappears, now naked. "He was no longer smiling; a murderous scowl clouded his face and the threat embedded in his countenance excited her." He orders her to turn around and kneel at the altar. She "knelt on hands and knees, heard a clattering of hoofs on the floor, smelled smoke, cried out with delight as the hairy belly and groin swarmed around her."

Alvin H. Rosenfeld has written a sensitive, passionate, and persuasive book on the literature of the Holocaust. The judgments of *A Double Dying* are based on the undeniable singularity of the concentration camp, the irrevocable change it produced in human consciousness, the impossibility but necessity of finding a language to fit its form, the limits of the imagination in dealing with events that have already reached beyond its limits—and, therefore, the necessity of remaining true to the facts. For Rosenfeld, *Sophie's Choice* transposes "erotic and aesthetic motives onto a landscape of slaughter." At best, it "reveals all too clearly the literary imagination . . . seduced by the erotic underside of totalitarian terror," readily accepting it "as a metaphor for what exists just beneath the normal life of social and sexual behavior." At worst, he argues, "by reducing the war against the Jews to sexual combat" Styron "has misappropriated Auschwitz and used it as little more than the erotic centerpiece of a new Southern Gothic Novel."

Rosenfeld is one of Styron's most formidable critics, and it is difficult to argue with the witnesses he summons. But he seems to overlook the need for a writer who is not a witness, trying in good faith to come to grips with the Holocaust over a distance of time and culture, to start somewhere in the world he knows. In *Sophie's Choice,* Auschwitz is not a metaphor for the dark underside of sexual experience, but this darkness may serve as a metaphor reaching toward a horror that must remain unimaginable and unutterable. I will not argue with what seems an incontrovertible fact, that in the camps "the central, most frustrated, and hence most abiding appetite was for food. Other passions were secondary and, it seems, for most were held in abeyance." Or that "Holocaust writings at their most authentic . . . are peculiarly and predominantly sexless" (Rosenfeld, p. 164). And I am fully aware of the dangers of taking liberties with the facts. But there are other facts—such as those associated with the psychology of submission and the guilt for even staying alive—that Sophie's dream can suggest for us to explore.

Sophie's guilt may stem from more than the accident of her survival, as might the guilt of any other survivor. In her case it also derives from her relationship with her father. For she did type and edit his manuscript, *Poland's Jewish Problem,* which dealt which "population transfer" and, finally, "total abolishment." Indeed, she admitted that "she may have even relished her virtually menial submission." True, she came to hate her father when she realized that he was prescribing murder in his rational, circumspect way. But it is interesting that this hatred becomes most pronounced when she sees him in contrast to Walter Dürrfeld, the director of IG Farben, who stopped by during his brief visit to Cracow in 1937. Handsome, healthy for his years, well groomed and well mannered, Dürrfeld makes her father seem "hopelessly dowdy," and a sycophant if not a buffoon. As he discreetly courts her during the conversation, she dismisses the almost certain knowledge that he is a Nazi and feels the erotic, "sweetly queasy sense of danger she once felt in Vienna years ago as a child at the very peak of the terrifying Prater Ferris wheel." In liberating herself from her father and her husband, who is only a poor copy of him, Sophie transfers her feelings to another father figure, one with the same principles (though she will not admit this to herself) but more power. And in her dream, the demonic lover turns out to be this same man.

I do not mean to "explain" Sophie through a Freudian analysis of her dream. For the dream also serves to reinforce the inescapable nightmare through which Sophie has been living—where the actual source of terror, though familiar and pervasive, cannot be fixed, and where the father embodies just the kind of rational but banal evil that Stingo can only recount from his readings of Arendt, Weil, and Rubenstein. But Sophie's dream also expresses, in ways I have only begun to explore, her inability to separate voluptuousness from evil, desire from submission, freedom from guilt, procreation from death, the power of her father from the power of the Nazis, and the chronicle of her life from the history that culminated in the death camps. And her meeting with the swollen caricature of her *Liebestraum* the next day, when she was expecting to see her son, illuminates the reality beneath her idealization and will contribute to the helplessness, guilt, and terror she feels when she is violated on the subway.

Sophie's dream also helps us understand her self-destructive relationship with Nathan Landau. Nathan is Sophie's only source of hope and escape. Although he is fatherly in his caring as well as command, he seems a genuine alternative to Professor Zbigniew Biegański, Distinguished Professor of Jurisprudence at the Jagiellonian University of Cracow and Doctor of Law *honoris causa,* Universities of Karlova, Bucharest, Heidelberg, and Leipzig. For Nathan is Jewish, vital, and mad. He can entertain Sophie and Stingo as they walk along Flatbush Avenue and startle the windowshopping Hadassah matrons by concocting "an entire southern Appalachian scenario, a kind of darkling, concupiscent Dogpatch in which Pappy Yokum was transformed into an incestuous old farmer." In the space of an hour, he can "with no gratuitous strain, weave together Lytton Strachey, *Alice in Wonderland,* Martin Luther's early celibacy, *A Midsummer Night's Dream* and the

mating habits of the Sumatran orangutan into a little jewel box of a . . . lecture." He can feed Sophie, restore her to health, bring music back into her life and laughter into her throat, make love to her day and night, rail at her for an imagined infidelity, beat her, reduce her to despair by calling her an Irma Griese who played footsie with the SS to get out of Auschwitz. And he can cry out "in a tone that might have been deemed a parody of existential anguish had it not possessed the resonances of complete, unfeigned terror: 'Don't . . . you . . . see . . . Sophie . . . we . . . are . . . dying!' "

Nathan is not a realistic character. He is a life force. But he is also, as Morris Fink says, "a golem," "a runaway f—in' *monster.*" That he is suffering from a degenerative disease does not reduce him to a clinical case, but makes him all the more responsive—like an enormous sounding board—to the Holocaust as well as to the change in human consciousness. His role in the novel is, on the one hand, to symbolize this change and, on the other, to raise Sophie to a character of tragic proportions. The young woman who typed and edited her father's anti-Semitic pamphlet, the mother who out of fear for her children would not join in the Resistance, even the desperate secretary to Rudolf Höss was, after all, quite ordinary. It is only after she commits herself to Nathan—and, dramatically, only in relation to Nathan—that Sophie develops the thirst for life, the capacity for guilt, and the attraction to death which give her such tragic stature. Nathan is an alternative to Sophie's father, indeed a substitute, as he brings her back to life in a new world. But rather than allow her to escape, he compels her to face in full consciousness the living death she has escaped from. Granted, she tells her story to Stingo and hides the dark facts from Nathan. But she tells Stingo more and more only as her relationship with Nathan becomes more and more threatening.

Styron's use of suspense is only in part gothic. Through her relationship with Nathan, Sophie is driven to confront more and more of her experience. Nathan's developing madness drives her to consciously confront the madness of the Holocaust as well as her own involvement in it. One of the most powerful sections of the novel is generated by Nathan's "raging insistence . . . that she justify to his satisfaction the way in which she survived Auschwitz while 'the others' (as he put it) perished." Styron amplifies the madness of this episode, and hence its effect on Sophie, first by suspending the story of her relationship with Höss, and then by fracturing the new storyline and leaping back and forth in space and time. Although the rest of the novel is relatively straightforward, alternating mainly between Stingo's present and Sophie's past, chapter eleven is broken into fifteen sections; indeed, there are actually twenty-two breaks in the continuity, each coming faster and more radically than the one before. The story cuts back and forth, leaps forward, digresses, or is arbitrarily broken by a space in the text—now recounting the visit of Stingo's father, now recalling the scene where Stingo fails to attend his dying mother, now taking us to the Maple Court where he pleads with Sophie to tell him about Nathan, now focusing on the suicide of Dr. Blackstock's alcoholic wife, on Dr. Blackstock embracing Sophie after the funeral while Nathan watches from the window, on Nathan telling Sophie about his breakthrough at the lab and listening to H. V. Kaltenborn's obituary of Hermann Göring, on the Danny Kaye movie and the newsreel of the Warsaw ghetto, the party where Nathan surprises Sophie with an announcement of their wedding, his frenzy the next morning over what he imagined was Sophie's infidelity with Dr. Blackstock, and—back and forth all out of sequence—the drive to Connecticut, as he calls her Irma Griese and kicks her in the ribs with his well-polished shoes and tries to urinate in her mouth, and the inn where they lie in bed and he wiggles a tiny cyanide capsule between his fingers and continues to taunt her about her prostitution while Mrs. Rylander knocks on their door to remind them of supper.

As we gradually learn, Nathan is not far off in his judgment of Sophie, though it may be wrongly based and intolerably severe. While Dr. Blackstock had other ideas, Sophie never entertained the thought of infidelity. Still, she had at least tried to prostitute herself in Auschwitz to save her son. And she had tried to use the anti-Semitic pamphlet that so disgusted her to save herself. What Styron does in the disorder of chapter eleven is to bring together a wide range of infidelities—Stingo's natural desire to play rather than chop wood for his mother, Sophie's innocent embrace of Dr. Blackstock, her selfless attempt to save her son, and her more ambiguous but no less desperate attempt to save herself. He also holds them up to an absolute though unreasonable standard of morality. It is indeed disturbing to see Nathan taking on the role of the God of the Old Testament, the stern Father and omniscient Judge, although it is in just this role that he compels Sophie to confront the actuality of her guilt and thus raises her from the level of ordinary woman to that of tragic heroine. And it is equally disturbing to recognize the Christ-like dimension of Nathan's character, for he is nonetheless compassionate; moreover, his madness reflects the human condition after the Holocaust, and his suffering may be seen as a propitiation for the sins of man. What makes these dimensions of his character so disturbing is, of course, the demonic role he plays in the novel.

For, while Nathan takes on the role of Sophie's father in the new world, he also takes on the role of a character who was far more threatening and destructive—the doctor Sophie encountered when arriving at Auschwitz, whom Stingo calls demand von Niemand. After all, despite the singular term in the novel's title, Sophie is compelled to make two impossible choices. The first choice is demanded by the Nazi officer who, while drunk and boorish, is nonetheless arrestingly handsome, aristocratic, "silkily feminine," and disturbingly attractive—whose first words are: "Ich möchte mit dir schlafen," or, as Stingo translates it, "I'd like to get you into bed with me." This is the doctor assigned to choose who will go to the labor camps and who will be killed. And, after he frightens Sophie into lying that she is a believer in Christ, he asks "in a thick-tongued but oddly abstract voice, like that of a lecturer examining the delicately shaded facet of a proposition in logic, . . . 'Did He not say, "Suffer the little children to come unto me"? . . . You may keep one of your children . . . The other one will have to go. Which one will you keep?'"

The sexual invitation and ironic use of the Christian parable carry the theme of submission, infidelity, betrayal, and violation to its limit—especially as it is associated with Sophie's father and her *Liebestraum*. Moreover, through the inescapability of the situation, the nature of the choice, and the gratuitousness of the demand Styron can illuminate the innocent side of Sophie's choice. And he can also suggest an experience of total domination, depersonalization, senseless guilt, and horror that are beyond the power of the imagination to picture. But Styron is also aware that Sophie's choice at Auschwitz fails to convey the reality of the concentration camp for another reason. Stingo quotes Simone Weil: "Imaginary evil . . . is romantic and varied, while real evil is gloomy, monotonous, barren, boring." Which is why Sophie's violation on the Flatbush subway, with its terrifying banality, is more telling. Styron's ambivalence between the power of imaginary evil and the demands of realistic fidelity is reflected in Stingo's need to fill out the character of Jemand von Niemand.

Stingo creates Jemand von Niemand from the clues in Sophie's story, some scraps of information she picked up later at Auschwitz, his readings on the Holocaust, and, no doubt, his reading in Dostoyevsky. The doctor had been a religious man; he had wanted to enter the ministry but was compelled by a mercenary father to go into medicine. But, "awaiting the arrival of countless trains from every corner of Europe, then winnowing out the fit and the healthy from the pathetic horde of cripples and the toothless and the blind, the feeble-minded and the spastic and the unending droves of helpless aged and helpless little children, he surely knew that the slave enterprise he served . . . was a mockery and a denial of God. Besides, he was at bottom a vassal of IG Farben. Surely he could not retain belief while passing time in such a place. He had to replace God with a sense of the omnipotence of business." When Himmler sent down the order that all Jews must be exterminated it must have been a kind of relief, for the doctor would no longer be responsible for the selection. But when there was a new need for slave labor at IG Farben and selections had to begin again, Dr. Jemand von Niemand lost control. He drank, became sloppy, and wondered about the absence of God, and his sense of sin. "He had suffered boredom and anxiety, and even revulsion, but no sense of sin. . . . All had been unutterable monotony. All of his depravity had been enacted in a vacuum of sinless and businesslike godlessness, while his soul thirsted for beatitude." So to restore his belief in God, he had to affirm his capacity for evil and commit the most intolerable sin he was able to conceive.

It is important to realize that Jemand von Niemand is Stingo's creation and fulfills Stingo's needs. He has learned from his readings about the "banality of evil" and has used this knowledge in motivating the doctor he calls Someone or Anyone from No one. But he has not assimilated his lesson and remains a romantic who needs to imagine an evil that still affirms the heroic possibilities of man, and still allows the possibility of redemption.

By making her choose one of her children for the gas chamber, the doctor initiates Sophie into the reality of Auschwitz and implicates her in the horror. Nathan brings Sophie back to life, awakens her consciousness, and offers her a second choice. But is this choice any different from the first? If the doctor at Auschwitz mocks the Christian parable, Nathan mocks the Trinity in his form of Father, Son, and Devil. If Nathan is a life force, he is also mad, and driven toward death. Sophie's final choice is between life and death. But if the only life force in the world of the novel is Nathan, where is the choice? Nor, at any time since Nathan took

on the roles of her father and the doctor at Auschwitz, did he ever offer her any new hope. Sophie is too much of a realist to choose Stingo and the peanut plantation. So, ultimately, she has been reborn into a world that offers no escape from the past, and she has been twice led to a knowledge of its senseless logic.

Source: Richard Pearce, "Sophie's Choices," in *The Achievement of William Styron*, rev. ed., edited by Robert K. Morris, with Irving Malin, University of Georgia Press, 1981, pp. 284–94.

Sources

Aldridge, John W., "Styron's Heavy Freight," in *Harper's*, September 1979, pp. 95–98.

DeMott, Benjamin, "Styron's Survivor: An Honest Witness," in *Atlantic Monthly*, Vol. 244, July 1979, pp. 77–79.

Review of *Sophie's Choice*, in *New Yorker*, Vol. 55, June 18, 1979, pp. 109–10.

"Riddle of a Violent Century," in *Time*, June 11, 1979, p. 86.

Styron, William, *Sophie's Choice*, Random House, 1992.

Further Reading

Asscher-Pinkof, Clara, *Star Children*, Wayne State University Press, 1946.
   Asscher-Pinkof, a Dutch Jewish teacher and novelist, taught in schools set up for Jewish children in Amsterdam during World War II. In this book, she presents first-person fictional short stories based on some of her students' experiences in detention centers, transit camps, and in concentration camps such as Bergen-Belsen.

Becker, Jurek, *Bronstein's Children*, University of Chicago Press, 1999.
   This novel tells the story of an eighteen-year-old German Jew who accidentally comes upon his father and two other men beating up an old man, a former Nazi guard from one of the concentration camps, who tortured them thirty years before. The novel explores the complicated relationship between victim and persecutor and demonstrates how sadism and prejudice persisted long after the end of World War II.

Blum, Jenna, *Those Who Saved Us*, Harcourt, 2004.
   Blum, who worked with Steven Spielberg's Shoah Foundation, takes an unsentimental look at the Holocaust. In this novel, the story alternates between the present-day story of a history professor in Minneapolis who is collecting oral histories from World War II German and Jewish survivors and her elderly mother's story of being a young woman in Weimar, Germany, near Buchenwald, one of the largest Nazi concentration camps.

The Woman in the Dunes

Kobo Abe

1962

Kobo Abe, one of Japan's most celebrated and frequently translated authors and playwrights, is often compared to the Czech writer, Franz Kafka, because both writers created novels that were built upon nightmarish allegories. Abe's *The Woman in the Dunes* is a prime example. With this novel, one of Abe's more popular works, Abe takes the reader into a very strange and isolated world in order to make a statement about the condition of modern civilization. His statement is fascinating, but not very glorifying, as the protagonist becomes trapped in a world of ceaseless and mindless labor.

The Woman in the Dunes and the subsequent movie based on the novel catapulted Abe into the international realm. After the popular success of this novel, Abe's works became the most often translated fiction of Japanese literature. And long since its publication, *The Woman in the Dunes*, which in 1960 won the Yomiuri Prize for literature, continues to retain its classification of being not only the best of Abe's extensive life work, but also one of the classic examples of modern Japanese fiction.

The story begins with a character, Niki Jumpei, who seems all but totally unaware of who he really is. He often describes himself and his actions as if he were a detached observer of his own actions. His imprisonment in a hole in the sand dunes tempers his psyche, however, and in the end he comes to an awakening in which he grasps a better understanding of his basic psychological makeup. As Wimal Dissanayake, writing for *Literary Relations, East and West: Selected Essays* put it: "What Kobo

Abe has sought to do is to remove his protagonist from his cultural environment and to probe deeper and deeper into his own psyche as a way of attaining his authentic selfhood." The story of a journey of inner discovery during which the protagonist remembers what it means to be human in a modern society that sometimes seems to have forgotten.

Author Biography

Kobo Abe, one of Japan's greatest writers, was born on March 7, 1924, in Tokyo. He followed in his father's footsteps to a certain extent, gaining a degree in medicine but quickly decided that he did not want to become a doctor. He much preferred storytelling. During his childhood, most of which was spent in the Manchurian city of Mukden, Abe entertained himself and his friends by reciting stories. Many of these tales came from the writings of Edgar Allan Poe; but Abe, even at an early age, created stories of his own. Having been raised outside of the main Japanese culture, Abe's writings and interests differed from those of many of his compatriots. He studied abstract painting instead of the traditional Japanese arts, and like his character in *The Woman in the Dunes*, Abe also studied insects.

Abe witnessed the atrocities and consequences of war, both in Mukden, and later, when he returned to Tokyo and read such Western writers as the German philosopher Martin Heidegger (1889–1976) and Czech novelist Franz Kafka (1883–1924) to find support for his own ideas against the militaristic Japanese government at that time, according to Raymond Lamont-Brown in his article in the *Contemporary Review*. But as Lamont-Brown states, "Abe's searches did not produce what he needed." When his father died, Abe felt released from his father's wishes that he become a doctor and decided to concentrate even harder on creating his own path. He dropped all efforts to pursue a medical profession and delved deeply into literature. If he could not find what he was looking for in the writings of others, he became determined to create what he was looking for on his own.

In 1951, Abe was awarded the Akutagawa literary prize for *The Crime of Mr. S. Karuma* and from this point, there was no turning back. His career was set, and his theme—that of alienation and loss of identity in modern society—was established and would be repeated throughout his life's work.

Kobo Abe   © Jerry Bauer. Reproduced by permission

Some of Abe's most important novels include: *Suna no Onna* (1962) (*The Woman in the Dunes*, 1964); *Tanin no Kao* (1964) (*The Face of Another*, 1966); *Moetsukita Chizu* (1967) (*The Ruined Map*, 1969); *Hako Otoko* (1973) (*The Box Man*, 1975); and his last novel, *Kangaru Noto* (1991) (*The Kangaroo Notebook*, 1960).

Abe was also well known for his work in theater. He created his own drama group, which produced at least one of Abe's plays each year. He is remembered for such productions as *Tomodachi, Enemoto Takeaki* (1967) (*Friends*, 1969), and *Bo ni Natta Otoko* (1969) (*The Man Who Turned into a Stick*, 1975).

Abe married the artist Machi Yamada in 1947. The couple had one child, Neri. On January 22, 1993, Abe died, in Tokyo, of heart failure.

Plot Summary

Part 1

Kobo Abe's *The Woman in the Dunes* begins with a short summary of the main action of the novel. In this summary, the reader is told that a man has disappeared and since seven years have passed,

Media Adaptations

- *The Woman in the Dunes* was adapted as a film in 1963, directed by Hiroshi Teshigahara and starring an all Japanese cast. The movie won the Jury Prize at Cannes in 1964. It was shot in black and white and can be viewed with subtitles. Image Entertainment recently converted the film to DVD format.

---

he has been presumed dead. After this statement, the story flashes back to the day that this so-far unnamed man began what he thought would be a brief adventure to the seaside, in his search for an unusual insect. His hope is that he will find a bug that has yet to be classified. If he is the first to categorize it, his name will be attached to the insect's scientific classification. This will give the protagonist a sense of self identity.

Upon arriving at the coast, the man discovers a village that is being all but buried by the drifting sand dunes. He does not pay much attention to the village, as he is focused on finding a particular beetle that he believes lives in the sand. As the sun sets, he is approached by one of the villagers, an old man, who asks if the protagonist is an inspector. Upon discovering that he is not, the old man asks where the protagonist plans to spend the night, as the last bus out of the village has already left. The protagonist suggests that he might stay at one of the villagers' houses, which the old man finally arranges.

The protagonist climbs down the steep slope of one of the sand dunes by way of a rope ladder and finds himself at the entrance of an old dilapidated house, which looks as if it could easily collapse under the weight of sand should a large enough amount blow onto it. Once on the sandy floor, a thirty-something-year-old woman greets him. She is not unpleasant to look at, he confesses, but he is a little disturbed by the rundown condition of her house and wonders if he is being taken as a fool. The woman feeds him dinner, but when he asks to take a bath, she informs him of her lack

of water. He will have to wait until the day after tomorrow, she says. The protagonist laughs at this, telling her that he will be gone by then.

There are a series of brief discussions between the man and woman in which the man thinks the woman ignorant because she makes statements that are counter to his beliefs. One such comment that the woman makes is that the sand is damp, which the man refutes but later realizes how wet sand can be. Slowly, the man's reality begins to change as he sees things differently than he had previously. As the night progresses, he becomes nervous, sensing some inherent danger in his situation. A shovel and two buckets are dropped down into the pit where the house stands, for example, and a suggestion is made that the man should help the woman with her nightly chores, which consist of digging out all the sand that has fallen into the pit during the day. By the next morning, the man is on the verge of panic when he discovers that the rope ladder is nowhere to be found. It has been taken away. He tries to calm his nerves, cautiously asking the woman questions in an attempt to discover if she has indeed planned his entrapment. As all clues point to this sadistic conclusion, the man plans his escape. He will dig at the base of the sand dune, forcing the sand to slowly move toward the house, thus easing the angle of the slope. Or so he thinks. His knowledge of sand is faulty, once again, and he is all but buried in the sand when he starts digging as the slope collapses on him, and he passes out.

Part 2

The protagonist wakes up to the sounds of the woman cooking. He has been put to bed in the woman's house, and she is caring for him. He is feigning his injuries, though, falsely believing that if he does not work, the woman will not be able to do all the work and take care of him too, and the captors will see how useless the man is and will let him go. He tests his captors' willingness to cope with him by requesting a newspaper. He also hopes to find a story about himself as a missing person in the newspaper. There is no such story when the newspaper arrives, and the man is disappointed. He asks the woman why she allows herself to be used as a slave and tries to tempt her into demanding her freedom. But the woman is content with her life. The man thinks back on his life, wondering why no one has reported him missing. He describes the lives of those who were once around him and talks about Mobius man, with whom he tries to have a conversation about his inner thoughts. He also refers to the "other" woman, a woman with whom he had some kind of relationship. It is not clear if this is his girlfriend or a prostitute.

When the villagers seem to pay little mind to the fact that the man does not work, the protagonist grabs the woman and ties her up, forcing her to join him in not working. The villagers do pay attention to this but not in the way the man had hoped. Instead of releasing him as he demands, they quit bringing them water. The man asks the woman if the villagers have ever kidnapped and enslaved other outsiders. The woman tells him about a postcard dealer who was also entrapped. That man eventually died. There was also a young student. But no one has ever escaped, the woman tells him. The man begins to strip the wood of the house to make a ladder. He will not give up hope of finding a way out. When he threatens to take down the main supports of the house, the woman, whom the man has by now untied, tackles him to stop him. As they wrestle, they both become sexually aroused but do not act on it. The man flashes back to other sexual encounters with the other woman. He thinks about a venereal disease that he once had and wonders if the other woman gave it to him. A little later, the man and woman do have a sexual encounter. The next day, the man gives in and begs for water. They must work, the woman tells him, before the villagers will bring water. The man talks to the old man who brings the water and tries to convince him that he must let him go. The protagonist still believes he has the upper hand in the situation. He believes he can con his way out. But the old man does not give in. And once again, the protagonist refers to the fact that he thinks he is being taken advantage of, being laughed at. It has not completely dawned on him, however, that this is the exact truth.

There are hints in the next passages that the man is not disliking his situation as much as he had originally. He begins to like the ordinary things of his life in the sand dunes, the shoveling of the sand, the routine, and the nearness of the woman. But he does not stop planning his escape. He finally succeeds in creating a rope, and one day, as the woman sleeps, he climbs to the top of the roof, throws the rope to the top of the dune, where it anchors onto a sand bag, and climbs out of the hole. A fog hides him until nightfall, when he fumbles in the dark, trying to find his way out of the village. Unfortunately, he falls into a bog and sinks into it up to his waist and must be rescued. The villagers than take him back to the hole.

Part 3

A couple of months have passed. The man has set a trap for crows. If he catches one, he will wrap a note around its leg and hope that someone, other than the villagers, will read it and rescue him. The trap does not work. But one day, he finds that water has collected in the bottom of the trap. This excites him. He realizes that the villagers can never threaten him again by not bringing water to him. However, he becomes very stir crazy and craves seeing a different view, if only for a few minutes. He pleads with a group of villagers to let him out for just a few minutes. They say they might consider this if he first lets them watch as the man and woman make love. The protagonist agrees to this but the woman fights him off.

Time passes, and it is spring, and the woman is pregnant. One night she begins to bleed and must be taken away. In their hurry, the villagers forget to take away the rope ladder that they used to lift her out. The protagonist sees this, but he decides there is no hurry, and he does not escape.

Characters

Niki Jumpei

The protagonist Niki Jumpei has such an undeveloped sense of self that throughout most of the novel that he is not even given a name, but rather referred to only through the pronoun *he*. In the first lines of the story, the reader is told that the protagonist has disappeared. And at the end of the story, legal papers are offered to the reader in which Jumpei has been declared dead. The remainder of the story takes Jumpei through a challenge in which he must first shed his normal way of looking at life, and at himself, in order to find new definitions. He is placed in circumstances that are stark and confining, minimizing the details of his life down to the bare essentials. Jumpei fights his rebirth as he insists on hanging onto the old information that he has gathered so far in his life. He is rather haughty, looking down on those around him. Because of this, he stands apart from everyone and feels alienated. He constantly misjudges circumstances and people who filter in and out of his life. He is blind to what is happening to him because he refuses to take things at face value. By becoming so completely absorbed in trying to second-guess everyone, he completely misses the cues they offer him. This concentration on others causes him to also fail to understand himself. Not until Jumpei has failed miserably at everything he attempts does he finally realize that what he was looking for outside of himself is actually found within.

Mobius Man

A Mobius strip is a slip of paper that has been twisted once and then taped together to create a form that has no beginning and no end. Jumpei has given this name to a colleague of his, a man to whom Jumpei comes the closest to opening his more inner thoughts. Mobius Man listens without ridiculing Jumpei. The men discuss their philosophies of life. Jumpei thinks about Mobius Man often while he is in captivity. He does not have many discussions with the woman and so Jumpei turns to his thoughts of Mobius Man when he has a need for a deeper conversation.

Old Man

The old man is the only person who is singled out among the people of the village at the sea. It is the old man who first talks to Jumpei at the sand dunes, asking him how he is going to get back to town since the last bus has already left. It is also the old man who negotiates Jumpei's subsequent capture. The old man returns to the hole in which Jumpei is held prisoner. It is to the old man that Jumpei pleads to be released. The old man listens to Jumpei's requests but never changes his mind. In the old man's world, he needs Jumpei to remain exactly where he is, for the sake of the community.

Woman

The woman who lives in the sand dune is never given a name. At first, as seen through the eyes of the protagonist, she comes across as very innocent and somewhat backward. She easily submits to the horrid living conditions she must deal with in which she accomplishes back-breaking labor each day and a gritty existence at all other times. She flirts with Jumpei quite easily but it is not certain that she is doing this to entice him to stay or if it is just her childlike behavior, having had little contact with the outside word. But as the story progresses, the woman comes across more strongly. She fights back when Jumpei tries to rape her in front of the villagers, for instance. And she wrestles with Jumpei when he threatens to bring down the house. She is grateful for his presence, however, and is tender with him. She nurtures him, washes him, and tends to him when he is sick or hurt. In the end, her submissiveness teaches Jumpei to adapt to his surroundings, to enjoy the simplicity and the routine of the confining environment, and to see himself as he truly is.

Themes

Alienation

One of the overall themes in Abe's *The Woman in the Dunes* is that of alienation. The protagonist feels out of step with his society and is eventually cast into a situation that exemplifies his feelings. He is tossed into a hole and held captive in an environment that consists, for the most part, of only sand—a substance in which little if anything will grow. His surroundings consist of drab colors, stale air, and a lack of water. He remains totally dependent on outsiders to keep him alive. His attitude toward the woman with whom he shares a house is abrupt at best, but for most of the time it is caustic. He cannot relate to her acceptance of her dull life. While he is held captive, he recounts incidents from his former life as a schoolteacher. Although he is anxious for his freedom, his recollections of what his life was like outside the hole in the sand are not much more pleasant. He does not relate to his fellow teachers. He had been in some kind of relationship with a woman but it is unclear whether that relationship was as a lover and friend or if it were a relationship with a prostitute. Either way, the comments he makes about the "other" woman do not indicate that he enjoyed it. She always disagrees with him, he says, no matter what he tries to discuss with her. He is alienated from everyone, it seems, even from himself. He often refers to himself in an objective manner as if he were talking about someone else.

Loss of Identity

At the start of the novel, the protagonist searches for insects not so much to learn about them in any scientific way but rather so he might find an insect that has not yet been named. If he is successful, his name will be forever attached to the description of this bug. This will give him a sense of identity. As the readers find out later, the protagonist's identity is very much in question. As the story develops, it becomes obvious that he is not only looking for insects to immortalize his name, he is also looking for a true sense of himself. He has no identity, readers learn, other than insurance papers, birth certificate, and other pieces of paper that have his name on them. When he thinks of reasons why it is wrong for him to be held captive, he does not state the obvious, but rather he says that he is "someone who had paid his taxes, who was employed, and whose family records were in order." He is so lacking in a concept of himself that he often laughs without knowing why he is

Topics For Further Study

- Since Abe is often compared to Franz Kafka, read Kafka's *Metamorphosis* and compare this with Abe's *The Woman in the Dunes*. Both of these works are allegories. What does each work represent? How do they differ from one another? How are they the same? How do the endings differ?

- Critics often refer to Abe's novel as being affected by the philosophy of existentialism. Research this mode of thought and define what existentialism is. Who were some of the most influential thinkers of this philosophy? What writers infused their work with existential thought? Then explain how Abe's novel explores this philosophy.

- Read Yasunari Kawabata's *Snow Country*, which was written before the war. Focus on the way Kawabata describes the female characters in this novel. How do they compare to the way that Abe describes his female characters? Then pay attention to the male protagonist's emotions in Kawabata's novel and compare them to those of Jumpei in *The Woman in the Dunes*. Does Kawabata's protagonist discover something new about himself at the end? Which of the stories is more uplifting? And why?

- There have been great changes in Japan's long history. Choose three different time periods and compare the literature, the economy, and the culture. How did they change? What were the influences that caused these changes? How were these changes reflected in the literature of the times?

---

laughing. He senses pain but only as if that pain belonged to someone else. And when he cries, it is described in this way: "He sobbed in a stifled voice. But he was not particularly sad. He felt quite as if someone else were crying." But it is not only his emotions that he does not claim. There are moments when his body does not even seem to belong to him. For instance, at one point, as he goes to light a cigarette he is holding, and as he looks at his hand, he states: "The fingers that held it trembled." A later section reads: "He felt that the hand he held to his face was floating free in the air." This was his own hand he was talking about. Even in his description of having sex, it is said: "It was not he who had satisfied his desires, but apparently someone quite different, someone who had borrowed his body."

And in case these concepts of a lack of self were not clear enough, the protagonist mentions a mirror that is hung in the house in the sand pit. The paint on the back of the mirror has chipped away, and when anyone looks into it, they see only disjointed parts of themselves. And when the woman mentions that she wants to buy a new mirror, the protagonists says a new mirror would be just as useless. "What use would a mirror be to someone who no longer could be seen?" This loss of oneself builds up in the novel until the very last section. In the last pages, after he realizes that the sand contains drinkable water, the narrator states: "The change in the sand corresponded to a change in himself. Perhaps, along with the water in the sand, he had found a new self." And thus, the ending of the story is a new beginning, one in which the protagonist begins to create a true image of himself.

Impotency

The protagonist fights to retain some kind of power throughout most of the story. He threatens his captors, but his threats are weak and have no effect. He tries to escape several times but his plans are thwarted by the sand. He tries to catch a crow in his trap, but the crow is too smart to fall for it. Only at the end of the story, when he discovers water in his crow trap does the protagonist finally taste success. It is an accidental success, but the thought of it fills him with joy. He finally has something that works in his favor. He has water, the basis of life. It is at this point, when the feeling of impotency is finally lifted from his shoulders, that he finds a purpose and meaning to life.

Submission

The woman who lives in the sand dunes represents, in many ways, submission. She does not totally lack a will, but she often submits to her circumstances. She does not question why she cannot leave her house. She believes her endless digging of the sand is done in the name of the community. Whereas the man has lost his identity in the shuffling of paperwork in the modern society, the woman has acquiesced her identity in the name of her fellow villagers. She does what she is told. She lives according to the rules set upon her by others. She seldom talks back to the man even though what he says is often wrong. When he demands that she stop working, she obeys him. When he feigns illness and injury, she waits on him. When he talks about escaping, she ignores him.

Through most of the story, the man, on the other hand, fights against his circumstances. He constantly looks for an escape. It is not until the end of the story that he begins to understand the other side of submission. In the end it did not matter that he was stuck in a hole. After a failed escape attempt, the narrator recalls: "He was still in the hole, but it seemed as if he were already outside." The protagonist begins to realize that he had been lost in the details of life, much like a viewer might be lost in a mosaic by trying to see it by standing too close to it. In his new revelations, he felt as if "perhaps the world had been turned upside down and its projections and depressions reversed." What he once saw as submission, in other words, he now saw as tranquility.

Misunderstanding

As much as the protagonist believes he knows about life, the environment, and the people around him, he is constantly off the mark. This begins with his statement, at the beginning of the novel, that sand is dry. He later learns, to the contrary, that sand, in fact, is very wet. It is so wet that he can extract water from it. But this is not the only concept that is mixed up inside his head. He also believes, in the first section of the story, that the woman's submissiveness is wrong. "In every way that position [of submission] of hers was exceedingly dangerous." And once again, he is proven wrong. By the end of the story, it is the protagonist's submission that brings him peace. Again and again, the protagonist misjudges situations. He asks for a newspaper and expects to find an article about himself, but there is

no such story. He threatens his captors by telling them: "You're going to be the ones in trouble if we're buried by the sand." Of course, this is ridiculous. He will be the one who is buried, and the villagers will find someone else to dig the sand. And when the villagers do not respond to him, the protagonist tells himself that "he was the one who held the fuse to the time bomb." He says this as if he truly believes he is the one with the power. His concepts of reality and psychology are almost always wrong. He often thinks the woman is backwards or stupid such as when she tells him that the sand rots the wood. And when he tries to wrestle the shovel out of her hands, a task which he believes will be a simple one, he is caught off guard by her strength.

Style

Irony

The construction of *The Woman in the Dunes* includes many instances of irony. The overall ironic structure of the novel is that of the tables being turned on the protagonist. He hunts down and traps bugs for a hobby. And then he becomes like a bug, trapped in a hole in the sand. "He was lured on by the feeling that in all probability his prey was there, and he made his way down the gentle slope," the narrator relates in the beginning of the story. There are also many other examples of irony, most of them on a much smaller scale. A little later, the protagonist states that he was in "no special hurry," as he makes his way through the dunes before his capture. This is ironic because as soon as he realizes he is trapped, time weighs down on him almost to the point of his breaking. Then a few lines later, the protagonist sums up the village people with the words: "With their sense of caution appeased, they were merely good, simple fisherfolk." He will soon learn the irony of his own words. These people were neither simple nor merely good. Once he is lowered into the woman's house, the protagonist looks around himself and sees what a dilapidated condition the house is in, and the narrator states: "He would have thought they were making a fool of him and would doubtless have gone back at once." This is ironic on two fronts. First, they were making a fool of him and second, there was no way he could have gone back even if he had realized how foolish he was. At a later point, he misjudges the woman's actions, then he corrects his interpretation, stating to himself that "he certainly wouldn't be taken in again." Of course, at this point, he still does not have any realization that he already has been taken. And so Abe creates one ironic statement after the other. The reader knows what is going on and can laugh at the protagonist's continual naïveté.

Foreshadowing

Abe also uses foreshadowing, allowing the reader to sense what is coming as well as to create a dramatic sense of foreboding. Examples of foreshadowing include some of the protagonist's ironic thoughts before he is captured. For instance, there is the statement he makes as he wanders through the sand dunes, searching for insects. He says, at one point, "There was really nothing yet that foretold danger." In using this statement, Abe implants the sense of danger in the reader's mind even if it was not yet in the protagonist's thoughts. Then a few sentences later, Abe has the man thinking: "What in heaven's name could it be like to live there? he thought in amazement, peering down into one of the holes." Again, this is a mix of irony and foreshadowing. The protagonist's question, although he does not yet realize it, will soon be answered. He will be given a first-hand experience of what it is like to live in a hole in the sand. Yet later, as he continues to wander through the sand dunes, the protagonist concludes that the dunes represent "a disturbing and unsettling landscape." He has no idea, at that point, how true his feelings are. And when he contemplates a fly, he makes an interesting statement about the insect's adaptability. "The fact that the fly showed great adaptability meant that it could be at home even in unfavorable environments in which other insects could not live—for example, a desert where all other living things perished." Much like the fly, the protagonist will also have to learn to adapt and to live in a hole in the sand.

Continuing his hunt for insects, the protagonist comments on the tactics of an entomologist, who "must concentrate his whole attention within a radius of about three yards around his feet." In a short time, that will be almost all the space that he will have, as the narrow space of the house in the hole will be all that is granted to him. And finally, just before he is captured, he makes the observation: "No matter what they did, he mused, there was no escaping the law of the sand." That law, the constant motion of the sand, and the inability to climb a steep cliff of sand, will also entrap him.

Scientific Details

Abe fills a lot of his narrative with scientific details. It is through these details that the protagonist seems to hold onto his sanity. His reality is filled with details. Most of these details, he has left behind in his former life. But the scientific ones have come with him and provide him with hope as he attempts to plan his escape. The scientific details also provide him with a mental stimulus that his rather barren surroundings do not allow. These details begin early in the story as he discusses the beetles that he has found and the ones he hopes to find. He talks about their body structure and their scientific names. He includes descriptions of the different types of vegetation he finds in the sand. And later, he makes the woman describe a bug she has seen. He asks several questions of her until he can name that particular beetle. But one of the major scientific discussions involves sand. The reader learns how sand is formed, what it is made of, how big its dimensions, how it drifts, etc. The protagonist later tries to create a theory of sand in order to imagine a particular construction of a house that might drift or float upon the sand, rather than be buried by it. He thinks in a scientific manner when he tries to scale the cliff of sand, digging at the bottom of the bank, calculating the angles of how the sand will fall and how much he will have to dig in order to make the cliff scalable. And then there are the scientific calculations that he uses to try and trap the crows, and his subsequent discovery of the capillary action of the sand in collecting water.

Allegory

The Woman in the Dunes is an allegory, a story that is symbolic of a specific point that the author is trying to make. The story serves as a way of expressing meanings other than those that first appear on the surface. The plot, setting, and characters merely represent abstractions that are the main focus of the author. In other words, the author wants the reader to feel or intuit what is actually behind these surface elements. Parables, many found in the Bible, and fables, as in children's stories, are allegories. Abe uses the forever-shifting sand, the entrapment, and the senseless and monotonous nightly labor of trying to save the woman's house as an allegory for the way he feels about the industrialized modern society and humankind's loss of meaning, self-worth, and identity.

Historical Context

Japan Immediately after World War II

On April 28, 1952, the official occupation of Japan by the United States ended. This did not,

Compare & Contrast

- **1960s:** Tokyo is considered to have experienced an economic miracle as it emerges from wartorn status, the results of World War II, to become the second-largest economy in the world.

  Today: Although the economic bubble that Tokyo enjoyed in the mid-twentieth century has burst, Tokyo remains one of the most modern and most thriving cities of all the industrial countries.

- **1960s:** Japanese literature in translation is studied in many U.S. universities, but the main focus of research is on ancient poetry, Noh drama, and classical literature such as *The Tale of Genji*, written in the eleventh century.

  Today: Japanese literature is considered one of the main components in the study of comparative literature as taught in U.S. universities. Modern Japanese novels, including those written

  by Japanese women, are now considered important topics of research.

- **1960s:** In 1968, Yasunari Kawabata becomes the first Japanese to win the Nobel Prize for literature.

  Today: Japan now has two Nobel Prize winners in literature, as Kenzaburo Oe joins Kawabata in winning the prize for his life's work.

- **1960s:** Japanese literature, which had previously been described in terms of its beautiful aesthetics and multiple references to female beauty and nature, takes up new themes of alienation, loss of identity, loss of purpose, and the sense of defeat.

  Today: The popularity of manga (Japanese comic books) has some critics worried that the younger Japanese generations will grow up without reading the more traditional forms of literature like novels and poetry.

---

however, end the American influence on Japan, as Japanese officials had signed an agreement with the United States that established American military bases in the country. This agreement stated that the United States would protect Japan against any military attack by another country. The presence of the military, other government officials, as well as American businessmen, created an ever-widening change on the lives of the people of Japan. From clothes to music, from food to department stores, the ancient culture was rapidly becoming westernized. Japan was ruled by a new constitution; the emperor became more of a figurehead than a leader; and the country, in which most of its major cities had been destroyed, relied on American aid to get back on its economic feet.

For many years, despite the fact that Japan was now a democracy, only one party ruled the country. This allowed a certain stability in the region; and with the foreign aid they received, the Japanese people worked hard and were rewarded with one of the strongest economies in the world. Rapid

rebuilding of its industries, which had almost been completely destroyed during World War II, was helped by the military needs during the United States involvement in the war with Korea in the 1950s. By the 1960s, Japan's economy had been quickly turned around.

Japan's Literature after World War II

Many Japanese authors were affected with feelings of loss and alienation after their country's defeat and subsequent occupation after World War II. Some of the more influential writers of the 1940s, 1950s, and 1960s included Osamu Dazai, whose pessimistic views and characters often contemplated suicide because they could not cope with the changes they must face. One of Dazai's most remembered novels is *Ningen Shikkaku*, 1948, which was translated and published as *No Longer Human* in 1958. After many failed attempts, Dazai committed suicide in 1948.

Another great writer of that time period was Yuko Mishima, author of *Gogo No Eiko* (1963), translated the same year as *The Sailor who Fell from Grace with the Sea*. Mishima often wrote about suicide also, and performed seppuku, or ritualized suicide with a sword, in a much publicized event in 1970.

After the war, Nobel Prize–winning Kenzaburo Oe often wrote about rootless young people, such as in his most influential novel, *Kojinteki Na Taiken (A Personal Matter)*, 1964. This story was influenced by the birth of his son, who was born with a congenital abnormality of the skull. In real life, doctors had suggested that Oe and his wife allow the child to die. Oe refused. Today, his son, Hikari, is a famous music composer. The birth of his son changed Oe's life and influenced his writing. He began to write against the use of nuclear weapons.

Japanese Educational System

Education is very important in Japan. The country enjoys high literacy rates, and a majority of high school students continue on to college. Although it has changed recently, during the post-War time period, getting into a secondary school in Japan was almost as difficult and challenging as it is today for a student in the United States to be accepted into college.

Although a form of education was present as early as the sixth century, the Japanese educational system was changed during the occupation by American forces. Education became compulsory until age sixteen, and schools were classified similar to the American system with elementary, middle, and secondary schools. Subjects taught are also similar to the school system in the United States, except that languages, especially English, are emphasized. Entrance exams are required in order to enter the last two years of secondary schools. And if a student does well on the exam and studies hard, he or she is all but guaranteed entrance into a well-respected college. The exams are tough, however, and schools specializing in studying for these exams are well attended. A popular term applied to this time of intense study is "examination hell." But almost half of all secondary students will eventually pass the exam and go on to college. Entrance exams into college, especially the more popular colleges, are also very difficult. But the rewards of gaining a degree from one of the more elite colleges is so profitable that prospective students will study for another year and retake the exam if he or she fails it the first time. Pressure to pass these exams begins as early as elementary school, during which time young students attend night classes to cram for the entrance exams they will one day have to take. This pressure has often been blamed for the emotional stress that many of Japan's children experience. This stress has been blamed for a rise in violence in school and in cases of suicide.

Critical Overview

The Woman in the Dunes remains a classic novel of Japanese literature almost half a century after it was published. As Myrna Oliver, writing for the *Los Angeles Times* put it, this first novel of Abe's "was considered a contender for the Nobel Prize for literature, but was not nominated, partly because the very private Abe studiously avoided the literary spotlight." Oliver continues her article by quoting Hisaaki Yamanouchi, who states one reason for Abe's popularity with Western readers: "He [Abe] is probably the first Japanese writer whose works, having no distinctly Japanese qualities, are of interest to the Western audience because of their universal relevance."

The Woman in the Dunes has been a popular favorite all over the world, sometimes bringing readers to their first experience of Japanese literature in translation. Abe's works, in general, are more easily translated because of their lack of allusions to traditional Japanese themes. *The Woman in the Dunes* focuses instead on problems that people all over the globe must face. Oliver continues her article on Abe by describing the protagonist, Niki Jumpei, as a man who "is first obsessed with the loss of his identity and with escape, but comes to realize that his sand prison gives him intellectual and spiritual freedom."

When *The Woman in the Dunes* was made into a movie, Brent Kliewer, of the *Santa Fe New Mexican* offered these comments. He wrote that it "is a haunting allegory probing the fundamental questions of existence and the meaning of freedom." Kliewer continued by stating: "Its in the man's surrender to his circumstances that captured the imagination of the existential thinkers of the 60s." Existentialists believe that life is purposeless, a point that is at the heart of the novel.

One other critic, Kevin Thomas of the *Los Angeles Times*, who also viewed the movie, commented: "The late Kobo Abe provided Teshigahara [the director of the movie] with a metaphor for the human condition endlessly rich in implications." In one more review of the movie version, William Arnold, for the *Seattle Post-Intelligencer* wrote

Eiji Okada as the entomologist Niki Jumpei trapped in the sand, still from the 1964 film version of the The Woman in the Dunes   © Teshigahara/The Kobal Collection. Reproduced by permission

that, although the story can be enjoyed just on a surface level, if taken deeper, it provides "an existential allegory" and works "as an unforgettable and almost perfect metaphor for man's plight in a hostile world, and a lesson in how the individual must find his own meaning—and limits—in what is, in the end, a futile existence." Another movie critic, Jay Carr of the *Boston Globe* refers to the story as one on a level with Albert Camus's *The Myth of Sisyphus*. Carr then adds: "It's one of the great postwar statements of existential isolation, on a par with Beckett, Camus, Sartre."

From *The Washington Post* comes an article written by Anthony Thwaite, who calls *The Woman in the Dunes* "a hypnotic story of a struggle for existence." Thwaite continues by stating that the novel is "full of hard-edged detail and circumstantial stuff, at the same time it's a sort of parable about losing an identity and perhaps finding a new one." And finally, Wimal Dissanayake adds: "*The Woman in the Dunes* deals with the themes of alienation and identity, themes which are explored with the power of a fabulist imagination." And a little later in his article, Dissanayake continues: "*The Woman in the Dunes* communicates powerfully the emergence of the protagonist's newer self." Dissanayake points out that the focus of the novel is on the relationship between self and place and "Kobo Abe has explored this with a great measure of sensitivity and concreteness. His powerful visual imagination has caught this interplay with subtlety and cogency."

Criticism

Joyce Hart

Hart is a freelance writer and author of several books. In the following essay, Hart examines the portrayal of the woman in Abe's novel, comparing it to the essence of the geisha as presented in Japanese novels written before World War II.

The character referred to only as "woman" in Abe's *The Woman in the Dunes* is a far cry from the portrayal of "woman as geisha" that was often presented in Japanese novels written before the devastation of World War II. And the author seems to almost go out of his way to make a statement contrary to the qualities for which geisha were known. For example, geisha were trained in the arts, were known for their grace and beauty, and were engaging in conversation. Whereas the woman in Abe's novel has a very limited scope of knowledge, and the narrator of the story mentions only her skill in shoveling sand. However, the aspects of geisha are not totally absent in Abe's female character. There remain hints of the geisha woman despite Abe's attempt to cast her aside.

The word *geisha* comes from two different Japanese characters. The first, *gei* stands for "the arts." The second *sha* means "person." Women who were chosen to become geisha were often raised in special schools, and these women sometimes began their studies as very early ages. The young girls were trained in many traditional Japanese arts including dancing, singing, enacting the ritual of the tea ceremony, creating artful flower arrangements, making calligraphy, writing poetry, and playing the shamisen (a stringed instrument). They were taught how to dress, how to walk, and how to maintain a stimulating conversation. They were known for the beautiful kimonos they wore and for the elegant hairstyles and formalized makeup, which featured a very white powder all over their faces, stylized, penciled-in eyebrows, and very bright red, painted lips. They were supposedly the epitome of feminine graces in their time. Their main purpose was to make men comfortable, to entertain them, and to provide them with an environment filled with beauty.

With this view of the geisha in mind, it is easy to see how Abe worked to create a woman in his novel who represented the exact opposite. Abe was raised amidst the ruins of war and westernized occupation. He was bitter about the changes he witnessed. So not only is the environment in which he throws his protagonist stark and hostile, so is his depiction of the female, at least up to a point.

When Jumpei, the protagonist in this story, first sets his eyes on the woman, he is less harsh. He had been expecting an older woman because the villagers had yelled to her, calling her granny. But when Jumpei sees her, one can hear just a tinge of the geisha in his description. She was a "nice sort of woman," the narrator informs the reader. Then he adds the fact that "perhaps she was wearing powder" on her face, because her skin looked unnaturally white for a woman who lived at the edge of the sea. Then, through her actions, the woman, though not necessarily gracefully, serves Jumpei a meal. She cooks for him, makes sure he is comfortable, and honors him by offering him the best seat at the dinner table. There is even a small attempt, on her part, of offering to make conversation. Unfortunately, Jumpei is arrogant and challenges much of what the woman says. He believes she is ignorant when she

> After dinner, the woman takes up the only instrument she owns. And Jumpei watches her, much as a man might have watched a geisha entertain him with music or dance. Except that Abe's woman goes outside to dig sand, fill buckets, and carry them to the lift."

tells him how damp the sand is and how it rots the wood. "Impossible," he exclaims. Sand cannot rot wood. Of course, Jumpei will later find out that the woman is correct about this fact, but for now, he feels he has put the stupid countrywoman in her place. He is in no way in awe of her intelligence, which he finds to be simple and limited.

After dinner, the woman takes up the only instrument she owns. And Jumpei watches her, much as a man might have watched a geisha entertain him with music or dance. Except that Abe's woman goes outside to dig sand, fill buckets, and carry them to the lift. The work is masculine, it is monotonous, and it is dirty. It makes the woman gritty, sweaty, and muscular (hard), whereas the geisha is soft and inspiring and stimulating. But despite the sweat and angularity, Abe's woman is not totally unable to arouse Jumpei.

"He was not particularly interested in what she had to say," the narrator states concerning Jumpei's feelings, "but her words had a warmth in them that made him think of the body concealed beneath the coarse work trousers." The woman, despite the fact that she has to do a man's work, flirts with Jumpei, poking a finger in his ribs and smiling at him in a way that ignites a physical passion inside of him. But nothing comes of his feelings, at least not that first night. And in the next morning, there is a startling sight for Jumpei to behold. An image so startling, he does not know what to make of it. There is the woman, sleeping stark naked in front of him. But what a mixed image she represents. On one hand he is drawn to her nudity; but on the other hand, she has covered her face with a towel,

What Do I Read Next?

- Abe's *The Box Man*, published in 1975 in English, tells the story of an unnamed protagonist who goes around the city wearing a box over his head and constantly describing the world through his scribblings inside the box. This is a fable-like story of the loss of identity, its wonders, and its worries.

- In his novel *Ruined Map* (first published in English in 1969), Abe creates a mystery of a missing person. Mr. Nemuro disappeared more than six months ago, and his wife finally hires a detective to find him. The reader follows the detective in his search as Abe delves into the psychology of this man.

- *The Wind-Up Bird Chronicle* (1998), by Haruki Murakami, is a fascinating journey as the reader follows the protagonist in search of his wife and his cat who have gone missing. There is a lot of comedy mixed in with the morbidity of some of its characters, which include a prostitute, an ex-soldier, and a nasty politician.

- Yasunari Kawabata's *Snow Country* (first published in English in 1957) is about wasted love. It stands in stark contrast to Abe's style, giving the reader a deeper understanding of how revolutionary Abe's style was.

- Kenzaburo Oe's *A Personal Matter* (1964) relates the tension and concern of a father as he deals with a son whose brain is damaged at birth. This is considered Oe's best writing. The protagonist leads a rather shiftless life until he must face the responsibilities of fatherhood.

- Franz Kafka's *The Metamorphosis* (1915) is a nightmarish tale of a young man who awakens one morning to discover the horrific fact that he has been turned into a beetle-like bug. Kafka's effect on Abe was significant, and this story might shed some light on that influence.

- *Geisha: The Life, the Voices, the Art* (1995), by Jodi Cobb, provides an interesting look into the history of this ancient tradition in Japan. Cobb details everything from the intricate hair styles and makeup requirements to the intense training in the arts that these young women undergo. She also provides information on how demanding this profession can be despite the large amounts of money that the women are capable of making. This will provide the reader with a contrasted view of Japanese women that Abe only hints at.

---

stripping her of any semblance of a soul. She is also covered with sand, taking away much of Jumpei's desire to touch her. But the sand does not totally distract him from her beauty. In fact, the sand "brought out the feminine lines; she seemed a statue gilded with sand" Here is the geisha beauty. A geisha was made up to look like a painting of a traditional beauty, much as Abe's woman represents that same beauty, at that moment at least. But something is wrong with this picture. "Suddenly a viscid saliva rose from under his tongue. But he could not possibly swallow it." The sand had gotten in the way, both in Jumpei's mouth, which prohibited him from swallowing and in his desire for the woman's body. "A sand-covered woman was perhaps attractive to look at but hardly to touch."

Jumpei makes his first attempt at an escape and fails miserably. He crawls back to the hut and at first calls out gently to the woman. When she does not respond, he yells at her. And when she finally stirs, she appears "annoyed," something a geisha should never do. Jumpei then tears the towel from her face and what he sees is far from a geisha image. "Her face was covered with blotches," and it was "gruesomely raw." Then the narrator adds: "Now the white stuff [powder on her face] had rubbed away, leaving bald patches that gave the impression of a cheap cutlet not cooked in batter." How much more contrary to a geisha's face can a description get?

But it does not take long for this vision of her to change. A short while later, after Jumpei has settled down and the woman has dressed in a "ki-mono," he looks at her with different eyes. "The color of her matching bluish-green kimono and work trousers gave him a sense of mintlike freshness." The woman is a hybrid, a mixture of both the geisha and the countrywoman. Jumpei also notices the natural-ness with which she waits on him. "Her solicitous manner was so natural that one would have thought she had spent her whole life with such an expression on her face." She is there to care for him, in other words. She helps him adjust to the sand environment, tells him how to dress, and then washes his clothes.

Jumpei listens to the woman sing as she cleans around the house. He watches her shadow dance in the flicker of the candlelight as she works at night. But he also recounts the foul smell of her body and her breath. And when he finally allows free reign to his sexual passion, it begins, not as a courtship or intriguing enticement. Rather, it begins as a physical fight. And it is the woman who starts it. Jumpei is caught off guard. He puts his arms up to protect himself. At first his sole role is that of de-fense. But he is surprised by her strength, and when he thinks he has pinned her down, she flips him over, and it is she who is on top. And he finds that "he no longer cared that his opponent was a woman." He would now treat her as if she were a man. And he takes the offensive. At this moment, with Jumpei back on top of the situation, he sees and feels her feminine sensuality. But they disen-gage before having sex, and the woman stands up and blows "her nose with her fingers" and rubs "her hands with sand." Not a pretty geisha sight.

But it is not over yet. Despite the fact that Jumpei thinks of the woman in terms of having rab-bit eyes (rimmed in red) and having "a strong smell like boiled gristle," he confesses that he "inwardly rubbed his hands in expectation" when he watched her go into her room and begin to undress. He then exclaims: "Such a woman was a real woman." Jumpei appears to be so confused. Much like the shedding of his old self for a new one, he is also shedding his images of what a woman is for him. Is she the artificial but artful beauty of the geisha? Or is she this simple, natural but base woman? Or is the perfect woman a combination of the two? And who is really base? During the moment before they share a sexual engagement, Jumpei is not thinking of love but rather he is considering rape. "The stage at which he could bargain for her body had long passed. Now, force had decided the situation," the narrator tells the reader. And while they join to-gether sexually, there is nothing geisha-like, noth-ing delicate here. In the course of the encounter, the woman laughs "in a husky voice," and when the man brushes his hand against her hair, he finds it "hard and rough to the touch."

Eventually though, a change comes over the man, not all at once, but in pieces. He has failed to escape again, and the woman nurses him back to health. She has taken up the art of beaded jewelry, and she opens up more of her more personal thoughts to him, making him feel as if she has dropped the mask that she had been wearing. And when she fights him off when he attempts to rape her for the sake of a village audience, he abandons himself to her fists. "It seemed that what remained of him had turned into a liquid and melted into her body." Soon after, the woman becomes pregnant. New life, a joint project between them, seems about to take root. But the woman miscarries. And as they wait for the truck to take her to the doctor, Jumpei rubs her "belly." This is the first sign of tenderness between them. It is with her departure that Jumpei finds a key to his release. The men have forgotten to take the rope ladder away. However, by this time, Jumpei discovers that rather than being repulsed by the woman and her environment, he quite likes it there. This woman, whatever her image, is grow-ing on him. He looks down into the hole where the house sits and thinks he sees someone. But it is only his shadow. And when he climbs down, he hears a voice singing on the radio, and he has "to stifle the sobbing that seemed about to burst from him." In finding himself, he has dropped all pre-suppositions about femininity—geisha and country-woman alike. The woman had entered inside of him, and they became one.

Source: Joyce Hart, Critical Essay on *The Woman in the Dunes*, in *Novels for Students*, Thomson Gale, 2006.

Donald Keene

In the following essay excerpt, Keene describes the influence of Abe's dual homelands—Manchuria and Japan—on his writing.

Abe was a maverick, incapable of aligning himself for long with any political movement or writing works in accordance with doctrinal lines. His independence and breadth of vision were often attributed by Japanese—who tend to emphasize ge-ographical considerations as determining factors in a man's life—to his having grown up in Manchuria rather than in the insular world of Japan.

Abe was born in Tokyo in 1924. At the time his father, a medical doctor, was a professor at the Medical University of Manchuria (Manshū ika daigaku) but was temporarily in Tokyo doing

> " ... it is probably no coincidence that the novel that established his reputation, *The Woman in the Dunes,* describes the part of Japan that most resembles the windswept dunes of Manchuria...."

research. The family moved to Mukden (Shenyang) in the following year, and Abe spent his childhood there, attending Japanese schools. Although such schools were products of the Japanese occupation of Manchuria and signified the Japanese intention of remaining there permanently, the official line taught to the pupils was not that the Japanese were superior to the other inhabitants but that the five constituent peoples—Japanese, Chinese, Manchus, Mongols, and Russians—must live on terms of equality and harmony. As a boy Abe believed in this ideal, although he also must have been aware that other Japanese, enjoying their privileged position, accepted as a matter of course their predominant role in the new country. Even though Abe seemed to be permanently domiciled in Manchuria, he never forgot that he was Japanese. I recall Abe saying that boys in his school wore gloves in winter to distinguish themselves from the Chinese boys who wore mittens, even though mittens were much warmer.

But such awareness of the distinction between the Japanese and the other peoples of Manchuria was probably less important to Abe than what he unconsciously absorbed from the place. If he did not become a Manchurian, he was quite unlike a typical Japanese schoolboy. The textbooks he read in school, intended for children in Japan, contained such sentences as "In our country, the streams are pellucidly clear and the mountains are green." But the streams in Manchuria were few and likely to be muddied, and there were no mountains in sight, only immense, dusty plains merging imperceptibly into the desert. The contradiction between the textbook descriptions of "our country" and the visible reality of sand dunes behind the school building made the boy question the veracity of the textbooks. It

inspired contradictory feelings: a yearning for Japan but also a sense of alienation from Japan. In later years, when he was actually living in Japan, such feelings kept him from identifying himself with Japanese landscapes. He told me once that he never could understand why Japanese were so fond of the ocean. More important, he developed a suspicion and even a hatred of manifestations of love of the soil—any soil—an emotion he came to associate with fascism.

In Abe's novel *The Woman in the Dunes,* the hero, a collector of rare insects that live in the dunes, finds himself as dusk comes on without a place to spend the night. He visits the village cooperative and asks their help. He notices a placard on the wall: "The Spirit of Love for One's Home-Place" (*aikyōseishin*). Later, he comes to understand that attachment to the soil, love of home-place, accounted for the villagers' determination to remain in the bleak dunes, eternally shoveling sand. The man appears just at a time when the villagers are in need of another hand to help shovel the sand. They lead him to a house buried in the dunes whose owner, a woman, welcomes him. Gradually he realizes that he is a prisoner, given enough to eat and provided with a woman, but compelled to keep shoveling the sand. Late in the novel the man, whose various attempts to escape have been frustrated, asks the woman why people go on living in such a place. She says it is because of the sand:

"The sand?" The man clamped his teeth together, rolling his head.

"What good is the sand? Outside of giving you a hard time, it doesn't bring in a penny."

[The woman answers,] "Yes, it does. They sell it."

"You sell it? Who do you sell such stuff to?"

"Well, to construction companies and places like that. They mix it with concrete...."

"Don't be silly. It'd be a fine mess if you mixed this sand with cement—it's got too much salt in it. In the first place, it's probably against the law or at least against construction regulations...."

"Of course, they sell it secretly. They cut the hauling charges in half too...."

"That's too crazy! Even if it was free, that wouldn't make it right when buildings and dams start to collapse, would it?"

The woman suddenly interrupted him with accusing eyes. She spoke coldly, looking at his chest, and her attitude was completely different.

"Why should we worry about what happens to other people?"

Eiji Okada as the entomologist Niki Jumpei with the woman in the dunes, still from the 1964 film version of the The Woman in the Dunes © Teshigahara/The Kobal Collection. Reproduced by permission

The woman is elsewhere portrayed as a sympathetic though very nearly mute character, but in this one scene she reveals her love of the soil, the place where (she says) the bones of her child are buried, so strong that she is indifferent to whether or not the sand causes people to die in other places. Abe, who had two homelands—Manchuria and Japan—was attached to neither. I can hardly imagine him feeling either nostalgia or local pride, but he never forgot Manchuria, his lost homeland. He did not describe his life in Manchuria in the kind of first-person novel that is typical of twentieth-century Japanese literature, but his early writings evoked experiences on the continent, and it is probably no coincidence that the novel that established his reputation, *The Woman in the Dunes,* describes the part of Japan that most resembles the windswept dunes of Manchuria. . . .

Other experiences in Manchuria directly or indirectly colored Abe's future writings. One came as a particular shock and affected not only his writings but also his outlook on life: it was seeing the lawless behavior of the Japanese troops in Mukden after the surrender. He felt such disgust on witnessing the crimes perpetrated by Japanese soldiers on Japanese civilians as to make him wish to renounce his identity as a Japanese. This disgust further developed into

a hatred of any form of nationalism or of the belief that one "belonged" to a nation. In later years he was sometimes accused of being a rootless cosmopolite, but he accepted the charge. I once asked him why he so seldom gave names to the characters in his novels or play's. (They are called instead "the mother," "the boxer," "the fiancée," or simply, as in *The Woman in the Dunes,* "the man" and "the woman"). He said it was because it made things more difficult if he gave them names. He did not elaborate, but I wonder if he was not reluctant to confine his characters within the limitations of being Japanese—or any other nationality. He asked that when his plays were staged abroad, there be no suggestion of their Japanese origins. . . .

Abe's novels have never been great favorites with people who seek from fiction nothing more than entertainment or with commuters hoping to make the two-hour journey to work pass more quickly, but he has had a solid following and could count on sales of at least 100,000 copies for his novels. It is amazing that avant-garde works should have sold so well. But as they became more difficult, many readers who bought them because of the prestige of Abe's name did not always read them to the end, and the critics often regretted that he had abandoned the easily followed narrative style of *The Woman in the Dunes* or *The Face of Another* for new experiments. But Abe was determined that his novels not be viewed merely as Japanese examples of some world trend in literature. Instead, he wanted to *make* the trends, even if this meant that his books would not be fully appreciated until some future time. When I casually mentioned to an editor that I had enjoyed *Kangaroo Notebook,* the story of a man with a strange malady—radish sprouts coming from his shins—he begged me to write an article for *Shinchō,* the literary monthly published by the company, because no one else had praised it. Probably my friendship with Abe had enabled me to understand, better than most critics, that this novel, so full of humor, is about death, and specifically about Abe's own death.

Source: Donald Keene, "Abe Kobo," in *Five Modern Japanese Novelists*, Columbia University Press, 2003, pp. 65–84.

David Pollack

In the following essay excerpt, Pollack explores how Abe's particular rendering of logic and deduction lead inevitably to the irrational in The Woman in the Dunes.

The detective genre plays against conventional expectations of logic, sending readers up blind alleys and forcing them to come to the wrong conclusions about the facts. Abé's works, as if set in a hall of mirrors, subject the ostensibly deductive method of the detective genre (*tantei shōsetsu* or *suiri shōsetsu*) itself to a kind of infinite regression, investigating the idea of investigation by making problematic its conventions, its assumptions, its procedures, its quandaries. What is thus actually at stake in such works is the validity of deductive logic as a way of arriving at ultimate truth, and so of the very underpinning of the scientific method itself.

In Abé's hands, deductive logic becomes something truly terrifying. He is concerned especially with the violent collisions that occur when the awesome instrumental power of cold, self-contained rationality—generally the sole stock-in-trade of the otherwise entirely fallible detective—is trained on the patent absurdity of human life and, even worse, with how the results of such collisions haunt the menacing corridors of inhuman bureaucracies: the offices, penal institutions, and hospitals where criminals and victims, perpetrators and lawyers, doctors and patients, jailers and prisoners are no longer clearly distinguishable from one another.

Abé's labyrinthine underworld is a faithfully detailed mirror image, only turned upside down, of the world we take for granted. The world of Raymond Chandler's novels, by way of contrast, may sometimes become considerably absurd, but it never lapses into the truly Kafkaesque nightmare; and even when good guys and bad guys in Chandler's stories look very much alike, there is always a bottom line of decency that clearly separates them. In Abé's stories, however, the all-too-human and the all-too-inhuman are not simply opposite sides of the same coin; after a while we realize that we have no idea which side of the coin we are seeing or, even worse, on which side our sympathies should lie.

The connective strand running through all of Abé's work is the idea that rationality, pursued logically to its logical endpoint, turns out to be insanely irrational. The most frightening thing about the world we live in is its power to rationalize itself to us as the only normality there is by its amazing trick of being able to account paranoically for everything down to the last tiny detail. And the name we give to the ability to perform this particular ideological accounting trick is "science." In Abé's hands, properly licensed and accredited scientific knowledge of the world proves not only as false as any other but even more so, and certainly more destructive in its consequences. And what is "logical" turns out to be the world we know turned on its head and made strange.

Jumpei Niki, the protagonist of *Woman in the Dunes,* is as ordinary a man as it is possible to be. Even the given name of this Japanese schoolteacher and amateur scientist means "obedient and average," suggesting the dreary ordinariness of a man who has no use at all for the imagination. Though entirely plausible as a Japanese name, it has something of the ring of Meade E. Oaker to it, if not simply Everyman—and even this ordinary name is withheld from the reader until chapter II, where it appears only as part of an imagined missing-person report. As in a Kafka tale, the protagonist Jumpei is known throughout simply as "the man" (*otoko*) or, more anonymously still, "he" (*kare*).

The narrative voice is deployed in the pseudo-objective tone of the official report which characterizes the detective genre and parodies the language of the police and bureaucracies everywhere. Raymond Chandler has a way of beginning sentences in a flat narrative voice that suddenly breaks into bizarre simile, and his detective, Philip Marlowe, occasionally begins what was intended as a quiet chuckle but almost accidentally rises into an inappropriate cackle or guffaw. But Abé's narrative voice never loses its careful modulations even as it lapses smoothly into absurdity, and when his narrative veers off on bizarre tangents, they diverge from the ordinary so gently as to pass almost unnoticed:

> The theory had been advanced that the man, tired of life, had committed suicide. One of his colleagues, who was an amateur psychoanalyst, held to this view. He claimed that in a grown man enthusiasm for such a useless pastime as collecting insects was evidence enough of a mental quirk. Even in children, unusual preoccupation with insect collecting frequently indicates an Oedipus complex. In order to compensate for his unsatisfied desires, the child enjoys sticking pins into insects, which he need never fear will escape. And the fact that he does not leave off once he has grown up is quite definitely a sign that the condition has become worse. Thus it is far from accidental that entomologists frequently have an acute desire for acquisitions and that they are extremely reclusive, kleptomaniac, homosexual.

This passage begins reasonably enough, and seems all the more reasonable in having been prepared for by the simple statement of the man's disappearance, his description, and speculation as to his possible motives. Yet, all the while continuing to deploy the same tone of detached objectivity, it drifts off unnoticed into absurdity. From the quite reasonable and accurate proposition that insect collecting is a common pastime among Japanese children, the logic simply marches inexorably onward, out of control; children who collect insects do so because they have Oedipus complexes and are insecure; insect collecting continued into adulthood it is a sign of mental peculiarity; adult entomologists are notable for their deviant behavior; and these deviants end up more fascinated by the cyanide in their collecting bottles than in collecting and are thus likely to commit suicide. Even if it is not the sort of logic we are used to, by the end of this passage we find ourselves simply accepting the proposition that children who collect insects for a hobby become adult candidates for suicide. Such a proposition allows the world around the entirely unremarkable jumpei to ignore his disappearance as just another unremarkable event.

In an essay on science fiction, Abé wrote that he first encountered this kind of logic in the work of Edgar Allan Poe. Tales such as "The Purloined Letter," "Descent into the Maelstrom," and "The Unparalleled Adventure of One Hans Pfaall," he wrote, are based on a logic of "bizarre reasoning that never leaves the realm of reason." Quoting a passage from "Hans Pfaall" in illustration, Abé remarks on the

> The connective strand running through all of Abé's work is the idea that rationality, pursued logically to its logical endpoint, turns out to be insanely irrational."

balloonist's discovery of a phenomenon which, though contrary to all reason, can yet be reasonably explained: "What mainly fascinated me, in the appearance of things below, was the seeming *concavity* of the surface of the globe." Poe's passage is worth quoting in full here, for it reveals the same logic that informs *Woman in the Dunes:*

> I had, thoughtlessly enough, expected to see its real *convexity* become evident as I ascended; but a very little reflection sufficed to explain the discrepancy. A line, dropped from my position perpendicularly to the earth, would have formed the perpendicular of a right-angled triangle, of which the base would have extended from the right-angle to the horizon, and the hypotenuse from the horizon to my position. But my height was little or nothing in comparison with my prospect. In other words, the base and the hypotenuse of the supposed triangle would, in my case, have been so long, when compared to the perpendicular, that the two former might have been regarded as nearly parallel. In this manner the horizon of the aëronaut appears always to be *upon a level* with the car. But as the point immediately beneath him seems, and is, at a great distance below him, it seems, of course, also at a great distance below the horizon. Hence the impression of concavity.

"Rather than ask how this discovery holds up under the test of fact," Abé suggests, "we should ask how it elicits a feeling of surprise from the reader. The degree of proximity to the inner rules of the behavior we call 'discovery' is far more significant, in a literary sense, than any relationship to fact." In the case of "Hans Pfaall," we need only accept that from the height of a balloon the base and hypotenuse of such a triangle would appear infinitely long; for all perceptual purposes, logic tells us that they would then for all intents and purposes be parallel, and the rest simply follows automatically.

Elsewhere in the same essay, Abé describes a novel by John W. Campbell, Jr., *The Moon Is Hell* (1951), as "a meticulously detailed depiction of a man who, having drifted to the moon, discovers a way of being able to live there and goes through the process of putting together a life." This plot not only continues the story of "Hans Pfaall" but also sounds very much like a thumbnail sketch for *Woman in the Dunes.* Abé's theme in this essay is that science fiction, which he regards as the most strikingly imaginative of all fiction, has little to do with either science or ghost stories (a genre of the Edo period continued into modern times by the popular author whose pen name, Edogawa Rampō, puns on "Edgar Allan Poe"). Rather, he says, it occupies a world of "pseudo-science" (science, that is, in which all hypotheses are equally possible) and represents ghost stories (the popular genre, that is, which Poe intentionally satirized and parodied) "but without the ghosts."

The operation of the entire plot of *Woman in the Dunes* recapitulates the early passage I have quoted concerning insect collectors and their fate. Almost without noticing it, we are led by the incremental addition of bizarre descriptive detail, the logic of step-by-step deduction somehow gone a few degrees awry, to conclusions that turn common sense on its head. Central to this revolution in logic is Jumpei's normal human curiosity about how things work, his all-too-human egotistical desire for mastery, and even his absurd ambition in life (though he does not turn into a cockroach like Gregor Samsa, he does yearn to have a beetle named after him)—all qualities that resonate plausibly enough in ourselves. It is not long before the reader too, most likely for the first time in his life, finds himself thinking of sand as "a very interesting substance."

Beginning with a dry but somehow slightly implausible encyclopedia entry that reads like a passage from one of Borges's imaginary books ("Sand: an aggregate of rock fragments. Sometimes including loadstone, tinstone, and more rarely gold dust. Diameter: 2 to 1/16 mm"), the narrator informs us that sand is everywhere uniform ("The size of the grains shows very little variation and follows a Gaussian distribution curve with a true mean of 1/8 mm") and that it has much the same aerodynamic properties as a fluid. The narrator then turns to a consideration of sand's corrosive properties—"The sands never rested. Gently but surely they invaded and destroyed the surface of the earth"—carefully building up an equation between the flow of sand and entropy. This notion "excites" the man just as a new intellectual discovery excites us: sand is inhospitable not because it is dry (and here we simply accept its dryness as

factual, although it is soon to be proved false) but rather because it is always in motion. Its entropic motion even affords the man a revelation of the truly moral life: "Didn't unpleasant competition arise precisely because one tried to cling to a fixed position? If one were to give up a fixed position and abandon oneself to the movement of the sands, competition would soon stop." People fail because they cling together; sand succeeds because it does not. The idea sounds quite Buddhist, or perhaps Taoist, yet the logic appears at this point to lead as inexorably to the desolation of alienation as to the exhilaration of enlightened liberation.

Solitary, friendless, unmarried, a tiny cog in a huge bureaucracy, Jumpei is the very personification of the alienation of modern life. To this point in his very modern life he has managed to associate love only with sex (he scorns the emotion as "soap opera"), sex only with venereal disease ("the very opposite of soap opera"), and—since being trapped in his sandpit—venereal disease only with his new-found moral entropy, the measure of things running down over time: "Venereal disease [was] stealthily imported by Columbus in his tiny ships into tiny harbors [and] spread so diligently by everyone throughout the world. All men were equal before death and venereal disease." In Jumpei's modern logic, love is equated with disease, disease with death, and death with sand.

This chain of associations does not end in the conclusion we are led to expect, however: in his new sandtrap world the sheer material fact of sand entirely preempts Jumpei's more usual neurotic obsession with venereal disease to become, as it were, a transcendent spiritual condition, the natural environment of life itself. For the first time in his life, he and "the woman" both covered with sand, Jumpei improbably finds real pleasure and fulfillment in sex (chapter 20) and, eventually, in love. His having been forced to live in nothing but sand, and thus fully in the flow of entropy, becomes for him the limiting condition within which human love becomes possible. We appear to be bordering here on the world of Mishima.

The world of the villagers who have trapped Jumpei and become his captors and tormentors, a world oddly normal *but entirely upside down,* is clearly a critique of the fate of the traditional rural village in modern, urban, capitalist Japan. These poor and remote farmers and fishermen have been abandoned by the state, which has given up on the impossible task of trying to prevent the constantly encroaching entropic sand from swallowing up their fields and homes (the story is set near the coastal city of Sakata, an area whose villagers' problems Abé became fascinated with after reading an article about them *Asahi Graph*). These peasants have therefore simply reinvented themselves in a new relationship to the state, surviving by selling their problematic sand to be made into the equally problematic concrete used in public highway and housing construction projects.

The woman and the others like her who live in these sandpits perform the dual and necessary function of any underclass. By constantly digging the ever flowing sand away from their homes only to find themselves at the bottom of ever deeper holes (Abé's Sisyphian metaphor for the everyday life of the proletariat), they serve as a front line of defense against the encroaching sand, which represents entropy, time, change, history. At the same time, they provide raw labor and material for the state. The villagers are well aware that their salt-laden sand is fatal to the structural integrity of any concrete in which it is used, yet when Jumpei objects that bridges, buildings, and dams made of such concrete will absorb too much water and eventually collapse, he is shocked by the apparent callousness of the woman's reply: "Why should we worry about what happens to others?"

Her response is both an indictment of the heartlessness and inevitability of the ruthless logic of capitalism and an accurate portrayal of the mentality of peasants anywhere toward the larger world beyond their own limited horizons. By much the same Keynesian logic that can justify the notion of a well-functioning economy, sadly though inevitably, leaving some of its members out of work, the Japanese economy has found it expedient simply to ignore these unfortunate but, in the end, expendable wretches. Their understandable response is that if, in order to survive, society can abandon them, they in turn are justified in poisoning society for the same purpose. Along with the generally suspicious nature of the villagers (who are at first certain that Jumpei is some sort of official up to no good), nothing sums up this provincial mentality as pointedly as the woman's phrase *tanin no koto:* "what happens to others" is certainly none of *their* business.

The moment is pivotal for Jumpei. Until now he has naturally taken the side of the "normal" outside world from which he came against these apparently demented brutes who have trapped him. Once he realizes the reason for their hostility, however, their entire enterprise suddenly takes on a new logic of its own: "It had never occurred to him to think of his relationship with the village in that light. It was natural that they should be confused and upset. But even if that were the case, and he conceded the point, it would be like throwing away his own justification." And then, recognizing that he has in fact already thrown it away ("Yes, of course. It's true about 'other people's business'"), Jumpei makes an about-face and simply accepts this new world and its logic built on shifting sand.

The idea that there is no such thing as an innocent victim pervades all of Abé's work. His stories seem predicated on the urban myth that if one repeatedly dials random phone numbers and yells, "Run, they're onto us," at least half of those who answer will flee town. Since *everyone* secretly feels guilty about *something,* what better premise with which to hook the reader? It is Abé's firm conviction that if you examine any life closely enough, you will find a crime—and from that starting point any good detective can reconstruct what will, inevitably, turn out all along to have been the criminal life.

The logic of Jumpei's insight is that of all accommodation in general: a logic of reversal, of the topsy-turvy. At first he is able to think of nothing but escape and spends all his time plotting it, only to fail at each more desperate attempt. The next stage occurs when, exhausted and ill from his efforts, he concludes that he must give at least the appearance of cooperating with his captors, both to lull their suspicions and to keep up his strength. In time, however, appearance inevitably becomes reality: needing something to do, like all men, he initiates little projects to keep himself busy. Among other projects, he fashions a trap from a wooden bucket sunk into the sand, hoping to catch a crow and tie a plea for help to its leg—even though he knows that the crows never fly farther than the nearby homes of the villagers who have trapped him. As he repeats this and other equally ludicrous quotidian tasks over and over, he comes to feel "a certain gentle contentment with the hand work which he performed daily and in the repeated battle with the sand." Karma is the weight of these accumulated moments of a mindless, time-killing, hopeless repetition that eventually drowns each individual in the sea of time. Like all moderns, Abé's characters are in some way victims of it; it is only Mishima's quixotic heroes who can literally "kill time" by their fanatical determination to become the perpetrators of their own fate. Like the rest of humankind, Jumpei seems doomed to succumb to it.

Jumpei's epiphany occurs with his miraculous discovery that although his trap fails to catch crows, it succeeds in trapping something even better: fresh water. Sand is hygroscopic, attracts water, a fact he had noted long before, though in an entirely different context. That fog rose from the sand at night, or that the sides of the sandpit kept their shape best when damp from the morning dew, had impinged on his awareness only in terms of how these facts either contributed to or hindered his attempts at *escape*. The need for water from the village had been a major reason for continuing to cooperate in shoveling sand every day (though only one among many reasons connected with other basic human needs: to keep the sand out, to keep busy, to obtain sexual favors from the woman). Now, having discovered that a leaky wooden bucket sunk into the sand will trap fresh water, he suddenly realizes he is freed from any compulsion to cooperate: "If he were successful in this experiment he would no longer have to give in to the villagers if they cut off his water. But more important, he had found that the sand was an immense pump."

"*But more important*" (*sore dokoro ka*): the sense of reversal in this conjunctive phrase is crucial, for it indicates that the logic of final accommodation has entirely replaced the earlier logic of escape. The sand, which he had thought to be destructive because it contained water that rotted everything it touched, now turns out *for exactly the same reason* to be constructive and so becomes the basis on which to construct a whole new world view and life: "The change in the sand corresponded to a change in himself. Perhaps, along with the water in the sand, he had found a new self" (236/142). His discovery has given him a purpose in life for the first time. When, soon afterward, the woman has a miscarriage, and the villagers, in their hurry to rush her to the hospital, leave a rope ladder dangling into his pit, he simply ignores the chance to escape and turns back instead to repair his water trap: "There was no particular need to hurry about escaping." He even hopes to impress the villagers with his new discovery; the logic of reversal is complete, his earlier ambition replaced with something resembling an ideal of communal endeavor. Gradually, step by step, we have been led to feel that the man trapped in this wretched topsy-turvy world is no longer alienated, anonymous, friendless, and without love. A much more content and fulfilled person than he was before he was trapped, he must acknowledge the truth that we are indeed our own jailers.

Source: David Pollack, "The Ideology of Science: Kobo Abe's *Woman in the Dunes*," in *Reading "Against" Culture: Ideology and Narrative in the Japanese Novel*, Cornell University Press, 1992, pp. 121–35.

Wimal Dissanayake

In the following essay excerpt, Dissanayake examines elements, including "self, place, and body," that contribute to a successful film adaptation of The Woman in the Dunes.

The Woman in the Dunes deals with the themes of alienation and identity, themes which are explored with the power of a fabulist imagination. Sand is the ruling trope of the novel; it is everywhere, pervading the thoughts, revelations, imaginings, ruminations and actions of the protagonist. As Currie aptly points out, sand is the novel's central metaphor, standing for the shifting reality in which the protagonist needs to come to terms with himself and his circumambient reality, in which he needs to sink roots to anchor his existence. Many literary critics and scholars have interpreted the significance of the symbolism of the sand in diverse ways. It is my conviction that Abe's symbolism is deeply rooted in Buddhism, according to which sand signifies *samsara* or worldly existence, and water signifies wisdom and insight.

Hiroshi Teshigahara has made a visually stunning and critically acclaimed film from Kobo Abe's novel. How does one account for this rare success—a great film born out of a great novel. One can argue that Teshigahara is a hugely talented director in the way that Kobo Abe is an outstanding novelist. One can also argue that the novel is visually conceived so that it made the task of the screenplay writer and the director that much lighter. It is also true that the director of the film worked very closely with the novelist. All these factors, in their different ways, no doubt, contributed to the successful animated transcreation of the novel. There is, I believe, yet another, and in some ways, deeper reason for this success, namely, the dialectic between self and place that is so crucial to the thematic and stylistic intent of the novel and its bearing on the art of cinematography.

Teshigahara has sought to stick as closely as possible to the novel; even the dialogue is, by and large, taken directly from the novel. He has added a few incidents like the rape scene and the scene dealing with his old girlfriend that occurs at the beginning of the film, and shortened the escape scenes which are much longer in the novel. But beyond these changes, the film adheres very faithfully to the novel.

A distinguishing feature of *The Woman in the Dunes* is the vital dialectic between self and place. Niki Jumpei is realized, defined and assessed in relation to place. First we are shown how he attempts to escape from the urban environment that he inhabits; next we see him against the background of the desolate and remote seaside village; the third stage, which constitutes the bulk of the novel is his encounter with the pervasive sand in the shack at the bottom of the sand pit; finally his struggle with the environment and his triumph over it with the discovery of water, resulting in the emergence of a newer self. The interplay between self and place, then, is pivotal to the meaning of the novel.

Interestingly, something that cinema does far more effectively and cogently than the other media of symbolic expression is capture the mutual interaction between self and place. It is almost a power invested with the art of cinema. Therefore, the fact that Kobo Abe's novel deals precisely with this aspect certainly helped to make it a literary work full of cinematic possibilities, and the director, Hiroshi Teshigahara, was quick to exploit them to the maximum advantage.

The central trope in the film, as in the novel, is sand. It is at once beautiful and frightening, attractive and repulsive. Director Teshigahara has captured with remarkable skill and power the various shapes, forms and patterns of the sand. At one point, he magnifies a single grain of sand so as to fill the entire screen; at another point, he shows how the sand flows on and on in a cascade-like manner. Throughout the film we are shown how Niki Jumpei's and the woman's bodies are covered with sand, investing their very being with its presence. Indeed, I can hardly think of any other film in which sand plays such a dominant role.

Hiroshi Teshigahara has an acute sensitivity to the sense of place. Niki walking all by himself across the dunes as the sun sinks beyond the horizon; the pitiful condition of the shack in which he is condemned to live with the woman; the woman holding up an umbrella to keep the sand from falling on the food as Niki eats his dinner, the torrential fall of sand on the shack; the shack as seen by the villagers from above; the faces of the villagers transformed into diabolic masks; how these sequences are presented through Teshigahara's wonderful use of the camera and editing bears testimony to this fact. Niki Jumpei's new awareness of himself is a direct consequence of his confrontation with his environment, and the film brings this out graphically.

As I mentioned earlier, *The Woman in the Dunes* communicates powerfully the emergence of the protagonist's newer self. This is accompanied by a significant shift in his cognitive style. It

> **The central trope in the film, as in the novel, is sand. It is at once beautiful and frightening, attractive and repulsive."**

demonstrates the proneness of human beings to adhere to specific cognitive styles and to structure and reify reality in accordance with that style. What the novel points out is the imperative need to get out of such a rigid cognitive style as a way of realizing one's self fully. Needless to say, these cognitive styles are products of, and embedded in, specific discourses.

Niki is a product of the modern, urban environment and the discourse which brought it into being. He may not be totally happy with all facets of this discourse, but he certainly operates within its parameters. He structures his reality in relation to the signification systems that he has inherited from his environment. In addition, he is a resolute insect collector, the entomological and scientific discourse has deeply penetrated his being. He has a rational and analytical frame of mind; he likes to reduce things to their basic constituent elements. He privileges reductionism over holism. As early on in the novel, we are told

> His head bent down, he began to walk following the crescent-shaped line of dunes that surround the village like a rampart and towered above it. He paid almost no attention to the distant landscape. An entomologist must concentrate his whole attention within a radius of about three yards around his feet.

Niki is used to classification and atomization rather than to seeing things holistically, as a consequence of his experiences in the shack with the woman, and as he becomes increasingly acquainted with her ways of thinking and perceiving, his cognitive style begins to change. As he says toward the end of the novel:

> He was still in the hole, but it seemed as if he were already outside. Turning around, he could see the whole scene. You can't really judge a mosaic if you don't look at it from a distance. If you really get close to it you get lost in detail. You get away from one detail only to get caught in another. Perhaps what he had been seeing up until now was not the sand but grains of sand.

As a consequence of Niki's experiences in the shack—as a consequence of the interaction between self and place—he acquires a new cognitive style which is more contextualized, holistic and experiential. This shift in the cognitive style is closely associated with his newly emergent self.

The dialectic between self and place is at the heart of *The Woman in the Dunes.* Kobo Abe has explored this with a great measure of sensitivity and concreteness. His powerful visual imagination has caught this interplay with subtlety and cogency. As I stated earlier, the dialectic between self and place is one that the art of cinema handles with undiminishing enthusiasm. This fact, more than anything else, in my judgment, has contributed to the stunningly successful cinematic transcreation of Kobo Abe's novel.

What Kobo Abe has sought to do is to remove his protagonist from his cultural environment and to probe deeper and deeper into his own psyche as a way of attaining his authentic selfhood. However, culture plays such a formidable role in the combination of self that by merely removing Niki from his familiar cultural surroundings, Kobo Abe is not able to achieve this. As a matter of fact the dialectic between self and place that is clearly a pervasive presence in the novel and the film gain much by way of force and definition from Niki's cultural reflexes.

When discussing the dialectic of self and place in *The Woman in the Dunes,* it is very important that we pay attention to the concept of body that is so central to the textual strategies of the novel and the film. Once Niki is imprisoned in the sand pit, the only reality is the ever present sand and his own body. Much of the communication, experience of diverse emotions, imaginings' ruminations are anchored in the body. Many of the most memorable passages in the novel are associated with the human body.

She was stark naked.

She seemed to float like a blurred shadow before his tear-filled eyes. She lay face up on the matting, her whole body, except her head, exposed to view; she had placed her left hand slightly over her lower abdomen, which was smooth and full. The parts that one usually covered were completely bare, while the face, which anybody would show, was concealed under a towel. No doubt the towel was to protect her nose, mouth, and eyes from the sand, but the contrast seemed to make the naked body stand out even more.

The whole surface of her body was covered with a coat of fine sand, which hid the details and brought out the feminine lines; she seemed a statue gilded

with sand. Suddenly a viscid saliva rose from under his tongue. But he could not possibly swallow it. Were he to swallow, the sand that had lodged between his lips and teeth would spread through his mouth. He turned toward the earthen floor and spat. No matter how much he ejected he could not get rid of the gritty taste. No matter how he emptied his mouth the sand was still there. More sand seemed to issue constantly from between his teeth.

Here Niki is experiencing the strange and bizarre situation into which he has found himself in terms of the body; indeed, the body becomes the instrument by which the strangeness and the abnormality that surrounds him is measured and assessed. Similarly, the attractions and antagonisms that Niki and the woman experience for each other are signified in terms of the body. The human body assumes the stature of a master signifier in the novel.

Without paying any attention, he poised his arms to strike, but the woman, screaming, rushed violently at him. He put out his elbow and twisted his body in an effort to ward her off. But he had miscalculated, and instead of the woman he himself was swung around. Instantly, he tried to counter, but she held on as if chained to the shovel. He did not understand. At least he could not be defeated by force. They rolled over two or three times, thrashing about on the earthen floor, and for a brief moment he thought he had pinned her down, but with the handle of the shovel as a shield she deftly flipped him over. Something was wrong with him; maybe it was the sake he had drunk. Anyway, he no longer cared that his opponent was a woman. He jabbed his bended knee into her stomach.

As he was being soaped he pretended to be aroused and pulled at her kimono. He would wash her in return. Caught between confusion and expectancy, she made a gesture of resistance, but it was not clear just what she was resisting. He quickly poured a bucket of warm water over her naked body and without a washcloth began to pass his soapy hands directly over her skin. He started with the earlobes and shifted down to the jaw, and as he passed over her shoulders he reached around and with one hand grasped her breast. She cried out and, sliding down his chest, crouched level with his stomach. Undoubtedly it was a posture of expectation. But the man was in no hurry. With measured cadence, his hands went on with their painstaking massaging from one part of her body to another.

Throughout the novel we find tropes, passages of description which suggest to us that the human body in the novel has become the measure of achievement of all things human. For instance, the author says that, "They say the level of civilization is proportionate to the cleanliness of the skin." When discussing the dialectic of self and place in *The Woman in the Dunes,* then, it is very important that we not lose sight of this very significant dimension of signification.

The last decade or so has witnessed a remarkable increase in the scholarly interest in the human body with a clear focus on the understanding of different modes in which the human body is constructed. The nature and significance of the human body as a reality that is being continually produced and reproduced in society is increasingly attracting scholarly attention. The mapping out of the modalities of construction of the human body, understandably enough, leads into discussions of politics, ethics and questions of power and knowledge. The pioneering work of Foucault, Elias, and Kantorawicz and the writings of Nietzsche from which they took their cue, have significantly inflected this newly generated interest.

The human body, it should be noted, is at the center of a plurality of discourses that produce and reproduce culture. It has, consequently, become a useful analytical tool with which to decode some of the cultural meanings embedded in fictional and filmic texts. For example, modern film theorists of a feminist persuasion are engaged in the task of symbolically reclaiming the body as a means of displacing patriarchal narratives that dominate filmic enunciation. Focusing on a hermeneutic of dominance and submission, they seek to call attention to the diverse ways in which women are situated as objects of male gaze and desire and how the female body is specularized as a rhetorical strategy of male domination over it.

In *The Woman in the Dunes,* the human body is portrayed as a central fact of self; this somatic facticity that runs through the novel inflecting all human emotions, perceptions and ratiocinations has a metaphysical dimension rooted in Japanese thought. It is interesting at this point, to compare the altitudes to body and mind in the Western and Eastern traditions of thought. The Western tradition, by and large, subscribing to a Cartesian duality, posit a definite separation of mind and body whereas the Eastern traditions posit a unity. This unity is perceived as an accomplishment, and wisdom, the highest achievement of human existence, is seen as a physical and intellectual attainment. Truth is not perceived merely as a way of examining the world, but is seen as a modality of being in the world, and a significant aspect of this has to do with our somatic existence. Their line of thinking has a direct bearing on Niki Jumpei's experience. As Yuasa Yasuo remarks, true knowledge cannot be obtained simply through theoretical thinking; it can be obtained only through "bodily recognition as realization" (*tainin* or *taitoku*), that is, through the utilization of one's entire body and mind.

The body and the somatic experiences associated with it play a central role in the novel bearing much of its existential meaning. And one thing that cinema in the hands of gifted filmmakers can do extremely well, is to capture the nuanced experiences and complex responses of the human body. Kobo Abe in writing his novel, has given much attention to questions of corporeality, embodiment, and somaticity. Hiroshi Teshigahara, in translating the literary experience into a cinematic experience has fully utilized the power and beauty of the human body. The centrality accorded to the human body in the novel is another reason that facilitated the transcreation of it in cinema by Teshigahara.

In discussing the relative success of the novel and the film, and the ways in which the novel had enabled its cinematic conversion, the question of male gaze, which is closely related to the representation of the human body, merits closer attention. *The Woman of the Dunes* is essentially a male-centered novel obeying all the laws of representation associated with patriarchy. The novel in essence charts the physical experiences and the ensuing cognitive metamorphosis of Niki, and the woman in the dunes is the catalyst that brings about the changes in Niki. Indeed, the focus of interest in Niki, and the woman is seen and evaluated through his eyes. This is, of course, a limitation of the novel. Once again this feature in the novel is one that ties in very nicely with the dictates and imperatives of the medium of cinema as we know it today.

In Western cinema—and Teshigahara is clearly following the conventions of Western cinema—the female is generally dichotomously and fetishistically constructed as a symbolic outcome of female desire. The female becomes an object of male gaze and her subjectivity is denied, entrapped as she is in the complex dictates of patriarchy. In cinematic representation, the woman being a product of the male gaze, continues to be an object devalued as the site of male voyeurism. She is relegated to a position of marginality and that marginality being vital to the ahistorical, essentialist, and negative image of women created by cinema. Feminist film critics like Laura Mulvery have argued persuasively that women as represented in cinema are entrapped within the economy of male libidinal pleasure obtained in the dark world of fantasy of theater. The woman in the film *The Woman in the Dunes* suffers a dual entrapment;

she is physically entrapped in the sand pits, and communicationally entrapped in the male gaze. And her plight serves to underline the mechanisms of scopophilia (the pleasure of looking) outlined by psychoanalytically-oriented film scholars. So what we find in the representation of the woman in the dunes in the film is the faithful adherence to the androcentric conventions of Western filmmaking. And once again, the built-in patriarchal biases in the novel helped the filmmaker immensely.

The relationship between the self and culture is another dimension that merits close analysis. Clearly, the distinction between society and culture is not an easy one to establish. Anthropologists such as Marcel Mauss who have pointed out the shaping role of society on the evolution of the human self have also talked about the importance of culture. Other anthropologists, like A. Irving Hallowell, who have placed emphasis on the role of culture in the creation of the self, have not ignored the crucial role played by society. The dividing line between society and culture is a finely drawn one, and it is really with shifts of emphasis that we are concerned here.

Of the many scholars who have pointed out the vital role played by culture, it is perhaps Hallowell who invites the closest attention. He pointed out the importance of what he termed the "behavioral environment" on the formation of the self, and this behavioral environment, as he sees it, is essentially culturally constituted. While agreeing with the notion that self-awareness is a generic human trait, Hallowell goes on to make the following observation:

The nature of the self, considered in its conceptual context, is a culturally identifiable variable. Just as different people entertain various beliefs about the nature of the universe, they likewise differ in their ideas about the nature of the self. And, just as we have discovered that notions about the nature of the beings and powers existent in the universe involve assumptions that are directly relevant to the understanding of the behavior of the individual in a given society, we must likewise assume that the individual's self-image and his interpretation of his own experience cannot be divorced from the concept of the self that is characteristic of his society. For such concepts are the major means by which different cultures promote self-orientation in the kind of meaningful terms that make self-awareness of functional importance in the maintenance of a human social order. In so far as the needs and goals of the individual are at the level of self-awareness, they are structured with reference to the kind of self-image that is consonant with other basic orientations that prepare the self for action in a culturally constituted world.

This passage brings out clearly Hallowell's orientation toward the self as a product of culture. As

Andrew Lock points out, culture constitutes man's behavioral environment and provides him with basic orientations that make him capable of acting intelligently in a world so constituted. All these are orientations for the self and facilitate giving it its particular structure. As he goes on to point out, culture provides a self-concept through the linguistic marking of self from non-self. He further remarks,

while one of the constant functions of all cultures . . . is to provide a concept of self along with other means that promote self-orientation, the individuals of a given society are self-oriented in terms of a provincial content of the self-image.

What this means, of course, is that while each culture provides the idiom for self-orientation, the idiom of one culture cannot be directly translated to another culture. This makes the role of culture in the formation of the self even more important.

Clifford Geertz, who did not totally endorse Hallowell's views of the self, nevertheless makes the point that becoming human is becoming individual, and we become individual under the guidance of cultural patterns, historically created systems of meaning in terms of which human beings impart form, order, point, and direction to their lives. Hence the role of culture and inherited history is crucial to Geertz. He then proceeds to note that as culture has shaped us as a single species, so too it shapes us as separate individuals. What we have in common, then, is neither an unchanging subcultural self nor an established cross-cultural consciousness. In his analysis of the Balinese person, he shows very clearly how cultural codings and presuppositions are vital to a proper understanding of the notion of self in that particular culture. In his exegesis of Balinese self, the concerns that come to the fore are not those of motivation, will, and individuation, which would figure very prominently in a similar discussion in the context of Western culture, but an entirely different set intimately linked to Balinese culture. In his essay, "Person, Time and Conduct in Bali," which seeks to delineate some of the cultural apparatus in terms of which the people of Bali define and perceive persons, Geertz starts out by categorically asserting:

Human thought is consummately social: social in its origin, social in its function, social in its focus, social in its applications. At base, thinking is a public activity—its natural habitat is the houseyard and the market place and the town square.

The implication of this fact for the understanding of self are vast and complex. In recent times, several studies have appeared that seek to uncover the cultural formulations of the self (Heelas and Lock; Shweder, and Levine; White and Kirkpatrick). With a justifiably greater interest being evinced in ethnopsychologies, more and more attention will be paid to the cultural codings of self.

The way in which different cultures across the face of the earth have sought to conceptualize, and thereby contribute to, the formation of self is indeed fascinating. For example, Alfred Smith, in an interesting essay on the self and experience of Moon culture, notes, employing a motoring metaphor, that if the self in the Western view can be seen as the driver of the car, then in the Moon view it must be seen as the passenger in its body.

Some of the concerns of Hallowell and Geertz have been fruitfully extended by modern ethnopsychologists who are interested in the cultural understanding and cultural formulation of the self and the processes and dynamics of interplay by means of which these formulations find expression in quotidian life. These ethnopsychologists are trying to rectify some of the deficiencies associated with earlier culture and personality studies, in which the emphasis was clearly on the motivational constructs of individuals and their centrality in shaping behavior. In these studies, very little attention was paid to the modalities of interpretation of the people regarding questions of self and how they have a direct bearing on the wider cultural discourse of a given society. Hence, the work of some of the new ethnopsychologists serves to open up a new and useful dimension of inquiry into the concept of self.

These discussions on the cultural construction of self have a direct bearing on *The Woman in the Dunes*. Kobo Abe has selected a middle-class character who grew up in the city and transfer him to a situation that is bizarre and cultureless. However, the way Niki behaves in that situation only foregrounds his cultural upbringing. The way his newer self emerges from his unanticipated encounters and the way his attitudes are inflected can best be understood against the background of his culture.

Another important area that merits close analysis is the relationship between the self and the psyche. In the case of the self and society, and of the self and culture, the emphasis was on exteriority; now it shifts to interiority. Here the writings of Freud and Jung and their respective followers are of paramount importance. Let us first consider the view of self expounded by Freud. In a sense, it is difficult to summarize Freud's view because over a period of more than four decades of conceptualizing and writing, it changed constantly. When analyzing Freud's views of the self, one can talk of three stages—the somatic, the psychological, and the metapsychologicala—depending on which area one chooses to emphasize. In the early period of his conceptualizations of self, during which he was primarily interested in the somatic nature of self, Freud saw the self as a function of the organism's physical drives, the sex-instinct and the ego-instinct. During the next stage, when his emphasis was on the psychological, the dualism between the sex-instinct and ego-instinct was transformed into twin manifestations of a unitary psychic energy, object-libido and ego-libido. In the metapsychological stage, these two concepts were transformed into Eros, the life-instinct, and Thanatos, the death-instinct.

As we examine the evolution of Freud's concept of self, one thing becomes clear: he conceived of the self in dualistic terms. He saw it as a relation between psychic reality and material reality. The concept of psychic reality was of supreme importance to him:

> The unconscious is the true psychic reality: in its inner nature it is just as much unknown to us as the reality of the external world, and just as imperfectly communicated to us by the data of consciousness as the external world by the reports of our sense-organs.

Freud was interested in getting behind the phenomenal self to its inner reality. For this purpose, he sought to analyze dream processes.

As Freud envisioned it, the self begins as an organism, and instinctual impulses dominate its behavior. However, for the purpose of social survival, it needs to find a mechanism whereby this libidinal expenditure is inhibited and directed toward realistic paths of gratification. This is achieved by investing the libido in the reality-ego. However, in certain specific cultures, certain forms of gratification are not allowed. The requisite libidinal inhibition and sublimation are achieved by means of a projected ego ideal which functions in the capacity of a censor. The energy that was originally invested in the reality-ego is now invested in the ideal-ego. Therefore, Freud saw the self to be a relation between the libidinal desires of the pleasure-ego and the transcendental norms of the ideal-ego. The stability of this relationship is always in danger. The repressed portion of the self, the unconscious, constantly threatens to upset this relationship. Therefore, according to Freud, if the self is to remain a self, it must endeavor to maintain this relationship.

In his book *The Ego and the Id,* Freud delineated clearly the nature of this interaction, using far more precise terminology than before. Instead of the three terms, pleasure-ego, reality-ego and ideal-ego, he now began to employ the terms id, ego, and superego. It is the dynamics among these three entities that result in the formation of the self. What is of interest in this early analysis of Freud, from our point of view, is his attempt to delineate self in terms of psychic reality. The highly stimulating lines of inquiry opened up by Freud have been further developed in newer directions by such influential theorists as Heinz Kohut, Jacques Lacan, Erik Erikson, and Roy Schafer.

Although Jung differed considerably from Freud in his general analysis of the inward behavior of human beings, he too sought to define the self in terms of inner experience. Jung saw the self as the totality of the psyche and distinguished it from the ego, which he saw as constituting only a small portion of the entire psyche.

According to Jung, the self is an inner guiding factor that is clearly different from the conscious personality. It can be grasped only by means of an investigation of one's own dreams. An analysis of dreams, in his opinion, will demonstrate the fact that the self is indeed the regulating center which serves to bring about an extension and maturation of the personality. At first this larger aspect of the psyche emerges as only a possibility. It may appear very dimly or in a more developed form later in life. Its development is largely contingent upon the inclination of the ego to listen to the signals and messages sent out by the self. Jung, then, saw the self as the totality of the psyche, which is the organizing center of the personality. Freud and Jung and many psychologists who have chosen to follow in their footsteps define the self in terms of the psyche and inward experience. This, of course, is not to suggest that they have totally ignored the social and cultural dimensions. However, their emphasis in seeking to define self has unmistakably been on the psychic as opposed to external reality.

These discussions on self and psyche, just like the discussion on self and culture, shed interesting light on the experiences of *The Woman in the Dunes*. The behavior of Niki in its most inwardness can best be understood in relation to the interplay between self and psyche. As a novelist, Kobo Abe has always been fascinated by this interplay, and *The Woman in the Dunes* bears ample evidence of this fact. Teshigahara's visual imagination and Kobo Abe's literary imagination met very productively on the terrain of self and psyche. What I have sought to do in this paper is to examine one of those rare instances in which a highly successful novel has been made into a highly successful film, and to examine some of the reasons that may have contributed to this productive venture. In this regard, I chose to focus attention on what I think are three key entities: self, place, and body, and to discuss them in relation to current intellectual discourse.

Source: Wimal Dissanayake, "Self, Place, and Body in *The Woman in the Dunes*: A Comparative Study of the Novel and the Film," in *Literary Relations, East and West: Selected Essays*, 1990, pp. 41–54.

Sources

Abe, Kobo, *The Woman in the Dunes*, Vintage International, 1991.

Arnold, William, "Years Enhance Eerie Feeling of Landmark Japanese Film *Woman in Dunes*," in *Seattle Post-Intelligencer*, January 23, 1998, p. 22.

Carr, Jay, "*Dunes*: An Allegory of Human Endeavor," in the *Boston Globe*, December 5, 1997.

Dissanayake, Wimal, "Self, Place, and Body in *The Woman in the Dunes*: A Comparative Study of the Novel and the Film," in *Literary Relations, East and West: Selected Essays*, edited by Jean Toyama and Nobuko Ochner, University of Hawaii Press, 1990, pp. 41–54.

Kliewer, Brent, "An Absurd View of Humanity," in *Santa Fe New Mexican*, December 19, 1997.

Lamont-Brown, Raymond, "Kobo Abe: Japan's Novelist of Alienation," in *Contemporary Review*, Vol. 263, No. 1530, July 1993, pp. 31–33.

Oliver, Myrna, "Kobo Abe, 68; Japanese Novelist and Playwright," in *Los Angeles Times*, January 23, 1993, p. 22.

Thomas, Kevin, "*Woman in the Dunes* an Erotic Masterpiece," in *Los Angeles Times*, September 5, 1997, p. 8.

Thwaite, Anthony, "Kobo Abe's Fables of Identity," in the *Washington Post*, April 21, 1991, sec. X, p. 6.

Further Reading

Henshall, Kenneth G., *A History of Japan: From Stone Age to Superpower*, Palgrave MacMillan, 2001.
  Through a study of politics, culture, literature, and economics, as well as other topics, Henshall provides a very spirited study of the history of Japan. Equal time is spent on both the classic periods as well as the modern.

Iles, Timothy, *Abe Kobo: An Exploration of His Prose, Drama, and Theatre*, European Press Academic Publishing, 2002.
  This is a critical study of Abe's life's work, including the influences that affected his writing.

Keene, Donald, *Five Modern Japanese Novelists*, Columbia University Press, 2003.

Donald Keene is one of the most respected translators of Japanese literature. In this book, he examines the work of Kobo Abe, Junichiro Tanizaki, Yasunari Kawabata, Yukio Mishima, and Ryotaro Shiba—five of the best Japanese authors of the past century.

Murray, Giles, *Breaking into Japanese Literature*, Kodansha International, 2003.

Giles Murray, an editor and writer living in Japan, has compiled a study of Japanese literature in both the original language and in translation. For students of Japanese, this is a great study tool. For others, it is a good way to sample some of Japan's best writing.

Shields, Nancy, *Fake Fish: The Theater of Kobo Abe*, Weatherhill, 1996.

Shields presents both a personal and a professional view of Kobo Abe's art as a playwright and director. This book is filled with anecdotes about Abe as well as a behind-the-curtain view of what it was like to work with Abe.

Varley, H. Paul, *Japanese Culture*, University of Hawaii Press, 2000.

From the effects of Zen Buddhism and the samurais to the modern influences of literature and comics, this is a comprehensive overview of what it might feel like to be brought up Japanese.

Glossary of Literary Terms

A

Abstract: As an adjective applied to writing or literary works, abstract refers to words or phrases that name things not knowable through the five senses.

Aestheticism: A literary and artistic movement of the nineteenth century. Followers of the movement believed that art should not be mixed with social, political, or moral teaching. The statement "art for art's sake" is a good summary of aestheticism. The movement had its roots in France, but it gained widespread importance in England in the last half of the nineteenth century, where it helped change the Victorian practice of including moral lessons in literature.

Allegory: A narrative technique in which characters representing things or abstract ideas are used to convey a message or teach a lesson. Allegory is typically used to teach moral, ethical, or religious lessons but is sometimes used for satiric or political purposes.

Allusion: A reference to a familiar literary or historical person or event, used to make an idea more easily understood.

Analogy: A comparison of two things made to explain something unfamiliar through its similarities to something familiar, or to prove one point based on the acceptedness of another. Similes and metaphors are types of analogies.

Antagonist: The major character in a narrative or drama who works against the hero or protagonist.

Anthropomorphism: The presentation of animals or objects in human shape or with human characteristics. The term is derived from the Greek word for "human form."

Antihero: A central character in a work of literature who lacks traditional heroic qualities such as courage, physical prowess, and fortitude. Antiheroes typically distrust conventional values and are unable to commit themselves to any ideals. They generally feel helpless in a world over which they have no control. Antiheroes usually accept, and often celebrate, their positions as social outcasts.

Apprenticeship Novel: See *Bildungsroman*

Archetype: The word archetype is commonly used to describe an original pattern or model from which all other things of the same kind are made. This term was introduced to literary criticism from the psychology of Carl Jung. It expresses Jung's theory that behind every person's "unconscious," or repressed memories of the past, lies the "collective unconscious" of the human race: memories of the countless typical experiences of our ancestors. These memories are said to prompt illogical associations that trigger powerful emotions in the reader. Often, the emotional process is primitive, even primordial. Archetypes are the literary images that grow out of the "collective unconscious." They appear in literature as incidents and plots that repeat basic patterns of life. They may also appear as stereotyped characters.

***Avant-garde*:** French term meaning "vanguard." It is used in literary criticism to describe new writing that rejects traditional approaches to literature in favor of innovations in style or content.

B

Beat Movement: A period featuring a group of American poets and novelists of the 1950s and 1960s—including Jack Kerouac, Allen Ginsberg, Gregory Corso, William S. Burroughs, and Lawrence Ferlinghetti—who rejected established social and literary values. Using such techniques as stream of consciousness writing and jazz-influenced free verse and focusing on unusual or abnormal states of mind—generated by religious ecstasy or the use of drugs—the Beat writers aimed to create works that were unconventional in both form and subject matter.

***Bildungsroman*:** A German word meaning "novel of development." The *bildungsroman* is a study of the maturation of a youthful character, typically brought about through a series of social or sexual encounters that lead to self-awareness. *Bildungsroman* is used interchangeably with *erziehungsroman,* a novel of initiation and education. When a *bildungsroman* is concerned with the development of an artist (as in James Joyce's *A Portrait of the Artist as a Young Man*), it is often termed a *kunstlerroman.* Also known as Apprenticeship Novel, Coming of Age Novel, *Erziehungsroman,* or *Kunstlerroman.*

Black Aesthetic Movement: A period of artistic and literary development among African Americans in the 1960s and early 1970s. This was the first major African-American artistic movement since the Harlem Renaissance and was closely paralleled by the civil rights and black power movements. The black aesthetic writers attempted to produce works of art that would be meaningful to the black masses. Key figures in black aesthetics included one of its founders, poet and playwright Amiri Baraka, formerly known as LeRoi Jones; poet and essayist Haki R. Madhubuti, formerly Don L. Lee; poet and playwright Sonia Sanchez; and dramatist Ed Bullins. Also known as Black Arts Movement.

Black Humor: Writing that places grotesque elements side by side with humorous ones in an attempt to shock the reader, forcing him or her to laugh at the horrifying reality of a disordered world. Also known as Black Comedy.

Burlesque: Any literary work that uses exaggeration to make its subject appear ridiculous, either by treating a trivial subject with profound seriousness or by treating a dignified subject frivolously. The word "burlesque" may also be used as an adjective, as in "burlesque show," to mean "striptease act."

C

Character: Broadly speaking, a person in a literary work. The actions of characters are what constitute the plot of a story, novel, or poem. There are numerous types of characters, ranging from simple, stereotypical figures to intricate, multifaceted ones. In the techniques of anthropomorphism and personification, animals—and even places or things—can assume aspects of character. "Characterization" is the process by which an author creates vivid, believable characters in a work of art. This may be done in a variety of ways, including (1) direct description of the character by the narrator; (2) the direct presentation of the speech, thoughts, or actions of the character; and (3) the responses of other characters to the character. The term "character" also refers to a form originated by the ancient Greek writer Theophrastus that later became popular in the seventeenth and eighteenth centuries. It is a short essay or sketch of a person who prominently displays a specific attribute or quality, such as miserliness or ambition.

Climax: The turning point in a narrative, the moment when the conflict is at its most intense. Typically, the structure of stories, novels, and plays is one of rising action, in which tension builds to the climax, followed by falling action, in which tension lessens as the story moves to its conclusion.

Colloquialism: A word, phrase, or form of pronunciation that is acceptable in casual conversation but not in formal, written communication. It is considered more acceptable than slang.

Coming of Age Novel: See *Bildungsroman*

Concrete: Concrete is the opposite of abstract, and refers to a thing that actually exists or a description that allows the reader to experience an object or concept with the senses.

Connotation: The impression that a word gives beyond its defined meaning. Connotations may be universally understood or may be significant only to a certain group.

Convention: Any widely accepted literary device, style, or form.

D

Denotation: The definition of a word, apart from the impressions or feelings it creates (connotations) in the reader.

Denouement: A French word meaning "the unknotting." In literary criticism, it denotes the resolution of conflict in fiction or drama. The *denouement* follows the climax and provides an outcome to the primary plot situation as well as an explanation of secondary plot complications. The *denouement* often involves a character's recognition of his or her state of mind or moral condition. Also known as Falling Action.

Description: Descriptive writing is intended to allow a reader to picture the scene or setting in which the action of a story takes place. The form this description takes often evokes an intended emotional response—a dark, spooky graveyard will evoke fear, and a peaceful, sunny meadow will evoke calmness.

Dialogue: In its widest sense, dialogue is simply conversation between people in a literary work; in its most restricted sense, it refers specifically to the speech of characters in a drama. As a specific literary genre, a "dialogue" is a composition in which characters debate an issue or idea.

Diction: The selection and arrangement of words in a literary work. Either or both may vary depending on the desired effect. There are four general types of diction: "formal," used in scholarly or lofty writing; "informal," used in relaxed but educated conversation; "colloquial," used in everyday speech; and "slang," containing newly coined words and other terms not accepted in formal usage.

Didactic: A term used to describe works of literature that aim to teach some moral, religious, political, or practical lesson. Although didactic elements are often found in artistically pleasing works, the term "didactic" usually refers to literature in which the message is more important than the form. The term may also be used to criticize a work that the critic finds "overly didactic," that is, heavy-handed in its delivery of a lesson.

Doppelganger: A literary technique by which a character is duplicated (usually in the form of an alter ego, though sometimes as a ghostly counterpart) or divided into two distinct, usually opposite personalities. The use of this character device is widespread in nineteenth- and twentieth-century literature, and indicates a growing awareness among authors that the "self" is really a composite of many "selves." Also known as The Double.

Double Entendre: A corruption of a French phrase meaning "double meaning." The term is used to indicate a word or phrase that is deliberately ambiguous, especially when one of the meanings is risqué or improper.

Dramatic Irony: Occurs when the audience of a play or the reader of a work of literature knows something that a character in the work itself does not know. The irony is in the contrast between the intended meaning of the statements or actions of a character and the additional information understood by the audience.

Dystopia: An imaginary place in a work of fiction where the characters lead dehumanized, fearful lives.

E

Edwardian: Describes cultural conventions identified with the period of the reign of Edward VII of England (1901–1910). Writers of the Edwardian Age typically displayed a strong reaction against the propriety and conservatism of the Victorian Age. Their work often exhibits distrust of authority in religion, politics, and art and expresses strong doubts about the soundness of conventional values.

Empathy: A sense of shared experience, including emotional and physical feelings, with someone or something other than oneself. Empathy is often used to describe the response of a reader to a literary character.

Enlightenment, The: An eighteenth-century philosophical movement. It began in France but had a wide impact throughout Europe and America. Thinkers of the Enlightenment valued reason and believed that both the individual and society could achieve a state of perfection. Corresponding to this essentially humanist vision was a resistance to religious authority.

Epigram: A saying that makes the speaker's point quickly and concisely. Often used to preface a novel.

Epilogue: A concluding statement or section of a literary work. In dramas, particularly those of the seventeenth and eighteenth centuries, the epilogue is a closing speech, often in verse, delivered by an actor at the end of a play and spoken directly to the audience.

Epiphany: A sudden revelation of truth inspired by a seemingly trivial incident.

Episode: An incident that forms part of a story and is significantly related to it. Episodes may be either self-contained narratives or events that depend on a larger context for their sense and importance.

Epistolary Novel: A novel in the form of letters. The form was particularly popular in the eighteenth century.

Epithet: A word or phrase, often disparaging or abusive, that expresses a character trait of someone or something.

Existentialism: A predominantly twentieth-century philosophy concerned with the nature and perception of human existence. There are two major strains of existentialist thought: atheistic and Christian. Followers of atheistic existentialism believe that the individual is alone in a godless universe and that the basic human condition is one of suffering and loneliness. Nevertheless, because there are no fixed values, individuals can create their own characters—indeed, they can shape themselves—through the exercise of free will. The atheistic strain culminates in and is popularly associated with the works of Jean-Paul Sartre. The Christian existentialists, on the other hand, believe that only in God may people find freedom from life's anguish. The two strains hold certain beliefs in common: that existence cannot be fully understood or described through empirical effort; that anguish is a universal element of life; that individuals must bear responsibility for their actions; and that there is no common standard of behavior or perception for religious and ethical matters.

Expatriates: See *Expatriatism*

Expatriatism: The practice of leaving one's country to live for an extended period in another country.

Exposition: Writing intended to explain the nature of an idea, thing, or theme. Expository writing is often combined with description, narration, or argument. In dramatic writing, the exposition is the introductory material which presents the characters, setting, and tone of the play.

Expressionism: An indistinct literary term, originally used to describe an early twentieth-century school of German painting. The term applies to almost any mode of unconventional, highly subjective writing that distorts reality in some way.

F

Fable: A prose or verse narrative intended to convey a moral. Animals or inanimate objects with human characteristics often serve as characters in fables.

Falling Action: See *Denouement*

Fantasy: A literary form related to mythology and folklore. Fantasy literature is typically set in non-existent realms and features supernatural beings.

Farce: A type of comedy characterized by broad humor, outlandish incidents, and often vulgar subject matter.

***Femme fatale*:** A French phrase with the literal translation "fatal woman." A *femme fatale* is a sensuous, alluring woman who often leads men into danger or trouble.

Fiction: Any story that is the product of imagination rather than a documentation of fact. Characters and events in such narratives may be based in real life but their ultimate form and configuration is a creation of the author.

Figurative Language: A technique in writing in which the author temporarily interrupts the order, construction, or meaning of the writing for a particular effect. This interruption takes the form of one or more figures of speech such as hyperbole, irony, or simile. Figurative language is the opposite of literal language, in which every word is truthful, accurate, and free of exaggeration or embellishment.

Figures of Speech: Writing that differs from customary conventions for construction, meaning, order, or significance for the purpose of a special meaning or effect. There are two major types of figures of speech: rhetorical figures, which do not make changes in the meaning of the words, and tropes, which do.

***Fin de siecle*:** A French term meaning "end of the century." The term is used to denote the last decade of the nineteenth century, a transition period when writers and other artists abandoned old conventions and looked for new techniques and objectives.

First Person: See *Point of View*

Flashback: A device used in literature to present action that occurred before the beginning of the story. Flashbacks are often introduced as the dreams or recollections of one or more characters.

Foil: A character in a work of literature whose physical or psychological qualities contrast strongly with, and therefore highlight, the corresponding qualities of another character.

Folklore: Traditions and myths preserved in a culture or group of people. Typically, these are passed on by word of mouth in various forms—such as legends, songs, and proverbs—or preserved in customs and ceremonies. This term was first used by W. J. Thoms in 1846.

Folktale: A story originating in oral tradition. Folktales fall into a variety of categories, including legends, ghost stories, fairy tales, fables, and anecdotes based on historical figures and events.

Foreshadowing: A device used in literature to create expectation or to set up an explanation of later developments.

Form: The pattern or construction of a work which identifies its genre and distinguishes it from other genres.

G

Genre: A category of literary work. In critical theory, genre may refer to both the content of a given work—tragedy, comedy, pastoral—and to its form, such as poetry, novel, or drama.

Gilded Age: A period in American history during the 1870s characterized by political corruption and materialism. A number of important novels of social and political criticism were written during this time.

Gothicism: In literary criticism, works characterized by a taste for the medieval or morbidly attractive. A gothic novel prominently features elements of horror, the supernatural, gloom, and violence: clanking chains, terror, charnel houses, ghosts, medieval castles, and mysteriously slamming doors. The term "gothic novel" is also applied to novels that lack elements of the traditional Gothic setting but that create a similar atmosphere of terror or dread.

Grotesque: In literary criticism, the subject matter of a work or a style of expression characterized by exaggeration, deformity, freakishness, and disorder. The grotesque often includes an element of comic absurdity.

H

Harlem Renaissance: The Harlem Renaissance of the 1920s is generally considered the first significant movement of black writers and artists in the United States. During this period, new and established black writers published more fiction and poetry than ever before, the first influential black literary journals were established, and black authors and artists received their first widespread recognition and serious critical appraisal. Among the major writers associated with this period are Claude McKay, Jean Toomer, Countee Cullen, Langston Hughes, Arna Bontemps, Nella Larsen, and Zora Neale Hurston. Also known as Negro Renaissance and New Negro Movement.

Hero/Heroine: The principal sympathetic character (male or female) in a literary work. Heroes and heroines typically exhibit admirable traits: idealism, courage, and integrity, for example.

Holocaust Literature: Literature influenced by or written about the Holocaust of World War II. Such literature includes true stories of survival in concentration camps, escape, and life after the war, as well as fictional works and poetry.

Humanism: A philosophy that places faith in the dignity of humankind and rejects the medieval perception of the individual as a weak, fallen creature. "Humanists" typically believe in the perfectibility of human nature and view reason and education as the means to that end.

Hyperbole: In literary criticism, deliberate exaggeration used to achieve an effect.

I

Idiom: A word construction or verbal expression closely associated with a given language.

Image: A concrete representation of an object or sensory experience. Typically, such a representation helps evoke the feelings associated with the object or experience itself. Images are either "literal" or "figurative." Literal images are especially concrete and involve little or no extension of the obvious meaning of the words used to express them. Figurative images do not follow the literal meaning of the words exactly. Images in literature are usually visual, but the term "image" can also refer to the representation of any sensory experience.

Imagery: The array of images in a literary work. Also, figurative language.

In medias res: A Latin term meaning "in the middle of things." It refers to the technique of beginning a story at its midpoint and then using various flashback devices to reveal previous action.

Interior Monologue: A narrative technique in which characters' thoughts are revealed in a way that appears to be uncontrolled by the author. The interior monologue typically aims to reveal the inner self of a character. It portrays emotional experiences as they occur at both a conscious and unconscious level. Images are often used to represent sensations or emotions.

Irony: In literary criticism, the effect of language in which the intended meaning is the opposite of what is stated.

J

Jargon: Language that is used or understood only by a select group of people. Jargon may refer to terminology used in a certain profession, such as computer jargon, or it may refer to any non-sensical language that is not understood by most people.

L

Leitmotiv: See *Motif*

Literal Language: An author uses literal language when he or she writes without exaggerating or embellishing the subject matter and without any tools of figurative language.

Lost Generation: A term first used by Gertrude Stein to describe the post-World War I generation of American writers: men and women haunted by a sense of betrayal and emptiness brought about by the destructiveness of the war.

M

Mannerism: Exaggerated, artificial adherence to a literary manner or style. Also, a popular style of the visual arts of late sixteenth-century Europe that was marked by elongation of the human form and by intentional spatial distortion. Literary works that are self-consciously high-toned and artistic are often said to be "mannered."

Metaphor: A figure of speech that expresses an idea through the image of another object. Metaphors suggest the essence of the first object by identifying it with certain qualities of the second object.

Modernism: Modern literary practices. Also, the principles of a literary school that lasted from roughly the beginning of the twentieth century until the end of World War II. Modernism is defined by its rejection of the literary conventions of the nineteenth century and by its opposition to conventional morality, taste, traditions, and economic values.

Mood: The prevailing emotions of a work or of the author in his or her creation of the work. The mood of a work is not always what might be expected based on its subject matter.

Motif: A theme, character type, image, metaphor, or other verbal element that recurs throughout a single work of literature or occurs in a number of different works over a period of time. Also known as *Motiv* or *Leitmotiv*.

Myth: An anonymous tale emerging from the traditional beliefs of a culture or social unit. Myths use supernatural explanations for natural phenomena. They may also explain cosmic issues like creation and death. Collections of myths, known as mythologies, are common to all cultures and nations, but the best-known myths belong to the Norse, Roman, and Greek mythologies.

N

Narration: The telling of a series of events, real or invented. A narration may be either a simple narrative, in which the events are recounted chronologically, or a narrative with a plot, in which the account is given in a style reflecting the author's artistic concept of the story. Narration is sometimes used as a synonym for "storyline."

Narrative: A verse or prose accounting of an event or sequence of events, real or invented. The term is also used as an adjective in the sense "method of narration." For example, in literary criticism, the expression "narrative technique" usually refers to the way the author structures and presents his or her story.

Narrator: The teller of a story. The narrator may be the author or a character in the story through whom the author speaks.

Naturalism: A literary movement of the late nineteenth and early twentieth centuries. The movement's major theorist, French novelist Emile Zola, envisioned a type of fiction that would examine human life with the objectivity of scientific inquiry. The Naturalists typically viewed human beings as either the products of "biological determinism," ruled by hereditary instincts and engaged in an endless struggle for survival, or as the products of "socioeconomic determinism," ruled by social and economic forces beyond their control. In their works, the Naturalists generally ignored the highest levels of society and focused on degradation: poverty, alcoholism, prostitution, insanity, and disease.

Noble Savage: The idea that primitive man is noble and good but becomes evil and corrupted as he becomes civilized. The concept of the noble savage originated in the Renaissance period but is more closely identified with such later writers as

Jean-Jacques Rousseau and Aphra Behn. See also Primitivism.

Novel of Ideas: A novel in which the examination of intellectual issues and concepts takes precedence over characterization or a traditional storyline.

Novel of Manners: A novel that examines the customs and mores of a cultural group.

Novel: A long fictional narrative written in prose, which developed from the novella and other early forms of narrative. A novel is usually organized under a plot or theme with a focus on character development and action.

Novella: An Italian term meaning "story." This term has been especially used to describe fourteenth-century Italian tales, but it also refers to modern short novels.

O

Objective Correlative: An outward set of objects, a situation, or a chain of events corresponding to an inward experience and evoking this experience in the reader. The term frequently appears in modern criticism in discussions of authors' intended effects on the emotional responses of readers.

Objectivity: A quality in writing characterized by the absence of the author's opinion or feeling about the subject matter. Objectivity is an important factor in criticism.

Oedipus Complex: A son's amorous obsession with his mother. The phrase is derived from the story of the ancient Theban hero Oedipus, who unknowingly killed his father and married his mother.

Omniscience: See *Point of View*

Onomatopoeia: The use of words whose sounds express or suggest their meaning. In its simplest sense, onomatopoeia may be represented by words that mimic the sounds they denote such as "hiss" or "meow." At a more subtle level, the pattern and rhythm of sounds and rhymes of a line or poem may be onomatopoeic.

Oxymoron: A phrase combining two contradictory terms. Oxymorons may be intentional or unintentional.

P

Parable: A story intended to teach a moral lesson or answer an ethical question.

Paradox: A statement that appears illogical or contradictory at first, but may actually point to an underlying truth.

Parallelism: A method of comparison of two ideas in which each is developed in the same grammatical structure.

Parody: In literary criticism, this term refers to an imitation of a serious literary work or the signature style of a particular author in a ridiculous manner. A typical parody adopts the style of the original and applies it to an inappropriate subject for humorous effect. Parody is a form of satire and could be considered the literary equivalent of a caricature or cartoon.

Pastoral: A term derived from the Latin word "pastor," meaning shepherd. A pastoral is a literary composition on a rural theme. The conventions of the pastoral were originated by the third-century Greek poet Theocritus, who wrote about the experiences, love affairs, and pastimes of Sicilian shepherds. In a pastoral, characters and language of a courtly nature are often placed in a simple setting. The term pastoral is also used to classify dramas, elegies, and lyrics that exhibit the use of country settings and shepherd characters.

Pen Name: See *Pseudonym*

Persona: A Latin term meaning "mask." *Personae* are the characters in a fictional work of literature. The *persona* generally functions as a mask through which the author tells a story in a voice other than his or her own. A *persona* is usually either a character in a story who acts as a narrator or an "implied author," a voice created by the author to act as the narrator for himself or herself.

Personification: A figure of speech that gives human qualities to abstract ideas, animals, and inanimate objects. Also known as *Prosopopoeia*.

Picaresque Novel: Episodic fiction depicting the adventures of a roguish central character ("picaro" is Spanish for "rogue"). The picaresque hero is commonly a low-born but clever individual who wanders into and out of various affairs of love, danger, and farcical intrigue. These involvements may take place at all social levels and typically present a humorous and wide-ranging satire of a given society.

Plagiarism: Claiming another person's written material as one's own. Plagiarism can take the form of direct, word-for-word copying or the theft of the substance or idea of the work.

Plot: In literary criticism, this term refers to the pattern of events in a narrative or drama. In its simplest sense, the plot guides the author in composing the work and helps the reader follow the work. Typically, plots exhibit causality and unity and have a beginning, a middle, and an end. Sometimes, however, a plot may consist of a series of disconnected events, in which case it is known as an "episodic plot."

Poetic Justice: An outcome in a literary work, not necessarily a poem, in which the good are rewarded and the evil are punished, especially in ways that particularly fit their virtues or crimes.

Poetic License: Distortions of fact and literary convention made by a writer—not always a poet—for the sake of the effect gained. Poetic license is closely related to the concept of "artistic freedom."

Poetics: This term has two closely related meanings. It denotes (1) an aesthetic theory in literary criticism about the essence of poetry or (2) rules prescribing the proper methods, content, style, or diction of poetry. The term poetics may also refer to theories about literature in general, not just poetry.

Point of View: The narrative perspective from which a literary work is presented to the reader. There are four traditional points of view. The "third person omniscient" gives the reader a "godlike" perspective, unrestricted by time or place, from which to see actions and look into the minds of characters. This allows the author to comment openly on characters and events in the work. The "third person" point of view presents the events of the story from outside of any single character's perception, much like the omniscient point of view, but the reader must understand the action as it takes place and without any special insight into characters' minds or motivations. The "first person" or "personal" point of view relates events as they are perceived by a single character. The main character "tells" the story and may offer opinions about the action and characters which differ from those of the author. Much less common than omniscient, third person, and first person is the "second person" point of view, wherein the author tells the story as if it is happening to the reader.

Polemic: A work in which the author takes a stand on a controversial subject, such as abortion or religion. Such works are often extremely argumentative or provocative.

Pornography: Writing intended to provoke feelings of lust in the reader. Such works are often condemned by critics and teachers, but those which can be shown to have literary value are viewed less harshly.

Post-Aesthetic Movement: An artistic response made by African Americans to the black aesthetic movement of the 1960s and early '70s. Writers since that time have adopted a somewhat different tone in their work, with less emphasis placed on the disparity between black and white in the United States. In the words of post-aesthetic authors such as Toni Morrison, John Edgar Wideman, and Kristin Hunter, African Americans are portrayed as looking inward for answers to their own questions, rather than always looking to the outside world.

Postmodernism: Writing from the 1960s forward characterized by experimentation and continuing to apply some of the fundamentals of modernism, which included existentialism and alienation. Postmodernists have gone a step further in the rejection of tradition begun with the modernists by also rejecting traditional forms, preferring the anti-novel over the novel and the antihero over the hero.

Primitivism: The belief that primitive peoples were nobler and less flawed than civilized peoples because they had not been subjected to the tainting influence of society. See also Noble Savage.

Prologue: An introductory section of a literary work. It often contains information establishing the situation of the characters or presents information about the setting, time period, or action. In drama, the prologue is spoken by a chorus or by one of the principal characters.

Prose: A literary medium that attempts to mirror the language of everyday speech. It is distinguished from poetry by its use of unmetered, unrhymed language consisting of logically related sentences. Prose is usually grouped into paragraphs that form a cohesive whole such as an essay or a novel.

Prosopopoeia: See *Personification*

Protagonist: The central character of a story who serves as a focus for its themes and incidents and as the principal rationale for its development. The protagonist is sometimes referred to in discussions of modern literature as the hero or antihero.

Protest Fiction: Protest fiction has as its primary purpose the protesting of some social injustice, such as racism or discrimination.

Proverb: A brief, sage saying that expresses a truth about life in a striking manner.

Pseudonym: A name assumed by a writer, most often intended to prevent his or her identification as the author of a work. Two or more authors may work together under one pseudonym, or an author may use a different name for each genre he or she publishes in. Some publishing companies maintain "house pseudonyms," under which any number of authors may write installations in a series. Some authors also choose a pseudonym over their real names the way an actor may use a stage name.

Pun: A play on words that have similar sounds but different meanings.

R

Realism: A nineteenth-century European literary movement that sought to portray familiar characters, situations, and settings in a realistic manner. This was done primarily by using an objective narrative point of view and through the buildup of accurate detail. The standard for success of any realistic work depends on how faithfully it transfers common experience into fictional forms. The realistic method may be altered or extended, as in stream of consciousness writing, to record highly subjective experience.

Repartee: Conversation featuring snappy retorts and witticisms.

Resolution: The portion of a story following the climax, in which the conflict is resolved. See also *Denouement.*

Rhetoric: In literary criticism, this term denotes the art of ethical persuasion. In its strictest sense, rhetoric adheres to various principles developed since classical times for arranging facts and ideas in a clear, persuasive, appealing manner. The term is also used to refer to effective prose in general and theories of or methods for composing effective prose.

Rhetorical Question: A question intended to provoke thought, but not an expressed answer, in the reader. It is most commonly used in oratory and other persuasive genres.

Rising Action: The part of a drama where the plot becomes increasingly complicated. Rising action leads up to the climax, or turning point, of a drama.

Roman a clef: A French phrase meaning "novel with a key." It refers to a narrative in which real persons are portrayed under fictitious names.

Romance: A broad term, usually denoting a narrative with exotic, exaggerated, often idealized characters, scenes, and themes.

Romanticism: This term has two widely accepted meanings. In historical criticism, it refers to a European intellectual and artistic movement of the late eighteenth and early nineteenth centuries that sought greater freedom of personal expression than that allowed by the strict rules of literary form and logic of the eighteenth-century neoclassicists. The Romantics preferred emotional and imaginative expression to rational analysis. They considered the individual to be at the center of all experience and so placed him or her at the center of their art. The Romantics believed that the creative imagination reveals nobler truths—unique feelings and attitudes—than those that could be discovered by logic or by scientific examination. Both the natural world and the state of childhood were important sources for revelations of "eternal truths." "Romanticism" is also used as a general term to refer to a type of sensibility found in all periods of literary history and usually considered to be in opposition to the principles of classicism. In this sense, Romanticism signifies any work or philosophy in which the exotic or dreamlike figure strongly, or that is devoted to individualistic expression, self-analysis, or a pursuit of a higher realm of knowledge than can be discovered by human reason.

Romantics: See *Romanticism*

S

Satire: A work that uses ridicule, humor, and wit to criticize and provoke change in human nature and institutions. There are two major types of satire: "formal" or "direct" satire speaks directly to the reader or to a character in the work; "indirect" satire relies upon the ridiculous behavior of its characters to make its point. Formal satire is further divided into two manners: the "Horatian," which ridicules gently, and the "Juvenalian," which derides its subjects harshly and bitterly.

Science Fiction: A type of narrative about or based upon real or imagined scientific theories and technology. Science fiction is often peopled with alien creatures and set on other planets or in different dimensions.

Second Person: See *Point of View*

Setting: The time, place, and culture in which the action of a narrative takes place. The elements of setting may include geographic location, characters' physical and mental environments, prevailing cultural attitudes, or the historical time in which the action takes place.

Simile: A comparison, usually using "like" or "as," of two essentially dissimilar things, as in "coffee as cold as ice" or "He sounded like a broken record."

Slang: A type of informal verbal communication that is generally unacceptable for formal writing. Slang words and phrases are often colorful exaggerations used to emphasize the speaker's point; they may also be shortened versions of an often-used word or phrase.

Cumulative Author/Title Index

Eliot, George
The Mill on the Floss: V17
Silas Marner: V20
Ellen Foster (Gibbons): V3
Ellis, Bret Easton
Less Than Zero: V11
Ellison, Ralph
Invisible Man: V2
Juneteenth: V21
Elmer Gantry (Lewis): V22
Emecheta, Buchi
The Bride Price: V12
The Wrestling Match: V14
Emma (Austen): V21
Empire of the Sun (Ballard): V8
The End of the Affair (Greene): V16
Ender's Game (Card): V5
Erdrich, Louise
Love Medicine: V5
Esquivel, Laura
Like Water for Chocolate: V5
Ethan Frome (Wharton): V5
Evelina (Burney): V16

F

Fahrenheit 451 (Bradbury): V1
Far from the Madding Crowd (Hardy): V19
Farewell My Concubine (Lee): V19
A Farewell to Arms (Hemingway): V1
Fathers and Sons (Turgenev): V16
Faulkner, William
Absalom, Absalom!: V13
As I Lay Dying: V8
The Sound and the Fury: V4
Fielding, Henry
Tom Jones: V18
Fitzgerald, F. Scott
The Great Gatsby: V2
This Side of Paradise: V20
Tender Is the Night: V19
The Fixer (Malamud): V9
Flagg, Fannie
Fried Green Tomatoes at the Whistle Stop Café: V7
Flaubert, Gustave
Madame Bovary: V14
Flowers for Algernon (Keyes): V2
Foden, Giles
The Last King of Scotland: V15
For Whom the Bell Tolls (Hemingway): V14
Forster, E. M.
Howards End: V10
A Passage to India: V3
A Room with a View: V11
The Fountainhead (Rand): V16
Fowles, John
The French Lieutenant's Woman: V21
Fox, Paula
The Slave Dancer: V12

Frankenstein (Shelley): V1
Frederic, Harold
The Damnation of Theron Ware: V22
The French Lieutenant's Woman (Fowles): V21
Fried Green Tomatoes at the Whistle Stop Café: (Flagg): V7
Fuentes, Carlos
The Old Gringo: V8

G

Gaines, Ernest J.
The Autobiography of Miss Jane Pittman: V5
A Gathering of Old Men: V16
A Lesson Before Dying: V7
A Gathering of Old Men (Gaines): V16
Giants in the Earth (Rölvaag): V5
García Márquez, Gabriel
Chronicle of a Death Foretold: V10
Love in the Time of Cholera: V1
One Hundred Years of Solitude: V5
Gardner, John
Grendel: V3
Gibbons, Kaye
Ellen Foster: V3
Gide, André
The Immoralist: V21
The Giver (Lowry): V3
Go Tell It on the Mountain (Baldwin): V4
The God of Small Things (Roy): V22
The Godfather (Puzo): V16
Golden, Arthur
Memoirs of a Geisha: V19
Golding, William
Lord of the Flies: V2
Gone with the Wind (Mitchell): V9
Gordimer, Nadine
July's People: V4
Grahame, Kenneth
The Wind in the Willows: V20
The Grapes of Wrath (Steinbeck): V7
The Grass Dancer (Power): V11
Graves, Robert
I, Claudius: V21
Great Expectations (Dickens): V4
The Great Gatsby (Fitzgerald): V2
Green, Hannah
The Dead of the House: V10
Greene, Bette
Summer of My German Soldier: V10
Greene, Graham
The End of the Affair: V16
Grendel (Gardner): V3
Guest, Judith
Ordinary People: V1
Gulliver's Travels (Swift): V6

Guterson, David
Snow Falling on Cedars: V13

H

Haley, Alex
Roots: The Story of an American Family: V9
Hammett, Dashiell
The Maltese Falcon: V21
The Handmaid's Tale (Atwood): V4
Hard Times (Dickens): V20
Hardy, Thomas
Far from the Madding Crowd: V19
The Mayor of Casterbridge: V15
The Return of the Native: V11
Tess of the d'Urbervilles: V3
Harris, Marilyn
Hatter Fox: V14
Hatter Fox (Harris): V14
Hawthorne, Nathaniel
The House of the Seven Gables: V20
The Scarlet Letter: V1
The Heart Is a Lonely Hunter (McCullers): V6
Heart of Darkness (Conrad): V2
Heller, Joseph
Catch-22: V1
Hemingway, Ernest
A Farewell to Arms: V1
For Whom the Bell Tolls: V14
The Old Man and the Sea: V6
The Sun Also Rises: V5
Herbert, Frank
Soul Catcher: V17
Herzog (Bellow): V14
Hesse, Hermann
Demian: V15
Siddhartha: V6
Hijuelos, Oscar
The Mambo Kings Play Songs of Love: V17
Hinton, S. E.
The Outsiders: V5
Rumble Fish: V15
Tex: V9
That Was Then, This Is Now: V16
The Hitchhiker's Guide to the Galaxy (Adams): V7
The Hobbit (Tolkien): V8
Høeg, Peter
Smilla's Sense of Snow: V17
House Made of Dawn (Momaday): V10
The House of Mirth (Wharton): V15
The House of the Seven Gables (Hawthorne): V20
The House of the Spirits (Allende): V6
The House on Mango Street (Cisneros): V2
How the García Girls Lost Their Accents (Alvarez): V5

Cumulative Nationality/Ethnicity Index

African American

Angelou, Maya
  *I Know Why the Caged Bird
    Sings:* V2
Baldwin, James
  Go Tell It on the Mountain: V4
Butler, Octavia
  Kindred: V8
  Parable of the Sower: V21
Cleage, Pearl
  *What Looks Like Crazy on an
    Ordinary Day:* V17
Ellison, Ralph
  Invisible Man: V2
  Juneteenth: V21
Gaines, Ernest J.
  *The Autobiography of Miss Jane
    Pittman:* V5
  A Gathering of Old Men: V16
  A Lesson before Dying: V7
Haley, Alex
  *Roots: The Story of an American
    Family:* V9
Hughes, Langston
  Tambourines to Glory: V21
Hurston, Zora Neale
  Their Eyes Were Watching God:
    V3
Johnson, James Weldon
  *The Autobiography of an
    Ex-Coloured Man:* V22
Kincaid, Jamaica
  Annie John: V3
Morrison, Toni
  Beloved: V6
  The Bluest Eye: V1
  Song of Solomom: V8
Sula: V14
Naylor, Gloria
  Mama Day: V7
  The Women of Brewster Place: V4
Shange, Ntozake
  Betsey Brown: V11
Toomer, Jean
  Cane: V11
Walker, Alice
  The Color Purple: V5
Wright, Richard
  Black Boy: V1

Algerian

Camus, Albert
  The Plague: V16
  The Stranger: V6

American

Agee, James
  A Death in the Family: V22
Alcott, Louisa May
  Little Women: V12
Alexie, Sherman
  *The Lone Ranger and Tonto
    Fistfight in Heaven:* V17
Allison, Dorothy
  Bastard Out of Carolina: V11
Alvarez, Julia
  *How the García Girls Lost Their
    Accents:* V5
Anaya, Rudolfo
  Bless Me, Ultima: V12
Anderson, Sherwood
  Winesburg, Ohio: V4
Angelou, Maya
  *I Know Why the Caged Bird
    Sings:* V2
Auel, Jean
  The Clan of the Cave Bear: V11
Banks, Russell
  The Sweet Hereafter: V13
Baum, L. Frank
  The Wonderful Wizard of Oz: V13
Bellamy, Edward
  Looking Backward: 2000–1887:
    V15
Bellow, Saul
  Herzog: V14
Borland, Hal
  When the Legends Die: V18
Bradbury, Ray
  Dandelion Wine: V22
  Fahrenheit 451: V1
Bridal, Tessa
  The Tree of Red Stars: V17
Brown, Rita Mae
  Rubyfruit Jungle: V9
Butler, Octavia
  Kindred: V8
  Parable of the Sower: V21
Card, Orson Scott
  Ender's Game: V5
Cather, Willa
  Death Comes for the Archbishop:
    V19
  My Ántonia: V2
Chandler, Raymond
  The Big Sleep: V17
Chopin, Kate
  The Awakening: V3
Cisneros, Sandra
  The House on Mango Street: V2

Japanese

Abe, Kobo
The Woman in the Dunes: V22
Ishiguro, Kazuo
The Remains of the Day: V13
Mori, Kyoko
Shizuko's Daughter: V15
Yoshimoto, Banana
Kitchen: V7

Jewish

Bellow, Saul
Herzog: V14
Seize the Day: V4
Kafka, Frank
The Trial: V7
Malamud, Bernard
The Fixer: V9
The Natural: V4
West, Nathanael
The Day of the Locust: V16
Wiesel, Eliezer
Night: V4

Mexican

Esquivel, Laura
Like Water for Chocolate: V5
Fuentes, Carlos
The Old Gringo: V8

Native American

Alexie, Sherman
The Lone Ranger and Tonto
Fistfight in Heaven: V17
Dorris, Michael
A Yellow Raft in Blue Water: V3
Erdrich, Louise
Love Medicine: V5
Marmon Silko, Leslie
Ceremony: V4
Momaday, N. Scott
House Made of Dawn: V10

Nigerian

Achebe, Chinua
Things Fall Apart: V3
Emecheta, Buchi
The Bride Price: V12
The Wrestling Match: V14

Norwegian

Rölvaag, O. E.
Giants in the Earth: V5

Peruvian

Allende, Isabel
Daughter of Fortune: V18

Polish

Conrad, Joseph
Heart of Darkness: V2
Lord Jim: V16
Kosinski, Jerzy
The Painted Bird: V12

Romanian

Wiesel, Eliezer
Night: V4

Russian

Bulgakov, Mikhail
The Master and Margarita: V8
Dostoyevsky, Fyodor
The Brothers Karamazon: V8
Crime and Punishment: V3
Nabokov, Vladimir
Lolita: V9
Rand, Ayn
Atlas Shrugged: V10
The Fountainhead: V16
Solzhenitsyn, Aleksandr
One Day in the Life of Ivan
Denisovich: V6

Tolstoy, Leo
War and Peace: V10
Turgenev, Ivan
Fathers and Sons: V16

Scottish

Grahame, Kenneth
The Wind in the Willows: V20
Spark, Muriel
The Prime of Miss Jean Brodie:
V22
Stevenson, Robert Louis
Treasure Island: V20

South African

Coetzee, J. M.
Dusklands: V21
Gordimer, Nadine
July's People: V4
Paton, Alan
Cry, the Beloved Country: V3
Too Late the Phalarope: V12

Spanish

Saavedra, Miguel de Cervantes
Don Quixote: V8

Swiss

Hesse, Hermann
Demian: V15

Uruguayan

Bridal, Tessa
The Tree of Red Stars: V17

West Indian

Kincaid, Jamaica
Annie John: V3

Subject/Theme Index